Interdisciplinary Studies in Human Rights

Human rights are one of the normative cornerstones of contemporary international law and global governance. Due to the complexities of actual or potential violations of human rights and in light of current crises, new and interdisciplinary research is urgently needed. The series Interdisciplinary Studies in Human Rights recognizes the growing importance and necessity of interdisciplinary research in human rights. The series consists of monographs and collected volumes addressing human rights research from different disciplinary and interdisciplinary perspectives, including but not limited to philosophy, law, political science, education, and medical ethics. Its goal is to explore new and contested questions such as the extraterritorial application of human rights and their relevance for non-state actors, as well as the philosophical and theoretical foundations of human rights. The series also addresses policy questions of current interest including the human rights of migrants and refugees, LGBTI rights, and bioethics, as well as business and human rights.

The series editors are Members of the Centre for Human Rights Erlangen-Nürnberg (CHREN), an interdisciplinary research center at Friedrich-Alexander-University Erlangen-Nürnberg. The Advisory Board brings together human rights scholars from a wide range of academic disciplines and regional backgrounds. The series welcomes suggestions for publications of academic research falling into the series subject matter.

Véronique Boillet • Sophie Weerts •
Andreas R. Ziegler
Editors

Sports and Human Rights

Springer

Editors
Véronique Boillet
Law School
University of Lausanne
Lausanne, Switzerland

Sophie Weerts
Swiss Graduate School of Public Administration
University of Lausanne
Lausanne, Switzerland

Andreas R. Ziegler
Law School
University of Lausanne
Lausanne, Switzerland

ISSN 2509-2960 ISSN 2509-2979 (electronic)
Interdisciplinary Studies in Human Rights
ISBN 978-3-031-56451-2 ISBN 978-3-031-56452-9 (eBook)
https://doi.org/10.1007/978-3-031-56452-9

This work was supported by University of Lausanne.

This Springer imprint is published by the registered company Springer Nature Switzerland AG
The registered company address is: Gewerbestrasse 11, 6330 Cham, Switzerland

Contents

Editors and Contributors

About the Editors

Véronique Boillet is a professor of public law at the Law School of the University of Lausanne. She was previously a lawyer at the Lausanne's Bar (2011–2013) and has just been elected to the Board of the Swiss Institution for Human Rights (2023–2027). As a scholar, she has in-depth knowledge of the European and Swiss constitutional system, which she has been teaching since 2010 and which she has analyzed in several contributions published in leading European and Swiss law journals. Her current research focuses on the link between human rights and the environment, and on the principle of non-discrimination.

Sophie Weerts is an associate professor of public law at the Swiss Graduate School of Public Administration, University of Lausanne. She holds a PhD in law from the University of Louvain and has a background in law and ethics. Sophie was previously a visiting professor at the University of Geneva and the University of St-Louis-Brussels and a lecturer at the University of Neuchâtel and the University of Louvain (Uclouvain). She practiced law for several years at the Brussels bar and worked as an expert for the federal government. Her research lies at the crossroads of legal theory, constitutional law, and European law. She is currently focusing on issues relating to digital transformation and its impact on public law. In this context, she is particularly interested in the business and human rights field for regulating the digital sector.

Andreas R. Ziegler is currently a Professor of International Law at the University of Lausanne and Director of its LLM Program in International Business Law. He holds a conjoint professorship at the Law School of the University of New South Wales (Sydney, Australia) as well as visiting appointments at the Universities of St. Gallen and of the Saarland (Saarbrücken) as well as ETH Zurich and the Geneva Academy. Previously, he was a civil servant working for several Swiss Ministries (Foreign Affairs, Trade) and international organizations (EFTA, EU). He has widely published on Swiss, international, and European law (including "Swiss LGBT Law",

2nd edn. 2017) and regularly advises Governments, International Organizations, NGOs, and private clients and has represented them before various domestic and international courts and arbitral tribunals. He is on the permanent roster of panelists of the WTO and a Member of the European Commission of Sexual Orientation Law (ECSOL). He is the President of the Swiss Chapter of the International Law Association (ILA) and on the Board of the Swiss and the German Societies of International Law and the European Law Faculties Association—ELFA). He founded and manages the blog "sogiesc.law.blog" on international and comparative SOGIESC law.

List of Contributors

Kim Barker Lincoln Law School, University of Lincoln, Lincoln, UK

Véronique Boillet Law School, University of Lausanne, Lausanne, Switzerland

Pieter Cannoot Department of Interdisciplinary Study of Law, Private Law and Business Law, Faculty of Law and Criminology, Ghent University, Ghent, Belgium

Ariël Decoster Human Rights Centre, Ghent University, Ghent, Belgium
FWO Flanders Research Foundation, Brussels, Belgium

Joseph Benjamin B. De Leon Las Pinas, Philippines

Antonio Di Marco University of Strasbourg, Strasbourg, France

Antoine Duval T.M.C. Asser Instituut, The Hague, The Netherlands

H. Burak Gemalmaz Faculty of Law, Istanbul University, Türkiye

Lena Holzer University of Cambridge, Faculty of Law, Cambridge, UK

Mark James Manchester Law School, Manchester Metropolitan University, Manchester, UK

Olga Jurasz Law School, The Open University, Milton Keynes, UK

Guy Osborn Westminster Law School, University of Westminster, London, UK

Seema Patel Nottingham Law School, Nottingham Trent University, Nottingham, UK

Claire Poppelwell-Scevak Human Rights Centre, Ghent University, Ghent, Belgium

Daniel Rietiker European Court of Human Rights, Strasbourg, France
Lausanne University, Lausanne, Switzerland
Suffolk University Law School, Boston, MA, USA

Sarah Schoentjes FWO Flanders Research Foundation, Brussels, Belgium

Cathérine Van de Graaf Academy for European Human Rights Protection, Faculty of Law, University of Cologne, Köln, Germany

Marjolaine Viret Institute of Sport Sciences, Faculty of Social and Political Sciences, University of Lausanne, Lausanne, Switzerland

Sophie Weerts Swiss Graduate School of Public Administration, University of Lausanne, Lausanne, Switzerland

William Thomas Worster The Hague University of Applied Sciences, The Hague, The Netherlands

Andreas R. Ziegler Law School, University of Lausanne, Lausanne, Switzerland

Introduction

Véronique Boillet, Sophie Weerts, and Andreas R. Ziegler

Contents

At the 1906 Olympic Games in Athens, the athlete Peter O'Connor protested the erasure of Ireland from the Olympics by climbing the flagpole during his medal ceremony, and replacing the Union Jack with the Irish flag. At the 1932 Olympic Games in Los Angeles, in the midst of the Great Depression, demonstrators denounced the economic injustice of the high cost of the Games. In 1968, at the Mexico City Olympics, Tommie Smith and John Carlos raised their fists in a Black Power salute when receiving their medals. More recently, the construction of infrastructure for the 2012 London Olympics and the 2016 Rio Olympics led to the displacement of marginalized communities, with the promise of access to new infrastructure, which has yet to materialize.[1] Whether concerning particular athletes, people involved in the organization of sporting events, or other causes, these various protests at the Olympics throughout history prove that attacks on human dignity, individual freedom, and equality between individuals also echo in sport. From this perspective, the sporting environment is not disconnected from major contemporary social issues: it constitutes a public space in which injustices can be denounced, but

[1] Boykoff (2017), p. 162.

V. Boillet (✉) · A. R. Ziegler
Law School, University of Lausanne, Lausanne, Switzerland
e-mail: veronique.boillet@unil.ch; andreas.ziegler@unil.ch

S. Weerts
Swiss Graduate School of Public Administration, University of Lausanne, Lausanne, Switzerland
e-mail: sophie.weerts@unil.ch

V. Boillet et al. (eds.), *Sports and Human Rights*, Interdisciplinary Studies in Human Rights 10, https://doi.org/10.1007/978-3-031-56452-9_1

also the theater in which prejudices are perpetuated against various parties, such as athletes or workers.

International human rights law (IHRL) commonly addresses attacks on individual dignity and social justice issues by guaranteeing rights to individuals and offering them protection mechanisms. Consequently, it becomes pertinent to inquire whether IHRL can solve the problems encountered in sporting practices and the sporting environment. This is the question that animates this volume, which seeks to explore the potential protection(s) that IHRL can offer to combat such abuse. Indeed, while its application is not self-evident due to the nature and status of stakeholders involved in human rights abuses, several changes in the field of IHRL show that Sports Governing Bodies (SGBs) can no longer afford not to comply with human rights standards. Recent cases, such as the European Court of Human Rights' (ECtHR) decision in *Caster Semenya*, reveals the application of human rights principles to international sports organizations, and the positive obligation of states to respect, protect, and promote human rights.[2]

Based on a series of themes and case studies, this book aims to illustrate the impact of sports policies and practices on individuals and their identities, and to analyze the potential solutions offered by IHRL for these infringements. It thus bridges the gap between IHRL and sports studies, and will be useful to scholars in both fields, especially those unfamiliar with each other's work. Conversely, by investigating the context of sport and its governance, this collection offers a series of valuable insights, enabling the development of an interpretation of 'law in context' for legal scholars in the field of human rights. As the governance and regulation of sport are seen as illustrations of other forms of normativity, this book also contributes to the conversation about the transnational dimension of law and legal orders.[3] In this respect, it illustrates that normative autonomy in the field of sport, associated with the idea of *lex sportiva*, tends to be relative regarding IHRL.[4]

In addition to the concrete examples that can be drawn from several chapters in this volume, three elements make it possible to call into question this idea of the autonomy of sport. The first is the evolution of IHRL itself; it should be noted that the international organizations responsible for human rights have broadened the range of their instruments in order to realize their commitment to respect, protect, and fulfil. Implementing this last obligation has led to the introduction of a series of actions structured within a public policy framework. From this perspective, the adopted texts constitute what jurists call 'soft law'. Including human rights in a public policy perspective makes it possible to go beyond the state as the sole interlocutor to include other stakeholders, such as civil society and business. The second element stems from the work on corporate social responsibility that began in

[2] ECtHR, *Semenya v. Switzerland*, req n°10934/21, 11 July 2023.

[3] See e.g. Peer Zumbansen, Transnational Law, CLPE Research Paper 09/2008; Cotterell (2012), pp. 500–524; Halliday and Schaffer (2015).

[4] Duval (2021), pp. 493–512; Di Marco (2022), pp. 244–268.

the 1990s,[5] which calls for companies to adopt an ethos that reconciles economic development with respect for social values. In this context, human rights are a particularly evocative discourse for organizations seeking to strengthen their legitimacy. Finally, the polycentric approach of IHRL is also illustrative of the object of regulatory studies, highlighting the shift from legislation to regulation, and from system of government to system of governance.[6] These three elements provide a fascinating framework for understanding the evolution of the issue of human rights in the sporting environment, which serves to elucidate the gradual rapprochement between IHRL and private sporting organizations. Considering this context, this book should be useful to SGBs who are under significant pressure to address human rights standards in their governance, and to provide athletes with advice regarding the legal mechanisms that can protect them before judicial authorities.

This book intentionally is centered on athletes.[7] The editors intended to highlight this relatively overlooked category of human rights beneficiaries: individuals who practice a sporting activity in a professional or semi-professional environment. Two prominent human rights topics are at the core of this collection: discrimination based on gender or nationality, and freedom of expression. This focus is a result of the proposals selected after the call of papers launched in December 2021. These topics are aligned with crucial social issues facing our increasingly digital society, which further proves that sport is an illustrative area of more general problems. From a legal point of view, several chapters deal with United Nations (UN) human rights law, but also devote considerable space to the case law of the ECtHR. This Eurocentric perspective is due to the current state of sport global governance, in which the ECtHR is involved through the establishment of the Court of Arbitration for Sport (CAS) in Lausanne, and its connection to Swiss law, which is in turn connected to the European Convention on Human Rights (ECHR). This book does not purport to provide a complete picture of all human rights issues in sport and all potential legal solutions. Other topics could have been more extensively addressed, such as freedom of religion or the right to privacy,[8] which has given rise to several cases in the fight against doping.[9] The situation of other beneficiaries, such as workers or people displaced in the construction of sports facilities, is also worthy of further analysis. The ECtHR decision in the Caster Semenya case deeply impacted the editorial process. Although the long-term effects of this decision will need to be addressed, several chapters explore different elements of the case. Finally, the importance of

---

[5] Carroll (2009), pp. 19–46.

[6] See e.g. Black (2001), p. 126.

[7] This book echoes the call for considering the status of athletes as human rights beneficiaries. See Schwab (2018), pp. 214–232.

[8] Both topics figure in the chapters Cannoot et al. "Hormonal Eligibility Criteria in Women's Professional Sports Under the ECHR: The Case of Caster Semenya v. Switzerland", and Holzer L "Gendered Athletes in Sports: CEDAW's Role in Tackling Heterosexist and Racialized Uniforms in Sports".

[9] ECtHR, Fédération nationale des Syndicats Sportifs (FNASS) and others v. France, 18 January 2018, req. n°s 48151/11 and 77769/13.

European human rights law in the field of sport is not without question, given the universalist vision promoted by global SGBs and the overshadowing of other legal systems that offer additional perspectives on solutions to protect vulnerable people. The limitations of the present volume are an invitation for other legal experts to explore these different areas and contribute to the dialogue that a universal human rights vision requires.

Before delving into the various chapters, some clarifications must be made regarding the context and approach of this book. First, the specific regulatory context of sports organizations will be discussed, which helps to understand the weaknesses of measures to protect, promote, and implement human rights in the field of sport. Second, the subject of sport will be placed in the context of IHRL. The growing economic power of global SGBs increases the vulnerability of athletes in sporting contexts, and thus strengthens the call for a complete application of human rights law to the field of sport. Finally, the editors will address questions concerning the legitimacy of the rise of European human rights law in sports governance.

1 The 'Autonomy' of Sports Governing Bodies

Historically, SGBs have been given significant autonomy when organizing sporting competitions as well as regarding their internal structure and regulations. One explanation for this is the idea that (international) sports should not be subject to the political influence of specific states, and that athletes should be free to organize their activities according to the specific needs of their chosen sport. Liberals would also add that the absence of state interference serves the idea of self-government in an area where the possibility of attracting sponsors and the general public is an important metric of success. While in some states, the interference with domestic sports associations may be more pronounced, there is hardly any international law related to SGBs and sports. A notable exception is the area of doping where a traditional international treaty[10] exists and an international body has been established, the World Anti-Doping Agency, although only in 1999 and with a hybrid character that falls short of a traditional international organization;[11] it is funded equally by the Olympic Movement and Member Governments.

[10] International Convention against Doping in Sport of 19 October 2005. It was negotiated under the auspices of UNESCO and has 191 State Parties (as of October 2023).

[11] The World Anti-Doping Agency is a foundation created through a collective initiative led by the International Olympic Committee (IOC) on 10 November 1999. WADA receives half of its budgetary requirements from the IOC, with the other half coming from various national governments. Its governing bodies are also composed in equal parts by representatives from the sporting movement (including athletes) and governments of the world. Government representation within WADA is allocated according to the five Olympic Regions. The membership allocation to WADA's Foundation Board (Board) was agreed by governments at the International Intergovernmental

Further, not only are international treaties and organizations absent from the field of sports, but also dispute settlement is largely left to the organizations themselves. The CAS was only created in 1984, and remains under the auspices of the International Olympic Committee (IOC) with little interference by the state or international courts and tribunals.[12] As the CAS is fundamental for safeguarding the (human) rights of athletes, it is a system that should be subject to close analysis, and many chapters of this volume directly address its structure and approach. Recent case law from the Swiss Federal Tribunal (which is the only national institution for challenging arbitral awards by the CAS), and national courts relating to disputes settled by the CAS have shown that the autonomy of this system could be further challenged in the near future. What is particularly interesting from an IHRL perspective is the fact that governments are bound by specific international obligations while the sports world is allowed to largely organize itself; this is relevant for the role of the ECtHR with regard to Switzerland where the CAS is located.[13]

2 Sport, Sports Governing Bodies and Athletes in International Human Rights

The second element that will now be addressed is the relationship between sport and IHRL; indeed, the topic of sport is not new regarding the agenda of public international organizations. Early perspectives on the topic treated sport as a means for personal development, and this has developed more recently in favor of recognizing the human rights of people who are impacted by sporting organizations and events. Several conventions and political declarations show that sport was first viewed as a vehicle for personal development at the universal level. In 1959, the UN adopted the Declaration on the Rights of the Child, which recognized sport as a fundamental right.[14] In 1978, in its International Charter of Physical Education, UNESCO

Consultative Group on Anti-Doping in Sport Meeting held in Cape Town, South Africa, in May 2001.

[12]The CAS Statute entered into force on 30 June 1984. See also the "Agreement concerning the constitution of the International Council of Arbitration for Sport of 22 June 1994", known as the "Paris Agreement". This was signed by the highest authorities representing the sports world, viz. the presidents of the IOC, the Association of Summer Olympic International Federations (ASOIF), the Association of International Winter Sports Federations (AIWF) and the Association of National Olympic Committees (ANOC).

[13]See below and Shinohara Tsubasa, Paving the Way for the Protection of Human Rights in Sports - The Case of Intersex and Transgender Female Athletes (2024).

[14]UN General Assembly, Resolution 1386 (XIV), 20 November 1959, https://digitallibrary.un.org/record/195831.

declared that sport and physical education are fundamental rights for all.[15] The recognition of sport as a factor in constructing identity and personal development is also reiterated in international conventions on the fight against racism, children's rights, and the rights of persons with disabilities.[16] From the 2000s onwards, the international approach to sport took on an institutional dimension. Within the UN, sport became a tool to help achieve the Millennium Development Goals (2000–2015) and the Sustainable Development Goals (2015–2030).[17] In 2001, the UN Secretary-General appointed a Special Adviser on Sport for Development and Peace; a task force of several UN agencies (including UNESCO, ILO, WHO, UNICEF, and UNDP) was also instituted. The UN General Assembly declared that 2005 was the 'International Year of Sport and Physical Education'.

In this regard, sport is not only a tool for helping people develop their autonomy and exercise their liberty, but it becomes an instrument of public policy. It is viewed as a means of achieving objectives in the fight against poverty and the promotion of peace, while also contributing to personal development. This instrumental and social understanding of sport led to it becoming an integral part of public policy that could be deployed at the international or national level. At the regional level, the Council of Europe was an active player for connecting sport and human rights. With its resolution on 'Principles for a Policy of Sport for All' in 1975, the European organization first promoted sport as a vehicle for improving individuals' rights to health, education, culture, and participation in the life of their community, and encouraged governments to develop policies in the field of sport. This resolution was updated in 1992, 2001, and 2021 as the 'European Sports Charter'.[18] Further, the Council of Europe adopted numerous recommendations in which the issue of sport is connected to other issues in the area of human rights protection. Some relevant resolutions here include the prevention of racism, xenophobia and racial intolerance in sport (Rec(2001)6), or in improving physical education and sport for children and young people in all European counties (Rec(2003)6). In its recommendation, the Committee of Ministers of the Council of Europe also expressed its sensitivity to governance issues, adopting two recommendations on the principles of good governance in sport (Rec(2005)8 and CM/Rec(2018)12), and also on the principle of autonomy of sport in Europe (CM/Rec(2011)3).

The rise of economic globalization and the arrival of transnational economic players changed the classic perspective on IHRL, and offered a new path for protecting human rights. Since thc 1990s, a new kind of actor emerged in the relationship between international organizations, states, and individuals: the

[15] Unesco General Conference, The Unesco Charter was revised in 2015 (Unesco General conference, International Charter of Physical Education, Physical Activity and Sport, SHS/2015/PI/H/14 REV).

[16] Hums et al. (2009), pp. 36–48.

[17] Beutler (2008), p. 360.

[18] Recommendation CM/Rec (2021) 5 of the Committee of Ministers to Member States on the Revised European Sports Charter (https://rm.coe.int/recommendation-cm-rec-2021-5-on-the-revision-of-the-european-sport-cha/1680a43914).

transnational private organization. These transnational players operate in a territorial, and therefore legal, environment distinct from the one in which they are based, and in this context can cause harm to people where public authorities are not in a position to protect them. In 2007, the Special Representative of the Secretary-General on Human Rights and Transnational Corporations and Other Business Enterprises, John Ruggie, recommended that transnational organizations adopt a human rights risks-based approach in their management.[19] The recommendation proposed to connect "elements of the state-centered international law not only to national law and legal institutions, but also to the forces of the market which drives many of the non-state business governance initiatives".[20]

In this context, the business and human rights perspective presents a cross-fertilized approach between the concepts and principles of human rights applicable in relations between states and individuals and those from organizational management; combining a 'goal-based approach', with the deployment of strategies and action plans, with a 'compliance approach', with implementation measures such as impact assessments. Indeed this kind of approach was adopted in 2011 by the UN Human Rights Council as the 'Guiding Principles on Business and Human Rights' (UNGP).[21] The UNGP offers a comprehensive catalogue of measures for states and business organizations to mitigate the negative effects of business on human rights. It echoes in the sporting field, particularly concerning the organization of mega-sporting events, which highlight the dark side of international sport competitions and their governance.[22] Involving a multitude of actors from international sports organizations to local contractors, such events blur the chain of responsibilities; some of these events have involved the expulsion of vulnerable populations and the exploitation of workers (i.e. London 2012 Summer Olympics, Rio 2016 Summer Olympics, FIFA World Cup Qatar 2022). Private sports organizations no longer remain off the radar of human rights defenders. The specific institutional architecture of sports organizations (often a decentralized and pyramidal structure) continues to generate controversy regarding legal status and obligations in terms of human rights.[23]

The comprehensive approach of the UNGP offers a solid way of encouraging sports organizations to commit to human rights.[24] Some of these organizations have followed this path: in 2016, the *Fédération internationale de football association* (FIFA) made such a commitment.[25] The International Olympic Committee (IOC)

[19] Aaranson and Higham (2011), pp. 333–364, spec. 337–345.

[20] Buhmann (2015), pp. 3099–3434, esp. 401.

[21] United Nations, Human rights Council, Resolution n°17/4 Human rights and transnational corporations and other business enterprises, 6 July 2011 (https://documents-dds-ny.un.org/doc/RESOLUTION/GEN/G11/144/71/PDF/G1114471.pdf?OpenElement).

[22] Amis (2017), pp. 135–141.

[23] Di Marco (2022), spec. p. 248.

[24] Schwab (2017), pp. 4–67.

[25] The organization adapted its statutes, hired a human rights manager, developed a human rights policy, and established an independent advisory board. Few years later, the organization took

followed suit in 2017.[26] A coalition of multi-stakeholders of international agencies, governments, sports bodies, and civil society, the Centre for Sport and Human Rights, was launched in 2018 to encourage all sports organizations to find solutions to the questions of applying human rights to the sporting field.[27]

However, the commitments made by international sports organizations to respect the UNGP cannot stand alone. While the UNGP was conceived as a tool to fight against the negative external effects of economic activity on populations, it was not specifically envisaged in terms of relations between sport organizations and individual athletes. It offers a useful perspective for thinking about this relationship, especially when considering the autonomy of sport organizations, but also contains weaknesses inherent in their ontology. This leads us to two separate conclusions: first, the need for athletes to have a territorial connection criterion enabling them to benefit from the classic legal principles and institutions of IHRL; and second, the importance of positive obligations in IHRL for guaranteeing the respect of human rights by private actors.[28]

3 The Swiss Connection of Sports Governing Bodies

The third element that will be explored in this introduction is the connection between the world of sports and public judicial authorities. The argument of the autonomy of the normative system of sports organizations is difficult to resist in the field of human rights. Indeed, as human rights monitoring bodies consider that states have a positive obligation to act to guarantee respect for human rights, it becomes imperative to delineate the criteria for imposing such obligations on sports organizations.

As a reminder, in the area of sports disputes, the CAS,[29] which is based in Lausanne, Switzerland, has primary jurisdiction, but appeal is possible to the FST. Concretely, it means that once the CAS has issued its decision, this is subject to Swiss jurisdiction, which makes it possible to create a link with the jurisdiction of the ECtHR.[30] Article 190 of the Swiss Federal Act on Private International Law notes

another position regarding its institutional commitment in favor of human rights. Nevertheless, some authors highlighted the positive trend. See Alfrey et al. (2022), pp. 311–318.

[26] Grell (2018), pp. 160–169; Ishida and Wada (2017), pp. 145–148.

[27] https://www.sporthumanrights.org/about-us/governance/.

[28] Heerdt and Ronda (2023), pp. 19–64, spec. p. 35.

[29] The question whether this Court is an appropriate body and well equipped to play a role in the protection of human rights is an important question that is dealt in chapter Duval A, Viret M "The Court of Arbitration for Sport under Human Rights Scrutiny: The role of the Swiss Federal Tribunal and the European Court of Human Rights".

[30] See ECtHR, *Semenya v. Switzerland*, § 90: "The Court notes that Switzerland played no part in the adoption of the DSD Regulations, which were issued by the IAAF, an association governed by Monegasque private law. It will therefore focus its examination of the complaints raised by the

that an arbitration decision, whether made by a sports organization or not, may be challenged before the FST, but only in cases determined by the legal provision. This involves, on the one hand, a breach of procedural rules and, on the other, a violation of Swiss public policy. Nevertheless, it must be noted that the FST has developed an extremely restrictive and sometimes rather cryptic interpretation of the notion of public policy. For illustration, in a particular tribunal ruling, it is noted that "a decision is incompatible with public policy if it disregards the essential and widely recognized values which, according to the prevailing conceptions in Switzerland, should form the basis of any legal order".[31] The ruling further states that "an award is contrary to substantive public policy when it violates fundamental principles of substantive law to such an extent that it can no longer be reconciled with the relevant legal order and system of values".[32] It continues: "it is not sufficient that a reason chosen by an arbitral tribunal offends public policy; it is the result to which the award leads that must be incompatible with public policy".[33] Finally, and in a particularly scathing manner, it is stated that "the incompatibility of the award with public policy, as referred to in Art. 190 Para. 2 let. e LPIL, is a more restrictive concept than that of arbitrariness".[34] The annulment of an international arbitral award on this ground of appeal is very rare.[35]

Regarding this right of appeal, the exceedingly narrow understanding of the public policy concept gives rise to concerns regarding the efficacy of the right of appeal to a judicial authority for issues beyond those related to the conduct of arbitration proceedings. The FST has explicitly signaled its intention not to create an avenue of redress beyond the procedural matters previously mentioned, even for individuals resorting to arbitration, including athletes. It should be noted that such an interpretation is not unexpected, given the chronic caseload burdening the FST.

Nevertheless, the ECtHR has already been tasked with adjudicating on the highly restrictive interpretation of public policy of the Swiss tribunal. In its three-judge ruling *Bakker v. Switzerland* in 2019, the European Court emphasized its limited authority in scrutinizing the application of domestic law by national judicial authorities. In this ruling, the Court acknowledged this stringent understanding of public policy while specifying its willingness to intervene if it detected arbitrary or manifestly unreasonable applications of domestic law. Although this interpretation had already raised concerns in *Ali Riza v. Turkey*, where the Court ruled that entrusting arbitration proceedings solely to private entities necessitates ensuring compliance with all aspects of Article 6 of the ECHR, it was deemed contrary to Article

applicant on the question of whether the review carried out by CAS and the Federal Court met the requirements of the Convention".

[31] FST 144 III 120, para. 5.1; FST 132 III 389, para. 2.2.3.

[32] FST 144 III 120, para. 5.1.

[33] FST 144 III 120, para. 5.1.

[34] FST 144 III 120 para. 5.1; judgments 4A_318/2018 of 4 March 2019 para. 4.3.1; 4A_600/2016 of 29 June 2017 para. 1.1.4.

[35] FST 132 III 389, para. 2.1.

13 ECHR in *Semenya v. Switzerland*. In the Semenya case, the Court also determined that "the Federal Court, primarily due to its severely limited review powers, had inadequately addressed the well-substantiated and credible claims, including allegations of discrimination, put forth by the applicant".[36] Consequently, the ECtHR concluded that,

> "in its capacity as a custodian of European public policy [...] the domestic remedies accessible to the applicant, when viewed comprehensively and in light of the specific circumstances of the case, could not be considered effective within the scope of Article 13 of the Convention."[37]

In essence, the Court acknowledged that the litigant was afforded incomplete protection, primarily because the FST adopts an overly narrow interpretation of the concept of public policy, construing it solely in procedural terms and as an exceptional grievance, thus obscuring its potential applicability.

Finally, it should be noted that despite restrictive interpretation of Article 190 of the Swiss Federal Act on Private International Law (which will have to change in light of the *Caster Semenya v. Switzerland* case law), this article does represent an important bridge between private law actors and responsibility for the protection of human rights. Moreover, it is precisely thanks to this type of legal mechanism that arbitration sentences can be brought into the realm of positive law and can then enter the system of conventional protection of human rights, since the ECHR allows appeals against national decisions rendered in the last instance.[38] In accordance with the notion of positive obligation developed in IHRL, states are responsible within their jurisdiction when there are human rights violations by private actors. In this regard, the ECtHR ruled that Switzerland was indeed responsible for human rights violations by the CAS, which makes it clear that the CAS is indirectly obliged to take human rights into account; this opens the possibility of addressing complaints to the ECtHR against Switzerland.

4 Overview of Chapters

The book consists of 11 chapters. Ten chapters were presented and discussed at a workshop held at the University of Lausanne on 30 June 2022. Regarding the key role of the CAS, based in Lausanne, the editors invited **Marjolaine Viret and Antoine Duval** to contribute with a chapter on CAS case law. The call for papers welcomed proposals for contributions adopting doctrinal or socio-legal approaches. The contributions thus reflect the diversity of legal research. Several chapters adopt a descriptive point of view and reveal the underlying ideological logic of power. Others take a normative approach, characteristic of legal dogmatics, and propose

[36] ECtHR, Semenya v. Switzerland, § 201.
[37] ECtHR, Semenya v. Switzerland, § 239.
[38] See ECtHR, Semenya v. Switzerland, § 103–113.

new normative developments. Some focus on the national context, while others examine the scope of international standards and the role of supervisory institutions. The result is a rich mix of contributions that illustrate the complexity of human rights in sports.

The first chapters are dedicated to discrimination and intersectionality, from national and international perspectives. Through several approaches, they investigate the potential and limits of IHRL to protect women athletes. In Chapter "But you're ok…' British South Asians and Regulatory Barriers to Participation in Sport', **Seema Patel** focuses on the regulatory barriers to participation from the perspective of British South Asian athletes in football and cricket. Based on an auto-ethnography, the socio-legal scholar emphasizes the double ambiguity of the law and sport, which act as barriers but are also effective tools for protecting marginalized groups. In Chapter 'Gendered Athletes in Sports: CEDAW's Role in Tackling Heterosexist and Racialized Uniforms in Sports', **Lena Holzer** dives into the Convention on the Elimination of All Forms of Discrimination Against Women (CEDAW) to assess the human rights implications of gendered and racialized clothing regulations. In Chapter '#MeToo, Sport, and Women: Foul, Own Goal, or Touchdown? Online Abuse of Women in Sport as a Contemporary Issue', **Olga Jurasz and Kim Barker** question the role of sport concerning online abuse against women and the limited impact of human rights protections. In Chapter 'Hormonal Eligibility Criteria in Women's Professional Sports Under the ECHR: The Case of Caster Semenya v. Switzerland', **Pieter Cannoot, Cathérine Van de Graaf, Ariël Decoster, Claire Poppelwell-Scevak and Sarah Schoentjes** use the Caster Semenya case for analyzing the hormonal eligibility criteria set by World Athletics in the light of the Articles 14, 3, and 8 ECHR.

The next chapters deal with the issue of nationality and its role in inclusion or exclusion for participation in elite sports. In Chapter 'Filipinos First? Exploring Xenophobia and Its Legal Remedies in Philippine Amateur Basketball', **Joseph Benjamin De Leon** analyzes the discriminatory practices against African student-athletes in Filipino national university competitions despite a series of human rights norms in Philippine law through a newspaper analysis. In Chapter 'Respecting the Right to Nationality in International Sport', **William Thomas Worster** addresses the issue of the right to nationality in international sports, highlighting the contradiction between Olympic regulations and IHRL surrounding nationality.

Chapters 'Athlete Activism at the Olympics: Challenging the Legality of Rule 50 as a Restriction on Freedom of Expression' to 'Freedom of Expression of Athletes and Players: The Current and Potential Role of the European Court of Human Rights as a Watchdog in Sport' are dedicated to the second key issue in this book: the question of freedom of expression for athletes. In this context, **Mark James and Guy Osborn** focus on Rule 50 of the International Olympic Committee, analyzing the provision and its evolution with the 2022 Tokyo Olympic Games in light of freedom of expression, and argue for a complete overhaul of Rule 50 to be compliant with human rights law standards. Chapters 'The Incompatibility of Banning Political Speech in Sports with the Right to Freedom of Expression Under the European Convention on Human Rights' and 'Freedom of Expression of Athletes and Players:

The Current and Potential Role of the European Court of Human Rights as a Watchdog in Sport' address athletes' freedom of expression in the ECtHR context. **H. Burak Gemalmaz** focuses on the context of the Turkish football cases, examining the Turkish authorities' response to the ECtHR's demands. **Daniel Rietiker** investigates the ECtHR's watchdog role in protecting athletes' freedom of expression.

Marjolaine Viret and Antoine Duval analyze how the ECHR has been employed by both the Swiss Federal Tribunal and the European Court of Human Rights to review CAS rulings.

In the final chapter, **Antonio Di Marco** proposes to go beyond current international human rights norms and athletes' perspectives to expand the human rights catalogue by including the right to sport for all. Adopting a conceptual and argumentative approach, the author considers that such a right will guarantee inclusive and non-discriminatory access to sporting activities and enhance the unity of fragmented claims rooted in other human rights, such as the right to participate in cultural life, the right to education, and the right to health.

The editors wish to address their warmest thanks to all of the authors who contributed to this collective book. Special thanks are also due to Doriana Ferreira, who was responsible for the administrative and logistical aspects of the project, and to Mathieu Fasel for his involvement in organizing the workshop. They would also like to thank the Faculty of Law, Criminal Justice and Public Administration at the University of Lausanne for its financial support, which made it possible to organize this international workshop and to publish this book in open access.

References

Aaranson SA, Higham I (2011) Re-righting business: John Ruggie and the struggle to develop international human rights standards for transnational firms. Hum Rights Q 35(2):333–364

Alfrey D, Amis L, Nickelsburg S, Rook W (2022) Candidate City Human Rights Proposal for the 2026 World Cup: the promise of a positive legacy. Bus Hum Rights J 7(2):311–318

Amis L (2017) Mega-sporting events and human rights – a time for more teamwork. Bus Hum Rights J 2(1):135–141

Beutler I (2008) Sport serving development and peace: achieving the goals of the United Nations through sport. Sport Soc 11(4):360

Black J (2001) Decentering regulation: understanding the role of regulation and self-regulation in a 'post-regulator world'. Curr Leg Probl:126

Boykoff J (2017) Protest, activism, and the Olympic games: an overview of key issues and iconic moments. Int J Hist Sport 34(3–4):162

Buhmann K (2015) Business and human rights: understanding the UN Guiding Principles from the perspective of transnational business governance interactions. Transnatl Leg Theory 6(2): 3099–3434

Carroll AB (2009) A history of corporate social responsibility: concepts and practices. In: Crane A (ed) The Oxford handbook of corporate social responsibility. Oxford University Press, Oxford, pp 19–46

Cotterell R (2012) What is transnational law? Law Soc Inq 37(2):500–524

Di Marco A (2022) Human rights in the Olympic movement: the application of international and European standards to the lex sportive. Neth Q Hum Rights:244–268
Duval A (2021) Transnational sports law: the living Lex Sportiva. In: Zumbansen P (ed) The Oxford handbook of transnational law. Oxford University Press, Oxford, pp 493–512
Grell T (2018) The International Olympic Committee and human rights reforms: game changer or mere window dressing. Int Sports Law J 17:160–169
Halliday TC, Schaffer G (eds) (2015) Transnational legal orders. Cambridge University Press
Heerdt D, Ronda L (2023) Lessons learned in Qatar: the role of the Netherlands and its business in addressing human rights abuses in mega-sporting events. Neth Int Law Rev:19–64
Hums MA, Moorman AM, Wolff EA (2009) Emerging disability rights in sport: sport as a human right for persons with disabilities and the 2006 UN convention on the rights of persons with disabilities. Cambr Law Rev 40:36–48
Ishida H, Wada H (2017) The implementation of the UN Guiding Principles into Daily Business Operations and the 2020 Tokyo Olympic ad Paralympic Games. Bus Hum Rights J 2(1): 145–148
Schwab B (2017) When we know better, we do better. Embedding the human rights of players as a prerequisite to the legitimacy of Lex Sportiva and sport's justice system. Md J Int Law 32:4–67
Schwab B (2018) Embedding the human rights of players in world sport. Int Sports Law J 17:214–232

Véronique Boillet is a professor of public law at the Law School of the University of Lausanne. She was previously a lawyer at the Lausanne's Bar (2011–2013) and has just been elected to the Board of the Swiss Institution for Human Rights (2023–2027). As a scholar, she has in-depth knowledge of the European and Swiss constitutional system, which she has been teaching since 2010 and which she has analyzed in several contributions published in leading European and Swiss law journals. Her current research focuses on the link between human rights and the environment, and on the principle of non-discrimination.

Sophie Weerts is an associate professor of public law at the Swiss Graduate School of Public Administration, University of Lausanne. She holds a PhD in law from the University of Louvain and has a background in law and ethics. Sophie was previously a visiting professor at the University of Geneva and the University of St-Louis-Brussels and a lecturer at the University of Neuchâtel and the University of Louvain (Uclouvain). She practiced law for several years at the Brussels bar and worked as an expert for the federal government. Her research lies at the crossroads of legal theory, constitutional law, and European law. She is currently focusing on issues relating to digital transformation and its impact on public law. In this context, she is particularly interested in the business and human rights field for regulating the digital sector.

Andreas R. Ziegler is currently a Professor of International Law at the University of Lausanne and Director of its LLM Program in International Business Law. He holds a conjoint professorship at the Law School of the University of New South Wales (Sydney, Australia) as well as visiting appointments at the Universities of St. Gallen and of the Saarland (Saarbrücken) as well as ETH Zurich and the Geneva Academy. Previously he was a civil servant working for several Swiss Ministries (Foreign Affairs, Trade) and international organizations (EFTA, EU). He has widely published on Swiss, international and European law (including "Swiss LGBT Law", 2nd edn. 2017) and regularly advises Governments, International Organizations, NGOs and private clients and has represented them before various domestic and international courts and arbitral tribunals. He is on the permanent roster of panelists of the WTO and a Member of the European Commission of Sexual Orientation Law (ECSOL). He is the President of the Swiss Chapter of the International Law Association (ILA) and on the Board of the Swiss and the German Societies of International Law and the European Law Faculties Association—ELFA). He founded and manages the blog "sogiesc.law.blog" on international and comparative SOGIESC law.

‘But you’re ok…’ British South Asians and Regulatory Barriers to Participation in Sport

Seema Patel

Contents

Abstract This chapter employs ethnographical research to examine the regulatory barriers to participation in the particular context of British South Asian athletes in sport. Recent racial tensions in English cricket have not only raised important regulatory questions about addressing discrimination and inequality in sport and beyond, but also emphasizes the limited coverage of British South Asian voices in sport. Adopting an ethnographic approach, this chapter centralizes the author’s lived experiences as a British South Asian female, to evaluate their intersectional identity. Alongside this, with two decades of academic research into discrimination in sport, the chapter provides a British South Asian academic view on the role of the law and sport regulation as both a barrier and an effective tool for the protection of marginalized groups in sport. Although it may be difficult to shift entrenched societal thinking about race, the chapter argues for a holistic collaboration between law and regulation, government, sport and society to apply pressure, alter behavior, and create conditions for effective anti-racism reforms. Change can also be achieved

The author is a member of the Cricket Disciplinary Commission (CDC).

The author would like to thank the editorial team and the attendees of the Sport and Human Rights workshop hosted by the University of Lausanne for their guidance on this chapter.

S. Patel (✉)
Nottingham Law School, Nottingham Trent University, Nottingham, England, UK
e-mail: seema.patel02@ntu.ac.uk

V. Boillet et al. (eds.), *Sports and Human Rights*, Interdisciplinary Studies in Human Rights 10, https://doi.org/10.1007/978-3-031-56452-9_2

through improved engagement with ethnographic research in law to better understand intersectional identity and the true impact of law and regulation upon marginalized individuals and groups.

1 Introduction[1]

Racial tensions in English cricket have recently been at the center of global attention following allegations of systemic racism in the sport.[2] The collision of three key developments has increased the focus on English cricket. Firstly, following the murder of George Floyd in 2020, there has been a global transformation of anti-racism movements and unified condemnation of racial discrimination. Sport has been significantly impacted by this uprising and athlete activism has intensified,[3] with increased pressure on sports governing bodies to eradicate racism through effective regulation and sanctioning. Secondly, tensions between inclusion and exclusion in sport are at their highest, particularly in the areas of marginalized athletes' rights, player welfare and well-being.[4] The capacity of sports bodies to adequately protect athletes and recognize human rights is under scrutiny. Thirdly, sports with long and complicated histories, such as cricket, are being challenged by the trend towards confronting rights and embracing diversity. English cricket has a close relationship with racism and discrimination, and is a site of exclusivity where the friction between race, gender and class has long served to distinguish between English white males and 'others'.[5] Cricket is heavily associated with its colonial origins and seeks to preserve the imagery and values of traditional 'Englishness', even where the modern game has shifted and evolved.

The global developments in anti-racism, shortfalls in the protection of athletes' rights, and the antiquated practices within English cricket, reached a crisis point in September 2020. Former professional South Asian cricketer Azeem Rafiq claimed that he experienced racial abuse during his time at the Yorkshire County Cricket Club (YCCC), one of the most historic and successful English county cricket teams. The allegations received international public attention and led to a series of responses, including counter allegations, a formal investigation by YCCC, legal proceedings, a parliamentary inquiry, the commencement of disciplinary

[1] This paper was finalised before the publication of the Independent Commission for Equity in Cricket (ICEC) Report in June 2023.

[2] Burnton S (2023) Azeem Rafiq and Yorkshire: timeline of a county cricket crisis. The Guardian, 31 March 2023, https://www.theguardian.com/sport/2023/mar/31/azeem-rafiq-and-yorkshire-timeline-of-a-county-cricket-crisis (last accessed 4 Jan 2023).

[3] See James M, Osborn G chapter in this book 'Athlete Activism at the Olympics: Challenging the legality of Rule 50 as a restriction on freedom of expression'.

[4] Patel (2021).

[5] Fletcher (2011).

proceedings by the England and Wales and Cricket Board (ECB), and finally a comprehensive scrutiny of inclusion and exclusion across cricket.[6]

Alongside conflicts between race, class, culture, and identity, this matter exposed key concerns about the relatively low representation of British South Asian athletes (those with Indian, Pakistani, Sri Lankan and Bangladeshi heritage, consistent with the literature)[7] in sport; a minority group that shares a symbolic yet difficult past with Englishness, the British Empire, national identity, and English cricket. The voices of British South Asian athletes represent a largely unheard perspective where the intersection between race, class, gender, culture, identity, and stereotyping manifests itself. Significant academic progress has been made using oral testimonies of British South Asians to illuminate their exclusion and underrepresentation in football and cricket,[8] but it must be noted that these largely focus on male athletes, with far less research into intersectional distinctions and the lived experiences of minority groups.[9] In response to this lacuna in the literature, this chapter combines law and ethnographic research to incorporate the author's personal stories in sport and social circles as a British South Asian female.[10] The author's intersectional perspective on gender and race offer a unique blend of both academic knowledge and personal experience.[11] Ethnographic research is employed here to emphasize the self-reflexive position of the researcher.[12] While there is of course limitations and challenges inherent in a research method grounded in personal experience,[13] it offers useful insights into this particular topic. To gain fresh insight, it is necessary to utilize the author's voice and consider less conventional ways of conducting legal research.

The title of the chapter reflects my experience growing up in predominantly 'white' communities where British Indians were a minority. Whilst my school days were largely pleasant, on certain occasions my inclusion into social circles and groups was legitimated on the condition that 'I hate Paki's, but you're ok Seema'. The term 'Paki' originates from the word Pakistani, and is commonly used in a derogatory and racist context to refer to individuals of Asian origin, regardless of background. This chapter will use this complex social context of conditional inclusion and 'honorary white' status,[14] to review the relationship

[6]Burnton S (2023) Azeem Rafiq and Yorkshire: timeline of a county cricket crisis. The Guardian, 31 March 2023, https://www.theguardian.com/sport/2023/mar/31/azeem-rafiq-and-yorkshire-timeline-of-a-county-cricket-crisis (last accessed 4 Jan 2023).

[7]Brown et al. (2021).

[8]Kilvington (2019); Bains and Johal (1998); Burdsey (2021); Lawless and Magrath (2021); Fletcher (2011, 2012).

[9]Ratna and Samie (2018); Ratna (2013).

[10]See Ratna and Samie (2018).

[11]Ratna (2013).

[12]Simmons and Feldman (2018); Pearson (2012), Chapter 1.

[13]Simmons and Feldman (2018); Burdsey (2021), p. 19.

[14]Garland and Chakraborti in Chakraborti and Garland (2004), p. 122.

between law/regulatory institutions and the individual/group, and the impact of legal/regulatory frameworks on my treatment.[15]

This chapter examines the role of law and sport regulation to assess whether it operates as an effective tool or ineffective regulatory barrier for combating race discrimination in sport. From this legal view, it will map out the legal framework that purports to guarantee equality, non-discrimination, and human rights. The framework will then be critiqued to assess its role in overcoming race discrimination in sport and offering a solution to the forms of discriminatory practices that I have personally experienced. Ethnographic research will be used to interrogate the rigid academic legal research and to better understand the true influence of law and regulation upon intersectional identity.

2 Race and Cricket

Differential treatment on the basis of race is systemic within society. A multitude of natural and environmentally-driven physical and non-physical similarities and differences distinguish our appearance and character, such as skin color, geographical location and environment, religion and culture, belief systems and practices, language and behavior. However, explanations for our differences are often entangled and begin to lack a real basis when described using over-generalized, misguided or even false assumptions about entire populations.[16] Biological and cultural notions of our differences become stretched and blurred to construct linear racial categories, which result in disparate treatments in the shape of racism or racial abuse.[17] Overt racial abuse isolates and excludes a specific group or community, with dangerous and harmful undertones. This may take place on an everyday level, through use of language or behavior between people, or institutionally, through structures and ideologies.[18] Racial thinking, which relates to the foundation upon which a racist act takes place, then "creates, organizes and sustains unequal power relationships between human groups along racial lines".[19]

Whilst overt racism may no longer be accepted in many societies, contemporary forms of race discrimination are surfacing in a range of alternative formats, and operating in a covert, less detectable manner.[20] For instance, racial microaggressions may be expressed subtly and unconsciously through day-to-day brief gestures, attitudes, glances or jokes.[21] 'Banter' refers to an exchange of jovial comments

[15] Griffiths (2017); Bens and Vetters (2018).

[16] Patel (2015).

[17] Patel (2015).

[18] Hylton (2010), p. 350.

[19] Collins (2022), p. 96.

[20] Burdsey (2021), pp. 11, 58; Patel (2015).

[21] Burdsey (2011), p. 268.

that may incorporate racist language and can be both offensive and inclusive.[22] Such behavior is excused on the basis that no harm is intended because it is a joke, but it can also act as a significant barrier to inclusion and acceptance. As the nature of racism mutates, there are indistinct shades of racism and inclusion/exclusion that function across a spectrum rather than as a binary.[23]

In 2020, the murder of George Floyd in Minneapolis, USA, ignited a wave of global activism and led to an explosion in conversations about modern experiences of overt and covert racial discrimination. Opposition to police brutality and racism united communities to participate in anti-racism demonstrations and form alliances around the Black Lives Matter movement. Most areas of society have been inspired by this public attack on racism, discrimination, and inequality, with a subtle shift towards celebrating and valuing difference.[24] The protests prompted a wider re-evaluation of the colonial history of various institutions and structures and how they may fuel racial disparity.[25]

Sport is no exception; it is a construct held together by its own structures that are soaked in traditional and long-standing values, with clear divisions between who can and cannot access the territory. Each sport carries with it its own exclusive cultural space and emotional expression, which has evolved to become its recognized heritage and charter of who is permitted to enter the dominant culture. It also reproduces ideologies and practices concerning race and difference, and is a site where racial biases are both expressed and challenged. Marginalized groups are forced to assimilate, often at the cost of their heritage. Consequently, racism and exclusion is a common and complex feature of sport,[26] which has created overt and covert barriers to participation for athletes, coaches, supporters and management staff, particularly where these traditional customs have not progressed, or where there is a denial of the existence of racism in sport.

English cricket is distinct from other English sports. It is deeply attached to its colonial past, and still treated as a quintessential English activity that preserves the imagery of the English countryside, as well as gentlemanly, white upper- and middle-class values.[27] Its notion of 'Englishness' is uniquely portrayed in literature, art and film, but has generated very specific conflicts when considering race, class, gender and discrimination. Historically played by wealthy aristocrats and in 'public schools' (i.e. fee-charging private schools), cricket spread throughout the British Empire and came to be shared by non-white participants, bringing together nations and classes. It is a popular sport in many countries, notably the West Indies and the Indian subcontinent. Throughout its journey, cricket showcased English authority,

[22] Lawless and Magrath (2021), p. 1496.

[23] Burdsey (2011), p. 268.

[24] Bekker et al. (2023).

[25] Selwyn (2019).

[26] Burdsey (2011).

[27] Greenfield and Osborn (1996).

identity, values and morals, which only strengthened as the sport expanded.[28] Although cricket unified the Empire, the essence of Englishness and sameness remained firmly intact, with disregard for other cultures and a possessive dominance over who plays the game and how it is played. There has always been a clear demarcation between the English and the outsiders with strict class, race and professional/amateur segregation.[29] Race and class prejudice is entrenched within the traditional foundation of the sport, and this has created friction for ethnic minority communities in post-colonial Britain who seek access and inclusion.

As society has become more diverse, the notion of English identity has come under threat, and has taken on an entirely different meaning in a modern Britain. The sport has transformed globally, with increased finance and authority afforded to other nations such as India, where cricket is even more popular than it is in England. With the overwhelming success of the Indian Premier League (IPL), India has become a cricket superpower. The shift of control is further illustrated by the transfer of the International Cricket Council (ICC) headquarters from Lord's Cricket Ground in London to Dubai.[30] There are encouraging adaptations to the varied formats of the game, with the introduction of the more accessible The Hundred.[31] The seemingly diverse nature of cricket, with highly visible non-white players, has led some to believe that cricket is a well-integrated sport, with no discrimination. However, the literature widely details the prevalence of racism and barriers to participation for marginalized groups in cricket, and this chapter argues that there has been a silent tolerance of racism amongst the senior members of cricket governance which has contributed to a denial of its existence.[32] There remains an underlying reluctance to modernize, and the legacy of the British Empire with an emphasis on 'Englishness' continues to haunt the game.

English cricket is currently embroiled in serious accusations of failing to address deep institutional inequities. Key conversations around the 'racial status quo'[33] of English cricket and its position in modern society began with a passionate contribution from retired West Indian cricketer and commentator Michael Holding, who shared his feelings on the mistreatment of non-white players. This attached cricket to the broader dialogue on racism taking place. Allegations of racist comments by high-profile cricketers received heightened public scrutiny,[34] and the ECB formed an Independent Commission for Equity in Cricket (ICEC) in 2020 to identify actions to address race, class and gender-based discrimination in the sport.

Exclusionary practices in cricket were further exposed in September 2020, when former professional cricketer Azeem Rafiq spoke publicly about his experience of

[28] Fletcher (2011).

[29] Collins (2022); Simons (1996).

[30] Fletcher (2011), p. 26.

[31] Fletcher et al. (2021).

[32] Burdsey (2011); Marqusee (1995); Nicholson in Ratna and Samie (2018), p. 130.

[33] Fletcher (2011), p. 23.

[34] Berkson (2021).

institutional racism during his career at YCCC.[35] This brought international attention to discrimination in cricket. Rafiq was born in Pakistan and has lived in England since he was 10 years old. He was one of a handful of British South Asian players at YCCC and expressed that he was close to taking his life because of the constant racist abuse he received about his Pakistani heritage. He detailed how he was frequently referred to as a 'Paki.' The location of this episode at YCCC is profound because of its status in English cricket history. As one of the most successful English cricket teams, cricket embodies Yorkshire identity. However, it is considered to be an 'insular' region that is troubled with historical racial difference and divide, particularly with South Asian communities.[36] Resistance to diversity is evidenced by previous racist incidents reported at the regional grounds,[37] and the institution of the YCCC birthright policy, in which only players born within the county were eligible to represent YCCC. Whilst such exclusionary rules were abandoned by other teams, YCCC insisted on the eligibility rule until 1992, which may have acted as a barrier to participation for ethnic minority players. Although the visibility of ethnic minority players at YCCC has improved, with the implementation of some inclusion strategies such as the Black and Ethnic Minority Cricket Forum in 1993,[38] and structural overhauls, the adequacy of these efforts to address systemic and subtle racism was under investigation at the time of writing.

In response to Rafiq's statement several events took place. First, in August 2021 YCCC completed a formal investigation and upheld some of the allegations but concluded that there was insufficient evidence to confirm that the club was 'institutionally racist', with no disciplinary action taken. Rafiq settled an employment tribunal case with YCCC in November 2021. In the same month, a Parliamentary Select Committee was convened to hear testimony from Rafiq about his racial abuse, with a follow-up in December 2022. In its findings, the Digital, Culture, Media and Sport (DCMS) Select Committee found evidence of 'deep-seated' racism in cricket and urged the Government to restrict public funding until there was demonstrable improvement in the game.[39] In June 2022, the ECB commenced disciplinary proceedings against seven players and the YCCC for alleged breaches of ECB Directive 3.3, which concerns conduct that may be prejudicial to the interests of cricket, or that brings the game into disrepute. The case was referred to the Cricket Disciplinary Commission (CDC) and a public hearing took place in March 2023. The YCCC admitted a failure to address the systemic use of racist and/or discriminatory language over a prolonged period and a failure to take adequate action in respect

[35] BBC, Azeem Rafiq: What England's cricket racism scandal is all about, 19 November 2021, https://www.bbc.co.uk/news/world-59316567 (last accessed 1 April 2023).

[36] Fletcher (2011); Fletcher (2012), p. 227; Fletcher and Swain (2016).

[37] Fletcher (2012).

[38] Fletcher (2011), p. 29.

[39] UK Parliament, Racism in Cricket, 14 January 2022, https://publications.parliament.uk/pa/cm5802/cmselect/cmcumeds/1001/report.html (last accessed 10 March 2023).

of allegations of racist and/or discriminatory behavior. The CDC judgment on the liability of each party is outlined elsewhere.[40]

The CDC Panel addressed the specific ECB charges brought before it. Beyond that, the case more widely offers valuable insights into the operation and function of internal sport disciplinary processes and its ability to effectively deal with discrimination matters. Sport is at a critical moment of reckoning in relation to the defense of marginalized rights, with more focus on the responsibility of sports governing bodies to eradicate racism through meaningful regulation and sanctioning, and with closer connection between political, social, legal and regulatory considerations.[41]

3 British South Asians

Alongside conflicts between race, class, culture, and identity, the episode raises prominent concerns about the exclusion of British South Asian athletes, a minority group who share a symbolic yet intricate history with Englishness, the British Empire, national identity, and English cricket.[42] The migration of the South Asian population in the UK mostly took place in the 1940s and they were both present and absent from British industry and culture.[43] Integration into the country was difficult for South Asians, who were perceived as a threat to Englishness and were often treated with hostility.[44] Although they made a positive impact and influence in some areas of British society, they have been subject to discrimination and exclusion in other aspects of a predominantly white culture, including sport. Quantitative research suggests that British South Asian participation and representation in English sports are generally lower than other groups, particularly for South Asian women.[45]

During the migration period, sport played an important role within South Asian communities. Cricket facilitated integration, cohesion and cultural mixing, signifying a common ground between migrants and established communities.[46] Cricket was a familiar and comforting setting for South Asian migrants which assisted with their settlement in a foreign land, and this enthusiasm for the sport has transferred to second- and third-generation British South Asians. A number of studies have

[40] England and Wales Cricket Board (ECB), ECB responds to Yorkshire Cricket Discipline Commission decisions, 31 March 2023, https://www.ecb.co.uk/news/3125588/ecb-responds-to-yorkshire-cricket-discipline-commission-decision (last accessed 10 April 2023).

[41] Patel (2021); Patel in Witcomb and Peel (2022).

[42] Burdsey (2011), p. 364.

[43] Burdsey (2011), p. 364.

[44] Burdsey (2013).

[45] Gov.UK, Physical Activity, 14 July 2022, https://www.ethnicity-facts-figures.service.gov.uk/health/diet-and-exercise/physical-activity/latest (last accessed 10 March 2023); Berkson (2021).

[46] Fletcher (2011).

identified a steady growth in British South Asian participation in English cricket, with an increased proportion playing cricket compared to the 7% population.[47] A small number of British South Asian cricket players, such as Monty Panesar, have successfully represented England, altering the identity of English cricket. Investigations have in fact revealed an over-representation of British South Asians at the youth level and in informal cricket settings, but a reverse effect at the formal and professional level.[48] One study found socioeconomic and racial biases in cricket, mostly favoring privately educated and white cricketers over British South Asian cricketers at both the youth and professional level.[49] There is also far less diversity and representation in the coaching, management, and governance realms of cricket.[50] Similarly, although the modern England football team may exemplify a new multicultural Britain, only a few British South Asians have competed in professional football. This is at odds with the popularity and importance of football within the British South Asian community and their success at a recreational and amateur level.[51] It is asserted that their marginalization is indicative of exclusion rather than under-representation, with consistent evidence of racism within the structure, culture and institution of football and with common critiques of the (in)-action taken to overcome this.[52]

Despite the presence of some British South Asian cricketers in English cricket, their overall invisibility is somewhat of a conundrum. In formulating a qualitative justification for potential barriers to sport, several lifestyle and personal preferences are attributed to the low participation rates, as well as wider structural constraints relating to income and wealth, working patterns, access to facilities, lack of role models, exclusion from attending sport events, language, culture, religion and racism.[53] English cricket organizations and scouts have been criticized for failing to seek out non-white talent, with racial barriers uncovered in the talent systems and at the grassroot level.[54] Research confirms that although cricket on its face displays a diverse pool of home and overseas players, those statistics are inconsistent with the experience of exclusion, unfair treatment and discrimination amongst ethnic minorities in sport.[55]

Contentious assumptions and myths about British South Asians also rationalize their overt and covert exclusion such as their physical unsuitability to sport, parent

[47] Fletcher et al. (2021), p. 1475; See Kilvington (2019).

[48] Brown et al. (2021); Burdsey (2011).

[49] Brown et al. (2021).

[50] Fletcher et al. (2021), p. 1476; Rankin-Wright and Norman in Ratna and Samie (2018), p. 204.

[51] Kilvington (2019).

[52] Burdsey (2021), p. 11; Fletcher (2011); Kilvington (2019); Bains and Patel (1996); Bains and Johal (1998); Hylton et al. (2015a, b).

[53] Fletcher and Swain (2016); Patel (2015); Hylton et al. (2015a, b); Brown et al. (2021).

[54] Fletcher (2011), p. 29; Fletcher et al. (2021), p. 1487; Burdsey (2011); Hylton et al. (2015a, b); Berkson (2021); Kilvington (2019).

[55] Burdsey (2011).

influence on education, diet and nutrition. The implication that particular races are naturally better suited to certain sports contributes towards pockets of over- and under-representation in sport. Asian cricketers have been characterized as aggressive, cheats, unintelligent and irrational, which is considered incompatible with the style and substance of the English game.[56] Research implies that varied playing styles are characterized and valued according to ethnicity.[57] These theories about differences between race, gender and culture have fueled further divides between English superiority and the 'other', and makes it more difficult to address the true inequalities at work.[58]

The colonial exclusion has had a lasting impact upon cricket and the perceived white exclusivity of the game. Consequently, all Asian teams and leagues have been established in cricket and football, separate to the mainstream structure. These have strengthened the British South Asian identity and provided a valuable space for players to reimagine cricket by participating in new and unorthodox styles away from the formal settings.[59] Breakaway leagues and teams have also been used as a means of asserting British South Asian identity, challenging the racial status quo and actively distinguishing themselves from the traditional Englishness of cricket. Although this is a positive opportunity for ethnic minority communities, it has fragmented cricket to some extent, and is not necessarily the solution to defeating racism in mainstream sport.[60]

There are several conscious and unconscious practices that, when combined, may act as exclusionary barriers for British South Asians in sport.[61] However, additional research is required to ensure that quantitative statistics, which can be misleading and limited in terms of intersectional data, are supported by qualitative data that examines the drivers behind over- and under-representation in cricket.[62] For instance, the voices of British South Asian athletes, particularly females, are rarely examined.[63] The Rafiq testimony emphasizes an absence of British South Asians speaking out about their experiences in sport and influencing anti-racism agendas. Minority groups have expressed that they avoid communicating about the racist treatment they face because they have little faith that their complaint will be dealt with, and they understand the risk of being labelled a troublemaker if they speak out.[64] With relatively little known about the experiences of British South Asians in sport the current cricket case and the academic literature highlights a pressing need

[56] Fletcher (2011), p. 19; Fletcher (2012), p. 236.

[57] Fletcher (2011), p. 28.

[58] Nicholson in Ratna and Samie (2018), p. 131; Ratna (2013).

[59] Fletcher (2011), p. 25.

[60] Fletcher (2011), p. 27; Malcolm (2002).

[61] Fletcher et al. (2021), p. 1477.

[62] Brown et al. (2021); Randwaha and Burdsey in Carter et al. (2018).

[63] Burdsey (2021), p. 59.

[64] Burdsey (2011).

for the development of an open environment where minority voices can be heard and used to inform future studies.

4 Lived Experience

This section seeks to remedy this gap in the field by using my lived experiences as a prism through which to explore British South Asian identity. Research into female experiences within sport has been largely neglected, with female cricketers rarely referred to in historical accounts of English cricket.[65] Although some valuable research exists in the field,[66] the participation and voices of British Indian women in sport is an overlooked area that is situated within a blurred economic, political and ideological framework of race and gender intersectionality. Whilst my experiences are by no means a representation of every British Indian female, it is critical that we interrogate intersectional lived experiences and reflect upon personal accounts in order to construct a better understanding of the relationship between gender and race within sport and regulation, and to foster alternative ways of researching law. Ethnographic research in this way is also valuable to intimately examine marginalized groups who have been generalized as the 'other' through linear and homogenous categories.[67]

I was born in Luton, which is situated in the Southeast of England. My parents were both born in India and moved to Luton in the 1970s following their arranged marriage. My older sister and I were raised as Hindu but were brought up in a very open environment. There is a perception that South Asian parents are concerned about culture safety, in other words, putting their children into British cultural positions that may threaten their Eastern values. I did not experience any such pressures, quite the opposite in fact; my parents placed me and my sister in situations where we were encouraged to integrate into the more dominant communities. For instance, we attended youth scout groups such as the Brownies and Guides, theatre school, and even went to Church every Sunday. Rather than for religious purposes this was a means of creating a sense of belonging to a community, which we achieved for the most part. As a result, I had a very happy, diverse and multicultural upbringing.

In the 1980s and 1990s, the culture in our area was predominantly white. In fact, I believe that we were the only Indian family on our street at the time. When I began school, I recall being a minority amongst my mostly white friends, but it never presented itself as an issue on the surface. I always felt very included. It was only when I got to secondary school that I became more aware of the impact of my color

[65] Nicholson in Ratna and Samie (2018), p. 126.

[66] Scraton et al. (2005); Ratna and Samie (2018), pp. 23, 119; Randhawa in Burdsey (2011); Mirza (2003), p. 121.

[67] Rana in Ratna and Samie (2018), p. 149; Randwaha and Burdsey in Carter et al. (2018), p. 160.

and difference on others. On various occasions, close friends in my social circles would say, 'I hate Paki's, but you're OK Seema'. This challenged whether I ever really was 'included' in the dominant culture. The racist slang term 'Paki' originates from the word Pakistani, and is commonly used in a derogatory and racist context to refer to all individuals of Asian origin, regardless of background. Essentially, it goes against everything that my parents tried to do for me. The statement reflects a type of conditional 'honorary white'[68] inclusion into a group, which operated in an exclusionary way. These references led me to hide my differences in order to assimilate and fit in with my friends.

Growing up in an Indian family, set amongst a predominantly Western community, sometimes proved a challenge for me as I felt I had a double identity. For instance, during my confused teenage years, I recall being embarrassed to have to wear Asian dress when attending a wedding or religious Hindu functions. I was never ashamed of who I was, but instead was concerned with how I may have been judged as the 'other' by my friends. The prevailing culture had a destructive impact on my own identity as I felt the need to 'trade off' my differences and background, in order to be included into British social structures such as sport. This led me consciously and unconsciously to distance myself from my family roots and drift between two cultures. British South Asian individuals are considered to be in conflict with their parents' ideals and their own religious practices and beliefs, which are said to affect participation in activities such as sport.[69] My parents were largely supportive of my pursuits, but I do recall some conflicts with my father about my strong allegiance to the England football team during international tournaments. Because of the color of my skin I did feel that I needed to shout louder to demonstrate my support for England.

British South Asian identity and national identity was previously scrutinized under the infamous 'Norman Tebbit Test' which questioned the support of British South Asian fans amidst concerns that cricket no longer belonged to the English or rather, England no longer belonged to the English in the 1990s. In 2001, former England captain Nasser Hussain questioned the national loyalty of British South Asian supporters.[70] British writer Robert Henderson's argument that England cricket players who were born abroad were less likely to want England to win, further perpetuated biological assumptions.[71] Henderson was widely challenged and the criticism prompted some anti-racism action in cricket.[72] Such statements fail to realize that supporting the national team of your ancestral homeland, is a means of

[68] Iftekhar R, The rebel tours: When black cricketers were awarded 'Honorary White' status, The Business Standard, 21 April 2020, https://www.tbsnews.net/sports/rebel-tours-when-black-cricketers-were-awarded-honorary-white-status-71989 (last accessed 1 April 2023).

[69] Valiotis (2009), p. 1792.

[70] Chaudhary V, A Question of Support, The Guardian 29 May 2001, https://www.theguardian.com/uk/2001/may/29/race.world (last accessed 1 April 2023).

[71] Henderson (1995).

[72] Greenfield and Osborn (1997).

reclaiming your heritage that, as a child, I dismissed in many ways in an attempt to be accepted. As a cricket fan my support for England and India is always split. I was aware that my identity is surrounded by stereotypical assumptions and pockets of cultural ignorance that make me question my inclusion when playing on a pitch or watching sport in a pub. I have always considered whether I have to pigeonhole my identity or compromise one culture over the other in order to assimilate with the dominant group.

Throughout the process of trying to fit in, I have encountered many instances of overt racial abuse growing up as a British Indian female in England, with the 'go back to your own country' and 'where are you really from' rhetoric firmly embedded within my memory. In my friendship groups at school, I also became accustomed to the covert banter relating to my Indian heritage, with little confidence to confront those who offended me. I am guilty of downplaying the jokes and ignoring them at times.[73] I did feel very alone trying to figure all of this out and although there were occasions where people would try to defend me, I realize now that it was not enough, and many were silent. My most heart-breaking moments as a child were witnessing my parents being racially abused and feeling completely helpless and confused. Those flashbacks hurt more than pebbles being thrown at my head at an English seaside, and I hope that my son will never have to endure such pain.

Some of these moments were aggressive, some ignorant, some from strangers, some from close friends. For better or worse, these critical moments have shaped my personality, my confidence and in my later years my parenting. My mistreatment on the basis of my race has prompted me to consider how I am truly perceived and to what extent the conditionally inclusive expression of 'but you're ok' has again determined my integration and acceptance. One of my early obsessions was sport, particularly football and cricket. I have played both ever since I was a child, but only ever with male friends on the school fields, in the park, or indoors. I was always the only female when I played and was considered 'quite good for a girl'. In parallel, I was often labelled as 'quite pretty for an Indian', which demonstrates the intersectional and conditional nature of my treatment.

At college I played for a football team and was one of three British Indian females. Our coach was a British Muslim male and we competed in a male college league. Interestingly, the teams were broadly diverse, with a range of ethnic backgrounds represented. We were only ever confronted with issues of gender but also gained a sense of respect when we played and were able to hold our own against boys. I was never very conscious of my color but I do recall being subject to racial slurs during those matches, targeted for being Indian.

My passion for cricket stems from my father; some of my fondest childhood memories include watching traditional four to five-day test cricket matches with him on television during the summer holidays. Fatherly influence on young females playing cricket is documented in other research.[74] Around the start of the 2009

[73]Burdsey (2011).

[74]Malcolm and Velija (2008).

cricket season, I joined a village women's cricket team. They were a relatively new side, looking to develop and establish themselves. My time there was illuminating. Aside from improving my ability through dedicated coaching and practice, I also encountered personal experiences that are significant to my academic research and that highlighted the struggle for acceptance as a female competing in cricket. Two incidents are notable. During a training session, I was bowling to a much younger girl than me, who was batting in the nets. She picked out my delivery very well and made a clean stroke that would have travelled to the boundary for four runs if we had been on a pitch. Instead, the ball got stuck at the top of the net and we struggled to retrieve it because it was so high above us. A senior figure, possibly a coach of the boys' team but nevertheless a clearly established member of the village club, approached us and told the young girl who was batting, 'How did you get the ball up there? That's not how you play cricket; it should be played on the ground'. He then walked away without attempting to assist us. The young girl seemed very upset and embarrassed by this comment. I tried to reassure her that she had played a very good shot.

On another occasion the women's team were training in the nets as we did every Sunday morning. A young boy asked his father if he could bowl in our net. The father immediately advised his son, 'Of course you can bowl in their lane, anyone can play if they want to', without asking for our permission. Our female coach then informed him that we were actually having a training session and his son could not join us. The father questioned this and appeared confused.

These incidents highlight some of the tensions that exist in female sports participation. While women's sport has dramatically advanced to achieve an important status of equality between men and women, mistreatment continues to be driven by traditional cultural and gender-based inequalities that can alienate girls and women rather than encourage them. My experiences are clearly a reflection of our team's position as 'outsiders' in this male space. We trained every Sunday morning on the village ground but would have to find an alternative place if there was a men's fixture. The alternative grounds were usually far way, in the middle of nowhere, with no formal access for us. In order to obtain entry, we had to climb over locked gates. On one occasion our training was interrupted by three men and a dog who forced us to move to a small area of the field because they wished to play a leisurely game of croquet on the pitch. Incidentally, they entered the space with a key to unlock the gate.

I was the only British Indian female on the team but I have found myself in that marginal position in many employment and leisure situations. I could say that throughout my life I have been met with both racism and sexism. This intersectional overlap has restricted access to sport for some South Asian women, with the traditional stereotype of being 'academic but not sporting' usually attached. They have been regarded as passive, experiencing difficulties in physical education because they are considered small and frail. Such attitudes have potentially limited their sport pursuits and their presence in the sport space.[75]

My account is my journey and my truth but certainly not a representation of all British South Asian women, who are a diverse, dynamic and heterogenous group.[76] That said, it does contribute to the limited field and offer some insight into my experiences of the many shades of inclusion and exclusion. I have spoken about a series of isolated events in my sporting experiences that are reflective of wider barriers to my integration in society generally. I have revealed how I negotiated my inclusion into those spaces and switched between an insider or outsider. I did have the opportunity to compete in sport and feel a sense of belonging, albeit under the conditional guise of 'but you're ok'. Sport has provided me with an identity, physical and mental wellbeing, motivation, focus and happiness. My personal experiences serve to knock down traditional sporting and societal attitudes towards British Indian women in sport. Upon reflection, my zest for theatre and performance provided me with the assurance and resilience to rise above race discrimination and develop a strong character, even though I may have been broken down by it all inside. I never labelled my experiences, but I knew that they were unjust. I could never quite understand why my white friends did not receive the same marginalization and I felt unprotected from any law or regulation. My experiences have inspired me to become an academic in this research field, as a way of taking control and making sense of my mistreatment. On a formal level, I am using my research as a platform to speak out and challenge discriminatory practices, and to advance reform.

5 Sport Inclusion Strategies

Having outlined my story, this section examines how sport regulatory strategies deal with such treatment and whether the measures in place go far enough to recognize lived encounters and protect minority groups. Sports bodies, clubs, teams, related organizations and stakeholders have affirmed their commitment to anti-racism in the form of disciplinary regulations, strategies, campaigns and events which have evolved over time and renewed periodically when race matters are thrust into the spotlight. Diversity and equality provisions are a core feature of sport documents, and a strong anti-racism culture is displayed, with support for equality amongst participants, spectators, coaches and managers within the operational structures. A consistent theme across the evaluation of these initiatives is that although advances have been made particularly in relation to overt forms of discrimination and abuse, there has been little effective change for ethnic minorities such as British South Asian athletes,[77] with far less understood about the inherent reasons for low

[75] Ismond (2003), p. 133.

[76] Fleming (1994).

[77] Randwaha and Burdsey in Carter et al. (2018).

participation and representation by policy makers.[78] The policies have certainly defined the race problems, but in order to be effective, they arguably need to extend further and engage with the contemporary forms of racism and inequities facing marginalized groups.[79]

In the context of disciplinary powers, racist spectator behavior at games falls within anti-social and disorderly conduct (such as chanting and abuse). Particularly in football, this has been tied to wider political and safety issues and governed by legislative provisions concerning public order, sport events and football specific offences.[80] Supporting these criminal offences, strict grounds controls have been enforced by football authorities to manage spectator conduct at matches. Racist behavior is tackled by some of those provisions. With the rise of discriminatory social media posts aimed at players, legal reforms for tackling online abuse are also being explored. While these measures relate to spectator behavior, and are not without their shortfalls, there is at least some evidence of a firm anti-racism approach. For matters concerning players and clubs, as evidenced by the recent ECB racism disciplinary proceedings, some sports bodies rely on their own independent commissions to invoke private internal disciplinary codes relating to misconduct and discrimination, leading to charges and, where proved, the imposition of sanctions. For example, in 2012, English footballer John Terry was found guilty of breaching Football Association (FA) rules on misconduct following allegations of racially abusing another player during a game. Terry was suspended from playing for four matches and fined.[81] When the ECB racism hearing is finalized, the sufficiency of the internal sport process to combat racism in this way will be closely examined.

In terms of broader initiatives to overcome racism, one of the most visible campaigns is Kick It Out, an organization established to fight racism and all forms of discrimination in football through raising awareness and education. Kick It Out has expanded beyond football, and following the cricket allegations, an exploratory partnership between Kick It Out and the ECB was announced in 2022, to examine inclusion and exclusion within cricket. Kick It Out has also launched a partnership with global broadcaster Sky to elevate its scope and reach. Given its public status in the sport anti-racism dialogue, significant attention has been placed on the impact of its initiatives. Kick It Out has raised awareness of anti-racism, provided education and progressed conversations about racism,[82] but its effectiveness has been debated. The key criticisms tend to be around the absence of practical reform and policy changes, slow developments, funding restrictions, limited independence, lack of real influence, and deficiencies in regulatory authority over sports bodies, spectators, athletes or other parties. Following high-profile racism incidents in football, professional players have opposed such organizations for their failure to actively support

[78] Dashper et al. (2019).

[79] Dashper et al. (2019).

[80] Greenfield and Osborn (2001), Chapter 5; Pearson and Stott (2022).

[81] Łukomski (2012).

[82] Kilvington (2019).

victims of racial abuse.[83] It is agreed that the nature of racism is rapidly changing, and this requires a refreshed regulatory approach.[84] With the rise of athlete activism, such as taking the knee and campaigning for anti-racism without reliance on external bodies (see England footballer Raheem Sterling), the utility of these organizations is under review.

British South Asian inclusion in sport has been considered in various ways. The Premier League and Kick It Out created the South Asian Action Plan in 2022, which acknowledges the under-representation of players with South Asian heritage in English football and seeks to end this disparity. As part of its many inclusion strategies, in 2019 The FA launched the Asian Inclusion Strategy (Bringing Opportunities to Communities), which seeks to improve Asian participation in all areas of English football. When I was younger, I particularly remember being drawn to Nike's 2005 "Stand Up Speak Up" anti-racism campaign and the symbolic interlocking wristbands that accompanied it. But for me it felt more like a trend than a meaningful movement.

Cricket campaigns have identified inequality in the sport and challenged the view that racism does not exist, but there has been limited progress. In 1996, Hit Racism for Six was an independent organization set up to oppose racism in cricket and force the governing bodies to design an anti-racism policy to tackle inequity.[85] The ECB responded with the establishment of a Racism Study Group which published a report, 'Going Forward Together: A Report on Racial Equality in Cricket'. Following wide consultation and a survey, the report reflected a majority belief that racism existed in English cricket at all levels, and many had experienced racism. The Racism Study Group encouraged clubs to be more inclusive in order to address these findings.

At a similar time, the 'Clean Bowl Racism' initiative was launched, which made several policy recommendations to increasing inclusivity and implemented funded development programs for marginalized groups and equality training for cricket staff.[86] In doing so, this aligned cricket more consistently with anti-racism campaigns in other sports such as football and rugby but it was not necessarily comprehensive enough.[87] In more recent years, the ECB has been associated with other initiatives to progress anti-racism such as those implemented by the International Cricket Council (ICC) and the Professional Cricketers' Association.[88] In addition, in 2017, in partnership with NatWest, the 'Cricket Has No Boundaries' campaign was rolled out which aimed to celebrate diversity and foster inclusion in cricket, but

[83] Gardner J (2020) Kick It Out admits Anton Ferdinand did not get proper support during racism case, The Independent, 1 December 2020, https://www.independent.co.uk/sport/football/news/anton-ferdinand-kick-it-out-john-terry-b1764449.html (last accessed 1 April 2023).

[84] Burdsey (2021), p. 32.

[85] Greenfield and Osborn (1997).

[86] Malcolm (2002).

[87] Malcolm (2002).

[88] Fletcher et al. (2021), p. 1474.

which arguably relayed contradictory messages given the existing racial barriers within English cricket.[89]

The ECB's current strategy for 2020–2024 ('Inspiring Generations') seeks to 'connect communities and improve lives by inspiring people to discover and share their passion for cricket'.[90] It sets six priorities to achieve this, which include improving accessibility for a wider cross section of people, such as South Asians, and transforming cricket for girls and women. Building upon this is the ECB Equity, Diversity and Inclusion Plan 2021 and the Engaging South Asian Communities Plan 2018. The South Asian Plan introduces 11 action points to increase engagement with South Asian communities across England and Wales.[91] The areas cover recreational, elite and professional cricket, attendance, media, marketing and communication and administration and culture, each with short, medium, and long-term outputs. The ECB has also refreshed its commitment to these plans in light of the current race tensions. In March 2021, the Independent Commission for Equity in Cricket (ICEC) was announced by the ECB, to examine the equity within cricket and to hear about the experiences of those involved in cricket. The ICEC final report was published in June 2023 and identified serious discrimination and underrepresentation issues in cricket.[92]

Although this is positive progress in terms of addressing disparities and participation in English cricket, the literature concludes that little has changed. Such policies do not reach the inherent issues, they neglect the individual stories of exclusion and fail to implement long term goals and objectives.[93] A number of persuasive alternative proposals for reform include shifting the focus from the prevailing quantitative statistics to the lived experiences of racism and exclusion for British Asians in cricket.[94] Failure to acknowledge those voices could ignore what is really needed, as opposed to what dominant stakeholders think is needed to remove barriers.[95] Change is also achieved by transforming the power relationships across all levels of sport and altering the dominant voices on issues of race within sport and academia.[96] It is argued that the ownership of these strategies should shift

[89] Powis and Velija (2021).

[90] ECB, Inspiring Generations- our 2020-24 Strategy for Cricket, 2020, https://resources.ecb.co.uk/ecb/document/2023/02/09/2f435e06-576b-4609-9609-0de3fb42da9d/Inspiring-Generations-FINAL-2020.pdf (last accessed 10 April 2023).

[91] ECB, Making Cricket a Game for Everyone: Engaging South Asian Communities. An ECB Action Plan, 2018, https://www.ecb.co.uk/south-asian-action-plan (last accessed 10 April 2023).

[92] This paper and its analysis was finalised before the publication of the Independent Commission for Equity in Cricket (ICEC) Report in June 2023. For coverage of the Report see, Morgan, T (June 27, 2023). English cricket branded 'racist, sexist and elitist' in damning report as ECB apologises. The Telegraph. https://www.telegraph.co.uk/cricket/2023/06/27/english-cricket-ecb-racist-sexist-elitist-report-commission/.

[93] Randhawa and Burdsey in Carter et al. (2018).

[94] Fletcher et al. (2021); Burdsey (2021).

[95] Rana in Ratna and Samie (2018), p. 163.

[96] Randhawa and Burdsey in Carter et al. (2018).

from stakeholders to the heart of British South Asian communities, encouraging a bottom-up approach that prioritizes increasing opportunities at grassroots levels, identifying role models and improving access to coaching and management vocations.[97] Stronger and sustainable links between clubs/teams and the Asian communities should be nurtured as part of the strategy process, in order to empower British South Asians and create pathways for inclusion in sport.[98]

In highlighting that most of these initiatives tend to concern increasing participation rather than exploring how to enhance skills for transitioning cricketers to the professional level, in 2020 the South Asian Cricket Association (SACA) was established to encourage more players of Asian origin into professional cricket in England and Wales by offering dedicated bursaries, education opportunities and coaching.[99] Rather than focus on participation levels, which appear to be stable at the recreational level, the SACA aims to increase the number of British South Asian players at the professional level of cricket. This goes some way to directly address exclusion and under-representation.

Criticism of these strategies and campaigns is legitimate since British South Asians continue to be invisible in most structures of sport, but it is emphasized that this does not necessarily portray the reality of the broader situation. For instance, Kick It Out defends its stance within this debate by clarifying that anti-discrimination organizations tend to have limited resources, with no decision-making powers and lack capacity.[100] The focus and blame placed on Kick It Out to some extent deflects attention from the role, responsibility, and authority of sports bodies, with vast resources, to eradicate racism, influence change, alter the dialogue and impose rules and sanctions. However, sports bodies have acted complacently on discrimination matters, failing to acknowledge that racism is at the core rather than the outskirts of sport.[101] Further research is also required to examine how effectively the internal sport disciplinary processes deal with discrimination, and how seriously such matters are taken.

With that said, my experiences reinforce the idea that race and inequality are not an isolated sport issue, and instead forms part of a widespread social and political problem. While sports bodies are well placed to attack racism with their financial power and regulatory autonomy,[102] this is only part of the solution. There needs to be a connection with legal frameworks and legislative reform in order to apply

[97] Randhawa and Burdsey in Carter et al. (2018).

[98] Kilvington (2019); Randhawa in Burdsey (2011).

[99] Brown et al. (2021).

[100] Magowan A (2012) Kick It Out caught in the crossfire as racism flares up again. BBC, 21 October 2012, https://www.bbc.co.uk/sport/football/20001544 (last accessed 10 April 2023).

[101] FRA (The European Union Agency for Fundamental Rights), Racism, Ethnic Discrimination and Exclusion of Migrants and Minorities in Sport: A Comparative Overview of the Situation in the European Union, October 2010, https://fra.europa.eu/en/publication/2012/racism-ethnic-discrimination-and-exclusion-migrants-and-minorities-sport-situation (last accessed 10 April 2023).

[102] Fletcher et al. (2021), p. 1488.

pressure, enforce rights and transform strategies into effective drivers for change.[103] Indeed, legal intervention has the potential to ensure a commitment to anti-racism in sport.[104] It is essential that the behavior of sports bodies in the fight against discrimination, the enforcement of law and human rights continues to be subject to analysis to ensure accountability.[105]

6 Law as an Effective Tool or Barrier

Since the issues facing sports are part of a broader race problem, this section examines whether the law provides an effective solution to such mistreatment, or alternatively, whether it represents a further barrier. The interdiction of race discrimination and the promotion of equality is an unambiguous and fundamental pillar of international law. Principal universal values of human dignity and bodily integrity are preserved within a wide range of international sources that condemn race discrimination. These include the Universal Declaration of Human Rights 1948 (UDHR), the International Covenant on Civil and Political Rights 1976 (ICCPR), the International Covenant on Economic, Social and Cultural Rights 1976 (ICESCR) and The United Nations Charter 1945. The rights and freedoms contained in those provisions are awarded without distinction of race, color, sex, language, religion, political or other opinion, national or social origin, property, birth or other status. Several ancillary international instruments provide specific protection such as the International Convention on the Elimination of All Forms of Racial Discrimination 1969 (ICERD) which reaffirms that discrimination between human beings on the grounds of race, color or ethnic origin is inconsistent with the ideals of any human society. The Convention aims to encourage states to adopt all necessary measures for elimination of racial discrimination in all its forms and manifestations, and to prevent and combat racist doctrines and practices in order to promote understanding between races and to build an international community free from all forms of racial segregation and racial discrimination. Although no specific reference to sport is made, Article 5(e) seeks to protect the enjoyment of economic, social and cultural rights, with specific reference to the rights to work and the right to equal participation in cultural activities.

The United Nations Educational, Scientific and Cultural Organization (UNESCO) conduct significant work in the fight against discrimination, using sport as a vehicle for change. The UNESCO Declaration on Race and Racial Prejudice (1978) states that 'all human beings belong to a single species and are descended from a common stock' (Article 1), with a 'right to be different' (Article 1). Article 2 condemns the assumption of superior or inferior racial groups, and

[103] Long and Spracklen (2011), p. 247.
[104] Long and Spracklen (2011), p. 247.
[105] Burdsey (2021), pp. 25–26; Patel (2021).

asserts that this theory has no scientific foundation and is contrary to the moral and ethical principles of humanity. It defines racism as including 'racist ideologies, prejudiced attitudes, discriminatory behavior, structural arrangements and institutionalized practices resulting in racial inequality as well as the fallacious notion that discriminatory relations between groups are morally and scientifically justifiable' (Article 2), and racial prejudice which is 'historically linked with inequalities in power, reinforced by economic and social differences between individuals and groups' (Article 2). It highlights the role of states in prohibiting and sanctioning racial discrimination through the enactment of legislation and education, reminding us that law is one of the foundational means of ensuring equality in dignity and rights among individuals (Article 7). Despite the value of international human rights law in prohibiting race discrimination, there remain shortfalls in ensuring compliance with the obligations and also dealing with entrenched problems in modern society relating to racism, racial thinking, covert expressions and racial bias.[106]

At the regional level, the basic human rights documents of the Inter-American system (the American Declaration of the Rights and Duties of Man 1948 and the American Convention on Human Rights 1978), the African Charter on Human and Peoples' Rights 1981 and Council of Europe European Convention on Human Rights 1950 (ECHR) protect human rights and apply those rights and freedoms to all persons equally without distinction on the grounds of characteristics including race or color. In the European Union (EU), discrimination based on race and ethnic origin is prohibited in the Race Equality Directive 2000/43. The provision has a wide scope, applying to public and private sectors. It instructs Member States to implement legislation to combat race discrimination in various areas relating to employment, vocational experience, social protection, education and access to and supply of goods and services. It states that the EU rejects 'theories which attempt to determine the existence of separate human races'. The 2008 Framework Decision on Combating Racism and Xenophobia instructs that particular acts of racism and xenophobia constitute an offence which can be punishable by firm penalties.[107]

Although these provisions have strengthened the legal framework for the prohibition of race discrimination at this level, the EU accepts that race discrimination persists within its member states.[108] For instance, in 2020 the European Union Agency for Fundamental Rights (FRA) identified an increase in racist and xenophobic attacks, particularly against the Asian community.[109] Furthermore, there remain challenges to enforcing these provisions.[110] In response to the global movement

[106] Spain Bradley (2019).

[107] de Groot (2022).

[108] de Groot (2022).

[109] FRA (European Union Agency for Fundamental Rights), Coronavirus Pandemic in the EU-Fundamental Rights Implications, April 2020, p. 33, https://fra.europa.eu/sites/default/files/fra_uploads/fra-2020-coronavirus-pandemic-eu-bulletin_en.pdf#page=33 (last accessed 10 April 2023).

[110] de Groot (2022).

against racial abuse, in 2021 the European Commission held an anti-racism summit and introduced a number of new actions to advance protection against race discrimination. This includes an EU anti-racism action plan which proposes a significant review of the EU legal framework, and the enactment of legislative and non-legislative measures where necessary to address race discrimination more effectively.[111]

The European Parliament Resolution of 8 March 2022 on the role of culture, education, media and sport in the fight against racism[112] highlights the important role that sports-governing bodies can play in eradicating racism and promoting equality and inclusion, particularly at a grassroots level to diversify representation. The Resolution highlights that although sport can foster unity between communities in social, cultural and educational life, there have been persistent cases of racism at sporting events, which must be addressed. It commands sports bodies to implement measures to address the underrepresentation of women and ethnic minorities in sport and places responsibility on Member States to ensure that sport is accessible to all, regardless of ethnicity or race. It insists on a zero-tolerance approach to racism, hate speech, violence and other racist behavior in sport and urges the Commission, the Member States and sports federations to develop measures to prevent such incidents, and to adopt effective penalties and measures to support victims, in addition to the space for athletes to speak out. Finally, the Resolution requires the Commission to implement guidance for sport to combat racism at all levels. It has been proposed that the European anti-racism provisions could be used to address racism in sport through binding commitments and as a basis for international agreements that are supported by international sports authorities, such as FIFA and the IOC.[113]

In the UK, race and identity are intricately tied up in its colonial history. Significant events such as Brexit, the Grenfell Tower fire in 2017, and the Windrush scandal in 2018 have all fueled a divisive atmosphere around immigration, citizenship and nationality, contributing to an exclusionary and fractured environment that is at odds with principles of inclusion and belonging.[114] In turn, this has impacted racial unrest in society and sport. The UK Government commissioned a series of reports on specific policy areas relating to race and ethnicity, which have included recommendations for improving outcomes for marginalized groups (Crick Report 1998, Parekh Report 2000, Ajegbo Report 2007). The most recent publication, The Report of the Commission on Race and Ethnic Disparities 2021, was criticized for, among other things, failing to identify the source of the adversities faced by minority

[111] European Commission, A Union of equality: EU anti-racism action plan 2020-2025, 18 September 2020, https://ec.europa.eu/info/policies/justice-and-fundamental-rights/combatting-discrimination/racism-and-xenophobia/eu-anti-racism-action-plan-2020-2025_en (last accessed 10 December 2022).

[112] European Parliament resolution of 8 March 2022 on the role of culture, education, media and sport in the fight against racism (2021/2057(INI) https://www.europarl.europa.eu/doceo/document/TA-9-2022-0057_EN.html.

[113] Long and Spracklen (2011), p. 247.

[114] Selwyn (2019).

groups in the UK.[115] Some positive action is demonstrated by the intervention of the Department for Digital Culture Media and Sport (DCMS), which has conducted independent committee inquiries into critical sport issues such as the allegations in cricket, racism in football, underrepresentation of ethnic minorities in sport, and concussions and player welfare. Recommendations to withdraw public funding from sport may encourage sports bodies to improve their standards and practices. With that said, the purpose, scope and impact of DCMS' inquires is unclear.

In terms of legislation, the UK has historically been advanced in the recognition of equality and non-discrimination, particularly in the areas of sex (Sex Discrimination Act 1975) disability (Disability Discrimination Act 1995) and race (Race Relations Act 1975). The Equality Act 2010 (EA) consolidates and repeals previous legislation in specific areas and shields protected characteristics, which includes race. It also outlines various types of discrimination that can be applied to race, such as racial harassment, direct and indirect discrimination, perceptive discrimination and associative discrimination. The EA also draws attention to combined discrimination and the intersectional relationship between the protected characteristics, such as gender and ethnicity, as illustrated by my experiences. The UK Human Rights Act 1998 (HRA) gives effect to the rights set out in the ECHR. Article 14 ECHR prohibits discrimination in the enjoyment of human rights based on characteristics including race (not a free-standing right, see Protocol No. 12 ECHR). As outlined above, spectator behavior and conduct at sporting events has required legal intervention and is governed by legislation that seeks to eradicate racist behavior and impose criminal sanctions.[116]

The international human rights framework credits the value of participation in sport as a means of enhancing and promoting human rights and overcoming race discrimination. It has played an important role in the construction of key sport documents, with explicit references made to human rights commitments, obligations and remedy mechanisms.[117] For instance, central sources of sport regulation proclaim that 'the practice of sport is a human right' which preserves human dignity and should be free from discrimination based on race and other characteristics.[118] International governing bodies explicitly condemn race discrimination and appear to support and respect the legal sanctions of such behavior, with disciplinary codes in place to reinforce this position. However, these rights are not absolute, and the complex regulation of sport inhibits the firm enforceability of human rights obligations and the translation of these obligations into sport policies beyond theoretical commitments.[119] The restricted application of the law to sport can create an

[115] Kaur R, Hague GM (2021) Race Commission Report: the rights and wrongs, The Conversation, 1 April 2021, https://theconversation.com/race-commission-report-the-rights-and-wrongs-158316 (last accessed 10 December 2022).

[116] Pearson and Stott (2022); Greenfield and Osborn (2001).

[117] Patel in Rook and Heerdt (2023).

[118] IOC Olympic Charter Principle 2; 4; 6.

[119] Patel (2021).

ineffective barrier to participation for minority groups. The intersection between marginalized groups in sport, human rights, sport regulation and law are under close evaluation. There is a renewed focus on the relationship between sport and human rights with an increased body of research navigating how to bind sport to the international human rights framework outlined above.[120] Accompanying this, the role of the judicial systems here is also being critiqued.

Overall, there is no ambiguity in the explicit prohibition of overt race discrimination within the rich international human rights framework, but modern covert microaggressions of racism remain systemic and embedded within many aspects of society, including sport. This questions the impact and effectiveness of these hard and soft law provisions. If engaged with, they can be promising tools for developing a harmonious approach and influencing shifts in racial thinking and covert practices. There is evidence of action at all levels of the legal framework to recognize the current regulatory shortfalls in eradicating racism and racial abuse from society, with efforts being made to refresh these provisions and align them with contemporary shades of racism, such as improved regulation of racism on social media platforms.[121] The law can have a transformative educational influence in sport to fight against race discrimination by exerting pressure on sports bodies.[122] Equally, sports bodies possess the power and authority to initiate effective change. An enhanced relationship between sport and the law could act as a driver for effective reform.

7 Conclusion

This chapter has experimented with the use of lived experience to examine the barriers to participation faced by British South Asians in sport. Using storytelling as part of my analysis, I have provided anecdotal evidence of being overtly and covertly included and excluded within various sport and social settings throughout my life. My experience of being a British South Asian in sport and in England are illustrative of a much wider narrative around race, Britain and South Asian identity. I hope that this will contribute to the current limited coverage of the British South Asian female perspective and offer some insight into the relationship between our intersectional identity and sport. As a British Indian female, I feel that my encounters challenge the traditional British Asian female stereotype and prompt a reformulation of what this identity represents today. Yet the notion of 'but you're ok' continues to haunt me and leads me to evaluate the legitimacy of my inclusion in sport and society.

[120] Rook and Heerdt (2023); Rietiker (2022); Patel (2021).

[121] FRA (The European Union Agency for Fundamental Rights), Racism, Ethnic Discrimination and Exclusion of Migrants and Minorities in Sport: A Comparative Overview of the Situation in the European Union, October 2010, p. 45, https://fra.europa.eu/en/publication/2012/racism-ethnic-discrimination-and-exclusion-migrants-and-minorities-sport-situation (last accessed 10 April 2023); Hylton et al. (2015a, b).

[122] Simmons and Feldman (2018), p. 128.

The participation of British South Asians in sport is currently being scrutinized in English cricket, and the complex tensions between the British Asian community and Englishness, racism, class and culture are being negotiated as cricket governing bodies seek a solution to exclusion and underrepresentation. In the aftermath of the CDC cricket hearing, the actions and practices of the cricket authorities are under close scrutiny. Sport anti-racism initiatives have been useful to identify the existence of racism and draw attention to the inequalities for British South Asians in sport. However, a common theme is that those efforts do not go far enough to overcome certain barriers. In order to construct effective tools, sports bodies must tackle the more contemporary expressions of racism and mistreatment at all levels of sport. In addition to promoting equality, the plans should celebrate and value difference by using the voices of minority athletes to directly inform any anti-racism agenda, and by redefining the traditional notions of cricket and Englishness.[123] Sport has a substantial platform to promote change and influence others by leading these positive shifts.[124] Indeed, diversity and inclusion provide key human rights and business benefits for sport, and this should be prioritized.[125]

However, sport alone cannot achieve this reform since racism is widely present across many aspects of society; and the law certainly does not provide an absolute solution.[126] Instead, a holistic approach is required, and at this key moment of diversity and inclusion, the symbiosis between law and regulation, sport, society, government and international organizations, play a crucial part in strengthening anti-racism strategies. The established international legal framework outlined above is being refreshed and there is evidence of a firmer commitment to addressing the more nuanced expressions of race and gender in society. If engaged with, the law can be an effective tool for applying pressure on sports bodies to achieve appropriate anti-racism legal standards and ensuring compliance with those relevant international, regional and domestic provisions.

This chapter suggests that independent organizations such as equality bodies, who monitor compliance of member states with legal provisions, are best placed to progress anti-racism and anti-discrimination despite their restricted legal authority and influence.[127] In previous work, I proposed the establishment of an International Anti-Discrimination in Sport Unit (IADSU), an enforcement body for the fight against discrimination in sport.[128] The enactment of an International Anti-Discrimination in Sport Charter could reinforce the IADSU to bind sport to human rights, and institute a relevant legal framework for the eradication of racism.[129]

[123] Bekker et al. (2023).

[124] Fletcher (2011).

[125] Fletcher et al. (2021), p. 1477.

[126] Greenfield and Osborn (2001), p. 165.

[127] de Groot (2022); Patel (2015).

[128] Patel (2015); Patel (2021); Patel in Rook and Heerdt (2023).

[129] Patel (2021).

Finally, as researchers in this field, we can improve our work by integrating ethnographic narratives into legal research to provide an accurate understanding of the true impact of law, regulation and intersectionality upon marginalized groups, such as British South Asians in sport. Including the voice of the British South Asian athletes will result in better academic legal research and foster meaningful inquiry.[130] In turn, this will assist in the fight against racism and cultivate positive actions for further inclusion.

References

Bains J, Johal S (1998) Corner flags and corner shops: the Asian football experience. Victor Gollancz, London

Bains J, Patel R (1996) Asians can't play football. Asian Social Development Agency

Bekker S, Storr R, Patel S, Mitra P (2023) Gender inclusive sport: a paradigm shift for research, policy, and practice. Int J Sport Policy Polit 15(1):177–185. https://doi.org/10.1080/19406940.2022.2161599

Bens J, Vetters L (2018) Ethnographic legal studies: reconnecting anthropological and sociological traditions. J Leg Plural Unoff Law 50(3):239–254. https://doi.org/10.1080/07329113.2018.1559487

Berkson S (2021) Is cricket 'for everyone'? Reflections on the 2021 Ollie Robinson scandal. Inst Race Relat 63(2):82–88. https://doi.org/10.1177/03063968211041498

Brown T, Khawaja I, Powell A, Greetham P, Gough LA, Kelly AL (2021) The sociodemographic profile of the England and Wales Cricket Board (ECB) talent pathways and first-class counties: considering the British South Asian player. Manag Sport Leis. https://doi.org/10.1080/23750472.2021.1949382

Burdsey D (2011) That joke isn't funny anymore: racial microaggressions, color-blind ideology and the mitigation of racism in English Men's First Class Cricket. Sociol Sport J 28:261–283

Burdsey D (2013) Monty Panesar and the new (sporting) Asian Britishness. In: Andrews DL, Carrington B (eds) A companion to sport. Wiley Blackwell. https://doi.org/10.1002/9781118325261.ch32

Burdsey D (2021) Racism in English Football. Routledge, London

Carter TF, Burdsey D, Doidge M (2018) Transforming sport: knowledges, practices, structures. Routledge, London

Collins M (2022) Cricket, Englishness and racial thinking. Polit Q 93(1):95–103

Dashper K, Fletcher T, Long J (2019) 'Intelligent investment'? Welsh sport policy and the (in)-visibility of 'race'. Leis Stud 38(6):762–774. https://doi.org/10.1080/02614367.2019.1653355

De Groot D (2022) EU legislation and policies to address racial and ethnic discrimination, European Parliamentary Research Service, May 2022. https://www.europarl.europa.eu/RegData/etudes/BRIE/2021/690525/EPRS_BRI(2021)690525_EN.pdf (last accessed 10 April 2023)

Fleming S (1994) Sport and South Asian youth: the perils of 'false universalism' and stereotyping. Leis Stud 13:159–177

Fletcher T (2011) The making of English cricket cultures: empire, globalization and (post) colonialism. Sport Soc 14(1):17–36. https://doi.org/10.1080/17430437.2011.530006

Fletcher T (2012) 'All Yorkshiremen are from Yorkshire, but some are more "Yorkshire" than others': British Asians and the myths of Yorkshire cricket. Sport Soc 15(2):227–245. https://doi.org/10.1080/17430437.2012.637735

[130] Patel in Rook and Heerdt (2023).

Fletcher T, Swain S (2016) Strangers of the north: South Asians, cricket and the culture of 'Yorkshireness'. J Cult Res 20(1):86–100. https://doi.org/10.1080/14797585.2015.1134062
Fletcher T, Piggott D, North J (2021) "The 'blazer boys' were getting all the chances": South Asian men's experiences of cricket coaching in England. Sport Soc 24(8):1472–1492. https://doi.org/10.1080/17430437.2020.1799979
Garland J, Chakraborti N (2004) Another country? Community, belonging and exclusion in rural England. In: Chakraborti N, Garland J (eds) Rural racism. Routledge, London. Chapter 6
Greenfield S, Osborn G (1996) Oh to be in England? Mythology and identity in English cricket. Soc Identities 2(2):271–292. https://doi.org/10.1080/13504639652330
Greenfield S, Osborn G (1997) Enough is enough: race, cricket and protest in the UK. Sociol Focus 31(4):373–383
Greenfield S, Osborn G (2001) Regulating football: commodification, consumption and the law. Pluto Press
Griffiths A (2017) Using ethnography as a tool in legal research: a anthropological perspective. Administrative Law. May
Henderson R (1995) Is it in the blood? Wisden Cricket Monthly
Hylton K (2010) How a turn to critical race theory can contribute to our understanding of 'race,' racism and anti-racism in sport. Int Rev Sociol Sport 45(3):335–354
Hylton K, Long J, Fletcher TE, Ormerod N (2015a) South Asian Communities and Cricket (Bradford and Leeds). Project Report. Yorkshire Cricket Foundation
Hylton K, Long J, Parnell D, Rankin AJ (2015b) 'Race', racism and participation in sport. Race Equality Foundation
Ismond P (2003) Black and Asian athletes in British sport and society. A sporting chance? Palgrave Macmillan
Kilvington DJ (2019) Two decades and little change: British South Asians, football and calls for action. Soccer Soc 20(4):584–601. https://doi.org/10.1080/14660970.2017.1366902
Lawless W, Magrath R (2021) Inclusionary and exclusionary banter: English club cricket, inclusive attitudes and male camaraderie. Sport Soc 24(8):1493–1509. https://doi.org/10.1080/17430437.2020.1819985
Long J, Spracklen K (2011) Sport and challenges to racism. Palgrave Macmillan, London
Łukomski J (2012) The John Terry Case - an overlap of criminal and disciplinary proceedings. Int Sports Law J 3–4:63
Malcolm D (2002) 'Clean bowled?' Cricket, racism and equal opportunities. J Ethn Migr Stud 28(2):307–325. https://doi.org/10.1080/13691830220124350
Malcolm D, Velija P (2008) Female incursions into crickets male preserve. In: Atkinson M, Young K (eds) Tribal play: subcultural journeys through sport. Research in the sociology of sport, vol 4. Emerald, Jai, Chapter 9
Marqusee M (1995) Anyone but England: cricket and the national malaise. Verso, London
Mirza HS (2003) 'All the women are white, all the blacks are men- but some of us are brave:' mapping the consequences of invisibility for black and minority ethnic women in Britain. In: Mason D (ed) Explaining ethnic differences. The Policy Press, Bristol
Patel S (2015) Inclusion and exclusion in competitive sport. Routledge, London
Patel S (2021) Gaps in the protection of athletes gender rights in sport- a regulatory riddle. Int Sports Law J. https://doi.org/10.1007/s40318-021-00182-2
Patel S (2022) Law and regulatory barriers to increasing inclusivity for trans athletes. In: Witcomb G, Peel E (eds) Gender diversity and sport interdisciplinary perspectives. Routledge, London, pp 34–56
Patel S (2023) Refreshing and reimagining the human rights framework to protect athletes' gender rights and remove risks at mega-sporting events. In: Rook W, Heerdt D (eds) The Routledge handbook of mega-sporting events and human rights. Routledge, London, Chapter 34
Pearson G (2012) An ethnography of English football fans: cans, cops and carnivals. Manchester University Press

Pearson G, Stott C (2022) A new agenda for football crowd management: reforming legal and policing responses to risk. Palgrave Macmillan

Powis B, Velija P (2021) Cricket has no boundaries with NatWest? The hyperreality of inclusion and diversity in English cricket. Sport Soc 24(8):1510–1525. https://doi.org/10.1080/17430437.2020.1789105

Randhawa K (2011) Marrying passion with professionalism: examining the future of British Asian Football. In: Burdsey D (ed) Race, ethnicity and football: persisting debates and emergent issues. Routledge, London, Chapter 16

Ratna A (2013) Intersectional plays of identity: the experiences of British Asian Female Footballer. Sociol Res Online 18(1):108–117. https://doi.org/10.5153/sro.2824

Ratna A, Samie SF (2018) Race, gender and sport: the politics of ethnic 'other' girls and women. Routledge, London

Rietiker D (2022) Defending athletes, players, clubs and fans. Council of Europe, Strasbourg

Rook W, Heerdt D (2023) The routledge handbook of mega-sporting events and Human Rights. Routledge

Scraton S, Caudwell J, Holland S (2005) 'Bend it like Patel': centring 'race', ethnicity and gender in feminist analysis of women's football in England. Int Rev Sociol Sport 40(1):71–88. https://doi.org/10.1177/1012690205052169

Selwyn T (2019) Post-home: dwelling on loss, belonging and movement. Ethnoscripts 21(1): 125–156

Simmons WP, Feldman L (2018) Critical ethnography and human rights research. In: McConnell L, Smith R (eds) Research methods in human rights. Routledge, London. https://doi.org/10.4324/9781315672632

Simons J (1996) The "Englishness" of English Cricket. J Pop Cult 29(4):41–50

Spain Bradley A (2019) Human rights racism. Harv Hum Rights J 32

Valiotis C (2009) Runs in the outfield: the Pakistani Diaspora and Cricket in England. Int J Hist Sport 26(12):1791–1822. https://doi.org/10.1080/09523360903172408

Seema Patel is Associate Professor in Sports Law at Nottingham Law School, Nottingham Trent University. With international leading expertise on discrimination in sport, Dr Patel has published and offered global media commentary on the legal and regulatory implications of the participation of gender diverse athletes in sport. Dr Patel has been involved in supporting legal teams on these issues, contributing to sport eligibility policies, and informing Government reviews on inclusion and exclusion in sport. In recognition of her wider expertise on discrimination in the context of race and sport, Dr Patel was appointed as a panel member for the Cricket Disciplinary Commission (CDC).

Gendered Athletes in Sports: CEDAW's Role in Tackling Heterosexist and Racialized Uniforms in Sports

Lena Holzer

Contents

Abstract This chapter examines the human rights implications of gendered and racialized clothing regulations in sports. It specifically uses the Convention on the Elimination of All Forms of Discrimination Against Women (CEDAW) as the framework to discuss how gendered and racialized clothing regulations contravene international human rights law. By analysing the applicability of CEDAW to the issue of heterosexist clothing regulations in sports, the chapter provides general insights into the protection of human rights in sports through reliance on existing international instruments.

I would like to thank the editors of this book for their support in writing this chapter.

L. Holzer (✉)
University of Cambridge, Faculty of Law, Cambridge, UK
e-mail: lh850@cam.ac.uk

V. Boillet et al. (eds.), *Sports and Human Rights*, Interdisciplinary Studies in Human Rights 10, https://doi.org/10.1007/978-3-031-56452-9_3

1 Introduction

Sports remains one of the few domains where women and men are often treated differently. Not only is sex segregation a highly normalized practice in sports, but athletes are also frequently subjected to different sporting rules based on their gender. This was exemplified by the fine that was imposed on the Norwegian women's beach handball team for violating clothing regulations in 2021. The team wore shorts instead of bikini bottoms in a game of the European Championship, which contravened the international beach handball rules prescribing that women must wear bikini tops and bikini bottoms while men must wear tank tops and shorts.[1] The imposed penalty of €1500 on the women's team for wearing attire that was only allowed for men shows how sporting regulations regularly reproduce sexist and heteronormative (heterosexist) norms. As many similar examples continue to exist in sports, this chapter examines gendered—and racialized—clothing regulations from a human rights perspective.

More specifically, this chapter analyses the obligations of states to address heterosexist and racialized clothing regulations in sports that derive from the Convention on the Elimination of All Forms of Discrimination Against Women (CEDAW). I am specifically interested in how CEDAW could be used to regulate the rules on clothing implemented by international sports federations, which are private organizations. This will be done by analysing a variety of clothing regulations in sports and examining the applicability of CEDAW to these regulations. For this task, I will examine the text of the CEDAW Convention as well as documents issued by the CEDAW Committee, notably general recommendations.

The rationale for this chapter is twofold. Firstly, it aims to shed light on the deeply gendered structure of the international sporting system. The chapter reveals that the gender binary, namely the assumption that women and men are dichotomous, are inherently different and have complementary identities, is reflected in several sporting rules. Sexism, homophobia, transphobia and intersexphobia are thus intimately connected, making it necessary to analyse these different axes of gendered oppression together. Moreover, the chapter makes clear that the gendered nature of sports must be understood in relation to other systems of inequality, such as racism and classism.

The second rationale of this chapter is that I aim to explore how an existing international human rights instrument, CEDAW, can be used to improve the human rights situations of athletes, in particular women athletes. CEDAW seems a promising instrument to overcome obstacles that the application of international human rights law to sports entails, since the Convention not only contains a broad meaning of "equality" but is also equipped to deal with discrimination carried out by private actors, such as sports federations. Analysing CEDAW's applicability to clothing

[1] Gross J, Women's Handball Players Are Fined for Rejecting Bikini Uniforms. The New York Times (20 July 2021), www.nytimes.com/2021/07/20/sports/norway-beach-handball-team.html (last accessed 4 April 2023).

regulations in sports will thus provide general insights into how existing human rights law is applicable to sports governance.

The chapter continues with an introduction to gender distinctions that exist in sports. It then goes on to analyse examples of heterosexist and racialized clothing regulations in international sports, before delving into an examination of CEDAW's applicability to the issue. In this examination, I will first lay out the mechanisms that are available to use CEDAW for tackling gendered clothing regulations, such as individual communications, before addressing the question whether CEDAW would even have jurisdiction to deal with regulations issued by private sports federations. This is followed by a discussion on states' obligations to act with *due diligence*, to work towards establishing *de facto* equality, to fight gender stereotypes and to address intersectional forms of discrimination in sports. The conclusions will embed my results into the broader field of examining sports from a human rights perspective.

2 The Gendered Sporting System

Gendered clothing rules in sports are part of the broader hierarchical international sports governance system that is infused with global inequalities. The International Olympic Committee (IOC) often depicts international sports as an apolitical field and considers itself as "strictly politically neutral at all times".[2] However, the apolitical image of the IOC and international sports more generally has been challenged by many sports commentators, athletes and scholars.[3] Specifically, Rule 50 of the Olympic Charter banning political protests at the Olympic Games has been criticized for presenting sports federations as politically neutral entities, even though they indirectly uphold systems of inequality by preventing protests against these inequalities.[4] The numerous instances of athletic activism at the Olympic Games,[5] despite the presumed political neutrality of the Games, show that international sports events have often been places of political struggle and contestation.[6] As this chapter discusses, these political struggles have included the

[2]Bach T, The Olympics Are about Diversity and Unity, Not Politics and Profit. Boycotts Don't Work. The Guardian (24 October 2020), www.theguardian.com/sport/2020/oct/24/the-olympics-are-about-diversity-and-unity-not-politics-and-profit-boycotts-dont-work-thomas-bach (last accessed 4 April 2023).

[3]Boykoff (2021).

[4]Boykoff (2021), p. 9.

[5]James M, The Re-Emergence of the Athlete Activist. Verfassungsblog (8 February 2022) verfassungsblog.de/the-re-emergence-of-the-athlete-activist/ (last accessed 4 April 2023).

[6]An example of this claim was presented in 2022 when the IOC called on international sports federations to not invite any Russian or Belarussian athletes to sports events due to Russia's invasion of Ukraine. See: International Olympic Committee (2022) IOC EB Recommends No Participation of Russian and Belarusian Athletes and Officials. www.olympics.com/ioc/news/ioc-

negotiation and re-negotiation of appropriate gender norms at international sports events.

The highly gendered character of international sports becomes clearly visible when looking at its history. Past sports events, such as the Ancient Olympic Games, sometimes excluded women entirely from competing or even attending the events.[7] Women were also excluded from competing in the first edition of the modern Olympic Games, and it was only in the second edition in Paris in 1900 that 22 women participated in tennis, sailing, croquet, equestrian and golf.[8] Since then, Olympic disciplines have gradually opened for women, with boxing being the last summer Olympic discipline opening for women in 2012 and ski jumping the last winter Olympic discipline opening in 2014.[9] Nevertheless, men still remained barred from competing in two traditionally "feminine" disciplines, synchronized swimming and rhythmic gymnastics, in the 2020 Olympic Games in Tokyo.[10] This shows how sports continue to shape the gender binary in which women and men are characterized as two dichotomous and inherently different entities.

In terms of numbers, women constituted for the first time 48.7% of all athletes in the 2020 Summer Olympic Games in Tokyo and 45% in the 2022 Winter Olympic Games in Beijing.[11] The Games in Tokyo were also the first ones in which non-binary athletes competed openly for the first time.[12] Moreover, the number of

---

eb-recommends-no-participation-of-russian-and-belarusian-athletes-and-officials (last accessed 4 April 2023).

[7]Wackwitz (2003), p. 553.

[8]Gender Equality through Time: At the Olympic Games, olympics.com/ioc/gender-equality/gender-equality-through-time/at-the-olympic-games (last accessed 4 April 2023).

[9]International Olympic Committee (2022), Key Dates in the History of Women in the Olympic Movement, www.olympic.org/women-in-sport/background/key-dates (last accessed 4 April 2023).

[10]Jenkin M, Synching Feeling: Male Synchronised Swimmers Bid to Be Taken Seriously. The Guardian (18 December 2013), www.theguardian.com/lifeandstyle/the-swimming-blog/2013/dec/18/male-synchronised-swimming-london-ots-angels (last accessed 4 April 2023); International Olympic Committee, Synchronized Swimming - Summer Olympic Sport, www.olympic.org/synchronized-swimming (last accessed 4 April 2023); Keng Kuek Ser K, See 120 Years of Struggle for Gender Equality at the Olympics. Public Radio International (17 August 2016), www.pri.org/stories/2016-08-17/see-120-years-struggle-gender-equality-olympics (last accessed 4 April 2023); International Olympic Committee (2017) Gymnastics Rhythmic - Summer Olympic Sport, www.olympic.org/gymnastics-rhythmic (last accessed 4 April 2023).

[11]International Olympic Committee (2022) Tokyo 2020 First Ever Gender-Balanced Olympic Games in History, Record Number of Female Competitors at Paralympic Games - Olympic News, olympics.com/ioc/news/tokyo-2020-first-ever-gender-balanced-olympic-games-in-history-record-number-of-female-competitors-at-paralympic-games (last accessed 4 April 2023); International Olympic Committee (2022) Women at the Olympic Winter Games Beijing 2022 – All You Need to Know, olympics.com/ioc/news/women-at-the-olympic-winter-games-beijing-2022-all-you-need-to-know (last accessed 4 April 2023).

[12]Bell B, Quinn, Alana Smith Represent Non-Binary Olympic Excellence. Outsports (9 August 2021), www.outsports.com/olympics/2021/8/9/22616378/quinn-alana-smith-nonbinary-2020-summer-olympics-soccer-skateboarding-canada-usa-lgbtq-ioc (last accessed 4 April 2023).

women acting as flag bearers in Tokyo rose to 39%,[13] and the Games included almost as many women-only events (46%) as men-only events (48.7%).[14] Despite these developments, there is still a long way to go to ensure gender-equal representation in sports, since women—and non-binary persons—continue to remain highly underrepresented in decision-making bodies and the technical administration (incl. coaches) in international sporting bodies. This is demonstrated by the fact that only 38% of all IOC board members were women in 2020,[15] while no data has been collected on non-binary persons.

Initiatives aimed at increasing the representation of all genders in international sports, such as the Olympics, have the potential to normalize certain bodies and gender expressions in sports. Yet, they reflect liberal approaches to equality, which often fail to address the structural root causes for the gender imbalances in the participation in sports.[16] The significant difference in the funding for women's and men's sports shows that gender continues to influence the material conditions for professional, semi-professional and amateur sports all around the world.[17] While more and more international sports federations equalize prize money for women's and men's competitions, the funding gap continues to persist in other types of remunerations, including sponsorship opportunities, as well as at the national, semi-professional, youth and amateur levels.[18] International sports are thus also deeply gendered because of the allocation of financial resources in sports, usually advantaging (cis)[19] men athletes.

Another important element in the discussion on the gendered nature of sports is that the gendered power inequalities lay the ground for the occurrence of sexual violence in sports. While sexual abuse in sports continues to remain under-investigated and under-researched, several scandals, such as the one concerning the US women's gymnastics team doctor Larry Nassar, have shown that sexual violence regularly occurs in sports.[20] Part of the problem that creates the risk of sexual violence in sports are the weak labour standards. As the International Labour

[13]The increase in women as flag bearers was mainly caused by the new IOC policy that allows every National Olympic Committee to nominate one woman and one man to jointly carry the flag at the Opening Ceremony.

[14]International Olympic Committee (n.d), 'Factsheet. Women in the Olympic Movement' pp. 4–6.

[15]International Olympic Committee (n.d), 'Factsheet. Women in the Olympic Movement' pp. 4–6.

[16]Prügl (1996), pp. 16–17.

[17]Prize Money in Sport - BBC Sport Study. BBC Sport (8 March 2021), www.bbc.com/sport/56266693 (last accessed 4 April 2023).

[18]Dans le sport professionnel, le long chemin des femmes vers l'égalité salariale. LVSF - Le Vent Se Lève (23 March 2021), lvsl.fr/dans-le-sport-professionnel-le-long-chemin-des-femmes-vers-legalite-salariale/ (last accessed 4 April 2023); Sportscotland, Barriers to Women and Girls' Participation in Sport and Physical Activity (2008), pp. 1–2.

[19]I use the term "cis" to refer to individuals who identify with the gender that was assigned to them at birth.

[20]Mergaert L et al., Study on Gender-Based Violence in Sport Final Report. European Union (2016).

Organization points out, weak labour protection for athletes can create strong economic dependencies of athletes on their coaches, clubs and sports federations, which generates risks for exploitation.[21] Furthermore, more and more studies show that child athletes, especially those competing at an elite level, are at a high risk of experiencing emotional and physical abuse from their coaches.[22] This generally creates an environment where abusive behaviour, including sexual abuse, is highly normalized and tolerated, especially given the fact that sports federations often lack effective prevention and protection mechanisms in this field.[23]

In the popular imagination, many sports disciplines continue to be seen as masculine fields, where ideas on hegemonic masculinity are manifested and reproduced.[24] Nevertheless, some sports disciplines are marked as "feminine", especially those that are seen as enhancing stereotypical and heterosexist understandings of female attractiveness.[25] Men entering those "feminine" disciplines are often perceived as transgressing gender norms even more than women participating in traditionally "masculine" sports.[26] This is exemplified by the above-mentioned fact that men still cannot compete in rhythmic gymnastics and synchronized swimming at the Olympics, while women are nowadays allowed to compete in all disciplines.[27] Hegemonic ideas on appropriate femininity and masculinity in sports are also reproduced due to the public broadcasting of sports, which usually shows more men's competitions than women's and often sexualizes and objectifies women athletes.[28] Moreover, studies have shown that sports education also often reproduces gender stereotypes in sports.[29]

While the media and the education sector create gendered cultural imaginations in sports, these are also (re)produced by the rules imposed by international sports federations. Athletes competing in women's and men's competitions are regularly subjected to different rules, such as in rules on sporting equipment and competition

---

[21] International Labour Organisation (2020), Report. Global Dialogue Forum on Decent Work in the World of Sport, para 27.

[22] Gervis and Dunn (2004); Wilinsky and McCabe (2021); Tofte S, Husain N and Worden M, I Was Hit so Many Times I Can't Count: Abuse of Child Athletes in Japan. Human Rights Watch (2020).

[23] Mergaert L et al., Study on Gender-Based Violence in Sport Final Report. European Union (2016), p. 72.

[24] Whitson (1990); Buzuvis (2007).

[25] Lenskyj (1990), p. 236.

[26] Messner (2011).

[27] Jenkin M, Synching Feeling: Male Synchronised Swimmers Bid to Be Taken Seriously. The Guardian (18 December 2013), www.theguardian.com/lifeandstyle/the-swimming-blog/2013/dec/18/male-synchronised-swimming-london-ots-angels (last accessed 4 April 2023); Keng Kuek Ser K, See 120 Years of Struggle for Gender Equality at the Olympics. Public Radio International (17 August 2016), www.pri.org/stories/2016-08-17/see-120-years-struggle-gender-equality-olympics (last accessed 4 April 2023).

[28] Representation Project, #RespectHerGameReport. Gender & Media Coverage of the Tokyo Summer Olympics (2021).

[29] Preece and Bullingham (2022).

formats. For instance, international women's and men's basketball competitions use differently sized balls, except for the recently created 3 × 3 basketball events. Furthermore, women play only three sets in Grand Slams, while men play five. In addition to these examples, gender-specific rules in sports also include clothing regulations, which will be further discussed in the following sections.

3 Heterosexist and Racialized Clothing Regulations

Gendered clothing regulations are normalized in the world of sports. Not only do schoolchildren often have to wear different sports uniforms, but also many international sports federations have different rules on attire for women and men. The above-mentioned case of the Norwegian women's beach handball team being fined for wearing shorts in 2021 is a telling example of the way international sports federations hold on to gender differences in uniform regulations, even when they are publicly challenged.

What happened in the case was that after having been fined for wearing shorts instead of bikini bottoms, the Norwegian women's beach handball team protested, with the support of the Norwegian Handball Federation, against the rules of the International Handball Federation. This eventually led to changes in the respective clothing regulations in the fall of 2021. The International Handball Federation then decided to allow women to wear "body fit tank top, short tight pants and eventual accessories".[30] While this satisfies some of the demands of the concerned athletes, these new clothing rules continue to make a difference between women and men, since the latter can wear *loose* tank tops and shorts in their competitions, while women must wear "body fit" attire.[31] Thus, even though the International Handball Federation changed its regulations after having received criticism of objectifying women's bodies, it continues to differentiate between women and men athletes by prescribing tight clothing for women only. Based on the current rules, women who do not want to wear the prescribed attire cannot participate in international beach handball events, which also generates intersectional effects since women may not want to follow the dress code for various reasons, including religious ones.

Another notable example of rules on gendered sporting attire can be found in the clothing regulations of the International Skating Union. According to these regulations, men must wear full-length trousers in single and pair ice dancing, while women must wear a skirt.[32] These clothing regulations fit the overall

[30] International Handball Federation, IX. Rules of the Game b) Beach Handball (2021), Rule 4.8.

[31] International Handball Federation, IX. Rules of the Game b) Beach Handball (2021), Rule 4.8.

[32] International Skating Union, Special Regulations & Technical Rules Single & Pair Skating and Ice Dancing (2021), Rule 501.

heteronormative nature of ice skating, given that pair dances must always include a man and a woman and that men lead the dances.

These examples of clothing regulations in beach handball and ice dancing show that ensuring safety in sports is rarely the reason for gender-specific differences in uniform regulations. Otherwise, the safety argument would apply to all participants across gender categories in the same manner. Instead, it seems that the gendered regulations follow the rationale that was once explicitly stated by Joseph Blatter, the former President of the *Fédération internationale de football association* (FIFA), namely that women athletes should expose their naked bodies to attract more spectators and sponsors.[33] This demonstrates that gendered clothing regulations often put the appearance of women's body into focus, instead of their athletic performance.

Attracting spectators and sponsors through the objectification of bodies is arguably not a *necessary* justification for the institutionalized difference between women and men in sports. Simply put, human rights bodies would have a hard time treating gendered clothing regulations, for example in beach handball or ice dancing, as having a legitimate aim. Instead, these regulations seem to restrict the autonomy of athletes to choose clothes that they feel comfortable wearing, and they can foster the sexualization and objectification of women athletes. While clothing regulations especially target women's bodies, men's bodies can also be subjected to heterosexist clothing regulations. This is clearly shown in the example of ice dancing, where men are obliged to wear trousers and cannot wear leggings, feeding into the image of elite masculinity.

Another example that highlights the fact that elitism influences clothing regulations in sports is the "catsuit" controversy involving Serena Williams. After having given birth in September 2017, Williams returned to the 2018 French Open in a tight full bodysuit, which reportedly helped address certain health issues she faced after childbirth, including the prevention of blood clots. Yet the President of the International Tennis Federation, Bernard Giudicelli, banned the catsuit, arguing that one has "to respect the game and the place".[34] This institutionalized governance of Williams' body presented one of the many racist and sexist comments that she has had to endure during her career.[35] As Nittle argues, it also reflects the elitist and white roots

[33]Longman J, Badminton's New Dress Code Is Being Criticized as Sexist. The New York Times (27 May 2011) www.nytimes.com/2011/05/27/sports/badminton-dress code-for-women-criticized-as-sexist.html (last accessed 4 April 2023); CBC Sports, Sexy Shorts Good Idea for Women's Soccer: Blatter (16 January 2004) www.cbc.ca/sports/sexy-shorts-good-idea-for-women-s-soccer-blatter-1.488140 (last accessed 4 April 2023).

[34]Nittle N, The Serena Williams Catsuit Ban Shows That Tennis Can't Get Past Its Elitist Roots. Vox (28 August 2018) www.vox.com/2018/8/28/17791518/serena-williams-catsuit-ban-french-open-tennis-racist-sexist-country-club-sport (last accessed 4 April 2023).

[35]McLaughlin EC, Why Serena Williams' Catsuit Ban Matters, and What It Says about Us. CNN (27 August 2018), www.cnn.com/2018/08/27/tennis/serena-williams-catsuit-ban-racism-misogyny/index.html (last accessed 4 April 2023).

of tennis, since tennis became popular during Victorian England, where the elite dressed in white to signal hygiene, privilege and wealth.[36]

The obligatory whiteness in tennis attire, such as in Wimbledon, has recently come under attack by women athletes and activists. In summer 2022, several women tennis players and tennis broadcasters started to speak out about the stress that the all-white dress code at Wimbledon generates for menstruating players.[37] This example demonstrates that clothing requirements can also constitute indirect forms of discrimination since the requirement of wearing white applies to all players regardless of their gender, but the impact of the clothing rules negatively affects menstruating players, who are predominately but not exclusively women. It further shows that sports continues to treat cis men as the *status quo*, and other experiences, such as those of menstruating players, remain unconsidered. This discussion also brought attention to the fact that menstruation remains a taboo in sports; competitions and facilities are often not designed to accommodate menstruating participants.

The elitism reflected in, for instance, a white tennis dress code highlights how gender discrimination in sports must always be understood in relation to other structures of inequality. The examples of the gendered beach handball rules, the ice dancing rules and the ban on Williams' catsuit all have intersectional effects that reflect inequalities based on gender, race, class and religion. The governance of bodies in international sports not only relies on heterosexist assumptions on body appearance, but these assumptions are also strongly shaped by historically and culturally specific norms. One must keep in mind that international sport is not only a heavily male-dominated field, but it is also strongly shaped by "Western" powers. The largest international federations are almost exclusively located in the Global North, especially in Switzerland,[38] and decision-makers within those federations as well as sports arbitrators are predominantly men from the Global North.[39] Moreover, only three Olympic disciplines have their roots outside of Europe or North America: judo, karate and taekwondo.[40] In addition, researchers increasingly point out that Christian norms on gender and modesty have influenced international

[36]Nittle N, The Serena Williams Catsuit Ban Shows That Tennis Can't Get Past Its Elitist Roots. Vox (28 August 2018) www.vox.com/2018/8/28/17791518/serena-williams-catsuit-ban-french-open-tennis-racist-sexist-country-club-sport (last accessed 4 April 2023). See also: Lake (2017), p. 53.

[37]BBC Sport, It's Time to Talk Tennis, Periods & Wimbledon Whites (21 June 2022) www.bbc.com/sport/tennis/61785521 (last accessed 4 April 2023).

[38]In summer 2022, 73 out of 104 listed international sport federations were registered as private associations in Switzerland. This is due to a favourable taxing system and other economic incentives for international federations in Switzerland. See: Think Sport, International Sports Organisations, www.thinksport.org/en/if-wall/ (last accessed 4 April 2023); Zintz and Winand (2013), pp. 11–12; Chappelet (2008), p. 108.

[39]While more quantitative research would be needed to further substantiate this claim, skimming through the Boards of international sports federations and the list of possible arbitrators at the Court of Arbitration for Sports provides a good indication for the validity of this claim.

[40]Besnier et al. (2018), pp. 46–50.

sports significantly, also caused by the colonial practices of European states that exported their sports to other parts of the world.[41]

While sports are often considered "a shared global 'monoculture'",[42] there is nothing universal about sporting rules. Instead, they are the product of historically contingent and specific circumstances, which always reflect power inequalities based on gender, race, religion, class, physical ability, colonial legacies and geographical position. The workings of gender norms in clothing regulations in sports can thus only be understood by taking into account power inequalities based on location, race and history in international sports.

Two other recent examples of clothing regulations in sports exemplify this point. First, the ban on religious veils in certain international sports events shows precisely how heterosexist norms intersect with religious discrimination and racism. For example, Zahra Lari was penalized for wearing a hijab when competing in figure skating in the 2012 European Cup. After this incident, she was able to successfully lobby the International Skating Union to change this rule, which now instructs the jury to not take any points away for the wearing of hijabs.[43] Yet while athletes are now able to wear a hijab *in practice*, the official clothing rules of the Union still do not mention that religious veils may be worn during competitions.[44]

The example of Zahra Lari lobbying the International Skating Union shows once more that changes in clothing regulations have often been the result of extensive activism by impacted athletes. Similarly, it was only after athlete activism that FIFA and the International Basketball Association (FIBA) started allowing players to wear a hijab in international competitions in 2014 and 2017.[45] Indeed, major changes have taken place in relation to the rules on hijabs over the last decade, and many international sports federations no longer categorically ban a veil from competitions. However, most of these federations have not yet explicitly addressed the veil in their rules;[46] it seems that they deal with the issue on a case-by-case basis when a relevant situation arises. This leaves athletes in situations of insecurity and frames them as the exception that needs special treatment.

Another example of a racialized rule in sports occurs in the debate as to whether so-called soul caps should be allowed at the Olympic Games in Tokyo. World Aquatics justified the banning of "soul caps", a specific kind of swim cap designed

---

[41] Carlson et al. (2022).

[42] Besnier et al. (2018), p. 228.

[43] Hosny B, How the Future of Hijabi Athletes Is Being Changed by a 23-Year-Old Emirati Figure Skater. SceneArabia (24 April 2018), www.SceneArabia.com/Life/Zahra-Lari-Hijabi-Athletes-Emirati-Figure-Skater (last accessed 4 April 2023).

[44] International Skating Union, Special Regulations & Technical Rules Single & Pair Skating and Ice Dancing (2021), Rule 501.

[45] Hosny B, How the Future of Hijabi Athletes Is Being Changed by a 23-Year-Old Emirati Figure Skater. SceneArabia (24 April 2018), www.SceneArabia.com/Life/Zahra-Lari-Hijabi-Athletes-Emirati-Figure-Skater (last accessed 4 April 2023).

[46] See e.g. FIVB - Fédération Internationale de Volleyball, Event Regulations Volleyball (2022), para A.3.1.

to fit "thick, curly, and voluminous hair",[47] from the Tokyo Olympics, arguing that they did not fit "the natural form of the head". This decision by World Aquactics presents another instance when clothing regulations in sports can *indirectly* discriminate against a certain group based on race and gender. It treats formally all swimmers the same. Yet in practice, the decision has largely negative effects on women since they tend to have longer hair than men, especially black women as their hair tends to be more "thick, curly, and voluminous".

The various examples of gendered and racialized clothing regulations discussed in this section show that international sporting rules are part of the transnationally circulating norms that normalize and (re)produce heterosexist, racialized, elitist and religion-specific notions of hegemonic femininity and masculinity. Rules on clothing in sports are thus part of the gendered sporting system which reproduced the gender binary by constructing women and men as different entities that are in a hierarchical relationship to another.

As intersex and trans activists have further pointed out, the gendered nature of uniforms also puts an extra burden on people whose gender identity and/or sex characteristics do not conform to the normative expectations of the gender binary. For example, activists have reported that clothing exposing body anatomy, such as tight clothing, can create anxiety and discomfort for trans and intersex persons.[48] Gender differences in sports uniforms involve a financial burden when people change the gender category in sports or start to compete in mixed sports because they must purchase new uniforms, creating an additional obstacle for people in precarious economic situations.[49] By enforcing the gender binary on people, heterosexist sports uniforms reflect the assumption that women and men are naturally opposite, complementary and fundamentally different entities. This also invisiblizes the existence of persons with gender identities and/or expressions outside of the binary.

The problematic nature of gendered clothing regulations has been increasingly noticed by international sports governance bodies. In its 2018 Report, the IOC Gender Equality Review Panel recognized that gendered clothing regulations could be contrary to the principle of gender equality, recommending that "competition uniforms reflect the technical requirements of the sport and do not have any unjustifiable differences".[50] To reach this goal, it recommended conducting a review

[47] Pavitt M, FINA Review Use of Swim Caps for Natural Black Hair as Not Permitted at Olympics, Inside the Games (3 July 2021), www.insidethegames.biz/articles/1109732/fina-swimming-soul-cap-review-olympics (last accessed 4 April 2023).

[48] Fluch (2017), p. 80; Barras (2021); Verity Smith, Trans Inclusion in Sports Manager at Mermaids, online interview, 11 March 2022; Spandler H et al., Non-Binary Inclusion in Sport. Specific Detriment Project (2020), p. 7.

[49] Verity Smith, Trans Inclusion in Sports Manager at Mermaids, online interview, 11 March 2022.

[50] International Olympic Committee, IOC Gender Equality Review Project. IOC Gender Equality Report (2018), p. 11.

of gender-specific clothing differences, consulting with international sports federations and identifying an oversight body to address gendered clothing rules.[51] The follow-up to these recommendations has yet to be made public. Until the IOC and international sports federations become more active in tackling gender-specific clothing regulations themselves, international human rights law could be a tool to support the de-gendering of clothing regulations in sports.

4 International Human Rights Law and Gendered Clothing Regulations

International sports law and international human rights law have long been considered two distinct legal regimes that hardly overlap each other. Yet, this volume shows that there is currently momentum to consider the interactions between these two regimes and how international human rights law can guide developments in the field of sports. This is also increasingly recognized in discussions on gender equality in sports. For instance, the Brighton Declaration adopted during the 6th World Conference on Women and Sport in 2014 holds explicitly that sports governance bodies should comply with international human rights law, including CEDAW.[52] Following this proposition, the remainder of this chapter will analyse how CEDAW can be applied to the issue of heterosexist and racialized clothing regulations in sports.

CEDAW was adopted by the UN General Assembly in 1979 and entered into force in 1981. After the Convention on the Rights of the Child, it is the most widely ratified treaty among the nine core international human rights treaties, but it is also the treaty with the most reservations.[53] It was drafted as a result of the dissatisfaction of women's rights activists with general international human rights treaties, which often failed to take into account experiences commonly made by women and thus applied a male-biased definition of human rights.[54] Similar to other UN human rights treaties, the implementation of CEDAW is monitored by a Committee composed of 23 experts from different geographical regions and with different backgrounds. The Committee issues concluding observations, individual communications, general recommendations and inquiry reports, which provide guidance on the substance of state obligations deriving from the Convention.

[51] International Olympic Committee, IOC Gender Equality Review Project. IOC Gender Equality Report (2018), p. 11.

[52] Brighton plus Helsinki 2014. Declaration on Women and Sport. Adopted during the 6th IWG World Conference on Women and Sport in Helsinki, Finland from June 12–15 (2014) Principle B (1).

[53] According to the UN Treaty Body Database, only eight UN member states have not ratified CEDAW at the end of 2022.

[54] Gaer (2009), p. 62.

Sports is mentioned in CEDAW in two different articles. Article 10(h) on the right to education holds that state parties shall take all appropriate measures to ensure, on the basis of the equality of women and men, "[t]he same Opportunities to participate actively in sports and physical education".[55] In addition, Article 13 (c) ensures women's "right to participate in recreational activities, sports and all aspects of cultural life" on the same terms as men.[56] These two references to sports show that the drafters of CEDAW were well aware that there are considerable gender inequalities in sports. However, even if the treaty text was silent on sports, the Convention could be used to fight gender inequalities in sports since it aims to eliminate "all forms of discrimination", including those that are not explicitly mentioned in the Convention.[57]

Even though the text of CEDAW gives consideration to sports, Pérez González argues that the CEDAW Committee has rarely dealt with issues of discrimination in this area.[58] This lack of engagement is partly due to the Committee's own blind spots,[59] but states and civil society have also largely failed to include sports as a substantive issue in state reporting procedures and individual communications. This also shows that international women's rights movements have long sidelined the field of sports in their human rights advocacy.

To better understand the possible applicability of CEDAW to gendered clothing regulations in sports, the next sections will look at available mechanisms provided by CEDAW (Sect. 4.1), the possibility of taking recourse to CEDAW in the specific subject matter (Sect. 4.2), the due diligence obligations deriving from CEDAW (Sect. 4.3), the state obligation to work towards *de facto* equality (Sect. 4.4), the use of CEDAW to fight gender stereotypes (Sect. 4.5) and the Convention's approach to intersectional forms of discrimination (Sect. 4.6).

4.1 Mechanisms: How to Use CEDAW to Address Gender Discrimination in Sports

CEDAW's state reporting procedure and individual complaint procedure are two of the mechanisms that could be specifically useful for upholding women athletes' rights. Aside from these two mechanisms, the CEDAW Committee also has the

---

[55] Convention on the Elimination of all Forms of Discrimination against Women (1979), Art. 10(g).

[56] Convention on the Elimination of all Forms of Discrimination against Women (1979), Art. 13(c).

[57] Freeman et al. (2012), p. 76.

[58] Pérez González (2020), p. 16. See also: Blakey (2018), pp. 269, 292.

[59] The Committee has mentioned sports in some of its documents, such as General Recommendations 25 and 36. The latter is further analysed in the section on gender stereotypes of this paper. See: CEDAW Committee, General Recommendation No. 25, on Article 4, Paragraph 1, of the Convention on the Elimination of All Forms of Discrimination against Women, on Temporary Special Measures (2004), para 38; CEDAW Committee, General Recommendation No. 36 on the Right of Girls and Women to Education (2017), paras 62–63.

option to start an inquiry procedure if it receives reliable information indicating grave or systematic violations and the state party has accepted the inquiry procedure under the Optional Protocol.[60] Moreover, to clarify how CEDAW applies to gender inequalities in sports, the Committee could issue a specific General Recommendation on the issue. I will focus this analysis on the state reporting and individual complaint procedure under CEDAW since this could help advocacy efforts concretely. It also seems rather unlikely that the Committee would trigger an inquiry procedure due to gendered clothing regulations since starting an inquiry procedure usually requires a high level of violence and urgency, and issuing a General Recommendation is usually a decision up to the Committee.

CEDAW's state reporting mechanism is established by Article 18 of the Convention, which creates the obligation of states to regularly submit reports on the progress of their implementation of the Convention to the Committee. These reports are considered during an interactive dialogue between the CEDAW Committee and state representatives, which takes place in Geneva. The outcome of the dialogue involves the Committee issuing Concluding Observations that record the concerned state's developments of implementing the Convention and make recommendations for further improvements. While civil society organizations cannot usually speak during the interactive dialogue, they can write so-called shadow reports, which the Committee members can consider in their questions to the state party. In addition, it has become common practice that Committee members meet members of civil society to discuss challenges in the implementation of the Convention as part of the state reporting procedure.[61] Sports could therefore receive more attention in the reporting procedure if civil society provide more input on the matter or if Committee members bring it up themselves.

Another mechanism through which gender inequalities in sports could be considered by the CEDAW Committee is through the individual communication procedure. The procedure is established under the Optional Protocol adopted in 1999 and allows individuals to send to the Committee complaints about alleged violations of their rights guaranteed by CEDAW. The Committee can consider the merit of these communications in cases where the state concerned has ratified the Optional Protocol, domestic remedies have been exhausted and the complaint is admissible.[62] Once the Committee has conducted its investigation and sought additional information from the concerned state and applicant, it will make its final decision on the merits of the complaint.[63] Despite the fact that the Committee's views on these

[60] Optional Protocol to the Convention on the Elimination of All Forms of Discrimination against Women (1999), Art. 8.

[61] CEDAW Committee, Rules of Procedure and Working Methods, www.ohchr.org/en/treaty-bodies/cedaw/rules-procedure-and-working-methods> accessed (last accessed 4 April 2023).

[62] Optional Protocol to the Convention on the Elimination of All Forms of Discrimination against Women (1999), Art. 4.

[63] Optional Protocol to the Convention on the Elimination of All Forms of Discrimination against Women (1999), Articles 6 and 7; OHCHR, Individual Complaint Procedures under the United Nations Human Rights Treaties. Fact Sheet No. 7/Rev.2 (2013), p. 10.

individual complaints become authoritative decisions on the interpretation of CEDAW and form part of the jurisprudence of the Committee, they are not legally binding.[64]

These individual communications could be a promising avenue for raising the issue of heterosexist clothing regulations with the CEDAW Committee. However, domestic remedies must first be exhausted before an individual can take recourse to CEDAW, which can be difficult in the realm of sports since most disputes are decided through arbitration and thus remain outside of a state's public justice system. As the next section addresses, identifying the exact state that can be held accountable for failing to protect the athlete from the harm committed by a sports federation can be challenging in itself.

4.2 *Recourse to CEDAW: Questions of Jurisdiction*

A major difficulty in addressing discrimination and inequalities in sports through CEDAW is that organizations that make sporting rules are usually non-state entities. CEDAW is a state-centric instrument that follows the traditional legal approach to considering states as the duty-bearer of human rights and as responsible for ensuring compliance with CEDAW. This traditional approach stands in contrast to the emerging view that private entities, such as businesses and sports federations, also have human rights responsibilities[65] The latter view underpins the currently negotiated draft treaty on transnational corporations and other business enterprises[66] and has been supported by the Guiding Principles on Business and Human Rights (2011).[67] Even though the emerging approach to consider non-state actors as duty-bearers of human rights could be useful for addressing human rights issues in sports, this chapter remains within the accepted parameters of CEDAW and aims to analyse the obligations of states to address gendered clothing regulations in sports.

There are two scenarios in which to use CEDAW for tackling heterosexist clothing regulations within a state-centric approach. The first scenario comes into play when public bodies themselves are involved in implementing gendered clothing regulations. In many regions of the world, such as North America, sports are mostly organized as part of scholastic activities, such as college or high school sports. These structures tend to be public institutions or, if they are private, they often receive

[64]OHCHR, Individual Complaint Procedures under the United Nations Human Rights Treaties. Fact Sheet No. 7/Rev.2 (2013), p. 11.

[65]Lane (2018), pp. 16–17, 24.

[66]OEIGWG Chairmanship, Third revised draft. Legally binding instrument to regulate, in international human rights law, the activities of transnational corporations and other business enterprises (2021).

[67]The Guiding Principles did not talk about human rights obligations but focused on the "human rights responsibilities" of private companies. See: OHCHR, Guiding Principles on Business and Human Rights (2011), p. 13.

public funding. If the state concerned has ratified CEDAW, then the Convention becomes directly applicable to the governance of sports organized publicly. A crucial provision in this regard is CEDAW Article 2(d), which mentions that states must "refrain from engaging in any act or practice of discrimination against women and to ensure that public authorities and institutions shall act in conformity with this obligation".[68]

The second scenario is the focus of this article. In this scenario, non-state entities, notably private sports federations, are mostly responsible for establishing and implementing the rules in sports competitions, including clothing regulations. This raises the question of whether the concerned state has any responsibility for regulating the actions of these federations. The answer to this question depends partly on the legal technicalities of each state and whether sports federations have been considered as carrying out a "public function", such as in India.[69] In this chapter, I aim to establish general principles, such as the principle of "due diligence", which requires states to undertake positive measures to protect individuals from harm committed by other private actors.[70] I chose to analyse this scenario precisely because CEDAW provides strong due diligence obligations and could thus shed light on avenues to regulate the norm-setting behaviour of sports federations through existing international human rights law.

I will discuss the nature of CEDAW's due diligence obligations further below, but another point regarding the recourse to CEDAW must be considered. Since disputes in international sports are often of a transnational nature, it can be difficult to ascertain which state has the responsibility for the actions of a sports federation. Is it the state where the relevant sports federation is legally registered, or is it the place where the actions are carried out (i.e. the host states of international sports events)? As Shinohara has analysed, the fact that disputes in sports are largely settled by means of arbitration further complicates the situation since the host state of relevant arbitration tribunals could also be responsible for ensuring that the settlement of disputes upholds human rights.[71] In fact, the approach of holding states that host respective arbitration tribunals accountable if the tribunals fail to uphold human rights is increasingly prevalent in cases concerning human rights in sports, such as the *Caster Semenya* case discussed in Chap. 5.[72] In this particular case, Switzerland is the respondent state before the European Court of Human Rights since the Swiss Federal Tribunal upheld the respective award issued by the Court of Arbitration for Sports (CAS).[73] This was

[68] Convention on the Elimination of all Forms of Discrimination against Women (1979), Art. 2(d).

[69] Bhogle (2016); Board of Control of Cricket v Cricket Association of Bihar and Ors [2016] Indian Supreme Court 3 SCC 251.

[70] Freeman et al. (2012), p. 87.

[71] Shinohara (2022).

[72] Mutu and Pechstein v Switzerland [2018] European Court of Human Rights Applications nos. 40575/10 and 67474/10 [paras 62–67]; Platini c la Suisse [2020] La Cour européenne des droits de l'homme Requête no 526/18 [paras 36–38]; Semenya v Switzerland (pending) European Court of Human Rights Application 10934/21.

[73] Semenya v Switzerland (pending) European Court of Human Rights Application 10934/21.

possible since the CAS is located in Switzerland and CAS awards can be appealed, under certain circumstances, at the Swiss Federal Tribunal.[74]

While a detailed discussion on jurisdictional issues in human rights cases concerning sports is outside the scope of this chapter, it is important to note that the transnational nature of international sports calls into question issues surrounding responsibility in terms of human rights protection. If one wants to take recourse to the CEDAW Committee to tackle heterosexist clothing regulations in sports, an effective link between the state and the regulations must be established. In other words, based on due diligence obligations, states can be held accountable under international human rights law if they fail to take necessary measures to prevent harm caused by non-state actors, such as international sports federations.

4.3 Due Diligence Obligations: Regulating the Actions of Sports Federations

Based on the discussion above, this section will look more closely at the due diligence obligations established by CEDAW. The Convention explicitly recognizes states' positive obligations to influence the actions of non-state actors by requiring states, in Article 2(e), to "take all appropriate measures to eliminate discrimination against women by *any person, organization or enterprise*".[75] The Committee has clarified that "Article 2 also imposes a due diligence obligation on States parties to prevent discrimination by private actors"[76] and that "[i]n some cases a private actor's acts or omission of acts may be attributed to the State under international law".[77] The strong due diligence obligations under CEDAW have proven to be particularly important in the fight against gender-based violence, which is mainly committed by private persons, such as family members, rather than state officials.[78]

CEDAW General Recommendations have further addressed the responsibility of states to regulate the actions of private organizations, notably private companies. For

[74] Code of Sports-related Arbitration 2023, R46 and R59. Federal Act on Private International Law 1987 Art. 191.

[75] Convention on the Elimination of all Forms of Discrimination against Women (1979), Art. 2 (e) (emphasis added).

[76] CEDAW Committee, General Recommendation No. 28 on the Core Obligations of States Parties under Article 2 of the Convention on the Elimination of All Forms of Discrimination against Women (2010), p. 13.

[77] CEDAW Committee, General Recommendation No. 28 on the Core Obligations of States Parties under Article 2 of the Convention on the Elimination of All Forms of Discrimination against Women (2010), p. 13.

[78] Sahide Goekce (deceased) v Austria [2007] Committee on the Elimination of Discrimination against Women CEDAW/C/39/D/5/2005; Fatma Yildirim (deceased) v Austria [2007] Committee on the Elimination of Discrimination against Women CEDAW/C/39/D/6/2005; CEDAW Committee, General Recommendation No. 19: Violence against Women (1992), para 24(a).

instance, General Recommendation 25 states that CEDAW Article 2 "imposes accountability on the State party for action by [the private sector, private organizations, or political parties]".[79] General Recommendation 28 holds that the obligations to protect women from discrimination "also extend to acts of national corporations operating extraterritorially".[80] While international sports federations are not "corporations", this reference could be applied by analogy to non-commercial organizations, including sports federations. This would indicate that states in which international sports federations are registered, such as Switzerland, must take necessary measures to prevent these federations from taking actions that generate extraterritorial effects and are contrary to CEDAW. This could be the case when their rules apply in international sports events, for instance World Cups or Olympic Games.

Discussions on CEDAW's due diligence obligations have rarely considered sports, but Freeman, Chinkin and Rudolf have explicitly analysed the use of CEDAW to regulate the actions of sports federations. They state in their commentary on CEDAW that

> the duty to protect obliges the State party to prevent private organizers of cultural and sports events from discriminating directly or indirectly against female participants, for example, by excluding women from certain sports because of gender-based stereotypes.[81]

Accordingly, CEDAW's due diligence obligations could make the Convention a useful instrument for tackling women's exclusion from sports, for example through heterosexist and racialized clothing regulations. The due diligence provision enshrined in CEDAW Article 2(e) must be read in conjunction with Article 2(a), (b) and (c), which establishes the obligation to outlaw gender discrimination through legislation.[82] Reading these provisions together suggests that state parties also have the obligation to prohibit horizontal discrimination against women, which is discrimination conducted by private actors, such as sports federations. However, strong state protection against horizontal discrimination in the field of sports runs counter to the principle that sports federations enjoy significant autonomy in their norm-setting activities.[83] The IOC Charter establishes that sports organizations "have the rights and obligations of autonomy, which include freely establishing and controlling the rules of sport".[84] Furthermore, most jurisdictions, such as Switzerland, grant sports federations vast autonomy and freedom in establishing the rules for their games and

[79] CEDAW Committee, General Recommendation No. 25, on Article 4, Paragraph 1, of the Convention on the Elimination of All Forms of Discrimination against Women, on Temporary Special Measures (2004), para 29.

[80] CEDAW Committee, General Recommendation No. 28 on the Core Obligations of States Parties under Article 2 of the Convention on the Elimination of All Forms of Discrimination against Women (2010), para 36.

[81] Freeman et al. (2012), p. 353.

[82] Freeman et al. (2012), p. 88.

[83] Chappelet (2016).

[84] Olympic Charter (2021), para 5.

internal governance structures.[85] A lack of strong protections from horizontal discrimination in the field of sports fosters the autonomy of international sports federations to establish gendered clothing rules. It indirectly allows those federations, such as the International Handball Federation, to avoid properly implementing the anti-discrimination clauses that are enshrined in their own statutes.[86]

The implementation of due diligence obligations by states can be especially critical in the field of sports because sports federations often hold a quasi-monopoly in their specific discipline.[87] Since there is usually one dominant federation organizing international competitions in a specific discipline, athletes are not in a position to freely consent to the federation's rules.[88] Chappelet argues in this regard that

> [w]ithin their respective sports, the IFs have "monopolistic powers" over the national federations (NFs) affiliated to them. Without recognition of the national federation by the IF of the sport in question, an athlete cannot envisage international-level competition.[89]

The monopolistic status of international sports federations makes it difficult for athletes to refuse the rules of international sports federations since this would make it impossible for them to compete internationally at all. As discussed in the *Mutu and Pechstein v. Switzerland* judgment of the European Court of Human Rights (ECtHR), if athletes decide not to subject themselves to the regulations of the respective federation, they may incur significant loss of their economic livelihoods. This makes their consent to the rules of sports federations of a "compulsory" nature instead of a "voluntary" one.[90]

In *Mutu and Pechstein*, the judges at the ECtHR decided that if the consent of athletes to accept the rules of sports federations is "compulsory" instead of "voluntary", the protections of the ECHR, specifically Article 6, apply.[91] While the case invoked rights under the ECHR and not CEDAW, it provides general insights into the nature of due diligence obligations in the field of sports, indicating that states have the obligation to act with due diligence, especially in cases where the athletes concerned do not have the option to freely consent to the sporting rules due to the respective federation's monopolistic status.

---

[85] Baddeley (2020).

[86] International Handball Federation, Statutes (2022), Art. 5.

[87] Cisneros (2020), p. 22.

[88] Mutu and Pechstein v Switzerland [2018] European Court of Human Rights Applications nos. 40575/10 and 67474/10 [paras 25, 77–115].

[89] Chappelet (2008), p. 70.

[90] Mutu and Pechstein v Switzerland [2018] European Court of Human Rights Applications nos. 40575/10 and 67474/10 [paras 77–115].

[91] Mutu and Pechstein v Switzerland [2018] European Court of Human Rights Applications nos. 40575/10 and 67474/10 [para 115].

4.4 De Facto Equality: Sports as an Unequal Practice

My discussion on due diligence obligations illustrated that CEDAW is based on a broad meaning of "discrimination", covering also actions taken by non-state actors. The Committee has recognized that the "Convention goes beyond the concept of discrimination used in many national and international legal standards and norms".[92] One important element that makes the Convention special is that it obliges states to work towards *de facto equality* or *substantive equality*, instead of ensuring only formal or *de jure* equality, which is the focus of most anti-discrimination laws.[93] The obligation to foster *de facto* equality involves changing societal structures, material conditions and the behaviour of non-state actors to achieve equality in outcome between women and men.

According to the CEDAW Committee, the overall objective and purpose of the Convention is to "eliminate all forms of discrimination against women with a view to achieving women's *de jure* and *de facto* equality with men".[94] Indeed, the call to work towards substantive equality is mainstreamed throughout almost all substantive CEDAW articles regularly obliging states to take "all appropriate measures" to tackle the discrimination experienced by women. Moreover, Article 2(f) urges states to "take all appropriate measures, including legislation, to modify or abolish existing laws, regulations, *customs* and *practices* which constitute discrimination against women".[95] The reference to customs and practices shows that states must go further than just eliminating any formal distinction between women and men and also address normalized patterns of social organizations that disadvantage women and reproduce inequalities.

The obligation to work towards substantive equality as enshrined in CEDAW could be useful for fighting inequalities in sports in various ways. It obliges states to create the material and social conditions that allow women to play sports on an equal footing with men. This could include making sure that women's sports receive the same funding as men's sports or undertaking educational projects to combat images of hegemonic masculinity in sports. It could further mean undertaking measures that ensure representation of women in decision-making bodies in sports, such as through

[92]CEDAW Committee, General Recommendation No. 25, on Article 4, Paragraph 1, of the Convention on the Elimination of All Forms of Discrimination against Women, on Temporary Special Measures (2004), para 5.

[93]CEDAW Committee, General Recommendation No. 25, on Article 4, Paragraph 1, of the Convention on the Elimination of All Forms of Discrimination against Women, on Temporary Special Measures (2004), para 4.

[94]CEDAW Committee, General Recommendation No. 25, on Article 4, Paragraph 1, of the Convention on the Elimination of All Forms of Discrimination against Women, on Temporary Special Measures (2004), para 4.

[95]Convention on the Elimination of all Forms of Discrimination against Women (1979), Art. 2 (f) (emphasis added).

"temporary special measures", commonly referred to as affirmative action, and explicitly allowed by CEDAW Article 4.[96]

CEDAW's strong commitment to foster *de jure* and *de facto* equality can also support the fight against indirect discrimination in sports. The CEDAW Committee has recognized on multiple occasions that the Convention prohibits direct and indirect discrimination.[97] Indirect gender discrimination occurs when rules or measures seem neutral as they apply to all people in the same manner regardless of their gender, but their effects end up being discriminatory. As discussed above, neutral clothing regulations in sports can constitute an indirect form of discrimination if their effects disproportionally harm women and/or non-white people. This is the case with the requirement to wear white in Wimbledon, which indirectly disadvantages people who menstruate. Likewise, the banning of soul caps in international swimming tournaments indirectly disadvantages black women since they are more likely than others to have "thick, curly, and voluminous hair". CEDAW's clear stance to prohibit indirect discrimination and work towards substantive equality by addressing structural inequalities in the distribution of power and resources could thus be used to tackle clothing regulations in sports that cause indirect discrimination.

4.5 Stereotyping: Tackling the Gender Binary in Sports Through CEDAW Article 5

Another issue reflected in international clothing regulations is that sporting rules are often underpinned by gender stereotypes that are infused with hetero-, cis- and endosexnormativity,[98] as well as racism, classicism and Islamophobia. For example, the international rules prescribing women to wear skirts and men to wear trousers in ice dancing also require athletes to wear attire that is "modest, dignified and appropriate for athletic competition—not garish or theatrical in design".[99] In practice, these requirements reproduce stereotypical and Western ideas of hegemonic

[96] See e.g.: CEDAW Committee, General Recommendation No. 25, on Article 4, Paragraph 1, of the Convention on the Elimination of All Forms of Discrimination against Women, on Temporary Special Measures (2004), para 8.

[97] CEDAW Committee, General Recommendation No. 25, on Article 4, Paragraph 1, of the Convention on the Elimination of All Forms of Discrimination against Women, on Temporary Special Measures (2004), para 7; CEDAW Committee, General Recommendation No. 28 on the Core Obligations of States Parties under Article 2 of the Convention on the Elimination of All Forms of Discrimination against Women (2010), paras 9, 16.

[98] The term endosexnormativity refers to the treatment of endosex people as the norm and of intersex people as "the Other" or the exception. Intersex persons are born with sex characteristics that do not correspond to normative medical definitions of binary sex, while endosex persons are usually described as being the opposite of intersex persons since their sex characteristics do correspond to normative medical sex definitions.

[99] International Skating Union, Special Regulations & Technical Rules Single & Pair Skating and Ice Dancing (2021), Rule 501.

femininity and masculinity. The rule that pair dances must include a man and a woman, and that men must lead the dances, further shows the heteronormative nature of some sports regulations, presuming that women and men are inherently different and complementary. Since CEDAW also creates the obligation to fight gender stereotypes, it could be a useful instrument to tackle these underlying stereotypical and binary ideas on appropriate gender norms in sports.

CEDAW Article 5(a) is particularly useful in the fight against gender stereotypes in sports. It obliges states

> [t]o modify the social and cultural patterns of conduct of men and women, with a view to achieving the elimination of prejudices and customary and all other practices which are based on the idea of the inferiority or the superiority of either of the sexes or on stereotyped roles for men and women.[100]

Even though the CEDAW Committee has rarely addressed issues on sports, it has recognized that gender stereotypes affect women's access to sports. General Recommendation 36 on the right to education urges states to address gender stereotypes in sports and in media representations of women athletes. It further raises other issues of discrimination in sports, such as the lack of funding for women's sports.[101] As Freeman, Chinkin and Rudolf point out in their CEDAW commentary, gender stereotypes ultimately rest upon a binary construction of gender, in which heterosexuality functions as a core determinant.[102] Thus, challenging gendered clothing regulations in sports by relying on CEDAW Article 5 has the potential to address not only the sexist nature of clothing regulations but also their hetero-, cis- and endosexnormative bases.

Indeed, the interpretation of CEDAW by its Committee increasingly recognizes that sexism is entangled with hetero-, cis- and endosexnormativity. The Committee has refuted the understanding that gender is an inherent, biologically determined and binary characteristic that creates two complementary sexes or genders. Instead, it has recognized the social construction of gender by defining it as "socially constructed identities, attributes and roles for women and men".[103] While this definition recognizes gender as a social system of inequality rather than as a biologically deterministic category, it continues to frame women as opposite to men, which recreates a binary understanding

---

[100] Convention on the Elimination of all Forms of Discrimination against Women (1979), Art. 5(a).

[101] CEDAW Committee, General Recommendation No. 36 on the Right of Girls and Women to Education (2017), para 63(i). The CEDAW Committee also mentions the effects of gender stereotypes on the sporting activities of girls and women in some concluding observations, such as the one in Haiti in 2008. See: CEDAW Committee, Combined Initial, Second, Third, Fourth, Fifth, Sixth and Seventh Periodic Reports of States Parties. Haiti' (2008) CEDAW/C/HTI/7, para 13.3.

[102] Freeman et al. (2012), p. 149.

[103] CEDAW Committee, General Recommendation No. 28 on the Core Obligations of States Parties under Article 2 of the Convention on the Elimination of All Forms of Discrimination against Women (2010), para 5.

of gender.[104] In fact, as Miller explains, issues on non-heterosexual sexualities and diverse sexual identities have long been controversial issues for the CEDAW Committee and have largely been excluded from its mandate.[105]

Yet in the last 15 years, the CEDAW Committee has started to consider the discrimination of women based on their sexual orientation, gender identity and sex characteristics. For example, it was the first UN Human Rights Treaty Body that recognized intersex persons in one of its concluding observations in 2009.[106] In a recent individual communication, it confirmed that "the rights enshrined in the Convention belong to all women, including lesbian, bisexual, transgender and intersex women, and that article 16 of the Convention applies also to non-heterosexual relations".[107] These references are in line with the Committee's approach to intersectionality, which, as discussed in the next section, considers sexual orientation and gender identity as intersecting statuses, possibly affecting women's experiences of discrimination.[108] The Committee's increasing consideration of issues of sexual orientation, gender identity and sex characteristics could make it a useful instrument for overcoming multi-layered gender stereotypes in sports.

4.6 *Intersectionality: Tackling Multiple Forms of Discrimination in Sports*

A related question to the previous discussion concerning gender stereotypes is how CEDAW could be used to tackle intersectional forms of discrimination presented by clothing regulations in sports. The Convention itself does not include provisions on intersectional forms of discrimination, but it does specifically address the situation of rural women in Article 14 and mentions the effects of poverty, racial discrimination and (neo-)colonialism on women's rights in the Preamble. Critics have pointed out that the absence of a specific provision on intersectional forms of discrimination in CEDAW fails to take account of the varied lived experiences of women. More specifically, the Convention has been criticized for presuming a monolithic and universally true category of "womanhood" whose definition has been shaped by the realities of white and middle- or upper-class women.[109]

---

[104] This binary understanding of gender has also been enshrined in the Convention by tackling discrimination against women instead of discrimination based on gender. This evaluates the treatment of women in comparison to those against men. See also: Miller (2012), p. 23.

[105] Miller (2012), p. 25.

[106] CEDAW Committee, Concluding Observation on Germany (2009) CEDAW/C/DEU/CO/6, paras 61–62.

[107] Rosanna Flamer-Caldera v Sri Lanka [2022] Committee on the Elimination of Discrimination against Women CEDAW/C/81/D/134/2018 [para 9.7].

[108] CEDAW Committee, General Recommendation No. 28 on the Core Obligations of States Parties under Article 2 of the Convention on the Elimination of All Forms of Discrimination against Women (2010), para 18.

[109] Bond (2003), p. 96; Rosenblum (2011), p. 128.

While the text of CEDAW only implicitly considers the intersection of gender discrimination with other relations of inequality, the Committee's interpretation of the Convention increasingly recognizes the complexity of different forms of gender discrimination. Most notably, General Recommendation 28 holds:

> Intersectionality is a basic concept for understanding the scope of the general obligations of States parties contained in article 2. The discrimination of women based on sex and gender is inextricably linked with other factors that affect women, such as race, ethnicity, religion or belief, health, status, age, class, caste and sexual orientation and gender identity.[110]

In fact, the Committee's commitment to tackle intersectional forms of discrimination has become visible in its more recent work, specifically in individual communications in which, among others, indigenous women, women with disabilities, Roma women and lesbian women have raised intersectional claims.[111] The Committee has further produced several General Recommendations on the rights of specific groups of women, such as migrant women, older women and women with disabilities.[112] As Sousa explains, by focusing on specific groups of women, the CEDAW Committee mainly applies a group-based approach to intersectionality,[113] instead of considering more generally how gender norms are shaped by other social statuses, such as race, class, disability and religion.

Despite the fact that intersectionality is only weakly enshrined in the CEDAW Convention itself, the increasing sensibilities to intersectional forms of discrimination by the CEDAW Committee is a promising development. If addressed with the issue of clothing regulations in sports, the Committee would likely be compelled to analyse the intersection between different social categories—such as gender, race and religion. This could help show the gendered *and* racialized effects of banning soul caps, hijabs and bodysuits from sports competitions.

[110] CEDAW Committee, General Recommendation No. 28 on the Core Obligations of States Parties under Article 2 of the Convention on the Elimination of All Forms of Discrimination against Women (2010), para 18.

[111] ON and DP v Russian Federation [2020] Committee on the Elimination of Discrimination against Women CEDAW/C/75/D/119/2017; LA et al v North Macedonia [2020] Committee on the Elimination of Discrimination against Women CEDAW/C/75/D/110/2016; Rosanna Flamer-Caldera v Sri Lanka [2022] Committee on the Elimination of Discrimination against Women CEDAW/C/81/D/134/2018 (Cecilia Kell v Canada 2012; R. P. B. v. the Philippines 2014).

[112] CEDAW Committee, General Recommendation No. 26 on Women Migrant Workers (2008); CEDAW Committee, General Recommendation No. 27 on Older Women and Protection of Their Human Rights (2010); CEDAW Committee, General Recommendation No. 18: Disabled Women' (1991) Contained in document A/46/38.

[113] Sosa (2017), p. 81.

5 Conclusion

While this chapter remains exploratory, it has shown that the existing international human rights law provides concrete tools to address (gender) inequalities in sports, such as heterosexist and racialized clothing regulations, which remain a widespread phenomenon in international sports. The regulations examined affect both women's and men's competitions, but women's bodies are especially often policed based on hegemonic gender norms. By reflecting the idea that women and men are the sole gender identities and are inherently different, complementary and in a hierarchical relationship to each other, the clothing regulations further reinforce hetero-, cis- and endosexnormativity and foster the invisibility of non-binary persons. As shown in several examples, gender norms often also intersect with norms on race and religion in sports, creating intersectional forms of discrimination.

Even though the CEDAW Committee has not yet considered heterosexist clothing regulations, I have shown that the Convention's broad definition of discrimination bears the possibility of addressing these rules within the CEDAW framework. CEDAW's strong due diligence obligations allow scrutinizing the obligations of states to ensure that international sports federations do not harm athletes and result in unjustified discrimination based on gender. Moreover, CEDAW prohibits direct and indirect forms of discrimination and obliges states to work towards ensuring substantive gender equality or equality in practice. It further creates the obligation to eliminate gender stereotypes, which is highly relevant for addressing gendered clothing regulations in sports, and the Committee increasingly considers intersectional forms of discrimination in its work.

This chapter set out conceptual considerations for using CEDAW to tackle gender inequalities in sports. The future will show how effective the protection of athletes' rights will be through existing international human rights instruments, such as UN Treaty Bodies. Until more clarity on the relationship between sports law and human rights law exists, women athlete activists, such as Zahra Lari and the Norwegian beach handball team, will continue to contest the imposition of heterosexist and racialized body norms that pervade international sports.

References

Baddeley M (2020) The extraordinary autonomy of sports bodies under Swiss law: lessons to be drawn. Int Sports Law J 20(1):3–17

Barras A (2021) The lived experiences of transgender and non-binary people in everyday sport and physical exercise in the UK. PhD thesis, University of Brighton

Besnier N, Brownell S, Carter TF (2018) The anthropology of sport: bodies, borders, biopolitics. University of California Press, Oakland

Bhogle S (2016) Amenability of Indian domestic sports governing bodies to judicial review. Marquette Sports Law Rev 27(1):153–170

Blakey E (2018) Women's participation in sport: how is it regulated in international human rights law, and is Australia meeting its international obligations? Aust J Hum Rights 24(3):292–306

Bond JE (2003) International intersectionality: a theoretical and pragmatic exploration of women's international human rights violations. Emory Law J 52:71–186

Boykoff J (2021) Athlete activism and the Olympic Games. In: Magrath R (ed) Athlete activism. Routledge, London, pp 8–19

Buzuvis E (2007) Reading the pink locker room: on football culture and Title IX. William Mary J Race Gend Soc Just 14(1):1–53

Carlson C, Putz P, Bolt B (2022) Introduction: sport-gender orthodoxy and muscular Christian values. Int J Hist Sport:1–7

Cecilia Kell v Canada (2012) Committee on the Elimination of Discrimination against Women CEDAW/C/51/D/19/2008

Chappelet J-L (2008) International Olympic Committee and the Olympic System (IOC): the governance of world sport. Routledge, London; New York

Chappelet J-L (2016) Autonomy and governance: necessary bedfellows in the fight against corruption in sport. In: de Olivera RSV (ed) Global Corruption Report: Sport. Routledge, pp 16–28

Cisneros B (2020) Challenging the call: should sports governing bodies be subject to judicial review? Int Sports Law J 20(1):18–35

Fluch A (2017) Auswirkungen des binären Geschlechterkonzepts auf das Sportverhalten von trans- und intergeschlechtlichen Personen. Master thesis, University of Vienna

Freeman MA, Chinkin C, Rudolf B (eds) (2012) The UN Convention on the elimination of all forms of discrimination against women: a commentary. Oxford University Press, Oxford, New York

Gaer F (2009) Women, international law and international institutions: the case of the United Nations. Women's Stud Int Forum 32(1):60–66

Gervis M, Dunn N (2004) The emotional abuse of elite child athletes by their coaches. Child Abuse Rev 13(3):215–223

Lake RJ (2017) Tennis in an English Garden Party: Wimbledon, Englishness and British Sporting Culture. In: Tom G, Dominic M (eds) Sport and English National Identity in a 'Disunited Kingdom'. Routledge

Lane L (2018) The horizontal effect of international human rights law in practice: a comparative analysis of the general comments and jurisprudence of selected United Nations human rights treaty monitoring bodies. Eur J Comp Law Gov 5(1):5–88

Lenskyj H (1990) Power and play: gender and sexuality issues in sport and physical activity. Int Rev Sociol Sport 25(3):235–245

Messner M (2011) Gender ideologies, youth sports, and the production of soft essentialism. Sociol Sport J 28(2):151–170

Miller A (2012) Fighting over the figure of gender. Pace Law Rev 31(3):837–8xx

Patel S (2021) Gaps in the protection of athletes gender rights in sport—a regulatory riddle. Int Sports Law J 21(4):257–275

Pérez González C (2020) Transformative equality, due diligence and female players' rights: CEDAW as an avenue for women's rights accountability in the world of football. NYU School of Law

Preece S, Bullingham R (2022) Gender stereotypes: the impact upon perceived roles and practice of in-service teachers in physical education. Sport Educ Soc 27(3):259–271

Prügl E (1996) Gender in international organization and global governance: a critical review of the literature. Int Stud Notes 21(1):15–24

R. P. B. v. the Philippines (2014) Committee on the Elimination of Discrimination against Women CEDAW/C/57/D/34/2011

Rosenblum D (2011) Unsex Cedaw, or what's wrong with women's rights. Columbia J Gend Law 20:98–194

Shinohara T (2022) Which states parties should be held responsible for the implementation of positive obligations under the ECHR in sports-related disputes? Int Sports Law J 22(4):332–342

Sosa L (2017) Intersectionality in the human rights legal framework on violence against women: at the centre or the margins? Cambridge University Press, Cambridge

Wackwitz L (2003) Verifying the myth: Olympic sex testing and the category "woman". Women's Stud Int Forum 26:553–560

Whitson D (1990) Sport in the social construction of masculinity. In: Messner MA, Sabo DF (eds) Sport, men, and the gender order: critical feminist perspectives. Human Kinetics Books, Champaign, Ill, pp 19–29

Wilinsky CL, McCabe A (2021) A review of emotional and sexual abuse of elite child athletes by their coaches. Sports Coach Rev 10(1):84–109

Zintz T, Winand M (2013) Les fédérations sportives. Courrier hebdomadaire du CRISP 2179(14): 5–52

Lena Holzer (she/her) is an Assistant Professor in Gender, Race and the Law at the University of Cambridge. Her research focuses on queer-feminist and intersectional examinations of international law, sports law and human rights law. She is also interested in counter-hegemonic ways of researching and teaching law that recognize and subvert law's relationship with unequal power and domination. In addition to her academic research, she has worked as a consultant for several European human rights organizations.

#MeToo, Sport, and Women: Foul, Own Goal, or Touchdown? Online Abuse of Women in Sport as a Contemporary Issue

Kim Barker and Olga Jurasz

Contents

Abstract Online violence against women (OVAW), and online gender-based abuse more broadly, have been acknowledged at an international level as an obstacle to gender equality as well as women's freedom of expression, positioning these phenomena as a concern from a human rights perspective. In particular, the scale, seriousness and the impact of social media abuse has raised questions about the appropriate legal protections for individuals from such forms of abuse and its harms. The world of sport has not been immune to the devasting impact of social media abuse, especially online hate, leading to a social media boycott within the British sport community in May 2021 as a protest against online hostility and discrimination. However, little action has been taken to date to address gender-based abuse and online misogyny directed at women in sport. Left unchecked and unaccounted for, instances of such online abuse reinforce the already existing structures and gender stereotypes that fuel gender-based hostility and violence against women. What is

K. Barker (✉)
Lincoln Law School, University of Lincoln, Lincoln, UK
e-mail: kbarker@lincoln.ac.uk

O. Jurasz
Law School, The Open University, Milton Keynes, UK
e-mail: olga.jurasz@open.ac.uk

V. Boillet et al. (eds.), *Sports and Human Rights*, Interdisciplinary Studies in Human Rights 10, https://doi.org/10.1007/978-3-031-56452-9_4

more, by being left unchallenged and allowed to play out in the very public context of professional sports, these behaviors become normalized, contributing to the continuum of violence against women, but doing so on a global and high-profile stage. While there have been controversial campaigns, such as taking the knee, there are few of any significance from the sporting world that address OVAW. Limited protections exist in terms of human rights, but little has been done by sporting bodies, sporting associations, and unions to add value to any initiatives aimed at tackling OVAW in sport. This chapter questions the role of sport in supporting the global action against violence against women, while also assessing the broader response to problems posed by online abuse, online harassment, and its gendered aspects. Do human rights protections go far enough? Is this an issue for sporting bodies, or is it an 'athlete-only' problem?

1 Introduction

Sport, especially at an elite and/or international level, is a multimillion-pound industry rooted not only in the 'spirit of sport' but also high-value commercial and political interests. Yet despite this, the image of the sport industry undermines women's equality, which ignores the problem of online abuse suffered by women in sport. The grievous consequences are not sustainable nor desired.[1]

Despite significant debates that have centered on why women and girls shy away from sport and why participation drops, little has been done to address the social media aspect of participation in sport, and especially the online abuse of women in sport. While there are initiatives designed to work towards gender equality in sport, their focus has tended to fall on the use of social media for business and/or sponsorship purposes, instead of addressing the potential for gender-based violence to occur via social media; something that the 2014–2020 strategic action plan by the European Commission failed to address.[2] The scale of online violence against women (OVAW) in sport is highly visible, yet it is frequently overshadowed by other forms of abuse in the context of sport, such as racist abuse.[3] As a result, the online abuse of women in sport has gone largely unaddressed. In light of the #MeToo movement, it is surprising that online abuse of women in sport remains so underdiscussed, underrecognized, and, most distressingly, under-addressed by sporting bodies.

This chapter offers an analysis of online abuse of women[4] in sport, and questions the appropriateness of (limited) responses to this contemporary issue. The discussion

[1] Jurasz (2021).

[2] European Commission (2014).

[3] 'Racist abuse' (2021).

[4] The authors recognize that there is an ongoing and controversial debate about whether transgender women should be allowed to compete in women's sports. This is not an issue that forms a part of

is placed within the broader context of regulation of online, gender-based abuse (online violence against women specifically), as well as human rights perspectives on women's rights in sport, with an emphasis on the issue within the United Kingdom. The discussion also rests on a socio-legal exploration of the measures taken to address other forms of abuse in sport and discusses the applicability or expandability of these to gender-based abuse on social media.

The position advanced here is that online abuse of women in sport is a matter which requires urgent attention, not only from sporting regulatory bodies but also from social media platforms, albeit in a holistic manner rather than a piecemeal one. Ultimately, this chapter argues that sport governance bodies have an opportunity to step up in the post-#MeToo era and challenge one of societies' most contemporary challenges: OVAW in sport.

2 Online Abuse of Women in Sport: The Problem

The data regarding the scale of incidents of online abuse of sportswomen is only starting to emerge, but it already shows that this is a serious problem. In 2020, 30% of British sportswomen were 'trolled' on social media,[5] a figure that has doubled since 2015, which shows the significant increase in OVAW. A recent study into experiences of women footballers in the North and North-East of Scotland revealed high levels of sexism and "sexist hate, sexualized comments, homophobia, body shaming and even death threats, with most abuse coming on social media".[6] Alarmingly, over 70% of female survey respondents reported having experienced sexism, with 68% having suffered hate—both on- and off-line—just for playing football.[7] The figures look equally alarming at a global level, where female athletes were the target of 87% of social media abuse at the 2020 Tokyo Olympics.[8] The frequency of online abuse received by some sportswomen over a prolonged period of time is equally concerning. For example, Naomi Osaka was found to be the most abused tennis player on social media receiving 32,415 abusive Tweets over a

---

analysis presented in this paper. However, where transgender women have been allowed to compete in women's sports and have subsequently experienced online abuse, these examples would fall within the scope of presented analysis.

[5] Grey et al. (2020).

[6] Stewart (2022).

[7] Ibid. (Stewart 2022).

[8] World Athletics (2021), "To gain an understanding of the level of online abuse in athletics, a sample of 161 Twitter handles of current and former athletes involved in the Tokyo Olympic Games (derived from a list of 200 athletes selected by World Athletics) was tracked during the study period, starting one week prior to the Olympic opening ceremony and concluding the day after the Olympic closing ceremony (15 July–9 August 2021). In this timeframe, 240,707 tweets including 23,521 images, GIFs and videos were captured for analysis".

12-month period (January–December 2021),[9] closely followed by Serena Williams (18,118 abusive Tweets).

This volume of online abuse was over two times more than that received by the most abused male tennis player, Novak Djokovic (15,793 abusive Tweets, over half of which were received following the COVID-19 vaccine controversy). Whilst the data above does not give a comprehensive picture of the scale and volume of abuse received by sportswomen across the world and across sport disciplines, it is a chilling indicator of the seriousness of this problem, which is also reflected in the kind of abuse that sportswomen receive. Online abuse directed at female athletes tends to be frequently sexualized, sexist, and often questions their professional commitments and values. For example, Indian women's cricket team captain, Mithali Raj, was trolled in 2017 for the way she dressed in a selfie that she posted on Twitter. Not only were her appearance and clothes criticized and called 'inappropriate', but her patriotism was questioned.[10] Similarly, Naomi Osaka faced a high volume of racist online abuse after announcing her decision to relinquish her American citizenship and to play for Japan in the Olympics.[11]

2.1 *Toxic, Masculine Culture*

Whilst the rise in popularity and common use of social media certainly contributes to the visibility of online abuse and its rapid spread, the underlying attitudes which lead to such abusive behaviors towards women in sport are rooted in factors that long pre-date social media. Sexism and gender stereotyping are firmly embedded in the way that sport is governed.[12] There are stark differences in the way that women's and men's sport is treated, with different expectations and double standards, despite pledged commitments to equality and non-discrimination.

Despite some progress in recent years, the sporting world is far from a level playing field for women. It is a space highly dominated by a masculine, and more often than not, toxic culture that perpetuates unequal power relations between men and women athletes. Women who try to occupy these spaces and be successful are met with challenges posed by misogyny and abuse, often sexual in nature, as well as structural hurdles, alongside public vilification through online abuse, almost all of which is gendered in nature. A 2019 study by Plan International Australia revealed that more than a quarter of comments directed at sportswomen were sexist, sexualized, belittling, or otherwise negative in nature.[13] Overall, women faced three times

[9] 'Social Media Abuse of Tennis Stars' (2022).

[10] 'Mithali Raj' (2017).

[11] Reid (2021).

[12] That said, Petty and Pope (2019) suggest that the manner in which women's football is covered in the media is gradually changing towards more equal and positive reporting.

[13] Plan International (2019).

as many negative comments as men (27% women, 9% men). No sportsmen received sexualized comments, these were directed only at women and constituted 14% of all negative comments received.

The perception that the media covers women's and men's sports differently is shared by sportswomen (86.2% of UK sportswomen agreed with that finding),[14] and the general public. In the context of Novak Djokovic's behavior surrounding his COVID-19 vaccination status, tennis fans questioned whether his treatment would have been equally lenient if similar behavior was committed by a female player, such as Naomi Osaka or Serena Williams.[15] The questions—albeit rhetorical in nature—nonetheless highlight the hypervisibility of different treatment of women and men in sports as well as the everyday sexism perpetuated against women in sport. The contrasts here are stark: a woman wearing a compression suit to a tennis game for medical reasons (i.e., Serena Williams at the 2018 Roland Garros) allegedly shows disrespect for the game,[16] whereas an unvaccinated male player is allowed to compete in championships as an exercise of his "freedom to choose".[17] Gender-biased media reporting of sport not only contributes to the lack of parity in the public visibility between women's and men's sports, but also provides fertile ground for the perpetuation of everyday sexism and gender stereotypes directed at sportswomen.

2.2 *The Impact of Online Abuse on Sportswomen*

Sportswomen's efforts to participate in these masculine spaces, and any milestones achieved in the process, are jeopardized, if not undone, by the barrage of online abuse that takes a toll on both physical and mental health. For example, Sydney McLaughlin, American 400m hurdles champion and Tokyo Olympic gold medalist, spoke openly on Instagram about online abuse she received during the Olympics, noting the severe impact it had on her mental health, creating feelings of anxiety and depression.[18] Sportswomen have described online abuse as "scary, threatening",[19] "overwhelming",[20] and emphasized the significant impact this continuum of abuse had on them as individuals. Former footballer, Alex Scott who has detailed the impact of online, intersectional abuse she experienced both in sport, and her media work, stated that, "I kind of lost myself with my personality because I knew everything that was going on around it. And it's not until I actually got to a stage

[14] Grey et al. (2020).
[15] McCallig (2022).
[16] "One must respect the game" (2018).
[17] Rajan (2022).
[18] Gijy (2021).
[19] Grey et al. (2020).
[20] 'Coco Gauff' (2021).

where I thought, 'I can't take this anymore. It is becoming too much for me' that I spoke out about it".[21]

Scott is not alone, with former footballers and hockey players amongst those emphasizing the scale of the problem and their experiences. Welsh rugby player, Elinor Snowshill, highlighted similar experiences that had a significant impact, indicating that the fear that is created through online abuse is profound: "It feels more threatening because if there ever was a situation where someone took it to the extreme, generally men have more power in a situation than women because they're stronger. It just has that different edge to it".[22]

This kind of online harassment has been experienced by women in other forms of public life, including but not limited to politics, especially those who have held public office. Jacinda Ardern, former Prime Minister of New Zealand,[23] is another example of a high-profile woman who opted out of public life because of the toll of the online abuse and persistence of the threats she received. However, as we argue elsewhere, the range of harms arising from online text-based abuse (which is typically perpetuated on social media) is expansive and not limited to 'merely' physical and/or psychological harms.[24] Importantly, harm can also be transferred, not only between the online and offline world (e.g., online threats of physical harm/violence materializing offline), but also onto individuals other than the victim. The personal toll of online abuse is harrowing and often underestimated; as is the broader social harm that comes with online abuse (be it in sport or otherwise) going unchecked. With online abuse of women in sport peaking yet largely unaddressed, sexist and abusive behaviors have become normalized, leading to further social and cultural harms.

2.3 Online Harms, OVAW and Sports Regulation: Towards a Level Playing Field?

The omnipresence of online abuse of women in sport, paired with the lack of attempts to remedy the situation by sport governing bodies, leads to important questions: What is the future of sport regulation in an era of unprecedented social media use, and what does this future hold for women in sport? Online abuse of women in sport is an issue that exemplifies a contemporary form of discrimination against women, which is explicitly prohibited in the core UN human rights treaties, including the Convention on Elimination of All Forms of Discrimination Against Women 1979 (CEDAW). States parties to CEDAW have due diligence obligations with respect to eliminating all forms of discrimination against women, as articulated

[21] Reddy (2020).

[22] Grey (2020).

[23] McClure (2023).

[24] Barker and Jurasz (2021a), pp. 256–258.

in Article 2 of the Convention. This covers both sex-based and gender-based forms of discrimination,[25] as well as both direct and indirect forms of discrimination.[26]

While CEDAW does not address violence against women and girls (online or offline) explicitly in the text of the convention, the nexus between gender-based violence and discrimination has been established by the CEDAW Committee in General Recommendation No. 19, where it affirmed that "*(t)he full implementation of the Convention requires States to take positive measures to eliminate all forms of violence against women*" (para 4).[27] More recently, this interpretation was reemphasized in General Recommendation No. 35,[28] with explicit recognition of "contemporary forms of violence occurring in the Internet and digital spaces".[29]

In the European context, the Council of Europe Group of Experts on Action against Violence against Women and Domestic Violence (GREVIO), explicitly recognized that due diligence obligations to prevent, investigate, punish, and provide reparation for acts of violence perpetrated by non-state actors[30] extends to "cover all expressions of violence against women, including digital expressions and violence perpetrated with the help of or through technology".[31] Outside of GREVIO's General Recommendation, the Council of Europe's approach to addressing the online abuse of women (albeit not specifically women in sport) has been largely to focus on gender stereotypes and sexist hate speech. For example, the Council of Europe Gender Equality Strategy[32] stresses the need to tackle violence against women (both online and offline) through combatting gender stereotypes and sexism, including sexist hate speech and violent and sexualized threats online, especially on social media platforms. This approach is also reflected in the 2019 Council of Europe Recommendation on Preventing and Combating Sexism, the first ever international legal instrument to combat sexism. However, while addressing sexism and gender stereotypes is useful to emphasize the root causes of these types of violence and the way(s) in which gender stereotyping reinforces unequal social power relations between men and women, it should not be the sole lens through which the online abuse of women is addressed. In particular, a more comprehensive approach, capturing the spectrum of online harms arising from OVAW is required.

The seriousness of OVAW is recognized at regional and international levels, by European bodies, as well as the UN. While this is in itself progress, fundamental

[25] Although the Convention only explicitly refers to sex-based discrimination, the CEDAW Committee clarified in *General Recommendation 28 on the core obligations of States parties under Article 2 of the CEDAW* that the Convention extends to gender-based discrimination too: UN CEDAW (2010) para.5.

[26] UN CEDAW (2010) para.16.

[27] CEDAW, General Recommendation 19 (1992), paras.1, 6.

[28] UN CEDAW (2017) para.21.

[29] UN CEDAW (2017) para.20.

[30] Article 5(2) of The Council of Europe Convention on Preventing and Combating Violence Against Women and Domestic Violence 2011 (Istanbul Convention).

[31] Council of Europe (2021) para.34.

[32] Council of Europe (2019).

questions remain as to the practicality of international regimes or treaty obligations to address online violence. High-level recognition is important, but to date, no treaty at regional nor international level includes provisions that impose obligations on states to address OVAW. This is reflective of the responsibility gap that exists between states, private actors (i.e., social networking platforms), and sporting organizations. Unless and until a treaty imposes obligations on states to address OVAW, and unless and until sporting organizations address it in the same way as they would injury-related issues, it is unlikely that platforms will be held responsible for their inaction in regards to the online abuse that female athletes receive. Online abuse of women in sport is not a one-dimensional challenge, and does not constitute a one-dimensional harm, with at least 13 spheres of harms having been recognized.[33] This necessitates collaborative measures to make the internet a safer place for women in sport.

3 A Safer Internet for Women: Responses, Reactions and Rehabilitation?

Despite the now long-standing, and increasingly visible, prevalent, and numerous incidents of online abuse of athletes, the responses have not led to meaningful change. There have been campaigns across sport designed to address elements of protest, responding to aspects of discrimination, although not without controversy; for example, taking the knee.[34] There are few campaigns of any significance from the sporting world that address social media abuse of women, and in particular women in sport. Similarly, there are no high-profile campaigns initiated by, or supported by sporting organizations to address the online abuse of women in sport. Even if such campaigns were to become popular, there is little evidence to suggest that this would make a meaningful difference to treaty obligations, or to legal mechanisms in individual jurisdictions; not least because women's sport rarely receives the same level of media coverage as men's sport. Limited protections exist for human rights, but little added value has been forthcoming by sporting bodies, sporting associations, federations or unions. Fewer initiatives still provide any element of joined up thinking in response to social media abuse, especially that of women in sport.

While numerous high-profile incidents have affected athletes and sportspersons from a range of sports, there have been very few specific mechanisms adopted or implemented by professional or regulatory bodies that have resulted in a reduction in the level or frequency of online abuse of women in sport. This, despite the "fatigue, burnout, and anxiety"[35] that elite athletes have reported, and the steps taken by

[33] Barker and Jurasz (2021a), pp. 256–258.

[34] Campbell (2021).

[35] George (2021).

national teams to protect their athletes when at major tournaments, including effectively opting out of exercising speech rights by choosing to disengage with social media as in the case of the England Women's Cricket team at the 2017 World Cup, following the lead of the women of Team GB Hockey during the 2016 Olympics. These are not the only 'in house'[36] responses that have been developed outside of platform or legal approaches. Despite the widespread recognition of the significant harm caused by online abuse of women in sport, the need for 'in house' support mechanisms, including so-called 'social media captains'[37] continues. This is in no small part due to the combined failure of human rights mechanisms, legal protections, and platforms through their own content moderation systems to address the problem and scale of abuse.

In contrast to the steps taken by some national teams, very few mechanisms or measures have been introduced that address the safety of women online, especially in sport. There have, in contrast, been measures adopted or proposed that seek to address other forms of discrimination in sport. The discussion here turns to how these could apply to gender and explores how these mechanisms have been developed on an ad-hoc basis; something reflective of the challenge posed by online abuse in sporting contexts more widely.

3.1 *Legal Responses vs. Governing Bodies' Obligations?*

While a significant number of incidents *could*[38] potentially result in criminal prosecutions and charges, this relies upon on both police investigation and resourcing. Given that, especially in the UK, such responses are unlikely, other responses are required, especially from the governing bodies of sports. This is especially the case where there are professional bodies that include in their remit the welfare and mental wellbeing of their members. Legal responses are outside of the remit of professional and sporting bodies, but there is scope within sporting regulatory bodies to address social media abuse. Similarly, there is potential to address internationally, regionally, and transnationally the harms caused by social media abuse directed at women in sport. Growing recognition and press coverage has exemplified and drawn public attention to the scale, breadth, and impact of social media abuse.[39] Where there have been breaches of standards within specific sports by specific sportspersons, governing bodies have been prepared to act, but the same cannot be said for broader

---

[36] Ehantharajah (2017).

[37] Batte (2022).

[38] It is also worth noting that, in England and Wales in particular, most legal provisions are not tailored for online specific behaviors. Rather criminal offences are designed to address the behavior, which means—in theory—they could be applicable to online or offline behavior, even though the former is highly unlikely to result in prosecutorial action.

[39] Doyle (2021); The FA (2021).

work more generally in tackling the root causes of social media abuse of women in sport.

Social media abuse is particularly prevalent among high-profile athletes, and is exacerbated when sportswomen are pitted against sportsmen, or are seen to be 'acting out' and contradicting male stars. England cricketer, Alex Hartley, suffered a backlash when she entered into a discussion on Twitter with England men's cricketer Rory Burns. Discussing the controversy, Hartley indicated that her Tweet was "singled out" because she is a woman.[40] More damagingly, this social media tension between the two England cricketers damaged the perception of the women's game, and perpetuated abuse of a woman cricketer, at the instigation of a men's cricketer in the national team. Beyond highlighting that the attitudes are problematic within sport generally, the Burns-Hartley incident also demonstrates the "deep-rooted negative attitudes"[41] women encounter, both online and off. In the aftermath of this social media incident, both Burns and Hartley were spoken to by the governing body, but no further action was taken, demonstrating that the problems stemming from social media abuse are downplayed and dismissed, even at the highest levels in professional sport when it relates to social media abuse against women.

The Burns-Hartley controversy was not a one-off. Other high-profile incidents of social media abuse have marred the reputation of cricket. For instance, the immediate suspension of England cricketer Ollie Robinson after his test match debut in 2021 for historic social media abuse[42] (albeit on the basis of racism and sexism) show that within sport there are actions taken to address elements of problematic social media abuse. That said, these tend to focus on the regulation, rehabilitation, or punishment of specific sportspersons rather than addressing issues more broadly within a particular sport. Even when there are sport-wide initiatives, such as wearing anti-discrimination shirts the day after Robinson fiasco,[43] they fall short of making a lasting impact and appear to be reactionary measures rather than initiatives with a lasting legacy; in this case, the Disciplinary Panel of the Cricket Discipline Commission of the England and Wales Cricket Board recognized the "extremely serious" conduct of Robinson in both sporting and societal contexts.[44] Such campaigns do not tackle the behaviors of those involved in the sport more broadly. Even when these initiatives do occur, they tend to happen in the context of men's sport, and do not extend beyond it. Ultimately, while they are a nice foil for public relations management and damage limitation, they do not constitute meaningful measures to address the root causes of the problem.

[40] Cricket News (2021).

[41] Gardner (2021).

[42] Burnton (2021).

[43] Ibid. (Burnton 2021).

[44] England & Wales Cricket Board (2021).

Some developments are worthy of note in challenging aspects of discrimination, harassment, and abuse though, albeit these tend to be attached to or funded by specific sports and sporting bodies. For instance, English football's 'Kick it Out' Campaign[45] focuses specifically on football, and while originally conceived as an anti-racism campaign within football in the late 1990s, it is now broader and claims to tackle "all aspects of discrimination, inequality and exclusion".[46] While this applies equally across all branches of the game, and covers all who play the game irrespective of gender, it is a targeted campaign that still presents as focusing on racism, rather than broader intersectional aspects of equality within football, including gender. Despite the fact that social media abuse relating to women in football is rampant, where sexist taunts are common, and even where women's teams dare to put themselves on show against the men's game, the women are the ones to suffer "vile sexist abuse" at the hands of trolls, such as the backlash that reached Manchester United W.F.C. when losing to the Salford youth team 9-0 in 2018.[47] In fact, even in its 2017 report,[48] the emphasis in reporting on Kick It Out's landmark achievements during the previous 25 years still falls on aspects of aggravated abuse incidents in describing the development of reporting systems.[49] This is perhaps not as inclusive as Kick it Out may otherwise claim to be given the aggravations referred to rely on the legal recognition of characteristics such as race and/or religion, but which (currently) in England and Wales, exclude sex/gender from such considerations.

While responsibility for the lack of inclusivity in categorizing aggravations cannot be laid on Kick It Out, other shortcomings, especially in respect of gender equality in football can. It is also problematic that the Kick It Out approach is limited when it comes to challenging problematic attitudes beyond racism and equality, but issues affecting women more broadly. The Raith Rovers debacle surrounding David Goodwillie is one particularly high-profile example which has been damaging to football in light of the prominence surrounding violence against women. It is the latest in a protracted history of football clubs putting their interests on-pitch before their broader social responsibilities to their communities and their fans, especially women, and society,[50] while also perpetuating the idea that sport, and football in particular, is (and should be) an environment toxic to, and for, women. Raith Rovers signed David Goodwillie despite a Scottish civil court finding him guilty of rape. This situation followed shortly after another footballer, Benjamin Mendy, was accused of seven counts of rape.[51]

---

45 Kick It Out (n.d.).

46 Ibid. (Kick It Out n.d.).

47 Tuckey (2018).

48 Kick It Out (2017).

49 Ibid. (Kick It Out 2017).

50 Dunn (2022).

51 BBC News (2022a).

These are not isolated incidents, with other high-profile players[52] having been found guilty of committing acts of violence against women. The difference with Raith Rovers was in the response from those within and outside the club, with high-profile sponsors, staff, and the entire women's and girls' teams separating from the club over the decision to re-sign Goodwillie.[53] Given the culturally embedded role of football, particularly in the UK, football clubs must do more to prevent similar issues happening again. In fact, there are increasing calls to broaden out the cultural responsibilities of football and footballers, and address systemic issues beyond racism, specifically including actions to address gender-based violence.[54] It is however, disappointing that this has not (yet) specifically extended to social media abuse too.

Campaigns such as Kick It Out predominantly focus on *an* aspect of abuse, to the detriment of their other social responsibilities, rather than either taking a holistic approach and including *all* forms of social media abuse and harassment, *or* have been developed in response to a specific issue which has arisen following particular high-profile sporting events or tournaments such as the Euro 2020 tournament, or the Olympic Games. This is particularly clear through the England and Wales Cricket Board response to the Burns-Hartley spat or the Ollie Robinson Tweets, with their 'Cricket is a Game for Everyone' campaign.[55] What is particularly notable is that there remains very little specific attention given to women in sport, and the abuse that women face.

In fact, while campaigns such as Kick It Out have attempted to focus on issues such as racism, (and none of, for example, intersectionality of discrimination and abuse) there have been some other legal mechanisms introduced. Notably—although specifically in the context of football—there are a number of laws that aim to address different elements of abuse in varying contexts in England and Wales. While the Football (Offences) Act 1991 specifically includes offences for racial or indecent chanting at matches under s3, no similar provisions exist for online abuse. Football Banning Orders were subsequently introduced through the Football Spectators Act 1989 and allow for individuals to be prohibited from attending certain locations or football matches or particular football grounds under s14A for a number of reasons, including indecent chanting, or making violent threats.

While these developments focus attention on offline or analogue forms of abuse, the law was extended in 2022 to cover behaviors that relate to online conduct. Section 190 of the Police, Crime, Sentencing and Courts Act 2022 amends Schedule 1 of the Football Spectators Act 1989 to allow football banning orders to be made in respect of any offence relating to sending malicious communications (as outlined in the Malicious Communications Act 1988), or where there is an improper use of a

---

[52] See e.g., accusations of rape, sexual assault and making threats to kill against footballer Mason Greenwood: BBC News (2022b).

[53] Courier Reporters (2022).

[54] End Violence Against Women Coalition (2022).

[55] ECB (2021).

public communications network (under the Communications Act 2003). It should however be noted that while Football Banning Orders can now be sought to prevent individuals from attending football events or matches on the basis of their online abuse, they are not a way to change culture, nor are they a way to specifically protect women in sport.

There is no gender lens attached to the communications offences, and this continues to be a lacuna in the law, particularly where the abuse is misogynistic in nature.[56] At best, the banning orders can offer some potential means of protection from physical and direct threats of violence or abuse made in proximity to women footballers; they do not extend coverage beyond football. Moreover, the offences are likely to require modification in light of the proposed online safety provisions which will all but repeal the malicious communications and communications offences from 1988 and 2003 respectively. At most, the extension of Football Banning Orders is a token gesture, but one which is little more than a sticking plaster on a severed artery. There is some potential that this could be developed to target other forms of discrimination and abuse, but no progress has been made here. There is—at the time of writing—no evidence of any plan to develop such mechanisms to address other forms of abuse and discrimination.

What is evident from this analysis of the capacity for responding to incidents of abuse in sport, is that the regulatory and governing bodies have some capacity and resources to address some elements. They have not—to date—prioritized the gendered aspects of social media abuse, despite the fact that this is now a well-recognized phenomenon. It is also evident from these limited examples, that there remains much work to be done, and there is some distance to go. In the UK for instance, there is work to be done in adopting the recommendations of the Duty of Care Review,[57] and ensuring that there are appropriate (and enforceable) boundaries between banter and bullying which respect equality, diversity and inclusion.[58] While it is reassuring to see the emphasis falling on the Duty of Care broadly with an emphasis on equality aspects, it too is lacking in its consideration of the wider context in which sport operates, with no mention of online abuse or social media abuse featuring in the report itself.

Similarly, the disciplinary codes of specific sports pay little, if any, attention to online abuse. They tend to refer to aspects of conduct that bring a sport into disrepute, or which damages the reputation of the game. While this is in some ways, very broad, it also has the potential added value of allowing, as in the ECB's example of Ollie Robinson, online conduct to be brought within the purview of disciplinary action for professional sportspersons within their particular sport. For instance, the disciplinary codes of the England and Wales Cricket Board make it very clear that "improper" acts which are "prejudicial to the interest of cricket" are

[56] Barker and Jurasz (2019a, b).

[57] Grey-Thompson (2017).

[58] Ibid. (Grey-Thompson 2017), pp. 2–3.

prohibited.[59] Similarly, the England and Wales Cricket Board Anti-Discrimination Code outlines the grounds upon which a "breach" will be found, and explicitly references the protected characteristics (under the law of England and Wales).[60] Unfortunately, disciplinary codes do not extend to fans of particular sports, something that is left to routes of redress outside of professional and governing bodies.

3.2 *Online Safety and Content Moderation*

The much awaited, and much debated, Online Safety Bill (OSB) (subsequently, the Online Safety Act 2023 (OSA)) has pledged to make the UK one of the safest places in the world to be 'online'.[61] That ambition was outlined in 2017. The proposed OSB outlines changes in UK law relating to online content. It is designed (at the time of writing) to introduce a new framework to ensure that online platforms including, but not limited to, social media platforms act to address illegal content that is shared via their services. This instrument is based around a new proposed framework which is harm-based, but with an extra onus on those platforms that will be accessed by children. The most contentious part of the OSB, similar to the Digital Services Act (DSA) in Europe, is the distinction between illegal content, and lawful but harmful content. The draft OSB only proposed to require action from platforms where there is harmful content, which is legal but, which is in contravention of the terms of service (or terms of use) of a particular platform. The OSB proposed to ensure that platforms act to remove this content. However, no specific provisions in the OSB are designed to protect women, despite the introduction of amended provisions that will require the UK regulator to pay greater attention to issues affecting women and girls, and provide guidance to platforms that "may, among other things—contain advice and examples of best practice for assessing risks of harm to women and girls from content and activity [which may disproportionately affect women and girls]".[62] The harms-based approach captures content that affects women, but crucially, there is no specific capture of any provisions designed to address OVAW, and no specific element of the proposed framework to tackle the gendered nature of the abuse women in sport suffer. The OSB is disappointing in this regard,[63] offering little in the way of protection or redress for women abused and harassed online.

The (proposed) legal framework to address online safety and online harms also fails to consider the nuances of different platforms, pursuing a model that is dominated by considerations of protecting children and the under-18s especially.[64]

[59] England and Wales Cricket Board Directives (August 2020). Directive 3.3.

[60] England and Wales Cricket Board Anti-Discrimination Code (2022). Paragraph 1.2.

[61] DCMS (2017).

[62] OSB 2023, s54(2).

[63] Barker and Jurasz (2021c), pp. 535–538.

[64] DCMS (2022).

More concerningly, the OSB mechanisms for dealing with platforms that do not "fulfil their own standards to keep people safe"[65] is to block the site and/or platform in the UK, thereby punishing the platform *and* the people using it, rather than the people who use it to abuse. This is also a failure to protect women: by blocking platforms that do not uphold terms of service (which are self-created and designed, usually to the benefit of the platforms themselves), the OSB proposed to all but limit participatory rights for women and women in sport. Without the use of social media platforms, the reach and participation of women in sport and women's sport generally would be significantly curtailed. Blocking is therefore not a solution, even one advanced through law reform proposals. It all but encourages people not to engage with online platforms. Above all else, there are free expression implications of blocking online platforms which do not uphold terms of service, which in the context of online abuse, seems to mask the problem rather than address it directly.

Furthermore, the OSB not only spectacularly fails women, but it also fails platforms. In proposing (or introducing) a framework that is based on the ultimate punishments of (i) fines and (ii) blocking sites, the OSB omits the potential and significance of platform content moderation systems. Content moderation is in and of itself a significant challenge, not least because of the delicate balance between moderating content, freedom of expression, and participatory rights.[66] The volume of content itself, together with its context,[67] are also significant challenges for each platform, let alone for all platforms when considered in combination. The OSB pays little real attention to this aspect of the role of platforms in responding to and addressing the online abuse of women in sport. While the majority of responses seem to rest on domestic criminal law provisions, or domestic legal innovations such as the Online Safety Act 2023, in the UK little has been done to comprehensively address the social media abuse of women in sport. There are indicators of a growing recognition that there is a need to address the phenomenon of online social media abuse, but meaningful steps and compliance with human rights obligations are yet to materialize in the context of professional sport.

4 Sport and #MeToo: A Watershed Moment?

The rise of #MeToo has been a watershed moment for speaking out against sexual harassment around the world, and has finally begun to reach women's sports, with many sportswomen speaking out about the harassment, sexual violence, and sexism they have faced, as well as emotional and psychological abuse.[68] While #MeToo has provided a platform and momentum for sportswomen to share their lived

[65] Ibid. (DCMS 2022).

[66] Oliva (2020).

[67] Barker and Jurasz (2021d), p. 14.

[68] Giles and Darroch (2020); BBC (2021).

experiences of sexual harassment and violence, it hardly highlighted a new phenomenon.[69] The experiences reported by women are not new, with sexist, violent, and discriminatory behaviors having been prevalent in women's sports for decades. An increase in public attention to the treatment of women in sport, has led to slow changes and actions against sexual harassment and abuse.

For example, as a result of investigations into sexual abuse in women's football by the Guardian,[70] FIFA has given life bans to the Afghan FA President (in 2018) and the Haitian FA President (in 2019). This subsequently led to the long-awaited announcement in December 2021 of plans to launch a global investigative network to tackle sexual abuse in sport, which would see collaboration between FIFA and the UN Office on Drugs and Crime.[71] That said, these actions come after a significant investigation of high-profile figures in sport; while any action taken is laudable, it is crucial to note that it likely represents the peak of an iceberg, and that so many instances of sexual harassment and abuse against sportswomen at lower levels remain under-investigated and unpunished. In principle, sport governing bodies have pledged to tackle discrimination in sport (i.e., FIFA has committed to anti-discrimination practices in accordance with international human rights standards),[72] but practice and lived experiences of women in sport are very divergent from this goal.

There is a parallel pandemic of abuse directed at women in sport that occurs online on social media. Sportswomen face online abuse on a scale vastly higher than men, and of a significantly different variety. The abuse is not only violent and hateful, but also deeply sexist and underwritten by gender stereotypes. This is the case for not only sportswomen but also women in the sport industry more broadly. For instance, female sport journalists have faced significant online abuse for merely reporting on sport,[73] and female football fans have suffered sexist social media abuse for simply tweeting about the sport.[74] Likewise, sportswomen who speak out about their experiences of sexual harassment and/or violence have suffered a backlash in the form of online abuse. While this is a pattern not specific to women in sport,[75] it highlights the precarious position occupied by women in professional and public life. The seriousness of the abuse and its lasting impact on women (as well as men) in sport has been highlighted by high-profile sport celebrities. For instance, Roger Federer indicated that the next generation of tennis players may need "help to prevent social media abuse affecting them",[76] suggesting we need a "revolution

[69] Brackenridge (1997).
[70] Wrack (2019); Aarons et al. (2020).
[71] Aarons and Molina (2021).
[72] FIFA (n.d.).
[73] See, for example: 'BBC's Sonja McLaughlan reveals online abuse' (2021); Antunovic (2019).
[74] 'Female football fan speaks out' (2022).
[75] Barker and Jurasz (2019a, b, 2020, 2021a, b).
[76] Latham-Coyle (2021).

[if not] evolution of where we are today";[77] while the rising star of women's tennis, Iga Świątek, called for social media users to "stop and think".[78]

5 Conclusion: Foul, Own Goal, Touchdown?

Coverage of men's sport is high-profile, commercially valuable, and widespread. Where there is attention paid to social media abuse, it tends to relate either to the misdeeds, or to racism or homophobic abuse suffered by male athletes, rather than online abuse of women. Equally, issues of violence against women seem to be brushed aside in the coverage of sports. This is not representative of the oft-stated aims of making sports inclusive and equal and serves to perpetuate harm to women. While there are clear intersectional issues affecting all involved in sport, the dominance of male professional sport is as evident in discussions and responses to social media abuse as it is in prominence, commercial value, salaries, and coverage. The #MeToo movement has yet to permeate professional sports as effectively as other areas of societal and cultural life, or has fallen on deaf ears, which is perhaps even more disappointing for women, and women's equality within professional sport more broadly.

Incidents of violence against women and intimate partner violence have been shown to increase on football match days during FIFA World Cups: increasing when teams win, and increasing still further when teams lose.[79] Similarly, given the correlation between sporting events and increases in gender-based violence, the importance of "situational dynamics"[80] cannot be underestimated either, nor can social media engagement around the time of high-profile sporting events. This is highly likely to exacerbate instances of social media abuse given the relative ease with which abuse, hostility, and violence can be disseminated online. The problem—and challenge of responding meaningfully—is not only one affecting those that engage in professional sports offline, but also impacts on eSports professionals too. Likewise, from a legal perspective, the emergence and commonplace nature of online abuse of women—in sport and more generally—prompts complex questions about the enforceability and usefulness of human rights frameworks in this context, as well as the role of states.

There is a clear and undisputed human rights dimension to the problem, albeit one that is unlikely to be resolved within the traditional, state-centered conception of human rights and the remedies available within it. This is predominantly due to the typology of actors involved in the regulation of sport (largely private, non-state) on the one hand, and the typology of spaces in which the abuse occurs (social media

[77] Heaf (2021).

[78] 'Iga Swiatek column' (2022).

[79] Kirby and Birdsall (2022), pp. 386–387.

[80] Kirby and Birdsall (2022), p. 385.

sites) on the other. While states have due diligence obligations under international (human rights) law that can extend to human-rights based accountability for acts committed by non-state actors, it is difficult to ignore other considerations surrounding the uneasy relationship between states as human rights duty bearers, online platforms, and sport governing bodies. Specifically, the economic power, resources, and highly specialized technical knowledge of those that work at online platforms stands in stark contrast to the capabilities of many states in these areas. Furthermore, both sport governing bodies and social media companies are private, non-state entities, with elaborate self-governance structures.

Regardless of the medium and mode of sport, there is an emerging consensus that #MeToo has not yet led to the cultural and societal shift required, and that actions such as introducing diversity committees are, at best, akin to putting sticking plasters on amputated limbs.[81] There is significant room for improvement in addressing social media abuse in sport, especially when it involves women. Using a sporting analogy, the professional and governing bodies have, to date, managed to commit a foul and are not far from scoring own goal. Scoring a touchdown in gender equality benchmarks, and in tackling social media abuse of women in sport, remains a significant challenge for *all* sports.

References

Aarons E, Molina R (2021) Fifa and UN agency plan global network to tackle sexual abuse in sport (2021, December 6), The Guardian. Retrieved from: https://www.theguardian.com/sport/2021/dec/06/global-network-to-tackle-sexual-abuse-in-sport-planned-by-fifa-and-un-agency

Aarons E, Molina R, Cizmic A (2020) Haiti FA president Yves Jean-Bart banned for life by Fifa over sexual abuse (2020, November 20), The Guardian. Retrieved from: https://www.theguardian.com/football/2020/nov/20/haiti-fa-president-yves-jean-bart-banned-for-life-by-fifa-over-sexual-abuse

Antunovic D (2019) "We wouldn't say it to their faces": online harassment, women sports journalists, and feminism. Fem Media Stud 19(3):428–442

Barker K, Jurasz O (2019a) Online Misogyny: a challenge for global feminism. J Int Aff 72(2): 95–113

Barker K, Jurasz O (2019b) Online Misogyny as a hate crime: a challenge for legal regulation? Routledge

Barker K, Jurasz O (2020) Gendered misinformation & online violence against women in politics: capturing legal responsibility? (2020, March 18) Co-Inform. Retrieved from: https://coinform.eu/gendered-misinformation-online-violence-against-women-in-politics-capturing-legal-responsibility/

Barker K, Jurasz O (2021a) Text-based (sexual) abuse and online violence against women: towards law reform? In: Bailey J, Flynn A, Henry N (eds) Technology-facilitated violence and abuse – international perspectives and experiences. Emerald Publishing, pp 247–264

Barker K, Jurasz O (2021b) Online violence against women: recognising democratic harms & participatory exclusion. Paper presented at Suffrage Now. International Conference on Gender and Democracy, Stockholm University, August 13-14, 2021 (on file with authors)

[81] Lorenz and Browning (2020); van Homrigh (2021).

Barker K, Jurasz O (2021c) Gender based abuse online: an assessment of law, policy and reform in England and Wales. In: Powell A, Flynn A, Suguira L (eds) The Palgrave handbook of gendered violence and technology. Palgrave MacMillan, pp 529–545

Barker K, Jurasz O (2021d) Online Misogyny as a hate crime: an obstacle to equality? (2021, November), GenIUS. Retrieved from: http://www.geniusreview.eu/wp-content/uploads/2021/11/Barker_Jurasz.pdf, 1–19

Batte K (2022) England appoint two senior squad members as 'social media captains' on how to deal with potential abuse they may receive during Women's Euro's as Rachel Day insists younger stars 'can lean on us for support' (2022, 23 June), Daily Mail. Retrieved from: https://www.dailymail.co.uk/sport/sportsnews/article-10946593/England-appoint-two-social-media-captains-deal-potential-abuse-Womens-Euros.html

BBC (2021) Nowhere to run: abused by our coach. Director: Helen Spooner

BBC News (2022a) Benjamin Mendy: rape-accused man city footballer faces new charge (2022, 2 February). Retrieved from: https://www.bbc.co.uk/news/uk-england-manchester-60216445

BBC News (2022b) Mason Greenwood: Man Utd footballer further arrested over sex assault (2022, 1 February 2022). Retrieved from: https://www.bbc.co.uk/news/uk-england-manchester-60202000

BBC's Sonja McLaughlan reveals online abuse over Owen Farrell interview (2021, February 27), The Guardian. Retrieved from: https://www.theguardian.com/sport/2021/feb/27/bbcs-sonja-mclaughlan-reveals-online-abuse-over-owen-farrell-interview

Brackenridge C (1997) 'HE OWNED ME BASICALLY...': women's experience of sexual abuse in sport. Int Rev Sociol Sport 32(2):115–130

Burnton S (2021) England's Ollie Robinson apologises after racist and sexist tweets emerge (2021, 2 June), The Guardian. Retrieved from: https://www.theguardian.com/sport/2021/jun/02/ollie-robinsons-england-debut-marred-by-emergence-of-racist-and-sexist-tweets

Campbell PI (2021) Taking the knee in football: why this act of protest has always been political (2021, 16 June), The Conversation. Retrieved from: https://theconversation.com/taking-the-knee-in-football-why-this-act-of-protest-has-always-been-political-16254

Coco Gauff warns Emma Raducanu about social media use (2021, October 7) ESPN. Retrieved from: https://www.espn.com/tennis/story/_/id/32353458/coco-gauff-warns-emma-raducanu-social-media-use

Council of Europe (2019) Recommendation on preventing and combating sexism, 27 March 2019. Retrieved from: https://rm.coe.int/prems055519-gbr-2573-cmrec-2019-1-web-a5/168093e08c

Council of Europe (2021) GREVIO General Recommendation No.1 on the digital dimension of violence against women, adopted on 20 October 2021. Retrieved from: https://rm.coe.int/grevio-rec-no-on-digital-violence-against-women/1680a49147

Courier Reporters (2022) Full list of Raith Rovers resignations over David Goodwillie signing (2022, 1 February), The Courier. Retrieved from: https://www.thecourier.co.uk/fp/news/fife/2966589/raith-rovers-resignations-david-goodwillie/

Cricket News (2021) Alex Hartley reveals online abuse following Twitter misunderstanding with England's Rory Burns (2021, 3 June), Sky Sports. Retrieved from: https://www.skysports.com/cricket/news/12123/12236512/alex-hartley-reveals-online-abuse-following-twitter-misunderstanding-with-englands-rory-burns

Decision of the Disciplinary Panel of the England and Wales Cricket Board against Ollie Robinson (2021, 30 June). Retrieved from: https://resources.ecb.co.uk/ecb/document/2021/07/02/97245365-2737-444c-801f-fa7e39a2240f/Decision_of_Disciplinary_Panel_ECB_and_Ollie_Robinson.pdf

Department for Culture, Media & Sport (2017) Internet Safety Strategy – Green Paper (2017, 11 October), gov.uk. Retrieved from: https://www.gov.uk/government/consultations/internet-safety-strategy-green-paper

Department for Culture, Media & Sport (2022) Online Safety Bill: factsheet (2022, 19 April), gov.uk. Retrieved from: https://www.gov.uk/government/publications/online-safety-bill-supporting-documents/online-safety-bill-factsheet#what-the-bill-does-to-protect-women

Doyle T (2021) England Rugby condemns online abuse directed towards its players after Wales Six Nations loss (2021, 28 February), Evening Standard. Retrieved from: https://www.standard.co.uk/sport/rugby/england-rugby-condemns-online-abuse-of-players-after-wales-six-nations-loss-b921577.html

Dunn C (2022) Football needs to stop condoning violence against women (2022, 4 February), openDemocracy. Retrieved from: https://www.opendemocracy.net/en/5050/raith-rovers-david-goodwillie-football-violence-against-women/

Ehantharajah V (2017) England women curtail social media activity during cricket World Cup (2017, 26 June), The Guardian. Retrieved from: https://www.theguardian.com/sport/2017/jun/26/england-women-social-media-blackout-world-cup

End Violence Against Women Coalition (2022) The Three Hijabis and Level Up Open Letter to CEOs of the Premier League and Football Association (2022, 5 February), evaw.org. Retrieved from: https://www.endviolenceagainstwomen.org.uk/open-letter-football-gender-based-violence/

England and Wales Cricket Board (2020) ECB Directives (2020, August). Retrieved from: https://resources.ecb.co.uk/ecb/document/2020/08/05/71a17d71-fce5-4667-84f5-8c4c67df3b8c/ECB-Directives-July-2020-vF.pdf

England and Wales Cricket Board (2021) Equity, Diversity and Inclusion – A Game for Everyone (2021). Retrieved from: https://www.ecb.co.uk/about/equity-diversity-and-inclusion/overview

England and Wales Cricket Board (2022) Anti-Discrimination Code (2022). Retrieved from: https://resources.ecb.co.uk/ecb/document/2022/03/17/36918e2a-b649-489a-9295-ea3bb6b5d433/ECB_Anti-Discrimination_Code_2022_v5-1-.pdf

European Commission (2014) Gender Equality in Sport – Proposal for Strategic Actions 2014-2020 (2014, February)

Female football fan speaks out over 'vile' social media abuse (2022, March 30) BBC News, Retrieved from: https://www.bbc.co.uk/news/uk-england-south-yorkshire-60921116

FIFA (n.d.) Human Rights and Anti-Discrimination. Retrieved from: https://www.fifa.com/social-impact/human-rights

Gardner B (2021) Hartley-Burns Twitter scuffle highlights deep-rooted negative attitudes towards women's cricket in England (2021, 1 March), Wisden. Retrieved from: https://wisden.com/stories/opinion/hartley-burns-twitter-scuffle-highlights-deep-rooted-negative-attitudes-towards-womens-cricket-in-england

George Z (2021) How social media is taking a toll on elite athletes (2021, 23 May), Stuff. Retrieved from: https://www.stuff.co.nz/sport/women-in-sport/300312925/how-social-media-is-taking-a-toll-on-elite-athletes

Gijy J (2021) 'It's Toxic'- Sydney McLaughlin Breaks Down in Tears Over Lack of Respect After Tokyo Olympics 2020 (2021, August 24). Retrieved from: https://www.essentiallysports.com/tokyo-olympics-athletics-news-its-toxic-sydney-mclaughlin-breaks-down-in-tears-over-lack-of-respect-after-tokyo-olympics-2020/

Giles AR, Darroch F (2020) We must pay attention to Canada's #MeToo moment in sports (2020, October 29), The Conversation. Retrieved from: https://theconversation.com/we-must-pay-attention-to-canadas-metoo-moment-in-sports-133309

Grey B, Lofthouse A, Oxley S, Thompson A (2020) Social media trolling affects almost a third of elite British sportswomen, BBC Sport survey finds (2020, August 9) BBC Sport. Retrieved from: https://www.bbc.co.uk/sport/53430686

Grey-Thompson T (2017) Duty of Care in Sport – Independent Report to Government (2017, April). Retrieved from: https://assets.publishing.service.gov.uk/government/uploads/system/uploads/attachment_data/file/610130/Duty_of_Care_Review_-_April_2017__2.pdf

Heaf J (2021) Roger Federer: 'Emma Raducanu's run has been incredible, but there is too much pressure on young players' (2021, September 27) GQ. Retrieved from: https://www.gq-magazine.co.uk/sport/article/roger-federer-emma-raducanu-2021

Iga Swiatek column: French Open favourite on online abuse & Ashleigh Barty advice (2022, May 25) BBC Sport. Retrieved from: https://www.bbc.co.uk/sport/tennis/61567160

Jurasz O (2021) Tackle online violence against women now: a call to the internet giants (2021, December 22) openDemocracy. Retrieved from: https://www.opendemocracy.net/en/north-africa-west-asia/tackle-online-violence-against-women-now-a-call-to-the-internet-giants/

Kick It Out (2017) Football in pursuit of Equality (E), Inclusion (I) and Cohesion (C) – A Brief Overview of Football's EIC Initiatives, Achievements, and Shortcomings 1993-2017 with an Outline of the Challenges Ahead (2017, November). Retrieved from: https://www.kickitout.org/Handlers/Download.ashx?IDMF=3b3d9537-cc5e-4cde-acb3-6febdecf19cc

Kick It Out (n.d.). Retrieved from: https://www.kickitout.org/about-us

Kirby S, Birdsall N (2022) Kicking off: is the association between the FIFA world cup and domestic abuse an international phenomenon? Police J 95(2):378–390

Latham-Coyle H (2021) Roger Federer: next generation of tennis stars need to be protected from social media abuse (2021, September 27) The Evening Standard. Retrieved from: https://www.standard.co.uk/sport/tennis/roger-federer-emma-raducanu-naomi-osaka-protect-social-media-abuse-b957440.html

Lorenz T, Browning K (2020) Dozens of women in gaming speak out about sexism and harassment (2020, 23 June) The New York Times. Retrieved from: https://www.nytimes.com/2020/06/23/style/women-gaming-streaming-harassment-sexism-twitch.html

McCallig E (2022) Tennis fans feel criticism would have been much worse if Serena Williams had done what Djokovic did (2022, January 14) Indy100. Retrieved from: https://www.indy100.com/sport/serena-williams-novak-djokovic-double-standard-b1993177

McClure T (2023) Jacinda Ardern: political figures believe abuse and threats contributed to PM's resignation (2023, January 20) The Guardian. Retrieved from: https://www.theguardian.com/world/2023/jan/20/jacinda-ardern-speculation-that-abuse-and-threats-contributed-to-resignation

Mithali Raj gets trolled for her dress, fans show massive support (2017, September 7) Times of India. Retrieved from: https://m.timesofindia.com/Mithali-Raj-gets-trolled-for-her-dress-fans-show-massive-support/videoshow/60408595.cms?mobile=no

Oliva TD (2020) Content moderation technologies: applying human rights standards to protect freedom of expression. Hum Rights Law Rev 20(4):607–640

'One must respect the game': French Open says 'non' to Serena's catsuit (2018, August 24) The Guardian. Retrieved from: https://www.theguardian.com/sport/2018/aug/24/serena-catsuit-french-open-dress-code

Online Safety Bill 2023 (OSB), HL Bill 164 as at July 2023

Petty K, Pope S (2019) A new age for media coverage of women's sport? An analysis of English Media Coverage of the 2015 FIFA Women's World Cup. Sociology 53(3):486–502

Plan International (2019) Snapshot analysis: social media commentary of sportswomen and sportsmen (2019, April 18). Retrieved from: https://www.plan.org.au/news/news/snapshot-analysis-social-media-commentary-of-sportswomen-and-sportsmen/

Racist abuse of England players Marcus Rashford, Jadon Sancho & Bukayo Saka 'unforgivable' (2021, July 12) BBC Sport. Retrieved from: https://www.bbc.co.uk/sport/football/57800431

Rajan A (2022) Novak Djokovic willing to miss tournaments over vaccine (2022, February 15) BBC News. Retrieved from: https://www.bbc.co.uk/news/world-60354068

Reddy M (2020) Alex Scott: 'There was a stage I lost myself and personality because of social media abuse' (2020, October 1) Independent. Retrieved from: https://www.independent.co.uk/sport/football/womens_football/alex-scott-interview-social-media-abuse-question-of-sport-between-the-lines-b721291.html

Reid A (2021) Naomi Osaka reveals disgusting backlash over Olympics decision (2021, July 19) Yahoo! Sports. Retrieved from: https://au.sports.yahoo.com/olympics-2021-naomi-osaka-representing-japan-tokyo-games-backlash-004646831.html

Social Media Abuse of Tennis Stars (2022) Pickswise. Retrieved from: https://www.pickswise.com/tennis/most-abused-tennis-players/

Stewart S (2022) Women in football: our investigation reveals scale of sexist abuse facing those who love the game (2022, February 16) The Press and Journal. Retrieved from: https://www.pressandjournal.co.uk/fp/pj-investigations/3946200/sexism-in-football-survey/
The Football Association (2021) A statement following the online abuse of England players following Euro 2020 final (2021, 12 July), thefa.com. Retrieved from: https://www.thefa.com/news/2021/jul/12/20210712-statement-online-abuse-of-england-player
Tuckey I (2018) PAN UTD Manchester United women beaten 9-0 by Salford youth team triggers vile sexist abuse on Twitter (2018, 27 July), The Sun. Retrieved from: https://www.thesun.co.uk/sport/football/6881715/manchester-united-women-beaten-9-0-by-salford-youth-team-triggers-vile-sexist-abuse-on-twitter/
UN CEDAW (1992) General Recommendation 19: Violence Against Women
UN CEDAW (2010) General Recommendation 28 on the core obligations of States parties under Article 2 of the CEDAW
UN CEDAW (2017) General Recommendation 35 on gender-based violence against women, updating general recommendation No. 19
van Homrigh M (2021) Rape threats and misogyny: Female gamers detail online abuse as industry tries to make amends (2021, 16 November), News.com.au. Retrieved from: https://www.news.com.au/technology/rape-threats-and-misogyny-female-gamers-detail-online-abuse-as-industry-tries-to-make-amends/news-story/90f697260244b9c05da353c984f924d0
World Athletics publishes Online Abuse Study covering Tokyo Olympic Games (2021, November 25) World Athletics. Retrieved from: https://worldathletics.org/news/press-releases/online-abuse-study-athletes-tokyo-olympic-games
Wrack S (2019) Afghanistan's football president banned for life for sexual abuse (2019, June 8), The Guardian. Retrieved from: https://www.theguardian.com/football/2019/jun/08/keramuudin-karim-banned-for-life

Kim Barker is Professor of Law at the University of Lincoln, and an expert in online violence against women, internet law, and online regulation. She is a founding co-director of Europe's first Observatory on Online Violence Against Women (ObserVAW). Kim is the co-author of *Online Misogyny as a Hate Crime: a challenge for legal regulation* (Routledge, 2019) and *Violence Against Women, Hate and Law: perspectives from contemporary Scotland* (Palgrave 2022), alongside numerous publications addressing online harms, violence against women, online misogyny, the regulation of online content/spaces and the law. Her expertise has informed law and policy making in the UK, Europe, and Asia.

Olga Jurasz is Professor of Law at the Open University. She specialises in legal and policy responses to violence against women (especially in relation to its online and technology-facilitated forms) and in feminist approaches to governance of online spaces. Professor Jurasz is co-founder and co-director of ObserVAW – Europe's first Observatory on Online Violence Against Women.

Hormonal Eligibility Criteria in Women's Professional Sports Under the ECHR: The Case of Caster Semenya v. Switzerland

Pieter Cannoot, Cathérine Van de Graaf, Ariël Decoster, Claire Poppelwell-Scevak, and Sarah Schoentjes

Contents

P. Cannoot (✉)
Department of Interdisciplinary Study of Law, Private Law and Business Law, Faculty of Law and Criminology, Ghent University, Ghent, Belgium
e-mail: pieter.cannoot@ugent.be

C. Van de Graaf
Academy for European Human Rights Protection, Faculty of Law, University of Cologne, Köln, Germany
e-mail: catherine.vandegraaf@uni-koeln.de

A. Decoster · S. Schoentjes
Human Rights Centre, Ghent University, Ghent, Belgium

FWO Flanders Research Foundation, Brussels, Belgium
e-mail: ariel.decoster@uantwerpen.be; sarah.schoentjes@ugent.be

C. Poppelwell-Scevak
Human Rights Centre, Ghent University, Ghent, Belgium
e-mail: claire.poppelwellscevak@ugent.be

V. Boillet et al. (eds.), *Sports and Human Rights*, Interdisciplinary Studies in Human Rights 10, https://doi.org/10.1007/978-3-031-56452-9_5

Abstract Although society is (slowly) evolving, rigid gender stereotypes still persist in the world of professional sports. In line with the creation of a strict binary division of athletes, sex-testing policies based on stereotypical considerations of womanhood have come to target 'overly masculine' women athletes with variations of sex characteristics (VSC), as elevated levels of testosterone are believed to constitute a competitive advantage.

Some international sports federations, such as World Athletics, have adopted hormonal eligibility criteria (HEC) for women's sports competitions, although the underlying scientific evidence has been strongly contested. Athletes are excluded if they do not comply with these requirements. The standard way of reducing testosterone levels is via the use of hormonal contraceptives, although irreversible surgical treatment also occurs. HEC for sports competitions raises important issues in respect of the fundamental rights of professional women athletes with VSC, and have been challenged before the Court of Arbitration for Sports (CAS).

In this chapter, we analyze the HEC set by World Athletics in light of the European Convention on Human Rights (ECHR), which is the relevant framework for addressing human rights concerns since Switzerland accepts jurisdiction for appeals against CAS decisions. We discuss the relevant societal background, argue how HEC for sports competitions violates the individual's right to bodily and mental integrity as protected by Article 3 ECHR, and explain that the scope of the state's positive obligations under Article 8 ECHR needs to be interpreted as encompassing a duty to ensure the effective protection of an athlete's bodily and psychological integrity. Finally, we set out why HEC directed at women athletes with VSC amounts to intersectional discrimination in breach of Article 14 ECHR in conjunction with Articles 3 and 8 ECHR.

1 Introduction

Should women with variations of sex characteristics (VSC) be excluded from professional women's sports?[1] In recent years, this question has spurred considerable controversy around the globe. In November 2021, the International Olympic Committee (IOC) released its new Framework on Fairness, Inclusion and

[1]This chapter was finalized in March 2023 and therefore before the European Court of Human Rights adopted its judgment in the case of Caster Semenya v. Switzerland (ECtHR, Semenya v. Switzerland, 11.07.2023). For an early analysis of the judgment, see Cannoot (2023).

Non-Discrimination on the Basis of Gender Identity and Sex Variations.[2] According to the IOC, "every person has the right to practise sport without discrimination and in a way that respects their health, safety and dignity. At the same time, the credibility of competitive sport – and particularly high-level organized sporting competitions – relies on a level playing field, where no athlete has an unfair and disproportionate advantage over the rest".[3] This need to find a balance in sports between, on the one hand, inclusion and non-discrimination, and on the other hand, fairness, is at heart of the issue that we will address in this chapter: namely, hormonal eligibility criteria (HEC) for the participation of athletes with VSC in women's professional sports competitions.

While the Framework is based on the acceptance that no athlete should be excluded from participating in sport based on their gender identity or sex characteristics, it allows the establishment of eligibility criteria that determine the participation conditions for male/female categories for certain contests in high-level organized sports competitions. However, according to the IOC, these criteria must not lead to physical or psychological harm, or targeted testing aimed at determining athletes' sex, gender identity, or variation in sex characteristics. Moreover, they should be based on robust and peer-reviewed research, and applied so as to respect the athlete's integrity and requirements of procedural fairness. According to the Framework, every athlete should be able to participate in a gendered category on the basis of self-determination.

The IOC Framework is not designed as a one-size-fits-all policy. Indeed, the IOC has recognized that it must be for each sport and its governing body to determine how exactly an athlete may have a disproportionate advantage, and which eligibility criteria for professional sports competitions are necessary to provide compensation for such an advantage. In response to the new Framework, the International Federation of Aquatics (FINA) adopted new eligibility criteria for participation in men's and women's competitions, excluding trans women and women with 46 XY chromosomes who had experienced 'male puberty' beyond Tanner Stage 2 or before age 12 (whichever is later).[4] Following FINA's decision, the International Rugby League

[2]This chapter will interchangeably make use of the terms 'persons with variations of sex characteristics' and 'intersex persons'. We recognize that these terms are often accompanied with distinct connotations and are not universally accepted by persons who have a variation of sex characteristics. In any case, no offense was intended by our terminological choices.

[3]International Olympic Committee (2021) IOC Framework on Fairness, Inclusion and Non-Discrimination on the Basis of Gender Identity and Sex Variations, https://stillmed.olympics.com/media/Documents/News/2021/11/IOC-Framework-Fairness-Inclusion-Non-discrimination-2021.pdf?_ga=2.126449807.389375767.1653928341-809039675.1653928341 (last accessed 20 October 2022), p. 1.

[4]The new regulations are available at https://resources.fina.org/fina/document/2022/06/19/525de003-51f4-47d3-8d5a-716dac5f77c7/FINA-INCLUSION-POLICY-AND-APPENDICES-FINAL-.pdf (last accessed 20 October 2022).

announced that it would also develop a new inclusion policy and banned trans women from competing in women's international competitions for the time being.[5]

In March 2023, World Athletics, the international federation for athletics, decided to update its controversial 'Eligibility Regulations for the Female Classification (Athletes with Differences of Sex Development)'—often referred to as the 'DSD Regulations'—so as to exclude all trans women who had experienced 'male puberty' either beyond Tanner Stage 2 or after age 12 (whichever comes first).[6] On the basis of the updated DSD Regulations, women athletes with a certain variation of sex characteristics that leads to levels of testosterone beyond the 'normal' female range, are excluded from all World Rankings events, unless they have reduced their level of testosterone to below 2.5 nmol/l for a continuous period of at least 24 months, and as long as they want to remain eligible to compete. Any relevant athlete has the duty to inform World Athletics when they might have such variation in sex characteristics, and can be asked to undergo testing on a suspicion-based model. While no athlete may be forced to undergo testing or certain forms of treatment, all relevant athletes have a duty to cooperate in good faith, and will be excluded from competition if they fail to reduce their level of testosterone to the required level or fail to cooperate with World Athletics.

Before the 2023 update, the DSD Regulations set by World Athletics excluded the affected women athletes from events such as 400m (hurdles) races, 800m (hurdles) races, 1500m races and one mile races, unless they reduced their level of testosterone to below 5 nmol/l for a continuous period of at least six months, and as long as they wanted to remain eligible to compete. Ever since they were adopted, these DSD Regulations have been strongly contested. Two affected athletes in particular, Dutee Chand and Caster Semenya, have challenged the regulations before the Court of Arbitration for Sport (CAS). In 2015, in the case of Chand, the CAS suspended World Athletics' (then called IAAF) 'Hyperandrogenism Regulations', for lack of sufficient evidence that the affected women athletes indeed had a disproportionate competitive advantage over fellow competitors who did not have elevated levels of testosterone.[7] Following the CAS ruling, in 2018 World Athletics repealed the 'Hyperandrogenism Regulations' and adopted new DSD Regulations, citing new evidence and data showing "that testosterone, either naturally produced or artificially inserted into the body, provides significant performance advantages in female athletes".[8] Caster Semenya challenged the new DSD Regulations before the

[5]The IRL's statement is available at https://www.intrl.sport/news/statement-on-transgender-participtiion-in-women-s-international-rugby-league/ (last accessed 20 October 2022).

[6]The newly updated version 3.0 of the DSD Regulations is available at https://worldathletics.org/about-iaaf/documents/book-of-rules (last accessed 28 March 2023), under Book C, C3.6. They entered into force on 31 March 2023. Since we focus on hormonal eligibility criteria for women athletes with variations of sex characteristics, we will not address the exclusion of trans women.

[7]CAS 2014/A/3759 Dutee Chand v. Athletics Federation of India (AFI) and The International Association of Athletics Federations (IAAF), 24 July 2015.

[8]https://www.worldathletics.org/news/press-release/eligibility-regulations-for-female-classifica (last accessed 20 October 2022).

CAS, which found the regulations discriminatory on the basis of sex and of 'innate biological characteristics', yet necessary and proportionate in light of the objective of maintaining fairness in women's professional sports.[9] The ruling was upheld by the Swiss Federal Tribunal, which found that the CAS award did not breach Swiss public policy.[10]

Caster Semenya brought her case before the European Court of Human Rights (hereafter 'the ECtHR' or 'the Court'), which communicated the case to the respondent State (Switzerland) in May 2021. Semenya *inter alia* claimed that the (then applicable) DSD Regulations set by World Athletics violate several provisions of the European Convention on Human Rights (ECHR), such as the prohibition of torture and inhuman or degrading treatment (Article 3 ECHR) and the right to respect for private life (Article 8 ECHR), taken alone and in combination with the prohibition of discrimination (Article 14 ECHR). In this chapter, we will focus on how—in our view—the DSD Regulations and their application to Caster Semenya (i.e., before the March 2023 update) should be substantively assessed under the ECHR, taking into account the ECtHR's case law and other standards of international human rights law. We will therefore not elaborate at length on the process through which the DSD Regulations were established, on the prior challenges of the regulations by other athletes such as Dutee Chand, or on the procedures that Semenya initiated before the CAS and the Swiss Federal Tribunal. For those analyses, we refer to the extensive body of work by other authors.[11]

While the involvement of the Swiss courts in the case of Caster Semenya is the formal anchor point for application of the ECHR and jurisdiction of the ECtHR, substantively the case is about rules that are part of the so-called *lex sportiva*, set by a private sports governing body. While ECtHR rulings necessarily focus on the facts of the case, their impact can be much broader. For private sports governing bodies, as well as for state courts monitoring them, the judgment in the case of Semenya is likely to become a central reference point concerning the role of human rights standards in sports. As such, it has the potential to strengthen, or disable, dynamics calling for increased human rights protection for athletes. Indeed, the inherent threat to human rights stemming from HEC set by sports bodies has also been stressed by several special procedures of the UN Human Rights Council. In their *amicus curiae* submission to CAS[12] in the Semenya case, the Special Rapporteur on the right of everyone to the enjoyment of the highest attainable standard of physical and mental health; the Special Rapporteur on torture and other cruel, inhuman or degrading treatment or punishment; and the Working Group on the issue of discrimination against women in law and in practice, signaled that both the World Athletics

[9] CAS 2018/0/5794 and 2018/O/5798 Mokgadi Caster Semenya and Athletics South Africa v. International Association of Athletics Federations, 30 April 2019.

[10] Swiss Federal Tribunal 25 August 2020, 4A_248/2019 and 4A_398/2019.

[11] See for recent analyses *inter alia* Holzer (2020), Karkazis and Jordan-Young (2018), Gilleri and Winckler (2021), Byczkow and Thompson (2019).

[12] The *amicus curiae* cannot be publicly consulted but is referenced in the CAS decision.

eligibility criteria as well as procedures for their implementation appear to contravene international human rights standards.[13]

Our contribution is based on our written third party intervention in Semenya's case before the Court, under the supervision of Professor Eva Brems. As academics who are affiliated with the Human Rights Centre at Ghent University—an academic center of expertise on European and international human rights law, which has a long tradition of submitting third party interventions in important cases before the ECtHR—we took on the task of assisting the Court by clarifying relevant legal standards that are applicable to the case.[14] In other words, we did not comment on the facts of the case, nor did we take on the role of Semenya's counsel. In this contribution, we first set out the societal background against which HEC should be assessed (Sect. 2). In Sect. 3, we argue that HEC for women sports competitions that apply to women with variations of sex characteristics, such as the DSD Regulations set by World Athletics, violate the prohibition of inhuman and degrading treatment as protected by Article 3 ECHR. We proceed to argue, in Sect. 4, that the scope of the state's positive obligations under Article 8 ECHR needs to be interpreted as encompassing a duty to ensure the effective protection of a professional athlete's physical and psychological integrity. Before concluding, we set out in Sect. 5 why HEC directed at women athletes with a variation of sex characteristics amounts to intersectional discrimination in breach of Article 14 ECHR in conjunction with Articles 3 and 8 ECHR.

2 Hormonal Eligibility Criteria in Women's Professional Sports in Context

2.1 Persisting Structural Sex and Gender Discrimination in Sports

While society is currently undergoing significant changes in the ways sex and gender identity are understood, recognized, and organized,[15] rigid culturally-constructed gender stereotypes still persist. This is also (and arguably especially) true for the world of professional sports. As the United Nations High Commissioner for Human Rights has pointed out, women and girls are structurally confronted with exclusion

[13] CAS 2018/O/5794 Mokgadi Caster Semenya v. The International Association of Athletics Federation (IAAF) and CAS 2018/O/5798 Athletics South Africa v. The International Association of Athletics Federation (IAAF), 30 April 2019, § 553.

[14] Our intervention is available at https://hrc.ugent.be/wp-content/uploads/2021/10/Final-Submission.pdf (last accessed 20 October 2022).

[15] Patel (2021).

and discrimination in sports.[16] According to the High Commissioner, the underlying reasons can be,

> both external to sport, such as discriminatory social norms or obstacles to reconciling the burdens of care, work and sport, and internal to sport, including the lack of programmes to create a gender sensitive and safe sporting environment or to address the harassment and other forms of gender-based violence in sport, including sexual exploitation and abuse.[17]

Importantly, the High Commissioner has also pointed out that broader sociocultural gender norms—such as culturally-constructed expectations about a woman's sex characteristics—hinder women and girls from participating in sport.[18] While this structural discrimination affects all women, trans and intersex women are especially vulnerable. Indeed, in their recent report on LBTI (lesbian, bisexual, trans and intersex) women in sport, ILGA Europe, OII Europe,[19] EL*C[20] and EGLSF[21] note that sport is "a social environment where sexism and misogyny are still present an deeply linked with the history, structure and dynamics of participation of women in sport".[22] They held that, bearing in mind this structural sexism in sports, it is "not surprising that women perceived as non-conforming in society at large, due their sexual orientation, gender identity and/or expression, or sex characteristics (SOGIESC), are exposed to additional stigma and societal pressure".[23]

The beginning of women's participation in international professional sports only dates back to the beginning of the twentieth century. Since then, women's full inclusion has been hindered by cultural expectations about women's bodies and appearance—from early concerns about the public exhibition of female bodies, physical exertion and risk, to gender stereotypes about women's appearances.[24] Moreover, the start of women's participation in professional sports also coincided with so-called sex verification tests, since the participation of women was managed

[16] UN High Commissioner for Human Rights, "Intersection of race and gender discrimination in sport", A/HRC/44/26, p. 2.

[17] UN High Commissioner for Human Rights, "Intersection of race and gender discrimination in sport", A/HRC/44/26, p. 2.

[18] UN High Commissioner for Human Rights, "Intersection of race and gender discrimination in sport", A/HRC/44/26, p. 3.

[19] Organisation Intersex International Europe.

[20] EuroCentralAsian Lesbian* Community.

[21] European Gay and Lesbian Sport Federation.

[22] ILGA Europe, OII Europe, EL*C and EGLSF (2021) "LBTI women in sport: violence, discrimination and lived experiences", https://oiieurope.org/wp-content/uploads/2021/08/20210810-violence-and-discrimination-against-LBTI-women-in-sport-2.pdf (last accessed 20 October 2022), p. 5.

[23] ILGA Europe, OII Europe, EL*C and EGLSF (2021) "LBTI women in sport: violence, discrimination and lived experiences", https://oiieurope.org/wp-content/uploads/2021/08/20210810-violence-and-discrimination-against-LBTI-women-in-sport-2.pdf (last accessed 20 October 2022), p. 6.

[24] UN High Commissioner for Human Rights, "Intersection of race and gender discrimination in sport", A/HRC/44/26, pp. 6–7.

through the creation of a strict binary division of athletes.[25] In other words, women's participation in professional sports has always co-existed with some degree of suspicion towards 'overly masculine' women athletes and the 'policing' of women's bodies.[26] While elements such as dominance, strength, and stamina are traditionally celebrated in sports, they are still predominantly associated with masculinity and are thus treated as an advantage in sports.[27] As Holzer has argued, the lack of any HEC for men's professional sports and the absence of sex verification procedures for men show that men can never be 'too masculine' or have too much androgens, while professional women athletes may be scrutinized for being too 'manly'.[28] Historic methods of sex verification of women athletes have been strongly criticized for their humiliating nature and inaccuracy.[29]

2.2 *Intersectionality and Racialized Constructions of Womanhood*

As soon as women were allowed to enter the world of sports, women athletes' bodies and gender were policed and met with suspicion. Eligibility criteria for women's sport competitions reflect (and participate in) the social regulation of who 'is', and 'is not', a woman. While this policing of womanhood applies to all women, it is a form of discrimination that is particularly familiar for Black women, who have throughout history been stereotyped as 'overly masculine' and have been denied being recognized as 'feminine' or even as 'women'.[30] Their marginalization occurs on the basis of both race and gender, so that they are confronted with specific forms of oppression that white women or Black men do not face. Black women are subjected to specific stereotypes—such as their perceived toughness, aggression and anger, tying into the 'Angry Black Woman' stereotype—which ensure that their femininity is constantly scrutinized.[31] Indeed, gender is constructed through a racialized lens: the social category of 'woman' is influenced by the ideal of the white woman.[32] This factor

[25] UN High Commissioner for Human Rights, "Intersection of race and gender discrimination in sport", A/HRC/44/26, p. 7.

[26] See also Holzer (2020), pp. 395–396 and 408.

[27] Patel (2021). As the Rapporteurs and Working Group Joint Letter points out: "natural physical traits associated with above-average performance by elite male athletes are applauded and admired", https://spcommreports.ohchr.org/TMResultsBase/DownLoadPublicCommunicationFile?gId=24087 (last accessed 20 October 2022), p. 4.

[28] Holzer (2020), p. 400. See also Karkazis and Jordan-Young (2018), p. 7.

[29] Holzer (2020), p. 400.

[30] Kauer and Rauscher (2019).

[31] Jones and Norwood (2017).

[32] Yuval-Davis (2006) and Olofsson et al. (2014).

played an important role in Semenya's exclusion from sporting competitions; her womanhood was first suspect by virtue of her Blackness, and then denied.

In this sense, it is no coincidence that the 2020 Summer Olympics in Tokyo saw two more Black women being disqualified from the running competitions, after three Black women (including Semenya herself) had already suffered the same fate in 2016.[33] It is telling that the testosterone rule has, to date, overwhelmingly been enforced against Black women; the definition of a woman in sports is built around, and for, white women.[34] Whenever applied to Black women, eligibility regulations that force women with variations in sex characteristics to lower their level of testosterone perpetuate a societal tendency to deny them their womanhood as they are not considered 'woman enough' to participate in women's sport competitions.[35] The fact that Semenya is lesbian is relevant as well, as lesbian womanhood is often considered suspect, due to the widespread conflation between gender and sexual orientation. The stereotype is that real women are (exclusively) attracted to men, so lesbians cannot be considered 'real' women.[36] Thus, the womanhood of a Black lesbian woman is considered suspect on the grounds of their race *and* their sexual orientation, and can lead to their exclusion from sporting events.

2.3 The Erroneous Universality of Binary Sex and Rising International Attention for the Bodily Integrity of Persons with VSC

While sex-testing policies based on stereotypical considerations of womanhood ultimately affect all women athletes, they predominantly target transgender athletes and women athletes with VSC. Although World Athletics has claimed that the DSD Regulations are "in no way [intended] as any kind of judgement on or questioning of the sex or the gender identity of any athlete",[37] it is still the case that 'non-conforming' athletes are challenged in their 'true' sex,[38] which is informed by stereotypical constructions of sex and gender. In most societies, human beings are discretely 'sexed' into two categories, male and female, leading to the construction of 'sex' as a binary notion. However, between at least 1–1.7% of the population are

[33] Zaccardi N (2021) "Top 400m sprinters ruled ineligible due to testosterone rule, officials say" OlympicTalk | NBC Sports, https://olympics.nbcsports.com/2021/07/02/namibia-400-christine-mboma-beatrice-masilingi-testosterone/ (last accessed 20 October 2022).

[34] Holzer (2020); see also Bruening (2005).

[35] Holzer (2020).

[36] Gonzalez-Salzberg (2018) and Theilen (2018).

[37] § 1.1.5 of the regulations.

[38] Karkazis and Jordan-Young (2018), p. 8.

born with one or more natural variations of sex characteristics.[39] Persons with VSC thus show that strict and universal sex bipolarity does not exist in human nature, even if it does exist in culture or cultural norms. In other words, standards for 'normality' and 'abnormality' regarding the presence of certain sex characteristics (such as hormonal levels) in males and females deny the natural, congenital variations that human bodies can show. While persons with VSC will have *physical sex characteristics* that fall outside of the male/female binary, the majority of people with this range of conditions still identify their gender within the binary, and therefore identify as either a man or a woman.[40]

Over the last decade, several institutional human rights actors have called attention to the human rights violations that many people with VSC have suffered; central to the discussion is the protection of bodily integrity.[41] Variations of sex characteristics cannot be explained satisfactorily under the essentialist binary theory of sex, revealing inner contradictions in the theoretical framework.[42] The dominant approach has therefore consisted of routinely subjecting persons with VSC to medical and surgical sex 'normalizing' treatments (shortly after birth or during adolescence), without their prior and informed consent, even though they do not usually face actual health problems due to their status.[43/44] Several UN bodies have expressed concerns about non-consensual treatment of persons with VSC, and called for a legal prohibition of deferrable surgical and other medical treatment on children with VSC until they reach an age when they can provide their full informed consent.[45]

The same concern for guaranteeing the human rights of persons with VSC, and especially their autonomy rights, can be found among European institutional human rights actors. In October 2017, the Council of Europe Parliamentary Assembly (PA) adopted a comprehensive and ground-breaking resolution, "Promoting the human rights of and eliminating discrimination against intersex people", which called for a legal prohibition of deferrable sex 'normalizing' treatment.[46] The resolution recognized the serious breaches of physical integrity for children or infants with VSC who have undergone non-consensual, medically unnecessary sex 'normalizing' treatment, based on considerations of 'social emergency'. The PA

---

[39] EU Fundamental Rights Agency (2020) "A long way to go for LGBTI equality", https://fra.europa.eu/en/publication/2020/eu-lgbti-survey-results (last accessed 20 October 2022), p. 58; Council of Europe Commissioner for Human Rights (2015) "Human Rights and Intersex People" https://rm.coe.int/16806da5d4 (last accessed 20 October 2022), p. 16.

[40] Richards et al. (2016), p. 95.

[41] Cannoot (2022), pp. 112–118.

[42] Weiss (2001), p. 163.

[43] Garland and Travis (2018).

[44] See also Holzer (2020), pp. 391–392.

[45] See Cannoot (2022), pp. 112–116.

[46] Parliamentary Assembly of the Council of Europe, Resolution 2191 (2017) "promoting the human rights of and eliminating discrimination against intersex people", http://assembly.coe.int/nw/xml/XRef/Xref-XML2HTML-en.asp?fileid=24232 (last accessed 20 October 2022).

therefore called for a legal prohibition of medically unnecessary sex 'normalizing' surgery, sterilization and other treatments practiced on children with VSC without their informed consent.

While the case of *Semenya v. Switzerland* does not concern non-consensual sex 'normalizing' treatment, attention to the autonomy rights of persons with VSC within the international human rights community, as well as the historical vulnerability of persons with variations of sex characteristics for violations of their bodily integrity is needed when assessing the case. In any case, as Holzer, referencing Camporesi, states, "singling out testosterone as the only physical factor that could potentially create a comparative advantage is 'based entirely on heteronormative standards for how a female athlete should look".[47]

2.4 HEC for Women's Sports Competitions and Their Scientific Basis

As Seema Patel points out, evolutions in modern understandings of human variation in sex characteristics and the recognition of human diversity from a human rights perspective has "created tensions with the traditional binary structures of sport", triggering "a global debate mostly framed around science and athletic advantage" that tends to overlook the human rights of the affected athletes.[48] It is within this context that eligibility criteria for women's sports competitions, like World Athletics' DSD Regulations have to be situated. As mentioned above, on the basis of the rules applicable until 31 March 2023, athletes with VSC[49] who wanted to compete in the women's category of a certain event,[50] not only needed to be legally recognized as female or 'intersex' (or equivalent), but also needed to reduce blood testosterone levels to below 5 nmol/l for a continuous period of at least six months, and as long as they wished to remain eligible to compete.[51] Since the 2023 update, in order to compete in any women's competition, athletes with VSC must reduce testosterone levels to below 2.5 nmol/l for a continuous period of at least 24 months, and as long

[47] Holzer (2020), p. 403; Camporesi (2019), p. 797.

[48] Patel (2021).

[49] See § 2.2 (a) (i) of the regulations (before the 2023 update).

[50] See § 2.2 (b) of the regulations (before the 2023 update). Note that experts have criticized the arbitrariness of the selection of the events for which the eligibility criteria apply. They point out that there is no scientific basis for such selection. See for instance Stebbings S, Herbert A, Heffernan S, Pielke Jr R, Williams A (2021) The BASES Expert Statement on Eligibility for Sex Categories in Sport: DSD Athletes, https://www.bases.org.uk/imgs/8931_bas_bases_tses_summer_2021_online_pg_12_130.pdf (last accessed 20 October 2022).

[51] See § 2.3 of the regulations (before the 2023 update).

as they wish to remain eligible to compete.[52] The standard way of reducing natural testosterone levels is the use of hormonal contraceptives.[53]

While the policy does not foresee the possibility of forced hormonal treatment, it does result in the exclusion of certain athletes so long as they do not comply with the requirements. The policy is justified on the basis that the affected athletes allegedly have a significant performance advantage over other women whose hormonal levels come within the 'normal' female range.[54] However, since the eligibility criteria were adopted, the underlying scientific evidence has been strongly contested.[55] For instance, in September 2021, the authors of a 2017 study paid for by World Athletics and cited by the latter as "peer-reviewed data and evidence from the field",[56] published a statement correcting their earlier conclusions. According to the authors, "there is no confirmatory evidence for causality in the observed relationships [between levels of testosterone and performance advantage] reported", and "our results cannot be used as confirmatory evidence for the causal relationship but can indicate associations between androgen concentrations and athletic performance".[57]

Other experts have stated that, while one's level of testosterone is connected to sporting advantages and women with VSC might have natural testosterone levels exceeding the 'typical' female range, the extent of any performance advantage remains unclear; indeed, due to genetic factors, the ability to process these higher levels of testosterone may be compromised.[58] Other genetic characteristics such as height, eye sight, lung capacity, and socio-economic factors such as wealth, access to nutrition and training facilities, and family support, can equally create a competitive advantage.[59] The absence of a demonstrated relationship of causality between high levels of natural testosterone in women and their sports performance was pointed out in a letter addressed to the president of World Athletics by the UN Special Rapporteur on the right of everyone to the enjoyment of the highest attainable standard of physical and mental health, the UN Special Rapporteur on torture and other cruel, inhuman or degrading treatment or punishment, and the UN Working Group on the

[52] See § 2.1 of the regulations.

[53] However, more invasive and irreversible procedures such as a surgical gonadectomy also occur.

[54] See § 1.1 (d) of the regulations (before the 2023 update) and § 1.1.2 of the currently applicable regulations.

[55] Indeed, the 2011 version of the regulation was suspended for two years by the Court of Arbitration for Sports in the case of Dutee Chand v. Athletics Federation of India and the IAAF, 2014/A/3759. See also Bermon and Garnier (2021). See also Karkazis and Jordan-Young (2018), p. 8, Pielke et al. (2019), pp. 18–26.

[56] See § 1.1 (d) of the regulations (before the 2023 update).

[57] Bermon and Garnier (2021).

[58] Stebbings S, Herbert A, Heffernan S, Pielke Jr R, Williams A (2021) The BASES Expert Statement on Eligibility for Sex Categories in Sport: DSD Athletes, available at https://www.bases.org.uk/imgs/8931_bas_bases_tses_summer_2021_online_pg_12_130.pdf (last accessed 20 October 2022).

[59] Holzer (2020), p. 402.

issue of discrimination against women in law and in practice (hereafter, Rapporteurs and Working Group Joint Letter).[60]

3 Hormonal Eligibility Requirements as Inhuman and Degrading Treatment Under Article 3 ECHR

In this section, we argue that HEC for women's sports competitions that apply to women with VSC, such as the DSD Regulations set by World Athletics, violate the prohibition of inhuman and degrading treatment as protected by Article 3 ECHR. When deciding on whether a certain practice or treatment falls within the scope of Article 3, the Court has held that the "ill-treatment must attain a minimum level of severity".[61] In assessing whether such treatment meets this threshold, the Court looks to "the nature and context of the treatment, its duration, its physical and mental effects and, in some instances, the sex, age and state of health of the victim".[62] Further, the Court held that "the infliction of psychological suffering [...] can be qualified as degrading when it arouses in its victims feelings of fear, anguish and inferiority capable of humiliating and debasing them".[63]

As outlined above, it remains common practice for persons with VSC to be targeted from birth as requiring medical procedures to 'normalize' them. A rapidly growing number of UN Member States, including Switzerland, have been notified that they must adopt a legal framework that addresses the multiple human rights violations experienced by those who have been forced to undergo sex 'normalizing' treatment. In this light, we argue that mandatory medical treatment, *in casu*, is an extension of this 'normalization' and results in stigmatization and psychological suffering.

It is not disputed that non-compliance with HEC leads to the effective exclusion from participation in several women's sports competitions. The affected women athletes with VSC still maintain the possibility to exercise their profession as long as they undergo (hormonal) medical treatment, predominantly by taking contraceptives.[64] In its judgment in *V.C. v. Slovakia*, which concerned the forced sterilization

[60] Letter by the Mandates of the Special Rapporteur on the right of everyone to the enjoyment of the highest attainable standard of physical and mental health, the Special Rapporteur on torture and other cruel, inhuman or degrading treatment or punishment, and the Working Group on the issue of discrimination against women in law and in practice, OL OTH 62/2018 (hereinafter: Rapporteurs and Working Group Joint Letter), https://spcommreports.ohchr.org/TMResultsBase/DownLoadPublicCommunicationFile?gId=24087 (last accessed 20 October 2022), p. 2.

[61] ECtHR, Identoba and Others v. Georgia, 12.05.2015, § 65.

[62] ECtHR, Identoba and Others v. Georgia, 12.05.2015, § 65.

[63] ECtHR, Identoba and Others v. Georgia, 12.05.2015, § 65.

[64] Sometimes irreversible surgeries, such as gonadectomies or even clitoridectomies, are performed. In the case of athlete Annet Negesa, a gonadectomy was performed without her full and prior informed consent. See the report by Human Rights Watch, https://www.hrw.org/sites/default/files/

of Roma women, the Court attached significant importance to the protection of meaningful informed consent ('free will') under Article 3 and Article 8 of the Convention,[65] especially taking into account the impact of the treatment concerned on the applicant's reproductive health status. In its assessment of the applicant's claim under Article 3, the Court noted that,

> sterilisation constitutes a major interference with a person's reproductive health status. As it concerns one of the essential bodily functions of human beings, it bears on manifold aspects of the individual's personal integrity including his or her physical and mental well-being and emotional, spiritual and family life. It may be legitimately performed at the request of the person concerned, for example as a method of contraception, or for therapeutic purposes where the medical necessity has been convincingly established.[66]

In the same case, the Court refuted the paternalistic actions on behalf of the hospital staff concerned, which meant that "in practice, the applicant was not offered any option but to agree to the procedure".[67] However, in the recent case of *Y.P. v. Russia*,[68] the Court seemed to bring nuance to its findings in *V.C. v. Slovakia*. Even though the former case also concerned the non-consensual sterilization of a woman in the absence of any pressing necessity to protect her life, the Court, surprisingly,[69] found that the case did not meet the threshold of severity of Article 3 ECHR. While it pointed out that the sterilization was clearly disrespectful of the applicant's autonomy, the Court paid particular attention to the circumstances of the case, such as the absence of any particular vulnerability of the applicant,[70] the lack of an intent of ill-treatment on behalf of the medical team, and the consultation of a panel of doctors that had backed the proposed treatment.

While mandatory hormonal treatment, in order to participate in a professional sports competition, does not necessarily amount to the same severity as an irreversible sterilizing surgery, we consider it vital that necessary parallels are drawn between the ECtHR's judgment in *V.C. v. Slovakia* and Semenya's case. Indeed,

---

media_2020/12/lgbt_athletes1120_web.pdf (last accessed 20 October 2022), as well as the report by ILGA Europe, OII Europe, EL*C and EGLSF, "LBTI women in sport: violence, discrimination and lived experiences", https://oiieurope.org/wp-content/uploads/2021/08/20210810-violence-and-discrimination-against-LBTI-women-in-sport-2.pdf (last accessed 20 October 2022), pp. 8–10.

[65] ECtHR, V.C. v. Slovakia, 08.11.2011, § 112.

[66] ECtHR, V.C. v. Slovakia, 08.11.2011, § 106–7.

[67] ECtHR, V.C. v. Slovakia, 08.11.2011, § 114.

[68] ECtHR, Y.P. v. Russia, 20.09.2022, § 31–38.

[69] See Tongue Z L and Graham L (2022) "Y.P. v. Russia: sterilisation without consent, Article 3, and weak reproductive rights at the ECtHR", *Strasbourg Observers,* https://strasbourgobservers.com/2022/09/30/y-p-v-russia-sterilisation-without-consent-article-3-and-weak-reproductive-rights-at-the-ecthr/ (last accessed 20 October 2022).

[70] Based on the concurring opinion by Judge Elósegui, it seems that the fact that the sterilisation of the applicant was not based on the same eugenic, racist logic applicable to the non-consensual sterilisation of Roma women was of importance to the majority's reasoning under Article 3 ECHR. To the contrary, dissenting Judges Serghides and Pavli pointed out that unconscious women undergoing sterilising treatment that they did not consented to are inherently in a condition of (situational) vulnerability.

women athletes with VSC who have a natural high level of androgens, a group that has suffered historical vulnerability,[71] have no other choice but to consent to long-lasting hormonal treatment during their careers, which negatively affects their reproductive health status and may also lead to unforeseen bodily or psychological side-effects. The Court has consistently observed that "the very essence of the Convention is respect for human dignity and human freedom",[72] and that medical treatment "without the consent of a mentally competent adult patient would interfere with his or her right to physical integrity".[73]

With respect to forced consent to take hormonal contraceptives, the temporal nature of contraceptive medication and its effect on persons with VSC has not been medically proven and, as such, there is no clear understanding of the effect that hormonal contraceptives could have on their reproductive system and bodies. In that regard, the Commission already held in *X v. Denmark* that there can be a violation of Article 3 if the "medical treatment [is] of an experimental character and [has been given] without the consent of the person involved".[74] Accordingly, we argue that forced consent to contraceptives for women athletes with VSC—in the absence of reliable research on the effects of such treatment—is a clear violation of a person's bodily integrity and therefore a violation of Article 3. The same conclusion was reached in the Rapporteurs and Working Group Joint Letter to the president of World Athletics.[75] Similarly, the UN High Commissioner for Human Rights noted that hormonal eligibility criteria for professional sports may violate the right to freedom from torture and other cruel, inhuman or degrading treatment or punishment.[76]

4 Positive Obligations Under Article 8 ECHR in the Context of Hormonal Eligibility Requirements

The case of *Semenya v. Switzerland* calls for a clarification of the nature and scope of the state's obligation to ensure the effective protection of the right to private life of professional athletes under Article 8 ECHR. In this section we will first elaborate on

[71]The need to show special consideration regarding the protection of the informed consent of persons with variations of sex characteristics to medical treatment due to vulnerabilities stemming from economic, social and cultural circumstances was also pointed out in the Rapporteurs and Working Group Joint Letter, https://spcommreports.ohchr.org/TMResultsBase/DownLoadPublicCommunicationFile?gId=24087 (last accessed 20 October 2022), p. 8.

[72]ECtHR, V.C. v. Slovakia, 08.11.2011, § 105.

[73]ECtHR, V.C. v. Slovakia, 08.11.2011, § 105.

[74]ECmHR, X. v. Denmark, 02.03.1983, 32 DR 282, at 293.

[75]Rapporteurs and Working Group Joint Letter https://spcommreports.ohchr.org/TMResultsBase/DownLoadPublicCommunicationFile?gId=24087 (last accessed 20 October 2022), p. 1.

[76]UN High Commissioner for Human Rights, "Intersection of race and gender discrimination in sport", A/HRC/44/26, p. 8.

the scope of the state's positive obligation and the state's margin of appreciation (Sect. 5.1), before addressing the elements that affect the balance between the general interests and the private interests in cases that concern HEC for participation in sports competitions (Sect. 6).

4.1 Scope of the State's Positive Obligation and Margin of Appreciation

The Court has held before that Article 8 ECHR may impose certain positive obligations on the state,[77] even in the horizontal relation between two private parties.[78] In *Hämäläinen v. Finland*, the Court mentioned several factors that have been considered relevant for the assessment of the content of positive obligations on states: the importance of the 'interests at stake', whether 'fundamental values' or 'essential aspects' of private life; the impact on an applicant of a discordance between the social reality and the law; the coherence of the administration and legal practices within the domestic system; and the impact of the alleged positive obligation on the state concerned.[79]

The case of Caster Semenya is arguably concerned with essential aspects of private life. Indeed, in the case of *A.P., Garçon, Nicot v. France*, which centered on the issue of compulsory sterilizing treatment as a precondition for legal gender recognition, the Court already held that cases that directly impact individuals' physical integrity have an essential aspect of an individual's intimate identity at their core.[80] In *Y.P. v. Russia*, the Court repeated that a person's reproductive status concerns one of the essential bodily functions of human beings, and bears on manifold aspects to personal integrity, including physical and mental well-being, as well as emotional, spiritual, and family life, as protected by Article 8 ECHR.[81]

The Court has previously found that Article 8 imposes on states a positive obligation to ensure the right to effective respect for a person's physical and psychological integrity.[82] In cases involving violence by private individuals, the Court has held that this positive obligation may include a duty to maintain and apply an adequate legal framework affording effective protection of an individual's physical integrity.[83] It is without question that HEC for women's sports competitions, which could lead to effectively mandatory hormonal or surgical treatment, directly

[77] ECtHR, Bărbulescu v. Romania, 05.09.2017, § 108.
[78] ECtHR, Evan v. United Kingdom, 10.04.2007, § 75.
[79] ECtHR, Hämäläinen v. Finland, 16.07.2014, § 66.
[80] ECtHR, A.P., Garçon, Nicot v. France, 06.04.2017, § 123.
[81] ECtHR, Y.P. v. Russia, 20.09.2022, § 51.
[82] ECtHR, Glass v. United Kingdom, 09.03.2004, § 74.
[83] ECtHR, Söderman v. Sweden, 12.11.2013, § 80.

impacts an athlete's physical and psychological integrity.[84] Such cases therefore fall within the scope of the state's positive obligations under Article 8 as earlier defined by the Court.

In cases concerning the Convention rights of persons with VSC, only a narrow margin of appreciation should arguably apply, especially when their right to bodily integrity is at stake. According to the Court's case law, the margin is substantially more narrow when restrictions apply to a particularly vulnerable group in society that has "suffered considerable discrimination in the past" and there must be weighty reasons to justify the restrictions.[85] It is hard to deny that persons with VSC form such a particularly vulnerable group in society, since they have suffered considerable discrimination and violations of fundamental rights on the basis of the perceived abnormality of their sex characteristics. The vulnerability of persons with VSC, and the stigmatization and discrimination they have face, has been raised by the Parliamentary Assembly of the Council of Europe in the aforementioned resolution 2191(2017).[86]

4.2 Balance Between General Interests and Private Interests in Cases Concerning HEC for Sports Competitions

In determining whether the state has abided by its positive obligation under Article 8 ECHR, the Court will determine whether a fair balance has been achieved between the competing interests of the individual and the community as a whole, taking into account the margin of appreciation enjoyed by the state.[87] In this section we discuss that, while protecting fairness in sports is a legitimate general interest, considerations of bodily and psychological integrity outweigh the need to create a level playing field in women's sports competitions.

[84] Next to the potential side-effects of hormonal treatment for a person's mental condition, qualitative research with intersex athletes has also indicated that the affected persons often suffer from intense public scrutiny, stress and psychological challenges stemming from the public suspicion and doubts concerning their gender identity and sex characteristics. See in particular the recent report by Human Rights Watch on DSD eligibility criteria, https://www.hrw.org/report/2020/12/04/theyre-chasing-us-away-sport/human-rights-violations-sex-testing-elite-women, (last accessed 20 October 2022).

[85] ECtHR Alajos Kiss v. Hungary, 20.05.2010, § 42.

[86] Parliamentary Assembly of the Council of Europe, Resolution 2191 (2017) "promoting the human rights of and eliminating discrimination against intersex people".

[87] ECtHR, Bărbulescu v. Romania, 05.09.2017, § 112.

4.2.1 The General Interest of Ensuring Fairness in Sports

The essence of professional sports is to test human difference. Indeed, if all athletes would perform in exactly the same way, no true competition would exist. In other words, differences in bodily characteristics, training opportunities, nutrition, and socioeconomic background, among others, are common and almost intrinsically related to the world of professional sports. Should athletes who differ in strength, stamina, height, weight, eye sight, lung capacity, wealth, be prevented from competing against each other? At the same time, fairness and the assurance of a level playing field are as central to professional sports as human difference.[88] The question then becomes what forms of difference can be considered as undermining the need for fairness, and indeed whether all (women) athletes are served by hormonal eligibility criteria in their needs for a level playing field.[89] In this light, we do not submit that the organization of sports along binary lines (women–men) is necessarily untenable from the perspective of the ECHR. Nevertheless, as the case of Semenya demonstrates, it needs to be questioned whether the highly contested use of a single bodily characteristic (i.e., the (natural) level of testosterone) in women's sports competitions meets the requirements of the ECHR; taking into account the impact on the bodily integrity, mental and physical health, professional life, and reproductive status of the athlete concerned (as well as its connection to outdated understandings of 'normality' of women's bodies). In the following section, we will elaborate on two important issues: the lack of meaningful informed consent to (hormonal) treatment aimed at reducing testosterone levels, and the impact of HEC on the athletes' professional life.

4.2.2 The Lack of Meaningful Informed Consent to Medical (Hormonal) Treatment

As we demonstrated above, non-compliance with HEC leads to the effective exclusion from participation in a number of women's sports competitions. The affected women athletes with VSC still maintain the possibility to exercise their profession as long as they forcibly undergo (hormonal) medical treatment (predominantly via

[88] Nevertheless, importantly, in September 2021 three major global women's sports organisations (WomenSport International, International Association of Physical Education and Sport for Girls and Women, and International Working Group on Women and Sport) called for action to immediately withdraw controversial DSD eligibility criteria by World Athletics and other Olympic movement sports bodies. See https://iwgwomenandsport.org/womens-sport-calls-for-global-action-on-flawed-female-eligibility-regulations/?fbclid=IwAR1jsZNx218Tp1k85mWBGPEaANuOKCEBeKCrw0XfWPJeHh6cbXcFkUjp-Ss#eng (last accessed 20 October 2022).

[89] Karkazis and Jordan-Young (2018), p. 10.

contraceptives).[90] We consider it necessary to draw parallels under Article 8 ECHR between the ECtHR's existing case law, and the case of Semenya. In the aforementioned judgment in *V.C. v. Slovakia*, which concerned the forced sterilization of Roma women, the Court attached importance to the protection of meaningful informed consent ('free will') under Article 3 and Article 8 of the Convention, especially taking into account the impact of the treatment concerned on the applicant's reproductive health status. In its assessment of the applicant's claim under Article 3, the Court noted that the imposition of such medical treatment without the consent of a mentally-competent adult patient is incompatible with the requirement of respect for human freedom and dignity as one of the fundamental principles on which the Convention is based.[91]

In the same case, the Court refuted the paternalistic actions on behalf of the hospital staff concerned, which meant that "in practice, the applicant was not offered any option but to agree to the procedure".[92] In *V.C. v. Slovakia*, the Court found that the state breached its positive obligations under Article 8 ECHR, on the basis of its failure to give special consideration to the reproductive health of the applicant as a Roma woman, taking into account the historical vulnerability and targeting of the Roma minority.[93] In the recent case of *Y.P. v. Russia*, the Court again stressed that, under Article 8 ECHR, sterilization cannot be routinely carried out unless the patient has given her express, free and informed consent to that particular procedure. The only exception to this rule is an emergency situation in which medical treatment cannot be delayed to obtain the appropriate consent.[94]

While the mandatory hormonal treatment in order to participate in a professional sports competition does not necessarily involve the same severity as an irreversible sterilizing surgery, a clear parallel can be drawn. Indeed, women athletes who have a naturally high level of androgens have no other choice but to 'consent' to medical (hormonal) treatment during their careers, which negatively affects their bodily and mental integrity, and their reproductive health status. It must therefore be strongly questioned whether any exercise of free will is possible in this context. As the Court similarly held in *A.P., Garçon, Nicot v. France* and *X. and Y. v. Romania*, the

[90] Sometimes irreversible surgeries, such as gonadectomies or even clitoridectomies, are performed. In the case of athlete Annet Negesa, a gonadectomy was performed without her full and prior informed consent. See the report by Human Rights Watch, https://www.hrw.org/report/2020/12/04/theyre-chasing-us-away-sport/human-rights-violations-sex-testing-elite-women, (last accessed 20 October 2022), as well as the report by ILGA Europe, OII Europe, EL*C and EGLSF (2021), "LBTI women in sport: violence, discrimination and lived experiences", https://oiieurope.org/wp-content/uploads/2021/08/20210810-violence-and-discrimination-against-LBTI-women-in-sport-2.pdf (last accessed 20 October 2022), pp. 8–10.

[91] ECtHR, V.C. v. Slovakia, 08.11.2011, § 106.

[92] ECtHR, V.C. v. Slovakia, 08.11.2011, § 114.

[93] ECtHR, V.C. v. Slovakia, 08.11.2011, § 138–155.

[94] ECtHR, Y.P. v. Russia, 20.09.2022, § 53.

athletes concerned are presented with an impossible dilemma:[95] either they undergo the required hormonal treatment against their wishes, thereby relinquishing the full exercise of their right to respect for their physical and psychological integrity (as protected under Articles 3 and 8 ECHR), or they waive the right to exercise their profession (which is also protected under Article 8 ECHR, see *infra*).[96] In the Rapporteurs and Working Group Joint Letter, it was concluded that the athletes are left with no real choice but to undergo medically unnecessary treatment in order to maintain their livelihoods.[97] This view is shared by the UN Human Rights Council,[98] and the UN High Commissioner for Human Rights, who stated that "female eligibility regulations may push some athletes to undergo investigations, tests and interventions, [. . .] which may have negative physical and mental health impacts".[99] They stressed that "particular care is required where there are power imbalances resulting from inequalities in knowledge, experience and trust between health-care providers and individuals, particularly those from vulnerable groups".[100]

4.2.3 Impact on an Athlete's Access to Chosen Profession

While the ECtHR has not recognized a general right to employment, or the right to freely choose a particular profession, Article 8 ECHR does not exclude activities of a professional nature from the notion of 'private life'.[101] A summary of the general principles of the case law in employment-related disputes can be found in the Court's judgment in *Denisov v. Ukraine*.[102] In particular, the Court held that,

> there are some typical aspects of private life which may be affected [. . .] by dismissal, demotion, non-admission to a profession or other similarly unfavourable measures. These aspects include (i) the applicant's "inner circle", (ii) the applicant's opportunity to establish and develop relationships with others, and (iii) the applicant's social and professional reputation.[103]

---

[95] In their 2018 paper, K. Karkazis and M. Carpenter also refer to the situation of the affected intersex athletes as a set of impossible 'choices'. See Karkazis and Carpenter (2018).

[96] ECtHR, A.P., Garçon, Nicot v. France, 06.04.2017, § 132; X. and Y. v. Romania, 19.01.2021, § 165.

[97] Rapporteurs and Working Group Joint Letter https://spcommreports.ohchr.org/TMResultsBase/DownLoadPublicCommunicationFile?gId=24087 (last accessed 20 October 2022), p. 5.

[98] UN Human Rights Council, Resolution 40/5 "Elimination of discrimination against women and girls in sport", A/HRC/RES/40/5.

[99] UN High Commissioner for Human Rights, "Intersection of race and gender discrimination in sport", A/HRC/44/26, pp. 8–9.

[100] UN High Commissioner for Human Rights, "Intersection of race and gender discrimination in sport", A/HRC/44/26, pp. 8–9.

[101] ECtHR, Bărbulescu v. Romania, 05.09.2017, § 71.

[102] ECtHR, Denisov v. Ukraine, 25.09.2018, § 115–117.

[103] ECtHR, Denisov v. Ukraine, 25.09.2018, § 115.

The Court has developed two different tests to assess the state's compliance with Article 8: a reasons-based approach and a consequence-based approach. On the basis of the latter, it is for the applicant to present evidence substantiating consequences of the impugned measure, as well as their level of severity. The Court will only accept that Article 8 is applicable where these consequences are very serious and affect the applicant's private life to a very significant degree.

In its admissibility decision in *Platini v. Switzerland*,[104] the Court, applying the criteria set out in *Denisov*, held that the level of severity under the consequences-based approach was reached in the case where the applicant had worked all his life in the world of football and was banned from any football-related professional activity for four years by FIFA. The Court accepted, first, that the negative consequences of the measure were likely to occur within the framework of the 'inner circle' of the applicant, who was provisionally prohibited from earning a living in the world of football, the only source of income throughout his life, a situation aggravated by the dominant position, even monopoly, of FIFA in the global organization of football and by his age. Secondly, it considered that the sanction could have a negative impact on the possibility of forming and developing social relations with others given the very broad nature of the sanction imposed, which extended to 'any' football-related activity. In this regard, the Court considered that it should be borne in mind that the applicant was commonly, in the public and in the media, identified in relation to football. Finally, the Court considered it probable that the sanction pronounced against the applicant had negative effects on his reputation in the sense of a certain stigmatization.[105]

Despite the clear contextual differences between the sanction imposed in *Platini v. Switzerland* and HEC for participation in a sports competition, parallels between the ECtHR's existing case law and the case of Caster Semenya can be drawn. Indeed, professional women athletes with VSC who choose to preserve their bodily integrity and reproductive status are effectively banned from their profession, which in many cases is their main or only source of income. Given the monopoly position of most international sports federations, these athletes have no other possibility but to agree to the required treatment or to engage in other professional activities. Indeed, the UN High Commissioner for Human Rights found that HEC for professional sports may violate the right to work and to the enjoyment of just and favorable conditions of work, since "they may constitute a barrier limiting disproportionally equal access to work for athletes with variations in sex characteristics".[106]

---

[104] ECtHR, Platini v. Switzerland, 05.03.2020.

[105] ECtHR, Platini v. Switzerland, 05.03.2020, § 57–58.

[106] UN High Commissioner for Human Rights, "Intersection of race and gender discrimination in sport", A/HRC/44/26, p. 8.

5 HEC and (Intersectional) Discrimination Under the ECHR

As mentioned above, sport regulations that impose forced hormonal treatment to determine eligibility to compete in women's sports competitions may also be in violation of the prohibition of discrimination (Article 14 ECHR), in conjunction with Articles 3 and 8 ECHR, when they are applied to women with VSC, and especially to intersex women of color as well as intersex lesbian women. In this section, we argue that these regulations can be characterized as both discrimination on the basis of sex characteristics (Sect. 7.1), as well as a specific form of intersectional discrimination on the basis of gender, race and, in Caster Semenya's specific case, sexual orientation (Sect. 8).

5.1 *Discrimination on the Basis of Sex Characteristics*

HEC that force women with VSC to lower their levels of testosterone in order to compete in women's sports competitions treat them differently than women without such variations (i.e. endosex women), precisely on the basis of their sex characteristics. Under such regulations, people who identify as women and whose bodies meet the normative medical and social expectations of women's bodies are allowed to participate in sports competitions without undergoing hormonal treatment. In contrast, women whose bodies have a variation of sex characteristics (such as high levels of androgens) are forced to undergo such treatment in order to participate in these sport competitions.

While Article 14 ECHR does not literally mention 'sex characteristics', it prohibits differential treatment on the basis on 'sex'. Even though the notion of sex has traditionally been understood as a binary, determined on the basis of an individual's genitalia, recent scientific insights have made clear that an individual's sex refers to their unique composition of several sex characteristics. It seems logical, therefore, to understand the prohibition of differential treatment *on the basis of sex* as meaning the prohibition of differential treatment *on the basis of sex characteristics*. The ECtHR has made clear in the past that the list of prohibited grounds of discrimination is not exhaustive.[107] The Court has extended protection to individuals treated differently on the basis of their sexual orientation and/or gender identity as inherently personal and intimate characteristics that relate to their sexual identity.[108] Thus, the case of Caster Semenya provides the opportunity to extend the prohibition of discrimination enshrined in Article 14 to differences in treatment on the basis of sex characteristics.

---

[107] ECtHR, Engel and others v. Netherlands, 08.06.1976, § 72.

[108] ECtHR Salgueiro Da Silva Mouta v. Portugal, 21.12.1999, § 28; Identoba and others v. Georgia, 12.05.2015, § 96.

Applicants bringing a claim under Article 14 ECHR need to show that they were not only treated differently than others on the basis of a specific ground of discrimination, but also that they are similarly situated compared to these other individuals. Under World Athletics regulations, women who present a variation in sex characteristics are forced to undergo hormonal treatment to lower their testosterone level if they wish to participate in women's sport competitions. In contrast, other women whose bodies conform to medical and societal expectations of a woman's body—for instance, endosex women, who are, however, diagnosed with polycystic ovary syndrome (PCOS)—are allowed to compete in women's sport competitions without having to undergo hormonal treatment. This is the case even if PCOS causes them to have 'androgen excess' or 'hyperandrogenism', that is, 'ovarian overproduction of testosterone'.[109] Although both categories of women are similarly situated, insofar as they have high levels of testosterone, women with VSC are subjected to invasive regulations and hormonal treatment whereas the right of the other women to compete in women's sport competitions is left unquestioned.

Comparing intersex and endosex women more generally, one should note that the Council of Europe's Commissioner for Human Rights, and the EU Agency for Fundamental Rights have recently pointed out that people whose bodies present a variation in sex characteristics face structural forms of exclusion in all areas of life.[110] This is because they defy normative binary understandings of sex and gender—arguing that women with VSC and women without VSC are not similarly situated in relation to sports competitions amounts to subscribing to precisely such a normative understanding of sex. It also amounts to perpetuating the structural oppression of people who present variations in sex characteristics. Indeed, forcing women with VSC to lower their levels of testosterone in order to participate in a women's sports competition reproduces the idea that a woman is a person whose level of testosterone does not exceed a certain threshold. However, the very existence of women with VSC demonstrates that all bodies, and thus all women, in fact differ. As a result, intersex and endosex women are actually, as women, similarly situated when it comes to their eligibility to compete in women's sport competitions.

Under Article 14 ECHR, differential enjoyment of Convention rights by similarly situated individuals on the basis of a prohibited ground of discrimination only becomes discrimination when it lacks an objective and reasonable justification. In order to assess whether such justification exists, the Court usually performs an assessment of the legitimate aim and the proportionality between the measure and the aim pursued. States often allow sports bodies to regulate the eligibility of individuals to compete in women's competitions with the aim of ensuring a fair competition. As noted above, ensuring fairness in sports is unquestionably a

[109] National Institutes of Health (2019) "Polycystic Ovary/Ovarian Syndrome (PCOS)" https://orwh.od.nih.gov/sites/orwh/files/docs/PCOS_Booklet_508.pdf (last accessed 20 October 2022).

[110] EU Fundamental Rights Agency 2020 "A long way to go for LGBTI equality" https://fra.europa.eu/en/publication/2020/eu-lgbti-survey-results (last accessed 20 October 2022); Council of Europe Commissioner for Human Rights (2015) "Human Rights and Intersex People" https://rm.coe.int/16806da5d4 (last accessed 20 October 2022).

legitimate aim, even if sport competitions are by essence about testing human difference. In that regard, one could argue that human rights issues arise not because of gender segregation in sports as such, but rather because of the disproportionate measure to determine admission to women's sport competitions based on a single bodily characteristic (i.e., level of testosterone); and the fact that this results in the exclusion of, or enforced hormonal treatment for, women with VSC.

With all of that said, relying on testosterone levels is not even a suitable method to achieve the desired aim. Although the World Athletics' eligibility criteria are adopted based on the assumption that the amount of testosterone is causally linked to performance, recent scientific studies contradict, or at the minimum, strongly question this assumption.[111] Even if one assumes that an athlete's level of testosterone is an adequate proxy for their performance (which is nevertheless doubtful), excluding women with VSC unless they undergo hormonal treatment to lower their level of testosterone does not achieve the aim pursued of ensuring fairness in sport competitions. This is because excluding women with VSC does not eliminate the natural variation in levels of testosterone observed in women without VSC. As a result, and under the assumption that testosterone and performance are causally related, women with higher levels of testosterone will still perform better (for instance, women with PCOS). The only effect of excluding women with VSC is to eliminate this category of woman (i.e., women who happen to have a variation in sex characteristics) rather than eliminating the advantage that high(er) levels of testosterone provide to *some* women athletes.

Related to this last observation is the fact that excluding people who identify as women and whose bodies display variations in sex characteristics from participating in women's sport competitions unless they undergo hormonal treatment questions their womanhood (see Sect. 2.2). Given that women's sport competitions are reserved for women, refusing women who present a variation in sex characteristics to participate in these competitions unless they lower their level of testosterone boils down to scrutinizing their gender. As such, allowing sports bodies to adopt eligibility regulations such as those of World Athletics jeopardizes their right to have their gender identity recognized at all.

Regarding the proportionality assessment, one can also not ignore that, as mentioned above, people with VSC continue to face considerable and structural stigma, prejudice, and discrimination. Based on the Court's own definition of vulnerability, people with VSC should be considered a vulnerable group in society and be subject to the 'very weighty reasons' principle.[112] This would narrow the state's margin of appreciation regarding differences in treatment of people without VSC and people with VSC.[113] As we have argued in the previous sections, the reasons invoked to justify intersex women's exclusion from women's sports competitions fail to stand up to scrutiny, and can consequently not be regarded as being sufficiently 'weighty'

[111] See Sect. 2.2.

[112] ECtHR, Alajos Kiss v. Hungary, 20.05.2010, § 42; Kiyutin v. Russia, 10.03.2011, § 63.

[113] ECtHR, Alajos Kiss v. Hungary, 20.05.2010, § 42.

to satisfy the proportionality test. Given the above, we argue that sport regulations that force women with VSC to undergo hormonal treatment to lower their levels of testosterone in order to be allowed to participate in women sport's competitions are discriminatory under the ECHR.

5.2 *Intersectional Discrimination on the Basis of Gender, Race, and Sexual Orientation*

Intersectional oppression refers to a situation in which multiple grounds of oppression interact to create a new situation that cannot be reduced to the simple sum of its parts.[114] The absence of an intersectional approach of inequalities and oppressions can result in a lack of attention to the least privileged members of a marginalized community, and to inadequate redress for the human rights violations they suffer.[115] In order to avoid this, it is important to pay attention to patterns of sameness and difference between individuals and communities.[116]

The concept of intersectionality has been increasingly recognized by international human rights monitoring bodies in the last few years, including by the ECtHR. In *B. S. v. Spain*, the Court stressed that the vulnerability of a person or a group may result from the interaction of several characteristics such as gender, social, and ethnic origins.[117] Moreover, the Court considered an intersectional subject of a *prima facie* case of discrimination in *S.A.S. v. France* when stating that the ban "has specific negative effects on the situation of Muslim women".[118] In *Carvalho Pinto de Sousa Morais v. Portugal*, the Court tackled an intersectional stereotype based on age and gender.[119] These developments offer a promising basis to develop a case law that does justice to intersectional vulnerability.

Semenya's positioning as a Black lesbian woman with VSC is inextricably tied to the intersectional discrimination she suffered. As argued above, her race, sexual orientation, and variation in sex characteristics combined to make her womanhood suspect to a normative society that links stereotypes of womanhood with whiteness, heterosexuality, and 'typical' female sex characteristics (i.e., endosex).[120] This led to her quite literal exclusion from the category of 'woman' in a core area of her life, impacting both her access to her preferred career, as well as her perceived identity as a woman in the eyes of the public, in a blatant form of intersectional discrimination. As a Black lesbian woman with VSC, Semenya combines at least three grounds

---

[114] Crenshaw (1989).

[115] Bouchard and Meyer-Bish (2016), p. 186.

[116] Atrey (2020), pp. 17–38.

[117] ECtHR, B.S. v. Spain, 24.07.2012, § 62.

[118] ECtHR, S.A.S. v. France, 01.07.2014, § 161. See Brems (2021).

[119] ECtHR, Carvalho Pinto de Sousa Morais v. Portugal, 25.05.2017, § 52–56.

[120] *Cf.* 2.2. Racialised constructions of womanhood.

related to 'vulnerable groups' as identified by the ECtHR in, among others, the Alajos Kiss and Kiyutin judgments: sex, race, and sexual orientation.[121] As argued above, people with VSC should be considered a vulnerable group in their own regard; the intersection of all of these characteristics puts Semenya in a particularly vulnerable position. It would considerably strengthen protection under Article 14 ECHR if the intersectional discrimination inherent in this case was recognized and it was confirmed that her differential treatment can only be justified by 'very weighty reasons'. We have already argued that justification of Semenya's exclusion is based on normative assumptions of sex and gender, and not, in fact, on any 'very weighty reasons'. Consequently, Semenya is the subject of intersectional discrimination.

6 Conclusion

As Holzer has argued, "being a woman who is affected by the testosterone rules means that one's athletic performance is valued according to so-called 'scientific' tests of womanhood, informed by stereotypical, white and intersexphobic notions of femininity".[122] In this chapter, we have explored how the case of *Semenya v. Switzerland*, in which Caster Semenya challenged the validity of the HEC set by World Athletics, should be assessed under the ECHR. We have demonstrated that there are compelling arguments, and sufficient parallels with existing case law, to find that HEC for the participation in women's professional sports competitions are incompatible with Articles 3 and 8 ECHR, read alone and in conjunction with Article 14 ECHR.

It is important to stress that the case of *Semenya v. Switzerland* does not challenge the binary organization of professional sports competitions as such. While the case could lead to an abolition of the *de facto* mandatory hormonal treatment that face women athletes with VSC who want to compete at the highest levels in their sport, it will not bring the policing of the boundaries of the 'male' and 'female' categories to an end. Given that this chapter established that the organization of sports competitions along the sex/gender binary is strongly related to persistent gender discrimination, racialized constructions of womanhood, and the erroneous universality of natural binary sex, a move away from HEC will no doubt evoke new challenges for athletes who do not meet the socially constructed normative standard in their sport. As mentioned in the introduction, the example set by FINA and World Athletics, which exclude all women who have experienced 'male' puberty beyond Tanner Stage 2 or before age 12, irrespective of their current levels of testosterone, shows that the inclusion of women with VSC in women's sports competitions will remain illusory in the near future.

[121] ECtHR, Alajos Kiss v. Hungary, 20.05.2010, § 42; ECtHR, Kiyutin v. Russia, 10.03.2011, § 63.
[122] Holzer (2020), p. 411.

References

Atrey S (2020) Beyond universality: an intersectional justification of human rights. In: Atrey S, Dunne P (eds) Intersectionality and human rights law. Hart Publishing, Oxford, pp 17–38
Bermon S, Garnier PY (2021) Correction: serum androgen levels and their relation to performance in track and field: mass spectrometry results from 2127 observations in male and female elite athletes. Br J Sports Med 55(17)
Bouchard J, Meyer-Bish P (2016) Intersectionality and interdependence of human rights: same or different? Equal Rights Rev 16:186–203
Brems E (2021) Hidden under headscarves? Women and religion in the case law of the European Court of Human Rights. Relig Hum Rights 16(2–3):173–200
Bruening JE (2005) Gender and racial analysis in sport: are all the women white and all the blacks men? Quest 57(3):330–349
Byczkow M, Thompson K (2019) Testosterone maketh the man or woman. Slowing down Caster Semenya. N Z Women's Law J 3:327–347
Camporesi S (2019) A question of 'fairness': why ethics should factor in the court of arbitration for sport's decision on the IAAF hyperandrogenism regulations. Br J Sports Med 53:797–798
Cannoot P (2022) The right to personal autonomy regarding sex, gender and sexual orientation: the case of Belgium. Eleven – Boom Juridisch Antwerpen, Antwerp
Cannoot P (2023) Semenya v Switzerland: divided ECtHR significantly advances the human rights protection for intersex athletes (and all professional sportspeople in general), Oxford Human Rights Hub Blog. https://ohrh.law.ox.ac.uk/semenya-v-switzerland-divided-ecthr-significantly-advances-the-human-rights-protection-for-intersex-athletes-and-all-professional-sportspeople-in-general-part-i/
Crenshaw K (1989) Demarginalizing the intersection of race and sex: a black feminist critique of antidiscrimination doctrine, feminist theory and antiracist politics. Univ Chic Leg Forum n°1, Article 8:139–167
Garland F, Travis M (2018) Legislating intersex equality: building the resilience of intersex people through law. Leg Stud 38(4):587–606
Gilleri G, Winckler M (2021) Of athletes, bodies and rules: making sense of Caster Semenya. J Law Med Ethics 49(4):644–660
Gonzalez-Salzberg DA (2018) An improved protection for the (mentally ill) trans parent: a queer reading of AP, Garçon and Nicot v France. Mod Law Rev 81(3):526–538
Holzer L (2020) What does it mean to be a woman in sports? An analysis of the jurisprudence of the court of arbitration for sport. Hum Rights Law Rev 20(3):387–411
Jones T, Norwood KJ (2017) Aggressive encounters & white fragility: deconstructing the trope of the angry black woman. Iowa Law Rev 102:2017–2069
Karkazis K, Carpenter M (2018) Impossible 'choices': the inherent harms of regulating women's testosterone in sport. J Bioeth Inq 15:579–587
Karkazis K, Jordan-Young RM (2018) The powers of testosterone: obscuring race and regional bias in the regulation of women athletes. Fem Form 30(2):1–39
Kauer KJ, Rauscher L (2019) Negotiating gender among LGBTIQ athletes. In: Krane V (ed) Sex, gender, and sexuality in sport: queer inquiries. Routledge, New York
Olofsson A, Zinn J, Griffin G, Girtli Nygren K, Cebulla A, Hannah-Moffat K (2014) The mutual constitution of risk and inequalities: intersectional risk theory. Health Risk Soc 16(5):417–430
Patel S (2021) Gaps in the protection of athletes gender rights in sport – a regulatory riddle. Int Sports Law J 21:257–275
Pielke R, Tucker R, Boye E (2019) Scientific integrity and the IAAF testosterone regulations. Int Sports Law J 19(18):18–26
Richards R, Bouman WP, Seal L, Barker MJ, Nieder T, T'Sjoen G (2016) Non-binary or genderqueer genders. Int Rev Psychiatry 28(1):95–102

Theilen JT (2018) Beyond the gender binary: rethinking the right to legal gender recognition. Eur Hum Rights Law Rev 3:249–257
Weiss JT (2001) The gender caste system: identity, privacy, and heteronormativity. Law Sex: Rev Lesbian Gay Bisex Transgender Leg Issues 10:123–186
Yuval-Davis N (2006) Intersectionality and feminist politics. Eur J Women's Stud 13(3):193–209

Pieter Cannoot is an assistant professor of law and diversity at the Faculty of Law and Criminology of Ghent University (Belgium). He defended his doctoral thesis on the autonomy rights of LGBTQI+ people in 2019. His research mainly concerns the relationship between sexual diversity, gender diversity and law. Together with his colleagues at the Human Rights Centre, Pieter regularly intervenes as a third party before the European Court of Human Rights. Before taking up his current position, he was a visiting professor at the University of Antwerp and a law clerk at the Belgian Constitutional Court. Pieter is the editor-in-chief of the Flemish Journal of Human Rights *(Tijdschrift voor Mensenrechten).*

Cathérine Van de Graaf is a post-doctoral researcher at the Academy for European Human Rights Protection (University of Cologne) founded by former German ECtHR Judge Angelika Nussberger. She completed her doctoral research entitled 'Procedural Justice in Cases of Perceived Discrimination' under the supervision of Eva Brems at the Human Rights Centre (Ghent University) to which she is still affiliated as a visiting professor. Her research has been published in journals such as Islamophobia Studies Journal and Netherlands Quarterly of Human Rights, among others. Additionally, Cathérine regularly blogs for Strasbourg Observers, has submitted several third party interventions to the ECtHR and is an editor at Völkerrechtsblog and Tijdschrift voor Mensenrechten.

Ariël Decoster is a doctoral researcher specialised in feminist legal theory and critical legal masculinity studies at the Universities of Antwerp and Ghent. Her FWO-funded dissertation, entitled "Masculinity as Property", sits at the intersection of legal studies, gender studies, and philosophy. She relies on the notion of property as a heuristic tool to make visible how masculinity and law interact in an increasingly gender-neutral legal system. Her research aims to rethink the way law, gender and power are intertwined. Ariël was previously a Fulbright student at the University of California, Los Angeles and a visiting researcher at King's College London as well as the University of California, Irvine.

Claire Poppelwell-Scevak is a PhD Researcher at the Human Rights Centre of Ghent University. She received her double bachelors in Law and International Studies at Macquarie University, Australia in 2013. She was admitted as a solicitor to the Roll of Solicitors in New South Wales in February 2014. Claire has an LLM (completed in 2016) from Oslo University with a focus on Public International Law and LGBTQI rights. Since 2022, she is an advocacy officer at the European Parliamentary Forum for Sexual and Reproductive Rights.

Sarah Schoentjes has been a doctoral researcher at the Ghent University Human Rights Centre since November 2020, following her appointment as a fellow at the FWO (Flanders Research Foundation). Her study, carried out under the supervision of Prof. Dr. Eva Brems and Prof. Dr. Pieter Cannoot, focuses on the implementation of intersectional reasoning in the decisions of international human rights monitoring bodies. She is one of the editors of the Strasbourg Observers academic blog.

Sarah holds a Bachelor and Master of Laws from Ghent University, and spent a semester of her Master's program studying at Fribourg University (Switzerland). Before starting her PhD, she worked for the legal department of the Belgian Institute for the equality of women and men.

Filipinos First? Exploring Xenophobia and Its Legal Remedies in Philippine Amateur Basketball

Joseph Benjamin B. De Leon

Contents

Abstract This chapter analyzes the discrimination that foreign student-athletes (FSAs) face through policies instituted by the Philippines' top collegiate amateur sports organizations, which restrict participation in competitions. These policies ostensibly uphold amateurism and develop local talent, but negatively impact student-athletes from Nigeria, Cameroon, and other African countries who tend to excel compared to local student-athletes. While these restrictions have been widely criticized as racist, and detrimental to basketball as a sport, it appears likely that they will remain in place. The ban on FSAs is reinforced explicitly and/or implicitly in law and league regulations, confirming a recurring nationalist theme within Philippine sports. To the extent that law and jurisprudence can have a positive normative effect on society, it is important to find legal avenues to resist these measures. This chapter argues that there is the possibility under Philippine law for affected FSAs to protect their freedom through litigation based on equal protection and non-discrimination, and discusses potential modes of action and evaluates elements that may affect their success.

The views here belong solely to the author and do not necessarily represent those of his employer/s or other associated institutions or persons. The author acknowledges the assistance extended by the Faculty of Law, Criminal Justice and Public Administration of the University of Lausanne for the opportunity to contribute to the field of sport and human rights.

J. B. B. De Leon (✉)
Las Pinas, Philippines

V. Boillet et al. (eds.), *Sports and Human Rights*, Interdisciplinary Studies in Human Rights 10, https://doi.org/10.1007/978-3-031-56452-9_6

1 Introduction

In 2005, the San Beda University Red Lions were the penultimate team in the Philippines' National Collegiate Athletic Association (NCAA) men's basketball tournament. The following year, the team recruited a new, promising player to end their 28-year title drought. Samuel Ekwe, a foreign student-athlete (FSA) from Nigeria,[1] helped the Red Lions win their first-ever NCAA men's basketball championship. From then onwards, assisted by a number of other FSAs, San Beda would go on to reach the finals every year until 2019, collecting 11 championships along the way.[2]

San Beda's success would influence the next 15 years of the NCAA and its rival league, the University Athletic Association of the Philippines (UAAP), as teams established their own FSA recruitment pipelines. While they catapulted college basketball to a new level of excitement and exposure, this influx of foreign students also became a referendum on the place of foreign talent in Filipino amateur sports and their impact on the Filipino identity. After a decade of this phenomenon, the UAAP capped FSAs to just one per basketball team,[3] while the NCAA banned all FSAs from its sporting events.[4] Both organizations claimed this preserves and improves amateur basketball.

Those policies restricting FSA participation rest on arguments concerning national origin and race; they are insufficient justifications to violate fundamental tenets of equal protection and freedom from discrimination. This chapter explores potential causes of action against the NCAA and UAAP, and sees this issue as an opportunity to use judicial action to influence social norms and reinforce state commitments to equality. Nevertheless, these paths are limited by the lack of precedent and contemporary developments, as well as the framework's intrinsic challenges.

Considering the connection between the role of basketball in Philippine culture and its role in validating and replicating cultural norms—including how Filipinos, through basketball, situate themselves in relation to the global community—the chapter argues that FSA restrictions are a manifestation of a protective and exclusionary attitude, which replicates features of the colonial relationships between the Philippines and Spanish and American colonizers, prioritizing the ruling class' sense

[1] Olivares, R., Sam Ekwe: Life after San Beda, ABS-CBN News, 27 March 2013, https://news.abs-cbn.com/blogs/opinions/03/26/13/sam-ekwe-life-after-san-beda (last accessed 30 May 2022).

[2] Sudan Daniel (United Sates), Ola Adeogun (Nigeria), Donald Tankoua (Nigeria) and Arnaud Noah (Nigeria).

[3] Alegre, M., & Gloria, G., Broad shoulders and huge expectations: Foreign student athletes in the UAAP. The Lasallian, 22 January 2017, https://thelasallian.com/2017/01/22/broad-shoulders-and-huge-expectations-foreign-student-athletes-in-the-uaap-2 (last accessed 30 May 2022).

[4] Naredo, C., No more foreign athletes in NCAA by 2020. ABS-CBN News, 19 July 2018, https://news.abs-cbn.com/sports/06/19/18/no-more-foreign-athletes-in-ncaa-by-2020 (last accessed 30 May 2022).

of worth[5] over a class comprised of persons of other descent. Despite the lack of precedents, the chapter considers that human rights legal instruments could protect FSAs and help combat the discriminatory and nationalistic dynamics that corrupt Philippine sport.

The chapter draws on news reports and commentaries that record the sentiments of key personalities in the industry; the historical and cultural attitudes towards Philippine basketball are also informed largely by the work of Rafe Bartholomew, Lou Antolihao, Satwinder Rehal, and Inez Ponce de Leon. Finally, the chapter examines these factual developments in light of the Philippine Constitution and existing laws addressing vulnerable persons, laws adjacent to FSA participation, Philippine commitments to equal protection and freedom from discrimination in international instruments, domestic legislation, and case law relevant to the topic.

This chapter leaves space to explore adjacent inquiries, such as a comparative analysis with other jurisdictions that either implement similar rules on foreigners (or have since rejected them), or the legal outcomes of intersections between the rule of law on the one hand, and nationality and race on the other. The chapter aims to serve as a baseline exploration that may assist policymakers and potential litigants towards reform. Necessarily, the chapter assumes that changes to law and policy through legal remedies can have a normative effect on social climates, which itself is a rich area of debate.

The first section of the chapter introduces Philippine basketball and Filipino identity, and traces their history and developments up to the FSA era. The second section highlights the impact of discriminatory practices on FSAs, identifies potential legal remedies, and evaluates their strengths and pitfalls While social change would be better serve to fully integrate FSAs into the Philippine basketball scene, legal remedies are worth exploring as another front to create change and uphold basic, universal human rights.

2 Introduction to Philippine Basketball

This section introduces the significance of basketball in Philippine history and culture, including its colonial past, and contextualizes the current dilemma as a reenactment of colonial dynamics in the modern day. The broader, sociological elements are drawn from the work of Bartholomew (2011), generally regarded as the broadest and most accessible ethnographic study of basketball as a cultural phenomenon in the Philippines. Antolihao's (2017) work examines the many entanglements between Filipinos and basketball through various lenses. The social

[5]Cuna, C., Ban This!, Inboundpass.com, 19 November 2010, https://web.archive.org/web/20140226063644/http://www.inboundpass.com/2010/11/19/ban-this/ (last accessed 30 May 2022). Gasgonia, D., 'Imports in UAAP, NCAA bad for PH basketball', ABS-CBN News, 14 January 2013, https://news.abs-cbn.com/sports/01/04/13/imports-uaap-ncaa-bad-ph-basketball (last accessed 30 May 2022).

dynamics of nationalism, race, and sport in the local context are also informed by the studies of Rehal (2020) and Ponce de Leon (2018) on the matter, as they delve into the specific treatment of Black bodies in Philippine media and the dynamics of having players of mixed ethnicities in the national football team, respectively.[6]

American colonizers introduced basketball to the "savage natives" of the Philippines in the early 1900s. The game began as a missionary schoolyard pastime in the 1910s, and steadily grew in popularity as the sport of choice in the smaller urban spaces populated by the social elite.[7] The Americans hoped that sports, in a multi-prong approach including modern infrastructure and social services, would lead to health and nutrition, as well as evangelization, discipline, teamwork, and nation-building for a people reeling from over 300 years of Spanish rule.[8]

The Philippine men's basketball team's fifth place finish during their Olympic debut in 1936 cemented the sport's status as a source of national pride.[9] As of 2022, the team has yet to return to the Olympics, and every iteration of the Summer Games renews debates on whether the country might win more medals if resources were diverted to other sports, like weightlifting or boxing, instead of basketball.[10]

Basketball was a unifying force in the Philippines through various milestones in the twentieth century: the modern sport of industrialization (versus the rurality of baseball, its brief rival); a salve for the wounds of World War II; an uncontested site in the Cold War propaganda battles; a spectacle for the masses propagated by (and a reflection of) the Marcos dictatorship; and a globalizing force in the country's Hollywoodization through the United States' National Basketball Association (NBA) and other popular media.[11]

Before Ekwe's arrival, the NCAA allowed up to 40 percent of an NCAA team to include foreigners.[12] In his wake, NCAA and UAAP teams raced to recruit FSAs at

---

[6] [citations from Rehal, PDL]. This chapter's discussion on FSA participation is also based on statements from important figures in amateur sports (e.g., players, coaches, and administrators), commentary from notable opinion leaders in that space, and media sources on policy changes in the UAAP and NCAA (the leagues heavily rely on the media to record and decree their rules, being without an official, comprehensive, and public repository). *See* Marquez, C., UAAP plans to publish rulebook this year, 1 September 2019, https://www.cnnphilippines.com/sports/2019/9/1/uaap-official-rulebook.html (last accessed April 7, 2023).

[7] Antolihao (2017), p. 21.

[8] Antolihao (2017), pp. 18–19; 36–40.

[9] Antolihao (2017), p. 3.

[10] Lao, G., Opinion: Why Filipinos bother with basketball (even though we're too short for it). CNN Philippines, 6 September 2018, https://www.cnnphilippines.com/life/culture/2018/09/06/basketball-medals-opinion.html (last accessed 18 October 2022).

[11] Antolihao (2017), pp. 78–86; 99–102; 107–120; and 170–176. Bartholomew (2011), pp. 57–63; 70–77; and 252–257.

[12] Sy, S., The NCAA has banned foreign student-athletes by 2020 and everyone loses. Multisport.ph, 4 July 2018, https://multisport.ph/28559/ncaa-banned-foreign-student-athletes-2020-everyone-loses/ (last accessed 30 May 2022).

the center position as scorers, rebounders and interior defenders.[13] Some FSAs became stars whose teams' fortunes rose and fell with them, and while having a good FSA did not guarantee wins, the association between them, and San Beda's trophy case and the string of UAAP champions,[14] persisted. Further, the NCAA MVP award went to FSAs five times since Ekwe's debut in 2006,[15] and five times from 2016 to 2022 in the UAAP.[16] Since 2012, at least one FSA made it to the UAAP and NCAA Mythical Five, peaking in 2016 with four FSAs in the NCAA's Mythical Five.[17]

Responding to the FSA trend, the UAAP reduced the number of FSAs (casually called "imports") per basketball team from two (though only one could play at a time) to just one.[18] Ahead of its 2018 season, the NCAA announced that FSAs were banned altogether from all events starting in 2020.[19] "As of the moment, [FSAs have] done more harm than good [to] basketball", said Fr. Vic Calvo, the NCAA management committee chair.[20]

---

[13] Alegre, M., and Gloria, G., Broad shoulders and huge expectations: Foreign student athletes in the UAAP. The Lasallian, 22 January 2017, https://thelasallian.com/2017/01/22/broad-shoulders-and-huge-expectations-foreign-student-athletes-in-the-uaap-2/ (last accessed 30 May 2022).

[14] The University of the Philippines (2022) and Malik Diouf (Senegal); Ateneo De Manila University Blue Eagles (2018, 2019, and 2022) and Ange Kouame (Côte d'Ivoire); the De La Salle Green Archers (2016) and Ben Mbala (Cameroon), and the National University Bulldogs (2014) and Alfred Aroga (Cameroon).

[15] Ekwe (2006 and 2008), Daniel (2010), and Alwell Oraeme (Nigeria) (2015 and 2016), and Prince Eze (Nigeria) (2018). NCAA Basketball Championship (Philippines) Most Valuable Players, Wikipedia, https://en.wikipedia.org/wiki/NCAA_Basketball_Championship_(Philippines)#Most_Valuable_Players (last accessed 30 May 2022).

There is a notorious lack of publicly available official sources for Philippine basketball records and statistics. Wikipedia is generally accepted as the best public available resource for this information.

[16] Mbala (2016, 2017), Bright Akhuetie (Nigeria) (2018), Soulémane Chabi Yo (Benin) (2019), and Kouame (2022). UAAP Basketball Championship Most Valuable Players, Wikipedia, https://en.wikipedia.org/wiki/UAAP_Basketball_Championship#Most_Valuable_Players (last accessed 30 May 2022).

[17] Akhuetie, Oraeme, Tankoua, and Laminou Hamadou (Cameroon). The NCAA and UAAP awards are based on player statistics and tend to favor scorers who play heavy minutes. While NCAA selects the top five point-getters for its Mythical Five, the UAAP filters for awardees by position (guard, forward, and center). If the UAAP had a positionless Mythical Five, more FSAs might make these lists.

[18] Alegre, M., & Gloria, G., Broad shoulders and huge expectations: Foreign student athletes in the UAAP. The Lasallian, 22 January 2017, https://thelasallian.com/2017/01/22/broad-shoulders-and-huge-expectations-foreign-student-athletes-in-the-uaap-2 (last accessed 30 May 2022).

[19] Naredo, C., No more foreign athletes in NCAA by 2020. ABS-CBN News, 19 July 2018, https://news.abs-cbn.com/sports/06/19/18/no-more-foreign-athletes-in-ncaa-by-2020 (last accessed 30 May 2022).

[20] Naredo, C., 'More harm than good': Foreign student-athletes still banned from NCAA. ABS-CBN News, 23 June 2020, https://news.abs-cbn.com/sports/06/23/20/more-harm-than-good-foreign-student-athletes-still-banned-from-ncaa (last accessed 30 May 2022).

FSA supporters argue that they improve the level of competition,[21] and they also suggest that smaller schools benefit more from FSA recruitment, as they offset the loss of local recruits to the more affluent programs.[22] From this perspective, banning FSAs would condemn the amateur game to stagnation,[23] and that arguments against FSAs are misguided by the belief that local talent are inherently more deserving of opportunities for further success.[24] Finally, it would be ironic to deny FSAs a chance to play in the country when many Filipinos celebrate their compatriots playing in more competitive leagues abroad.[25]

Arguments against FSAs include the fact that they stunt the development of local talent in the sense that they take scholarships, roster spots and playing time from locals at the same position.[26] FSA recruitment shifts collegiate leagues away from proving grounds for local upstarts towards win-at-all-costs enterprises.[27] FSAs are allegedly hired guns, loyal only to the highest bidder, which disturbs the leagues' amateur status.[28] In that sense, there is an argument that there is a higher prestige to winning championships without FSAs, like how the Philippine Basketball Association (PBA), the leading local professional league, regards its all-Filipino tournament as more prestigious than those "reinforced" with imports.[29]

These discussions center on deeper questions that extend beyond the games played on the court. Who belongs in the Philippine basketball community? For whom is Philippine basketball, and who gets to decide? Antolihao theorizes that

---

[21] Terrado, J., Scottie Thompson on NCAA foreign student-athletes ban. The Manila Bulletin, 7 August 2020, https://mb.com.ph/2020/08/07/thompson-on-ncaa-foreign-student-athletes-ban/ (last accessed 30 May 2022).

[22] Naredo, C., UAAP: For Adamson coach Pumaren, foreign-student athletes a big help in college hoops. ABS-CBN News, 6 August 2020, https://news.abs-cbn.com/sports/08/06/20/uaap-for-adamson-coach-pumeran-foreign-student-athletes-a-big-help-in-college-hoops (last accessed 30 May 2022).

[23] Ganglani, N., Mbala: NCAA decision to ban foreign players feels harsh, racist. Rappler, 21 June 2018, https://www.rappler.com/sports/205460-ben-mbala-ncaa-ban-foreign-players-imports/ (last accessed 30 May 2022).

[24] Cuna, C., Ban This!, Inboundpass.com, 19 November 2010 https://web.archive.org/web/20140226063644/http://www.inboundpass.com/2010/11/19/ban-this/ (last accessed 30 May 2022).

[25] Sy, S., The NCAA has banned foreign student-athletes by 2020 and everyone loses. Multisport.ph, 4 July 2018, https://multisport.ph/28559/ncaa-banned-foreign-student-athletes-2020-everyone-loses/ (last accessed 30 May 2022).

[26] Terrado, J., Scottie Thompson on NCAA foreign student-athletes ban. The Manila Bulletin, 7 August 2020, https://mb.com.ph/2020/08/07/thompson-on-ncaa-foreign-student-athletes-ban/ (last accessed 30 May 2022).

[27] Castillo, M., Excess imports. Inquirer.net, 16 October 2016, https://sports.inquirer.net/227715/ncaa-uaap-excess-imports (last accessed 18 October 2022).

[28] De La Cruz, C., Out From The Box: Fr. Calvo reveals 10 reasons why NCAA banned 'imports. Tiebreaker Times, 24 June 2020, https://tiebreakertimes.com.ph/tbt/box-fr-calvo-reveals-10-reasons-ncaa-banned-imports/185837 (last accessed 30 May 2022).

[29] Jugado, M., JRU coach okay with ban on foreign players. Malaya Business Insight, 14 August 2020, https://malaya.com.ph/news_sports/jru-coach-okay-with-ban-on-foreign-players/ (last accessed 30 May 2022).

Filipinos did not passively receive basketball into their culture as inevitable from colonial relations, otherwise, the Americans' love for baseball should have also taken root. Rather, Filipinos vernacularized basketball which, like the Indians' experience with cricket and the British empire, gave literacy of a foreign cosmopolitan culture, which in turn is hybridized into the Filipino identity.[30]

On a related note, Bartholomew suggests that the strongest evidence of basketball's deep cultural embeddedness and integration is the difficulty in articulating its importance in Filipinos' lives, "as difficult to define as one's core".[31] On the international stage, the national team rallies around the cry of *puso*, which literally translates into "heart", but also connotes a determination to exceed one's limits, to triumph against overwhelming odds, whether in sport or in life, through the indomitable force of will.[32] In the Philippines it can seem that every alley, empty lot, park, plaza, pier, roof deck, warehouse, churchyard or mountainside is improvised as, if not eventually renovated into, a space for a pickup basketball game.[33] Bartholomew observes, however, that this nationwide passion has been leveraged not only into strong communal bonds, but also into corporate and political empires as conglomerates and politicians (including many ex-players) funnel money into goods, apparel, merchandise, professional teams and basketball courts as a cost-effective marketing and patronage strategy.[34]

Filipinos collectively transformed basketball into a unique cultural phenomenon, part and parcel of themselves and the modernity of Filipino life. Ponce de Leon observes a parallel with Philippines' national football team where Filipinos of mixed nationalities or ethnicities spark similar conversations on exclusion, belonging, and identity.[35] FIFA eligibility rules aside, players were judged by fans as either "Filipino enough" by the fact of their mixed heritage and decision to represent the country,[36] or "invaders" due to differences in ethnic features, geographical origin, and cultural upbringing.[37] Her study deconstructs the ways in which Filipinos perceive identity and belonging through sport.

But if basketball's cultural assimilation was conscious and intentional, then its negative aspects are also there by design, whether consciously or otherwise. Ponce de Leon notes that sports is a site for conflating "nationalism (placing one's country

---

[30] Antolihao (2017), pp. 19–24.

[31] Bartholomew (2011), p. 79.

[32] Antolihao (2017), pp. 132–146. Ramos, N., We are Gilas, Pilipinas. Slam Philippines, 11 August 2013, https://slamonlineph.com/in-case-you-missed-it-we-are-gilas-pilipinas/ (last accessed 30 May 2022). Bartholomew, R., Their Dinner with Andray. Grantland, 28 August 2014, https://grantland.com/features/andray-blatche-fiba-world-cup-philippines/ (last access 18 October 2022).

[33] Bartholomew (2011), pp. 178–179. Philippines: Home of the makeshift basketball court. BBC News, 23 May 2014, https://www.bbc.com/news/world-asia-27379716 (last accessed 30 May 2022).

[34] Bartholomew (2011), pp. 249–252.

[35] Ponce de Leon (2018), pp. 1308–1316.

[36] Ponce de Leon (2018), pp. 1309–1311.

[37] Ponce de Leon (2018), pp. 1312–1313.

above others)... with national pride (a personal emotion linked to self-esteem), and national identity".[38] This gives rise to situations in sport wherein structures are adopted which "transform [...] race prejudice through the exercise of power against a racial group defined as inferior, by individuals and institutions with the intentional or unintentional support of the entire culture".[39]

3 Philippine Basketball Policies and Regulation

The anti-foreigner sentiments of the UAAP and NCAA were stoked by the events preceding the enactment of the Student-Athletes Protection Act (SAPA),[40] a law that curbed excessive residency rules on transferring athletes because universities wanted to "protect" their recruits from other programs who "pirate" their investments".[41] The law set a compromise of a one-year residency due to UAAP officials' appeals to counterbalance the allegedly exorbitant transfer offers and packages.[42] Thus, under the SAPA, schools also cannot give benefits "which are contrary to the nature of amateur sports and which may result in the commercialization of a student-athlete".[43]

Against this backdrop, the FSA bans were seen as an extension of the financial excesses that the SAPA sought to curb. Clamping down on FSA recruitment went hand-in-hand with curbing excessive amateur sports spending. As one columnist noted after UAAP MVP Ben Mbala led the De La Salle Green Archers to the championship in 2016:

[38] Ponce de Leon (2018), p. 1302.

[39] Anderson (1996), p. 358.

[40] Rep. Act No. 10676 (2015).

[41] Lim, F., The Pingoy Rule of the UAAP. Inquirer.net, 3 April 2013 https://business.inquirer.net/115307/the-pingoy-rule-of-the-uaap (last accessed 30 May 2022). Inocencio, J., Free Jerie Pingoy! ABS-CBN News, 14 March 2013 at https://news.abs-cbn.com/blogs/insights/03/14/13/free-jerie-pingoy (Last accessed on 30 May 2022).

[42] Verora, L., Senate hearing: New rules for UAAP, student athletes sought. Rappler, 10 April 2014, https://www.rappler.com/sports/55164-senate-hearing-pia-cayetano-uaap-malpractices/ (Last accessed on 30 May 2022). There's a lack of detailed reporting on these offers, but rumors persist of cars, condominiums, cash, and employment given to family members. Commercialization of college sports. Business Mirror, 12 September 2022, https://businessmirror.com.ph/2022/09/12/commercialization-of-college-sports/ (last accessed 18 Oct 2022).

[43] Section 5 of the SAPA limits these to tuition and school fees, board and lodging, sports equipment, reasonable allowances, medical and insurance, and "reasonable similar benefits." Since the SAPA's enactment, there is no public record of any complaints filed for improper benefits. This, plus the one-year residency rule, has led some to argue that the SAPA formalizes and facilitates piracy. Pia Cayetano law promotes athlete piracy. The Varsitarian, 15 September 2015, https://varsitarian.net/sports/sports/20150925/pia_cayetano_law_promotes_athlete_piracy (last accessed 30 May 2022). It is worth noting, however, that nothing prohibits college players from profiting through brand endorsements and appearances based on their name, image and likeness, even if in most cases their market value is almost entirely based on their status as an amateur player.

> Philippine college basketball has become so highly commercialized, so deeply committed to winning at all cost[s] that schools have thrown away any semblance of decency and sportsmanship to win championships. Blame San Beda for unleashing this monster, starting with the "hiring" of Sam Ekwe in 2006. San Beda had been without an NCAA title for 28 years until some of the school's officials had this bright idea of bringing in an "import."[44]

FSAs were scapegoated for the national team's winless performance in the 2019 FIBA World Cup. The squad was mostly composed of professional veterans, yet per House representative Michael Odylon L. Romero, amateur programs should have spent fewer resources recruiting FSAs to win tournaments, and instead reallocated efforts to developing local players to avoid future international embarrassment.[45]

Representative Romero filed a resolution calling for a law that would prohibit all collegiate and university leagues from recruiting and fielding FSAs.[46] To him, local players are "victims" of FSAs who deserve "the chance to improve and compete to the best of their ability".[47] No further action appears to have been taken on the measure, but Romero remains an influential voice, not only in the House of Representatives, but as one of the wealthiest people in the Philippines according to Forbes in 2020,[48] the owner of PBA team NorthPort Batang Pier, and a national polo athlete. In the context of how the sports community moves forward, his words carry deep significance.

Even the Senate seemed indirectly concerned with the effect of FSAs on the competitive balance in the UAAP. In 2019, the Samahang Basketbol ng Pilipinas (SBP), the national basketball federation, lobbied to grant Philippine citizenship to Angelo Kouame so he could join the national team as a naturalized player under FIBA rules.[49] Kouame was targeted because his stellar performance propelled the Ateneo de Manila University Blue Eagles to two championships. Yet Senator Edgardo Angara, SBP chair and sponsor of Kouame's naturalization bill, asked, "If [Ateneo] were to get another import, would that not be fair to the rest of the

---

[44] Marcelo, D., Imports make winning college titles hollow. The Manila Bulletin, 9 December 2016, https://www.pressreader.com/philippines/manila-bulletin/20161209/page/20/textview (Last accessed on 30 May 2022).

[45] House Resolution 388, 18th Cong., 1st Sess. (2019) (H. Res. 388), pp. 1–2. The Philippines' last major international successes are probably qualifying for the 1972 Olympics (13th) and peaking at 3rd at the 1954 FIBA World Championships. The country were runners-up in the 2013 and 2015 FIBA Asia Cups but placed only 21st and 32nd in the 2014 and 2019 FIBA World Cups, respectively.

[46] H. Res. 388, p. 1.

[47] Solon files resolution prohibiting colleges from using foreign student-athletes. ESPN Philippines, 30 September 2019, https://www.espn.com/basketball/colleges/story/_/id/27733899/romero-files-resolution-prohibiting-colleges-using-foreign-student-athletes (last accessed 30 May 2022).

[48] Michael Romero. Forbes.com, https://www.forbes.com/profile/michael-romero/?sh=15663948330e (last accessed 30 May 2022).

[49] Castillo, M., With Kouame now Filipino, Gilas program has front-line cornerstone it can build on. Inquirer.net, 19 May 2021, https://sports.inquirer.net/423543/size-boost (last accessed on 30 May 2022).

league?" during the Senate's deliberations.[50] The following season, the UAAP classified the newly 'Filipinized' Kouame as an FSA.[51] The extent to which Senator Angara's remarks influenced the UAAP's policy is unclear, but it furthers the theory of a common perception that foreigners, notwithstanding the legal fiction of citizenship, should be treated differently.

4 Impact of Discriminatory Treatment on FSAs

This section examines the impact of this discriminatory treatment of FSAs, combining media reports of these incidents with media analysis forwarded by Satwinder Rehal. This section also applies relevant legal principles to the factual background illustrated in Sect. 2. Using descriptive and interpretative analyses, it identifies the promising and challenging aspects of legal remedies to assist FSAs.

This chapter takes the view that Philippine basketball belongs to anyone who wishes to play, and arbitrary barriers against the free participation of FSAs should be dismantled. Race and/or national origin are not good enough reasons to deny anyone's freedom to join a team and play, considering international law commitments to upholding human rights, including the principle of equality and freedom from discrimination; the constitutional guarantee of equal protection and strict scrutiny in favor of protected classes of persons, such as the youth; and equal protection-based actions against private persons. However, these cases either go beyond current developments in Philippine jurisprudence or legal theory, and/or are subject to countervailing principles which may be deployed to defend FSA restrictions.

Although they are the most affected by the UAAP and NCAA restrictions, many FSAs do not feel that they can speak freely on the issue. For example, Alfred Aroga, UAAP MVP and star of the National University Bulldogs' championship run in 2014, declined to comment at the time that rumors of FSA bans were circulating because as a foreigner, what he says or does "has no impact".[52] While at least one

---

[50] Sen. Angara questions classification of Kouame in UAAP once naturalized. Tiebreaker Times, 10 March 2021, https://tiebreakertimes.com.ph/tbt/sen-angara-questions-classification-of-kouame-in-uaap-once-naturalized/203051 (last accessed 18 October 2022).

[51] Li, M., Naturalized Filipinos by Congress to remain as FSAs in UAAP. Tiebreaker Times, 18 May 2021 https://tiebreakertimes.com.ph/tbt/naturalized-filipinos-by-congress-to-remain-as-fsas-in-uaap/208326 (last accessed 30 May 2022).

[52] Ganglani, N., Banning foreign student-athletes from the UAAP isn't right. Retrieved from Rappler, 7 December 2014 https://www.rappler.com/sports/77196-banning-uaap-foreign-student-athletes/ (last accessed 30 May 2022).

FSA has gone on record to call out these rules as racist,[53] others are just grateful for the scholarship, which they value above their playing experience.[54]

Casual racism is not an uncommon experience for foreign players in the Philippines. In 2018, a group chat between members of a university-based fraternity was leaked. The messages revealed a picture of Bright Akhuetie, who debuted that year for the University of the Philippines Fighting Maroons, and a message referring to him as the team's "pet gorilla", with another member noting that he would make Akhuetie his ball boy if he was part of the fraternity.[55] Days before the conversation leaked, the UAAP named Akhuetie as the season MVP.

Black basketball players in the Philippines have experienced some form of racism.[56] Overt violence is rare, but there have been instances of hate speech and harassment from fans, competitors, and opposing coaching staff, including taunting words and gestures, and occasionally the n-word.[57] Support at the league level also seems insufficient, as leagues generally forbid detrimental conduct but have no specific prohibitions against discriminatory or racist behavior.[58] In 2014, the NCAA excluded FSAs from their All-Star game altogether, because allowing them to play would lead to an imbalanced exhibition game.[59] San Beda's Ola Adeogun (who months earlier was verbally abused by an opposing staff member using a banana and animal gestures)[60] then Tweeted sarcastically that he and other FSAs

---

[53] Ganglani, N., Mbala: NCAA decision to ban foreign players feels harsh, racist. Rappler, 21 June 2018, https://www.rappler.com/sports/205460-ben-mbala-ncaa-ban-foreign-players-imports/ (last accessed 30 May 2022).

[54] Sarmenta, Y., Perpetual Help's Prince Eze thinks NCAA ban not good for local players. ESPN Philippines, 28 June 2018, https://www.espn.ph/basketball/colleges/story/_/id/23932673/perpetual-eze-says-ncaa-ban-not-good-idea (last accessed 18 October 2022).

[55] UAAP: Bright Akhuetie responds to alleged racist talk in viral frat chat. ABS-CBN News, 23 November 2018, https://news.abs-cbn.com/sports/11/23/18/uaap-bright-akhuetie-responds-to-alleged-racist-talk-in-viral-frat-chat (last accessed 30 May 2022).

[56] Iñigo, T., The Reality of Racism in Philippine Sports. Batas Sportiva, 12 July 2022, https://batassportiva.com/2020/07/12/the-reality-of-racism-in-philippine-sports/ (last accessed 30 May 2022).

[57] Iñigo, T., The Reality of Racism in Philippine Sports. Batas Sportiva, 12 July 2022, https://batassportiva.com/2020/07/12/the-reality-of-racism-in-philippine-sports/ (last accessed 30 May 2022).

[58] Ingles, M., Racism in Philippine Sports: Who's Got Next? Batas Sportiva. 21 August 2019, https://batassportiva.com/2019/08/21/racism-in-philippine-sports-whos-got-next/ (last accessed 30 May 2022).

[59] Ganglani, N., NCAA explains why there are no foreign players in the All-Star game. Rappler, 11 August 2014, https://www.rappler.com/sports/65920-ncaa-foreign-players-all-star-game/ (last accessed 30 May 2022).

[60] For waving banana at NLEX's Adeogun, team staff suspended. ABS-CBN News, 7 February 2014, https://news.abs-cbn.com/sports/02/07/14/waving-banana-nlexs-adeogun-team-staff-suspended (last accessed 30 May 2022).

"will be having [their] own [All-Star] game in Manila Zoo".[61] Adeogun finished the year with Mythical Five honors, and San Beda a fifth straight championship.

Rehal argues that Philippine sports media is complicit in thematically reinforcing racism against FSAs and Black people in general.[62] Undertaking his own survey of sports reporting, Rehal notes that stories essentialize Black athletes by their "animalistic" physical prowess and other traits, in contrast to the diminutive Filipinos who take an intellectual, refined approach to basketball; FSAs are "tall and beefy", possessing "limited basketball know-how", and are "snared" to play under "patient Filipino coaches" against "graceful, high-flying and sharp shooting Filipino players".[63] Rehal posits that this discourse is a redirection of the colonial discrimination that Filipinos suffered by the Spanish, Americans, and Japanese, and symptomatic of an attempt to assert racial and financial dominance through hypermasculinity.[64] As Filipinos now occupy the dominant, West-adjacent cultural position in basketball, they perpetuate the same methods of subjugation, "border [ing] on both fear and fantasy of African student-athletes".[65]

4.1 *Legal Remedies for FSA Discrimination*

Legal remedies, beyond creating a more inclusive environment in amateur basketball, could have a normative effect that reduces, if not eliminates, discrimination and mistreatment against FSAs. First, we identify international human rights instruments, constitutional litigation, and tort actions as key areas of law that may apply to the FSA situation. Second, we use descriptive analysis to illustrate the current state of those areas of law, including relevant cases decided by the Philippine Supreme Court. Third, considering that the FSA situation is novel in this jurisdiction, we provide interpretative analysis of their applicability to FSA exclusion by relying on the emerging analysis and/or synthesis of other scholars, and through a textual examination of these legal sources based on the current state of the law.

The Philippines generally regards itself as a dualist jurisdiction with regard to its treaty obligations, and thus requires legislation to make them applicable in the country.[66] The Philippines recognizes the inherent equality among all people and commits itself to realizing their equal treatment without distinction on the basis of immutable factors, including their national origin. The country considers itself

[61] Dy, A., Ola Adeogun is not happy about the NCAA's "no foreigners" All-Star Game. SLAM Philippines, 9 August 2014, http://web.archive.org/web/20151126020808/http://slamonlineph.com/ola-adeogun-happy-ncaas-foreigners-star-game/ (last accessed 30 May 2022).

[62] Rehal (2020), p. 134.

[63] Rehal (2020), pp. 134–137.

[64] Rehal (2020), pp. 139–145.

[65] Rehal (2020), pp. 137–143; 145.

[66] Casis (2020), pp. 130–136.

bound by relevant instruments such as the Universal Declaration of Human Rights (UDHR),[67] the International Covenant on Civil and Political Rights (ICCPR),[68] and the International Convention on the Elimination of All Forms of Racial Discrimination (CERD).[69]

Article 26 of the ICCPR exhorts each state-party to ensure that all persons within its jurisdiction are entitled to "equal and effective protection" against discrimination on any ground, including race or national origin. It is concerned with legal or factual discrimination in any field regulated by public authorities (i.e., legislation), such that

[67]UDHR, Article 1: All human beings are born free and equal in dignity and rights. They are endowed with reason and conscience and should act towards one another in a spirit of brotherhood.

UDHR, Article 7: All are equal before the law and are entitled without any discrimination to equal protection of the law. All are entitled to equal protection against any discrimination in violation of this Declaration and against any incitement to such discrimination.

[68]ICCPR, Article 2(1): Each State Party to the present Covenant undertakes to respect and to ensure to all individuals within its territory and subject to its jurisdiction the rights recognized in the present Covenant, without distinction of any kind, such as race, colour, sex, language, religion, political or other opinion, national or social origin, property, birth or other status.

Article 26: All persons are equal before the law and are entitled without any discrimination to the equal protection of the law. In this respect, the law shall prohibit any discrimination and guarantee to all persons equal and effective protection against discrimination on any ground such as race, colour, sex, language, religion, political or other opinion, national or social origin, property, birth or other status.

[69]CERD, Article 1(1): In this Convention, the term "racial discrimination" shall mean any distinction, exclusion, restriction or preference based on race, colour, descent, or national or ethnic origin which has the purpose or effect of nullifying or impairing the recognition, enjoyment or exercise, on an equal footing, of human rights and fundamental freedoms in the political, economic, social, cultural or any other field of public life.

Article 2: 1. States Parties condemn racial discrimination and undertake to pursue by all appropriate means and without delay a policy of eliminating racial discrimination in all its forms and promoting understanding among all races, and, to this end: (a) Each State Party undertakes to engage in no act or practice of racial discrimination against persons, groups of persons or institutions and to en sure that all public authorities and public institutions, national and local, shall act in conformity with this obligation; (b) Each State Party undertakes not to sponsor, defend or support racial discrimination by any persons or organizations; (c) Each State Party shall take effective measures to review governmental, national and local policies, and to amend, rescind or nullify any laws and regulations which have the effect of creating or perpetuating racial discrimination wherever it exists; (d) Each State Party shall prohibit and bring to an end, by all appropriate means, including legislation as required by circumstances, racial discrimination by any persons, group or organization; (e) Each State Party undertakes to encourage, where appropriate, integrationist multiracial organizations and movements and other means of eliminating barriers between races, and to discourage anything which tends to strengthen racial division.

2. States Parties shall, when the circumstances so warrant, take, in the social, economic, cultural and other fields, special and concrete measures to ensure the adequate development and protection of certain racial groups or individuals belonging to them, for the purpose of guaranteeing them the full and equal enjoyment of human rights and fundamental freedoms. These measures shall in no case entail as a consequence the maintenance of unequal or separate rights for different racial groups after the objectives for which they were taken have been achieved.

any laws passed by state-parties should not contravene Article 26.[70] It is understood that "racial discrimination" in this context has the same definition as that under Article 1 of the CERD.[71] As the UAAP and NCAA are regulated by law (by the SAPA and the Commission on Higher Education),[72] it falls to Congress to prevent discrimination in law or in fact in that sphere of social or cultural life in line with the state's obligation not to sponsor, defend, or support racial discrimination in any way, and to review, rescind or nullify contrary laws.[73] Under the CERD, differential treatment will constitute discrimination "if the criteria for such differentiation, judged in the light of the objectives and purposes of the Convention, are not applied pursuant to a legitimate aim, and are not proportional to the achievement of this aim".[74]

The CERD may be used to scrutinize FSA restrictions, similar to how the CERD has been invoked to challenge racial quotas in South African rugby (where quotas intended to encourage minority participation may lead to questioning the merits of those players counted under the quota).[75] One can argue that FSA restrictions do not seem legitimate as they boil down to Filipino exclusivity for its own sake. Assuming, *arguendo*, that legitimate aims exist, then these restrictions disproportionately affect FSAs of African origin—as it was their on-court excellence that prompted the FSA restrictions in the first place—and deny them the opportunity to participate in university-level sports. This is evidence of discrimination and shows that Congress has not complied with its ICCPR and CERD obligations.

Non-discrimination on this level, however, does not appear to be a priority. For over 50 years, the Philippines has implemented law that criminalizes the discriminatory acts in Article 4 of the CERD, but punishes them by only up to a year's imprisonment—hardly a sign of commitment or a strong deterrence.[76] There are no Supreme Court decisions that cite the CERD or its implementing law to nullify racist policies or elaborate on its scope or application. In this regard, Ignatius Michael D. Ingles, a prominent sports law practitioner and observer in the Philippines, notes that the very provisions of the SAPA are evidence of discrimination in law; Sect. 4 states that the one-year residency rule is explicitly "without prejudice to the

[70] OHCHR, *General Comment No. 18*, 37th Sess., HRI/GEN/1/Rev.9 (Vol. I), adopted 10 November 1989, paras. 1, 12.

[71] OHCHR, *General Comment No. 18*, 37th Sess., HRI/GEN/1/Rev.9 (Vol. I), adopted 10 November 1989, paras. 6–8.

[72] SAPA, § 7.

[73] Arguably, participation in sports, given its significance in the Philippine context, falls under the right to equal participation in cultural activities per Articles 5 of the CERD. At any rate, that enumeration is regarded as not exhaustive of the rights protected by the convention (McDonnel, G., *Introductory Note to the CERD*, United Nations, 21 December 1965, https://legal.un.org/avl/ha/cerd/cerd.html (last accessed 18 October 2022).

[74] McDonnel, G., *Introductory Note to the CERD*, United Nations, 21 December 1965, https://legal.un.org/avl/ha/cerd/cerd.html (last accessed 18 October 2022).

[75] Louw (2019), pp. 407–408.

[76] Pres. Dec. No. 966 (1976) and Pres. Dec. No. 1350-A (1978).

respective residency rules of athletic associations on student-athletes who are foreign imports".[77] Ingles warns that this leaves the door open to justify other bans and restrictions, since the law explicitly allows for distinctions regarding residency, and implies that FSAs may be treated differently from Filipino student-athletes.[78]

Ongoing attempts to codify the rights of student-athletes do not appear to include FSAs. For example, Senate Bill No. 286 ("An Act Providing for the Magna Carta of Student-Athletes") proposes the following regarding equality for student-athletes and schools' correlative duties:

> Section 5.4(f): It is the right of the Student-Athlete to be treated with respect and dignity and be free from any form of discrimination on account of age, sex, gender, language, ethnicity, religion, ideology, disability, education and status.
>
> Section 7.16: It is the duty of the schools and their officials to ensure that no Student-Athlete shall, on account of age, sex, gender, language, ethnicity, religion, disability, education and status, be excluded from participation in, be denied the benefits of, or be subjected to discrimination under any athletic program or activity.[79]

The bill adopts the SAPA's definition that a student-athlete may be someone who "has an intention to represent the school in an inter-school athletic program or competition",[80] which should extend its coverage to FSAs. However, it may be argued that the bill could, ironically, reinforce the different treatment of FSAs: Senate Bill No. 286 does not recognize equality based on national or geographical origin which, unlike equality based on ethnicity, is recognized in other laws like the Magna Carta of Women.[81]

It can also be said that the bill was meant only to strengthen the SAPA and did not intend to go so far as to recognize FSA equality. Considering this, it could be argued that, following the rule that ambiguities in a law's intent and scope may be ascertained by examining contemporaneous events, legislative deliberations, and prior laws on the same subject matter,[82] an FSA has no demandable right to play in the NCAA or UAAP; whether under the SAPA, or if Senate Bill No. 286 should become law, since Congress only sought to expound on existing legislation and did not intend to recognize equality on the basis of national origin.

---

[77] SAPA, § 4.

[78] Ingles, M., Banning Foreign Student-Athletes, Legal or Not? Batas Sportiva, 21 June 2018 at https://batassportiva.com/2018/06/21/banning-foreign-student-athletes-legal-or-not/ (last accessed 30 May 2022). Ingles notes that the counterargument is that the differentiation may apply only to residency rules and not any other kind of right or entitlement, especially since there is no textual basis for other FSA-specific restrictions.

[79] S. No. 286, 18th Cong, 1st Sess., §§ 5.4(f), 7.16 (2019).

[80] S. No. 286, 18th Cong, 1st Sess., § 4.4 (2019).

[81] Rep. Act No. 9710 (2009). Section 2 reads, in part: "All individuals are equal as human beings by virtue of the inherent dignity of each human person. No one, therefore, should suffer discrimination on the basis of ethnicity, gender, age, language, sexual orientation, race, color, religion, political, or other opinion, national, social, or geographical origin, disability, property, birth, or other status as established by human rights standards."

[82] Gatmaytan (2016), pp. 351–357.

The extent and application of international human rights obligations to FSA discrimination is relevant as the Supreme Court of the Philippines cites several to buttress its decisions protecting and enhancing human dignity and reducing inequality, and the equal treatment of persons.[83] The Bill of Rights declares that no person "shall be deprived of life, liberty, or property without due process of law, nor shall any person be denied the equal protection of the laws".[84] "All persons subjected to legislation shall be treated alike, under like circumstances and conditions, both in the privileges conferred and in the liabilities imposed, to prevent undue favor on the one hand, and hostile discrimination on the other".[85]

"A law or measure seeking to impose a classification must (1) rest on substantial distinctions; (2) be germane to the purposes of the law; (3) not be limited to existing conditions only; and (4) apply equally to all members of the same class."[86] The Philippines' equal protection jurisprudence reserves the highest level of scrutiny for classifications affecting suspect classes,[87] or fundamental rights:[88]

> There are three levels of scrutiny at which the Court reviews the constitutionality of a classification embodied in a law: a) the deferential or rational basis scrutiny in which the challenged classification needs only be shown to be rationally related to serving a legitimate state interest; b) the middle-tier or intermediate scrutiny in which the government must show that the challenged classification serves an important state interest and that the classification is at least substantially related to serving that interest; and c) strict judicial scrutiny in which a legislative classification which impermissibly interferes with the exercise of a fundamental right or operates to the peculiar disadvantage of a suspect class is presumed unconstitutional, and the burden is upon the government to prove that the classification is necessary to achieve a compelling state interest and that it is the least restrictive means to protect such interest.[89]

The Supreme Court goes further, applying strict scrutiny to acts affecting "persons accorded special protection by the Constitution",[90] as determined by specific recognitions or guarantees pertaining to them.[91] These are sectors of society for which the Constitution professes regard in their development, well-being, and protection,

[83] *Int'l. Sch. Ass'n of Educators v. Quisumbing*, G.R. No. 128845, 1 June 2000. *Cent. Bank Emp. Union v. Bangko Sentral ng Pilipinas*, G.R. No. 148208, 15 December 2004.

[84] 1987 Const. Article III, §1

[85] *Dumlao v. Comm'n on Elections*, G.R. No. L-52245, 22 January 1980.

[86] *People v. Vera*, G.R. No. L-45685 16 November 1937). Magalang (2014), pp. 506–507.

[87] A suspect class is defined as "a class saddled with such disabilities, or subjected to such a history of purposeful unequal treatment, or relegated to such a position of political powerlessness as to command extraordinary protection from the majoritarian political process" (*Zomer Dev't. Co., Inc. v. Ct. of Appeals*, G.R. No. 194461, 7 January 2020). Classifications warranting strict scrutiny include those based on race or national origin, alienage, and religion (*Cent. Bank Emp. Union v. Bangko Sentral ng Pilipinas*, G.R. No. 148208, 15 December 2004, Carpio-Morales, J., Dissenting Opinion).

[88] Magalang (2014), pp. 506–509.

[89] *Serrano v. Gallant Maritime Services, Inc.*, G.R. No. 16714, 24 March 2009. (Citations omitted.)

[90] *Cent. Bank Emp. Union v. Bangko Sentral ng Pilipinas*, G.R. No. 148208, 15 December 2004.

[91] Magalang (2014), p. 513.

including women, indigenous peoples, workers, and the urban poor.[92] The youth[93] also enjoys an explicit constitutional guarantee in Article II, § 13, which declares that the State "recognizes the vital role of the youth in nation-building and shall promote and protect their physical, moral, spiritual, intellectual, and social well-being. It shall inculcate in the youth patriotism and nationalism, and encourage their involvement in public and civic affairs".[94] Those provisions are traditionally regarded as "state policies" or simple instructions to the legislature to enact laws following those outlines, but not as independent sources or rights.[95]

Nonetheless, the Supreme Court has occasionally declared or treated several state policies as self-executing.[96] These developments are the premise of Efren Resurreccion's call to abandon the traditional view that reduces state policies to "mere platitudes".[97] Rather, state policies should be seen as indicative of the intent with which the Constitution was ratified, and accorded with at least one of the following functions: to nullify state actions for affirmative protection; to complement other constitutional provisions from which a right invoked is derived; or to validate state actions consistent with constitutional mandates.[98] Those policies with nullifying functions are classified as "first-order state policies", because they carry commands (e.g., "protect") to the state from which individuals can claim a direct injury from an infringement of a constitutional right.[99] Resurreccion's analysis is appealing to potential constitutional litigants because it implies that the words of the Constitution can provide powerful relief for a broad range of matters without further legislative enactment; he proposes that Article II, § 13, which contains the word "protect", is one such policy.[100]

Resurreccion cites *Soriano v. Laguardia*,[101] as an instance where Article II, § 13 was treated as self-executing. There, the petitioner's daytime television show was suspended because he made obscene remarks. Soriano argued, *inter alia*, that the suspension constituted prior restraint. In its discussion on speech and censorship, the Supreme Court factored the state interest's in protecting the youth under Article II, § 13 in determining that there was a permissible infringement on Soriano's right to free speech:

---

[92]For example, for women, 1987 Const. Article II, § 14, Article XIII, 3 14; indigenous peoples, Article II, § 22; workers, Article II, § 18, Article XIII, § 3; urban poor, Article XIII, §§ 9–10.

[93]Magalang (2014), pp. 513–514.

[94]1987 Const. Article II, § 13.

[95]*Manila Prince Hotel v. Gov't Serv. Ins. Sys.*, G.R. No. 122156, 3 February 1997.

[96]*Legaspi v. Civil Serv. Comm'n*, G.R. No. L-72119 29 May 1987; *Oposa v. Factoran*, G.R. No. 101083, 30 July 1993; *Province of North Cotobato v. Republic of the Phils.*, G.R. No. 183591, 14 October 2008, *Manila Prince Hotel v. Gov't Serv. Ins. Sys.*, G.R. No. 122156, 3 February 1997.

[97]Resurreccion (2016), pp. 61–62.

[98]Resurreccion (2016), pp. 63–65.

[99]Resurreccion (2016), pp. 63–71.

[100]Resurreccion (2016), pp. 64–67.

[101]G.R. No. 1964785, 29 April 2009.

> Indisputably, the State has a compelling interest in extending social protection to minors against all forms of neglect, exploitation, and immorality which may pollute innocent minds. It has a compelling interest in helping parents, through regulatory mechanisms, protect their children's minds from exposure to undesirable materials and corrupting experiences. The Constitution, no less, in fact enjoins the State, as earlier indicated, to promote and protect the physical, moral, spiritual, intellectual, and social well-being of the youth to better prepare them fulfil their role in the field of nation-building. In the same way, the State is mandated to support parents in the rearing of the youth for civic efficiency and the development of moral character.[102]

The Supreme Court did not explicitly declare the right of the youth to protection as self-executing, but Resurreccion notes that it relied heavily on this state policy to dismiss Soriano's claim that his rights were violated. Resurreccion further observes that while Article II, § 13 was invoked to validate the state's suspension and censorship power, the Supreme Court did not deny its nullifying function, which may yet be demonstrated in a future case. For now, the fact that this state policy was weighed against the fundamental right to free speech is a sign that the youth's right to protection has a "heightened importance" under the Constitution.[103]

In this vein, it would seem that FSAs fall under the 'youth' protected by Article II, § 13. The Youth in Nation-Building Act (YNBA) states that "youth" may include persons in the 15- to 30-year-old range,[104] which would include FSAs. Thus, anti-FSA rules, with distinctions made based on race or national origin, can be seen as detrimental to the youth's moral, intellectual, and social well-being; anti-FSA rules in educational institutions do not aid the youth for involvement in public and civic affairs. Following Resurreccion's reading of *Soriano v. Laguardia*,[105] the nullifying functions of Article II, § 13 could be invoked to strike down FSA restrictions.

However, it should be noted that *Soriano v. Laguardia*[106] primarily dealt with the state's power to penalize on-air obscenities. The case could have been resolved within the framework of free speech, and any pronouncements regarding the right of the youth to state protection should be treated as *obiter dicta*. Moreover, the 'youth' should arguably be defined on a case-to-case basis by Congress,[107] and not by reference to existing laws such as the YNBA. Any argument to include student-athletes and FSAs under the "youth" category in Article II, § 13 hinges on a liberal

---

[102] *Soriano v. Laguardia*, G.R. No. 1964785, 29 April 2009. (Citations omitted.)

[103] Resurreccion (2016), p. 67.

[104] Rep. Act No. 8044 (1995) § 4(a). The YNBA created the National Youth Commission, a government body generally tasked to develop the youth for nation-building by encouraging youth organizations to participate in government agenda-setting and relevant projects, and restates Article II, § 13 in its mandate to "enable the youth to fulfill their vital role in nation-building," to "promote and protect their physical, moral, spiritual, intellectual, and social well-being." (Rep. Act No. 8044 (1995) §§ 2–3.)

[105] G.R. No. 1964785, 29 April 2009.

[106] G.R. No. 1964785, 29 April 2009.

[107] For example, youth welfare and criminal laws (e.g., child abuse and child pornography) applicable to legal minors, also cite or reference Article II, § 13 as among their policy bases.

interpretation of the term, before proceeding to convince the courts of the merits of Resurreccion's theory on the actionability of state policies.

Article 32 of the Civil Code provides a tort action against private individuals who directly or indirectly obstruct, defeat, violate, or in any manner impede or impair the rights and liberties of another person, including "the right to the equal protection of the laws" and other rights under the Bill of Rights.[108] This provision deters the "subtle, clever and indirect" rights violations outside of penal laws, recognizing that, "it is in these cunning devices of suppressing or curtaining freedom, which are not criminally punishable, where the greatest danger to democracy lies".[109] Article 32 adopts the common law elements of this action:

1. A duty or obligation recognized by law, requiring a person to conform to a certain standard of conduct, for the protection of others against unreasonable risks;
2. Failure on the person's part to conform to the standard: a breach of a duty;
3. A reasonably close causal connection between the conduct and resulting injury; (i.e., legal or proximate cause); and
4. Actual loss or damage resulting to the interests of another.[110]

As discussed above, FSA restrictions fall along the lines of race, national origin, or alienage, and should be evaluated under strict scrutiny. In applying strict scrutiny, the usual presumption of the constitutionality of a law or other regulation is reversed. The government must demonstrate that the law is (1) necessary to achieve a *compelling* (i.e., beyond merely reasonable) government interest, and (2) the least restrictive means to achieve that result.[111] That standard, however, applies to acts of the state. There is no precedent of the test applied to private persons since the Civil Code's effectivity in 1950.

One case has applied equal protection analysis to private acts affecting a constitutionally protected class. In *Int'l. Sch. Ass'n of Educators v. Quisumbing*,[112] the petitioner was a teacher's union that, in a bargaining dispute, assailed the discrepancy in the salaries between its Filipino and foreign teaching staff. Apart from citing labor laws on equal work for equal pay, the Supreme Court emphasized the constitutionally protected status of workers to nullify the school's policy:

> In this case, we find the point-of-hire classification employed by respondent School to justify the distinction in the salary rates of foreign-hires and local hires to be an invalid classification. There is no reasonable distinction between the services rendered by foreign-hires and

[108] Article 32. Any public officer or employee, or any private individual, who directly or indirectly obstructs, defeats, violates or in any manner impedes or impairs any of the following rights and liberties of another person shall be liable to the latter for damages: [...] (8) The right to the equal protection of the laws; [...].

[109] *Silahis v. Soluta*, G.R. No. 163087, 20 February 2006.

[110] Casis (2012), pp. 17–24.

[111] *Samahan ng mga Progresibong Kabataan v. Quezon City*, G.R. No. 255442, 8 August 2017.

[112] G.R. No. 128845, 1 June 2020.

> local-hires. The practice of the School of according higher salaries to foreign-hires contravenes public policy and, certainly, does not deserve the sympathy of this Court.[113]

This case is a starting point for different lines of analysis. First, Casis suggests that *Int'l. Sch. Ass'n of Educators v. Quisumbing*,[114] which cites the UDHR, ICCPR and CERD, is evidence that courts recognize non-discrimination as customary international law, which the Constitution then incorporates as part of the law of the land,[115] and therefore directly actionable before Philippine courts.[116] However, this is susceptible to differing, sometimes conflicting, approaches to locating international law within the Philippine domestic legal order.[117]

Second, one could extend *Int'l. Sch. Ass'n of Educators v. Quisumbing*[118] to argue a claim for damages under Article 32, such that the salary classification burdened the constitutionally-protected worker class, and requires the school to show a compelling state interest to justify the classification and show that it was narrowly tailored. Applying this to FSAs, schools and athletic associations may be asked to defend why their classifications creating a suspect class (e.g., based on race or nationality distinctions) should be maintained under strict scrutiny. Nonetheless, schools and athletic associations can claim to only be furthering the state's interest in regulating immigration and education, which generally already impose different standards and requirements on foreigners (e.g., the SAPA and immigration laws),[119] and are not at fault for acting within law. Moreover, they can forward their own qualitative and quantitative analyses, as to how FSAs negatively impact local athletes or development programs to justify an interest in excluding FSAs in favor of Filipino student-athletes.

Third, Article 32 is a potential vehicle to operationalize international non-discrimination obligations in domestic law. For example, plaintiffs in Japan have convinced Japanese courts to use the CERD as a supplementary reference in equality and minority rights tort claims.[120] Like the Philippines, Japan ratified the CERD but has no anti-discrimination legislation, leading its courts to take a freer hand in resolving discrimination disputes by applying the treaty's standard of discrimination to interpersonal relationships.[121] In this regard, nothing prevents Philippine courts from taking a similar approach, as decisions of foreign courts

---

[113] *Int'l. Sch. Alliance of Educators v. Quisumbing*, G.R. No. 128845, 1 June 2020. (Citations omitted.)

[114] G.R. No. 128845, 1 June 2020.

[115] Article II, § 2.

[116] Casis (2020), pp. 134; 151–152.

[117] Casis (2020), pp. 139–152.

[118] G.R. No. 128845, 1 June 2020.

[119] Calsado-Amoroso and Balisong (2019), pp. 785–787.

[120] According to Article 709 of the Japanese Civil Code, a "person who violates intentionally or negligently the right of another is bound to make compensation for damage arising therefrom". Webster (2007), p. 347.

[121] Webster (2010), pp. 245–246; 259–266.

have persuasive authority domestically.[122] A case could be made that, to arrive at a standard for equal protection in private relations, international non-discrimination principles should be consulted. Adopting the discussion on the CERD above should lead to a similar conclusion here.

Japanese precedents, however, have ruled against non-discrimination plaintiffs based on reasonableness, analogous to rational basis scrutiny in American jurisprudence. They have also found that the freedoms of assembly and association justify excluding persons of different ethnic backgrounds.[123] This would lower the threshold to justify the FSA rules, and would anchor it to another constitutional right. Necessarily, this approach would add the question of balancing associative interests and the state interest in eradicating discrimination,[124] adding to the list of constitutional questions that have hitherto not been resolved by Philippine courts.

5 Conclusion

It is not clear if there is any incentive within the Philippine basketball scene to keep FSAs, as they seem to be merely a desirable and not an intrinsic feature of the sport. To illustrate, the FSA pool is not a national team recruitment pipeline, notwithstanding Kouame's naturalization; in the past, the national team has recruited professional journeymen from overseas to fill roles. For similar reasons, PBA teams, which can field foreigners in certain tournaments, would rather recruit professional journeymen to make an immediate impact rather than develop an FSA into a professional-caliber player.[125] Schools have also pivoted to recruiting more Filipinos with mixed heritage, particularly those who have US amateur experience, to upgrade their rosters and whose heritage shields them from the "foreigner" label. Fans may ultimately accept moving on from FSAs, who may not have been around long enough to be considered integral to the basketball community.[126] If anything, the "mercenary" narrative and the Kouame situation suggest that many Filipinos view foreigners' place in the sport as mostly transactional and not core to its fabric.

[122] *Ient v. Tullet Prebon (Philippines), Inc.*, G.R. No. 189158, 11 January 2017.

[123] Webster (2010), pp. 264–265. Webster (2008), pp. 228–236.

[124] Generally, *New York State Club Association, Inc. v. City of New York*, 487 U.S. 1 (1988) and *Boy Scouts of America v. Dale*, 530 U.S. 640 (2000).

[125] Asis, M., What makes a great PBA import? Manila Times, 6 November 2021, https://www.manilatimes.net/2021/11/06/sports/what-makes-a-great-pba-import/1821159 (last accessed 30 May 2022).

[126] Antolihao (2017), p. 65. Villar, J., NCAA sticks with ban on foreign recruits. The Philippine Star, 24 June 2020, https://www.philstar.com/sports/2020/06/24/2023029/ncaa-sticks-ban-foreign-recruits (last accessed 30 May 2022). Jacinto, L., & Lichauco, J., 10 Questions for a UAAP Board Member. The Lasallian, 22 December 2014, https://thelasallian.com/2014/12/22/10-questions-for-a-uaap-board-member/ (last accessed 30 May 2022).

These signs, however, should not mean that advocating for FSAs is a lost cause, especially when popular foreign athletes identify or are welcomed as "Filipino at heart",[127] a connection that Senator Angara highlighted, ironically, to campaign for Kouame's naturalization.[128] This shows that Filipinos are able to welcome foreign athletes. Moreover, it is conveniently omitted in the popular discourse that not all FSAs came to the Philippines specifically to play sports like basketball. Anti-FSA policies would deny a contingent of foreign students in other sports the opportunity to not only play and excel, but also to fully embrace the collegiate, academic experience.[129]

At the very least, challenging institutional barriers to the movement of foreign talent, such as the case of *Union Royale Belge des Societes de Football Association ASBL v. Bosman*,[130] can propel amateur basketball to new competitive heights, such as that of European football.[131] As Calsado-Amoroso and Balisong argue, "a xenophobic league breeds xenophobic fans".[132] The UAAP and NCAA should be seen as valuable partners to contest regressive perspectives on race. It is hoped that, insofar as laws are tools to encourage or discourage behavior,[133] this chapter supports the idea that sport is an area that embraces equality and non-discrimination.

References

Anderson P (1996) Racism in sports: a question of ethics. Marq Sports Law J 6(2):357–408

Antolihao L (2017) Playing with the big boys: basketball American imperialism, and subaltern discourse in the Philippines. Ateneo De Manila University Press, Quezon City

Bartholomew R (2011) Pacific rims: Beermen Ballin' in flip-flops and the Philippines' unlikely love affair with basketball. New American Library, USA

Bliz K, Nadler J (2014) Law, moral attitudes, and behavioral change. In: Zamir E, Teichman D (eds) The Oxford handbook of behavioral economics and the law. Oxford University Press, Oxford, pp 241–266

[127] Leongson, R., American Sudan Daniel a Filipino at heart, say San Beda teammates. Spin.ph, 26 December 2020, https://www.spin.ph/basketball/sudan-daniel-tributes-a2437-20201226 (last accessed 18 October 2022). De Leon, J., Naturalization hopeful Andray Blatche embraces being 'half-Filipino'. GMA News Online, 10 June 2014, https://www.gmanetwork.com/news/sports/basketball/365081/naturalization-hopeful-andray-blatche-embraces-being-half-filipino/story/ (last accessed 18 October 2022).

[128] Leongson, R. Ange Kouame a true-blue Filipino on and off court, says Angara. Spin.ph, 24 February 2021, https://www.spin.ph/basketball/fiba/ange-kouame-a-true-blue-filipino-on-and-off-court-says-angara-a2437-20210224 (last accessed 18 October 2022).

[129] Kuku, I., A foreigner's thoughts on imports in the UAAP. GMA News Online, 15 July 2013, https://www.gmanetwork.com/news/sports/content/317501/a-foreigner-s-thoughts-on-imports-in-the-uaap/story/ (last accessed on 30 May 2022).

[130] ECJ Case No.: C-415/93 (1995) ECR I-4921.

[131] Calsado-Amoroso and Balisong (2019), pp. 796–797.

[132] Calsado-Amoroso and Balisong (2019), p. 797.

[133] Bliz and Nadler (2014), pp. 241–266.

Calsado-Amoroso A, Balisong P (2019) In or out: gaps in Philippine immigration law in relation to foreign athletes and sports leagues regulations as migration and human rights issues. Ateneo Law J 63(3):777–806

Casis R (2012) An analysis of Philippine law and jurisprudence on torts and quasi-delicts. University of the Philippines College of Law, Quezon City

Casis R (2020) Domesticating international law: resolving the uncertainty and incongruence. Phil Yearb Int Law 19:128–156

Gatmaytan D (2016) Legal method essentials 3.0. University of the Philippines College of Law, Quezon City

Louw A (2019) Affirmative (measures in) action: revising the lawfulness of racial quotas (in South African (professional) team sports). De Jure Law J 52:380–414

Magalang S (2014) Legitimizing illegitimacy: revisiting illegitimacy in the Philippines and arguing for declassification of illegitimate children as a statutory class. Phil Law J 83(3):467–538

Ponce de Leon M (2018) Of half-bloods and street dogs, Arnold Clavio vs. the Azkals: discourses and definitions of national identity. Sport Soc 21(9):1302–1318

Rehal S (2020) Shifting the 'White Gaze' on Black bodies in Philippine collegiate basketball. Soc Transform J Glob S 8(2):125–156

Resurreccion E (2016) Charting the waters of constitutional construction: a function-based framework for appreciating our constitutional state policies. Phil Law J 90(1):1–83

Webster T (2007) Mcgowan v. narita. Aust J Asian Law 9(2):346–364

Webster T (2008) Reconstituting Japanese law: international norms and domestic litigation. Mich J Int Law 30(1):211–250

Webster T (2010) International human rights law in Japan: the view at thirty. Colum J Asian Law 23(2):241–268

Joseph Benjamin B. De Leon is a legal associate of Cignal TV, Inc., the leading pay TV and sports broadcaster in the Philippines, where his responsibilities include handling the company's sports, entertainment, and intellectual property matters.

Job previously lectured at the University of Muntinlupa and the University of the Philippines College of Law. After his admission to the bar in 2019, Job joined the law firm of Gatmaytan Yap Patacsil Gutierrez & Protacio where he focused on employment law, dispute resolution and arbitration. He obtained his juris doctor degree from UP Law in 2018, where he served as an associate editor of the Philippine Law Journal (Volume 90). Prior to his law practice, Job covered the basketball beat for GMA News Online.

Respecting the Right to Nationality in International Sport

William Thomas Worster

Contents

Abstract International sports pledge to eradicate discriminatory practices, yet paradoxically continue to support discrimination on the grounds of nationality. Athletes compete as part of a national team. This requires sporting associations and the International Olympic Committee (IOC) to make distinctions among athletes merely on the grounds of nationality. The Olympic Charter does this. Because of this need to make nationality distinctions, those associations must also develop nationality rules. These rules force choices of nationality and place restrictions on the ability to compete for the new national team. When athletes wish to change nationality, they risk falling into a nationality limbo, where they cannot compete, for lack of a sports nationality.

In contrast to international sporting rules and the Olympic Charter, international human rights law takes a different approach to nationality as a human right. Every

W. T. Worster (✉)
The Hague University of Applied Sciences, The Hague, The Netherlands
e-mail: w.t.worster@hhs.nl

V. Boillet et al. (eds.), *Sports and Human Rights*, Interdisciplinary Studies in Human Rights 10, https://doi.org/10.1007/978-3-031-56452-9_7

individual has a right to a nationality. This nationality is often the source of other rights, such as political participation, employment and education. In addition, this right includes the right to change nationality. However, the IOC limits recognizing nationality changes. The result is that athletes who do not satisfy nationality rules can be deemed *de facto* stateless for sport, even though the creation of statelessness is largely prohibited. For these reasons, IOC rules on change of nationality do not live up to the Committee's own human rights aspirations and the Olympic Charter must be amended to respect the rights to nationality.

1 Introduction

International sports are not in compliance with international human rights law in regards to nationality. This is exemplified by the Olympic Games, which are entirely structured around the concept of nationality, both ceremonially and substantially. Olympic athletes must be members of a National Olympic Committee (NOC), in addition to the relevant International Sports Federation (IF) governing their particular sport (e.g., the International Tennis Federation (ITF)). In order to join an NOC, each athlete must have the nationality of the state with which the NOC is affiliated. Athletes then compete on the basis of nationality, generally on teams composed entirely of co-nationals; should they win a medal, they do so in the name of the state and its NOC. If an athlete possesses more than one nationality, or loses their nationality to acquire another, then the NOC faces a challenge, since changes to nationality require changes to NOC membership. In order to provide for orderly transitions, the Olympic Charter includes rules related to changes of nationality. However, these rules do not fully respect international human rights on nationality.

As a whole, states have significant freedom to prescribe rules on nationality; international law covers the right to have, acquire, and change nationality, as well as rights against discrimination on the basis of nationality or national origin. While there is no particular right to possess multiple nationalities, there is a right to one nationality, and states cannot render individuals stateless. States can, however, refuse to respect grants of nationality from other states, as expressed in the famous *Nottebohm* case at the International Court of Justice (ICJ), although the actual application of *Nottebohm* is not as broad as often claimed. As such, states are limited in their ability to refuse nationality, except for situations of multiple nationality, where there are stronger connections to one state compared to another. Beyond this narrow exception, states must respect the individual's freedom to change their nationality. States are permitted to make some distinctions among individuals based on nationality, but again, those situations are very limited. In all of these situations, when states propose to withdraw nationality, curtail nationality changes, or make nationality distinctions, they must act only to achieve legitimate aims through proportionate measures.

International law on nationality applicable to states stands in partial opposition to nationality rules at the Olympics. For one, the Olympics classifies athletes by nationality, yet nationality discrimination is prohibited by international law. The

Olympics also limits the ability to change nationality, yet changing nationality is a protected right and treating athletes on the basis of former nationality implicates discrimination on the basis of national origin. Athletes also face the assimilation of dual nationality to nationality change, ignoring which state has stronger connections. During the lengthy process of nationality change, the Olympics can treat an athlete as if they were stateless, which is forbidden by international law. The question, then, is whether the Olympics has any underlying justification for these measures that can pass scrutiny. While several justifications can be identified, they are surprisingly weak, and the blanket nationality rules are far too broad to support them. Therefore, nationality rules at the Olympics constitute a violation of international human rights.

This is perhaps a surprising thesis given that the International Olympic Committee (IOC) claims to respect and protect human rights. The Olympic Charter and other Olympic documents contain language that strongly rejects discrimination on numerous grounds. Yet the problematic rules on nationality, as the basic organizing principle of the Olympics and international competition, tend to go unnoticed. One can imagine the international uproar were the Olympic Charter to discourage freedom of thought or bodily integrity. Nationality should be no less protected as a fundamental human right. This chapter suggests an amendment to the Olympic Charter that would abolish the nationality classification scheme or at least permit a freer change of nationality, thus avoiding the creation of *de facto* statelessness.

Throughout this chapter, it is assumed that international legal standards, such as those enshrined in the International Covenant on Civil and Political Rights (ICCPR) and other human rights instruments, constitute the relevant standard. This chapter will not analyze whether the IOC is formally bound to follow human rights law in a manner comparable to states, resulting in responsibility. The Court of Arbitration for Sport (CAS) has determined that international human rights law on nationality is applicable to sports, unless otherwise specified.[1] For example, the CAS has applied international law on nationality to determine whether an athlete is stateless, in spite of the views of the IOC and NOC.[2] Ultimately, CAS decisions on sport arbitration fall under the jurisdiction of the European Court of Human Rights due to Switzerland's judicial oversight. This chapter argues that the Olympics should at least follow the spirit of international human rights since the IOC has pledged to comply with these standards.[3] However, for the sake of clarity in the analysis, the chapter will apply human rights law to the actions of the IOC, in a manner similar to how human rights would apply to a state, as if the IOC were formally bound. As such, the chapter will describe the nationality classification system and the rules on election and change of nationality; it will clarify the law on nationality-based discrimination, the right to a nationality, and the right to change nationality,

[1] See CAS 94/132 Puerto Rico Amateur Baseball Federation (PRABF)/USA Baseball (USAB) [in re C.], 15 March 1996.

[2] See CAS 00/005 Perez/International Olympic Committee (IOC), 19 September 2000, paras. 19, 27.

[3] See Zeid and Davis (2020), pp. 12, 20–21.

following *Nottebohm* and other recent case law from the ICJ, CAS, and other authorities. Because of the partial overlap between nationality-based discrimination and national origin discrimination, it will also clarify this distinction. Finally, it will note where Olympic practices deviate from international law, critique those practices, and recommend changes to bring those practices into compliance.

The structure of the chapter proceeds as follows. After the introduction, Sect. 2 identifies and critiques the nationality classification system at the Olympics. Section 3 compares multiple nationality and change of nationality rules under international law and the rules of the Olympics. Having concluded in those sections that the Olympics violates international human rights standards, Sect. 4 tests whether those nationality rules can nonetheless be justified as proportionate to legitimate aims. The final section concludes with recommendations for changes to the rules and practices of the Olympics.

2 Classification on the Basis of Nationality

At its core, the Olympic Games maintain a discriminatory regime on the basis of nationality categorization. The IOC argues that it is autonomous[4] and independent[5] from state governments, and while it cooperates with them, it maintains it is politically neutral.[6] But there is one area where this independence and neutrality does not apply: nationality. The IOC encourages and enforces laws from state governments regarding nationality and fundamentally supports the current political world order that separates people into states by nationality. An athlete must fall into some state citizenship classification category in order to compete, and if they do not, they may be excluded. In the rare situation that an athlete is permitted to compete as stateless, their participation is nonetheless still classified by their exclusion from the state citizenship scheme. Peter Spiro has argued forcefully for the end of the use of nationality in the Olympics based on the increasingly widespread adoption of dual nationality laws, the realities of athletes' international life, and the arbitrariness inherent in the nationality system.[7] This section argues that, in addition to these considerations, the nationality system in international sport is potentially discriminatory and contrary to contemporary human rights law.

[4] See International Olympic Committee, Olympic Charter, 2021, Fundamental Principles of Olympism, para. 5; International Olympic Committee, [Code of] Ethics, January 2022, art. 1, https://stillmedab.olympic.org/media/Document%20Library/OlympicOrg/Documents/Code-of-Ethics/Code-of-Ethics-ENG.pdf#page=14&_ga=2.159102330.1177896064.1618845860-971153820.1601050134.

[5] See International Olympic Committee, Olympic Charter, 2021, Rule 2 Mission and role of the IOC.

[6] See International Olympic Committee, Olympic Charter, 2021, Rule 2 Mission and role of the IOC.

[7] See generally Spiro (2012), p. 6.

2.1 The Nationality Classification System in International Sport

According to the Olympic Charter, athletes may only participate if they meet certain qualifications: they must respect the Olympic Charter;[8] they must have a nationality that has an NOC;[9] and their nationality must be from a state recognized by the international community. The Charter states that a "country" is a state recognized by the international community[10] in alignment with the recognized name and territory of that state.[11] It is doubtful that this latter requirement is still applied with such strict rigor,[12] as the CAS has held that Puerto Rico was a valid nationality for participation,[13] and Taiwan has been permitted to participate as "Chinese Taipei" on several occasions,[14] even though neither is recognized as a 'state' by the international community. Nevertheless, these unusual situations still largely follow the general intent of the rule that an athlete must participate in a category of some territorial-based, political, quasi-state entity.

In addition, even if an athlete has a qualifying nationality, they must also comply with potentially more burdensome qualification criteria of their respective NOC[15] and IF.[16] These requirements are strange, considering the fact that the Charter declares the NOC only serves the purpose of selecting athletes to compete in the

[8] See International Olympic Committee, Olympic Charter, 2021, Rule 40 Participation in the Olympic Games.

[9] See International Olympic Committee, Olympic Charter, 2021, Rule 41 Nationality of competitors, para. 1. Also see CAS 98/209 Spanish Basketball Federation/FIBA [in re Zassoulskaia], 6 January 1999, para. 8 (regarding the comparable FIBA rules).

[10] See International Olympic Committee, Olympic Charter, 2021, Rule 30 Country and name of an NOC, para. 1.

[11] See International Olympic Committee, Olympic Charter, 2021, Rule 30 Country and name of an NOC, para. 2.

[12] *See* CAS 2014/A/3776 Gibraltar Football Association (GFA) v. Fédération Internationale de Football Association (FIFA), 27 April 2016, paras. 298–299, 301, 307. Also see Court of Appeal, England and Wales, Reel v. Holder and another, [1981] 1 WLR 1226 (26 June 1981) (interpreting the meaning of "country" under International Amateur Athletic Federation rules as territory over which there is authority, not necessarily the same as the meaning of state or nation).

[13] *See* CAS 94/132 Puerto Rico Amateur Baseball Federation (PRABF)/USA Baseball (USAB) [in re C.], 15 March 1996.

[14] *See* International Olympic Committee, "Chinese Taipei," https://olympics.com/ioc/chinese-taipei.

[15] See International Olympic Committee, Olympic Charter, 2021, Rule 40 Participation in the Olympic Games.

[16] See International Olympic Committee, Olympic Charter, 2021, Rule 40 Participation in the Olympic Games, Bye-Law to Rule 40, para. 1; CAS 2001/A/357 Nabokov & Russian Olympic Committee (ROC) & Russian Ice Hockey Federation (RIHF)/International Ice Hockey Federation (IIHF), 31 January 2002, paras. 18–19.

Olympics,[17] as well as promoting the Olympics in their country,[18] and that IFs are only meant to contribute "technical direction" to competition.[19] Although in other contexts, the Charter declares that NOCs "represent . . . their respective countries at the Olympic Games".[20] In any event, every athlete must be qualified by having a nationality, and the Charter permits distinctions between athletes on the basis of their nationality.

The IOC has shown that these rules on nationality can be applied flexibly. For example, while the Charter is quite clear that an athlete must have nationality in a recognized state, represented by a NOC, non-state entities have been admitted as NOCs, and the IOC has just recently permitted a new non-state "Refugee Team".[21] However, the Refugee Team includes participating athletes who have a nationality *de jure* but whose state and/or NOC will not support or protect them.[22] This concept is quite distinct from a truly stateless person who is lacking any nationality *de jure*.[23] Nonetheless, the entire system of the Olympic Games is based on a structure where nationality, or lack thereof, is the central organizing principle, rather than purely individual competitiveness in sport.

2.2 The Prohibition of Discrimination on the Basis of Nationality

This system of classifying and qualifying athletes by nationality creates and supports a system of discrimination; specifically, discrimination on the basis of nationality, and potentially also on the basis of national origin. In its numerous documents, the IOC repeatedly affirms that it prohibits discrimination "of any kind" without limitation.[24] Examples are provided regarding the kinds of discrimination that is

[17] See International Olympic Committee, Olympic Charter, 2021, Rule 6 Olympic Games, para. 1.

[18] See International Olympic Committee, Olympic Charter, 2021, Rule 27 Mission and role of the NOCs, para. 1.

[19] See International Olympic Committee, Olympic Charter, 2021, Rule 6 Olympic Games, para. 1.

[20] See International Olympic Committee, Olympic Charter, 2021, Rule 27 Mission and role of the NOCs, para. 3.

[21] See International Olympic Committee, IOC Refugee Olympic Team Tokyo 2020, https://olympics.com/ioc/refugee-olympic-team-tokyo-2020.

[22] See International Olympic Committee, IOC Refugee Olympic Team Tokyo 2020, https://olympics.com/ioc/refugee-olympic-team-tokyo-2020.

[23] See CAS 00/005 Perez/International Olympic Committee (IOC), 19 September 2000, paras. 19–20, 27.

[24] See International Olympic Committee, Olympic Charter, 2021, Fundamental Principles of Olympism, paras. 4, 6. Also see UN Educational, Scientific and Cultural Organization, "International Charter of Physical Education, Physical Activity and Sport," UN Doc. SHS/2015/PI/H/14 REV (2015), https://unesdoc.unesco.org/ark:/48223/pf0000235409, preamble, para. 2, art. 1.1.

prohibited, including "race, colour, sex, sexual orientation";[25] discrimination on the basis of "national origin"[26] any "other status",[27] is also explicitly prohibited. The IOC maintains that sport is a "human right"[28] and conducted for the benefit of "humankind,"[29] not for the states concerned.[30] With that said, the Charter appears to narrow this absolute prohibition to "discrimination affecting the Olympic Movement",[31] suggesting that the forms of prohibited discrimination must have some bearing on the conduct of international sport.

The UNESCO International Charter of Physical Education, Physical Activity and Sport permits only one kind of discrimination: on the basis of sporting ability.[32] Indeed, this is a form of meritocratic discrimination that is defensible in the context of sport and, as such, could be the only form of discrimination that is inherently necessary for the purpose of the Olympic Movement.[33] However, given that the Olympic Charter simultaneously prescribes distinctions on the basis of nationality, it is difficult to imagine that the Charter can prohibit nationality-based discrimination. There are other sources of international human rights law that do prohibit nationality discrimination. Both nationality and national origin discrimination are addressed by a number of international human rights treaties; many cover "national origin" explicitly, some include "nationality,"[34] and others have been interpreted to cover nationality, though they might only specify national origin and/or "other status".[35] In addition, there is a

---

[25] See International Olympic Committee, Olympic Charter, 2021, Fundamental Principles of Olympism, para. 6.

[26] See International Olympic Committee, Olympic Charter, 2021, Fundamental Principles of Olympism. Also see UN Educational, Scientific and Cultural Organization, "International Charter of Physical Education, Physical Activity and Sport," UN Doc. SHS/2015/PI/H/14 REV (2015), https://unesdoc.unesco.org/ark:/48223/pf0000235409, preamble, para. 2, art. 1.1.

[27] See International Olympic Committee, Olympic Charter, 2021, Fundamental Principles of Olympism, para. 6. Also see UN Educational, Scientific and Cultural Organization, "International Charter of Physical Education, Physical Activity and Sport," UN Doc. SHS/2015/PI/H/14 REV (2015), https://unesdoc.unesco.org/ark:/48223/pf0000235409, preamble, para. 2, art. 1.1.

[28] See International Olympic Committee, Olympic Charter, 2021, Fundamental Principles of Olympism, para. 4.

[29] See International Olympic Committee, Olympic Charter, 2021, Fundamental Principles of Olympism, para. 2.

[30] See International Olympic Committee, Olympic Charter, 2021, Rule 6 Olympic Games, para. 1.

[31] See International Olympic Committee, Olympic Charter, 2021, Rule 2 Mission and role of the IOC.

[32] See UN Educational, Scientific and Cultural Organization, "International Charter of Physical Education, Physical Activity and Sport," UN Doc. SHS/2015/PI/H/14 REV (2015), https://unesdoc.unesco.org/ark:/48223/pf0000235409, art. 1.6.

[33] See International Olympic Committee, Olympic Charter, 2021, Rule 2 Mission and role of the IOC, para. 6.

[34] *See* International Convention on the Protection of the Rights of All Migrant Workers and Members of Their Families, UNGA Res. 45/158 (18 December 1990), 2220 UNTS 3, arts. 1(1), 7.

[35] See e.g. Human Rights Committee, Gueye et al. v France, Comm No. 196/1985 (3 April 1989) para. 9.4 interpreting the International Covenant on Civil and Political Rights, Dec. 16, 1966, 999 UNTS 171.

nuanced distinction between discrimination by a state against foreigners, and discrimination between foreigners who possess nationalities of different states.[36] Because the IOC is not a state, and it is impossible for it to discriminate between citizens and non-citizens, this section will only address discrimination among nationalities. As is apparent in the interpretation of the following treaties, nationality-based discrimination is implicit in virtually any anti-discrimination regime.

The ICCPR, much like the Olympic Charter, prohibits "discrimination of any kind", listing the protected grounds of "race, colour, sex, language, religion, political or other opinion, national or social origin, property, birth or other status".[37] In Article 26, on the right to equality before the law, the above list of protected grounds is referenced, and it states that this protection applies to "any discrimination" against "all persons".[38] However, in Article 13, on expulsion, and Article 25, on civil and political participation, the ICCPR refers to "citizens" and "alien[s]" as distinct categories,[39] so it can be understood that the Covenant provides an exemption to the usual rule against discrimination, including on the basis of nationality. The UN Human Rights Committee has concluded that the rights in the ICCPR apply to persons regardless of nationality.[40] Thus, any such distinctions that invoke nationality would need to be justified as legitimate and proportionate.[41]

The International Covenant on Economic, Social and Cultural Rights (ICESCR) contains the same language as the ICCPR, prohibiting "discrimination of any kind" against persons on the basis of various characteristics or "other status".[42] This instrument, considering its content, prohibits nationality discrimination with only one exception,[43] demonstrating that discrimination on the basis of nationality was otherwise prohibited. The Committee on Economic, Social and Cultural Rights has stated that the ICESCR prohibits discrimination on the basis of nationality.[44]

---

[36] See generally Worster (2022a).

[37] See International Covenant on Civil and Political Rights, Dec. 16, 1966, 999 UNTS 171, arts. 2(2).

[38] See International Covenant on Civil and Political Rights, Dec. 16, 1966, 999 UNTS 171, art. 26.

[39] See International Covenant on Civil and Political Rights, Dec. 16, 1966, 999 UNTS 171, arts. 13, 25. Also see Human Rights Committee, General Comment 15: The Position of Aliens Under the Covenant (1986), paras. 5–7; Human Rights Committee, A v. Australia, Comm No. 560/1993 (30 April 1997), paras. 9.3–9.4.

[40] See Human Rights Committee, General Comment 15: The Position of Aliens Under the Covenant (1986), para. 7; Human Rights Committee, Sipin v Estonia, Comm No 1432/2005 (9 July 2008), para. 7.2; Human Rights Committee, Gueye et al. v France, Comm 196/1985 (3 April 1989), paras. 9.4–9.5.

[41] See Human Rights Committee, General Comment 15: The Position of Aliens Under the Covenant (1986), paras. 7.5, 8.

[42] See International Covenant on Economic, Social and Cultural Rights, 16 December 1966, 999 UNTS 3, art. 2(2).

[43] See International Covenant on Economic, Social and Cultural Rights, 16 December 1966, 999 UNTS 3, art. 2(3); Chetail (2019), p. 160.

[44] See Committee on Economic, Social and Cultural Rights, General Comment 20: Non-discrimination in economic, social and cultural rights (art. 2, para. 2) (May 2009), para. 30.

Both the European Convention on Human Rights (ECHR) and American Convention on Human Rights (ACHR) prohibit nationality discrimination. The ECHR covers "everyone",[45] and prohibits discrimination on various grounds "such as" sex, race, and so on, including "national or social origin" and "other status".[46] In a few areas, it permits nationality discrimination.[47] The ECHR notes that these are deviations from the general rule prohibiting nationality discrimination,[48] and has been interpreted to prohibit nationality discrimination insofar as such treatment also infringes on an individual's right to their identity.[49] Thus, measures that discriminate on the basis of nationality must be justified[50] and only "very weighty reasons" would suffice.[51] For example, discrimination between EU and non-EU citizens for purposes of deportation law was justifiable,[52] but nationality discrimination for social security benefits was not.[53]

The ACHR also protects individuals from nationality discrimination. It covers "all persons ... without any discrimination" on the grounds of "race, color, sex, language, religion, political or other opinion, national or social origin, economic status, birth, or any other social condition".[54] Although it does not use the phrase "such as", it does include "any other social condition".[55] The ACHR refers to nationality in several places, with some of the references more aligned with national origin,[56] and others with citizenship (such as the "right to a nationality").[57] By its

[45] See [European] Convention for the Protection of Human Rights and Fundamental Freedoms, 4 November 1950, 213 UNTS 222, CETS. No. 5.

[46] See [European] Convention for the Protection of Human Rights and Fundamental Freedoms, 4 November 1950, 213 UNTS 222, CETS. No. 5, art. 14.

[47] See [European] Convention for the Protection of Human Rights and Fundamental Freedoms, 4 November 1950, 213 UNTS 222, CETS. No. 5, art. 16.

[48] See [European] Convention for the Protection of Human Rights and Fundamental Freedoms, 4 November 1950, 213 UNTS 222, CETS. No. 5, art. 16; ECtHR, Bah v UK, 27.09.2011, § 45; ECtHR, Koua Poirrez v France, 30.12.2003, §§ 36–42; ECtHR, Gaygusuz v Austria, 16.09.1996, § 43.

[49] See e.g. ECtHR, Mennesson v France, 26.06.2014, §§ 97–99.

[50] See ECtHR, Koua Poirrez v France, 30.12.2003, §§ 36–42; ECtHR, Gaygusuz v Austria, 16.09.1996, § 42.

[51] See ECtHR, Gaygusuz v Austria, 16.09.1996, § 42; ECtHR, Andrejeva v Latvia, 18.12.2009, § 87.

[52] See ECtHR, C v Belgium, 07.08.1996, §§ 37–38.

[53] See ECtHR, Koua Poirrez v France, 30.12.2003, §§ 38–39.

[54] See American Convention on Human Rights, 22 November 1969, 1144 UNTS 123, OASTS No. 36, art. 1(1).

[55] See American Convention on Human Rights, 22 November 1969, 1144 UNTS 123, OASTS No. 36, art. 1(1).

[56] See American Convention on Human Rights, 22 November 1969, 1144 UNTS 123, OASTS No. 36, arts. 13(5), 22(8).

[57] See American Convention on Human Rights, 22 November 1969, 1144 UNTS 123, OASTS No. 36, arts. 20(1)–(3), 22(5)–(6).

terms, few rights may be limited on the basis of nationality,[58] and the instrument is understood to generally prohibit nationality discrimination.[59] The Inter-American Court of Human Rights has upheld this protection, demanding that distinctions on the basis of nationality be legitimate and proportionate,[60] although some measures may survive this scrutiny.[61]

The Convention on the Elimination of All Forms of Racial Discrimination (CERD) also covers nationality discrimination, though this coverage has recently been challenged by the International Court of Justice (ICJ).[62] The CERD largely follows the format of the other treaties, prohibiting "any distinction, exclusion, restriction or preference based on race, colour, descent, or national or ethnic origin".[63] However, it also exempts "distinctions ... between citizens and noncitizens",[64] which led the ICJ to conclude that the CERD does not cover discrimination on the basis of nationality.[65] While other tribunals have determined that "national origin" in other treaties can mean the same thing as "nationality",[66] the ICJ took the position that the CERD did not consider such a definition.[67] This interpretation was met with discomfort by the CERD Committee, because it held that nationality discrimination was clearly covered by the CERD.[68] The ICJ did, however, agree

[58] See American Convention on Human Rights, 22 November 1969, 1144 UNTS 123, OASTS No. 36, art. 23(1)(a)–(c); Inter-American Court of Human Rights, Juridical Conditions and Rights of the Undocumented Migrants, OC-18/03 (17 September 2003), paras. 118–119, 135.

[59] See Inter-American Court of Human Rights, Juridical Conditions and Rights of the Undocumented Migrants, OC-18/03 (17 September 2003), paras. 118–124, 133, 136.

[60] See Inter-American Court of Human Rights, Juridical Conditions and Rights of the Undocumented Migrants, OC-18/03 (17 September 2003), para. 118.

[61] See Inter-American Court of Human Rights, Juridical Conditions and Rights of the Undocumented Migrants, OC-18/03 (17 September 2003), paras. 85, 89; Inter-American Court of Human Rights, Proposed Amendments to the Naturalization Provisions of the Constitution of Costa Rica, OC-4/84 (19 January 1984), paras. 52, 57–61.

[62] See generally Worster (2022a, b).

[63] See International Convention on the Elimination of All Forms of Racial Discrimination, UN GA Res. 2106 (XX) (21 December 1965), 660 UNTS 195, art. 1.

[64] See International Convention on the Elimination of All Forms of Racial Discrimination, UN GA Res. 2106 (XX) (21 December 1965), 660 UNTS 195, art. 1(2).

[65] See International Court of Justice, Application of the International Convention on the International Convention on the Elimination of All Forms of Racial Discrimination (Qatar v UAE), Preliminary Objections, Judgment, 2021 ICJ Reps 71, paras. 83–97.

[66] See International Criminal Tribunal for Rwanda, Prosecutor v Akayesu, Case No. ICTR-96-4-T, Judgment (2 September 1998), paras. 510–511.

[67] See International Court of Justice, Application of the International Convention on the International Convention on the Elimination of All Forms of Racial Discrimination (Qatar v UAE), Preliminary Objections, Judgment, 2021 ICJ Reps 71, paras. 83–97.

[68] See International Convention on the Elimination of All Forms of Racial Discrimination, UN GA Res. 2106 (XX) (21 December 1965), 660 UNTS 195, preamble, art. 1(2); Committee on the Elimination of Racial Discrimination, General Recommendation XXX on discrimination against non-citizens (2005), para. 3.

that the CERD prohibits national origin discrimination, which it viewed as an immutable characteristic of descent and heritage acquired at birth,[69] as opposed to nationality or citizenship which was changeable.[70]

All of the treaties discussed in this section cover national origin, and most cover nationality, with the single exception being the contested interpretation of the CERD. Nationality discrimination is well founded in international human rights law and derogations must be legitimate and proportionate. Insofar as the IOC has pledged to comply with human rights, including protection from nationality-based discrimination, its engagement with human rights and anti-discrimination must cover nationality-based discrimination. The only question that remains is whether those nationality-based measures can be justified. Before assessing nationality discrimination for proportionality, the next section will consider other nationality issues that arise under human rights law.

3 Multiple Nationalities and Change of Nationality

Based on the general issue of classification, and thus discrimination, on the basis of nationality, the Olympic Charter also includes rules on change of nationality and dual nationality to enforce the nationality system. In international competition, an athlete is treated as having one nationality.[71] The rules on holding a single "sport nationality" at a time have been adopted in turn by NOCs and IFs.[72] As such, under IF rules an athlete could have a "football nationality,"[73] a "basketball nationality,"[74] an "ice hockey nationality"[75] or a "swimming nationality".[76] This rule is only necessary because the Olympics is organized by nationality; a different structure

[69] See International Court of Justice, Application of the International Convention on the International Convention on the Elimination of All Forms of Racial Discrimination (Qatar v UAE), Preliminary Objections, Judgment, 2021 ICJ Reps 71, para. 81.

[70] See International Court of Justice, Application of the International Convention on the International Convention on the Elimination of All Forms of Racial Discrimination (Qatar v UAE), Preliminary Objections, Judgment, 2021 ICJ Reps 71, para. 81.

[71] See generally CAS 94/132 Puerto Rico Amateur Baseball Federation (PRABF)/USA Baseball (USAB) [in re C.], 15 March 1996.

[72] See CAS 92/80 B./Fédération Internationale de Basketball (FIBA), 25 March 1993, para. 13; CAS 98/215, International Baseball Association (IBA), 4 January 1999, para. 17.

[73] See CAS 2010/A/2071, Irish Football Association (IFA) v. Football Association of Ireland (FAI), Kearns & Fédération Internationale de Football Association (FIFA), 27 September 2010.

[74] See CAS 98/209 Spanish Basketball Federation/FIBA [in re Zassoulskaia], 6 January 1999, para. 8; CAS 94/123, Fédération Internationale de Basketball (FIBA)/W. & Brandt Hagen e. V., 12 September 1994.

[75] See CAS 2001/A/357 Nabokov & Russian Olympic Committee (ROC) & Russian Ice Hockey Federation (RIHF)/International Ice Hockey Federation (IIHF), 31 January 2002.

[76] See CAS 08/002, Simms v. Fédération Internationale de Natation (FINA), 1 August 2008.

would render nationality, change of nationality, dual nationality and even no nationality, as concepts only relevant for the administrative purpose of securing visas. The CAS has declined to explain the precise relationship between nationality and sports nationality.[77] While it has acknowledged that the concepts of nationality and citizenship have a nuanced distinction in international law,[78] it has failed to make this distinction in the realm of international sports.

3.1 Election and Change of Nationality Rules

As some athletes discover, the Olympic Charter takes no view on changing nationality under domestic law but may place restrictions on the athlete's ability to compete for the new national team. First, the individual would need to have the nationality of the relevant state under domestic laws. The CAS has repeatedly determined that domestic laws on nationality cannot be reviewed,[79] though it has examined the application of domestic nationality laws to determine whether an individual qualifies as a national.[80] In short, international sport will look to a state's laws for determining nationality.[81] Even when states discriminate between nationals who acquired nationality by birth or by naturalization—a distinction generally avoided by human rights law[82]—the CAS has recognized the independence of the state to prescribe nationality laws.[83]

Second, if an athlete has the nationality of the state, then the next question is whether they have the "sports nationality" sufficient to be selected by an NOC for competition. The CAS has ruled that sports nationality need not directly follow from nationality in a state.[84] As for cases of multiple nationality, the Olympic Charter states that the athlete must select one nationality for competition; should they wish to change to another nationality in a future competition, they must comply with the

[77] See CAS 08/002, Simms v. Fédération Internationale de Natation (FINA), 1 August 2008, 9.

[78] See CAS 00/003, Miranda/International Olympic Committee (IOC), 13 September 2000, para. 21; CAS 94/132 Puerto Rico Amateur Baseball Federation (PRABF)/USA Baseball (USAB) [in re C.], 15 March 1996, 6.

[79] See CAS 00/001, United States Olympic Committee (USOC) and USA Canoe/Kayak/International Olympic Committee (IOC) [in re Perez], 13 September 2000, para. 11; CAS 94/132 Puerto Rico Amateur Baseball Federation (PRABF)/USA Baseball (USAB) [in re C.], 15 March 1996.

[80] See CAS 00/001, United States Olympic Committee (USOC) and USA Canoe/Kayak/International Olympic Committee (IOC) [in re Perez], 13 September 2000, paras. 10, 15.

[81] See CAS 00/001, United States Olympic Committee (USOC) and USA Canoe/Kayak/International Olympic Committee (IOC) [in re Perez], 13 September 2000, para. 14.

[82] See Inter-American Court of Human Rights, Proposed Amendments to the Naturalization Provisions of the Constitution of Costa Rica, OC-4/84 (19 January 1984), para. 62.

[83] See CAS A2/2016, Lim v. Synchronised Swimming Australia Inc. (SSAI), 5 July 2016, para. 86.

[84] See e.g. CAS 92/80 B./Fédération Internationale de Basketball (FIBA), 25 March 1993, paras. 3, 14.

same change of nationality rules that apply to situations where an athlete has acquired a new nationality and lost a previous one.[85] If an athlete has ever competed for a national team, then they are prohibited from competing for the new national team for 3 years.[86] While the CAS has previously shown flexibility in interpreting the term "nationality"[87] and "change",[88] it has concluded that the 3-year waiting period rule is "clear"[89] and "straightforward",[90] leaving little room for ambiguity. By comparison, under *Fédération internationale de football association* (FIFA) rules, the first election of nationality can be tested by registration with a club,[91] and cannot be reversed without showing bad faith in the initial registration.[92] The FIFA test has not been applied by to the Olympics, so it may not be possible to reverse an election of nationality to circumvent the 3-year ban.

In addition to the 3-year wait, other rules may restrict a change in sports nationality. In some cases, the 3-year period can vary; for example, if the state granting the naturalization had any delay in processing.[93] The IF might also have more onerous nationality rules,[94] distinguishing between particular forms of nationality acquisition the federation views as legitimate. While applying the *Fédération Internationale de Basketball* (FIBA) rules, the CAS ruled against automatically designating a person as having a sports nationality based on place of birth, regardless of whether the athlete has competed for the national team.[95] It has previously upheld nationality rules limiting nationality qualification to the traditional means of *jus soli*,

[85] See International Olympic Committee, Olympic Charter, 2021, Rule 41, Bye-law to Rule 41, para. 1. Note that some nationality regimes contemplate a "shared nationality" and may have slightly differing application, see e.g. CAS 2010/A/2071, Irish Football Association (IFA) v. Football Association of Ireland (FAI), Kearns & Fédération Internationale de Football Association (FIFA), 27 September 2010 (22 July 2010), paras. 48, 51.

[86] See International Olympic Committee, Olympic Charter, 2021, Rule 41, Bye-law to Rule 41, para. 2.

[87] See CAS 00/005 Perez/International Olympic Committee (IOC), 19 September 2000, para. 27.

[88] See CAS 00/005 Perez/International Olympic Committee (IOC), 19 September 2000, para. 32.

[89] See CAS 00/003, Miranda/International Olympic Committee (IOC), 13 September 2000, para. 18; CAS 00/001, United States Olympic Committee (USOC) and USA Canoe/Kayak/International Olympic Committee (IOC) [in re Perez], 13 September 2000, para. 26.

[90] See CAS 00/001, United States Olympic Committee (USOC) and USA Canoe/Kayak/International Olympic Committee (IOC) [in re Perez], 13 September 2000, para. 26.

[91] See CAS 2020/A/6933, Faure v. Al Salam Zgharta Club & Fédération Internationale de Football Association (FIFA), 26 January 2021, para. 16.

[92] See CAS 2020/A/6933, Faure v. Al Salam Zgharta Club & Fédération Internationale de Football Association (FIFA), 26 January 2021, para. 66.

[93] See CAS A2/2016, Lim v. Synchronised Swimming Australia Inc. (SSAI), 5 July 2016, paras. 123–125.

[94] See CAS 2001/A/357 Nabokov & Russian Olympic Committee (ROC) & Russian Ice Hockey Federation (RIHF)/International Ice Hockey Federation (IIHF), 31 January 2002, paras. 18–19.

[95] See CAS 94/123, Fédération Internationale de Basketball (FIBA)/W. & Brandt Hagen e. V., 12 September 1994, paras. 20–22.

jus sanguinis, and "[s]ome other exceptional legal concept".[96] In addition, the CAS upheld an IF demanding that an athlete reside for a certain period of time in the state in order to claim its nationality.[97]

The 3-year waiting period can be reduced in two particular situations. One option is for a waiver of the rule by exclusive discretion of the IOC,[98] with the agreement of the relevant IFs and NOCs.[99] The CAS has confirmed that the refusal of those bodies to agree is not reviewable by any authority. The IOC does not produce statistics on the agreement of IFs and NOCs, so the actual possibility of such a waiver, based on historical data, is unclear. The only other exception is that the 3-year waiting period does not apply in the case of states acquiring independence. In these cases, the athlete may choose, and only choose once, which national team to join, either the prior state or the newly independent state, and skip the waiting period.[100] Any subsequent decision to change nationality will result in the 3-year waiting period under the normal rules on changing nationality.

This system means that an athlete who has lost their nationality and acquired a new one, cannot compete for the prior team because they no longer have that state's nationality, and cannot compete for the new team unless they wait 3 years. Effectively, the athlete is 'stateless' for the purpose of sport. Although the person might hold *de jure* nationality in relation to the state, the individual cannot exercise one of the benefits of having a nationality: the ability to compete under that state's flag.

3.2 *The Right to a Nationality*

Nationality is widely protected under a range of sources of international human rights law, and the interpretation of that law informs the IOC of the practices it should adopt. Most major human rights instrument provide for the right to a nationality, including the ICCPR,[101] CERD,[102] the Convention on the Elimination

---

[96] See CAS 94/123, Fédération Internationale de Basketball (FIBA)/W. & Brandt Hagen e. V., 12 September 1994, para. 15.

[97] See CAS 2010/A/2071, Irish Football Association (IFA) v. Football Association of Ireland (FAI), Kearns & Fédération Internationale de Football Association (FIFA), 27 September 2010 (22 July 2010), para. 19.

[98] See International Olympic Committee, Olympic Charter, 2021, Rule 41, Bye-law to Rule 41, para. 4.

[99] See International Olympic Committee, Olympic Charter, 2021, Rule 41, Bye-law to Rule 41, para. 2.

[100] See International Olympic Committee, Olympic Charter, 2021, Rule 41, Bye-law to Rule 41, para. 3.

[101] See International Covenant on Civil and Political Rights, 16 December 1966, 999 UNTS 171, art. 24(3).

[102] See International Convention on the Elimination of All Forms of Racial Discrimination, UN GA Res. 2106 (XX) (21 December 1965), 660 UNTS 195, art. 5(d)(iii).

of All Forms of Discrimination Against Women (CEDAW),[103] the International Convention on the Rights of All Migrant Workers (Migrant Workers Convention),[104] and the Convention on the Rights of Persons with Disabilities (Disabilities Convention).[105] This development in the law, providing for a right to a nationality, arose in parallel to the associated movement to abolish statelessness. Several treaties prohibit the creation of statelessness,[106] and the prohibition of statelessness has become a norm of customary international law.[107] Some regional treaties also protect the right to a nationality (e.g., the ACHR).[108] The ECHR does not protect a right to a nationality as such,[109] though protection against statelessness is indirectly protected through other rights in the Convention.[110] More directly, the European Convention on Nationality protects the right to a nationality,[111] although it has fewer parties than the ECHR (21 compared to 46). Similarly, the African Charter on Human and Peoples' Rights does not expressly cover nationality,[112] but has been interpreted

[103] See Convention on the Elimination of Discrimination Against Women, 18 December 1979, 1249 UNTS 13, art. 9; CEDAW General Recommendation No. 21: Equality in Marriage and Family Relations (1994), art. 9.

[104] See International Convention on the Protection of the Rights of All Migrant Workers and Members of Their Families, UNGA Res. 45/158 (18 December 1990), 2220 UNTS 3, art. 29; Human Rights Committee and UN Secretary-General, Human rights and arbitrary deprivation of nationality (19 December 2012).

[105] See Convention on the Rights of Persons with Disabilities, UNGA Res. 61/106 (12 December 2006), 2515 UNTS 3, art. 18.

[106] See Convention on the Reduction of Statelessness, 13 December 1975, 989 UNTS 175, art. 8.

[107] See generally Worster (2019), p. 441.

[108] See American Convention on Human Rights, 22 November 1969, 1144 UNTS 123, OASTS No. 36, art. 20(2); Inter-American Court of Human Rights, Proposed Amendments to the Naturalization Provisions of the Constitution of Costa Rica, OC-4/84 (19 January 1984), paras. 32–35; Inter-American Court of Human Rights, Yean & Bosico Children v. Dominican Republic, Ser. C, Case 130, Judgment (8 September 2005), paras. 140–142, 154–158; Inter-American Court of Human Rights, Castillo Petruzzi et al. Case (30 May 1999), para. 101; Inter-American Court of Human Rights, Bronstein v Peru (6 February 2001), para. 88; Inter-American Court of Human Rights, Case of Expelled Dominicans & Haitians v Dominican Republic, Ser. C No 282 (28 August 2014), paras. 253–264.

[109] See [European] Convention for the Protection of Human Rights and Fundamental Freedoms, 4 November 1950, 213 UNTS 222, CETS. No. 5; ECtHR, Poenaru v. Romania, 13.11.2001; ECtHR, Makuc v Slovenia, 31.05.2007, § 160.

[110] See ECtHR, K2 v UK, 09.03.2017; ECtHR, Labassee v. France, 26.06.2014; ECtHR, Genovese v. Malta, 11.10.2011; ECtHR, Kuric and Others v. Slovenia, 13.07.2010; ECtHR, Ciubotaru v. Moldova, 27.04.2010.

[111] See European Convention on Nationality, 6 November 1997, CETS No. 166, arts. 3–4. Also see Convention on the Avoidance of Statelessness in relation to State Succession, 19 May 2006, CETS No. 200.

[112] See African Charter on Human and Peoples' Rights, 27 June 1981, OAU Doc. CAB/LEG/67/3 rev. 5; Protocol to the African Charter on Human and Peoples' Rights on the Rights of Women in Africa, 11 July 2003, https://au.int/sites/default/files/treaties/37077-treaty-charter_on_rights_of_women_in_africa.pdf, art. 6(g)–(h). Also see African Charter on the Rights and Welfare of the Child, 11 July 1990, art. 6, OAU Doc CAB/LEG/24.9/49.

by the African Commission on Human and Peoples' Rights to cover it.[113] In addition, the right to nationality has been reaffirmed in non-treaty declarations, such as the Universal Declaration of Human Rights (UDHR),[114] and United Nations Declaration on the Rights of Indigenous Peoples (UNDRIP).[115] Some authorities, such as the Inter-American Court of Human Rights, have gone so far as to argue that the right to a nationality is a non-derogable right.[116] Holding multiple nationalities, however, has not been widely understood to constitute a right.[117] It has previously been concluded that when individuals possess more than one nationality their state of nationality is free to regard them as only having one nationality vis-à-vis the state.[118]

Nationality is therefore protected and states may not deprive individuals of their nationality arbitrarily.[119] If an individual has only one nationality, then that nationality may not be revoked at any time;[120] deprivation that is discriminatory is also arbitrary and prohibited.[121] Nationality laws may not prescribe or be applied in a manner that discriminates on the basis of race, color, gender, religion, political opinion, or national

[113] See African Commission on Human and Peoples' Rights, Malawi African Association, Amnesty International, Ms Sarr Diop, Collectif des Veuves et Ayant-droit et Association Mauritanienne des droits de l'homme v. Mauritania, 11 May 2000, para. 126; African Commission on Human and Peoples' Rights, John K. Modise v. Botswana, 6 November 2000, para. 88; African Committee of Experts on the Rights and Welfare of the Child, IHRDA and Open Society on behalf of Children of Nubian Descent in Kenya v. Kenya (Nubian Children case), 22 March 2011, paras. 46, 57.

[114] See UNGA Res. 217 A(III), Universal Declaration of Human Rights, UN Doc. A/810 (10 December 1948), art. 15(1).

[115] See UN Declaration on the Rights of Indigenous Peoples, UNGA Res. 61/295 (13 September 2007), art. 6.

[116] See Inter-American Court of Human Rights, Case of Expelled Dominicans & Haitians v Dominican Republic, Ser. C No 282 (28 August 2014), para. 253; Inter-American Court of Human Rights, Yean & Bosico Children v. Dominican Republic, Ser. C, Case 130, Judgment (8 September 2005), paras. 136–138.

[117] But see generally Spiro (2010), p. 111.

[118] See generally Worster (2009), p. 423.

[119] See UNGA Res. 217 A(III), Universal Declaration of Human Rights, UN Doc. A/810 (10 December 1948), art. 15(2); UN Secretary-General, Arbitrary Deprivation of Nationality: Report of the Secretary-General, UN Doc. A/HRC/10/34 (26 Jan. 2009).

[120] See UN Secretary-General, Arbitrary Deprivation of Nationality: Report of the Secretary-General, UN Doc. A/HRC/10/34 (26 Jan. 2009).

[121] See e.g. African Committee of Experts on the Rights and Welfare of the Child, IHRDA and Open Society on behalf of Children of Nubian Descent in Kenya v. Kenya (Nubian Children case), 22 March 2011, paras. 57, 263; Inter-American Court of Human Rights, Yean & Bosico Children v. Dominican Republic, Ser. C, Case 130, Judgment (8 September 2005), paras. 136, 139, 141; Inter-American Court of Human Rights, Case of Expelled Dominicans & Haitians v Dominican Republic, Ser. C No 282 (28 August 2014), para. 263; Human Rights Council, Draft report of the Working Group on the Universal Periodic Review: Austria UN Doc. A/HRC/WG.6/23/L.10 (11 November 2015), paras. 5.4, 5.5; Human Rights Council, Draft report of the Working Group on the Universal Periodic Review: Myanmar, UN Doc. A/HRC/WG.6/23/L.9 (10 November 2015), paras. 7.54, 7.55, 7.66.

or ethnic origin.[122] Other deprivations may also be arbitrary when they are not proportionate to a legitimate purpose.[123] For example, the Eritrea-Ethiopia Claims Commission held that revocation of nationality was acceptable when it was undertaken for security purposes or when a person had another nationality.[124]

In conclusion, international law forbids depriving an individual of nationality on an arbitrary basis. The creation of statelessness should always be considered arbitrary, but actions based on discrimination, such as national origin discrimination, are also arbitrary; states may not restrict change of nationality in an arbitrary manner. For the Olympics, the question is whether the 3-year waiting period, and possible additional restrictions by IFs, constitute an arbitrary limitation on the right to change one's nationality, and an arbitrary deprivation of a 'sport nationality' resulting in 'sports statelessness'. Where an athlete was completely prohibited from competition due to *de facto* 'sports statelessness', the CAS has found that this constitutes a loss of nationality.[125]

3.3 The Right to Change Nationality

The right to a nationality also includes the right to change nationality.[126] In the *Nottebohm* case at the ICJ, the Court held that states did not have to give effect to a claim of diplomatic protection when the nationality of the individual was not supported by a "genuine connection" with that state.[127] However, the Court did not question the underlying grant and change of nationality. The Court explicitly stated that states are free to grant their nationality as they see fit,[128] and that it did not seek to make any determination of the validity of the individual's nationality.[129] The question in the case was whether there were any international effects of that valid

---

[122] See Committee on the Elimination of Racial Discrimination, General Recommendation XXX on discrimination against non-citizens (2005); Inter-American Court of Human Rights, Yean & Bosico Children v. Dominican Republic, Ser. C, Case 130, Judgment (8 September 2005), para. 141.

[123] See Human Rights Committee, CCPR General Comment No. 27: Article 12 (Freedom of Movement) UN Doc. CCPR/C/21/Rev.1/Add.9 (2 November 1999), para. 21.

[124] See Eritrea-Ethiopian Claims Commission (Permanent Court of Arbitration), Civilian Claims (Eritrea v Ethiopia), Partial Award, International Legal Materials, vol. 44, 601, paras. 57–78 (2004).

[125] See CAS 00/005 Perez/International Olympic Committee (IOC), 19 September 2000, paras. 16, 18, 26.

[126] See UNGA Res. 217 A(III), Universal Declaration of Human Rights, UN Doc. A/810 (10 December 1948), art. 15(2).

[127] See International Court of Justice, Nottebohm Case (Liechtenstein v Guatemala), Second phase, Judgment, 1955 ICJ Reps 4, 20.

[128] See International Court of Justice, Nottebohm Case (Liechtenstein v Guatemala), Second phase, Judgment, 1955 ICJ Reps 4, 20.

[129] See International Court of Justice, Nottebohm Case (Liechtenstein v Guatemala), Second phase, Judgment, 1955 ICJ Reps 4, 30 (Klaestad, Judge, dissenting opinion, para. IV(1), (5)), 36 (Read, Judge, dissenting opinion), 57–58 (Guggenheim, Judge *ad hoc*, dissenting opinion, sec. II, para. 10).

grant of nationality.[130] In the more recent Preliminary Objections Judgment in the *Interpretation and Application of the International Convention on the Elimination of All Forms of Racial Discrimination* case,[131] brought by Qatar against the UAE, the Court affirmed its views in *Nottebohm* that nationality is a changeable political-legal status.[132] In his dissent, Judge Robinson also noted that *Nottebohm* must be read in harmony with the development of human rights law in the years since the judgment.[133]

Nottebohm is dubious authority for international sport. Insofar as it proposes to apply its 'genuine connection test' to an individual with one nationality, the Court's conclusion in the case has since been proved to have been incorrect. The Court relied on an analogy to situations of dual nationality,[134] to which the dissenting judges objected.[135] In its holding, the Court observed that its decision addressed whether the individual was "more closely connected with the population of the State conferring nationality than with that of *any other State*",[136] which suggests that the ICJ may have considered the individual to have had a *de facto*, though not *de jure*, alternative nationality. Thus, the decision may have been wrong on its face.

Nottebohm has not fared well since 1955, with most authorities in the law of nationality having rejected its central premise,[137] or at least that the case should be limited to only situations of diplomatic protection.[138] Several authorities concluded that *Nottebohm* is only applicable to situations of diplomatic protection of individ-

---

[130] See International Court of Justice, Nottebohm Case (Liechtenstein v Guatemala), Second phase, Judgment, 1955 ICJ Reps 4, 20.

[131] See International Court of Justice, Application of the International Convention on the International Convention on the Elimination of All Forms of Racial Discrimination (Qatar v UAE), Preliminary Objections, Judgment, 2021 ICJ Reps 71.

[132] See International Court of Justice, Application of the International Convention on the International Convention on the Elimination of All Forms of Racial Discrimination (Qatar v UAE), Preliminary Objections, Judgment, 2021 ICJ Reps 71, paras. 81–82.

[133] See International Court of Justice, Application of the International Convention on the International Convention on the Elimination of All Forms of Racial Discrimination (Qatar v UAE), Preliminary Objections, Judgment, 2021 ICJ Reps 71 (Robinson, J., Diss. Op.), para. 9. In this regard, see Macklin (2017), p. 492.

[134] See International Court of Justice, Nottebohm Case (Liechtenstein v Guatemala), Second phase, Judgment, 1955 ICJ Reps 4, 22.

[135] See International Court of Justice, Nottebohm Case (Liechtenstein v Guatemala), Second phase, Judgment, 1955 ICJ Reps 4, 41 (Read, Judge, dissenting opinion), 57–58 (Guggenheim, Judge *ad hoc*, dissenting opinion, sec. II, para. 10).

[136] See International Court of Justice, Nottebohm Case (Liechtenstein v Guatemala), Second phase, Judgment, 1955 ICJ Reps 4, 23.

[137] See e.g. Kochenov (2012); Kochenov (2010); Spiro (2019).

[138] See Weis (1979), p. 179. Also see Brownlie (2008), pp. 417–418; Shaw (2008), pp. 813–814. While the International Criminal Tribunal for Rwanda (ICTR) cited *Nottebohm* in the *Akayesu* case to interpret the meaning of "national" in the Genocide Convention, it carefully omitted any reference to "genuine connection," see International Criminal Tribunal for Rwanda (Chamber I), Prosecutor v Akayesu, Case No. ICTR-96-4-T, Judgment (2 September 1998) para. 510.

uals with multiple nationalities.[139] The International Law Commission rejected *Nottebohm* out of hand for situations of single nationality,[140] finding that, even after *Nottebohm*, the genuine connection test was only ever applied by other authorities to situations of multiple nationality.[141] This was applied to weigh the relative connections between two or more states, and support diplomatic protection by the state with the strongest connection.[142] In fact, the Court of Justice of the European Union (CJEU) in *Micheletti*[143] went even further to reject *Nottebohm* by finding that, under the EU legal order, EU member states may not apply the genuine connection test to individuals with multiple nationalities as a basis for refusing to recognize nationality from another EU member state.[144] The Court did not even cite to *Nottebohm* as a relevant precedent.[145] These developments support a narrow reading of *Nottebohm*.

The CAS has only ambiguously discussed the application of *Nottebohm* to cases of sport nationality. In *United States Olympic Committee (USOC) and USA Canoe/Kayak/International Olympic Committee (IOC)* [*in the matter of Perez*] (*USOC & USA Canoe/Kayak/IOC* [*Perez*]), the CAS merely noted that *Nottebohm* "may be relevant" for disregarding a valid grant of nationality and rejecting sport nationality.[146] However, the CAS also stated that *Nottebohm* "may also be relevant" for resolving situations of multiple nationality.[147] In the end, the CAS concluded that neither of those situations were relevant in the *USOC & USA Canoe/Kayak/IOC* [*Perez*] case.[148] In the *Miranda* case, the CAS also mentioned the "effective nationality" concept in international law, without specifically invoking *Nottebohm*.[149] It distinguished its application to situations of refusing to recognize state grant of nationality but not, as was the case in *Miranda*, for recognizing nationality where the state had not acted. It seems then that CAS' position on the applicability of *Nottebohm* remains unclear.

---

[139] *See generally* Macklin (2017), p. 492.

[140] See International Law Commission, Draft Articles on Diplomatic Protection with Commentaries, UN Doc A/61/10 (2006), 29–34, art. 4, cmty (5).

[141] See e.g. Italian-US Conciliation Commission, Flegenheimer (US v. Italy), UNRIAA vol. 14, 327, 375–376 (1958).

[142] See e.g. Iran-US Claims Tribunal, Case No. A/18 (Iran v. US), Iran-US Claims Tribunal Reporter vol. 5, 251, 263 (184). Also see Marian (2011), p. 313; Sironi (2013), pp. 53, 57.

[143] See CJEU, case C-369/90, Micheletti v. Delegación del Gobierno en Cantabria.

[144] See CJEU, case C-369/90, Micheletti v. Delegación del Gobierno en Cantabria, paras. 10–11.

[145] See CJEU, case C-369/90, Micheletti v. Delegación del Gobierno en Cantabria. Note that the Advocate General did cite to *Nottebohm* in his opinion to the Court, only to reject its application.

[146] See CAS 00/001, United States Olympic Committee (USOC) and USA Canoe/Kayak/International Olympic Committee (IOC) [in re Perez], 13 September 2000, paras. 19–20.

[147] See CAS 00/001, United States Olympic Committee (USOC) and USA Canoe/Kayak/International Olympic Committee (IOC) [in re Perez], 13 September 2000, paras. 19–21.

[148] See CAS 00/001, United States Olympic Committee (USOC) and USA Canoe/Kayak/International Olympic Committee (IOC) [in re Perez], 13 September 2000, para. 22.

[149] See CAS 00/003, Miranda/International Olympic Committee (IOC), 13 September 2000.

From the above discussion we can conclude that *Nottebohm* must be interpreted far more narrowly, in line with its original terms and in line with contemporary international human rights law. While it is doubtful that *Nottebohm* can be safely applied outside of diplomatic protection for people with multiple nationality, even if it can be applied by analogy, it is limited to dual nationals and requires an assessment of genuine connection. Thus, states and the IOC must give effect to nationality whenever an individual has one nationality, and in cases when an individual has more than one nationality they may only require a showing of genuine connection to select the operative nationality. A 3-year waiting period does not in itself test for genuine connection.

A highly unusual case, where a state might wish to refuse to recognize an athlete's nationality, could include situations when the grant of nationality was itself unlawful and the principle of *jus non oritur*[150] operates to deny its validity. However, the exception to this rule expressed in the *Namibia* advisory opinion by the International Court of Justice requires the recognition of nationality despite *jus non oritur* where such disregard would be to the disadvantage of the individual.[151] Instead, an athlete with more than one nationality may only be prohibited from changing their 'sport nationality' if they have a genuine connection to the other state of nationality. For this, there is no derogation or proportionality test, so the 3-year wait under Olympic rules cannot be justified. It also means that international law would permit the IOC and NOCs to prohibit an athlete with multiple nationalities from electing a sport nationality in a state with which they do not have genuine connection. The fact that the Olympic Charter presently does not impose this condition on first election is more liberal than human rights require and is thus acceptable. But it also means that a change to a new sport nationality, to a state where the athlete has genuine connection, cannot be refused.

For an athlete with only one nationality, who has lost a nationality and acquired another, the *Nottebohm* genuine connection test does not apply, and human rights law would demand that the new nationality be given international effect immediately. Any limitation on this respect for a change of nationality must be legitimate and proportionate.[152]

---

[150] See generally e.g. Permanent Court of International Justice, Nationality Decrees Issued in Tunis and Morocco (French Zone) on November 8th, 1921, Advisory Opinion, 1923 PCIJ, Ser. B, No. 4 (7 February); Worster (2020), p. 767; Open Society Justice Initiative, "Human Rights in the Context of Automatic Naturalization in Crimea" (2018), https://www.opensocietyfoundations.org/sites/default/files/report-osji-crimea-20180601.pdf.

[151] See International Court of Justice, Legal Consequences for States of the Continued Presence of South Africa in Namibia (South West Africa) Notwithstanding Security Council Resolution 276 (1970), Advisory Opinion, 1971 ICJ Reps. 16, 55–56 (June 21).

[152] Also see CAS 2007/A/1377, Rinaldi v. Fédération Internationale de Natation (FINA), 26 November 2007, paras. 49–52 (leaving the question open whether a refusal of change of nationality infringed personality rights).

3.4 *Change of Nationality and the Prohibition of National Origin Discrimination*

International human rights law forbids discrimination on the basis of national origin. This ground would largely prevent the Olympics from prohibiting an athlete from participating on a new Olympic team on the basis of having their origin in another state. This possibility will not be discussed in detail because its full implications are outside the scope of this chapter, but it is relevant in its relationship to nationality discrimination.

In the previous section, this chapter discussed the prohibition of discrimination on the basis of nationality with reference to multiple instruments. Most of these same instruments also prohibit national original discrimination: the UDHR,[153] ICCPR,[154] ICESCR,[155] Migrant Workers Convention,[156] ECHR,[157] and ACHR.[158] While the ICJ has interpreted the CERD to not prohibit nationality discrimination (although the CERD Committee understands the opposite),[159] the ICJ expressly affirmed that the CERD covers national origin discrimination.[160] In reaching this conclusion, the Court defined 'national origin discrimination' as an immutable characteristic, akin to the other characteristics in the CERD such as "race, colour and descent".[161]

Turning to the Olympics, in cases where an athlete is receiving less favorable treatment than other comparable athletes on the basis that they are "from" another state, there may be a valid claim of national origin discrimination. Consider that the IOC or an NOC blocking the quick transfer of an athlete to a new NOC is treating this athlete differently from other athletes on the basis of that athlete's origin. When the athlete wishes to transfer and retain their original nationality, discrimination is sometimes more difficult to identify; but when the athlete loses the prior nationality

[153] See UNGA Res. 217 A(III), Universal Declaration of Human Rights, UN Doc. A/810 (10 December 1948), art. 2.

[154] See International Covenant on Civil and Political Rights, 16 December 1966, 999 UNTS 171, arts. 2(2).

[155] See International Covenant on Economic, Social and Cultural Rights, 16 December 1966, 999 UNTS 3, art. 2(2).

[156] See International Convention on the Protection of the Rights of All Migrant Workers and Members of Their Families, UNGA Res. 45/158 (18 December 1990), 2220 UNTS 3, art. 1(1).

[157] See [European] Convention for the Protection of Human Rights and Fundamental Freedoms, 4 November 1950, 213 UNTS 222, CETS. No. 5, art. 14.

[158] See American Convention on Human Rights, 22 November 1969, 1144 UNTS 123, OASTS No. 36.

[159] See International Convention on the Elimination of All Forms of Racial Discrimination, UN GA Res. 2106 (XX) (21 December 1965), 660 UNTS 195, preamble.

[160] See International Convention on the Elimination of All Forms of Racial Discrimination, UN GA Res. 2106 (XX) (21 December 1965), 660 UNTS 195, art. 1.

[161] See International Court of Justice, Application of the International Convention on the International Convention on the Elimination of All Forms of Racial Discrimination (Qatar v UAE), Preliminary Objections, Judgment, 2021 ICJ Reps 71, paras. 81–82.

and acquires the new nationality, it is more obvious. To illustrate, an NOC demands that a foreign national athlete be blocked from participation in the Olympics because they have a national origin from a particular state. The athlete cannot change their former nationality, as it is immutable in the past. Yet, they are blocked from participation due to this immutable characteristic. The possibility that national origin discrimination might be at issue for individuals changing their sports nationality also argues in favor of a proportionality assessment.

4 Legitimacy and Proportionality of Nationality Rules

The sections above concluded that provisions in the Olympic Charter infringe on the right to a nationality (including the obligation to prevent statelessness), the right to change nationality, and the right to be free from discrimination on the basis of nationality and national origin. For these reasons, the infringing provisions must be justified by having a legitimate aim and being proportionate to that aim. Although each of these human rights provisions calls for specialized proportionality assessment, for the sake of brevity this chapter consolidates the assessments into a single section.

4.1 Identifying Possible Legitimate Aims of Nationality Rules

The IOC, CAS and other bodies have submitted a variety of reasons for the nationality regime at the Olympics, and in international sport generally, although the Olympic Charter itself says very little about the purpose of such a regime. This section will assess only those arguments that sport authorities have actually submitted, and will thus exclude other speculative arguments. While the Olympics are organized to promote the "harmonious development of humankind, with a view to promoting a peaceful society concerned with the preservation of human dignity", this aim does not specifically focus on classification by nationality, the denial of nationality ('sports statelessness'), limitations on acquisition and change of nationality, and national origin considerations.[162] While the Charter proclaims that sport is a human right,[163] it seems only concerned with human rights infringements (e.g., discrimination) "affecting the Olympic Movement",[164] leading one to wonder

[162] See International Olympic Committee, Olympic Charter, 2021, Fundamental Principles of Olympism, para. 2.

[163] See International Olympic Committee, Olympic Charter, 2021, Fundamental Principles of Olympism, para. 4.

[164] See International Olympic Committee, Olympic Charter, 2021, Rule 2 Mission and role of the IOC.

whether the objective of the rules is the protection of the interests of athletes or the interests of the Olympic Games. Most of the interests that follow are largely incoherent, and it is difficult to identify any interest important enough to justify infringing international human rights.

In some instances, the existence of nationality rules has been presumed as a foregone conclusion. The CAS has supported the change of nationality rules without seeing a need to explain their purpose,[165] or has simply stated that an athlete's request to change nationality was not compatible with the "spirit" of the Olympic Charter.[166] In a case under international baseball rules, the International Baseball Federation (IBAF) argued that it was "unthinkable" to engage in international sport without nationality classifications.[167] In a somewhat less conclusory manner, the *Fédération Internationale de Natation* (FINA) has argued that it is simply reality that international sports function with the concept of nationality;[168] the FIBA argued that it is merely tradition.[169] Even more questionable arguments have been submitted. FIBA stated that without nationality rules they might suffer a loss of spectator interest.[170] In *Liang Ren-Guey v. Lake Placid 1980 Olympic Games Inc.*, the US State Department submitted a statement of interest, arguing that the US had strong foreign policy interests in the Olympic Games,[171] a direct repudiation of the Olympic Charter's objective of political neutrality. In one case before the CAS, the Court concluded that the motivation for the change of nationality rules was strangely to inconvenience athletes and, presumably, chill attempts to change.[172] Obviously none of these statements can serve as justifications for infringing human rights.

In other cases, the IOC or IFs have appealed to a form of compulsory patriotism. The IBAF has argued that international sport is best served when athletes have close

[165] See CAS 00/001, United States Olympic Committee (USOC) and USA Canoe/Kayak/International Olympic Committee (IOC) [in re Perez], 13 September 2000, para. 24.

[166] See CAS 08/006 Moldova National Olympic Committee (MNOC) v. International Olympic Committee (IOC) [in re Gutu], 9 August 2008, para. 8.

[167] See CAS 94/132 Puerto Rico Amateur Baseball Federation (PRABF)/USA Baseball (USAB) [in re C.], 15 March 1996, 4.

[168] See CAS 2007/A/1377, Rinaldi v. Fédération Internationale de Natation (FINA), 26 November 2007.

[169] See CAS 2009/A/1788, UMMC Ekaterinburg v. FIBA Europe e. V., 29 October 2009.

[170] See CAS 2009/A/1788, UMMC Ekaterinburg v. FIBA Europe e. V., 29 October 2009, para. 25. Also see Alexandre Miguel Mestre (2009), The Law of the Olympic Games 75–76 ("It seems clear that the IOC, in its guise as 'guardian of the temple,' is trying to restrict these changes of nationality, both on ideological (national identity) and commercial grounds (international contests are of great interest to the viewer, which is reflected in the television rights paid for by television stations), and out of a desire to preserve a territorial dimension to sport.")

[171] But see USDOJ Statement of Interest in Liang Ren-Guey v. Lake Placid 1980 Olympic Games Inc., 424 N.Y.S.2d 535 (3d Dep't NY, 1980), affirmed, 403 N.E.2d 178 (1980).

[172] See CAS 08/006 Moldova National Olympic Committee (MNOC) v. International Olympic Committee (IOC) [in re Gutu], 9 August 2008, para. 8.

ties to their sports nationality.[173] In attempting to understand the underlying justification for Olympic sports nationality rules, Peter Spiro concluded that their purpose must be to require a connection between sport nationality and personal identity.[174] Of course, such a purpose assumes that an athlete's personal identify can be easily deduced from his or her nationality. The *Federación de Béisbol Aficionado de Puerto Rico* argued that an individual should not be permitted to compete against their true state of nationality.[175] This assertion runs contrary to the Olympic Charter that proclaims that the competition is between athletes and not countries.[176]

Others have argued that the purpose of nationality rules is to prevent "nationality shopping".[177] The IBAF has referred to this practice as a "commerce of nationalities".[178] The International Ice Hockey Federation (IIHF) sees it as "national team tourism",[179] while FINA refers to such athletes as "mercenaries".[180] By and large these complaints invoke "romantic" notions of nationality,[181] and run contrary to the notion that competition is between athletes and not states.[182] Surprisingly, in its criticism of some EU Member States' Citizenship-by-Investment schemes, the European Commission actually supported the long-standing practice of granting nationality to athletes on the extraordinary basis of "national interest".[183]

The argument against 'nationality shopping' does have certain important implications, most significantly, an economic argument. The IBAF[184] and FINA[185] have argued that they need to safeguard their economic investment in 'their' athletes, and that changes of nationality create a loss of investment. Some IFs argue that nationality rules simply prevent change, which can be interpreted to include such a loss of

---

[173] See CAS 98/215, International Baseball Association (IBA), 4 January 1999, para. 25.

[174] See Spiro (2020), pp. 374, 376.

[175] See CAS 94/132 Puerto Rico Amateur Baseball Federation (PRABF)/USA Baseball (USAB) [in re C.], 15 March 1996, 4.

[176] See CAS 00/005 Perez/International Olympic Committee (IOC), 19 September 2000, para. 26.

[177] See CAS 2007/A/1377, Rinaldi v. Fédération Internationale de Natation (FINA), 26 November 2007, para. 36.

[178] See CAS 98/215, International Baseball Association (IBA), 4 January 1999, para. 32.

[179] See Oberste Gerichtshof (OGH), Austria, Emanuel V. v. Austrian Ice Hockey Association & International Ice Hockey Federation (IIHF), 2 Ob 232/98a (24 September 1998).

[180] See CAS 2007/A/1377, Rinaldi v. Fédération Internationale de Natation (FINA), 26 November 2007, para. 55.

[181] Compare CJEU, Case C-369/90, Micheletti v. Delegación del Gobierno en Cantabria, Opinion of Advocate General Tesauro, ECR I—4253 (30 January 1992) 5 with European Commission, Press release, "Investor citizenship schemes: European Commission opens infringements against Cyprus and Malta for 'selling' EU citizenship" (20 October 2020).

[182] See CAS 00/005 Perez/International Olympic Committee (IOC), 19 September 2000, para. 26.

[183] See European Commission, "Investor Citizenship and Residence Schemes in the European Union," EU Doc. COM(2019) 12 final (SWD(2019) 5 final) (23 January 2019).

[184] See CAS 98/215, International Baseball Association (IBA), 4 January 1999, paras. 32, 39–42, 51.

[185] See CAS 2007/A/1377, Rinaldi v. Fédération Internationale de Natation (FINA), 26 November 2007.

investment. FIBA noted that the athlete "has to be put into one of two possible baskets because otherwise, he would be able to jump from one 'athletic nationality' to the other at his sole discretion".[186] The IBAF also argued for the importance of choosing one nationality,[187] emphasizing that unexpected changes of nationality should be prevented.[188] However, the CAS has explicitly ruled that for the Olympic Games, membership in an NOC does not create any property interest in the athletes.[189]

Another worry is that less restrictive nationality rules would encourage poaching athletes and introduce a 'financial arms race' into sport.[190] Poaching does have anti-competitive implications, and few would doubt that competitions should be won by talent and not by a bank account. According to the CAS, the modern implementation of more restrictive nationality rules at FIFA was largely triggered when Qatar began hiring and naturalizing Brazilian players, which other teams regarded as an unfair advantage.[191] Previously, FIFA had far less restrictive nationality rules and poaching was not considered problematic.[192] Linked to this concern, FINA has also argued in the *Rinaldi* case, that more liberal nationality rules would negatively impact the equal opportunity of athletes.[193] FINA did not explain how nationality rules operate to promote equal opportunity, although we can assume that if athletes were free to change nationality, then the free movers might take competition opportunities away from others. However, this argument is difficult to sustain because presumably those opportunities would go to athletes who performed better, and discrimination on performance is not a problem.[194] But poaching also has an alternate side which is providing more opportunity for athletes who are not selected by an NOC for competition. While NOCs have condemned nationality shopping for the purposes

---

186 See e.g. CAS 92/80 B./Fédération Internationale de Basketball (FIBA), 25 March 1993, para. 2.

187 See CAS 98/215, International Baseball Association (IBA), 4 January 1999, para. 26.

188 See CAS 98/215, International Baseball Association (IBA), 4 January 1999, paras. 32, 38, 42, 52.

189 See CAS 00/005 Perez/International Olympic Committee (IOC), 19 September 2000, para. 26; CAS 94/132 Puerto Rico Amateur Baseball Federation (PRABF)/USA Baseball (USAB) [in re C.], 15 March 1996, 6.

190 See CAS 2010/A/2071, Irish Football Association (IFA) v. Football Association of Ireland (FAI), Kearns & Fédération Internationale de Football Association (FIFA), 27 September 2010 (22 July 2010).

191 See CAS 2010/A/2071, Irish Football Association (IFA) v. Football Association of Ireland (FAI), Kearns & Fédération Internationale de Football Association (FIFA), 27 September 2010 (22 July 2010), para. 40.

192 See CAS 2010/A/2071, Irish Football Association (IFA) v. Football Association of Ireland (FAI), Kearns & Fédération Internationale de Football Association (FIFA), 27 September 2010 (22 July 2010), para. 39.

193 See CAS 2007/A/1377, Rinaldi v. Fédération Internationale de Natation (FINA), 26 November 2007.

194 See CAS 2007/A/1377, Rinaldi v. Fédération Internationale de Natation (FINA), 26 November 2007, para. 30.

accessing international competitions as “opportunistic” behavior,[195] the very argument presumes that excluding athletes is a legitimate goal.

A strong argument in favor of the nationality regime is that the objective of the Olympics, and other international sport competitions, is to promote international engagement and thus the competition needs to be international in character. The Olympic Charter states that sport promotes the “harmonious development of humankind, with a view to promoting a peaceful society”.[196] The UNESCO International Charter of Physical Education, Physical Activity and Sport further articulates this objective, stating that sports promotes “stronger bonds between people, solidarity, mutual respect and understanding, and respect for the integrity and dignity of every human being”,[197] partly through exposure to cultural diversity.[198] FIBA has argued that without nationality regulations, it would be more difficult to maintain the international character of the competitions.[199] Indeed, it could be that organizing the Olympics by nationality protects the games from being dominated by nationals from certain well-funded states. Without promoting more teams from different states,[200] there is a risk of less diversity and less international, intercultural engagement.[201]

It is the view of this author that there are few arguments for the IOC, and international sport in general, to impose nationality regulations. Some of the arguments above are easily dismissed, although the fact that these arguments were even offered lends some doubt as to their good faith. It is difficult to understand how the IOC has any legitimate interest in tradition, spectator interest, foreign policy of states, or compulsory patriotism, which leads them to infringe human rights. The derogatory language that refers to athletes who change nationality as “mercenaries”,[202] or

195 See UN Educational, Scientific and Cultural Organization (UNESCO), “International Charter of Physical Education, Physical Activity and Sport,” UN Doc. SHS/2015/PI/H/14 REV (2015), preamble (10). Also see CAS 08/006 Moldova National Olympic Committee (MNOC) v. International Olympic Committee (IOC) [in re Gutu], 9 August 2008, para. 8.

196 See International Olympic Committee, Olympic Charter, 2021, Fundamental Principles of Olympism, para. 2.

197 See UN Educational, Scientific and Cultural Organization (UNESCO), “International Charter of Physical Education, Physical Activity and Sport,” UN Doc. SHS/2015/PI/H/14 REV (2015), preamble, arts. 10, 12.1.

198 See UN Educational, Scientific and Cultural Organization (UNESCO), “International Charter of Physical Education, Physical Activity and Sport,” UN Doc. SHS/2015/PI/H/14 REV (2015), preamble (5), arts. 1.5, 5; International Olympic Committee, Olympic Charter, 2021, Fundamental Principles of Olympism, para. 1.

199 See CAS 2009/A/1788, UMMC Ekaterinburg v. FIBA Europe e. V., 29 October 2009, paras. 22–23.

200 See CAS 2009/A/1788, UMMC Ekaterinburg v. FIBA Europe e. V., 29 October 2009, para. 25.

201 See CAS 2009/A/1788, UMMC Ekaterinburg v. FIBA Europe e. V., 29 October 2009, para. 25.

202 See CAS 2007/A/1377, Rinaldi v. Fédération Internationale de Natation (FINA), 26 November 2007, para. 55.

mocking them for their hardship,[203] also casts doubt on the legitimacy of these interests. Arguments against 'nationality shopping' are also weak, especially when the European Commission appears to support the practice as a well-established, traditional way for states to promote their national interests.[204]

The argument that there is an economic investment in athletes in reliance on their continued nationality, though standing in contrast to the prohibition on property interests in athletes, does have some validity. After all, athletes cannot compete, and the Olympics cannot function, without funding. Discouraging poaching is dubious because it is unclear why the IOC has an interest in preventing athletes seeking out opportunities for support. The argument in favor of retaining the traditional nationality rules often has the effect of locking athletes into poorly-funded training support on the basis of their nationality. Perhaps the strongest argument in support of the IOC's nationality regime is in order to maintain the 'international character' of international sports competitions. This interest could be stronger for team sports where each team has a more unified character compared to individual sports. In order to pursue its aims of international cooperation and exchange, one could understand that the IOC would want to involve as diverse a group of athletes as possible, competing at the same level.

4.2 *Assessing the Proportionality of Nationality Rules*

This section will consider whether nationality rules are proportionate to their aims, and whether there are less restrictive ways to achieve legitimate aims. Throughout all arguments for nationality rules, the sport authority is clearly subordinating the interests of the athlete in favor of another interest, be it the NOC, IF, IOC, or even the state involved. FIBA has even argued that sport nationality should not depend on "goodwill or interests of the players".[205] These arguments all run counter to the Olympic Charter's statement that sport is a human right and that the interests of athletes are "fundamental".[206] As such, even by the terms of the Charter, and certainly under human rights law, nationality rules that infringe on nationality rights should be as limited and narrow as possible to achieve the aims of the IOC. After all, as noted by the Austrian Supreme Court, sporting federations are monopolies with

[203] See CAS 2007/A/1377, Rinaldi v. Fédération Internationale de Natation (FINA), 26 November 2007, para. 44 ("Consequently, if Ms Rinaldi failed to seek clarification or took the risk of relying on her own interpretation of the word 'resided' which is different from its common use, she would be the 'victim' of her own choice and not of an unpredictable rule, especially since in case of doubt, the natural or at least more prudent and easiest approach would have been to enquire with FINA.")

[204] See *e.g.* European Commission, "Investor Citizenship and Residence Schemes in the European Union," EU Doc. COM(2019) 12 final (SWD(2019) 5 final) (23 January 2019).

[205] See e.g. CAS 92/80 B./Fédération Internationale de Basketball (FIBA), 25 March 1993, para. 16.

[206] See CAS 00/005 Perez/International Olympic Committee (IOC), 19 September 2000, para. 26.

considerable market power.[207] Some IFs have nationality rules that are even harsher than the Olympic Charter,[208] and in some cases, the formal 3-year wait was far lengthier,[209] so those rules should also fail should the underlying Olympic rules fail.

The strict nationality rules have come under criticism on grounds of being disproportionate. The CAS held that the need for an 'international character' of sport can justify some rules on nationality,[210] and a 3-year wait is an incidental hardship.[211] The CAS noted, however, that in the context of IF nationality rules, a hardship of 3 years is only acceptable if the athlete may continue to participate as a foreigner on their sports team.[212] The Court criticized NOCs that oppose all requests for a waiver of the 3-year rule as unduly harsh.[213] In fact, 22 years ago, it strongly suggested that the IOC review and reconsider the inflexibility of the change of nationality rules.[214] The Austrian Supreme Court was not impressed that an athlete would be barred from competing for a state with which they had the strongest connection,[215] although the CAS reasonably believes that any genuine connection with a state for nationality needs objective tests rather than subjective feelings.[216] The CAS has also suggested to some IFs that they change their more onerous change

---

[207] See Oberste Gerichtshof (OGH), Austria, Emanuel V. v. Austrian Ice Hockey Association & International Ice Hockey Federation (IIHF), 2 Ob 232/98a (24 September 1998) ("Aus den dargelegten, zum Kontrahierungszwang entwickelten Grundsätzen ist aber auch abzuleiten, daß es dem Monopolisten ganz allgemein verwehrt ist, seine faktische Übermacht in unsachlicher Weise auszuüben. Die Monopolstellung beider beklagten Parteien ist hier aber eindeutig und auch nicht strittig. [However, it can also be deduced from the principles presented and developed for the compulsory contracting that the monopolist is generally prohibited from exercising his de facto superior power in an unobjective manner. The monopoly position of both defendant parties is clear and not controversial.]").

[208] See CAS 2010/A/2071, Irish Football Association (IFA) v. Football Association of Ireland (FAI), Kearns & Fédération Internationale de Football Association (FIFA), 27 September 2010 (22 July 2010), para. 46.

[209] See CAS 00/003, Miranda/International Olympic Committee (IOC), 13 September 2000, para. 3.

[210] See CAS 2009/A/1788, UMMC Ekaterinburg v. FIBA Europe e. V., 29 October 2009, paras. 26–27.

[211] See CAS 00/003, Miranda/International Olympic Committee (IOC), 13 September 2000, para. 44; CAS 92/80 B./Fédération Internationale de Basketball (FIBA), 25 March 1993, para. 17; CAS 00/001, United States Olympic Committee (USOC) and USA Canoe/Kayak/International Olympic Committee (IOC) [in re Perez], 13 September 2000, paras. 16, 19, 21–22.

[212] See e.g. CAS 92/80 B./Fédération Internationale de Basketball (FIBA), 25 March 1993, paras. 18–19.

[213] See CAS 00/003, Miranda/International Olympic Committee (IOC), 13 September 2000, para. 44.

[214] See CAS 00/003, Miranda/International Olympic Committee (IOC), 13 September 2000, para. 44.

[215] See Oberste Gerichtshof (OGH), Austria, Emanuel V. v. Austrian Ice Hockey Association & International Ice Hockey Federation (IIHF), 2 Ob 232/98a (24 September 1998).

[216] See CAS 2007/A/1377, Rinaldi v. Fédération Internationale de Natation (FINA), 26 November 2007, paras. 32–35.

of nationality rules because of their potential "invalidity",[217] and further speculated that economic reimbursement for the costs borne by the NOC could be a viable alternative to strict nationality rules.[218] This view suggests that a 3-year ban, without any flexibility or opportunity to compete, would always be disproportionate. The Austrian Supreme Court agreed that an inflexible 3-year ban is disproportionate,[219] and suggested that these concerns can be satisfied by changes to domestic nationality laws,[220] or by requiring a period of competition in the new state[221] rather than a ban on all competition.

The CAS also concluded that the decision by the NOC to refuse to waive the 3-year ban was contrary to the spirit of the Olympic Charter,[222] even though the Court was not empowered to reverse the decision.[223] The rules themselves are also fundamentally arbitrary. Peter Spiro observed that nationality rules depend entirely on the luck of birth and family descent, and even with the change regulations, can be manipulated.[224] Athletes who never competed for a national team can change nationality freely.[225]

---

[217] See CAS 2001/A/357 Nabokov & Russian Olympic Committee (ROC) & Russian Ice Hockey Federation (RIHF)/International Ice Hockey Federation (IIHF), 31 January 2002, para. 14.

[218] See CAS 98/215, International Baseball Association (IBA), 4 January 1999, para. 32.

[219] See Oberste Gerichtshof (OGH), Austria, Emanuel V. v. Austrian Ice Hockey Association & International Ice Hockey Federation (IIHF), 2 Ob 232/98a (24 September 1998). However, note that the athlete ultimately withdrew his request to the IIHF for waiver of the rule and application to compete, missing the competition, see CAS 2001/A/357 Nabokov & Russian Olympic Committee (ROC) & Russian Ice Hockey Federation (RIHF)/International Ice Hockey Federation (IIHF), 31 January 2002, para. 11.

[220] See Oberste Gerichtshof (OGH), Austria, Emanuel V. v. Austrian Ice Hockey Association & International Ice Hockey Federation (IIHF), 2 Ob 232/98a (24 September 1998).

[221] See Oberste Gerichtshof (OGH), Austria, Emanuel V. v. Austrian Ice Hockey Association & International Ice Hockey Federation (IIHF), 2 Ob 232/98a (24 September 1998).

[222] See CAS 00/001, United States Olympic Committee (USOC) and USA Canoe/Kayak/International Olympic Committee (IOC) [in re Perez], 13 September 2000, para. 26.

[223] See CAS 98/215, International Baseball Association (IBA), 4 January 1999, para. 53; CAS 2010/A/2071, Irish Football Association (IFA) v. Football Association of Ireland (FAI), Kearns & Fédération Internationale de Football Association (FIFA), 27 September 2010 (22 July 2010), paras. 19, 39; CAS 00/003, Miranda/International Olympic Committee (IOC), 13 September 2000, paras. 27, 32–37, 44; CAS 00/001, United States Olympic Committee (USOC) and USA Canoe/Kayak/International Olympic Committee (IOC) [in re Perez], 13 September 2000, para. 26.

[224] See Spiro (2020), pp. 374, 376. Note that athletes such as Eileen Gu and members of the Chinese Hockey Team at the recent 2022 Winter Olympic Games in Beijing appear to have benefitted from China's willingness to openly adopt policies contrary to its own nationality laws, which strictly prohibit multiple nationality. See e.g. Baker and Tracy (2022); "Olympic skier Eileen Gu sparks a debate about dual nationality: China does not allow it. But there may be loopholes," The Economist (17 February 2022), https://www.economist.com/china/2022/02/17/olympic-skier-eileen-gu-sparks-a-debate-about-dual-nationality.

[225] See Oberste Gerichtshof (OGH), Austria, Emanuel V. v. Austrian Ice Hockey Association & International Ice Hockey Federation (IIHF), 2 Ob 232/98a (24 September 1998).

For the economic reliance argument that NOCs may invest in athletes on the basis of nationality and unexpectedly lose the benefit of their investment should the athlete change nationality, this rule could be narrower than regulating change of nationality. In essence, the NOC could request some form of compensation for any investment rather than block the change of nationality. For the sake of brevity, this chapter will not venture to propose a precise valuation scheme, but some accounting of the funding paid out by the NOC and the benefit that it received leading up to the change of nationality could be appropriate. Any payment that exceeds the value added by the NOC would be punitive, resembling a claim to property interest in the athlete, thus leading to a chilling effect regarding a change of nationality. It is clear that the economic argument can be addressed with far narrower rules that do not infringe on human rights.

For the argument that the Olympic Games seek to retain an international character, and to some degree the argument of reducing poaching, the question is over the value of nationality diversity in the Games. The Olympic Charter appears to focus on both the international and intercultural character of the Games as benefitting cooperation and respect. One could surmise that the interaction of persons with differing nationalities forces engagement across nationality lines. Deliberately matching people with different backgrounds exposes people to different ways of acting and behaving, but matching two individuals with different nationalities does not necessary achieve any political dialogue, especially as the Olympics are meant to be apolitical, so the interaction is more likely to be cultural. However, nationality rules do not necessary achieve the aim of intercultural engagement. The assumption is that athletes with different political nationalities will have differing cultures, but that assumes that different passports equals cultural difference and engagement.

It is certainly possible that athletes active on the international stage have more in common culturally with their competitors from other countries than they might have with their fellow nationals. In fact, more liberal rules on change of nationality could achieve far more international and intercultural engagement. The Brazilian athletes poached by Qatar for its national team could have bridged far more cultural divides than they would have by staying in Brazil; immigration inherently fosters intercultural exchange. These are all speculative observations, but serve to demonstrate that nationality rules may not have sufficient justification so as to infringe human rights. At a minimum, if the change of nationality rules permitted immediate change to the state with which the individual has the closest connection, then athletes representing states would be far more genuine representatives, and would not need a 3-year waiting period. That being said, one could imagine that a team sport might have an even stronger need for all athletes to have the same nationality, and for that nationality to be the one with which they have a genuine connection, in order to present a more unified cultural representation.

5 Conclusion

Following from the conclusions of this chapter, if the IOC seeks to comply with international human rights, then it must comply with the laws on nationality and discrimination. It is probably already bound to these rules, but, as this cannot be determined with certainty, we can at least rely on the IOC's repeated intentions to comply with human rights law and the provisions of various instruments, such as the Olympic Charter. In this and other documents, the IOC engages with and draws upon the discourse over human rights law as a benchmark for its actions. In order to comply with international law prohibiting nationality and national origin discrimination, the Olympic Charter must be amended to largely abolish nationality discrimination. This discrimination could only be justified in the rarest of cases, such as team sports where all players would need to have a common nationality.

Alternatively, if the IOC wishes to retain nationality classification for individual competitors as well as for team sports, then the Olympic Charter must at least be amended to alter the terms on change of nationality. For an individual with one nationality, the athlete may join the national team of their nationality without a genuine connection test. If that athlete were to lose nationality and acquire a new one, then the athlete must be permitted to join the team of their new nationality immediately, without any waiting period. Any other limitation would infringe on the right to change nationality, creating 'sports statelessness' and potentially discriminating on the basis of national origin. It would be permissible for the prior team to request some form of compensation, which must be offset by the benefit that the athlete provided to the team during the term of membership, and not be designed to constitute a punishment with the effect to chill the decision to change nationality; such compensation would therefore end up being minimal.

For an athlete with more than one nationality, the Olympic Charter might limit changes of national team membership within narrow parameters. It could limit the initial election of sport nationality to the state with which the individual has the closest connection, although human rights law would not require this practice. The terms on change of membership could restrict change to a state with which the athlete could show a stronger connection. If the athlete could show a stronger connection, then the change should be effective immediately, with similar terms on compensation as discussed above. A mandatory waiting period would not be acceptable under any circumstances as it could risk 'sports statelessness'.

If the athlete cannot show a stronger connection to the other state, then human rights would permit the IOC to refuse the change, but that would not prevent them from allowing those changes in limited circumstances. The athlete would, of course, be free to renounce their nationality and join the new team immediately even without a genuine connection. The rules could permit change to a new NOC without renunciation after a 3-year waiting period, or even longer, following the request, even lacking a genuine connection, but human rights law would not demand this option. If the IOC chose this option, then it is already doing more than human rights on nationality require. However, refugee law and the right to leave any state might be relevant to support a nationality change without genuine connection, but such considerations are outside the scope of the present chapter. If there were to be a waiting period, the athlete should be permitted to continue participating for the original team to avoid experiencing 'sports statelessness'. A veto by either NOC would also be unacceptable because they may be interested in retaining the athlete. The decision on genuine connection must be *bona fide*. In this case, the right to an impartial tribunal and the right to appeal became relevant, though this is also outside the scope of the chapter. There should be a mechanism to decide issues of genuine connection, although this proposal does not preclude decision-making by the IOC, provided it complies with the right to impartial decision-making, and is based on a good faith assessment of genuine connection.[226]

Abolishing the NOC system and nationality classification entirely would avoid most of these problems, bypassing human rights concerns and promoting international understanding. Without NOC funding of athletes, replaced by direct IF or IOC funding, investment expectations in athletes would be irrelevant and athletes would not be trapped in poorly-funded situations due solely to their nationality. Instead, funding issues would only arise if athletes changed IFs, which is far less likely, and does not implicate any human rights issues. Abolishing the nationality classification would also prevent poaching concerns, to the degree that those are even valid, because there would be no NOC organization. Strangely enough, as Spiro has argued, spectator interest might even increase as the Olympics would be limited to only the most qualified athletes.[227] Abolishing nationality regulations could actually *improve* the international character of the Olympics, taking the focus away from nationalities, medals rankings, flags and anthems; and also avoiding the whispered disputes over geopolitics. The spotlight would be placed solely on the athletes.

For a wide variety of sporting competitions around the world, nationality is already irrelevant. From Wimbledon to the Boston Marathon, the nationality of the competitors is more of a curiosity, and not a qualification. Should the Olympics also abandon its nationality regime, athletes would interact as individuals, pushing each other to the heights of physical and mental excellence, rather than as proxies for national governments. This is a remarkable sporting ideal, and indeed a social ideal, to present to the world.

Cases and Documents

African Charter on Human and Peoples' Rights, 27 June 1981, OAU Doc. CAB/LEG/67/3 rev. 5

[226] See CAS 98/215, International Baseball Association (IBA), 4 January 1999, para. 51; CAS 00/003, Miranda/International Olympic Committee (IOC), 13 September 2000, paras. 38–41.
[227] See Spiro (2020), pp. 374, 378.

African Charter on the Rights and Welfare of the Child, 11 July 1990, OAU Doc CAB/LEG/24.9/49
African Commission on Human and Peoples' Rights, Malawi African Association, Amnesty International, Ms Sarr Diop, Collectif des Veuves et Ayant-droit et Association Mauritanienne des droits de l'homme v. Mauritania, 11 May 2000
African Commission on Human and Peoples' Rights, John K. Modise v. Botswana, 6 November 2000
African Committee of Experts on the Rights and Welfare of the Child, IHRDA and Open Society on behalf of Children of Nubian Descent in Kenya v. Kenya (Nubian Children case), 22 March 2011
American Convention on Human Rights, 22 November 1969, 1144 UNTS 123, OASTS No. 36
Committee on Economic, Social and Cultural Rights, General Comment 20: Non-discrimination in economic, social and cultural rights (art. 2, para. 2) (May 2009)
CEDAW General Recommendation No. 21: Equality in Marriage and Family Relations, 1994
Committee on the Elimination of Racial Discrimination, General Recommendation XXX on discrimination against non-citizens (2005)
Convention on the Avoidance of Statelessness in relation to State Succession, 19 May 2006, CETS No. 200
Convention on the Elimination of All Forms of Discrimination against Women, 19 December 1979, 1249 UNTS 13
Convention on the Reduction of Statelessness, 13 December 1975, 989 UNTS 175
Convention on the Rights of Persons with Disabilities, UNGA Res. 61/106 (12 December 2006), 2515 UNTS 3
CAS 92/80 B./Fédération Internationale de Basketball (FIBA), 25 March 1993
CAS 94/123, Fédération Internationale de Basketball (FIBA)/W. & Brandt Hagen e. V., 12 September 1994
CAS 94/132 Puerto Rico Amateur Baseball Federation (PRABF)/USA Baseball (USAB) [in re C.], 15 March 1996
CAS 98/209 Spanish Basketball Federation/FIBA [in re Zassoulskaia], 6 January 1999
CAS 98/215, International Baseball Association (IBA), 4 January 1999
CAS 00/001, United States Olympic Committee (USOC) and USA Canoe/Kayak/ International Olympic Committee (IOC) [in re Perez], 13 September 2000
CAS 00/003, Miranda/International Olympic Committee (IOC), 13 September 2000
CAS 00/005 Perez/International Olympic Committee (IOC), 19 September 2000
CAS 2001/A/357 Nabokov & Russian Olympic Committee (ROC) & Russian Ice Hockey Federation (RIHF)/International Ice Hockey Federation (IIHF), 31 January 2002
CAS 2007/A/1377, Rinaldi v. Fédération Internationale de Natation (FINA), 26 November 2007
CAS 08/002, Simms v. Fédération Internationale de Natation (FINA), 1 August 2008

CAS 08/006 Moldova National Olympic Committee (MNOC) v. International Olympic Committee (IOC) [in re Gutu], 9 August 2008
CAS 2009/A/1788, UMMC Ekaterinburg v. FIBA Europe e. V., 29 October 2009
CAS 2010/A/2071, Irish Football Association (IFA) v. Football Association of Ireland (FAI), Kearns & Fédération Internationale de Football Association (FIFA), 27 September 2010
CAS 2014/A/3776 Gibraltar Football Association (GFA) v. Fédération Internationale de Football Association (FIFA), 27 April 2016
CAS A2/2016, Lim v. Synchronised Swimming Australia Inc. (SSAI), 5 July 2016
CAS 2020/A/6933, Faure v. Al Salam Zgharta Club & Fédération Internationale de Football Association (FIFA), 26 January 2021
Court of Appeal, England and Wales, Reel v. Holder and another, [1981] 1 WLR 1226 (26 June 1981)
CJEU, case C-369/90, Micheletti v. Delegación del Gobierno en Cantabria
"Olympic skier Eileen Gu sparks a debate about dual nationality: China does not allow it. But there may be loopholes," The Economist (17 February 2022), https://www.economist.com/china/2022/02/17/olympic-skier-eileen-gu-sparks-a-debate-about-dual-nationality
Eritrea-Ethiopian Claims Commission (Permanent Court of Arbitration), Civilian Claims (Eritrea v Ethiopia), Partial Award, International Legal Materials, vol. 44 (2004)
European Commission, Infringement decisions (9 June 2021), https://ec.europa.eu/commission/presscorner/detail/en/inf_21_2743
European Commission, "Investor Citizenship and Residence Schemes in the European Union," EU Doc. COM(2019) 12 final (SWD(2019) 5 final) (23 January 2019)
European Commission, Press release, "Investor citizenship schemes: European Commission opens infringements against Cyprus and Malta for 'selling' EU citizenship" (20 October 2020), https://ec.europa.eu/commission/presscorner/detail/en/ip_20_1925
European Commission, "On progress towards effective EU citizenship 2013-2016," EU Doc. COM(2017) 32 final (24 January 2017)
European Parliament, European Parliament resolution of 10 July 2020 on a comprehensive Union policy on preventing money laundering and terrorist financing—the Commission's Action Plan and other recent developments (2020/2686(RSP)), EU Doc. P9_TA(2020)0204
[European] Convention for the Protection of Human Rights and Fundamental Freedoms, 4 November 1950, 213 UNTS 222, CETS. No. 5
European Convention on Nationality, 6 November 1997, CETS No. 166
ECtHR, Andrejeva v Latvia, 18.12.2009
ECtHR, C v Belgium, 07.08.1996
ECtHR, Ciubotaru v. Moldova, 27.04.2010
ECtHR, Gaygusuz v Austria, 16.09.1996
ECtHR, Genovese v. Malta, 11.10.2011
ECtHR, K2 v UK, 09.03.2017

ECtHR, Koua Poirrez v France, 30.12.2003
ECtHR, Kuric and Others v. Slovenia, 13.07.2010
ECtHR, Labassee v. France, 26.06.2014
ECtHR, Makuc v Slovenia, 31.05.2007
ECtHR, Mennesson v France, 26.06.2014
ECtHR, Poenaru v. Romania, 13.11.2001
Human Rights Committee, A v. Australia, Comm No. 560/1993 (30 April 1997)
Human Rights Committee, General Comment 15: The Position of Aliens Under the Covenant (1986)
Human Rights Committee, CCPR General Comment No. 27: Article 12 (Freedom of Movement) UN Doc. CCPR/C/21/Rev.1/Add.9 (2 November 1999)
Human Rights Committee, Gueye et al. v France, Comm 196/1985 (3 April 1989)
Human Rights Committee, Sipin v Estonia, Comm No 1432/2005 (9 July 2008)
Human Rights Committee and UN Secretary-General, Human rights and arbitrary deprivation of nationality (19 December 2012)
Human Rights Council, Draft report of the Working Group on the Universal Periodic Review: Austria UN Doc. A/HRC/WG.6/23/L.10 (11 November 2015)
Human Rights Council, Draft report of the Working Group on the Universal Periodic Review: Myanmar, UN Doc. A/HRC/WG.6/23/L.9 (10 November 2015)
Inter-American Court of Human Rights, Bronstein v Peru (6 February 2001)
Inter-American Court of Human Rights, Castillo Petruzzi et al. Case (30 May 1999)
Inter-American Court of Human Rights, Case of Expelled Dominicans & Haitians v Dominican Republic, Ser. C No 282 (28 August 2014)
Inter-American Court of Human Rights, Juridical Conditions and Rights of the Undocumented Migrants, OC-18/03 (17 September 2003)
Inter-American Court of Human Rights, Proposed Amendments to the Naturalization Provisions of the Constitution of Costa Rica, OC-4/84 (19 January 1984)
Inter-American Court of Human Rights, Yean & Bosico Children v. Dominican Republic, Ser. C, Case 130, Judgment (8 September 2005)
International Convention on the Elimination of All Forms of Racial Discrimination, UN GA Res. 2106 (XX) (21 December 1965), 660 UNTS 195
International Convention on the Protection of the Rights of All Migrant Workers and Members of Their Families, UNGA Res. 45/158 (Dec. 18, 1990), 2220 UNTS 3
International Convention on the Protection of the Rights of All Migrant Workers and Members of Their Families, UNGA Res. 45/158 (18 December 1990), 2220 UNTS 3
International Covenant on Civil and Political Rights, 16 December 1966, 999 UNTS 171
International Covenant on Economic, Social and Cultural Rights, 16 December 1966, 999 UNTS 3
International Court of Justice, Application of the International Convention on the International Convention on the Elimination of All Forms of Racial Discrimination (Qatar v UAE), Preliminary Objections, Judgment, 2021 ICJ Reps 71

International Court of Justice, Legal Consequences for States of the Continued Presence of South Africa in Namibia (South West Africa) Notwithstanding Security Council Resolution 276 (1970), Advisory Opinion, 1971 ICJ Reps 16
International Court of Justice, Nottebohm Case (Liechtenstein v Guatemala), Second phase, Judgment, 1955 ICJ Reps 4
International Criminal Tribunal for Rwanda, Prosecutor v Akayesu, Case No. ICTR-96-4-T, Judgment (2 September 1998)
International Law Commission, Draft Articles on Diplomatic Protection with Commentaries, UN Doc A/61/10 (2006)
International Olympic Committee, "Chinese Taipei," https://olympics.com/ioc/chinese-taipei
International Olympic Committee, [Code of] Ethics, January 2022, https://stillmedab.olympic.org/media/Document%20Library/OlympicOrg/Documents/Code-of-Ethics/Code-of-Ethics-ENG.pdf#page=14&_ga=2.159102330.1177896064.1618845860-971153820.1601050134
International Olympic Committee, IOC Refugee Olympic Team Tokyo 2020, https://olympics.com/ioc/refugee-olympic-team-tokyo-2020
International Olympic Committee, Olympic Charter, 2021
Iran-US Claims Tribunal, Case No. A/18 (Iran v. US), Iran-US Claims Tribunal Reporter vol. 5, (1984)
Italian-US Conciliation Commission, Flegenheimer (US v. Italy), UNRIAA vol. 14 (1958)
New York, Liang Ren-Guey v. Lake Placid 1980 Olympic Games Inc., 424 N.Y. S.2d 535 (3d Dep't NY, 1980), affirmed, 403 N.E.2d 178 (1980)
Oberste Gerichtshof (OGH), Austria, Emanuel V. v. Austrian Ice Hockey Association & International Ice Hockey Federation (IIHF), 2 Ob 232/98a (24 September 1998)
Open Society Justice Initiative, "Human Rights in the Context of Automatic Naturalization in Crimea" (2018), https://www.opensocietyfoundations.org/sites/default/files/report-osji-crimea-20180601.pdf
Permanent Court of International Justice, Nationality Decrees Issued in Tunis and Morocco (French Zone) on November 8th, 1921, Advisory Opinion, 1923 PCIJ, Ser. B, No. 4
Protocol to the African Charter on Human and Peoples' Rights on the Rights of Women in Africa, 11 July 2003, https://au.int/sites/default/files/treaties/37077-treaty-charter_on_rights_of_women_in_africa.pdf
UN General Assembly Res 217 A(III), Universal Declaration of Human Rights, UN Doc. A/810 (10 December 1948), art. 15(1)
UN Educational, Scientific and Cultural Organization, "International Charter of Physical Education, Physical Activity and Sport," UN Doc. SHS/2015/PI/H/14 REV (2015), https://unesdoc.unesco.org/ark:/48223/pf0000235409
UN Secretary-General, Arbitrary Deprivation of Nationality: Report of the Secretary-General, UN Doc. A/HRC/10/34 (26 Jan. 2009)

State of the Union Address by President von der Leyen at the European Parliament Plenary, (16 September 2020), https://ec.europa.eu/commission/presscorner/detail/en/SPEECH_20_1655

References

Baker K, Tracy J (2022) Team China's foreign-born Olympians. Axios, 17 February 2022. https://www.axios.com/2022/02/17/team-china-olympic-import-athletes
Brownlie I (2008) Principles of international law
Chetail V (2019) International migration law
Kochenov D (2010) Citizenship without respect: the EU's troubled equality ideal. Jean Monnet paper no. 8/10
Kochenov D (2012) Two sovereign states vs. a human being: ECJ as a guardian of arbitrariness in citizenship matters. In: Talani LS (ed) Globalisation, migration, and the future of Europe
Macklin A (2017) Is it time to retire Nottebohm? AJIL Unbound 111
Marian C (2011) Who is afraid of Nottebohm?: Reconciling the ICSID nationality requirement for natural persons with Nottebohm's 'Effective Nationality' test. J Int Arbitr 28(4)
Shaw MN (2008) International law
Sironi A (2013) Nationality of individuals in public international law: a functional approach. In: Annoni A, Forlati S (eds) The changing role of nationality in international law
Spiro PJ (2010) Dual citizenship as human right. Int J Constitutional Law 8
Spiro PJ (2012) The end of Olympic nationality. In: Rubenstein K (ed) Allegiance and identity in a globalised world
Spiro PJ (2019) *Nottebohm* and 'Genuine Link': anatomy of a jurisprudential illusion. Investment migration working papers IMC-RP2019/1. https://investmentmigration.org/wp-content/uploads/2020/10/IMC-RP-2019-1-Peter-Spiro.pdf
Spiro PJ (2020) Problematizing Olympic nationality. AJIL Unbound 117
Weis P (1979) Nationality and statelessness in international law
Worster WT (2009) International law and the expulsion of individuals with more than one nationality. UCLA J Int Law Foreign Aff 14
Worster WT (2019) The obligation to grant nationality to stateless children under customary international law. Mich State Int Law Rev 27
Worster WT (2020) European Union citizenship and the unlawful denial of Member States nationality. Fordham Int Law J 43
Worster WT (2022a) Discrimination on the basis of nationality under the convention on the elimination of racial discrimination. Pace Int Law Rev 35(1)
Worster WT (2022b) The divergence between the International Court of Justice and the Committee on the Elimination of Racial Discrimination regarding Nationality-Based Discrimination. Am Soc Int Law Insight 25(13)
Zeid, Davis R (2020) Independent Expert Report, "Recommendations for an IOC Human Rights Strategy", International Olympic Committee. https://stillmed.olympics.com/media/Document%20Library/OlympicOrg/News/2020/12/Independent_Expert_Report_IOC_HumanRights.pdf. Last accessed 13 Oct 2022

William Thomas Worster teaches public international law, the law of international organizations, and international migration and nationality law at The Hague University of Applied Sciences and the University of Missouri-Kansas City. He earned a JD from Chicago-Kent College of Law and an LLM in Public International Law from Leiden University. He is also currently an external PhD candidate at the University of Amsterdam. His research interests focus on his areas of teaching with a particular focus on international legal actors, sources of international law, and nationality law.

Athlete Activism at the Olympics: Challenging the Legality of Rule 50 as a Restriction on Freedom of Expression

Mark James and Guy Osborn

Contents

The authors would like to thank the editorial team and everyone who attended the workshop on Sport and Human Rights hosted by the University of Lausanne for their comments and advice on developing this chapter.

M. James (✉)
Manchester Law School, Manchester Metropolitan University, Manchester, UK
e-mail: mark.james@mmu.ac.uk

G. Osborn
Westminster Law School, University of Westminster, London, UK
e-mail: g.osborn@westminster.ac.uk

V. Boillet et al. (eds.), *Sports and Human Rights*, Interdisciplinary Studies in Human Rights 10, https://doi.org/10.1007/978-3-031-56452-9_8

Abstract Since Colin Kaepernick began taking the knee during the American national anthem to protest social injustice and inequality in the USA in 2016, athletes across a range of sports and from diverse national backgrounds have used their high media profiles to draw attention to the causes that they support. The International Olympic Committee, however, has maintained its stance that politics and sport should not mix, and that human rights should not be used as a tool to undermine the political autonomy of sport. Rule 50(2) of the Olympic Charter states that, "No kind of demonstration or political, religious or racial propaganda is permitted in any Olympic sites, venues or other areas". Anyone in breach of this provision may be disqualified from their event and have their Olympic accreditation removed, a position that was reinforced by the guidance issued to athletes prior to the Tokyo 2020 Olympic Games.

Using examples of athlete activism at Tokyo 2020 as case studies, this chapter will analyze whether any of these exercises of the right to freedom of expression were in breach of Rule 50(2). It will then examine whether the application of Rule 50(2) at Tokyo 2020 is compatible with Article 10 European Convention of Human Rights and the likely outcome of any challenge before the Court of Arbitration for Sport, the Swiss Federal Tribunal, and the European Court of Human Rights. It concludes by arguing for a complete overhaul of Rule 50(2) so that it promotes, rather than prohibits, freedom of expression.

1 The Rise of Athlete Activism

For the first time since the Black Power salute at the Mexico 1968 Olympic Games,[1] there has been a dramatic increase in activist athletes around the world engaging in protests to promote their support for a range of social justice causes. From the National Football League's Colin Kaepernick taking the knee during the American national anthem to protest social injustice and inequality in the United States of America, to wearing rainbows to support LGBTQI+ rights, athletes across a range of sports and from diverse social and national backgrounds have used their high profile and moments in the spotlight to draw attention to the causes that they support. In response, the International Olympic Committee (IOC) has sought to reassert its control over athlete behavior by providing additional guidance on how Rule 50(2) of the Olympic Charter (Rule 50) operates to prohibit demonstrations and propaganda in support of political, religious, and racial causes. The question addressed by this chapter is whether the prohibitions and restrictions on athletes' ability to exercise their freedom of expression is infringed by the operation of Rule 50.

---

[1] From this point, each edition of the Olympic Games is referred to by its 'City + Year' format, for example, Mexico 1968.

The IOC justifies the need for Rule 50 by stating that the Olympic Games should be politically neutral, with the world's focus solely on the sporting performances of the athletes. To achieve this, all acts of athlete activism are prohibited, or severely restricted, to ensure that athletes do not exploit their moment in the spotlight for non-sporting causes. Here, the legality of Rule 50 will be interrogated using the framework of protections for free expression provided by Article 10 of the European Convention on Human Rights (ECHR). By analyzing these restrictions through a human rights lens, this chapter will explain how Rule 50 lacks the necessary clarity, serves no legitimate aim, and is neither a necessary nor a proportionate response to the activities that attract the opprobrium of the IOC.

The aim of this chapter is to demonstrate that, despite the IOC's ideal of a politically neutral Olympics, the means by which it has sought to achieve this cannot withstand legal analysis. It argues that freedom of expression, and in particular the freedom of political expression, is a necessary part of a democratic society, and that any restrictions on the operation of Article 10 ECHR should not be imposed on a section of society, Olympic athletes, at the whim of a non-state actor, the IOC. In concluding that Rule 50 in its current form is an unlawful infringement of Article 10 ECHR, practical advice is offered to the IOC, and the Olympic Movement more generally, on how a more inclusive approach to athletes' human rights can be developed.

To conduct this analysis, the chapter draws on a wide variety of instances of athlete activism that occurred at Tokyo 2020. This was the first Olympic Games to take place under the specific new guidance on the interpretation and operation of Rule 50, with a number of athletes taking the opportunity to exploit the lack of clarity of the new regime. These acts of activism are first analyzed to determine whether they were in breach of Rule 50 and the accompanying guidance. Having determined the scope of the operation of Rule 50 through its application to the real-life examples from Tokyo 2020, a hypothetical challenge to a finding that an athlete should be disciplined for exercising their freedom of expression is undertaken. This demonstrates that an athlete is likely to succeed in a claim that Rule 50 infringes Article 10 ECHR in either the Court of Arbitration for Sport (CAS), the Swiss Federal Tribunal (SFT), and/or the European Court of Human Rights (ECtHR).

The chapter begins with an analysis of the evolution of athlete activism and the restrictions that have been imposed on athletes' ability to display in public their views on issues of social, racial, and political justice. It will move on to examine how Rule 50 was applied at Tokyo 2020 and the precedents that this could set for athletes at future editions of the Games, before analyzing the ways in which an athlete could bring a human rights challenge to any punishment imposed on them for exercising their freedom of expression. Finally, the chapter will examine the IOC's indirect law-making capabilities to demonstrate how it could require host nations to provide specific protections for athletes' human rights. This will contrast the approach of the IOC towards the protections required of hosts in respect of its intellectual property and commercial rights, and its claimed inability to influence legal change to increase human rights protections. It concludes that the forced transplantation of Olympic Laws from one host jurisdiction to the next, a technique that has been used to regulate ambush marketing, could be used in a positive way as a template for ensuring that universally accepted human rights are embedded in the host jurisdiction as a condition of hosting the Games.

2 Athlete Activism at the Olympic Games

Sport and politics have long had an uneasy relationship. Whilst most major sports bodies, including in particular the IOC, claim to be apolitical or politically neutral, international sport is regarded by many as inherently political.[2] The relationship between sport and politics is particularly strained when athletes themselves engage in moments of activism. Mexico 1968 witnessed a step-change in the impact that athlete activism could have in a mediated world. The Black Power salute of US athletes John Carlos and Tommie Smith, supported by Australian Peter Norman wearing an Olympic Human Rights Project badge, and Czech gymnast Vera Čáslavská's looking away whilst the Russian national anthem was played during the gymnastics medal ceremony, are now considered to be iconic moments of athlete activism that rightly deserve to be celebrated. Such overtly political demonstrations are rarely condoned and regularly condemned by sports administrators, fans, and the media, who still consider that sport and politics should not mix. Only with the benefit of hindsight are these activists celebrated for their bravery; Carlos and Smith were inducted into the United States Olympic and Paralympic (USPOC) Committee Hall of Fame in 2019,[3] Norman was posthumously awarded Olympic Order of Merit by the Australian Olympic Committee in 2018,[4] and Čáslavská became President of the Czech Olympic Committee and, in 1995, a member of the IOC.[5]

Since 1956, the Olympic Charter has contained a specific prohibition on athletes 'profiting politically' from their participation in the Games.[6] Any breach of this provision could be punished under what was then Rule 23 of the Charter, which stated that, as the Supreme Authority, the IOC was the final arbiter on all questions concerning the Olympic Games and the Olympic Movement. Rule 23 provided the IOC with absolute discretion on how to deal with anything that it considered to be

[2]For an overview of sport and politics see Kelly and Lee (2020), and for further detail on specific issues see Boykoff (2017), Hoberman (2011) and Kidd (2013).

[3]Hall of fame biographies for Carlos: https://www.teamusa.org/Hall-of-Fame/Hall-of-Fame-Members/John-Carlos and Smith: https://www.teamusa.org/Hall-of-Fame/Hall-of-Fame-Members/Tommie-Smith (last accessed 2 March 2022).

[4]Australian Olympic Committee, 'Peter Norman's family to accept Olympic Order of Merit tonight' https://www.olympics.com.au/news/peter-normans-family-to-accept-olympic-order-of-merit-tonight/ (last accessed 2 March 2022).

[5]Čáslavská's Olympic biography: https://www.olympedia.org/athletes/29115 (last accessed 2 March 2022).

[6]IOC (1956), p. 77.

inappropriate behavior, with no right of appeal available to any athlete punished under this power.

The IOC's response to the activism at Mexico 1968, led by its then President Avery Brundage, was to reaffirm the absolute prohibition on athletes demonstrating or engaging in 'propaganda' whilst at the Olympics. Over the next 10 years,[7] this prohibition was given increasing visibility in the 'Instructions to Athletes' section of the Charter. Following further protests by US athletes Vincent Matthews and Wayne Collett at Munich 1972,[8] the prohibition was elevated to the main body of the Olympic Charter as part of Rule 55, which placed restrictions on athletes' ability to exploit their participation in the Games commercially or politically. The prohibition has remained largely unchanged, resulting in what is now Rule 50.

Technically, any athlete in breach of Rule 50, or any of its predecessor Rules and Instructions, ran the risk of disqualification from their event, removal of their Olympic accreditation and expulsion from the Athletes' Village. Although rarely used to its fullest extent, the threat of being sanctioned under Rule 50 has resulted in Olympic athletes rarely having tested its limits, and generally backing down in response to a threat from the IOC that their conduct might be in breach.[9]

Since Colin Kaepernick first took the knee in 2016, athlete activism and its relationship with freedom of expression has been increasingly under the spotlight, becoming a particular concern of the IOC's in the months leading up to Tokyo 2020. For the first time, it issued detailed guidance on how Rule 50 was to be interpreted and applied at an Olympics, making clear that it had no intention of allowing the Games to become a platform for political expression. Although later amended, and in some ways relaxed by subsequent guidance, the ground rules had been set for a clash between the IOC's determination to keep the Olympic Games free from politics, and athletes' determination to use perhaps the highest profile stage of their career to demonstrate their support for a specific cause.

3 The Evolution of the Restrictions Imposed on Athlete Activism at the Olympic Games[10]

One of the founding and fundamental principles of the modern Olympic Movement was an avowed adherence to the concept of amateurism. This prevented any athlete from profiting commercially from competing at the Games, as well as preventing professional athletes and others who earned a living from sport from becoming

---

[7] For more detail on the evolution of Rule 50 see James and Osborn (2024) and Terraz (2014).

[8] See Tomizawa (2016).

[9] James and Osborn (2014), and the protest by US 400m gold medallists Lee Evans, Larry James and Ron Freeman, who wore Black Panther style berets raised their fists, but stopped protesting as the medal ceremony began: Anon (2021).

[10] On the evolution of Olympic governance more generally, see Chappelet (2016).

Olympians. In the 1956 edition of the Olympic Charter, this general prohibition was extended to prevent all individuals, organizations, and nations from profiting from the Games both commercially *and politically*. This prohibition was, at first, not part of the main body of the Charter, but constituted 'General Information' about the Games, found under the section, 'The Olympic Games are Amateur'.[11] Anyone breaching this prohibition could be punished under Rule 23 of the Olympic Charter, which stated that, as the Supreme Authority, the IOC was the final arbiter on all questions concerning the Olympic Games and the Olympic Movement. It was this power that enabled IOC President Avery Brundage to demand the expulsion of Tommie Smith and John Carlos from Mexico 1968.

There is a long and rich tradition of athlete activism at, or around, the Olympic Games. Cottrell and Nelson have identified several characteristics that help to explain why the Olympics are such an attractive platform for activism:[12] that the Olympics are accessible and high-profile, with almost all states invited to attend, ensuring that any protest is likely to attract significant and worldwide media attention; that activists can expect to forge new alliances with like-minded others as a result of their activism (as was seen when Peter Norman supported Tommie Smith and John Carols at Mexico 1968); and that, as the Olympics are attributed special symbolic meaning, there is a resultant widening of political opportunity. It is, therefore, no surprise that athletes have used these high-profile and highly mediated opportunities to draw attention to the causes that they support when the Olympic spotlight is on them.

Mexico 1968 took place against a backdrop of political turmoil around the world. Europe had witnessed the Prague Spring and student riots in Paris. In the USA, Martin Luther King Jr and Robert Kennedy were both assassinated, and in Mexico, the Tlatelolco Massacre saw more than 200 students killed when the army opened fire on a protest against the Government's spending on the Olympics instead of on social and welfare programs. Mexico 1968 saw some of the most iconic instances of athlete activism: Smith and Carlos' Black Power salutes, the support of the Black Panther movement by Lee Evans, Larry James and Ron Freeman, and the subtle act of defiance by Czech gymnast Vera Čáslavská, who looked down and away from the flags when the Russian national anthem was played for the controversial award of joint gold medals in the beam and floor exercises. These acts of activism triggered the rapid evolution of what had been a general prohibition on athlete activism into the Rule 50 that is applicable today, as the IOC determined that further action was needed to protect the political neutrality of the Olympic Games and the wider Olympic Movement.

The 1971 edition of the Olympic Charter gave greater prominence to the prohibition by placing it in a new section of the Instructions titled, 'The Olympic Games are not for Profit', though without changing the wording first introduced in 1956.[13]

---

[11] IOC (1956), p. 77.

[12] Cottrell and Nelson (2010), p. 733.

[13] IOC (1971), p. 48.

Following further protests by US athletes Vincent Matthews and Wayne Collett at Munich 1972,[14] the prohibition was finally included in Rule 55 of the Olympic Charter, under the subheading, 'Advertising, propaganda':

> Every kind of demonstration or propaganda, whether political, religious or racial, in the Olympic areas is forbidden.[15]

In 1978, Rule 55 was broken down into separate issues, resulting in the prohibition on athlete activism being elevated to the status of a Rule of the Olympic Charter in its own right:

> 57 Propaganda and advertising
>
> Every kind of demonstration or propaganda, whether political, religious or racial, is forbidden in the Olympic areas.[16]

Finally, in 2011, we see the current version of Rule 50 for the first time, becoming Rule 50(2) in 2015: No kind of demonstration or political, religious or racial propaganda is permitted in any Olympic sites, venues or other areas.[17]

Throughout this period, there was no specific justification for the prevention of athlete activism, except the IOC's claim that that politics should be kept away from sport to protect its political neutrality. Further, there were no prescribed procedures for the investigation and prosecution of suspected breaches of Rule 50 or any of its predecessors. This left the IOC with an incredibly wide-ranging discretion on whether and how to punish an athlete using its powers as the Supreme Authority of the Olympic Movement under Rule 23. More recently, a similarly wide explanation of the IOC's powers to investigate athletes for breaches of the Olympic Charter now can be found in Rule 59, supplemented by Bye-law 1. If found in breach, Rule 59(2.1) gives the IOC Executive Board, or its delegate, the power to punish athletes with:

> Temporary or permanent ineligibility or exclusion from the Olympic Games, disqualification or withdrawal of accreditation; in the case of disqualification or exclusion, the medals and diplomas obtained in relation to the relevant infringement of the Olympic Charter shall be returned to the IOC. In addition, at the discretion of the IOC Executive Board, a competitor or a team may lose the benefit of any ranking obtained in relation to other events at the Olympic Games at which he or it was disqualified or excluded; in such case the medals and diplomas won by him or it shall be returned to the IOC (Executive Board).

Further, Rule 59(2.5) enables the IOC to impose a financial penalty in addition to any punishment imposed in Rule 59(2.1). Finally, Rule 61(2) of the Olympic Charter provides that any appeal against a decision of the IOC made in respect of the Olympic Games can only be made to the CAS. Although the range of punishments and route of appeal is now clear, the investigatory process and powers of the IOC to

[14] Tomizawa (2016).

[15] IOC (1975), p. 35.

[16] IOC (1978), p. 31.

[17] IOC (2015), p. 93.

determine whether an athlete is in breach of Rule 50 (or any other Rule) remains opaque.

4 The Re-Emergence of the Athlete Activist and the IOC's Rule 50 Guidance

The re-emergence of the high-profile activist athlete began in 2016, with American footballer Colin Kaepernik 'taking the knee' when the US national anthem was played before San Francisco 49ers games.[18] At the 2019 Pan-American Games, US hammer thrower Gwen Berry and fencer Race Imboden raised a fist and took the knee on the medal podium respectively.[19] The high-profile nature of their demonstrations, and their status as prospective participants at Tokyo 2020, caused IOC President Thomas Bach to state that, "The Olympic Games [. . .] are not, and must never be, a platform to advance political or any other potentially divisive ends".[20]

The current iteration of Rule 50 of the Olympic Charter states that, "No kind of demonstration or political, religious or racial propaganda is permitted in any Olympic sites, venues or other areas".[21] Without further gloss, Rule 50 provides for an absolute prohibition on all demonstrations and political propaganda. The IOC Executive Board is the sole arbiter of whether or not an athlete's expression constitutes a prohibited demonstration or other form of propaganda, and is therefore in breach of Rule 50, and the type and severity of the punishment that will be imposed on them.

In January 2020, the first Rule 50 Guidelines were published by the IOC Athletes' Commission.[22] This stated unequivocally that all protests and/or demonstrations taking place during an event, in the Olympic Village, or during the opening, closing, and medal ceremonies were prohibited. A non-exhaustive list of what would constitute a prohibited protest, as opposed to a legitimate expression of an athlete's views, included: displaying any political messaging, including signs or armbands; gestures of a political nature, like a hand gesture or kneeling; and refusing to follow the Ceremonies' protocols.[23]

If an athlete was suspected of acting in breach of Rule 50, the incident would be evaluated by their respective NOC, ISF and the IOC, with disciplinary action taken on a case-by-case basis as necessary, which could include the disqualification of the athlete and the removal of their Olympic accreditation. Although this guidance was

[18] Kotecha (2020).

[19] Anon (2019).

[20] Bach (2020).

[21] IOC (2021), p. 94.

[22] IOC Athletes' Commission (2020).

[23] IOC Athletes' Commission (2020), p. 2.

later modified, it set the tone for the IOC's approach to athlete activism: it is not welcome at the Olympic Games.

Following a survey of athletes conducted by the IOC Athletes' Commission,[24] revised Guidelines were published in July 2021.[25] This new guidance relaxed the original Guidelines by allowing Olympic participants to make 'expressions' (including gestures) in the playing arena before the start of an event. Demonstrations were still prohibited, as were expressions, demonstrations, and propaganda during all official ceremonies. This change of approach allowed athletes, for example, to take the knee on the pitch before the start of a football match.[26] To comply with Rule 50, the Guidelines require that an 'expression' must:

(i) be consistent with the Fundamental Principles of Olympism;
(ii) not target, directly or indirectly, people, countries, organizations and/or their dignity;
(iii) not be disruptive [for example, it must not interfere with other athletes' concentration on and/or preparation for the event, physically interfere with the introduction of another athlete, or risk causing, or actually cause, physical harm to persons or property); and
(iv) not be prohibited or otherwise limited by the rules of the relevant National Olympic Committee and/or the competition regulations of the relevant International Federation.[27]

Further, any expression must also be compliant with the laws of the host nation.

The four requirements that any such expression must fulfil provide the most detailed guidance to date on what is, and what is not, an acceptable expression. First, an interesting development in the Tokyo 2020 Guidelines is the reference to the Fundamental Principles of Olympism (FPOOs). Found at the beginning of the Olympic Charter, the FPOOs have evolved over time into a mission statement and guiding ethos for the Olympic Movement. Of the seven FPOOs, three are of particular importance here and can be summarized as requiring athletes to: act with social responsibility and respect for universal fundamental ethical principles (Principle 1); promote a peaceful society concerned with the preservation of human dignity (Principle 2); and act at all times without discrimination of any kind (Principle 6).[28]

A novel approach to athlete activism was used by a number of athletes at Sochi 2014 as part of the 'Principle 6 Campaign'.[29] Instead of criticizing directly Russia's

---

[24] IOC Athletes' Commission (2021a).

[25] IOC Athletes' Commission (2021b).

[26] Both FIFA and World Athletics had supported athletes' right to take the knee before the start of an event. See for example, Steinberg (2020) and BBC (2020).

[27] IOC Athletes' Commission (2021b), p. 3.

[28] IOC (2021), p. 8.

[29] Athlete Ally statement on the Principle 6 Campaign and its impact: https://www.athleteally.org/p6-campaign-continues-make-difference/.

'anti-gay' laws, athletes supported LGBTQI+ rights by promoting the anti-discrimination agenda defined in Principle 6 FPOOs, ultimately resulting in the addition of sexual orientation to the list of protected characteristics.[30] By requiring that any expression complies with the FPOOs, the range of causes that can be supported by activist athletes has the potential to be expanded dramatically as, it will be argued, occurred at Tokyo 2020.

Secondly, an important limitation on athletes' freedom of expression is that it must not target people, countries, and/or organizations. This prevents both direct and indirect comment on the behavior, policies and politics of identifiable others, as occurred on three occasions at Tokyo 2020, ensuring that only expressions of support for generic causes should be tolerated. The third criterion will rarely come into play, as it is justifiable on the grounds that it is needed to promote the integrity of sport and/or prevent what is likely to be unlawful conduct of some kind. The fourth criterion adds little, as any additional prohibition required by an NOC or ISF that goes beyond the restriction on freedom of expression imposed by Rule 50 itself is unlikely to be justifiable legally.

As both the IOC and the CAS, where appeals against the IOC's decisions on conduct at the Olympic Games are heard, are located in Lausanne, Switzerland, the application and legality of Rule 50 will be analyzed against the right to freedom of expression as protected by Article 10 ECHR.[31] Following *Platini v Switzerland*,[32] the SFT has the power to review both procedural and substantive complaints raised under the ECHR. This in turn will allow athletes to bring actions against Switzerland where their freedom of expression has been unlawfully restricted by a sports organization headquarterd there.[33]

The legality of the Rule 50 restrictions on athletes' freedom of expression under Article 10 ECHR is determined by addressing the following criteria: is Rule 50 an interference with athletes' freedom of expression; is that interference prescribed by law; does the interference serve a legitimate aim; and is the interference necessary and proportionate in a democratic society? Despite Rule 50 being watered down by the Tokyo 2020 Guidelines, its application appears to be a *prima facie* restriction on athletes' freedom of expression because: it prevents them from expressing political opinions that, under normal circumstances, they would be free to express; it lacks sufficient clarity, accessibility, and predictability to be considered 'law' and appears to operate as an unfettered exercise of the IOC's discretion; and it is neither a necessary nor proportionate restriction that operates in furtherance of one of the acknowledged legitimate aims. Before examining whether the operation of Rule

---

[30]The Olympic Charter was updated on 8 December 2014 to reflect the additional of sexual orientation to Principle 6 FPOOs, IOC (2014).

[31]For how other human rights instruments could apply to this issue, see Shahlaei (2017).

[32]Federal Supreme Court, *Platini v Switzerland* 5 March 2020, no. 526/18, (dec.).

[33]For more detail on this issue see, Rietiker, D, 'Freedom of Expression of Athletes and Players: The Current and Potential Role of the ECtHR as a Watchdog in Sport' and the introduction to this book. On identifying the appropriate state party see further, Shinohara (2021).

50 is in breach of Article 10 ECHR, it is necessary to analyze how it has been interpreted and applied to incidents of athlete activism in light of the new guidance.

5 The application of Rule 50 at Tokyo 2020

Tokyo 2020 saw more varied instances of athlete activism than at any other edition of the modern Olympic Games. The athletes supported a wide range of causes, using a variety of innovative expressions and gestures. In each case, the expression was made by means of a gesture, sign or other non-verbal behavior. In none of the cases could the expression be considered to be disruptive, as defined by the Guidelines, nor were they otherwise in breach of any additional rules of the relevant NOC or ISF, nor were they in breach of Japanese national law. Prior to the publication of the Guidelines, each of these gestures would have been in breach of Rule 50 and could have resulted in punitive action being taking against the athlete. At the same time, each of these gestures, whether in support of political, social, racial or religious causes, would be protected under Article 10 ECHR if performed anywhere other than at the Olympic Games. The Tokyo 2020 expressions can be divided into three categories: those that were clearly in breach of Rule 50 and the accompanying Guidelines; those that appeared to be in breach; and those that were permitted under the Guidelines.

5.1 *Clear Breaches of Rule 50*

There were three demonstrations or protests that could be considered overtly political at Tokyo 2020. First, before the Games started, the South Korean delegation protested that the IOC and Tokyo organizing committee had refused to take formal steps to prohibit the flying of the Rising Sun flag, which is associated with Japan's colonial past and was used by the Japanese Imperial Army during the Second World War. As the Rising Sun is not an official flag of Japan, and therefore should not be flown in any Olympic venue, a prohibition was considered unnecessary. In response, a banner was hung from the South Korean accommodation in the Olympic Village quoting the sixteenth Century Korean Admiral Yi Sun-sin, who led 12 warships to an unlikely victory over the 300-strong Japanese Navy: "I still have support from 50 million Korean people". The IOC officially requested the removal of the banners as a potential breach of Rule 50. The Korean Sport and Olympic Committee removed the banners after the IOC agreed to treat any display of the Rising Sun flag in the same way.[34] As a politically motivated demonstration aimed at a specific country or people, the banner was a clear breach of Rule 50.

[34] Berkeley (2021).

Secondly, Algerian judoka Fethi Nourine withdrew from his event at Tokyo 2020 to avoid the possibility of facing Israeli competitor Tohar Butbul in the second round.[35] At his subsequent disciplinary hearing, Nourine was suspended from all International Judo Federation sanctioned events for 10 years, as his conduct was contrary to the Federation's Statutes, its Code of Ethics, and Rule 50. Nourine, who was the only athlete punished for his protest, was making a politically- and religiously-motivated expression in the belief that that his support for the Palestinian cause was bigger "than all of this" and that it was the right decision to retire.[36]

Thirdly, Chinese cyclists Bao Shanju and Zhong Tianshi were warned about their behavior after wearing badges depicting the former Chairman of the Chinese Communist Party, Mao Zedong, at their gold medal ceremony.[37] Although a clear breach of Rule 50 as a political expression, or propaganda, the IOC accepted the Chinese Olympic Committee's assurance that this would not be repeated so no further action was taken.[38] In all three cases, the actions of the athletes would be considered protected political expression in most other circumstances, providing clear examples of IOC exceptionalism.

5.2 *Apparent Breaches of Rule 50, But No Action Taken*

The next group of examples concern situations where the athletes' expressions not only appear to breach Rule 50, but do not conform with the criteria provided for allowable expressions under the Guidelines. During their initial pre-event introductions, three of the US men's fencing team wore pink face masks whilst the fourth, Alen Hadzic, wore a black one. Hadzic had not been informed that his teammates would be demonstrating their solidarity with survivors of sexual assault. Without further context, a pre-event demonstration of general support for survivors of sex crimes would fall into the same category of expression as taking the knee and could be interpreted as supporting Principles 1 and 2 of the FPOOs. However, as Hadzic was at the time being investigated for committing sexual assault against three women,[39] this could have been considered to be a protest targeted at an individual and therefore a breach of Rule 50.

Three other expressions appear in breach of Rule 50 because they were performed during the course of an event or during an official ceremony. Costa Rican gymnast Luciana Alvarado incorporated both raising her fist and taking the knee into the finale of her gymnastics floor routine. As this formed part of the artistic content of

---

[35] Ingle (2021).

[36] Decision of the IJF available at: https://www.ijf.org/news/show/fethi-nourine-and-amar-benikhlef-disciplinary-decision (last accessed 27 May 2022).

[37] Reuters (2021).

[38] BBC (2021).

[39] Niesen (2021).

her routine, the IOC did not take action against what would have been a clear breach of Rule 50 in any other sport. Alvarado justified her anti-discrimination and inclusion message as being, "because we're all the same. We're all beautiful and amazing".[40] Similarly, US discus thrower, Sam Mattis, competed with a cross surrounded by a circle drawn on his arm.[41] Technically, as this was an expression performed during the event, without prior permission from the IOC, and not forming part of an artistic element of the performance, it was in breach of Rule 50.[42] The same expression was made by US fencer, Race Imboden, when receiving his bronze medal, contrary to the absolute prohibition on making any expression during a medal ceremony. The cross surrounded by a circle drew inspiration from the actions of Raven Saunders (discussed below), drawing attention to social and racial injustices in the USA.

In each of these cases, the expressions could be said to support Principles 1, 2 and 6 of the FPOOs and do not in any other respect breach the Guidelines except for where they took place. In all four cases, expressing support for these causes in these ways would be considered a lawful exercise of the right to freedom of expression in non-Olympic settings.

5.3 No breach of Rule 50

The final examples illustrate where athletes were allowed to express themselves freely, though the precise reasons for why they were not in breach of Rule 50 are not always clear. The first group of athletes to avail themselves of the more relaxed approach to athlete activism permitted by the Tokyo 2020 Guidelines were footballers in the women's competition. As the Guidelines, supported by FIFA, allowed for expressions to be made on the pitch prior to the start of the game, footballers from a number of countries took advantage of this new approach by taking the knee before kick-off. The first to do so were Team GB, who were joined by their Chilean opponents and the match officials, who wanted "to fight all forms of discrimination and inequality, not just within sport but in the world".[43] Similarly, the Australian women's football team stood behind the Aboriginal flag, instead of the Australian national flag, before their first group game against New Zealand.[44] Their justification was one of inclusion and anti-discrimination from a uniquely Australian perspective,

[40] Adams (2021).

[41] For the reaction to the same expression performed during a medal ceremony, see below.

[42] Contrast this reaction with that of the USATF and USOPC who prevented Nick Symmonds from competing in the US trials for Rio 2016 with the logo of a personal sponsor drawn on his arm: *Gold Medal LLC v US Track & Field and US Olympic Committee*, US District Court for the District of Oregon, Civ. No.6:16-cv-00092-MC.

[43] Kyodo News (2021).

[44] NITV (2021).

again ensuring compliance with the new guidance. In both cases, the expressions can be said to support Principles 1, 2 and 6 of the FPOOs and so do not breach Rule 50 *at some events*. It should be noted that expressions of this nature were expressly prohibited by World Swimming,[45] demonstrating an ongoing lack of consistency and transparency in how the same actions can be treated differently by different ISFs, and potentially, NOCs.

Raven Saunders was initially investigated for performing a gesture at the end of the women's shot put medal ceremony. After the flags had been raised, the anthem had finished, and the protocols were completed, she crossed her arms above her head in solidarity with all oppressed people: "[The cross is] the intersection of where all people who are oppressed meet".[46] The IOC demanded that the USOPC conduct an investigation into the incident, which resulted in a finding that Saunders had not breached its code of conduct.[47] The IOC only dropped its investigation when Saunders had to return to the USA following the death of her mother. This incident raises a number of issues. First, did the expression take place during a medal ceremony? There is no recognised endpoint to a medal ceremony, so it is unclear whether her expression took place during (which is prohibited), or after its conclusion (which may not be prohibited). Secondly, if the expression was performed after the completion of the medal ceremony, not during competition on the field of play, and not in the Olympic Village, is it in breach of Rule 50 because it was performed in an Olympic Venue? Although Rule 50 itself prohibits demonstrations at Olympic venues, there is no additional guidance on the acceptability of post-event, as opposed to pre-event, protests. The lack of explanation from the IOC of both why Saunders was investigated, and why the investigation was ultimately dropped, again leaves the application of Rule 50 unclear and inconsistent.

Finally, German field hockey captain, Nike Lorenz, was permitted by the IOC to wear a rainbow band on her socks in support of LGBTQI+ rights, inclusion and anti-discrimination, a position clearly in support of Principle 6 FPOOs.[48] Under normal circumstances, an expression of this nature performed on the field of play during the course of an event would be absolutely prohibited. In this case, however, the athlete was granted permission to express her support for her chosen cause, which although laudable, creates further difficulties in terms of the need for transparency and consistency of application of Rule 50 and its accompanying Guidelines. There is no published process for requesting permission, and no guidance on what sort of expressions might be permitted, or why such permission might be granted or denied.

In conclusion, the approach taken to the enforcement of Rule 50 at Tokyo 2020 has created further confusion as to how and why it is applied to instances of athlete activism. Despite explicit prohibitions on expressions being performed during events and medal ceremonies, both were allowed at Tokyo 2020. The range of

---

[45] FINA (2021).

[46] The Guardian (2021).

[47] Ganguly (2021).

[48] Welt (2021).

expressions allowed suggests that almost anything in support of a general cause promoting social and/or racial justice, inclusion and anti-discrimination will be permitted. Only the most overt displays of political advocacy remain prohibited, despite the wording of Rule 50 and its interpretative Guidelines. If an activist athlete is punished for their expressions in the future, it can be almost guaranteed that any penalty imposed will be challenged.

6 The Different Routes to Challenging a Punishment for Breaching Rule 50

If an athlete has breached Rule 50, there are two potential sources of punishment. First, the IOC can investigate and prosecute the breach, or delegate such powers to the relevant NOC and/or ISF, as happened in the case of Raven Saunders. If found in breach, the IOC has the power to disqualify and/or remove the accreditation of the offending athlete. Secondly, the athlete's ISF can impose sanctions, as happened with Fethi Nourine. In either case, a first appeal can be made to CAS, either to its Ad Hoc Division that sits at each edition of the Games, or to the full tribunal in Lausanne under Rule 61 of the Olympic Charter. From here, there are limited opportunities of appeal to the SFT, and ultimately, the ECtHR.[49]

As CAS has its seat in Switzerland, its arbitrations are governed by Swiss arbitration law, specifically Chapter 12 of the Swiss Private International Law Act. Following *Pechstein v Switzerland*,[50] as CAS is required to adhere to the requirements of Article 6(1) ECHR then, by analogy, CAS could decide that all claims founded on breaches of Convention rights are also within its jurisdiction.[51] Alternatively, as Swiss law is the governing law of disputes involving the IOC, then the ECHR can be applied, or its values taken into consideration, when interpreting the grounds for appeal.[52] In either case, CAS could determine whether the protection of

[49]An alternative route for an athlete could be to go directly against the state in which their NOC is based, or against Switzerland, as the host jurisdiction of the IOC, as states are under a positive obligation to create an environment in which everyone is able to express their opinions and ideas without fear. This includes a positive obligation to protect that person's freedom of expression against attacks by non-state actors, *Dink v Turkey*, 14 September 2010, application nos. 2668/07, 6102/08, 30079/08, 7072/09 and 7124/09, par. 106 et seq. As a challenge beginning with an appeal to CAS is the most likely path for this litigation, and the ultimate reasoning of the ECtHR would be the same, only this route is discussed here. For further information on alternative challenges, see Shahlaei (2017).

[50]ECtHR, *Mutu and Pechstein v. Switzerland*, 2 October 2018, application nos. 40575/10 and 67474/10. See further, Goertz (2020).

[51]For a discussion of when CAS has discussed ECHR issues, see de la Rochefoucauld and Reeb (2021).

[52]CAS 2013/A/3139 *Fenerbahce SK v. UEFA* 5 December 2013, par. 88–89.

political neutrality in sport is a legitimate aim for restricting athletes' freedom of expression.

The most closely analogous case that has been heard before CAS,[53] *Josip Šimunić v FIFA*,[54] found that no protection could be founded on Article 10 ECHR where a Croatian professional footballer led fans in chants evoking the Ustaše, a Croatian fascist organization responsible for atrocities against various ethnic groups during WWII. It was legitimate for FIFA to restrict references to the Ustaše regime and fascism on the basis of its discriminatory connotations, and the 10-match ban imposed was appropriate in the circumstances. In a separate appeal to the ECtHR following his criminal conviction for inciting hatred on the basis of race, nationality, and faith, it was held that the restriction on his Article 10 rights,

> struck a fair balance between the applicant's interest in free speech, on the one hand, and the society's interests in promoting tolerance and mutual respect at sports events as well as combating discrimination through sport on the other hand, thus [the state was] acting within their margin of appreciation.[55]

Thus, CAS would have the jurisdiction to hear a case brought on the basis that Rule 50 breaches Article 10 ECHR.

If CAS either declines jurisdiction, or upholds the restrictions in Rule 50 as lawful, then an athlete has a limited ground of appeal to the SFT under Article 190(2)(e) of the Swiss Private International Law Act. The athlete will need to demonstrate that the CAS decision is contrary to Swiss public policy, such that Rule 50 is an unlawful restriction on free speech or offends the prohibition against discrimination on the grounds of their political opinions. The prohibition on discrimination has been interpreted extremely narrowly, with the SFT holding that Article 14 ECHR is not directly applicable as a ground for setting aside an international arbitral award in Switzerland.[56] A final appeal to the ECtHR could be brought against Switzerland on the grounds that a Swiss-based tribunal has failed to uphold the athlete's Convention rights.[57]

A possible alternative approach could be to bring proceedings directly against Switzerland on the basis of the state's failure to protect athletes' freedom of expression from interference by a non-state actor; the IOC.[58] The United Nations Guiding Principles on Business and Human Rights (UNGPs) apply, "to all States and to all business enterprises, both transnational and others, regardless of their size, sector, location, ownership and structure".[59] Thus, the

[53] For a history of CAS opinions on Article 10 ECHR see Abanazir (2022).

[54] CAS 2014/A/3562 *Josip Šimunić v FIFA* 29 July 2014.

[55] ECtHR, *Josip Šimunić v. Croatia,* 22 January 2019, application no. 20373/17, para. 48.

[56] Federal Supreme Court, *Leeper v World Athletics* 2 June 2021, 4A_618/2020 (dec).

[57] Schwab (2018), pp. 179–181.

[58] For more detail on the application of the UNGPs to sport see the introduction to this volume and further, Schwab (2019).

[59] United Nations Human Rights (2012), p. 1.

> UNGPs apply to [International Sports Organisations] and all sporting organizations within the world of professional sport, including leagues, clubs, national associations, academies, dispute resolution services, regulatory and enforcement agencies. [...] It can also be safely said that the UNGPs include the human rights of the players within their purview.[60]

Thus, the UNGPs apply to the IOC in the same way that they apply to all businesses.[61] Indeed, in its Strategic Framework on Human Rights, the IOC, "affirms its commitment to respecting human rights within its remit in accordance with the UNGPs".[62] As one of its Foundational Principles, the UNGPs state that, "Business enterprises should respect human rights. This means that they should avoid infringing on the human rights of others and should address adverse human rights impacts with which they are involved".[63]

This requires the IOC to respect the human rights of those affected by its Rules, in this case, the freedom of expression of Olympic athletes. As states are under a positive obligation to protect individuals from human rights abuses committed by businesses located within their jurisdiction, the ECtHR would have jurisdiction over an action brought by an athlete where their freedom of expression has been unlawfully restricted by the operation of Rule 50.[64] This would enable the ECtHR to examine the legality of the restrictions imposed by a non-state actor in a horizontal relationship with an individual, including that between the IOC and athletes competing at the Olympic Games. In particular, the ECtHR has determined that Article 10 ECHR protects political comment and acts of protest or expression on matters of public interest and debate from restrictions imposed by horizontal relationships,[65] including making gestures and wearing badges expressing affiliation with an issue or political group.[66] If the Swiss state is unable to justify why the IOC's restrictions are legitimate, necessary and proportionate, the Swiss government could be found to have violated Article 10 ECHR by its failure to protect athletes from the effects of Rule 50.

7 Does the Application of Rule 50 to Athlete Activism at Tokyo 2020 Breach Article 10 ECHR?

As noted above, the legality of any restrictions on an athlete's freedom of expression under Article 10 ECHR is determined by addressing the following criteria: is Rule 50 an interference with athletes' freedom of expression; is that interference

[60] Schwab (2017).

[61] Ruggie (2016).

[62] IOC (2022).

[63] United Nations Human Rights (2012), p. 13.

[64] ECtHR, *Mutu and Pechstein v. Switzerland*, 2 October 2018, applications nos. 40575/10 and 67474/10.

[65] Faut (2014), p. 256.

[66] ECtHR, *Vajnai v. Hungary*, 8 July 2008, application no. 33629/06, para. 47.

prescribed by law; does the interference serve a legitimate aim; and is the interference necessary and proportionate in a democratic society? These will now be examined in more detail.

7.1 *Is Rule 50 an Interference with the Athlete's Freedom of Expression?*

The Rule 50 prohibition on any kind of demonstration and all political, religious and/or racial propaganda is a clear restriction on athlete activism and athletes' exercise of their right to free expression. Although neither 'demonstration' nor 'propaganda' are defined in the Olympic Charter or the accompanying Guidance, it is clear from the actions of the IOC in the past,[67] and comments by President Thomas Bach more recently,[68] that any comment, gesture, item of clothing, or badge that projects support for a political, social, racial, or religious message can breach Rule 50. Without good reasons for the restriction, and despite the spatial and temporal limitations provided by Rule 50 and the Guidelines, preventing athletes' ability to comment on political issues and matters of public importance and debate is a *prima facie* restriction on their Article 10 ECHR rights.

7.2 *Is the Interference Caused by Rule 50 Prescribed by Law?*

Any restrictions on freedom of expression must be clear, accessible, predictable, and not operate as an unfettered exercise of discretion.[69] The lack of specificity of its definitions and transparency of its application runs the risk of Rule 50 being found to be insufficiently precise to be considered 'law', and both unnecessary and disproportionate.

Neither Rule 50 nor the Guidelines provide definitions of what constitutes a demonstration, propaganda, or an expression, although a 'gesture' is provided as an example of an expression in the Guidelines. Prior to Tokyo 2020, unacceptable gestures included: raising a fist; taking the knee; wearing a black armband as a mark of respect or bereavement; crossing one's arms at the finish line; waving an unofficial flag; looking away from the winner's flag during a medal ceremony; and covering one's medal whilst the anthem of another country was playing.[70] Conversely, gestures that have not been investigated by the IOC include: crossing oneself or genuflecting

---

[67] James and Osborn (2014).

[68] Bach (2020).

[69] For discussion of this issue in the sporting context, see Goh (2021), p. 23, and the shorter opinion piece version, Goh (2022).

[70] James and Osborn (2024), ch. 2.

before, during, or after an event; saluting one's flag; and placing one's hand on one's heart during a medal ceremony or whilst the national anthem is being played. Each of these gestures could be considered either an unacceptable political, religious or racial demonstration, or an acceptable expression of religion, nationality, or support for an issue of social justice and inclusion. This position was confused further by the lack of explanation of why the various gestures performed at Tokyo 2020 were neither investigated nor punished. This lack of clarity is exacerbated by the lack of explanation of why this wide range of gestures attracts such variable treatment.

The lack of definitional clarity leads to a lack of accessibility. As athletes cannot ascertain in advance with any degree of certainty which expressions are permitted and which demonstrations are prohibited, they are unable to adjust their behavior accordingly. This concomitant lack of predictability in the application of Rule 50 is compounded by the Guidance stating that expressions must comply with the Fundamental Principles of Olympism. Much of the athlete activism at Tokyo 2020 promoted diversity, tolerance, fairness, anti-discrimination, and inclusion. Conformity with the FPOOs should mean that such an expression is no longer a prohibited demonstration, protest, or propaganda stunt, as the IOC considers the Olympic Charter to be an inherently apolitical document.[71] However, it remains unclear where the line is drawn between promoting Olympism and acting politically.[72] The lack of clear definitions for the key behaviors leads to a rule that is open to inconsistency of both interpretation and application, resulting in unfairness to athletes engaging in activism in and around the Olympic Games. Further, the enforcement of Rule 50 appears to be an unfettered exercise of the IOC's discretion, as it has the ultimate power to determine whether a breach has occurred. This shows that the IOC has lost control of the interpretation of Rule 50, and, therefore, that it needs to be reframed through a human rights lens to ensure its future legitimacy.

7.3 Does the Interference Caused by Rule 50 Serve a Legitimate Aim?

Article 10(2) ECHR lists the circumstances in which freedom of expression can be restricted legitimately: in the interests of national security, territorial integrity or public safety; for the prevention of disorder or crime; for the protection of health or morals; for the protection of the reputation or rights of others; for preventing the disclosure of information received in confidence; or for maintaining the authority and impartiality of the judiciary. The principle of legitimacy is interpreted narrowly, leaving the preservation of sporting neutrality unlikely to be considered as necessary for the functioning of society.[73] Following the highly politicized responses of many

[71] See also Anmol (2020), p. 71.

[72] James and Osborn (2014).

[73] For a more detailed analysis of the meaning of legitimate aims in sport, see Goh (2021), although her conclusions that Rule 50's claims to promote political neutrality are valid is disputed.

ISFs to the Russian invasion of Ukraine, including in particular the IOC, it will be all the more difficult to sustain an argument that athlete activism should be restricted to protect sport's political neutrality.[74]

Rule 50 should make clear that freedom of expression is protected, except in cases analogous to the legitimate aims, not that it is prohibited except in specific limited circumstances. The Guidance states that expressions must not be: targeted, directly or indirectly, against people, countries, organizations and/or their dignity; disruptive ... [in that they are capable of] causing or risking physical harm to persons or property; discriminatory, promote hatred or hostility, or have the potential to incite violence; illegal in the host country.[75]

These restrictions align with the legitimate aims of preventing disorder or crime, protecting the reputation or rights of others, and preventing the disclosure of confidential information, and, by analogy, could be justified as situations in which free expression could be limited. Although the ECtHR has held that restrictions on hate speech are incompatible with Article 10 ECHR,[76] a spatially and temporally limited restriction could perhaps be justified on the grounds of preventing disorder or crime.[77] The expressions made by Olympic athletes rarely breach these aims or the Guidance, providing little justification for prohibiting all demonstrations and propaganda in the name of maintaining the Olympic Movement's political neutrality. For example, only the conduct of the Korean Sport and Olympic Committee, Nourine, and the Team USA fencers could be said to have been targeted at a specific person or country.

7.4 Is the Interference Caused by Rule 50 Necessary and Proportionate in a Democratic Society to Achieve the Legitimate Aim?

The breadth of interpretation of Rule 50 and the punishments imposed for its breach are not proportionate to its stated aim of preserving the political neutrality of sport. Restrictions on freedom of expression must meet a pressing social need, involve the least possible interference to meet the legitimate aim, and be underpinned by relevant and sufficient reasons for their imposition.[78] Without an underpinning 'legitimate aim' there is no acknowledged pressing social need for the restrictions

[74] Lindholm (2022), p. 1.

[75] IOC Athletes' Commission (2021b), p. 3.

[76] ECtHR, *Vejdeland and ors v Sweden*, 9 May 2012, application no. 1813/07.

[77] ECtHR, Application no. 20373/17, *Josip Šimunić v. Croatia*. See also Di Marco (2021), where the point is made that freedom to express criticism of superiors has been allowed, if not the more general freedom of expression under discussion here.

[78] Summarised in ECtHR, *Stoll v. Switzerland,* 10 December 2007, application no. 69698/01, para. 101, and restated in ECtHR *Morice v. France*, 23 April 2015, application no. 29369/10, para. 124.

imposed by Rule 50. On the contrary, it could be argued that there *is* a pressing social need for athlete activists to act as role models and use their platform to challenge structural injustices and discrimination of all kinds.[79]

Further, the punishments that can be imposed on athletes for breaching Rule 50 need to be clarified to ensure that they do not amount to a form of censorship, and that any penalties imposed are proportionate.[80] With no clear punishment structure in place and an inconsistent approach to explaining how and why an athlete has breached Rule 50, any penalty imposed appears to be arbitrary. To be proportionate, any restriction of athletes' freedom of expression must be the least restrictive means of achieving Rule 50's aim. Thus, freedom of expression, and in particular political expression, should be permitted, except in the circumstances highlighted in Article 10(2), not prohibited and allowed only in specific circumstances permitted by the IOC. Finally, no clearly articulated reasons for the imposition of the restrictions have ever been provided, beyond the argument that the rule is there to protect the political neutrality of the Olympic Games. Reasons that align with the legitimate aims, not simply a statement of the IOC's desire, must be provided.

7.5 Does Rule 50 Unlawfully Interfere with Athletes' Freedom of Expression?

The application of Rule 50 appears to be an unfettered exercise of the IOC's discretion, rather than a justifiable, necessary, and proportionate response to a specifically identified, pressing social need. The lack of clarity of the sanctioning framework reinforces this conclusion. Athletes simply do not know whether they are acting in accordance with Rule 50, or will be investigated (Saunders), warned (Bao and Zhong), expelled (Carlos and Smith), or banned (Nourine).

In its current form, Rule 50 appears incompatible with Article 10 ECHR. The justification for its existence lacks clarity and is inconsistently applied by the IOC itself. As can be seen from the approach undertaken at Tokyo 2020, Rule 50 lacks definitional clarity and its application lacks consistency and is without an underpinning rationale, making it difficult to justify either its legitimacy of purpose or inherent legality. Save for the most extreme and targeted demonstrations or expressions, it will be difficult to show that there is a compelling social need for Rule 50 that is necessary in a democratic society.[81] If the Swiss state is unable to justify why the IOC's restrictions are legitimate, necessary, and proportionate, it could be found to have violated Article 10 by its failure to protect athletes from the effects of

---

[79] See further, Di Marco (2021), p. 636.

[80] ECtHR, *Vereinigung Bildender Künstler v. Austria*, 25 April 2007, application no. 68354/01, para. 37.

[81] ECtHR, *Palomo Sanchex and others v. Spain*, 8 December 2009, application nos. 28955/06, 28957/06, 28959/06 and 28964/06.

Rule 50. A finding that Rule 50 is unlawful would allow athletes greater scope to exercise their freedom of expression, provided that, as role models, they do so responsibly.[82] The IOC would have a narrow margin of appreciation on expressions of public interest, but a much greater one where expressions are targeted at specific individuals, organizations, or countries.

8 Conclusion

The IOC's position on regulating athlete activism post-Tokyo 2020 is in many ways more confusing than it was when Rule 50 provided for an absolute prohibition on demonstrations and propaganda. The application of Rule 50 at Tokyo 2020 was inconsistent, did not always follow the interpretative Guidelines, and lacked transparency because of the IOC's lack of explanations for why it approached each incident in the way that it did. Further, any claim of sport's political neutrality has been decimated by the responses of many ISFs to Russia's invasion of Ukraine, making reliance on ostensible apoliticality to justify imposing restrictions on athlete activism even more problematic.[83] Expressions made in support of generic causes related to issues of social justice, inclusion, anti-discrimination and LGBTQI+ rights no longer appear to breach Rule 50, as in most cases the athletes can also be said to be promoting the FPOOs. Even expressions that were not covered by the relaxed interpretations provided by the Guidelines, including those that took place during an event or medal ceremony, were not investigated or punished. However, expressions that targeted a particular person or country will not meet the second of the Guidance criteria, although this was not used as a justification to penalize the Team USA fencing team, whilst those that are overtly political remain absolutely prohibited.

From a legal perspective, Rule 50 appears to breach Article 10 ECHR. The restrictions that it imposes on athlete activists do not support one of the acknowledged legitimate aims, cannot be justified as either necessary or proportionate, and lack clarity, accessibility, and transparency in both their definition and application. The result of this analysis is that Rule 50 either needs to be repealed or rewritten in a way that protects freedom of expression by narrowing the scope of its application, and is underpinned by a clear, coherent, and legally robust justification.

The IOC Strategic Framework on Human Rights provides a route towards how human rights will be protected, respected, and remedied throughout the Olympic Movement in the future, with a series of measures planned to be operative by 2030.[84] At present, however, future editions of the Olympics are required to protect and respect human rights only in respect of those activities conducted in the execution of the Olympic Host Contract that are linked to the organization of the Games.[85]

---

[82] ECtHR, *Josip Šimunić v. Croatia*, 22 January 2019, application no. 20373/17.

[83] Lindholm (2022).

[84] IOC (2022).

[85] IOC (2018), para. 27.

Further, only those human rights that are applicable in the host country are covered by this requirement, rather than requiring new rights to be protected by the host. The IOC has repeatedly claimed that it is powerless to require host countries to change their laws to provide greater protections for human rights. Such a claim is undermined by the IOC's requirement that specific legislation is implemented to protect its commercial rights, and those of the host organizing committee from ambush marketing,[86] and ignores Rule 33(3) of the Olympic Charter, which requires that:

> 33 Election of the host of the Olympic Games
>
> 3 The national government of the country of any candidature must submit to the IOC a legally binding instrument by which *the said government undertakes and guarantees that the country and its public authorities will comply with and respect the Olympic Charter* (emphasis added).[87]

At present, the restrictions imposed on the ability of athletes to speak freely on political, religious, or racial issues remains subject to Rule 50 and its interpretative Guidelines. If it wants to avoid challenges to the legality of Rule 50, it is our specific recommendation that the IOC urgently takes a number of proactive steps. It needs to ensure that it has a clear and understandable rationale for the existence of Rule 50, and that it is applied consistently and transparently to each incident. Although some restrictions on targeted expressions may be justifiable, the IOC needs to be aware that their necessity will be interpreted narrowly.

First, the IOC must revisit whether there is a need for Rule 50. At present, there is only a commitment to, "review the wording of Rule 50.2 to reflect the IOC Guidelines",[88] not to review its inherent need and purpose. Although the restrictions have wide-ranging support from parts of the athlete community,[89] that is not sufficient justification for their continued existence in breach of Article 10 ECHR. If some restrictions are still considered necessary, then Rule 50 will need to be recalibrated so that it protects athletes' freedom of expression,[90] and to ensure that its application is in compliance with Article 10 ECHR. It is particularly important for the IOC to ensure that expressions in support of the FPOOs are not captured by a new Rule 50, and that there is a clear and transparent process for ensuring that support for causes aligned to Olympism can be promoted as part of the Olympic ideal. This 'relativization' of sporting neutrality may be a convenient compromise,[91]

---

[86] Ambush marketing is a highly contested term. In essence, it is a marketing technique used by brands that are not sponsoring an event that makes unauthorized associations with the event that either make it look like an official sponsor, or undermine the marketing campaigns of official sponsors. See further James and Osborn (2024), ch. 3.

[87] IOC (2021), p. 73.

[88] IOC (2022), Objective 1, Action 1.2, p. 27.

[89] IOC Athletes' Commission (2020).

[90] For more on the argument that the IOC needs to recalibrate its relationships with key stakeholders, see James and Osborn (2024).

[91] Di Marco (2021), p. 636.

but would need to be managed carefully to ensure clarity and consistency of interpretation and application of any revised Rule 50. Alongside of any revisions to Rule 50 and the Guidelines, the procedures for investigation, prosecution, and punishment will need to be stated clearly and accessibly, as will the process to be followed for applications for permissions to make an expression.

Secondly, the IOC must require the enforcement of the recalibrated Rule 50 in all host countries. Rule 33 requires that all host governments act in compliance with the Olympic Charter. If a new Rule 50 operated to protect and promote freedom of expression, instead of limiting or prohibiting it, then the IOC could require the host country to amend its laws to ensure that it has a suitably robust human rights framework in place to be able to host the Olympic Games. Objective 2, Action 2.1 of the Strategic Framework on Human Rights states that the IOC will finalize the creation and effective operation of the Human Rights Advisory Committee.[92] The aim of this Committee is to support the IOC to meet its commitments under the Strategic Framework, and to help monitor and evaluate its implementation. This should help to ensure that all bodies within the Olympic Movement, including the host nation, are human rights compliant.[93]

Thirdly, this requirement can be enforced using the transplant framework, which protects the IOC and the local organizing committees from ambush marketing,[94] by making adherence to appropriate fundamental human rights instruments a condition of hosting the Olympics. Despite its claims that it cannot require hosts to change their laws, the IOC has a long history of requiring law creation for the benefit of itself and its sponsors. In particular, the Olympic Host Contract requires legal protections for its intellectual property rights and those associated with the specific edition of the Games by means of laws to prevent and criminalize ambush marketing. Following this framework, the IOC creates its own internal legal norms, a *lex Olympica*, which it then requires by a clause in the Olympic Host Contract to be enacted into the law of the host of each edition of the Olympic Games. After the event's conclusion, the effectiveness of the enacted legislation is reviewed, creating changes to the *lex Olympica*, which then in turn is transplanted in an amended form into the law of the next host country. A failure to adhere to the legislative requirements can result in the withdrawal of the invitation to host the Games.[95]

Not only is there long precedent of the IOC requiring this indirect form of law creation, its ubiquity is reflected in more generic legislation on offer in some states for these protections to apply to events other than the Olympic Games.[96] Thus, the IOC is in a position, both under Rule 33 of the Olympic Charter, and by analogy with the anti-ambush marketing requirements, to demand that hosts allow athlete activists

[92] IOC (2022), p. 27.
[93] IOC (2022), p. 46.
[94] James and Osborn (2016).
[95] IOC (2021), Rule 36(2).
[96] James and Osborn (2019).

to express themselves in accordance with general human rights standards and/or in accordance with a recalibrated Rule 50.

Finally, CAS will also need to be aware of these potential developments. If complex human rights issues are likely to come before its panels covering not only cases under Article 10 ECHR but other relevant Convention rights, then it will need to ensure that at least some of its pool of arbitrators are suitably qualified to hear these cases.[97]

The reality is that the IOC is willing and able to use its leverage over an Olympic host to force national, regional, and city legislatures to enact laws on its behalf. The IOC's law creating ability is exerted through its influence over domestic legislatures, resulting in a corpus of Olympic Law that both enables the Games to take place and provides novel and extensive protections for the Olympic Properties.

There is no reason why the IOC could not impose similar legislative requirements for the protection of athletes' freedom of expression, and of human rights more generally. This could take a number of forms: the host country is required to be a signatory of relevant regional or transnational instruments; the required rights are incorporated into domestic law; or specific constitutional or other legislative protections are enacted. This would mean that all competitors, and anyone else associated with the Games, would have their human rights protected. To do so is not the conceptual leap of imagination that it is sometimes considered to be. It is instead simply enforcing the *lex Olympica* defined in Rule 33 of the Olympic Charter.

The IOC has had an ambivalent attitude towards the protection of human rights at the Olympic Games and throughout the Olympic Movement. It claims to respect human rights for all and considers the practice of sport itself to be a human right.[98] However, when faced with the practicalities of human rights protections, it has been slow to show the leadership required of it. The Strategic Framework is the start of a journey towards the greater protection of human rights in the Olympic Movement, but one where there are no guarantees of what the destination will be. Despite a specific requirement that the host government must comply with the Olympic Charter, there is no evidence that the IOC is enforcing Rule 33(3). If the IOC begins to enforce its own *lex Olympica*, then the Olympic Charter in general, and the FPOOs in particular, must be respected and complied with by the host country. This justifies the application of our transplantation framework to embed human rights protections in the law of each Olympic host on threat of the removal of the invitation to host the Games where such protections are not offered. The approach described above to embed freedom of expression into athletes' rights at the Olympic Games can be extended to all fundamental rights throughout the Olympic Movement. At that point, *lex Olympica* and *lex sportiva* can begin to claim that they are legitimate additions to the transnational legal space.[99]

---

[97] de la Rochefoucauld and Reeb (2021).

[98] IOC (2021) Principle 4 FPOOs.

[99] Schwab (2017).

Case List

Court of Arbitration for Sport

CAS 2013/A/3139 *Fenerbahce SK v. UEFA* 5 December 2013
CAS 2014/A/3562 *Josip Šimunić v FIFA* 29 July 2014

European Court of Human Rights

Morice v. France, 23 April 2015, application no. 29369/10
Mutu and Pechstein v. Switzerland, 2 October 2018, application nos. 40575/10 and 67474/10
Palomo Sanchex and others v. Spain, 8 December 2009, application nos. 28955/06, 28957/06, 28959/06 and 28964/06
Josip Šimunić v. Croatia, 22 January 2019, application no. 20373/17
Stoll v. Switzerland, 10 December 2007, application no. 69698/01
Vajnai v. Hungary, 8 July 2008, application no. 33629/06
Vejdeland and ors v Sweden, 9 May 2012, application no. 1813/07
Vereinigung Bildender Künstler v. Austria, 25 April 2007, application no. 68354/01

Swiss Federal Supreme Court

Leeper v World Athletics 2 June 2021, 4A_618/2020 (dec.)
Platini v Switzerland 5 March 2020, no. 526/18, (dec.)

US District Court for the District of Oregon

Gold Medal LLC v US Track & Field and US Olympic Committee, US District Court for the District of Oregon, Civ. No.6:16-cv-00092-MC

References

Abanazir C (2022) The court of arbitration for sport's multifarious views on freedom of expression. Verfassungsblog, Freedom of Expression in the Olympic Movement, 23 February, https://verfassungsblog.de/category/debates/freedom-of-expression-in-the-olympic-movement/. Accessed 15 Mar 2022

Adams E (2021) Costa Rica's Luciana Alvarado raises fist during gymnastics floor routine in support of Black Lives Matter. USA Today 26 July, https://eu.usatoday.com/story/sports/olympics/2021/07/26/olympic-gymnast-luciana-alvarado-raises-fist-black-lives-matter/5374945001/. Accessed 2 Mar 2022

Anmol J (2020) Political speech in sports: a case for non-prohibition. J Sports Law Policy Gov 2(1): 61–73

Anon (2019) US Olympic medal list faces discipline for taking knee after winning Pan-Am gold. The Guardian, 11 August 2019, https://www.theguardian.com/sport/2019/aug/10/race-imboden-kneels-national-anthem-pan-am-games. Accessed 27 May 2022

Anon (2021) Lee Evans, Olympic Runner Who Protested Racism, Dies at 74. New York Times, 19 May 2021, https://www.nytimes.com/2021/05/19/sports/olympics/lee-evans-olympic-runner-who-protested-racism-dies-at-74.html. Accessed 21 Oct 2022

Athlete A (2014) P6 campaign continues to make a difference. Athlete Ally., https://www.athleteally.org/p6-campaign-continues-make-difference/. Accessed 29 May 2022

Bach T (2020) New year's message 2020. IOC Media 1 January 2020, https://olympics.com/ioc/news/new-year-s-message-2020. Accessed 27 May 2022

BBC (2020) Tokyo Olympics: Lord Coe supports athletes right to take a knee. BBC Online 8 October, https://www.bbc.co.uk/sport/athletics/54460521. Accessed 29 May 2022

BBC (2021) China says no more Mao badges after IOC warning. BBC Online 7 August, https://www.bbc.co.uk/news/world-asia-china-58127804. Accessed 29 Mar 2022

Berkeley G (2021) South Korea told to remove banners at Tokyo 2020 Athletes' village by IOC. Inside the Games 17 July, https://www.insidethegames.biz/articles/1110306/south-korea-remove-banners-village. Accessed 2 Mar 2022

Boykoff J (2017) Protest, activism, and the Olympic games: an overview of key issues and iconic moments. Int J Hist Sport 34(3–4):162–183

Chappelet JL (2016) From Olympic administration to Olympic governance. Sport Soc 19(6): 739–751

Cottrell MP, Nelson T (2010) Not just the games? Power, protest and politics at the Olympics. Eur J Int Relat 17(4):729–753

De la Rochefoucauld E and Reeb M (2021) Sport and human rights: overview from a CAS perspective. CAS, 16 April, https://www.tas-cas.org/fileadmin/user_upload/Human_Rights_in_sport__CAS_report_updated_16.04.2021_.pdf. Accessed 5 Oct 2022

Di Marco A (2021) Athletes' freedom of expression: the relative political neutrality of sport. Human Rights Law Rev 21:620–640

Faut F (2014) The prohibition of political statements by athletes and its consistency with Article 10 of the European Convention on Human Rights: speech is silver, silence is gold? Int Sports Law J 14:253–263

FINA (2021) FINA Confirms Athlete Expression Opportunities For Tokyo 2020. FINA 7 July, https://www.fina.org/news/2185484/fina-confirms-athlete-expression-opportunities-for-tokyo-2020///. Accessed 2 Mar 2022

Ganguly S (2021) IOC says looking into gesture used by U.S. athlete Saunders on podium. Reuters 2 August, https://www.reuters.com/lifestyle/sports/olympics-ioc-says-looking-into-gesture-used-by-us-athlete-saunders-podium-2021-08-02/. Accessed 27 May 2022

Goertz D (2020) Recap of the Pechstein Saga: a hot potato in the hands of the sports arbitration community. Kluwer Arbitration Blog, 1 February, http://arbitrationblog.kluwerarbitration.com/2020/02/01/recap-of-the-pechstein-saga-a-hot-potato-in-the-hands-of-the-sports-arbitration-community/

Goh CL (2021) Rule 50 of the Olympic Charter and the Right to Freedom of Expression. SSRN, https://ssrn.com/abstract=3833327. Accessed 16 Mar 2022

Goh CL (2022) Rule 50 of the Olympic Charter and the Right to Freedom of Expression. Regulatory Review, 22 March, https://www.theregreview.org/2022/03/22/goh-rule-50-of-the-olympic-charter-and-freedom-of-expression/. Accessed 29 Mar 2022

Hoberman J (2011) The myth of sport as a peace-promoting political force. SAIS Rev Int Aff 31(1): 17–29

IJF (2021) Decision on Fethi Nourine, https://www.ijf.org/news/show/fethi-nourine-and-amar-benikhlef-disciplinary-decision. Accessed 27 May 2022

Ingle S (2021) Algerian judoka sent home from Olympics after refusing to face Israeli. The Guardian 24 July, https://www.theguardian.com/sport/2021/jul/24/algerian-judoka-sent-home-from-olympics-after-refusing-to-compete-against-israeli. Accessed 18 Feb 2022

IOC (1956) Olympic Charter 1956, https://stillmed.olympic.org/media/Document%20Library/OlympicOrg/Olympic-Studies-Centre/List-of-Resources/Official-Publications/Olympic-Charters/EN-1956-Olympic-Charter.pdf. Accessed 15 Feb 2022

IOC (1971) Olympic Charter 1971, https://library.olympics.com/Default/doc/SYRACUSE/70242/olympic-rules-and-regulations-international-olympic-committee. Accessed 12 Sept 2023

IOC (1975) Olympic Charter 1975, https://library.olympics.com/Default/doc/SYRACUSE/70266/olympic-rules-bye-laws-and-instructions-international-olympic-committee. Accessed 12 Sept 2023

IOC (1978) Olympic Charter 1978, https://library.olympics.com/Default/doc/SYRACUSE/172262/olympic-charter-1978-provisional-edition-international-olympic-committee. Accessed 12 Sept 2023

IOC (2014) Olympic Charter 2014, https://library.olympics.com/Default/digital-viewer/c-172429. Accessed 27 May 2022

IOC (2015) Olympic Charter 2015, https://library.olympics.com/Default/doc/SYRACUSE/172431/olympic-charter-in-force-as-from-2-august-2015-international-olympic-committee. Accessed 12 Sept 2023

IOC (2018) Host City Contract Operational Requirements, https://stillmed.olympic.org/media/Document%20Library/OlympicOrg/Documents/Host-City-Elections/XXXIII-Olympiad-2024/Host-City-Contract-2024-Operational-Requirements.pdf. Accessed 27 May 2022

IOC (2021) Olympic Charter 2021, https://stillmedab.olympic.org/media/Document%20Library/OlympicOrg/General/EN-Olympic-Charter.pdf. Accessed 27 May 2022

IOC (2022) IOC Strategic Framework on Human Rights, https://stillmed.olympics.com/media/Documents/Beyond-the-Games/Human-Rights/IOC-Strategic-Framework-on-Human-Rights.pdf. Accessed 6 Oct 2022

IOC Athletes' Commission (2020) Rule 50 Guidelines, https://stillmedab.olympic.org/media/Document%20Library/OlympicOrg/News/2020/01/Rule-50-Guidelines-Tokyo-2020.pdf. Accessed 19 May 2022

IOC Athletes' Commission (2021a) Recommendations on Rule 50 and athlete expression, https://olympics.com/athlete365/voice/ioc-athletes-commissions-recommendations-on-rule-50-and-athlete-expression/. Accessed 27 May 2022

IOC Athletes' Commission (2021b) Rule 50.2 Guidelines - Olympic Games Tokyo 2020, https://olympics.com/athlete365/app/uploads/2021/07/Rule-50.2-Guidelines-Olympic-Games-Tokyo-2020-Final.pdf. Accessed 19 May 2022

James M, Osborn G (2014) IOC rules at Sochi go too far with ban on black armbands. The Conversation, 21 February, https://theconversation.com/ioc-rules-at-sochi-go-too-far-with-ban-on-black-armbands-23555. Accessed 18 Feb 2022

James M, Osborn G (2016) The Olympics, transnational law and legal transplants: The International Olympic Committee, ambush marketing and ticket touting. Legal Stud 36(1):93–110

James M, Osborn G (2019) Pliant Bodies: Generic event laws and the normalisation of the exceptional. Aust New Zealand Sports Law J 12(1):77–95

James M, Osborn G (2024) Olympic laws: culture, values, Tensions. Routledge, Oxford

Kelly J, Lee JW (eds) (2020) Routledge handbook of sport and politics. Routledge, Oxford

Kidd B (2013) The myth of the ancient games. Sport Soc 16(4):416–424

Kotecha T (2020) Colin Kaepernick: How taking a knee started after NFL quarterback met Nate Boyer. Skysports, 30 December, https://www.skysports.com/nfl/news/12118/12170048/colin-

kaepernick-how-taking-a-knee-started-after-nfl-quarterback-met-nate-boyer. Accessed 27 May 2022
Kyodo News (2021) Britain, Chile women's Olympic soccer teams take knee before games opener. 21 July, https://english.kyodonews.net/news/2021/07/d2ac575d4ad7-britain-chile-womens-olympic-soccer-teams-take-knee-before-games-opener.html. Accessed 2 Mar 2022
Lindholm J (2022) How Russia's invasion of Ukraine shook sports' foundation. Int Sports Law J 22:1–4
Niesen J (2021) US fencer Alen Hadzic kept apart from team in Tokyo after sexual misconduct claims. The Guardian, 23 July, https://www.theguardian.com/sport/2021/jul/23/us-fencer-alen-hadzic-sexual-impropriety-tokyo-olympics-allegations. Accessed 27 May 2022
NITV (2021) Matildas hold up Aboriginal flag ahead of Olympic win over New Zealand. 22 July, https://www.sbs.com.au/nitv/article/2021/07/22/matildas-hold-aboriginal-flag-ahead-olympic-win-over-new-zealand. Accessed Mar 2022
Reuters (2021) Chinese champions wear Mao badges on cycling podium. 2 August, https://www.reuters.com/lifestyle/sports/chinese-champions-wear-mao-badges-cycling-podium-2021-08-02/. Accessed 29 Mar 2022
Ruggie J (2016) "For the game. For the world." FIFA and human rights. Corporate Responsibility Initiative Report No. 68. Harvard Kennedy School, Cambridge, MA. https://www.hks.harvard.edu/centers/mrcbg/programs/cri/research/reports/report68. Accessed 31 Jan 22
Schwab B (2017) "When We Know Better, We Do Better." Embedding the Human Rights of Players as a Prerequisite to the Legitimacy of Lex Sportiva and Sport's Justice System. Maryl J Int Law 32(1) 4, https://digitalcommons.law.umaryland.edu/mjil/vol32/iss1/4/?utm_source=digitalcommons.law.umaryland.edu%2Fmjil%2Fvol32%2Fiss1%2F4&utm_medium=PDF&utm_campaign=PDFCoverPages. Accessed 16 Mar 2022
Schwab B (2018) "Celebrate Humanity": reconciling sport and human rights through athlete activism. J Legal Aspects Sport 28(2):170–207
Schwab B (2019) Protect, respect and remedy: global sport and human rights'. Int Sports Law Rev 3:52–65
Shahlaei F (2017) When sports stand against human rights: regulating restrictions on athlete speech in the global sports arena. Loy Los Angeles Entertain Law Rev 38(1):99–120
Shinohara T (2021) Which states parties should be held responsible for the implementation of positive obligations under the ECHR in sports-related disputes? Int Sports Law J Online, https://link.springer.com/article/10.1007/s40318-021-00202-1#citeas. Accessed 6 Oct 2022
Steinberg J (2020) FA unlikely to discipline players for taking a knee as FIFA urges leniency. The Guardian, 2 June, https://www.theguardian.com/football/2020/jun/02/fa-will-take-common-sense-approach-to-players-taking-a-knee-in-matches
Terraz T (2014) '(A)Political Games? Ubiquitous Nationalism and the IOC's Hypocrisy. Asser Sports Law Blog, https://www.asser.nl/SportsLaw/Blog/post/a-political-games-ubiquitous-nationalism-and-the-ioc-s-hypocrisy. Accessed 2 Mar 2022
The Guardian (2019) US Olympic medalist faces discipline for taking knee after winning Pan-Am gold. 11 August, https://www.theguardian.com/sport/2019/aug/10/race-imboden-kneels-national-anthem-pan-am-games. Accessed 27 May 2022
The Guardian (2021) Raven Saunders throws up X on podium to represent where the 'oppressed meet'. 1 August, https://www.theguardian.com/sport/2021/aug/01/raven-saunders-x-gesture-olympic-podium-tokyo-2020-shot-put. Accessed 18 Feb 2022
Tomizawa R (2016) Vincent Matthews and Wayne Collett: a most casual protest with most striking consequences. The Olympians, 18 November 2016, https://theolympians.co/2016/11/18/vincent-matthews-and-wayne-collett-a-most-casual-protest-with-most-striking-consequences/. Accessed 18 Feb 2022

United Nations Human Rights, Office of the High Commissioner (2012) Guiding Principles on Business and Human Rights. HR/PUB/11/4

Welt D (2021) "The only right thing": Hockey's Nike Lorenz allowed to wear rainbow band. 22 July, https://www.dw.com/en/the-only-right-thing-hockeys-nike-lorenz-allowed-to-wear-rainbow-band/a-58610913. Accessed 2 Mar 2022

Mark James is Professor of Sports Law at Manchester Law School. He is one of the UK's leading sports lawyers and an expert in Olympic law. He is the author of *Sports Law* (Palgrave Macmillan), co-author of *Olympic Laws* (Routledge) and the Editor in Chief of the International Sports Law Journal.

Guy Osborn is Professor of Law at Westminster Law School and a Director of the Centre for Law, Society and of Popular Culture at the University. He is a founding editor of the Entertainment and Sports Law Journal and editor of the Routledge Monograph series Studies in Law, Society and Popular Culture. He is Co-Artistic Director at the Soho Poly, a recently restored theatre in central London.

The Incompatibility of Banning Political Speech in Sports with the Right to Freedom of Expression Under the European Convention on Human Rights

H. Burak Gemalmaz

Contents

Abstract The SGBs and the CAS have created principles specific to the realm of sports based on the assumption that sports has a specific legal order and dispute resolution mechanisms independent from the state, namely, *lex sportiva*. In fact, sports law has specific principles, rules, and applications that diverge from International Human Rights Law.

I would like to thank my doctoral students Zeynep Günler and Egemen Esen for their valuable research, and Sare Karacan for her contribution in translating latest Turkish football legislation into English.

H. B. Gemalmaz (✉)
Faculty of Law, Istanbul University, Istanbul, Türkiye

V. Boillet et al. (eds.), *Sports and Human Rights*, Interdisciplinary Studies in Human Rights 10, https://doi.org/10.1007/978-3-031-56452-9_9

But the aforementioned *lex sportiva* assumption cannot be extended to totally exclude human rights concerns in the field of sports, especially after the recent ECtHR rulings, starting with *Mutu & Pechstein Case*. Through those rulings, human rights standards infiltrate into sports law.

This article particularly focusses on one of the most contested sports law rules, namely prohibition on political statements of sportspersons, adopted by all SBGs, in the light of recent judgments of ECtHR against Turkey concerning freedom of expression under Article 10 of the ECHR, and asserts that categorical universal ban on political speech in sports is not in conformity with the right to freedom of expression. However, after analysing relevant ECtHR judgments in detail, the article argues that by confining its review strictly to procedural grounds, the ECtHR missed the opportunity to rule the incompatibility of a blanket ban on political speech in sports with freedom of expression at an abstract level.

The article concludes that the ECtHR's acceptance that sportspersons have the freedom of speech in political matters and that such a right cannot be suspended categorically due to the sole fact that they belong to sports community, nevertheless, indicates that blanket ban on political speech cannot be sustainable any more.

1 Introduction

In 2016, Colin Kaepernick, an American footballer, took a knee during the singing of the national anthem before the match, as part of a protest against the oppression of African American people and police brutality.[1] Since then, the gesture has become a statement against racism, and a political symbol in the sports world. In 2017, then President Donald Trump made several speeches accusing American Football players who kneeled during the national anthem of disrespecting the flag, and encouraged NFL team owners to fire those players, and for fans to leave the stadium in counter-protest.[2] This tension between protesting NFL players and President Trump went beyond the borders of American football and spread to all major sports leagues. For example, one of the most famous NBA players, Lebron James, showed support to another NBA player Stephen Curry who refused the invitation to the White House.[3] Similarly, baseball player Bruce Maxwell from the Oakland Athletics mirrored the protests by NFL players against racial injustice and kneeled during the national

[1] What's taking the knee and why is it important?, 21 November 2022, BBC News, https://www.bbc.com/news/explainers-53098516 (last accessed 4 December 2022).

[2] Graham B A, Donald Trump blasts NFL anthem protesters: 'Get that son of a bitch off the field', 23 September 2017, The Guardian, https://www.theguardian.com/sport/2017/sep/22/donald-trump-nfl-national-anthem-protests (last accessed 4 December 2022).

[3] Jennings P and Kaepernick C, From one man kneeling to a movement dividing a country, 11 October 2017, BBC Sport, https://www.bbc.com/sport/american-football/41530732 (last accessed 4 December 2022).

anthem.[4] Most recently, the world has witnessed several political actions from football players at the FIFA World Cup in Qatar. In a joint statement, the football associations of England, Wales, Belgium, the Netherlands, Switzerland, Germany, and Denmark brought forward that their intent to wear OneLove armbands had to be abandoned because of the risk of sporting sanctions by FIFA.[5] The OneLove armbands were originally launched in 2020 by the Royal Dutch Football Association (KNVB) as part of a campaign against all forms of discrimination.[6] In response, FIFA revealed its 'No Discrimination' campaign, which allows team captains to wear a No Discrimination armband for the duration of the tournament.[7]

These salient examples of political actions in sports bear on the human rights responsibilities of sports governing bodies (SGBs). While there is an assumption that the field of sports has a specific legal order and dispute resolution mechanisms independent from the state—so-called *lex sportiva*—this chapter discusses whether one of the specific principles and rules of such an order, namely, the prohibition of political statements, can be considered sustainable *vis-a-vis* human rights law standards developed by the European Court of Human Rights (ECtHR). The recent judgment of ECtHR (*Naki et. Amed Sportif Faaliyetler Kulübü Derneği c. Turquie,* Req. 48924/16, 18/05/2021 [henceforth referred to as *Naki*]) is an opportunity to scrutinize the ban on political statements adopted by almost all SBGs.

The purpose of the chapter is to draw attention to human rights concerns in the discourse and practice of SGBs. Although SGBs are subject to private law—due to their private legal personality, autonomous organizational structure, self-validating power, and contractual obligations—the aforementioned *lex sportiva* assumption cannot be extended in a fashion that excludes human rights concerns in the field of sports. This is because considerations of traditional International Human Rights Law (IHRL)—that public agents using public power/authority in order for human rights norms to be applied to the dispute—cannot be considered sustainable since the influence of SGBs over other stakeholders of sports (i.e., athletes, trainers, and clubs) has become overwhelming due to their monopolistic status. In fact, sports law has specific principles, rules, and applications that diverge from IHRL.

---

[4]Bruce Maxwell kneels during first national anthem away from Oakland, 30 September 2017, ESPN, https://www.espn.com/mlb/story/_/id/20864958/bruce-maxwell-oakland-athletics-takes-knee-booed-some-texas (last accessed 4 December 2022).

[5]European Teams Abandon One Love Armband Protest At 2022 World Cup in Qatar After FIFA Pressure, 21 November 2022, EUROSPORT, https://www.eurosport.com/football/world-cup/2022/with-a-heavy-heart-european-teams-abandon-one-love-armband-protest-under-fifa-pressure_sto9237838/story.shtml (last accessed 4 December 2022).

[6]World Cup 2022: what is the OneLove armband and why did FIFA ban it?, 29 November 2022) Reuters, https://www.reuters.com/lifestyle/sports/world-cup-2022-what-is-onelove-armband-why-did-fifa-ban-it-2022-11-24/ (last accessed 4 December 2022).

[7]FIFA, *No Discrimination campaign made available for entire FIFA World Cup Qatar 2022™*, 21.11.2022, https://www.fifa.com/social-impact/campaigns/no-discrimination/media-releases/no-discrimination-campaign-made-available-for-entire-fifa-world-cup-qatar (last accessed 4 December 2022).

Unbalanced bargaining and the vulnerable position of other stakeholders against the monopolistic powers of SGBs necessitate states' positive obligations, which include the duty to prevent and/or redress violations, even in relations between private parties (horizontal application).[8] Thus the human rights responsibility of states can be triggered by positive obligations doctrine and the horizontal effect doctrine.[9] This chapter aims to put forward human rights obligations of SGBs via a thorough examination of the *Naki* ruling so as to highlight the incompatibility of the blanket ban on sportspersons' political speech with their freedom of expression. It should be noted that the ECtHR's response to the problem of the blanket ban on political statements has implications for Türkiye as well.

As in many academic studies in the field of law, doctrinal legal research methodology was used in our study. The main argument is built upon the ECtHR's *Naki* ruling because it had the potential to lead SGBs to revise their policy concerning the categorical ban, as it cannot be considered sustainable under IHRL in general, and the European Convention on Human Rights (ECHR) in particular. In addition, as a member of the Council of Europe, Türkiye is a part of the ECHR system, and is one of the states with the highest number of applications to the ECtHR.[10] The *Naki* ruling was not the only application against Türkiye before the ECtHR regarding sports[11], and it has particular importance because the decisions of the Court are indicative for all Turkish courts and the decisions of the Turkish Football Federation.

In this regard, the chapter will start with posing the problem by putting forward the nature and the extent of the blanket ban on political statements in sports. This section will scrutinize the issue in two main categories in the international arena and in Turkish football. This section will assess the categorical political statement ban as a universal standard of sports governance. Next, the ECtHR's response to the issue will be addressed, with a focus on the judgment of *Naki et. Amed Sportif Faaliyetler Kulübü Derneği c. Turquie*. The judgment will be analyzed in detail, and subjected

---

[8] Schabas (2015), p. 105.

[9] For instance, see Haas (2012), pp. 45–47; Faut (2014), pp. 253–263, especially 257–262; cf., Schönwald (2016), pp. 346–347.

[10] See European Court of Human Rights, Analysis of Statistics 2021, January 2022, https://www.echr.coe.int/Documents/Stats_analysis_2021_ENG.pdf (last accessed 4 December 2022).

[11] See, *Adnan Yüksel Gürüz v. Türkiye*, App. No. 51563/20, Communicated on 15 November 2022 (pending as of 23/9/2023); *Ali Nihat Yazıcı v. Türkiye*, App. No. 38976/18, Communicated on 15 November 2022 (pending as of 23/9/2023); *Serkan Çınar v. Türkiye*, App. No. 35314/20, Communicated on 15 November 2022 (pending as of 23/9/2023); *Koç et Autres c. Türkiye*, Requête nos 80/21 et 2 autres requêtes, Decision of 06 October 2022 (Consists of three seperate cases: *Fenerbahçe Futbol Anonim Şirketi et Alper Pirşen c. Turquie*, Requête no 33702/21, Communicated on 28 January 2022; *Ali Yıldırım Koç et Fenerbahce Futbol Anonim Sirketi c. Turquie*, Requête no 80/21, Communicated on 28 January 2022; *Galatasaray Sportif Sınai ve Ticari Yatırımlar Anonim Şirketi c. Turquie*, Requête no 52186/21, Communicated on 28 January 2022); *Sedat Doğan c. Turquie*, Requête no 48909/14, Judgment of 18 May 2021; *Naki et Amed Sportif Faaliyetler Kulübü Derneği c. Turquie*, Requête no 48924/16, Judgment of 18 May 2021; *İbrahim Tokmak c. Turquie*, Requête no 54540/16, Judgment of 18 May 2021; *Ali Rıza and Others v. Turkey*, App. Nos. 30226/10 and 4 others, Judgment of 28 January 2020.

to criticism, especially for the insufficiency of the procedural review of the Court. Following that, the chapter will argue that a total ban on political speech not only fails to meet the clarity and certain foreseeability criteria, but also the legitimate aim criteria of the Court. The proportionality of the interference will also be discussed. The final section of the chapter will explore the implications of the *Naki* ruling both for Türkiye and the international sports world in general.

2 The Nature and Extent of the Blanket Ban on Political Speech in Sports

Political and ideological statements by athletes during sports competitions are explicitly prohibited by almost all institutions and federations that govern sports in the international arena, as well as by national federations. For practical reasons, this section is confined to analysis of football and the Olympic Movement.

2.1 The International Arena

The Olympic Charter, issued by the International Olympic Committee (IOC), prohibits the use of political, religious and racial expressions in Olympic venues; punishment for violation of this rule includes the possibility of disqualification from the Games. Article 50.2 of the recent version of Olympic Charter, in force as from 8 August 2021, states that "No kind of demonstration or political, religious or racial propaganda is permitted in any Olympic sites, venues or other areas".[12] Article 50 is based on the mission and role of the IOC in managing world Olympics enshrined in Article 2.11 of the Charter, which states that the role of IOC is "to oppose any political [...] abuse of sport and athletes". The mission and role attributed to the IOC clearly reveals its approach against the concept of politics and explains the rigid political statement ban as regulated in Article 50.2.[13] The fifth paragraph of Article 2 of the Charter also authorizes the IOC to monitor and enforce this prohibition under the terms of political neutrality.[14]

[12] International Olympic Committee, Olympic Charter, 08 August 2021, https://stillmed.olympics.com/media/Document%20Library/OlympicOrg/General/EN-Olympic-Charter.pdf?_ga=2.193254574.2014879585.1669735357-1665792665.1669735357 (last accessed 4 December 2022).

[13] IOC also has a duty to prevent discrimination based on political opinion. The fundamental principles of Olympism in the Olympic Charter states in paragraph 6 that: "6. The enjoyment of the rights and freedoms set forth in this Olympic Charter shall be secured without discrimination of any kind, such as race, colour, sex, sexual orientation, language, religion, political or other opinion, national or social origin, property, birth or other status."

[14] I shall question the validity of the rationale of IOC for categorical political statement ban in the following sections.

Bye-law to Rule 50 elaborates the framework of the ban in more concrete terms, by explicitly prohibiting any form of political propaganda that may appear on persons and on any article of clothing or equipment whatsoever worn or used. The bye-law also notes that infringement of the political statement ban may result in sanctions, disqualification of the person or delegation concerned, or withdrawal of the accreditation of the person or delegation concerned. In addition to disqualification and accreditation withdrawal, other sanctions and measures can also be implemented. The IOC Athletes' Commission has prepared a 'Guide on Article 50',[15] and has applied the Guide to particular occasions (the most recent versions of the Guide: Rule 50.2 Guidelines–Olympic Games Tokyo 2020, and Rule 50.2 Guidelines–Olympic Winter Games Beijing 2022). The Guide explains in a detailed manner when, where, and how political statement bans are implemented, and how this impacts athletes' freedom of expression.[16]

FIFA, overseeing the football sport worldwide, also forbids political statements.[17] The FIFA Disciplinary Code 2019 (FDC) has even more detailed provisions on the matter. Article 11, entitled "Offensive behaviour and violations of the principles of fair play", expresses that disciplinary measures may apply in cases of non-sportive demonstrations, which includes political expressions.[18] Article 12 of the FDC explains the sanctions will be applied in cases of a discriminative occurrence. These sanctions may come as match suspensions or other disciplinary measures; they can vary from limiting spectator numbers and imposing fines if there is involvement by the supporters of an association or a club. Article 16.2 of the FDC imposes objective liability on all associations and clubs for cases of political and ideological statements of their supporters. Similar provisions can be found with regard to UEFA. Article 11 of the 2022 version of the UEFA's Disciplinary Regulations (UEFA DR) states that those who use sporting events for manifestations of a non-sporting nature may face disciplinary sanctions. The concept of manifestations of non-sporting nature includes political expressions.[19]

---

[15] Rule 50 Guidelines Developed by the IOC Athletes' Commission, https://stillmedab.olympic.org/media/Document%20Library/OlympicOrg/News/2020/01/Rule-50-Guidelines-Tokyo-2020.pdf (last accessed 4 December 2022).

[16] The Guide shall be discussed in detail below.

[17] FIFA Statutes 2021 has a provision outlawing discrimination in general in Article 4, which includes discrimination on the basis of political opinion.

[18] FDC 2019 also restricts expressions that publicly incite others to hatred or violence. Article 12 declares that "A player or official who, in the context of a match (including pre-and post-match) or competition, publicly incites others to hatred or violence will be sanctioned." Since these restrictions do not exclusively relate to political statements, and involve usual disclaimer on freedom of expression, we shall not deal with them separately in this article.

[19] UEFA, UEFA Disciplinary Regulations, Edition 2022, 02 June 2022, https://documents.uefa.com/v/u/r7fXo9v2XH9Uhi4VzO57qw (last accessed 4 December 2022).

2.2 *Turkish Football*

As a member of FIFA and UEFA, the Turkish Football Federation (TFF) has several provisions concerning speech and expressions, including political and ideological propaganda. The ban on unsportsmanlike statements can be considered the first provision that pertains to political speech. Under Article 36 of the current Turkish Football Federation's Professional Football Disciplinary Directive of 2017 (TFF FDD) amended in 2021,[20]

> (1) Acting against sportsmanship or sports ethics, harming the reputation of TFF with one's attitudes and behaviors, or taking actions that devalue football, or promoting violence or disorder in sports by means of the press and media or social media, or making statements or declarations contrary to sportsmanship, sports ethics or fair-play that may yield in fan activities, (. . .are sanctioned).
>
> (. . .)
>
> (d) If the actions mentioned in the first paragraph are conducted through the press organs (especially official websites, club televisions) or social media accounts of the clubs, the clubs shall be sanctioned a penalty from 400,000.-TL to 1,200,000.-TL for the Super League, from 220.000.-TL to 600.000.-TL for the 1st League, from 120.000.-TL to 220.000.-TL for the 2nd League, from 60.000.-TL to 120.000.-TL for the 3rd League. In addition, if the statement is made without citing any name or using the term 'board of management', the president of the club which made the statement will also be punished according to subparagraph (b) of this paragraph.
>
> (2) Where the Disciplinary Board deems necessary, merely the fine defined in paragraph 4 of Article 35 for the violations specified in paragraph 1 of this article could be applied. [21]

In practice, as will be demonstrated below, organs of TFF use this provision to apply sanctions against persons who make political statements. Furthermore, Article 38 prohibits that if and when any stakeholder of Turkish football makes statements that exceed the limits of criticism, threatening, insulting, offensive, discriminatory or abusive statements about referees and other competition officials shall be punished. This provision, which was included in 2021, and intents to protect the reputation and independence of referees and other competition officials, may also provide a basis to restrict political statements of sportspersons, despite the fact that there is no known implementation of this provision for political statements yet. Moreover, Article 42 of the TFF FDD, entitled "Discrimination and Ideological Propaganda", states that "It is forbidden to make any and all kinds of ideological propaganda before, during and after the competition. In case of non-compliance with this prohibition, the penalties specified in this article will be applied". This provision is the primary clause that is implemented against persons who make political expressions. Finally, the TFF FDD also prohibits "ugly and bad cheering" in its Article 53. According to that provision,

---

[20] Turkish Football Federation, Futbol Disiplin Talimatı, August 2017, https://www.tff.org//Resources/TFF/Documents/TALIMATLAR/Futbol-Disiplin-Talimati.pdf (last accessed 22 September 2023).

[21] Translated by Ms. Sare Karacan.

"Humiliating, inciting, or harassing cheering with words, actions, or similar means in the stadiums is prohibited without applying the criterion of continuity". Although there is no clear example of any sanction based on this provision for political statements, it may be used in order to implement sanctions when the spectators' political expressions are considered to be provocative or abusive.

2.3 Categorical Ban on Political Statements as a Universal Standard of Sports Governance

The aforementioned regulations clearly demonstrate that a ban on political speech in sports has become a universal standard of sports governance. Therefore, it should be addressed accordingly when it comes to human rights analysis, which this chapter argues, the ECtHR failed to do so properly in its *Naki* judgment. The next section will analyze the scope and ramifications of the political statement ban in sports, so as to discuss its compatibility with the right to freedom of expression under the ECHR.

2.3.1 Personal Scope of Ban

The first component of universality can be seen with regard to persons bound by the prohibition. First and foremost, the personal subject of the prohibitions is obviously the athletes. But it also covers every sportsperson who is involved in a particular sporting event, such as trainers, coaches, and club officials. While Bye-law to Rule 50 explicitly refers to team officials, other team personnel and all other participants regardless of their position, the Guide on Article 50.2 of the IOC explicitly refers to these persons in an exemplary manner, labelling them as participants (accredited persons). Both Bye-law to Rule 50 and the Guide state that they are all bound by the ban.[22] Moreover, Article 16 of the Olympic Charter has a provision for its members: a member should take the oath before commencement of his or her duty as a member of the IOC, and should swear to act independently of political interests. The ban on political speech also covers the leaders of SGBs, at least with regard to the IOC.

Similarly, FIFA's ban also covers almost every figure involved in the game of football. In addition to footballers, Article 11 of the FDC includes national associations/federations, clubs, officials, and any other member and/or person carrying out a function on their behalf as responsible persons to obey the legislation of FIFA (Laws of the Game, the FIFA Statutes and FIFA's regulations, directives, guidelines, circulars and decisions). All of the above persons are bound by FIFA legislation to

[22] Bye-law to Rule 50: "9. The OCOG, all competitors, team officials, other team personnel and all other participants in the Olympic Games shall comply with the relevant manuals, guides, regulations or guidelines, and all other instructions of the IOC Executive Board, in respect of all matters subject to Rule 50 and this Bye-law."

respect the ban on political speech. Here FIFA takes another step and widens prohibition on political statements to the spectators, under Article 16 of the FDC. In order to implement the prohibition effectively to persons who are not bound by its legislation directly, FIFA creates an objective liability regime for all associations and clubs for the political and ideological acts of their supporters.

UEFA has similar provisions with regard to the personal scope of prohibition. Article 11 of the 2022 version of the UEFA DR mentions national associations/ federations, clubs, their players, officials and all persons assigned by UEFA to exercise a function as responsible persons to respect the legislation of UEFA (Laws of the Game, UEFA's Statutes, regulations, directives and decisions).

It is not surprising that the Turkish Football Federation follows FIFA and UEFA with regard to the personal scope of political statement ban. In Articles 36 and 42 of its TFF FDD, the Federation indicates footballers and club managers in terms of responsibility for ideological propaganda and unsportsmanlike statements, which includes political speech. TFF also covers spectators in this regard (Article 42), and like FIFA, creates an objective liability regime for clubs for the political and ideological acts of their supporters and members.

These provisions indicate that any person involved in sport activity is bound by the political statement ban, irrespective of their position or capacity. With regard to personal scope, one can conclude that a ban on political speech in sports governance possesses universal coverage.

2.3.2 Material Scope of Ban

Secondly, one should pay attention to the material or substantive aspect of prohibition. Prohibition forbids any kind of political or ideological statements, expressions, gestures, demonstrations, which reach the level of propaganda. In fact, almost all expressions and statements that have any political or ideological component fall within the ambit of this prohibition. For example, Bye-law to Rule 50 blatantly forbids any political content by stating "No form of publicity or propaganda, commercial or otherwise". Similarly, the Guide on Article 50 of IOC explicitly mentions the principle of political neutrality and therefore shows the real purpose of Rule 50.2, namely prohibition of any kind of political expressions. In fact, when giving examples of how the host city's political officers are excluded from the Games, the Guide treats the concept of political expressions in the pejorative sense of the word and considers them to be an interference with sport at the Olympics.

Here the Guide on Article 50 distinguishes expressing views (acceptable form of speech) from protest and demonstrations (unacceptable form of speech), and leaves out the term 'propaganda', which is explicitly used in the Olympic Charter, thus lowering the threshold for applicability of the prohibition. At this point, the Guide prefers to list unacceptable examples of protest, as opposed to expressing views in a non-exhaustive manner, which includes displaying any political message or gestures of a political nature, such as kneeling.[23] Thus, the concept of politics cannot be considered within the scope of freedom of expression under the Olympic regime, a right acknowledged and recognized in the Athletes' Rights and Responsibilities Declaration.[24]

Similar terms can be observed in the field of football regulation. FIFA, UEFA, and TFF all forbid the use of gestures, words, objects or any other means to transmit a message that is not appropriate for a sports event, which explicitly covers political and ideological statements (Article 16 of the FDC of 2019; Article 16 of the 2022 version of the UEFA DR; Article 42 of TFF FDD of 2017). Again, using sporting events for manifestations of a non-sporting nature is also prohibited by FIFA (Article 11 of the FDC and Article of 11 the UEFA DR), which is likely to cover political expressions, gestures and demonstrations. Here one can observe that there is no 'propaganda' threshold for a political expression or gesture in order to fall within the ambit of prohibition in the FIFA regulations. But the UEFA regulations still maintain a threshold or a quality, namely 'provocative', and TFF regulations still maintain a 'propaganda' threshold for a political expression or gesture in order to fall within the ambit of prohibition.

With regard to the material scope of a ban on political speech, it can be observed that the terms and concepts used here—such as political, ideological and propaganda—are so wide that they lack clarity and certainty. It is possible to include almost any expression or gesture within the ambit of the 'political' or 'ideological' from a certain point of view. Therefore, I shall discuss the nature and meaning of these terms *vis-a-vis* freedom of expression under the ECHR in the following subsections.

2.3.3 Medium and Form-Related Scope of Ban

Closely linked to the material scope of ban, the third aspect of the universality of the prohibition of political statements in sports governance is the form of the expressions themselves. How the ideas, thoughts, or emotions are expressed or disseminated is equally as important as the substance of the expressions themselves.[25] In this regard, one can fairly say that sports law covers almost all forms of expressions. For example, Bye-law to Rule 50 of the Olympic Charter emphasizes the medium coverage of the ban by explicitly stating "no form of [...] propaganda", and lists different means through which political propaganda can be expressed, such as persons and any article of clothing (sportswear, accessories) or equipment worn or used. The Guide on Article 50 of the IOC also gives examples of what would

---

[23] Beside these examples, it is not clear what constitutes politics or protest or propaganda.

[24] On the other hand, it is contradictory that Rule 50 Guidelines Developed by the IOC Athletes' Commission gives its support to freedom of expression highlighted in the Athletes' Rights and Responsibilities Declaration (see, Gürcüoğlu (2020), p. 324).

[25] Gürcüoğlu (2020), p. 332.

constitute an unwarranted political expression in a non-exhaustive manner, such as wearing signs or armbands, hand gestures or kneeling, and refusal to attend the ceremonies. Through Bye-law to Rule 50 and the Guide, the IOC categorically excludes political expressions from acceptable and permissible speech. However, the Olympic rules concerning political expressions does permit athletes to express their opinions on digital or traditional media, or on other platforms like social media.[26]

Similar medium and form coverage can be seen with regard to football regulation (including FIFA, UEFA and TFF regulations). Thus, all forms of gestures, words, objects or other means to transmit a political message are prohibited categorically, irrespective of the medium through which they are conveyed.[27]

2.3.4 Spatial Scope of Ban

The fourth indicator that reveals the universal acceptance of the political statement ban by SGBs is the consensus with regard to its spatial dimension. When one looks at the places where the political statement prohibition applies, one observes the very wide coverage of spaces; starting from stadiums and competition sites, and expanding to almost all locations connected to the event (including but not limited to matches or competitions). These are all considered forbidden venues for political expression.[28]

For example, Article 50 of the Olympic Charter reveals that the prohibition on political speech is applicable in any Olympic sites, venues, and other areas. These locations include the field of play, the Olympic Village, and all places in which ceremonies are held (Guide to Rule 50). On the other hand, the IOC permits political manifestations where they are expressed in mixed zones, in the International Broadcasting Centre or the Main Media Centre, and places where team meetings are held (Guide to Rule 50). There are some differences between the Guide and its implementation in particular Olympics. In Rule 50.2 Guidelines–Olympic Games Tokyo 2020, it was permissible to express political manifestations on the field of play *prior to the start of the competition*, a regulation that was different than its counterpart in the Guide, on the basis of time factor (not during competition).

In football regulations, the national associations and clubs are responsible for order and security both inside and around the stadium before, during, and after

---

[26] Rule 50 Guidelines Developed by the IOC Athletes' Commission, https://stillmedab.olympic.org/media/Document%20Library/OlympicOrg/News/2020/01/Rule-50-Guidelines-Tokyo-2020.pdf (last accessed 4 December 2022).

Also see, Rule 50.2 Guidelines –Olympic Games Tokyo 2020 and Rule 50.2 Guidelines – Olympic Winter Games Beijing 2022.

[27] For example, Articles 38 of TFF FDD of 2017 clearly envisages sanctions to "Those who make statements contrary to sportsmanship, sports ethics or fair-play understanding through the press and media or social media" when their statements are considered unsportsmanlike.

[28] Gürcüoğlu (2020), p. 333.

matches. When a football-related sporting event takes place, manifestations or messages of a non-sporting nature, including political/ideological gestures, words, or objects are forbidden, regardless of the venue (Articles 11 and 16 of the FDC, Article of 11 and 16 of the UEFA DR and Articles 42 and 53 of TFF FDD of 2017). In Article 12 of the FDC, misconduct of players and officials is included, "in the context of a match (including pre- and post-match)", where political statements can easily fall within its ambit.

2.3.5 Temporal Scope of Ban

The fifth indicator for the universality of the ban on political speech in sports governance is the temporal dimension of the prohibition, which is closely related to the spatial aspect. In some regulations, regardless of the place, the event that is going on is decisive for the applicability of the prohibition. As a rule, the main event that triggers the applicability of the ban is the competition itself. In football, prohibitions with regard to political statements apply "before, during and after matches" (i.e., Article 42 of TFF FDD), bringing a considerable level of uncertainty as to how much time constitutes 'before' and 'after' matches. Similar problems arise with regard to players conduct as they are responsible for their behavior pre- and post-match.

At the Olympics, political statements are forbidden, "During Olympic medal ceremonies or During the Opening, Closing and other official Ceremonies" (Guide to Rule 50), and "during competition on the field of play" (Rule 50.2 Guidelines–Olympic Games Tokyo 2020). However, the Olympic regime does in facet permit expressions of a political nature during press conferences at the venue, interviews, or while speaking to the media.

2.3.6 SGBs That Have Adopted a Ban on Political Speech

The final indicator for the universality of a ban on political statements in sports governance is the variety of SGBs who have adopted such a prohibition into their regulations. Unsurprisingly, almost all major international SGBs have adopted similar prohibitions concerning the political speech of stakeholders, including the International Basketball Federation (FIBA) in their Internal Regulations, Book 1, Article 110(b);[29] the International Gymnastics Federation (FIG), in their Code of Conduct, Section I, Paras. 4,7;[30] the International Volleyball Federation (FIVB),

[29] International Basketball Federation (FIBA), Internal Regulations - Book 1 General Provisions, 25 August 2022 https://www.fiba.basketball/internal-regulations/book1/general-provisions.pdf (last accessed 4 December 2022).

[30] International Gymnastics Federation (FIG), FIG Code of Conduct For all Participants in Gymnastics - Edition 2022, 03 June 2022 https://www.gymnastics.sport/publicdir/rules/files/en_Code%20of%20Conduct%20-%20Edition%202022.pdf last accessed 4 December 2022).

in their Disciplinary Regulations, Chapter 2, Article 8.3;[31] World Athletics, in their Integrity Code of Conduct, Rule 3, Para. 3.3.14;[32] the International Swimming Federation (FINA), in its FINA Constitution, Article C 4;[33] and the International Tennis Federation (ITF), in its 2022 World Tennis Tour Code of Conduct, Article IV, Para. L, and Article IV, Para. C3d.[34]

These SGBs are not only the leading international bodies in sports governance, but they also control the most important sports in the world in terms of popularity, money, and stakeholder participation. It is safe to assume that, when one takes into account the functioning of transnational sports law or *lex sportiva*, national member associations/federations and clubs incorporate political statement bans into their national sports law and regulations.

2.3.7 Intermediate Result

As a result, political statements in sports are totally prohibited irrespective of the persons who express them, their content, the medium through which they are conveyed, and the place they are expressed at. SGBs consider political and ideological statements as an enemy of the political neutrality of sport, and prohibit them without any concern for freedom of expression. On the basis of its personal, material, medium and form-related, spatial, temporal scopes, and variety of SGBs that have adopted this ban, it can be concluded that a ban on political speech in sports has a universality in sports governance without any meaningful exception.

It should be emphasized that the political statement ban as a universal standard of sports governance is not considered a limitation to athletes' freedom of expression within the meaning of human rights law since it constitutes a total, categorical blanket ban for freedom of expression. Here, one should distinguish between limitation/restriction and total prohibition in terms of their consequences with regard to the right they interfere with.

[31] International Volleyball Federation (FIVB), Disciplinary Regulations, 21 March 2022 https://www.fivb.com/-/media/2022/coorporate/fivb/legal/regulations/fivb%20disciplinary%20regulations%202022_clean%20version_website_26042022.pdf?la=en&hash=39B9E7BE72278022EA54BD3ADAD6C929 (last accessed 4 December 2022).

[32] World Athletics, Integrity Code of Conduct, 01 November 2019, https://worldathletics.org/download/download?filename=ba923b86-b605-4e1f-9123-a4fa83793443.pdf&urlslug=D1.1%20-%20Integrity%20Code%20of%20Conduct (last accessed 4 December 2022).

[33] International Swimming Federation (FINA), FINA Constitution, 18 December 2021, https://resources.fina.org/fina/document/2022/01/13/f21af7d9-dc04-45f5-90f6-711f67453b61/23_FINA-Constitution_18.12.2021.pdf (last accessed 4 December 2022).

[34] International Tennis Federation (ITF), 2022 World Tennis Tour Code of Conduct, https://www.itftennis.com/media/7285/09-2022-wtt-code-of-conduct-v2.pdf (last accessed 4 December 2022).

3 Response of ECtHR to the Problem: *Naki* Case

This section will analyze the issue of the political statement ban from the angle of human rights law, and question its compatibility with the freedom of expression enshrined in various human rights instruments and constitutions, first and foremost the ECHR. After being silent on sports matters for decades, ECHR's supervisory organ, the ECtHR, has recently delivered several judgments and decisions on the freedom of expression in a sporting context against several state parties to the Convention. *Naki* is one of the leading cases concerning freedom of expression in sports, which will be discussed in detail below as it is directly related to the ban on political speech in sports governance.

3.1 Freedom of Expression Cases Before ECtHR in the Context of Sport

Before exploring the *Naki* case, there are other cases that have been adjudicated by the ECtHR related to freedom of expression in sports that are worth mentioning.

3.1.1 Kevin Maguire v. The United Kingdom

This case is relatively unknown to sports and human rights circles and concerns the historically-deep conflict between the Scottish football teams, Rangers and Celtic. The applicant, who is a Celtic fan and attended a football match between the two teams at Ibrox Stadium in Glasgow, home to Rangers, was sentenced to a two-year football banning order by the court, due to a breach of peace under the Police, Public Order and Criminal Justice Act 2006 (Scottish law) for wearing a black shirt during a football match between Rangers and Celtic, which, in bright green letters approximately three to four inches in size, displayed on the front the letters "INLA", and on the back the slogan, "FUCK YOUR POPPY REMEMBER DERRY". While initials INLA refer to the 'Irish National Liberation Army', which is a proscribed organization in terms of the Terrorism Act 2000, the poppy symbolizes remembrance of the members of the armed forces who died in the line of duty (also known as "Remembrance Day"). The word Derry refers to a town in Northern Ireland where thirteen civil rights protesters and bystanders were killed by soldiers of the British Army during a civil rights march in January 1972 (known as "Bloody Sunday").[35]

Under these circumstances, the ECtHR found that the sanction (two-year football banning order instead of custodial sentence of up to one year's imprisonment) was

[35] *Kevin Maguire v. The United Kingdom*, App. No. 58060/13, Admissibility Decision of 3 March 2015, para.4.

not excessive in terms of proportionality,[36] given the context of the gesture in question, historical sectarian violence between fans of the two football clubs, which is still ongoing, and the volatile atmosphere surrounding football matches between the two team. These factors called for pressing social need in order for limitation. Although the status of Northern Ireland, the historic role of British soldiers in Northern Ireland, and the events of Bloody Sunday are matters of general public interest, the Court nevertheless reminded that alongside the right to freedom expression comes duties and responsibilities under Paragraph 2 of Article 10 of the Convention; the scope of which depends on the situation of the applicant and the technical means the applicant used with regard to assessing the necessity of the interference. In the case at hand, the Court found that the slogan on the back of the applicant's top was likely to cause distress or alarm, give rise to a substantial risk of violence and disorder, and would offend and upset members of the public; the public would also be subjected to the risk of violence once the applicant engaged with Rangers supporters (thus sharing the findings of police officers under the margin of appreciation doctrine). The ECtHR mostly deferred to domestic authorities and courts' reasoning as to whether these reasons were relevant and sufficient in order to justify the interference.[37]

For the reasons discussed in the case above, the *Maguire* decision of the ECtHR cannot be considered to be a typical example of the universal political statement ban in sports governance. The material scope of the statement/gesture in the *Maguire* case is closely linked to inciting violence, a type of expression not widely protected and open to wide restrictions under Article 10 of the Convention. Secondly, the sanction imposed for the applicant's gesture was based on criminal law, even though it was a two-year football banning order, not disciplinary law of the relevant SGBs. The distinctive factor of the political statement ban in sports governance is its universal acceptance by the SGBs as a disciplinary regulation.

3.1.2 *Simunic v. Croatia*

The second case relevant here concerns a footballer who shouted "For Home" to spectators, who in turn replied back "Ready", four times consecutively, at end of the match (approximately 40 minutes after its conclusion) between Croatia and Iceland; the footballer was on the pitch with a microphone, and the spectators were still in the stands. Domestic judicial authorities considered this chant to be fascist in nature, since it had been used as an official greeting of the Ustaše movement and totalitarian regime of the Independent State of Croatia. According to domestic courts, the Ustaše

[36] Even though the applicant was an avid football fan and Celtic season-ticket holder.

[37] *Kevin Maguire v. The United Kingdom*, App. No. 58060/13, Admissibility Decision of 3 March 2015. According to the present author's knowledge, in the vast literature on the political statement ban in sports governance, this case has never been mentioned or cited. This includes the semi-official Fact Sheet on Sport and the ECHR, January 2022, prepared by the press division of ECtHR, https://www.echr.coe.int/documents/fs_sport_eng.pdf (last accessed 22 September 2023).

movement was based on racism and symbolized hatred towards people of different religious or ethnic identities, and a manifestation of racist ideology.[38]

The applicant footballer was fined 25,000 Croatian kunas (about 3300 euros at the time) by domestic courts of instances, and was found guilty of "addressing messages to spectators, the content of which incited to hatred on the basis of race, nationality and faith" under the Act on Prevention of Disorder on Sport Competitions. Although the footballer ultimately argued before the Croatian Constitutional Court in a domestic judicial process that his freedom of expression had been violated, as the lower courts considered any use of the incriminating expression in front of any spectators absolutely unacceptable and left no room for meaningful proportionality assessment, the Constitutional Court rejected this argument since the fine imposed on him had a legitimate aim of punishing behavior that expressed or incited hatred on the basis of racial or other identity at a sports competition; this in turn protects the dignity of others and the basic values of democratic society. The Croatian Constitutional Court stressed that freedom of expression also bears duties and responsibilities, and the fine imposed on the applicant footballer, as a last line of defense of society's values, was found to be proportional.[39]

When the case was brought before the ECtHR, the Court found that the gesture of the applicant footballer in question (i.e., shouting) falls within the ambit of Article 10, but the interference was legitimate and proportional due to the modest nature of the fine imposed to the applicant and the gesture's deeply controversial context. Again, the ECtHR deferred to domestic authorities and courts' reasoning as to whether these reasons were relevant and sufficient in order to justify the interference, and concluded that domestic courts diligently analyzed the words used by the applicant footballer and their contextual background. Underlining that the applicant is a famous footballer and therefore a role model for football fans, the ECtHR imposed the obligation on him to be aware of, and avoid the possible negative effects of, provocative chanting towards spectators. As a result, the ECtHR concluded that domestic authorities acted within their margin of appreciation when assessing whether a pressing social need exists under the necessity test of proportionality review, and thus the interference "[in] question struck a fair balance between the applicant footballer's interest, on the one hand, and the society's interests in promoting tolerance and mutual respect at sports events as well as combating discrimination through sport on the other hand".[40]

Similar considerations may be valid for the *Simunic* case as to its relevance to the universal prohibition of political statements, since the material scope of the statement in question was clearly an incitement to violence and hatred, a variety of expression not normally considered to fall within the ambit of freedom expression under ECHR. By virtue of Article 17, the ECtHR may exclude expressions that are

---

[38] *Simunic v. Croatia*, App. No. 20373/17, Admissibility Decision of 22 January 2019, paras.5 and 44.

[39] *Simunic v. Croatia*, App. No. 20373/17, Admissibility Decision of 22 January 2019, paras.5–7.

[40] *Simunic v. Croatia*, App. No. 20373/17, Admissibility Decision of 22 January 2019, paras.38–49.

incompatible with the values proclaimed and guaranteed in the Convention from the very protection of freedom expression under Article 10 of the Convention, particularly when these expressions are directed against Convention values, such as inciting hatred or violence. The footballer in question attempted to rely on freedom of expression in order to engage in an activity aimed at the destruction of the very existence of the Convention rights. In fact, the ECtHR in *Simunic* discussed the applicability of Article 17 as a last resort, and saw no need to recourse to that Article since the complaint of the footballer was considered inadmissible as the interference in question was found legitimate and proportional in any way.[41] Discriminatory, hateful speech, words and gestures cannot be equalized to mere political statements. And as a last note on *Simunic* case, the fine as a sanction imposed for the applicant footballer's words and gestures was based on criminal law, not the disciplinary law of relevant SGBs.[42]

3.1.3 *Sedat Doğan v. Turkey, İbrahim Tokmak v. Turkey, and A. M. v. Turkey*

Regarding freedom of expression cases before the ECtHR in the context of sport, there are three judgments related to Türkiye delivered on 18 May 2021: *Sedat Doğan v. Turkey*; *Naki et Amed Sportif Faaliyetler Kulübü v. Turkey*; and *İbrahim Tokmak v. Turkey*.[43] All three originated from the TFF's disciplinary sanctions against the applicants for statements made to media or shared on social media. These cases have some importance for the general compatibility of *lex sportiva* with human rights law, as this was the first time that the ECtHR ruled on disciplinary sanctions of an SGB. While the *Sedat Doğan* and *İbrahim Tokmak* cases are related to ordinary statements critical of TFF management or involved insults to the memory of a third person, the

[41] *Simunic v. Croatia*, App. No. 20373/17, Admissibility Decision of 22 January 2019, paras.37–39.

[42] It is interesting to note that FIFA also imposed ten match suspension (except national team) and 30,000 CHF fine on the applicant footballer due to the same event under Article 58 of the FIFA DC which prohibits discrimination, another prohibition apart from political statement ban. After very detailed analysis of the all words and gestures used by the Simunic and spectators, the CAS panel found that the words and gestures in question were discriminatory and the sanction imposed to the footballer were proportional in respect of the severity of the offence committed. Although the footballer and FIFA mentioned the ECHR several times, the CAS panel never mentioned freedom of expression in its reasoning (*Josip Simunic v FIFA,* CAS Award of 29 July 2014, 2014/A/3562).

Since the award of CAS was not brought before the ECtHR against Switzerland after Swiss Federal Tribunal's possible approval, the ECtHR's decision for the same event still concerns only his criminal conviction, and therefore not directly related to political speech ban in sports governance. Of course, ECtHR's decision is very important and has precedential value with regard to conflict between hate speech and freedom of expression.

[43] *Sedat Doğan c. Turquie*, Requête no 48909/14, Judgment of 18 May 2021; *Naki et Amed Sportif Faaliyetler Kulübü Derneği c. Turquie*, Requête no 48924/16, Judgment of 18 May 2021*; İbrahim Tokmak c. Turquie*, Requête no 54540/16, Judgment of 18 May 2021.

Naki case concerns purely political statements.[44] The next section shall focus solely on the *Naki* case. Before that, the particulars of the other Turkish cases, and their differences with the *Naki* case, should be explored.

In the *Sedat Doğan* case, the applicant, who was a member of the board of directors of Galatasaray S.K. (a football club based in in Istanbul) at the time of event, was sanctioned by TFF because of statements he made on a television program about the referral of two footballers to the Professional Football Disciplinary Committee of the TFF because they wore shirts under their official jersey in which a message was displayed paying tribute to Nelson Mandela (who had died the day before the match). In his televised statement, the applicant emphasized the anti-racist content of the shirts and the importance of Mandela to the struggle against racism, criticizing TFF management in general. The Professional Football Disciplinary Committee held that the statements by the applicant were excessive, disproportionate and not necessarily required to be used. The Professional Football Disciplinary Committee also thought that the applicant's words devalued the image of football, incited violence and disorder, destroyed the peaceful atmosphere in sports, escalated tension which put spectators at risk of violence and protests.

Accordingly, the Professional Football Disciplinary Committee considered that the applicant's statements constituted unsportsmanlike remarks enshrined in Article 37 of the Football Disciplinary Directive (FDD), and imposed a disciplinary sanction of removing the rights attached to his duties for sixty days, together with a fine of approximately 15,753 euros at the time. The Arbitration Board approved the decision of the Professional Football Disciplinary Committee since it found the applicant's assertions went beyond the acceptable limits of criticism, and aimed at harming and demeaning the TFF and its managers, although the Board reduced the sanctions to removal of the rights attached to his duties for thirty days, and a fine of approximately 7876 euros. Meanwhile, the applicant made several Tweets accompanied by the hashtag *#GoodbyeTFF* after the Professional Disciplinary Committee's first decision imposing the more severe sanctions on him. Using similar reasons, the Professional Disciplinary Committee once again held that the Tweets of the applicant constituted unsportsmanlike statements within the meaning of Article 37 of the Football Disciplinary Directive, and imposed another sanction on him: removing the rights attached to his duties for forty-five days, and a fine of approximately 11,750 euros. The Arbitration Board approved the sanction, adding

[44] In all cases, the applicants also claimed that the Arbitration Board is not independent or impartial, with regard to its indistinct legal personality from the TFF, appointment of its members etc. The ECtHR, cited the *Ali Rıza and Others* case (*Ali Rıza and Others v. Turkey*, App. Nos. 30226/10, 17880/11, 17887/11, 17891/11 and 5506/16, Judgment of 28 January 2020) where it has concluded in semi-pilot judgment that the Arbitration Board have structural problems capable of diminishing its independence and impartiality, decided that Article 6 of the ECHR had been violated again. In this regard, see the present author's article entitled "Applicability of human rights standards in Turkish football arbitration: the contribution of the European Court of Human Rights": H. Burak Gemalmaz (2019), pp.38–58 before *Ali Rıza and Others* case delivered by the ECtHR. Therefore, I shall not deal with the fair trial aspect of *Sedat Doğan v. Turkey, Naki et Amed Sportif Faaliyetler Kulübü v. Turkey* and *İbrahim Tokmak v. Turkey* cases in this chapter.

that the statements of the applicant in his Tweets could not be regarded as negative value judgments or criticism protected by the right to freedom of expression.[45]

When the case was brought before the ECtHR, the Court held that the reasoning adopted by the Professional Football Disciplinary Committee and the Arbitration Board did not indicate anything that showed that they carried out an adequate balancing—in accordance with the criteria developed by the ECtHR—between the applicant's right to freedom of expression and the right of TFF leadership to have their private lives respected, as well as other interests at stake, such as maintaining order and peace in the football community. According to the Court, the Professional Football Disciplinary Committee and the Arbitration Board simply cited the relevant provisions of the FDD and the statements in question, and provided no reasoning as to whether the interference with the applicant's right to freedom of expression was justified; particularly considering the context of the applicant's comments made during the television program—namely, referring to the disciplinary committee of two players from his club for having paid tribute to Nelson Mandela—and the Tweets that he posted in reaction to the disciplinary sanctions that he had received. It was not shown in the decisions of both the Professional Football Disciplinary Committee and the Arbitration Board that the applicant's statements—both on television and on Twitter—did appear likely to incite supporters to commit acts of violence. The ECtHR concluded that the sanctions imposed on the applicant by the Professional Football Disciplinary Committee and the Arbitration Board were neither relevant nor sufficient; accordingly, the sanctions were deemed unnecessary in a democratic society.[46]

However, the *Sedat Doğan* case is in fact not directly related to the political statement ban as a universal standard in sports governance, since the statements of the applicant in question did not involve political expressions, despite the fact that his statement on television program concerned the referral of two footballers to the Professional Football Disciplinary Committee for having paid tribute to Mandela through their t-shirts under their official jersey. Even the applicant himself particularly and plainly insisted that displaying anti-racist messages could not be considered political message and that the two footballers did not mean to be political when they displayed their tribute.[47] This is why the applicant was sanctioned under the 'unsportsmanlike behavior' ban (Article 37 of the FDD at the time) and not under the 'political statement' ban (Article 42 of the FDD). In fact, the two footballers who paid tribute to Mandela were not sanctioned at all by the Professional Football Disciplinary Committee since it had decided that there was no reason for sanctioning two footballers for wearing t-shirts with slogans commemorating Nelson Mandela

[45] *Sedat Doğan c. Turquie*, Requête no 48909/14, Judgment of 18 May 2021, paras.5–10.

[46] *Sedat Doğan c. Turquie*, Requête no 48909/14, Judgment of 18 May 2021, paras. 35–44.

[47] *Sedat Doğan c. Turquie*, Requête no 48909/14, Judgment of 18 May 2021, para.3 (Statements of the applicant on TV program).

following his death.[48] It would be an exaggeration to connect the *Sedat Doğan* case with the universal ban on political speech and its underlying principles in sports governance.

The *İbrahim Tokmak* case is another leading case against Türkiye, concerning the place of freedom of expression in sports governance. The applicant İbrahim Tokmak, a professional football referee, had shared a third-party Facebook post commenting on the death of a columnist in Saudi Arabia, allegedly due to the use of a drug for erectile dysfunction. When sharing the post, he added the text, "He was a real son of a bitch [. . .] Thanks to those who invented Viagra!" which he deleted two hours later. Because of this post, the Professional Football Disciplinary Committee imposed a disciplinary sanction of removing the rights attached to his duties for three months under Article 46 (1) of the FDD and Article 38 (a) of the Central Referee Committee Directive, which was subsequently approved by the Arbitration Board. The TFF Arbitration Board approved the sanction, deeming it relevant and proportionate. The TFF Arbitration Board considered that referees should be careful in their social lives as they represent the TFF on the field, and also because of the public importance of football. The social acts of referees would be attributed to TFF, damaging its reputation, which should be non-political, objective, and impartial. Thus, the referees should act by the fair-play principle, beyond any political concerns. The Arbitration Board considered that there were disrespectful expressions to the deceased columnist's memory in the applicant's post, which constituted a disciplinary offense as per Article 38 (a) of the Central Referee Committee Guidelines—against national culture, morals, and sports.[49] It should be emphasized that the three-month sanction automatically had the effect of the revocation of his license as referee in Turkish football.

The ECtHR first observed that the Professional Disciplinary Committee and the Arbitration Board, by not making any detailed examination apart from mentioning the letter of the applicable internal law, failed to balance the applicant's freedom of expression and the interests relevant to the TFF. In fact, the Disciplinary Committee and the Arbitration Board did not give detailed reasoning as to the existence of legitimate aims (of prevention of disorder and crime) and the proportionality of the sanction with these legitimate aims, if they existed. The two TFF organs did not note why the appellant's Facebook post could have impacted the peace in the football arena, especially considering it was removed within two hours; they did not give attention to the nature and severity of the sanction, which revoked the applicant's referee license and its deterrent effect for the freedom of expression of football professionals. Therefore, the ECtHR concluded that the necessity of the sanction could not be shown by the relevant and sufficient reasons, and the proportionality of

[48] TFF Professional Football Disciplinary Committee, PFDK Kararları (PFDK Decisions) - 17 December 2013, Meeting no. 44, https://www.tff.org/default.aspx?pageID=246&ftxtID=19648 (last accessed 4 December 2022). Also see, Anadolu Agency, Drogba ve Eboue'ye ceza yok (No sanction for Drogba and Eboue), 17 December 2013, https://www.aa.com.tr/tr/spor/drogba-ve-eboueye-ceza-yok/196965 (last accessed 4 December 2022).

[49] *İbrahim Tokmak c. Turquie*, Requête no 54540/16, Judgment of 18 May 2021, paras.5–8.

the sanction was not justified on the legitimate aims of prevention of disorder and crime by the reasons given by the TFF organs.[50]

As shown from the facts of the case and the judgment of the Court, the *İbrahim Tokmak* case does not have anything to do with the political speech of sportspersons within the context of the conflict between freedom of expression and the universal ban on political speech in sports governance. The applicant's post insulted the memory of third parties and had very little political content, despite the fact that deceased third party was known to the public because of his provocative writings. Consequently, the sanction imposed on the applicant was based on a specific directive applicable to referees due to his disrespectful statement that was considered immoral. In fact, the applicant's statement on social media does not even fall within the ambit of TFF regulations, as it was not posted before, during, or after a match, and was not related to sports activity; the only aspect that might have relevance for the ban on political speech was not been examined by the ECtHR in detail.[51]

The fourth case, *A.M. v. Turkey,* delivered several months later by the ECtHR, concerns a video recording of the applicant, who is a certified yoga trainer, that was uploaded to YouTube on 6 July 2014. The video recording shows the applicant talking about the number of wives of the Prophet Muhammad and his huge sword, and expressed his surprise as to why people are not surprised by these things. Although YouTube removed the video upon the request of the applicant, the applicant was nevertheless convicted by the Ankara Criminal Court of General Jurisdiction for publicly degrading religious values of a section of the public, and was convicted to one-year's imprisonment since the video was uploaded several times to YouTube after its removal. Disciplinary proceedings were initiated against the applicant under Articles 16 (breach of national honor) and 17 (discrimination) of the Disciplinary Regulation of the Turkish Federation of Sports for All (THİSF) of 24 January 2017.[52]

The Disciplinary Committee noted that the one-year prescription should begin to run from the date on which the disciplinary body in question became aware of the wrongful act, rather than the date of the commission of the act, and decided to deprive the applicant of his rights for three years, a sanction automatically revoking his license to perform yoga instruction in Turkish sports law. The General Directorate of Sport Arbitration Board upheld the decision of the Disciplinary Committee by making an analogy with the provisions of the Criminal Code in which it is enshrined that no prescription period applies for genocide and crimes against humanity, and consequently jumped to the conclusion that the prescription rule cannot be applied for acts of offending the Prophet Muhammad either. The General Directorate of Sport Arbitration Board thought that offending the Prophet Muhammad should be qualified as an act aimed at humiliating 'Turkishness', thus falling within the scope of Articles 16 and 17 of the Disciplinary Regulation of the THİSF (a generic

[50] *İbrahim Tokmak c. Turquie*, Requête no 54540/16, Judgment of 18 May 2021, paras.30–38.

[51] *İbrahim Tokmak c. Turquie*, Requête no 54540/16, Judgment of 18 May 2021.

[52] *A.M. v. Turkey*, App. No. 67199/17, Judgment of 19 October 2021, paras.9–23.

provision that all Turkish sports federations under the auspices of the General Directorate of Sport have in their disciplinary regulations). Ultimately, the General Directorate of Sport Arbitration Board found the disciplinary measures proportionate.[53]

When the case was brought before the ECtHR, the Court focused on the lawfulness of the interference within the terms of the second paragraph of Article 10. In this regard, the ECtHR underlined the fact that the Disciplinary Regulation that constituted the basis for the sanction imposed on the applicant entered into force (5 September 2016) after the applicant's statements in question were uploaded to YouTube, and the respondent Turkish Government's failure to submit or show any previous provision capable of sanctioning the same or similar violations in force when the YouTube video was uploaded or any other disciplinary regulation applicable to certified THİSF yoga trainers. Moreover, the Court thought that the prescription analogy of the Arbitration Board was unforeseeable because Article 30 of the Disciplinary Regulation provided no exceptions for the one-year prescription rule, which starts to run from the day of the event. Therefore, the ECtHR found that the interference at issue was not "prescribed by law" within the meaning of Article 10 (2) of the Convention and violated the applicant's right to freedom of expression.[54]

As seen above, the *A.M. v. Turkey* case does not relate to political expressions of sportspersons within the normal meaning of the term, since the statements in the uploaded YouTube video have an obvious religious and discriminatory dimension, which could even be considered under the terms of hate speech. Thus, like the *Maguire* and *Simunic* cases, the material scope of the statements in question is closer to inciting hatred, a kind of expression not normally considered to fall within the ambit of freedom of expression under ECHR. Discriminatory and hateful words and gestures cannot be equated to mere political statements—even if they may have political context or may be expressed in order to contribute to political debate. While the *A.M.* case was solved from the angle of lawfulness of the interference with the right to freedom of expression, the ECtHR's argumentation was strictly limited to the particular implementation of disciplinary laws and principles applied by the Disciplinary Committee of THİSF and General Directorate of Sports Arbitration Board, and did not cover the question of compatibility of the universal ban on political speech with all aspects (lawfulness, legitimate aim and proportionality of the interference, known as the 'tripartite test') of freedom of expression under Article 10 of the Convention. Nevertheless, the *A.M.* case is still important with regard to the concept of lawfulness under sports disciplinary law.

[53] *A.M. v. Turkey*, App. No. 67199/17, Judgment of 19 October 2021, paras.20–23.

[54] *A.M. v. Turkey*, App. No. 67199/17, Judgment of 19 October 2021, paras.36–41.

3.2 Naki *Case*

The *Naki* case is different from all of the aforementioned cases, as it is the only case in which the sanction imposed on a sportsperson by an SGB under its internal disciplinary regulations directly concerns the universal ban on political speech in sports governance. Hence, it deserves more attention than the others for the purposes of this chapter.

The fourth paragraph of Article 42 of the TFF Professional Football Disciplinary Directive (FDD) dated July 2015 (in force at the time of events) includes a provision under the title "discrimination" that, "It is forbidden to make any and all kinds of ideological propaganda before, during and after the competition. In case of non-compliance with this prohibition, the penalties specified in this article will be applied".[55]

On 31 January 2016, after his team had won a Ziraat Turkish Cup football match, Mr. Deniz Naki, a football player from Amed Sportif Faaliyetler Kulübü (henceforth referred as to 'Amedspor'), posted the following message on his personal Facebook account:

> Very important victory for us today. Dirty play from the team across the way, but we did [flawlessly]! Happy and proud to be able to be a beacon of hope for our people at this difficult time. [Amed Sportif] has not bowed and never will. We entered the field with our faith in freedom and we won. We have [sowed the seeds] of Freedom and Hope! Thank you to all our politicians, artists, intellectuals, and to our people. They haven't abandoned us. We dedicate and offer this victory to those who have lost their lives or been injured during the persecutions that have [befallen] our land for more than fifty days! Long live freedom.

Since these statements were considered "unsportsmanlike and ideological propaganda" within the meaning of Article 38 and 42 of the Football Disciplinary Directive, Mr. Naki was referred to the TFF Professional Football Disciplinary Committee. On 4 February 2016, The Committee decided that Mr. Naki's remarks violated the ban on making ideological propaganda and unsportsmanlike statements (i.e., Article 42/4 and Articles 35/4, 38/1(a) and 10/2 of the Football Disciplinary Directive respectively). The Committee believed that sentences and words used by Mr. Naki in his above statement devalued the image of football, incited violence and disorder, destroyed the peaceful atmosphere in sports, escalated tension and threatened spectators with violence and protests. The Committee also held that expressions in this statement were excessive and disproportionate and were not necessarily required to be used; Mr. Naki was sanctioned with a ban for twelve official matches and a fine of 19,500 Turkish liras.

Mr. Naki and Amedspor appealed this decision to the Arbitration Board, maintaining that Mr. Naki had a peaceful aim and in no way intended to incite violence. His remarks were protected by Articles 9 and 10 of the ECHR, and the decision of the Disciplinary Committee did not contain sufficient and relevant

[55]The TFF Disciplinary Directive of 2017 in force today still has the same provision as explained in detail above.

reasons. Moreover, Mr. Naki and Amedspor argued that the decision of the Disciplinary Committee did not precisely indicate specific and concrete acts or events caused by Mr. Naki's statements. They also alleged that the fact that the Committee punished Mr. Naki for two different offenses for just the one message was contrary to Article 7 of the European Convention. However, the Arbitration Board approved the decision of the Committee, simply stating that the contested decision was in accordance with the procedure, the law and the Directives with regard to both the assessment of facts and evidence and legal nature of the statements. As a cliché, the Arbitration Board stated that Mr. Naki's statements went beyond admissible criticism, that they had no connection with football, and that they aimed to disseminate ideological propaganda which would destroy the peaceful atmosphere of sports in Türkiye.

The ECtHR confined its review strictly to procedural grounds and found that the impugned interference had legal basis in domestic law and pursued legitimate aims. The ECtHR avoided the applicants' argument that the legal provisions in force (Disciplinary Directive of TFF) did not meet the quality of law requirement, since it reached that the interference was not necessary in terms of proportionality. Likewise, the ECtHR assumed that the interference in question was aimed at legitimate objects under Article 10/2 of the Convention, namely the prevention of disorder and/or crime in the context of Turkish football, despite the fact that the Court admitted that there may be doubt as to the validity of aims pursued by the sanction imposed on Mr. Naki in terms of legitimacy.

Accordingly, the ECtHR only dealt with the proportionality of the impugned interference on the basis of its necessity. The Court looked at the decisions of the Disciplinary Committee and Arbitration Board as to whether they contained relevant and sufficient reasons. In this regard, the Court came to the conclusion that the reasoning of the TFF bodies did not contain sufficient response to the question whether the interference had been justified. Neither the Disciplinary Committee nor the Arbitration Board had specified which parts of the Facebook message were problematic, and they had not examined the circumstances around the publication, namely the victory by Mr. Naki's team in a football match following violent incidents in the region over the preceding month. Nor had these decisions made it possible to ascertain the potential harm of Mr. Naki's statement; they did not show that it had encouraged spectators or would likely encourage them to commit acts of violence in the future.[56]

[56] *Affaire Naki et Amed Sportif Faaliyetler Kulübü Derneği c. Turquie*, Req. No: 48924/16, Judgment of 18 May 2021. The ECtHR also examined the independence and impartiality of the Arbitration Board under Article 6 of the Convention and held that Türkiye violated this obligation as well.

4 Insufficiency of the ECtHR's Procedural Review Approach in the *Naki* Case

4.1 Weakness of the Procedural Review

As in the other cases concerning freedom of speech in sports law analyzed above, in the *Naki* case, the ECtHR confined its review strictly to procedural grounds, focusing on the reasoning of the TFF bodies (especially the Arbitration Board). This approach prevented the ECtHR to deal with the substance of the issue (i.e., the compatibility of a universal ban on political speech with freedom of expression). Procedural review[57] can be seen mainly in relation to decision-making by national courts. If a case reveals a lack of inadequate proportionality or procedural care by national authorities, the ECtHR may evaluate the overall reasonableness of the interference. Here it can be understood that the Court focuses on the inadequate arguments of national authorities, as opposed to its own judicial review process.[58]

Since tests of necessity and fair balance are related to the substance of the review, the ECtHR's procedural review method, and its increasing implementation in nearly all its cases, has been heavily contested. It has been argued that by replacing substantive review with procedural review as a supplementary type of review, the ECtHR undermines its own standards and leads to window-dressing on the national level.[59] Even some of the strongest advocates of "shared responsibility" admit that the judicial techniques used in procedural review methods help the Court avoid substantive and moral choices in delicate cases,[60] issues normally dealt with under tests of necessity and fair balance.

With that said, instead of dealing with the substance of cases and developing generic principles in hard cases, the Court's procedural review does have some merits, as it may encourage national authorities to increase the quality of the national decision-making process. In this regard, the ECtHR tends to give more weight to the *quality* of the national authorities' decisions. The ECtHR particularly focuses on the national courts, with a view towards democratic process, in determining whether a violation of the Convention exists. Moreover, the Court expects relevant and competent national authorities to apply its case-law standards developed for a particular human rights issue, as if those national authorities act like its agent at the national

[57] Also known as evidence-based review or process-based review, or sometimes labeled as procedural turn. See further about procedural review e.g. Gerards (2019), p. 258; Huijbers (2017), pp. 177–201; Gerards and Brems (2017), pp. 1–15; Brems (2017), pp. 17–39; Gerards (2017), pp. 127–160; Popelier (2012), pp. 249–269; Popelier and Van de Heyning (2013), p. 260; Spano (2018), pp. 473–494.

[58] Gerards (2014), p. 52.

[59] For critiques on procedural review as a "risky game" and dangers of micro justice see Nussberger (2017), p. 162. As an opposing view on procedural review's contributions, especially more effective protection see Kleinlein (2019), pp. 91–110.

[60] See Gerards (2014), p. 52.

level. The Court implements procedural review both as a judicial interpretive technique and as a tool of 'shared responsibility', related to the interrelationship between the Court and national authorities.[61]

The procedural review appears to have two different guises: (1) procedural obligations for the member states, a procedural rights approach, and (2) procedural review *stricto sensu*, increasingly taking account of procedural shortcomings at the domestic level when determining whether a right has been violated.[62] As an international human rights mechanism, the ECtHR has important functions of standard-setting and maintaining constitutional justice as well as individual justice. The Court has the potential to contribute to the development of a more 'constitutional' system for the protection of human rights in Europe, as opposed to being a 'weak' body that can be criticized for being too intrusive on the national margin of appreciation and thus not recognized at the national level; and in extreme cases, receive threats from states to leave the Convention altogether.[63]

Nevertheless, when there are major deficiencies of national law in the meaning of lawfulness, legitimate aims, and the necessity test, the ECtHR cannot ignore its own standards. This is especially valid when the issue in question relates to blanket bans, a type of interference that leaves no room for balancing exercise.[64] Procedural review presupposes a national authority/court to exercise balancing between competing interests of the applicant and public or third parties, while using criteria developed by the ECtHR for that matter. The procedural review thus only becomes effective when the ECtHR has *already* developed criteria for a particular issue under the Convention, and consequently it can be argued that procedural review is meaningful for repetitive cases. But blanket bans never offer any kind of proportionality analysis by their very nature; that is to say, the current practices of procedural review have uncontrolled contents in sports law, and procedural review ought to be approached cautiously so as not to facilitate judicial restraint.

Here one could argue that the ECtHR should use a 'mixed-type review', which includes procedural and substantive review at the same time, to address the compatibility of blanket bans with the freedom of expression. Referred to as 'substance-flavored' procedural review, a mixed-type review could have the capacity to examine the quality of the human rights scrutiny performed at the domestic level by taking into account the substance of the issue as well.[65] In the subsequent subsections, the

[61] Gerards (2014), p. 52. Also see High-level Conference on the "Implementation of the European Convention on Human Rights, our shared responsibility", Brussel Declaration, 27 March 2015, https://www.echr.coe.int/documents/d/echr/brussels_declaration_eng (Accessed 22.09.2023).

[62] See Arnardóttir (2017), p. 33.

[63] See Arnardóttir (2015), p. 23.

[64] Cumper and Lewis (2019), pp. 611–638.

[65] Developed from Brems' explanations on the four rationales to implement the procedural review and different types of procedural review derived from these rationales. Brems tries to align the different rationales with the core business of the ECHR system, the human rights scrutiny of domestic measures, and prefers substance-flavoured procedural control instead of solely procedural scrutiny. See Brems (2017), pp. 17–39.

consequences of the ECtHR's procedural review in the *Naki* case (and indirectly in other freedom of expression cases concerning sports law) with regard to the universal ban of political speech in sports governance will be analyzed through the lens of 'mixed-type' review, revealing inconsistencies of such a universal ban with the right to freedom of expression under Article 10 of the Convention.

4.2 Total Ban on Political Speech Does Not Meet Clarity, Certainty, and Foreseeability Criteria

The first test that the ECtHR applies in order to determine the compatibility of interference with the right to freedom of expression is lawfulness criteria.[66] This test requires that the interference in question must have a legal basis in domestic law; mere existence of the provisions cannot automatically satisfy the clarity, certainty, and foreseeability criteria.[67] The ban on 'ideological statements' and 'political propaganda' regulated according to the regulations of various SGBs does not provide legal clarity, certainty and foreseeability. The nature, scope and context of such a ban on political speech leads to vagueness, and includes a broad spectrum of actions, behaviors, gestures, clothing, slogan, cheering, and statements. There is not a single element in the regulations of SGBs that explicitly details the kind of actions, behaviors, or clothing to be included in the scope of such a ban. For example, the statements that reach the threshold of 'propaganda' and, at the same time, fall within the scope of the concept of 'ideological', are completely undeterminable. Should statements made before, during, or after a sports competition that do not reach the limit of 'propaganda' but could be described as 'ideological' fit within the ban? Should a political statement that is not ideological be deemed legitimate under this regulation?

It is not possible to give satisfactory and consistent answers to these questions; it is evident that the national bodies that conducted legal proceedings, imposed, and

[66] *Sunday Times v. The United Kingdom,* App. No. 6538/74, Judgment of 26 April 1979, para. 49; *Huvig v. France,* App. No.11105/84, Judgment of 24 April 1990, paras.27–28; *Kruslin v. France,* App. No. 11801/85, Judgment of 24 April 1990, paras. 28–36; *Chauvy and Others v. France,* App. No. 64915/01, paras. 43–45; *Lindon, Otchakovsky-Laurens and July v. France*, App. No 21279/02 36448/02, GC Judgment of 22 October 2007, paras.41–43; *Satakunnan Markkinapörssı Oy and Satamedia Oy v. Finland*, App. No. 931/13, GC Judgment of 27 June 2017, paras.142–154; *Magyar Kétfarkú Kutya Párt v. Hungary,* App. No. 201/17, GC Judgment of 20 January 2020, paras. 93–101; *Nit S.R.L. v. The Republic of Moldova*, App. No. 28470/12, GC Judgment of 5 April 2022, paras.157–161. The Court has held that the law must indicate the scope of any such discretion conferred on the competent authorities and the manner of its exercise with sufficient clarity, having regard to the legitimate aim of the measure in question, to give the individual adequate protection against arbitrary interference. See *Malone v. The United Kingdom,* App. No. 8691/79, Judgment of 2 August. 1984, para. 68.

[67] It is accepted as "the rule of law test" Greer (1997), pp. 9–13. For lawfulness criteria see further e.g. Lautenbach (2013), pp. 70–124; Gerards (2019), pp. 198–220.

upheld particular sanctions possessed absolute and arbitrary power of appreciation. The legal proceedings and investigations conducted by the relevant authorities to determine whether a statement violated the ban on 'ideological' or 'political' propaganda were based on completely vague criteria. SGBs do not have a standardized background of judicial opinions regarding a ban on ideological or political speech. Even if a statement or gesture is deemed political, it is essential to determine whether such a statement or gesture is an emotional statement or a systematic and complete thought within the meaning of standards required by linguistics for reaching "the threshold of being ideological". Therefore, regulations that contain a ban on political or ideological propaganda would not be applicable in most cases.

It is also worth mentioning that the foreseeability criterion is assessed depending on the status of the persons to whom the text in dispute is addressed. In this context, the need for legal assistance/consultation in order to understand the legislation that forms the basis for the interference does not contravene the legality requirement if it is considered reasonable under the circumstances. This is especially the case in the case of persons whose profession requires them to be very attentive. Such persons may be expected to exercise special care in assessing the risks involved in their professional activities.[68] Against this background, specific diligence cannot be expected from sportspersons, who generally come from uneducated and poor segments of the society[69], in assessing the legal and technical risks which his/her profession includes. Similarly, since hiring a legal counsel for assessing the consequences of their statements and gestures posts cannot be expected from sportspersons, such excessive sanctions enshrined in accordance with disciplinary regulations of SGBs interpreted arbitrarily by internal institutions of SGBs and even by CAS are not foreseeable.

4.3 *Interference (Total Ban) Does Not Pursue Legitimate Aims*

In order to justify the existence and application of categorical bans on ideological/political speech, SGBs generally offer three aims: (1) protecting the political neutrality of sport (general legitimate aim),[70] (2) preventing disorder and crime (general legitimate aim), and (3) protecting the relevant sports communities (special

[68] *Cantoni v. France*, App. No. 17862/91, Judgment of 15 November 1996, para. 35; *Spacek v. Czech Republic*, App. No.26449/95, Judgment of 9 November 1999, para.59; *Chauvy and others v. France*, App. No. 64915/01, Judgment of 29 June 2004, paras. 44-49; *Soros v. France*, App. No.50425/06, Judgment of 6 October 2011.

[69] For this assumption, at least for American sports context, see Kelly (2016), pp. 231, 217.

[70] See Di Marco (2021), pp. 621–622, 633–635.

legitimate aim).[71] The validity of these abstract justifications is doubtful since the matter at hand pertains to a total and categorical ban of political speech, not simply a limitation of it. Provisions that contain clauses such as, "making any kind of ideological propaganda before, during or after a competition" (i.e., Article 42 of the TFF FDD), do not pursue a legitimate purpose as the clause suggests an absolute and categorical ban on political speech. The reason for prescribing such provisions in disciplinary regulations is isolating football from politics and propaganda. However, abolishing the freedom of expression of sportspersons or stakeholders in political matters on such grounds cannot be deemed valid. It should be emphasized that this ban is categorical, and the statement or gesture itself is punished without connecting the behavior to any other factor such as damage (or similar elements like violence), regardless of the medium it is expressed through. As there are no restrictions, the right itself is abolished and the essence of the right is infringed, it will not be possible to speak about any legitimate ground for restriction.

Sportspersons, like any other human being, have freedom of speech in political matters, and this right cannot simply be suspended categorically due to the fact that they belong to the sports community.[72] Falling under the category of 'being a sportsperson' is not a valid reason for abolishing their freedom of speech. Sportspersons may have opinions on political matters and seek to express those opinions in a way that they deem appropriate. Here it is essential to distinguish between a categorical ban and merely a limitation of speech. With that said, the followers or fans of successful sportspersons may indeed wonder about their role model's political opinions; a categorical ban on political speech not only violates the rights of the sportsperson, but also those of their followers. Moreover, statements made via social media should belong completely to the sportsperson, and not to the relevant SGBs. After all, a system respecting human rights cannot exclude freedom

[71] The Court focuses on necessity and proportionality review instead of legitimate aim. See Gerards (2019), pp. 220–229. Especially see "The Court doubts whether any of the legitimate aims listed under Article 10 § 2 of the Convention was pursued in the specific circumstances of the applicants' demonstrations. However, for the sake of argument and with the same reservations as in paragraph 140 above, the Court will proceed on the assumption that the applicants were taken to police stations for the purpose of 'prevention of crime'." *Novikova v. Russia,* App. No. 25501/07, Judgment of 26 April 2016, para. 143. Exceptionally the assessments of legitimate aims, see *Bayev and others v. Russia,* App. No. 67667/09 44092/12 56717/12, Judgment of 20 June 2017, paras. 65–83.

[72] The ECtHR accepts the idea that a sportsperson has the right to freedom of expression like everyone. In *Naki* Case, the ECtHR focused on national authorities' assessments related to the necessity of interference. The ECtHR held that the Government had failed to demonstrate that the reasons invoked by the national authorities to justify the impugned measure were relevant and sufficient and that this measure was necessary in a democratic society. The ECtHR did not rule on "quality of law" and "legitimate aim" elaborately in accordance with the procedural-review. The Court agreed to have doubts about the legitimate aims pursued by the measures taken in respect of the applicant, but the Court started from "the assumption" that the interference in question pursued the legitimate aims of the prevention of the order and crime prevention. See *Affaire Naki et Amed Sportif Faaliyetler Kulübü Derneği c. Turquie*, Req. No: 48924/16, Judgment of 18 May 2021, paras. 32–39.

of speech for certain categories of people or certain categories of statements/gestures; indeed, all statements (except hate speech variations,[73] and expressions that incite violence)[74] are protected under Article 10 ECHR.

As role models, sportspersons should use their right to freedom of political speech in a manner consistent with human rights standards, including responsibilities within the meaning of Article 10 ECHR. Their right may be limited if and when there are valid reasons to do so in accordance with Paragraph 2 of Article 10 ECHR. However, a total and categorical ban does not pursue any legitimate aim. One should note that sportspersons have to accept all rules and procedures imposed upon them by national or international SGBs in order to participate in the relevant sport. This kind of imposition increases the severity of the categorical ban in question.

4.4 Proportionality of Total Ban on Political Speech

The final test that the ECtHR applies as to whether an interference with the right to freedom of expression violates Article 10 ECHR is the proportionality test. If and when the Court finds that the impugned measure has legal basis and pursues legitimate aim, it also examines its proportionality to the aim pursued.[75] States have positive obligations to prevent violations as well as negative obligations not to violate them. Factors such as the nature of the expression in dispute, its contribution to a public debate, the scope and nature of the limitation, and whether the same legitimate aim can be achieved with less restrictive measures are taken into account. Preventing threats to freedom of expression from individuals is a positive obligation

[73] See, *Simunic v. Crotia*, App. No. 20373/17, Admissibility Decision of 22 January 2019, §38-49. The ECtHR found that the gestures of the applicant footballer in question (shouting Ustasha march to spectators which is considered to be fascist) falls within the ambit of Article 10, but the interference was legitimate and proportional due to the modest nature of the fine imposed to the applicant (about three thousand three hundred euros fine) and gesture's controversial context.

[74] *Kevin Maguire v. The United Kingdom*, App. No. 58060/13, Admissibility Decision of 3 March 2015.

[75] For summary see e.g. *Stoll v. Switzerland,* App. No. 69698/01, Judgment of 10 December 2007, para. 101; *Hertel v. Switzerland,* App. No. 25181/94, Judgment of 25 August 1998, para. 46; *Steel and Morris v. the United Kingdom,* App. No. 68416/01, Judgment of 15 February 2005, para.87; *Morice v. France*, App. No. 29369/10, GC Judgment of 23 April 2015, para.124; *Pentikäinen v. Finland,* App. No. 11882/10, GC Judgment of 20 October 2015, para.87; *Bédat v. Switzerland,* App. No. 56925/08, GC Judgment of 29 March 2016, para. 48. See further *Romanenko and Others v. Russia,* App. No. 11751/03, Judgment of 8 October 2009, para.49; *OOO Izdatelskiy Tsentr Kvartirnyy Ryad v. Russia,* App. No. 39748/05, Judgment of 25 April 2017, para.46; *Cheltsova v. Russia,* App. No. 44294/06, Judgment of 13 June 2017, para.100; *Skudayeva v. Russia,* App. No. 24014/07, Judgment of 5 March 2019, para.39; *Nadtoka v. Russia (no. 2),* App. No. 29097/08, Judgment of 8 October 2019, para.50; *Tolmachev v. Russia,* App. No. 42182/11, Judgment of 2 June 2020, para.56; *Timakov and OOO ID Rubezh v. Russia,* App. Nos. 46232/10 and 74770/10, Judgment of 8 September 2020, para.71.

of the state.[76] Thus, the categorical ban on political/ideological speech in sports is disproportionate as such, and infringes Article 10 ECHR regardless of the nature of the sanction applied, since it can lead to sportspersons refraining from expressing political/ideological opinions, which are protected under Article 10 in the broadest sense.[77] The only legitimate restriction of political speech is that which incites hatred or violence.[78]

In addition, it is vital for the competent authorities (in this case SGBs) to analyze whether the statement or gesture in question is just a declaration or has a performative aspect. The ECtHR does not consider sanctions proportional when the competent authorities of SGBs have construed a mere declaration/statement as an action. Further, the very assumptions lie within the heart of the political/ideological speech ban, namely "decreasing the value of sport, breaking neutrality of SGBs, promoting violence and disorder in sports and leading to supporters' movements",[79] cannot be considered proportional since they constitute 'irrebuttable' presumptions as such. These 'irrebuttable' presumptions make the search for a pressing social need requiring a sanction to be imposed on sportspersons when they declare their political and ideological views meaningless, which is a vital criterion for the ECtHR to determine whether the interference in question is proportional in a democratic society.

In order for the sanction to be considered proportional, the relevant SGBs have to give concrete examples of how the statements/gestures in question decrease the value of the sport, break neutrality, promote violence and disorder, and/or lead to unrest among supporters. Imposing automatic or semi-automatic sanctions when the statement/gesture in question is found to be political and/or ideological constitutes "disproportionate and excessive" interference with the right to freedom of

[76] *Özgür Gündem v. Turkey*, App. No. 23144/93, Judgment of 16 March 2000; *Dink v. Turkey*, App. Nos. 2668/07, 6102/08, 30079/08, 7072/09 and 7124/09, Judgment of 14 September 2010; *Fuentes Bobo v. Spain*, App. No. 39293/98, Judgment of 29 February 2000; *Khurshid Mustafa and Tarzibachi v Sweden*, App. No. 23883/06, Judgment of 16 December 2008.

[77] Prebensen (1998), pp. 14–15. See e.g. *Ceylan v. Turkey*, App. No. 23556/94, Judgment of 8 July 1999, para. 34; *Teslenko and others v. Russia*, App. Nos. 49588/12 65395/12 49351/18, Judgment of 5 April 2022, para.133.

[78] *Kevin Maguire v. The United Kingdom*, App. No. 58060/13, Admissibility Decision of 3 March 2015. In case of an incitement to violence against an individual or a public official or a sector of the population, state authorities enjoy a wider margin of appreciation when examining the need for an interference with freedom of expression. Therefore, it can be said that the ECtHR may evaluate where and when incitement to violence begins by taking into account the specific circumstances of cases. See *Sürek v. Turkey (No 3)*, App. No. 24735/94, GC Judgment of 8 July 1999, para.37; *Mariya Alekhina and Others v. Russia*, App. No. 38004/12, Judgment of 17 July 2018, para. 217 ("The Court reiterates that it has had regard to several factors in a number of cases concerning statements, verbal or non-verbal, alleged to have stirred up or justified violence, hatred or intolerance where it was called upon to decide whether the interferences with the exercise of the right to freedom of expression of the authors of such statements had been 'necessary in a democratic society' in the light of the general principles formulated in its case-law.")

[79] See, Sects. 2 and 4.3 of this Chapter.

expression under the ECHR.[80] Since the ban is blanket and categorical, there is no context analysis concerning the violated interests legitimizing the restriction (i.e., public order, public security, rights and freedoms of others, national security), and the balance provided between such violated interests and freedom of speech.

5 Implications of ECtHR's Rulings Concerning Freedom of Expression in Sports

Despite the failure of the ECtHR in its approach and method concerning freedom of expression cases in sports, the *Naki* ruling may still have important implications for all SGBs regarding the sustainability of a categorical political speech ban. The ECtHR implicitly indicates that sportspersons have freedom of speech in political matters, and that such a right cannot be suspended categorically due to the sole fact that they belong to sports community, or expressed their political views in or around the pitches.

5.1 *Rulings Involving Türkiye*

An infringement ruling of the ECtHR has two effects: one is subjective and provides redress to the victim of an already detected violation; the other is objective and prevents subsequent violations. In human rights law in general, and particularly European human rights law, it is expected that a judgment or decision in which a violation is detected has an objective impact on all segments of national authorities responsible, with a view to prevent subsequent violations for the same reason. These national authorities include all governmental branches (i.e., legislature, administrative, judiciary) and quasi-governmental agencies (i.e., TFF). In order to reveal the effects of the Court's rulings on freedom of expression cases against Türkiye in a sports law context, including the *Naki* case, one should take into account both the subjective and objective components together.

[80] There is little scope under Article 10/2 of the Convention for restrictions on political speech or on public interest. See *Castells v. Spain,* App. No. 11798/85, Judgment of 23 April 1992, para. 43; *Wingrove v. The United Kingdom,* App. No 17419/90, Judgment of 25 October 1996, para.58; *Magyar Helsinki Bizottság v. Hungary,* App. No. 18030/11, Judgment of 8 November 2016, para.163.

5.1.1 Subjective Effects: Rulings of ECtHR as a Retrial Reason in Turkish Sports Law

The main tool to give effect to the judgments of the ECtHR is the retrial mechanism enshrined in the code of procedures for main fields of law, such as Turkish Procedural Law, Turkish Administrative Law, and Turkish Criminal Procedure Law. Turkish Procedural Law is particularly important for sports law in Türkiye since it is applicable when there is no special provision in the legislation of internal sport regulations proclaimed by the relevant federations. According to Turkish Procedural Law, retrial may be requested against judgments which has the effect of *res judicata* if and when certain developments happened and certain conditions have been met.[81] One of the reasons for retrial is the final judgment or decisions of the ECtHR, including amicable settlements and unilateral declarations in which it has been determined that the domestic decision in question was made in violation of the ECHR.[82] This provision of Turkish Code of Civil Procedure is applicable to the Turkish sports law context in which retrial is also regulated, both for disciplinary proceedings under the heading of "retrial of disciplinary proceedings",[83] and final decisions of the Arbitration Board in which it is stated that, "The provisions of the Code of Civil Procedure and the Code of Criminal Procedure regarding the announcement of decisions, correction of factual errors, and retrial are reserved" when it comes to final decisions of the Arbitration Board.[84]

Against this legal background, on 27 May 2021, the TFF Arbitration Board accepted for the first time that the ECtHR's violation judgments concerning the final decisions of the Arbitration Board had provided a basis for retrial[85] upon the application of Serkan Akal, who was an applicant before the ECtHR where it was found that the Arbitration Board of TFF was neither independent nor impartial

---

[81] Article 374 of the Turkish Code of Civil Procedure, Law No. 6100; Enacted on 12 January 2011; (Official Gazette, Date 04 February 2011, no. 27836).

[82] Article 345 (1) (i) of the Turkish Code of Civil Procedure.

[83] Article 91 of the Turkish Football Federation's Professional Football Disciplinary Directive of 2017 (https://www.tff.org//Resources/TFF/Documents/TALIMATLAR/Futbol-Disiplin-Talimati.pdf).

[84] Articles 14 and 15 of the TFF Arbitration Board Instructions, August 2017. (https://www.tff.org/Resources/TFF/Documents/TALIMATLAR/Tahkim-Kurulu-Talimati.pdf).

[85] Turkish Football Federation (TFF), "Tahkim Kurulu Kararları (Arbitration Board Decisions)", 27 May 2021, https://www.tff.org/Default.aspx?pageId=200&ftxtId=35214. Whether retrial process is effective for the applicant Serkan Akal is another story. The Arbitration Board pointed out that re-trial should be made by the Central Referee Committee because of the applicant Serkan Akal was a referee and his grievances were concerning downgrading his status from super league to first league. The Arbitration Board sent the file to the Central Referee Committee who examined on its merits and decided to reject. The Arbitration Board later upheld this refusal (K.2021/363). Also see, Communication from Türkiye concerning the cases of Ali Riza and Others v. Turkey, Eksioglu v. Turkey, Sedat Dogan v. Turkey, Naki and AMED Sportif Faaliyetler Kulübü Dernegi v. Turkey, Ibrahim Tokmak v. Turkey (Application Nos. 30226/10, 2006/13, 48909/14, 48924/16, 54540/16), DH-DD(2022)937, 08/09/2022), para.15.

within the meaning of Article 6 ECHR.[86] This led to a series of retrial claims directed either to the Professional Disciplinary Committee or the Arbitration Board. For example, İbrahim Tokmak, the applicant in the *Tokmak* case whose right of freedom of expression was violated because of his statements posted on his Facebook account concerning a deceased columnist, also applied for retrial and his claim was granted by the Professional Football Disciplinary Board by a majority of votes on 4 November 2021. The Committee also accepted the ECtHR's authority over the dispute resolution processes (both procedural and substantive) within the TFF and abolished the previous sanctions by referring to a fundamental right (freedom of expression in the present cases) with these decisions.[87]

With regard to the *Naki* case, however, no change can be observed in terms of subjective effects of the ECtHR ruling in favour of the applicant footballer, Mr. Naki since he did not apply for retrial.[88] In fact, Mr. Naki faced considerable difficulties with regard to his professional football life. When his application for infringement of the political statement ban was pending before the ECtHR, TFF imposed another three-and-a-half year ban and a fine of 273,000 Turkish liras on Mr. Naki for a different political statement made which ultimately prevented him to ever play football for any club in Türkiye.[89] In this second sanction, the Disciplinary Board and the Arbitration Board took into account his first sanction for breaching the ban on political speech (which was the subject matter of the ECtHR ruling in the *Naki* case discussed in this chapter) as an aggravating factor in expelling him from playing professional football in Türkiye. The applicant was also tried by the criminal court and was found guilty of making propaganda for a terrorist organization, and was sentenced to 18 months and 22 days of imprisonment, which was subsequently

[86] *Ali Rıza and Others v. Turkey*, App. Nos. 30226/10, 17880/11, 17887/11, 17891/11 and 5506/16, Judgment of 28 January 2020.

[87] Turkish Football Federation (TFF), "Tahkim Kurulu Kararları (Arbitration Board Decisions)", 04 November 2021, https://www.tff.org/default.aspx?pageID=246&ftxtID=36371.

The PFDK also abolished two other persons sanction who received a judgment in their favour from the ECtHR concerning their private life under Article 8 because of the illegitimate use of allegedly illegal evidence in disciplinary proceedings before TFF organs taken in criminal investigations despite the fact that there is no legal provision which provides evidence transfer from criminal investigations to disciplinary proceedings (*Ekşioğlu and Mosturoğlu v. Turkey*, App. Nos. 2006/13 and 10857/13, Judgment of 15 June 2021).

[88] Communication from Türkiye concerning the cases of Ali Riza and Others v. Turkey, Eksioglu v. Turkey, Sedat Dogan v. Turkey, Naki and AMED Sportif Faaliyetler Kulübü Dernegi v. Turkey, Ibrahim Tokmak v. Turkey (Application Nos. 30226/10, 2006/13, 48909/14, 48924/16, 54540/16), DH-DD(2022)937, 08/09/2022), para.17.

[89] Final decision of the Arbitration Board, E.2018/36 - K.2018/33, delivered on 1 February 2018. (http://www.tff.org/default.aspx?pageID=247&ftxtID=28677).

adjourned for five years.[90] Consequently, Mr. Naki was excluded from pursuing professional football and left Türkiye.[91]

One could consider compensation schemes included in the judgment or decisions of the ECtHR as another tool for the subjective effect of ECtHR rulings. In all cases in which a violation of freedom of expression has been found, the ECtHR has also ruled for pecuniary and non-pecuniary compensation and expenses incurred at least before it.[92] According to the present author's knowledge, Türkiye has paid those amounts in due time.[93]

Similarly, one can observe that the road opened by the judgments of ECtHR concerning freedom of expression cases against Türkiye in the context of sports disciplinary, is now used by clubs. Fenerbahçe, its president and its managers, and Galatasaray have applied to the ECtHR for the sanctions imposed by the Professional Football Disciplinary Board and approved by the Arbitration Board due to their statements criticizing the TFF and its managers both on television and on social media. Recently, the applications resulted in an amicable settlement with an agreement reached between the applicants and Türkiye by the ECtHR. In the amicable settlement text, Türkiye undertakes to pay compensation (approximately 78,000 euros in total for pecuniary damages, non-pecuniary damages, and expenses).[94] The compensation and expenses undertaken by the respondent state can therefore be considered another means for the subjective effect of the ECtHR rulings.

5.1.2 Objective Effects of ECtHR Rulings

After the Court's rulings on the three freedom of expression cases against Türkiye in a sports law context, little change can be observed in terms of objective effects of ECtHR judgments. Following judgments of the ECtHR on 18 May 2021, the

[90] According to Mr. Naki's lawyer, Mr. Neşet Giresun, who represented the applicant in the first proceedings before the ECtHR, Mr. Naki did not bring his second, separate, and ultimate disciplinary sanctions, and his criminal conviction for his first statements which was later found in violation with the freedom of expression, to the attention of the ECtHR (Interview with Mr. Neşet Giresun on 01 November 2022 in İstanbul).

[91] According to the latest news, Mr. Naki has been arrested in Germany due to his alleged involvement in the drug trade and organized crime. (https://www.aa.com.tr/en/sports/germany-arrests-ex-footballer-on-criminal-charges/2088083). He was released in May 2023. (https://l24.im/SDZPu).

[92] *İbrahim Tokmak c. Turquie*, Requête no 54540/16, Judgment of 18 May 2021; *Sedat Doğan c. Turquie*, Requête no 48909/14, Judgment of 18 May 2021; *Naki et Amed Sportif Faaliyetler Kulübü Derneği c. Turquie*, Requête no 48924/16, Judgment of 18 May 2021; *A.M. v. Turkey*, App. No. 67199/17, Judgment of 19 October 2021.

[93] Communication from Türkiye concerning the cases of Ali Riza and Others v. Turkey, Eksioglu v. Turkey, Sedat Dogan v. Turkey, Naki and AMED Sportif Faaliyetler Kulübü Dernegi v. Turkey, Ibrahim Tokmak v. Turkey (Application Nos. 30226/10, 2006/13, 48909/14, 48924/16, 54540/16), DH-DD(2022)937, 08/09/2022), para.18.

[94] *Koç et Autres c. Türkiye*, Requête nos 80/21 et 2 autres requêtes, Decision of 06 October 2022. https://hudoc.echr.coe.int/eng?i=001-220621.

Arbitration Board unanimously, having explicitly taken into account the aforementioned judgments, and the concept of freedom of expression, lifted the sanctions imposed on the President of Samsunspor, the managers of Beşiktaş, and the Fenerbahçe Sports Club and its managers for their statements that were considered 'unsportsmanlike' under Article 38 of the FDD of 2017 (in force at the material time) by the Professional Disciplinary Committee.[95] But there is no other example publicly available that displays objective effect of ECtHR rulings in a similar context.

Further, the TFF Executive Board, other responsible national authority in providing objective effect to ECtHR judgments, has not made the necessary changes in the relevant statutes, codes, and instructions with a view to incorporate freedom of expression (and other human rights) concerns into the TFF *acquis*. On the contrary, the TFF Executive Board, on 10/08/2021 at its 95th meeting, first abolished Article 38 of the FDD (unsportsmanlike statements) and envisaged much more detailed provisions in Article 36 of FDD. Moreover, new Article 38 contains additional limitations on free speech that punish certain statements of sportspersons against referees and other officials.[96] Although these changes occurred after the ECtHR gave its rulings on *Doğan*, *Naki* and *Tokmak* cases in 18 May 2021, the TFF Executive Board did not take into account human rights concerns when making these changes.

In fact, the Government of Türkiye believes that changes made after *Ali Rıza* judgment with regard to impartiality and independence of the Arbitration Board also provides enough protection concerning freedom of expression in terms of equality of arms etc.[97] But in reality, the TFF and the State of Türkiye have not made the necessary structural changes sought by the ECtHR itself in its judgment pertaining to the impartiality and independence of the Arbitration Board. One should remember that the ECtHR, with its semi-pilot decision, decided that the TFF Arbitration Board was not independent and impartial, and invited Türkiye to take the necessary measures since the problem was of a structural/systemic nature.[98] The Act on TFF numbered 5894, promulgated by the Turkish Grand National Assembly (the legislative organ of Türkiye, GNAT), and the TFF Statute had to change after this semi-pilot judgment, but so far TFF and the State of Türkiye have only made window-dressing reforms, such as making an oath obligatory for the members of the Professional Disciplinary Committee and the Arbitration Board. Even the GNAT recently promulgated a new Act on sports clubs and federations, which also has

---

[95] Turkish Football Federation (TFF), "Tahkim Kurulu Kararları (Arbitration Board Decisions)", 20 May 2021. The Arbitration Board, https://www.tff.org/default.aspx?pageID=247&ftxtID=35150.

[96] Turkish Football Federation, Futbol Disiplin Talimatı, August 2017, https://www.tff.org//Resources/TFF/Documents/TALIMATLAR/Futbol-Disiplin-Talimati.pdf.

[97] Communication from Türkiye concerning the cases of Ali Riza and Others v. Turkey, Eksioglu v. Turkey, Sedat Dogan v. Turkey, Naki and AMED Sportif Faaliyetler Kulübü Dernegi v. Turkey, Ibrahim Tokmak v. Turkey (Application Nos. 30226/10, 2006/13, 48909/14, 48924/16, 54540/16), DH-DD(2022)937, 08/09/2022), paras.71–77.

[98] *Ali Rıza and Others v. Turkey*, App. Nos. 30226/10 and 4 others, Judgment of 28 January 2020. https://hudoc.echr.coe.int/eng?i=001-200548.

problematic clauses as to the independence and impartiality of the Arbitration Board from the Executive Board and President of TFF.[99] However, Committee of Minister of CoE, political organ of CoE in charge with supervising the implementation of the judgments of the ECtHR said nothing about these shortcomings while processing the execution of *Doğan*, *Naki* and *Tokmak* cases, and closed the case accordingly.[100]

Elsewhere, I have suggested that the TFF and its legal boards should internalize, by immediately adding specific clauses into relevant internal regulations, the standards enshrined under the relevant and applicable provisions of the ECHR and ECtHR judgments. In these modified regulations it should be stated that human rights principles, rules, and standards derived from the Turkish Constitution of 1982 and international conventions are part of Turkish substantive law to be applicable to the disputes. I also claimed that the reasoned decisions, which should include sufficient and relevant reasoning and concretization, should be published regularly and made accessible to public.[101] Unfortunately, despite my prediction about forthcoming ECtHR judgments concerning freedom expression, none of these suggestions have been taken into account, even after ECtHR rulings.

5.2 *Effects on General Sports Law and Governance*

Objective effects of the ECtHR judgments against Türkiye should also be expanded beyond the territory of Türkiye and reach Europe, since almost all major SGBs are established and operate within European states, and thus fall under the ambit of material, personal and territorial jurisdiction of ECtHR after the *Mutu & Pechstein*[102] and *Semanya*[103] judgments, and *Platini* decision.[104]

But by confining its review strictly to procedural grounds, the ECtHR missed the opportunity to rule the incompatibility of a blanket and categorical ban on political speech in sports with freedom of expression at an abstract level. Unfortunately, the ECtHR did not deal with the issue within its real context and made no remarks, despite the fact that the applicants explicitly raised their objections to the illegality and illegitimacy of blanket and categorical bans within the meaning of Article 10 ECHR. Had the ECtHR explicitly found that a blanket ban on political speech

[99] Law on Sports Clubs and Federations, No. 7405, dated 22/04/2022 (Published in the Official Gazette on 26/04/2022, No.31821).

[100] See, Resolution CM/ResDH(2022)427 Execution of the judgments of the European Court of Human Rights Four cases against Türkiye, *Adopted by the Committee of Ministers on 14 December 2022 at the 1452nd meeting of the Ministers' Deputies.*

[101] Gemalmaz (2019), p. 56.

[102] *Mutu and Pechstein v. Switzerland*, App. Nos. 40575/10-67474/10, Judgment of 2 October 2018, paras. 65–67.

[103] *Affaire Semanya c. Suisse*, Req. No.10934/21, Arret, 11 julliet 2023, paras.100–113 (not final).

[104] *Platini v. Swizerland*, App. No. 526/18, Admissilibity Decison of 11 February 2020, paras. 36-38.

in sports violates freedom of expression, SGBs would have had to revise their policy concerning this categorical ban, as it cannot be considered sustainable under IHRL in general and the ECHR in particular.

However, this chapter argues that the ECtHR's *Naki* ruling may still have important implications for all SGBs regarding the sustainability of this categorical political speech ban, since the ECtHR implicitly indicates that sportspersons have the freedom of speech in political matters and that such a right cannot be suspended categorically due to the sole fact that they belong to sports community or expressed their views in or around sports venues. As the above analyses suggests, categorical universal ban on political speech in sports is not in conformity with the right to freedom of expression. In any case, this judgment will provide important support for already pending campaigns and efforts against this categorical ban.

6 Conclusion: Opening Pandora's Box for Sports Law

The SGBs and the Court of Arbitration for Sport (CAS) are hesitant to apply human rights norms derived from international treaties and constitutions, emphasizing the difference between direct human rights and indirect ones. The CAS has also created principles specific to the realm of sports that may have divergent aspects with human rights law based on the assumption that the realm sports has a specific legal order and dispute resolution mechanisms independent from the state, namely, *lex sportiva*. But the aforementioned *lex sportiva* assumption cannot be extended to totally exclude human rights concerns in the field of sports, especially after the recent ECtHR rulings.

Through those rulings, human rights standards infiltrate into sports law thus opening Pandora's Box for *lex sportiva*. From the sports law point of view (i.e., the perspective of SGBs), it can be said that by opening Pandora's Box, human rights standards are unleashed as an evil thing that diminish the specificity of sport governance, the autonomy of SGBs, and their self-validating powers. However, one may interpret the story differently and see that opening the box also unleashes human rights as a positive power, since rights of other stakeholders are systematically ignored in global and domestic sports organization. Therefore, it may be considered that the ethical, normative and structural aspects of human rights provide "hope" for respect for human rights in sports law; and this hope, the infiltration of human rights standards into sports law through ECtHR rulings, may shed light on whether specific sports law principles and rules, such as the strict liability principle and the validity of illegally obtained evidence in disciplinary match fixing proceedings, can be considered sustainable. There is also the hope that human rights standards could provide guidelines to enable the wider compliance of SGBs and the CAS with international human rights law.[105]

[105] Also see, *Affaire Semanya c. Suisse*, Req. No.10934/21, Arret, 11 julliet 2023 (not final).

References

Arnardóttir OM (2015) Organised retreat? The move from 'substantive' to 'procedural' review in the ECtHR's case law on the margin of appreciation. ESIL Conf Pap Ser 5(4):1–23

Arnardóttir OM (2017) The "procedural turn" under the European Convention on Human Rights and presumptions of convention compliance. I•CON 15:9–35

Brems E (2017) The 'logics' of procedural-type review by the European Court of Human Rights. In: Gerards J, Brems E (eds) Procedural review in European Fundamental Rights Cases. Cambridge University Press, pp 17–39

Cumper P, Lewis T (2019) Blanket bans, subsidiarity and the procedural turn of the European Court of Human Rights. Int Comp Law Q 68:611–638

Di Marco A (2021) Athletes' freedom of expression: the relative political neutrality of sport. Human Rights Law Rev 21:620–640

Faut F (2014) The prohibition of political statements by athletes and its consistency with article 10 of the European Convention on Human Rights: Speech is silver, silence is gold? Int Sports Law J 14:253–263

Gemalmaz B (2019) Applicability of Human Rights standards in Turkish football arbitration: the contribution of the European Court of Human Rights. The Int Sports Law J 9(1):38–58

Gerards JH (2014) The European Court of Human Rights and the national courts–giving shape to the notion of 'shared responsibility'. In: Gerards JH, Fleuren JWA (eds) Implementation of the European Convention on Human Rights and of the Judgments of the ECtHR in National Case Law. A comparative analysis. Intersentia, Antwerp, pp 13–94

Gerards JH (2017) Procedural review by the ECtHR: A typology. In: Gerards J, Brems E (eds) Procedural review in European Fundamental Rights Cases. Cambridge University Press, pp 127–160

Gerards JH (2019) General principles of the European Convention on Human Rights. Cambridge University Press, Cambridge

Gerards JH, Brems E (2017) Introduction. In: Gerards J, Brems E (eds) Procedural review in European Fundamental Rights Cases. Cambridge University Press, pp 1–13

Greer S (1997) The exceptions to articles 8 to 11 of the European Convention on Human Rights. Council of Europe Publishing, Strasbourg

Gürcüoğlu B (2020) Olimpiyatlar ve Madde 50 Çerçevesinde Sporcuların İfade Özgürlüğü. In: Mehmet Polat Kalafatoğlu (ed). Olimpiyat Oyunları ve Hukuk, İstanbul, Oniki Levha, pp 315–354

Haas U (2012) Role and application of Article 6 of the European Convention on Human Rights in CAS procedures. Int Sports Law Rev 12(3):43–60

Huijbers LM (2017) The European Court of Human Rights' procedural approach in the age of subsidiarity. Cambridge Int Law J 6(2):177–201

Kelly B (2016) An overview of socioeconomic status's impact on college athletes, and the regulations and impact that can revolutionize the amateurism world. Pace Intell Prop Sports Entertain Law Forum 6:212–224

Kleinlein T (2019) The procedural approach of the European Court of Human Rights: between subsidiarity and dynamic evolution. Int Comp Law Q 68:91–110

Lautenbach G (2013) The concept of the rule of law and the European Court of Human Rights. Oxford University Press, Oxford, pp 70–124

Nussberger A (2017) Procedural review by the ECHR: view from the Court. In: Gerards J, Brems E (eds) Procedural review in European fundamental rights cases. Cambridge University Press, pp 161–176

Popelier P (2012) The Court as regulatory watchdog: the procedural approach in the case-law of the European Court of Human Rights. In: Popelier P, Mazmanyan A, Vandenbruwaene W (eds) The role of constitutional courts in multilevel governance, Intersentia, pp 249–269

Popelier P, Van de Heyning C (2013) Procedural rationality: giving teeth to the proportionality analysis. Eur Const Law Rev 9:230–262

Prebensen SC (1998) The margin of appreciation and articles 9, 10 and 11 of the Convention. Human Rights Law J 19(1):13–17

Schabas W (2015) The European convention on human rights – a commentary. Oxford University Press, Oxford

Schönwald L (2016) 'For the game, for the world'—and also for human rights? Analysing human rights obligations of international sports associations. In: Reinisch A, Footer ME, Binder C (eds) International law and...: select proceedings of the European Society of International Law. Hart Publishing, Oxford

Spano R (2018) The future of the European Court of Human Rights-subsidiarity, process- based review and the rule of law. Human Rights Law Rev 18(3):473–494

H. Burak Gemalmaz is a professor of human rights law at the Faculty of Law, İstanbul University. He is the Director of İstanbul University Center for Practice and Research in Human Rights Law and Head of Human Rights Law Department of the Faculty of Law, İstanbul University.

He also teaches human rights in sports law and arbitration at the Kadir Has University and serves as national and international consultant in various EU/CoE joint projects. He served as an arbitrator in Dispute Resolution Board of Turkish Football Federation (February 2012–June 2015) and still serves as an arbitrator in İstanbul Arbitration Centre in sports law matters. He regularly presents papers in sports law and human rights conferences. His piece entitled "Applicability of Human Rights Standards in Turkish Football Arbitration: The Contribution of the European Court of Human Rights" has been published in The International Sports Law Journal, Vol.19, Issue 1–2, 2019.

Freedom of Expression of Athletes and Players: The Current and Potential Role of the European Court of Human Rights as a Watchdog in Sport

Daniel Rietiker

Contents

Abstract Professional athletes enjoy many privileges, but their special status in society imposes on them duties that go far beyond the responsibilities of ordinary citizens. For example, they are generally expected to abstain from certain political statements (principle of political neutrality) and might face disciplinary sanctions for infringing that prohibition. This chapter focuses on the European Court of Human Rights' current and future contribution as a watchdog with a view to protect the right of athletes to freedom of expression (Article 10 ECHR).

He expresses his strictly personal views. See also, for the topic of human rights in sports more broadly, from the same author: Defending Athletes, Players, Clubs and Fans, Manual for human rights education and litigation in sport, in particular before the European Court of Human Rights. Council of Europe Publishing, Strasbourg (2022).

D. Rietiker (✉)
European Court of Human Rights, Strasbourg, France

Lausanne University, Lausanne, Switzerland

Suffolk University Law School, Boston, MA, USA
e-mail: daniel.rietiker@unil.ch

V. Boillet et al. (eds.), *Sports and Human Rights*, Interdisciplinary Studies in Human Rights 10, https://doi.org/10.1007/978-3-031-56452-9_10

In Part 1 of this chapter, cases that have already been decided by the Court in the field of sport will be analyzed. The case of *Šimunić v. Croatia* indicates that freedom of expression, within Article 10 ECHR, is not unlimited. Three recent judgments related to Turkey, delivered in 2021, will also be addressed; these concern sports sanctions and financial penalties imposed by the Turkish Football Federation on account of statements made by athletes to the media or messages posted and/or shared on social media.

In Part 2, the chapter will discuss the potential role of the ECtHR in securing the freedom of expression of athletes in the future in light of the principle of political neutrality in sport, which has yet to be addressed by the Court.

1 Introduction

Professional athletes and players are, in spite of their superhuman performances, not unthinking machines or robots. Like everybody else in society, they have personal opinions they may want to express and share publicly. In practice, however, significant obstacles exist to an effective exercise of this foundational human right. This chapter is focused on the European Court of Human Rights' ("ECtHR" or "Court") current and future contribution to freedom of expression in sport. It identifies the issues that have already been dealt with by the Court as well as one that has yet to be addressed: namely, the principle of political neutrality in sport.[1]

The question at the heart of this chapter is whether the sacrosanct principle of political neutrality of sport can be justified in light of recent human rights developments. Indeed, under the strict rules of sport-governing bodies, athletes and players are expected to abstain from certain political statements and might face disciplinary sanctions for infringing that prohibition. For example, recent tributes by athletes to the Black Lives Matter movement, triggered by the death of George Floyd by a Minneapolis police officer,[2] have brought to light a human rights challenges that the world of sport is currently facing: the freedom of expression of athletes and players. Even though these protests have generally been tolerated by the relevant sport-governing bodies, the International Olympic Committee (IOC) has nevertheless confirmed that athletes are still banned from protesting at the Games.[3] The IOC had announced well before the Summer Games in Tokyo that athletes who staged protests would face sanctions. Moreover, China's Olympic organizing committee

[1] See, for an overview of the already decided cases by the Court in the field of sport as well as for topics that could potentially be addressed by the Court in future, Rietiker (2022a).

[2] Di Marco (2021), p. 622.

[3] Bloom (2020).

warned that foreign athletes may face punishment for speech that violates Chinese law at the 2022 Winter Games in Beijing.[4]

This chapter follows the following structure: Part 1 will summarize the cases that the Court has already decided in the field of freedom of expression in sport, namely, the case of *Šimunić v. Croatia*,[5] and three very similar cases against Turkey, decided by the Court on 18 March 2021.[6] These cases concern sports sanctions and financial penalties imposed on the applicants by the Turkish Football Federation on account of statements made by athletes to the media, or messages posted on social media. In these judgments, the Court affirmed its recent trend towards a more procedural approach for this kind of case, which has its advantages and drawbacks, as will be discussed further on.[7] In Part 2, an issue that has yet to be addressed by the Court will be analyzed: namely, the principle of political neutrality in sport. The first section contains preliminary observations (Sect. 2.1), followed by an explanation of the principle of political neutrality (Sect. 2.2), and finally some theoretical considerations, with particular emphasis on the margin of appreciation doctrine (Sect. 2.3). The chapter will conclude with some final remarks.

2 The Issues Decided by the ECtHR so Far

2.1 The Šimunić Case: The Limits of Freedom of Expression

Article 10 ECHR guarantees freedom of expression, one of the fundamental rights protected by the Convention. Paragraph 1 of Article 10 ECHR sets out the right while Paragraph 2 details the limitation to that right; this is a comparable structure to Articles 8, 9 and 11 of the Convention. A limitation is justifiable if the interference is "prescribed by law", if it pursues a legitimate aim, and if it is "necessary in a democratic society" within the meaning of Paragraph 2 of Article 10. Overall, the Court's case law focuses on the third test, which is the most demanding of the three standards. The Court occasionally uses the "positive obligation" approach instead of the interference test, in particular when acts or omissions of private actors are at stake. This concept will be detailed further below.[8]

There are limits to freedom of speech under Article 10 ECHR. The Court's case law reveals a variety of values that have been considered contrary to the values of the Convention. Apart from typical examples of (neo-)Nazism,[9] fascism, racism, anti-

[4]Dou (2022). See also Duval and Heerdt (2022).

[5]ECtHR, Šimunić v. Croatia (dec.), 22.01.2019.

[6]ECtHR, Sedat Doğan v. Turkey, 18.05.2018, ECtHR, Naki and AMED Sportif Faaliyetler Kulübü Derneği v. Turkey, 18.05.2021, and ECtHR, İbrahim Tokmak v. Turkey, 18.05.2021.

[7]Below, 1.2.

[8]See below, 2.3.1.

[9]See, for instance, EComHR, W., P. and K. v. Austria (dec), 12.10.1989.

Semitism and (Stalinist) communism, the Court has addressed variations of expression linked to Islamic "fundamentalism"[10] and to aggressive forms of Kurdish nationalism, involving expressions of hatred and incitement to violence.[11]

The Court's overall approach seems to include most forms of free speech, including hideous and appalling ones, in the scope of protection of Article 10 § 1 ECHR, but that they may be lawfully restricted in light of Paragraph 2 of this provision.[12] When confronted, however, with blatant anti-Semitism and Holocaust denial, it might exceptionally find with reference to Article 17 ECHR, prohibiting the abuse of rights,[13] that such speech is not protected at all by Article 10 ECHR because it seeks to exploit that provision for ends that are incompatible with the letter and spirit of the Convention. This is the case where comments challenge the category of "clearly established historical facts", such as the Holocaust.[14] Apart from negationist or revisionist speech, the Court has considered that other types of speech might also fall under Article 17 ECHR insofar as they have the potential to also stir up violence or hatred.[15] This is the case, *inter alia*, with incitement to ethnic,[16] racial,[17] or religious[18] hate, or with incitement to violence and support for terrorist

[10] See, for instance, ECtHR, Refah Partisi (the Welfare Party) and Others v. Turkey [GC], 03.10.2000, §§ 94 and 123, and ECtHR, Erbakan v. Turkey, 06.07.2006, §§ 62 and 65 (in French only); and for a case concerning freedom of religion (Article 9 ECHR) ECtHR, Kalaç v. Turkey, 01.07.1997, §§ 8, 24 and 25.

[11] See, for instance, ECtHR, Sürek v. Turkey (no. 1) [GC], 08.07.1999, §§ 61–65.

[12] Harris et al. (2018), p. 602. In the case ECtHR, Féret v. Belgium, 16.07.2009 (only in French), dealing with a conviction of president of extreme right-wing party for inciting the public to discrimination or racial hatred in leaflets distributed in electoral campaign, the Court did not find that the application of Article 17 was justified (§ 82). In ECtHR, Vejdeland and Others v. Sweden, 09.02.2012, regarding convictions for circulating homophobic leaflets at school, the ECtHR did not bring into play Article 17 ECHR neither.

[13] Article 17 ECHR reads as follows: "Nothing in this Convention may be interpreted as implying for any State, group or person any right to engage in any activity or perform any act aimed at the destruction of any of the rights and freedoms set forth herein or at their limitation to a greater extent than is provided for in the Convention."

[14] See, in particular, ECtHR, M'Bala M'Bala v. France (dec.), 20.10.2015, § 41, ECtHR, Garaudy v. France (dec.), 24.06.2003, and Witzsch v. Germany (dec.), 13.12.2005.

[15] In this sense, ECtHR, Perinçek v. Switzerland [GC], 15.10.2015, §§ 113–115.

[16] See, inter alia, the case ECtHR, Pavel Ivanov v. Russia (dec.), 20.02.2007 (publication of articles portraying the Jews as the source of evil in Russia and call for their exclusion from social life).

[17] See, in particular, EComHR, Glimmerveen and Hagenbeek v. the Netherlands (dec.), 11.10.1979 (conviction for possessing leaflets with incitement to racial hate).

[18] See, in particular, ECtHR, Norwood v. the United Kingdom, 16.11.2004 (conviction for displaying a poster representing the Twin Towers in flame and accompanied with the words "Islam out of Britain – Protect the British People."), and ECtHR, Belkacem v. Belgium, 27.06.2017 (conviction for remarks the applicant made in YouTube videos concerning non-Muslim groups and Sharia).

activities.[19] In such cases, the Court declares a case inadmissible for being incompatible *ratione materiae* with the ECHR.

One situation of extreme speech has taken place in the domain of football, a sport that has seen recurrent instances of homophobic and other discriminatory chants in stadiums, which FIFA has attempted to deter through the use of regulation and disciplinary sanctions.[20] This restriction has collided with the right to freedom of expression. In the case *Šimunić v Croatia*, the applicant, a Croatian football player, was convicted by the Croatian authorities of a minor criminal offence for addressing messages to spectators at a football match, the content of which expressed or incited hatred on the basis of race, nationality, and faith.[21] In fact, he used an official greeting of the Ustasha movement, the totalitarian fascist regime of the Independent State of Croatia. The event at issue took place at Maksimir Stadium (Zagreb), after the official end of the match against the national team of Iceland on 19 November 2013, when the accused took the microphone, walked out onto the middle of the pitch and turned towards the spectators, addressing them by shouting "For Home", provoking some spectators to reply "Ready!"[22]

Before the Court, he submitted in particular that his right to freedom of expression (Article 10 ECHR) had been violated. The ECtHR declared the applicant's complaint inadmissible and manifestly ill-founded, finding that the interference with his right to freedom of expression had been supported by relevant and sufficient justifications, and that the Croatian authorities had struck a fair balance between his right to free speech, and society's interest in promoting tolerance and mutual respect at sports events, as well as combating discrimination in the sport.[23] It did, however, not find it necessary to apply Article 17 ECHR and exclude the applicant's speech from the scope of Article 10 ECHR.[24]

One of the decisive arguments invoked by the Court for the inadmissibility of the case was that the applicant, as a famous footballer and role-model for many young fans and players, should have been aware of the possible negative impact of provocative chanting on spectators' behavior, and should have abstained from such conduct.[25]

---

[19] See, in particular, ECtHR, Roj TV A/S v. Denmark (dec.), 17.04.2018 (broadcast company convicted for support to PKK's terror operation).

[20] Ruggie (2016), pp. 24–25.

[21] See, for a summary and brief analysis of the case, Rietiker (2022a), pp. 100–102.

[22] Šimunić, cited above, § 3. In parallel, there were also disciplinary proceedings engaged against Šimunić with a CAS award: CAS 2014/A/3562 Josip Simunic v. Fédération Internationale de Football Association (FIFA), 29 July 2014.

[23] ECtHR, Šimunić v. Croatia (dec.), 22.01.2019, § 48.

[24] ECtHR, Šimunić v. Croatia (dec.), 22.01.2019, § 39.

[25] ECtHR, Šimunić v. Croatia (dec.), 22.01.2019, § 45.

2.2 *Three Judgments Against Turkey Delivered on 18 May 2021: Confirmation of a Procedural Approach*

Aside from *Šimunić*, the Court delivered three judgments related to Turkey on 18 May 2021.[26] All three cases concerned sports sanctions and financial penalties imposed on the applicants by the Turkish Football Federation (TFF) on account of statements made to the media or messages posted on social media, and the appeal proceedings lodged against those sanctions by the applicants before the Federation's Arbitration Committee.[27] In all three cases, the Court found violations of Article 10 ECHR.[28]

In the case of *Sedat Doğan v. Turkey,* the applicant was a member of the management board of Galatasaray football club.[29] While participating via telephone in a televised sports event, he made comments about the referral to the Professional Football Disciplinary Committee of the TFF of two players from his club who, at a football match on the day following Nelson Mandela's death, had worn shirts paying tribute to him. Following the Disciplinary Committee's delivery of a decision imposing a sanction on the applicant, he published several messages on his Twitter account.[30] Holding that these tweets amounted to unsportsmanlike language capable of debasing the image of football, inciting violence and disorder in the sport, and giving rise to protests by supporters, the Disciplinary Committee sentenced Mr. Doğan to disciplinary sanctions.[31] These sanctions were upheld by the TFF Arbitration Committee.

In the case of *Naki and AMED Sportif Faaliyetler Kulübü Derneği v. Turkey,* the first applicant was a professional football player and was employed at the time by the applicant club, which competed in the first division of the Turkish professional league (Süper Lig). The second applicant was *Amed Sportif Faaliyetler Kulübü Derneği,* a Turkish association operating as a sports club based in the Kurdish town of Diyarbakır.[32] In January 2016, after his team's victory in a football match in the Turkish championship, Mr. Naki published a message on his Facebook account where he dedicated the victory of the match to those who had lost their lives or sustained injuries during the persecutions that had been occurring in Turkey

---

[26] See, for a summary and brief analysis of the three cases, Rietiker (2022a), pp. 95–100, 103–104.

[27] See Press Release of the Court, 18 May 2021, Sports and financial sanctions imposed on the applicants by the Turkish Football Federation: violations of the Convention.

[28] In all of the cases, the Court also found a violation of Article 6 § 1. Referring to the case ECtHR, *Ali Rıza and Others v. Turkey,* 28.01.2020, the Court noted structural deficiencies in the Arbitration Committee of the Turkish Football Federation and the lack of adequate safeguards to protect the members of the Committee from outside pressure. It concluded, unanimously, that the Arbitration Committee lacked independence and impartiality.

[29] ECtHR, Sedat Doğan v. Turkey, 18.05.2018, §§ 2 and 4.

[30] ECtHR, Sedat Doğan v. Turkey, 18.05.2018, § 8.

[31] ECtHR, Sedat Doğan v. Turkey, 18.05.2018, § 9.

[32] ECtHR, Naki and AMED Sportif Faaliyetler Kulübü Derneği v. Turkey, 18.05.2018, §§ 2–4.

for over fifty days.[33] The TFF's Professional Football Disciplinary Committee held that the applicant's comments breached the ban on ideological propaganda and amounted to unsportsmanlike language capable of debasing the image of football, inciting violence and disorder in the sport, and giving rise to protests by supporters. The Committee imposed a disciplinary sanction on the applicant.

In the case of *İbrahim Tokmak v. Turkey,* the applicant was a football referee at the time of the events in question.[34] In January 2016, Mr. Tokmak shared on his Facebook account a post from another person about H.K., a commentator and publisher of a daily newspaper, who had died two days previously in a hotel room during a trip to Saudi Arabia. Press reports indicated that this person had died from a heart attack caused by a drug used to address erectile dysfunction.[35] When sharing this publication, the applicant added his own commentary: "He was a real son of a bitch [...] Thanks to those who invented Viagra!"[36] In February 2016, the TFF's Professional Football Disciplinary Committee imposed on Mr. Tokmak the disciplinary sanction of a three-month withdrawal of the rights attached to his functions.[37] This measure had the effect of cancelling his license automatically.[38]

In all three cases, the Court noted that there had been an interference in the applicants' right to freedom of expression, that the interference in question had a legal basis and pursued the legitimate aims of the prevention of disorder, crime and the protection of the reputation and rights of others. However, the Court considered that the national authorities had not carried out an appropriate analysis, giving regard to all the criteria laid down and applied in its case-law concerning freedom of expression. In the Court's view, the Government had not shown that the reasons given by the national authorities to justify the contested measures had been relevant and sufficient, and that those measures had been necessary in a democratic society. It followed that for each of the three cases, there had been a violation of Article 10 ECHR.[39]

It is suggested here that the Court's analysis, very similar in all three cases, follows a new general trend towards a more procedural approach of the ECtHR, as a reaction to the call for subsidiarity and margin of appreciation, not only under Article

---

[33] ECtHR, Naki and AMED Sportif Faaliyetler Kulübü Derneği v. Turkey, 18.05.2018, § 5.

[34] ECtHR, İbrahim Tokmak v. Turkey, 18.05.2018, §§ 2–4. The Court does not explicitly state whether he was a professional football referee. Such a presumption flows however from paragraph 16 of the judgment, where the Court held that Article 6 § 1 is applicable to disciplinary proceedings where the right to exercise a profession was at stake.

[35] ECtHR, İbrahim Tokmak v. Turkey, 18.05.2018, § 5.

[36] ECtHR, İbrahim Tokmak v. Turkey, 18.05.2018, § 5.

[37] ECtHR, İbrahim Tokmak v. Turkey, 18.05.2018§ 7.

[38] ECtHR, İbrahim Tokmak v. Turkey, 18.05.2018, § 9.

[39] Press release of the three cases, "Sports and financial sanctions imposed on the applicants by the Turkish Football Federations: violations of the Convention", 18 May 2021.

10 ECHR.[40] In other words, the Court did not conduct its own assessment on the measures imposed on the applicants, but found that the balancing exercise of the TFF had not been sufficient in light of its jurisprudence concerning Article 10 ECHR. Such a procedural approach might be an appropriate compromise in sensitive cases insofar as the ECtHR can avoid dealing with or defining controversial concepts, such as extremism, terrorism, and hooliganism. At the same time, the Court opens itself to the reproach of not being willing to reply to the key issues of a case, including the legitimate question whether the principle of political neutrality can be maintained in light of Article 10 ECHR; particularly in situations where speech contributes to a political debate or to a discussion that is in the public interest.

2.3 Conclusion of Part 1

The ECtHR's decision in *Šimunić* follows the usual line of jurisprudence in cases where the limit of legitimate speech has been overstepped and, as a result, where the Court refuses to protect freedom of expression. Moreover, it reinforces FIFA's commitment to combat discrimination and confirms that the sanctions it is imposing on clubs and players for discriminatory conduct are likely to be deemed compliant with the ECHR.

For practical reasons, an in-depth analysis of the three cases against Turkey has not been made here, but it can nevertheless be added that the Court applied the usual Article 10 ECHR tests to sport-related situations. While the outcome of the first two cases explained above is unsurprising, the conclusions drawn by the Court in the *İbrahim Tokmak* case is less expected considering the limited value of the comments made by the applicant for a constructive public debate. On the other hand, the serious consequence, consisting of the cancellation of the license as a referee, might have been the decisive factor for the Court. It must be kept in mind that Article 10 ECHR also applies to information and ideas that "offend, shock or disturb the state or any sector of the population".

In the next section, a controversial principle that has not yet been addressed by the Court—the political neutrality of sport—will be introduced and discussed.

[40] See, for the same trend under Article 8 ECHR, for instance ECtHR, Z. v. Switzerland, 22.12.2020, § 60: "In recent cases concerning the expulsion of settled migrants, the Court declined to substitute its conclusions for those of the domestic courts, which had thoroughly assessed the applicants' personal circumstances, carefully balanced the competing interests and taken into account the criteria set out in its case law, and reached conclusions which were 'neither arbitrary nor manifestly unreasonable'."

3 Political Neutrality in Sport and Potential Conflicts with Article 10 ECHR

3.1 Preliminary Observations

A topic that has not yet been addressed by the Court—neither in *Šimunić*, nor in the three cases against Turkey—is the principle of political neutrality in sport and its conformity with Article 10 ECHR. Freedom of expression has historically been limited by the sport-governing bodies in line with the commitment of the IOC to remain "strictly politically neutral" at all times. It is pure speculation, and the question can therefore be left open, whether the Court would also have found violations of Article 10 ECHR if it had embarked on a substantive examination of the complaints in the three cases of Turkey instead of a procedural approach. It is suggested here that in the case *Naki and AMED Sportif Faaliyetler Kulübü Derneği v. Turkey*, the principle of political neutrality of sport was, at least, an underlying ground for the sanctions imposed on the applications. In the case of *Sedat Doğan,* the sanctions imposed on the applicant's players for paying tribute to Nelson Mandela were at the origin of the dispute, and certainly inspired by the principle of political neutrality. The question remains to what extent the generally comprehensive protection of freedom of expression by the Court would accommodate or challenge the principle of political neutrality in sport.

This section of the chapter will discuss whether this principle leads to problems under Article 10 ECHR, and assesses the Court's approach.

3.2 The Principle of Political Neutrality

The principle of political neutrality in sport, sometimes referred to as the "golden rule", is expressed in Rule 50 of the IOC Charter, according to which "no kind of demonstration or political, religious or racial propaganda is permitted in any Olympic sites, venues or other areas."[41] The prohibition for athletes to express political ideas in the sporting area is aimed at protecting the moral force of sport-governing bodies and at guaranteeing the autonomy of sport.[42] The principle must be distinguished from the freedom of athletes and players to criticize sporting authorities, which generally involves a greater degree of tolerance because good faith criticism against those in positions of power might allow acts and practices of mismanagement to be exposed.[43]

[41] Rule 50 § 1 of the IOC Charter. See, for an overview, Krieger (2022).

[42] Chappelet (2016).

[43] Di Marco (2021), pp. 626–630, with case law from the CAS. See also Abanazir (2022).

The IOC and the main international sports federations envisage this principle as part of their "universal fundamental ethical principles".[44] The principle has traditionally been imagined as 'absolute' without mitigation or balancing.[45] For instance, the famed 'black power salute' of the Olympic athletes Tommie Smith, John Carlos, and Peter Norman at the 1968 Mexico City Olympic Games became an icon for human rights and democracy.[46] Athlete activism has increased recently,[47] and so too have sanctions and disciplinary investigations for provocative political behavior.[48] This has given rise to criticism in respect of athletes' freedom of expression. The principle of political neutrality appears to be in conflict with the political engagement of the IOC to promote human rights and "peaceful society concerned with the preservation of human dignity".[49] This potential contradiction has recently been become more evident by athletes' symbolic tributes to the Black Lives Matter movement.[50]

There have been recent criticisms against a strict application of the principle of neutrality,[51] and as a reaction, the IOC Athletes' Commission issued guidelines to clarify the purpose and goals of Rule 50 of the IOC Charter.[52] The IOC argues that Rule 50 does not imply an extensive restriction of the right to free speech of athletes; they should have the opportunity to express their opinion, including during press conferences, interviews or on social media. Protests and demonstrations are banned because they could be divisive and "drive a wedge between individuals, groups and nations" at all Olympic venues, contrary to the image of peace and harmony propagated by the Olympics.[53] The guidelines add that incidents will be evaluated by their respective National Olympic Committee, International Federation and the IOC, and that disciplinary measures shall be taken on a case-by-case basis as necessary.[54]

---

[44] See, for instance, IOC, Code of ethics, edition 2020, Article 1.2, FIFA, Code of ethics, edition 2018, Article 14, Fédération Internationale d'Automobile (FIA), Code of ethics, edition 2017, Article 3.

[45] Di Marco (2021), p. 621.

[46] Boykoff (2016), p. 240.

[47] According to James (2022), the 2020 Tokyo Summer Games saw more instances of athlete activism than at any other Olympic Games.

[48] Di Marco (2021), pp. 621–622, with examples in footnote 12.

[49] Fundamental Principles of Olympism, § 2. Shahlaei (2017/2018) rightly points out that major sport-governing bodies, such as FIFA, have become more and more engaged themselves in human rights topics, such as the fight against racism (pp. 103–104).

[50] Di Marco (2021), p. 622.

[51] See, among others, Schwab (2018), in particular pp. 179–181, and Lindholm (2017).

[52] Rule 50 Guidelines, Tokyo 2020, available at: https://stillmedab.olympic.org/media/Document%20Library/OlympicOrg/News/2020/01/Rule-50-Guidelines-Tokyo-2020.pdf.

[53] Rule 50 Guidelines, Tokyo 2020. As examples are given displaying any political messaging, including signs and armbands, gestures of a political nature, like a hand gesture or kneeling, and refusal to follow the Ceremonies protocol.

[54] Rule 50 Guidelines, Tokyo 2020.

3.3 Theoretical Considerations

3.3.1 Margin of Appreciation Doctrine

A key concept used by the Court is the 'margin of appreciation' doctrine. The margin of appreciation is the leeway given to a state in determining the necessity of an interference into the rights at stake in a given situation, including the proportionality of the impugned measure.[55] It is the expression of the principle of subsidiarity imposes on the Court the duty to apply restraint in assessing the domestic tribunal's decisions, and to limit its own control (the so-called "European control") to the question of whether a fair balance has been struck between the different interests at stake.[56] It would be one of the decisive factors in a potential examination by the Court of the conformity of the principle of political neutrality with Article 10 ECHR.

If the impugned measure has been imposed by a private actor, the "interference" approach normally does not apply, and the only question to be examined is whether the state has complied with its "positive obligations".[57] In a leading case on positive obligations in the domain of freedom of expression, the Court held that:

> 43. The Court recalls the key importance of freedom of expression as one of the preconditions for a functioning democracy. Genuine, effective exercise of this freedom does not depend merely on the state's duty not to interfere, but may require positive measures of protection, even in the sphere of relations between individuals [...] In determining whether or not a positive obligation exists, regard must be had to the fair balance that has to be struck between the general interest of the community and the interests of the individual, the search for which is inherent throughout the Convention.[58]

However, the distinction between "interference" and "positive obligations" has become more and more blurred. In the *Šimunić* case, the situation was easy for the Court because the applicant was sanctioned by the state based on criminal law, a typical interference; the three Turkish freedom of expression cases are more ambiguous on this point. It is worth mentioning that, in all three cases, the Court applied the "interference" test, and in its conclusions under Article 10 referred to "national authorities" ("*autorités nationales*") when addressing those bodies. This is in spite of the private nature of the arbitration bodies having rendered final decisions on the disciplinary sanctions against the applicants.[59]

It should also be said that it may not actually matter which test is applied because, even under the positive obligation test, the question to be resolved is whether a fair balance has been struck between the competing interests at stake. In both contexts,

[55] Rietiker and Levine (2022).

[56] See, among others, ECtHR, Lacatus v. Switzerland, 19.01.2021, § 99.

[57] See on the human rights duties of private actors, Clapham (2018), and on the concept of positive obligations, Lavrysen (2016), Madelaine (2014), Mowbray (2004) and Shinohara (2021).

[58] ECtHR, Özgür Gündem v. Turkey, 16.03.2020, § 43.

[59] See, for example, ECtHR, Sedat Doğan v. Turkey, 18.05.2018, §§ 41–43.

the state enjoys a certain margin of appreciation.[60] The most significant difference between the two tests is the fact that there is generally no legal basis inquiry necessary in the positive obligation test. As a result, the question of which test to use might in practice turn out to be relevant, insofar as it has been claimed that Rule 50 is not precise enough to serve as a legal basis for an interference in such a fundamental right as enshrined by Article 10 ECHR.[61]

The element "necessary in a democratic society" requires a balancing exercise; considering the importance of freedom of expression for the political process in a healthy democracy, the standard to be applied must be a strict one.[62] If the principle of political neutrality is applied in an absolute fashion, not allowing for a fair balancing of the relevant interests at stake, as generally suggested by sport-governing bodies, this might already raise a problem under Article 10 ECHR. The Court has shown in the cases against Turkey that such a balancing exercise is indispensable in order to comply with freedom of speech.[63] Another relevant recent example, even if dealing with Article 8 ECHR (right to respect for private life) and not with freedom of expression, is the case of *Lacatus v. Switzerland*,[64] in which the applicant challenged a Geneva law criminalizing begging in an absolute fashion. In its judgment, the Court held:

> [. . .] the applicable legislation precluded a genuine balancing of the interests at stake and penalized begging in blanket fashion, irrespective of who was begging and whether he or she was vulnerable, the nature of the begging and whether or not it was aggressive, the location where it was carried out and whether or not the person concerned was part of a criminal network.[65]

This absolute nature of the ban on begging was one of the decisive reasons for the Court to find that the criminal sanction imposed on the applicant was disproportionate.[66] Finally, unlike Articles 8, 9 and 11 ECHR, Article 10 § 2 refers to "duties and responsibilities" of persons exercising their rights. Such an inclusion is unusual for the Convention,[67] however, this does not mean that this wording suggests an inherently greater limitation to the freedom of expression or room for implied limitations in Article 10.[68] The notion of "duties and responsibilities" has been invoked in relation to different functions and professions. It is one of the elements

---

[60] See, mutatis mutandis, ECtHR, Platini v. Switzerland (dec.), 11.02.2020, § 60, with further references. See also, for an analysis of this case, Rietiker (2022c).

[61] Shahlaei (2022).

[62] Harris et al. (2018), p. 593.

[63] See, in this sense, Schwab (2018), pp. 180–181.

[64] ECtHR, Lacatus v. Switzerland, 19.01.2021.

[65] ECtHR, Lacatus v. Switzerland, 19.01.2021, § 102 (unofficial translation from the French original).

[66] See, for a case note on this judgment, Rietiker and Levine (2022).

[67] Harris et al. (2018), p. 660.

[68] Harris et al. (2018), p. 660.

that might influence the broadness of the margin of appreciation relied upon by the states; this will be addressed further in Sect. 3.3.3.

3.3.2 Narrow Margin of Appreciation Regarding Matters of Public Interest

The Court has repeatedly held that interference with freedom of expression can be justified only by "imperative necessities", and that exceptions to this right must be interpreted narrowly.[69] Considering the importance of freedom of expression for the political process in a healthy democracy, the standard to be applied must be a strict one, "necessity in democratic society" supposing a "pressing social need".[70] There is, in particular, little scope under Article 10 § 2 of the Convention for restrictions on freedom of expression in two fields: political speech, and matters of public interest.[71] Accordingly, a high level of protection of freedom of expression, with authorities possessing a narrow margin of appreciation, will normally be accorded where the remarks concern a matter of public interest.[72]

A difficulty with the principle of political neutrality lies in the definition of "political";[73] in particular, its distinction from acts and expression of solidarity with victims of human rights abuse or social inequalities, such as ethnic minorities. Faraz Shahlaei raises the question whether athletes' gestures against racism, conflict, war, xenophobia, or in favor of inclusion, peace, and human rights, can really be recognized as a threat to public interest or a harm to the reputation of others.[74] The recent discussion on the rainbow, 'One Love', armband during the FIFA World Cup in Qatar (2022) is just one example illustrating the dilemma caused by the current legal regime.[75]

---

[69] Harris et al. (2018), p. 592, referring, *inter alia*, to the case ECtHR, Vereinigung demokratischer Soldaten Österreichs and Gubi v. Austria, 19.12.1994, § 37.

[70] Harris et al. (2018), p. 593.

[71] See ECtHR, Sürek v. Turkey (no. 1) [GC], 08.07.1999, § 61, ECtHR, Lindon, Otchakovsky-Laurens and July v. France [GC], 22.10.2007, § 46, ECtHR, Axel Springer AG v. Germany [GC], 07.02.2012, § 90, and ECtHR, Morice v. France [GC], 23.04.2015, § 125.

[72] This is, for instance, the case for remarks on the functioning of the judiciary, even in the context of proceedings that are still pending (see, mutatis mutandis, ECtHR, Roland Dumas v. France, 15.07.2010, § 43, ECtHR, Gouveia Gomes Fernandes and Freitas e Costa v. Portugal, 29.03.2011, § 47, 29, and Morice v. France [GC], 23.04.2015, § 125).

[73] See, in this sense, Shahlaei (2017/2018), p. 113.

[74] Shahlaei (2022).

[75] See, for a brief analysis on the rainbow armband discussion in Qatar, Rietiker (2022b).

3.3.3 Increased 'Duties and Responsibilities' of Athletes Due to Their Social Status

Article 10 ECHR guarantees freedom of expression, one of the key rights protected by the Convention. It follows from the wording and structure of Article 10 ECHR that—comparable to Articles 8, 9 and 11—Paragraph 1 of the provision sets out the right and Paragraph 2 the limitation to that right. Unlike Articles 8, 9 and 11 however, Article 10 § 2 refers to "duties and responsibilities" of persons exercising their rights. The notion of "duties and responsibilities" has been invoked in relation to different bearers of rights, including elected municipal officials,[76] civil servants,[77] lawyers, or the press, journalists, and editors.[78] The question is whether a new category, namely one covering athletes, has already been established by the Court or will be shaped in future.

In the *Šimunić* case, the Court stressed that the applicant, as a famous footballer, should have been aware of the possible negative impact of provocative chanting on spectators' behavior, and should have abstained from such conduct.[79] This has been interpreted as an acknowledgement by the ECtHR of the role of athletes as political actors, as the main 'vehicles' of the social and political function of sport.[80] For this reason, the UN has suggested that sport-governing bodies should encourage athletes and players to use their influence and experience as role models and to be "leaders who contribute to promote peace and human understanding through sport".[81] This paragraph suggests that famous athletes are role models, and as a result of their special status in society, must be particularly careful about what they say publicly.

The role model function of athletes was also referred to by the Court in the *Fédération Nationale des Associations et Syndicats Sportifs (FNASS) and Others v. France.*[82] The case concerned the requirement that certain sports professionals provide information detailing their whereabouts for the purposes of unannounced anti-doping tests. The Court held:

> 176. [...] The Court also attaches weight to the impact which doping among professional athletes has on the amateur sporting world. It is widely recognized that young people identify with elite athletes, who act as role models for them. The UNESCO Convention clearly demonstrates the concerns surrounding the impact of doping on the sporting community in general, and in particular on the young. For that reason it stresses the importance of

---

[76] See, for example, ECtHR, Willem v. France, 16.07.2009, § 37 (official version only in French).

[77] See, for example, ECtHR, Vogt v. Germany, 26.09.1995, § 60, or ECtHR, Karapetyan and Others v. Armenia, 17.11.2016, §§ 54–62.

[78] See, for example, ECtHR, Sürek v. Turkey (no. 1) [GC], 08.07.1999, § 63, or ECtHR, Leempoel & S.A. ED. Ciné Revue v. Belgium, 09.11.2006, § 66 (official version only in French).

[79] ECtHR, Šimunić v. Croatia (dec.), 22.01.2019, § 45.

[80] Di Marco (2021), p. 636, with further references in footnote 105.

[81] UNGA Resolution, 26 October 2015, Building a peaceful and better world through sport and the Olympic ideal (GA Res. 70/4//A/70/4).

[82] ECtHR, National Federation of Sportspersons' Associations and Unions (FNASS) and Others v. France, 18.01.2018. See Marguénaud (2019).

> educational programs on the subject [...] According to the Medical Academy, prevention requires the involvement of top-level athletes [...] *In the Court's view, the fact that the conduct of elite athletes is liable to have a major influence on young people is further justification for the requirements imposed on them while they are registered in the testing pool.*[83]

Finally, the special nature of a career in professional sport was also stressed by the Court in the case of *Michel Platini v. Switzerland*, who was handed by CAS a four-year suspension from all football-related activities on the national and international level, and was fined for having allegedly accepted a salary supplement of 2 million CHF via a verbal contract with the President of FIFA, for activities as an advisor between 1998 and 2002. In this case, the Court took account of the specificity of the applicant's situation, in that he had freely chosen a career in football, first as player then coach, and then in official capacities in football's governing bodies, which were private entities and not directly bound by the Convention. The Court held, "while that career had no doubt endowed him with many privileges and benefits, it had nevertheless involved waiving certain rights, provided any contractual restrictions were agreed freely, and the applicant had not claimed the contrary."[84]

Judging from the assessment of the Court in these cases, it cannot be excluded that the special role model position of athletes and players imposes increased "duties and responsibilities", and as a result, lowers their protection under the ECHR. This could lead to a new category of persons in relation to whom the states enjoy a wider margin of appreciation due to the special relationship that they maintain with their employers and the sport-governing bodies, imposing on them a '*réserve de fonction*' comparable to that of municipal officials, civil servants, lawyers, or the press.

3.4 Case Study: Comparison Between the CAS and the ECtHR Approach Regarding Calls for Boycott

In the absence of directly relevant case law of the ECtHR in the field of sport, it is appropriate to analyze jurisprudence in related fields in order to find inspiration and to draw conclusions for potential applications concerning the principle of political neutrality.

An example of an application of this principle brought before the CAS is the case of *Jibril Rajoub v. FIFA*, in which the President of the Palestinian Football Association was fined 20,000 CHF and was banned from attending matches for 12 months due to inciting a blatant protest during a match between Argentina and Israel in Jerusalem.[85] Mr. Rajoub publicly called for members of the Argentinian national

[83] Emphasis added.

[84] See ECtHR, Fernández Martínez v. Spain [GC], 12.06.2014, §§ 134–135.

[85] CAS 2018/A/6007 Jibril Rajoub v. Fédération Internationale de Football Association (FIFA), 18 July 2019.

team to boycott this match. Mr. Rajoub was understood by the CAS to be intentionally targeting the football icon Lionel Messi:

> [. . .] we will launch, as of today, a campaign targeting the Argentinian Federation, and in particular targeting Messi, who has tens of millions of fans in Arab and Islamic countries. [For his fans] he used to be a symbol and big deal. We are going to target Messi, and we are going to ask everybody to burn their Messi T-shirts and pictures, and to wash their hands of him.[86]

While CAS implicitly admitted the right of the appellant to declare publicly his political opinion, by affirming that "FIFA's interest in sanctioning such conduct should be balanced against Mr. Rajoub's interest to exercise his freedom of speech",[87] it nevertheless concluded that:

> [. . .] an association – based on the special contractual legal relationship – may impose stricter duties on its members than the ones imposed on citizens by criminal law [. . .] associations in general have large freedom to manage their own affairs and Mr. Rajoub can freely opt-out of his obligations as a FIFA official by resigning from any role that subjects him to FIFA's rules and regulations.[88]

Mr. Rajoub has, according to our knowledge, not appealed to the Swiss Federal Tribunal, followed by an appeal to the ECtHR. It is noteworthy to mention, however, that in similar circumstances, the Court has held against the applicant, namely in *Willem v. France*.[89] In this case, a left-wing mayor of a small French commune proposed to boycott Israeli products, in particular, fruit juice, as a protest against the policy of Ariel Sharon, the then Prime Minister, in the occupied Palestinian territories.[90] His proposal was featured in a local newspaper and he added more details on the website of the commune.[91] He was later convicted of provocation and discrimination. According to the ECtHR, the interference was pursuant to the protection of the rights of others, in particular the rights of Israeli producers.[92] In the Court's view, calling on the municipal services to boycott Israeli products amounted to discrimination.[93]

It is suggested here that the position of Mr. Willem, as a mayor of a French municipality, is comparable with the relationship that Mr. Raoub, the President of a national football association, maintains with FIFA, which enjoys a monopoly

---

[86] CAS 2018/A/6007 Jibril Rajoub v. Fédération Internationale de Football Association (FIFA), 18 July 2019, statement of Rajoub of 3 June 2018 (translation), as cited in § 5 of the award.

[87] CAS 2018/A/6007 Jibril Rajoub v. Fédération Internationale de Football Association (FIFA), 18 July 2019, § 92.

[88] CAS 2018/A/6007 Jibril Rajoub v. Fédération Internationale de Football Association (FIFA), 18 July 2019, § 94.

[89] ECtHR, Willem v. France, 16.07.2009 (only in French).

[90] ECtHR, Willem v. France, 16.07.2009, § 6.

[91] ECtHR, Willem v. France, 16.07.2009, §§ 7–8.

[92] ECtHR, Willem v. France, 16.07.2009, § 29.

[93] ECtHR, Willem v. France, 16.07.2009, §§ 35–39.

position in football.[94] As a result, the CAS judgement seems compatible with the ECtHR's findings in the *Willem* case, even more so considering the extreme nature of the language used by Mr. Rajoub. However, Harris, O'Boyle and Warbrick consider it conceivable that the Court would have given greater protection to free speech in the case of a private citizen or NGO, instead of a municipal official, and would have found a violation.[95] If this also applies to athletes and players calling for a boycott, the outcome might be at odds with the CAS' ruling in the *Rajoub* case.

The Court went exactly in this direction in a more recent case where the call for a boycott against products from Israel came from civil society. In the case of *Baldassi and Others v. France*,[96] the applicants, who were members of a local collective supporting the Palestinian cause (they were part of the international campaign "Boycott, Divestment and Sanctions" launched by NGOs in 2005) were prosecuted for calling on customers in a market not to purchase products from Israel. The prosecution followed a subsection of the Law on Freedom of the Press, prohibiting incitement to discrimination against a group of persons on account, *inter alia*, of their origin or belonging to a specific nation.[97] The applicants were acquitted at first instance – on the grounds that the subsection on which the prosecution had been based did not apply to the facts of the case – but on appeal, a suspended fine of one thousand euros was imposed on them, and they were ordered to pay damages to the associations appearing as civil parties.[98]

In its judgment of 11 June 2020, the ECtHR held that a boycott is primarily a means of expressing a protest and, as a result, a call for a boycott, which is aimed at communicating protest opinions while calling for specific protest actions, is in principle covered by the protection set out in Article 10 of the Convention.[99] The

[94] According to CAS, "there is an obvious parallel between a public authority and a sports federation, who make their own rules and regulations and reach their own decisions by following a similar process and with a similar impact on those affected" (CAS 2010/A/2058 British Equestrian Federation v. Fédération Equestre Internationale (FEI), 13 July 2010, § 16). In similar fashion, the CAS also held that there is "an evident analogy between sports-governing bodies and governmental bodies with respect to their role and functions as regulatory, administrative and sanctioning entities" (CAS 98/2000 AEK Atene and S.K. Slavia Praga v. Union of European Football Associations (UEFA), 20 August 1999, § 58). See also the Swiss Federal Tribunal in the *Semenya* case: « La recourante fait cependant valoir, non sans pertinence, que les relations entre un athlète et une fédération sportive mondiale présentent certaines similitudes avec celles qui lient un particulier à l'État. Il est vrai que le Tribunal fédéral a relevé que le sport de compétition se caractérise par une structure très hiérarchisée, aussi bien au niveau international qu'au niveau national. Établies sur un axe vertical, les relations entre les athlètes et les organisations qui s'occupent des diverses disciplines sportives se distinguent en cela des relations horizontales que nouent les parties à un rapport contractuel (...). [Federal Supreme Court, 25 August 2020, A4_248/2019, 25 August 2020, § 9.4 (unpublished decision)].

[95] Harris et al. (2018), p. 661. See also the dissenting opinion of Judge Jungwiert.

[96] ECtHR, Baldassi and Others v. France, 11.06.2020. See Bass (2020), Meyer-Ladewig (2021a, b), Dubuisson (2020).

[97] ECtHR, Baldassi and Others v. France, 11.06.2020, §§ 5–9.

[98] ECtHR, Baldassi and Others v. France, 11.06.2020, §§ 12–17.

[99] ECtHR, Baldassi and Others v. France, 11.06.2020, § 63.

Court recognized that the present case was different from the *Willem* case, in that the applicants here were ordinary citizens who were not restricted by the duties and responsibilities arising from a mayoral mandate and whose influence over consumers was not comparable to that of a mayor over his municipal services. Moreover, the applicants had not been convicted of making racist or antisemitic remarks or inciting hatred or violence, or of being violent themselves or causing damage. Nor had the market claimed damages before the domestic courts.[100]

The Court further held that, in convicting the applicants, the domestic court had failed to analyze the actions and remarks prosecuted in light of those factors and had concluded, broadly, that the call for a boycott had amounted to incitement to discrimination and, "was in no way covered by the right to freedom of expression".[101] It also held that the actions and remarks of the applicants had concerned a subject of public interest (compliance with public international law by the state of Israel and the human rights situation in the occupied Palestinian territories), and had been part of a contemporary debate in France and throughout the world. Secondly, the actions and remarks in question had fallen within the ambit of political or militant expression. It was in the nature of political speech to be controversial and often virulent. That did not diminish its public interest, provided that it did not cross the line and turn into a call for violence, hatred, or intolerance.[102] The Court ultimately concluded that there *had* been a violation of Article 10 ECHR.[103]

The question remains whether, in the case of a call for a boycott coming from a high official of a national or international sports federation, the Court would confirm its approach in the *Willem* case, and whether, if such a call was made by an athlete or player, it would follow its approach in the *Baldassi and Others* case, and be tougher on states in applying and respecting freedom of expression.

4 Conclusion

The *Šimunić* case is significant insofar as it stresses that there are limits to the freedom of expression that are applicable to the field of sport. As has been mentioned above, the Court did not engage in a substantive discussion on the principle of political neutrality in the three cases against Turkey, but chose to adopt a procedural approach by limiting itself to hold that the assessment made by the bodies of the TFF had not complied with the requirements of Article 10 ECHR; future cases might show whether the Court is willing to address the conformity of this principle with Article 10 ECHR. A future case may also reveal to what extent the generally broad

[100] ECtHR, Baldassi and Others v. France, 11.06.2020, §§ 71–72.

[101] ECtHR, Baldassi and Others v. France, 11.06.2020, § 76.

[102] ECtHR, Baldassi and Others v. France, 11.06.2020, §§ 78–79.

[103] ECtHR, Baldassi and Others v. France, 11.06.2020, §§ 80–81.

protection of freedom of expression by the Court would accommodate or challenge the principle of political neutrality in sport.[104]

This chapter has argued that the Court's decision would likely depend on the broadness of the margin of appreciation that is granted to states in their supervision of the sport-governing and arbitration bodies in assessing matters of freedom of expression in disciplinary proceedings (as well as criminal proceedings) of their ordinary courts. In both situations, the special responsibilities of athletes and players as role models in society would have to be taken into consideration. Famous athletes are heroes, especially in the eyes of the youth and thus have to assume a particular role model responsibility. In other words, as a result of their particular social position, they might have to accept a higher degree of "duties and responsibilities" under Article 10 ECHR than normal citizens. The sport-related case law seems to indicate a certain trend of the Court to consider professional athletes as falling into a category where the States Parties to the ECHR enjoy a broader margin of appreciation; in other words, their protection under Article 10 ECHR might be reduced.

Another relevant dimension is the practice of the ECtHR to grant only a narrow margin of appreciation to States Parties in matters of public interest or regarding the expression of political opinions and views. Moreover, the circumstances of each individual case and the relative weight of the interests of the athlete or player, on the one hand, and the sport-governing body, on the other, would have to be considered and balanced against each other.[105] In this regard, the interests of a restriction might carry more weight when the athlete expresses during a competition, rather than outside the arena or on social media, or in a situation where the athlete acts as a representative of a team or a nation.[106] Other factors to be considered include whether speech or gestures are at stake, the actual content of the message conveyed, as well as the severity of the sanction and its nature (i.e. criminal or only disciplinary). If it is disciplinary, will the sanction involve a fine or a ban? If there is some form of ban, should it be for life or a temporary suspension?

A key difficulty with political neutrality lies in the ambiguous definition of "political";[107] in particular, its distinction from acts and expressions of solidarity with victims of human rights abuse or social inequalities, such as ethnic minorities. It is suggested here that symbolic tributes to the Black Lives Matter movement, for instance, can hardly be qualified as "political" statements, but are rather expressions of sympathy and humanitarian concerns over certain events. In such circumstances, it is questionable whether sport-governing bodies can invoke this principle at all. In other words, can one remain neutral when facing human rights abuses,

---

[104] James (2022) argues that, save for the most extreme and targeted of demonstrations or expressions, it would be difficult to show that there is a compelling social need for Rule 50 that is necessary in a democratic society.

[105] Lindholm (2017), p. 2.

[106] Lindholm (2017), p. 2.

[107] See, in this sense, Shahlaei (2017/2018), p. 113.

discrimination, and other inequalities? The recent discussion on the rainbow armband during the FIFA World Cup in Qatar has shifted this issue to the forefront of sport news.

In a case where the principle of neutrality is applied in a strict fashion by sport-governing bodies, not leaving room for any appropriate balancing of the relevant interests at stake, the Court could find this problematic in light of the procedural (formal) requirements of Article 10 ECHR; as in the three cases against Turkey, or the *Lacatus* case. The conclusions of the Court in the latter case indicate that an absolute ban, here on begging, without taking into account the specificities of the individual case, might lead to a violation of the Convention.

The current state of affairs with regards to international sport involves an imbalance between the rights and obligations of athletes. One the one hand, professional athletes face increased "duties and responsibilities" due to their position as role models in society; on the other, they have no choice but to adhere to the principle of political neutrality imposed on them by powerful sport-governing bodies, which often benefit from monopoly positions within their sport and have the power to impose severe disciplinary sanctions. In addition, athletes might feel a tension between general calls to increase public speech, encouraging them to use their influence to promote peace,[108] and the principle of political neutrality in sport, which has the tendency to restrict public speech. Finally, the position of athletes is further weakened in practice by their duty to adhere to contract clauses that generally exclude the possibility to complain before ordinary courts in favor of the jurisdiction of CAS for potential disputes with a national or international federation.[109]

This chapter argues there is no compelling reason that would prevent the Court to close this protection gap in the future and play an even more significant role in these domains with the aim of finding a fair balance between the rights and duties of athletes and players. The Court's role might turn out to be even more significant in light of the fact that CAS's jurisdiction is not limited to European athletes. Thanks to the appeal open to the Swiss Federal Tribunal for well-defined complaints,[110] CAS could potentially become a global watchdog for human rights in sport, including for important questions related to freedom of speech.[111]

[108] See above, Sect. 3.3.2.

[109] See, for example, ECtHR, *Mutu und Pechstein v. Switzerland*, 02.10.2018, §§ 109–115, and for a case note, De Marco (2018).

[110] Section 190 § § of the Swiss Private International Law Act (PILA).

[111] See, *e.g.*, the case of Semenya v. Switzerland (no. 10934/21), currently pending before the Court. In this case, the applicant, an athlete from South Africa, complains about suspension from competition imposed by the IAAF (now World Athletics) due to her naturally increased testosterone levels.

References

Abanazir C (2022) The Court of Arbitration for Sport's Multifarious Views on Freedom of Expression. Verfassungsblog, 23 February 2022. Available: https://verfassungsblog.de/category/debates/freedom-of-expression-in-the-olympic-movement/. Accessed 5 Apr 2023

Bass T (2020) La répression pénale des appels au boycott de produits israéliens en droit européen des droits de l'homme. Revue trimestrielle des droits de l'homme 31(124):835–850

Bloom B (2020) Athletes taking a knee at Tokyo 2021 Olympics and Paralympics face bans. Telegraph, 9 June 2020

Boykoff J (2016) Power games. A political history of the Olympia. Verso, London

Chappelet J-L (2016) Autonomy and governance: necessary bedfellows in the fight against corruption in sport. In: Sweeney (ed) Global corruption report: sport, 16–28

Clapham A (2018) Non-state actors. In: Moeckli D et al (eds) International human rights law, 3rd edn. Oxford University Press, Oxford, pp 557–579

De Marco N (2018) The Right to a Fair Hearing in Sports' Cases: Lessons from the ECtHR's Decision in Mutu and Pechstein. LawinSport, 15 October 2018; Available: https://www.lawinsport.com/topics/item/the-right-to-a-fair-hearing-in-sports-cases-lessons-from-the-ecthr-s-decision-in-mutu-pechstein. Accessed 5 Apr 2023

Di Marco A (2021) Athletes' freedom of expression: the relative political neutrality of sport. Human Rights Law Rev 21:620–640

Dou E (2022) China warns foreign Olympic athletes against speaking out on politics at Winter Games. The Washington Post, 19 January 2022. Available: https://www.washingtonpost.com/sports/olympics/2022/01/19/china-winter-olympics-politics-speech/. Accessed 5 Apr 2023

Dubuisson F (2020) L'appel au boycott est protégé par la liberté d'expression: CEDH, 11 juin 2020, no. 15271/16 et al., Baldassi et al. C. France. La Semaine Juridique (JCP) 94(37):1531–1533

Duval A, Heerdt D (2022) Speaking up in Beijing or not? Debating (Un)Freedom of Expression in the Olympic Movement. Verfassungsblog, 4 February 2022; Available: https://verfassungsblog.de/category/debates/freedom-of-expression-in-the-olympic-movement/. Accessed 5 Apr 2023

Harris D, O'Boyle M, Warbrick (2018) Law of the European Convention on Human Rights, 4th edn. Oxford University Press, Oxford

James M (2022) The Re-Emergence of the Athlete Activist, Rule 50 and the Precarious Position of Free Speech under the IOC's Guidelines. Verfassungsblog, 8 February 2022; Available: https://verfassungsblog.de/the-re-emergence-of-the-athlete-activist/. Accessed 5 Apr 2023

Krieger J (2022) Keeping Politics Out, A Short History of Regulating Free Speech in the Olympic Movement. Verfassungsblog, 7 February 2022; Available: https://verfassungsblog.de/category/debates/freedom-of-expression-in-the-olympic-movement/. Accessed 5 Apr 2023

Lavrysen L (2016) Human rights in a positive state: rethinking the relationship between positive and negative obligations under the European Convention on Human Rights. Intersentia

Lindholm J (2017) From Carlos to Kaepernick and beyond: athletes' right to freedom of expression. Int Sports Law J 17:1–3

Madelaine C (2014) La technique des obligations positives en droit de la Convention européenne des droits de l'homme. Dalloz, Paris

Marguénaud J (2019) Les contrôles antidopages inopinés devant la Cour européenne des droits de l'homme ou le lancement de la course à la réification des sportifs de haut niveau. Revue trimestrielle des droits de l'homme 117:147–159

Meyer-Ladewig J (2021a) Aufruf zum Boykott israelischer Waren aus Palästina: EGMR (V. Sektion), Urt. V. 11.6.2020, 15271/16 u.a. (Baldassi u.a. gegen Frankreich). Neue Zeitschrift für Verwaltungsrecht 40(3):137–140

Meyer-Ladewig J (2021b) Sperre und Geldbusse für UEFA-Präsidenten: EGMR (III. Sektion), Entscheid vom 11.2.2020, 526/18 (Platini gegen Schweiz). Neue Zeitschrift für Verwaltungsrecht 40(7):465–469

Mowbray AR (2004) The development of positive obligations under the European Convention on Human Rights. Hart, Oxford

Rietiker D (2022a) Defending athletes, players, clubs and fans, manual for human rights education and litigation in sport, in particular before the European Court of Human Rights. Council of Europe Publishing, Strasbourg

Rietiker D (2022b) To Speak, or not to Speak: Freedom of Expression under the Lex Sportiva and Human Rights Law at the 2022 World Cup in Qatar, Verfassungsblog, 15 December 2022; Available: https://verfassungsblog.de/to-speak-or-not-to-speak/. Accessed 5 Apr 2023

Rietiker D (2022c) Football-related corruption as a human rights issue: the case of Michel Platini v. Switzerland before the European Court of Human Rights (Inadmissible, 11 February 2020). Hague YBIL 33:297–313

Rietiker D, Levine M (2022) Begging the Question: Lacatus v. Switzerland and the European Court of Human Rights' Recognition of Begging as a Human Rights Issue. Harv Int Law J (online); Available: https://harvardilj.org/2022/04/begging-the-question-la%cc%86ca%cc%86tus%cc%a7-v-switzerland-and-the-european-court-of-human-rights-recognition-of-begging-as-a-human-rights-issue/. Accessed 5 Apr 2023

Ruggie JG (2016) For the Game. For the World. FIFA and Human Rights; Available: https://www.hks.harvard.edu/centers/mrcbg/programs/cri/research/reports/report68. Accessed 5 Apr 2023

Schwab B (2018) "Celebrate Humanity": reconciling sport and human rights through athlete activism. J Legal Aspects Sport 28(2):170–207

Shahlaei F (2017/2018) When sports stand against human rights: regulating restrictions on athlete speech in the Global Sports Arena. Loyola Los Angeles Entertain Law Rev 38(1):99–120

Shahlaei F (2022) Athletes and the human right to freedom of expression, is it just "Shut Up and Play"? Verfassungsblog, 10 February 2022; Available: https://verfassungsblog.de/athletes-and-the-human-right-to-freedom-of-expression/. Accessed 5 Apr 2023

Shinohara T (2021) Which states parties should be held responsible for the implementation of positive obligations under the ECHR in sports-related disputes? Int Sports Law J. Available: https://www.researchgate.net/publication/356114512_Which_states_parties_should_be_held_responsible_for_the_implementation_of_positive_obligations_under_the_ECHR_in_sports-related_disputes. Accessed 5 Apr 2023

Daniel Rietiker PhD (University of Lausanne) Senior Lawyer at the European Court of Human Rights, Strasbourg; Part-time lecturer at Lausanne University, Faculty of Law; Adjunct Professor at Suffolk University Law School (Boston MA). Recent book: Defending Athletes, Players, Clubs and Fans – Manual for human rights education and litigation in sport, in particular before the European Court of Human Rights, Council of Europe Publishing, 2022.

The Court of Arbitration for Sport under Human Rights Scrutiny: The Role of the Swiss Federal Tribunal and the European Court of Human Rights

Antoine Duval and Marjolaine Viret

Contents

Abstract This chapter sets out to map how human rights (and more specifically, the ECHR) have been applied by the Swiss Federal Tribunal (SFT) and the European Court of Human Rights (ECtHR) to the CAS and its awards. It is based on a comprehensive review of the decisions of both courts related to the CAS. In doing so, the chapter traces the morphing role of the ECHR as a normative resource to check the CAS' judicial authority. Section 2 is dedicated to analyzing more than 20 years of the SFT's case law on appeal against CAS awards, and to showing how the supreme court of Switzerland has been conferring (limited) relevance to the ECHR in the framework of this control. Section 3 provides an analysis of the more

A. Duval
T.M.C. Asser Instituut, The Hague, Netherlands
e-mail: a.duval@asser.nl

M. Viret (✉)
Institute of Sport Sciences, Faculty of Social and Political Sciences, University of Lausanne, Lausanne, Switzerland
e-mail: marjolaine.viret@unil.ch

V. Boillet et al. (eds.), *Sports and Human Rights*, Interdisciplinary Studies in Human Rights 10, https://doi.org/10.1007/978-3-031-56452-9_11

recent case-law of the ECtHR on the compatibility of the CAS and its awards with the ECHR.

1 Introduction

The Court of Arbitration for Sport (CAS) is a central institution for the transnational governance of international sports. It is the private judicial body in charge of deciding the most important disputes involving international sports and, in particular, the Olympic Movement.[1] CAS panels are tasked, in particular, with the responsibility to review the final decisions of Sports Governing Bodies (SGBs), which have introduced CAS arbitration clauses in their statutes, licenses or entry forms. While it is formally recognized as an arbitral tribunal based in Lausanne, Switzerland, and run by a Swiss foundation, the International Council of Arbitration for Sport (ICAS), in practice, its jurisdiction tends to be imposed through the private and often monopolistic power of SGBs.[2] Unlike commercial arbitration, CAS arbitration (at least in its appeal arbitration procedure)[3] is not based on the consent of the parties to the arbitral process, but *de facto* imposed by one party, the governance entity, onto the other. As will be discussed later in the chapter, this idiosyncrasy plays an important role in determining how the European Convention for Human Rights (ECHR) applies to, and at, the CAS.

Another specificity of the CAS is connected to the applicable law in CAS appeal arbitration proceedings. Indeed, the CAS panels primarily apply the rules and regulations of SGBs when deciding disputes, and have recourse to state law (most frequently Swiss law, as the country of the seat of the SGB) only subsidiarily.[4] This does not mean that the CAS never considers other types of laws,[5] but in general its decisions are based primarily on the private regulations of SGBs and subsidiarily Swiss law as interpretative support when the former are unclear or incomplete. In turn, this raises the question of the human rights compatibility of CAS awards. There is the risk that individuals forced to submit their cases to the CAS could be deprived of their ability to argue the incompatibility of the decisions of SGBs with human rights. In fact, the CAS is not ignorant of the existence of the ECHR, nor of its potential relevance for the disputes it has to decide.[6] Nonetheless, until now, it has rarely referred to human rights in its decisions and seldomly considered their

[1] The Olympic Movement is composed of three main constituents: the International Olympic Committee (IOC), the International Sports Federations (IFs) and the National Olympic Committees (NOCs).

[2] Duval (2020a).

[3] Art. R47 et seq. CAS Code.

[4] Art. R58 CAS Code.

[5] See Duval (2015) and Duval (2021).

[6] Duval (2022).

application in a comprehensive fashion. It has concluded that a decision or regulation of an SGB violated the ECHR only in exceptional circumstances.[7] In short, while present in rare instances, human rights remain sidelined at the CAS, and impotent as a legal argument to challenge the decisions or regulations of the SGBs.

In this context, this chapter sets out to map how human rights (and more specifically, the ECHR) have been applied by the Swiss Federal Tribunal (SFT) and the European Court of Human Rights (ECtHR) to the CAS and its awards. It is based on a comprehensive review of the decisions of both courts related to the CAS. In doing so, the chapter traces the morphing role of the ECHR as a normative resource to check the CAS's judicial authority. Section 2 is dedicated to analyzing more than 20 years of the SFT's case law on appeal against CAS awards, and to showing how the supreme court of Switzerland has been conferring (limited) relevance to the ECHR in the framework of this control. Section 3 provides an analysis of the more recent case-law of the ECtHR on the compatibility of the CAS and its awards with the ECHR.

2 The SFT's Handling of Human Rights Claims with Respect to CAS Awards

This section gives an overview of the jurisprudence of the SFT related to human rights claims in sports arbitration matters, with a focus on the ECHR, from 2000–the present (July 2023).[8]

2.1 *Setting the Scene: SFT's Review of International Arbitral Awards*

Before the SFT, the impact of human rights on disputes decided in CAS arbitration is modulated by the limitative list of grounds available for setting aside an international arbitral award, as well as the strict requirements on pleadings applicable in proceedings before Switzerland's Supreme Court. The grounds that can be invoked in an application to set aside an international arbitral award are listed in Art. 190(2) of the Swiss Private International Law Act (SPILA), in Chapter 12, devoted to international arbitration. An arbitral award may be set aside only:

---

[7] On human rights at the CAS, see Maisonneuve (2017) and Duval (2022).

[8] The original full reference number of the case is used, regardless of whether the case has subsequently been published in the official ATF records. Where direct quotes are translated into English for this article, the original text of the quote (in French or German, as applicable) is provided in footnote.

a. where the sole member of the arbitral tribunal was improperly appointed or the arbitral tribunal improperly constituted;
b. where the arbitral tribunal wrongly accepted or declined jurisdiction;
c. where the arbitral tribunal ruled beyond the claims submitted to it, or failed to decide one of the claims;
d. where the principle of equal treatment of the parties or their right to be heard in an adversary procedure were violated;
e. where the award is incompatible with public policy.[9]

Requirements on substantiation are high (Art. 77(3) Federal Tribunal Act, LTF).[10] The applicant must outline precisely how the arbitral tribunal breached one of the grounds listed, and, especially for claims of breach of public policy aimed at the merits, how this affected the outcome reached by the arbitrators.[11] According to the description traditionally provided in SFT decisions, an award is only in breach of public policy "if it disregards fundamental principles of law and is therefore as such irreconcilable with the essential, generally recognised system of values, that should form the foundation of any legal order according to the views prevailing in Switzerland".[12] It is apparent from this definition that the ground of public policy overlaps with essential values protected by human rights instruments, and thus forms the primary juncture between the Swiss system of review of international arbitral awards and the protection of human rights.

Over the past two decades, the SFT has repeatedly faced arguments by applicants that the list of grounds should either be expanded or interpreted more generously in the context of sports arbitration. However, the SFT has thus far refused to extend its review, stressing that the restrictions "apply to all international arbitration proceedings, and thus equally to the domain of sport".[13] Specifically, the SFT judges have systematically rejected arguments that would lead to a notion of public policy specific to sports arbitration, a recognition of a *lex sportiva*.[14]

Prior to the ECtHR's *Semenya v. Switzerland* decision, the SFT assessed on several occasions the modalities of review of CAS awards, finding these modalities compliant with the ECHR in light of ECtHR jurisprudence in arbitration matters.[15]

---

[9] English version available at RS 291 - Loi fédérale du 18 décembre 1987 sur le droit international privé (LDIP) (admin.ch).

[10] 4A_564/2021, 2 May 2022, para. 4.2.

[11] 4A_564/2021, 2 May 2022, para. 6.1.1; 4A_406/2021, 14 February 2022, para. 7.1.

[12] E.g., most recently in sports arbitration: 4A_184/2023, 5 June 2023, para. 6.1 (in French); 4A_528/2023, 13 March 2023, para. 4.1 (in German).

[13] 4A_43/2010, 29 July 2010, para. 3.6.1 (our translation from German): "gilt für sämtliche Verfahren der internationale Schiedsgerichtsbarkeit, so auch im Bereich des Sports" ; see also 4A_320/2009, 2 June 2010, para. 1.5.3.

[14] E.g. 4A_488/2011, para. 6.2, confirmed in 4A_312/2017, para. 3.3.2 and 4A_248/2019, para. 9.8.3.3.

[15] Latest reference in 4A_10/2022, 17 May 2022, para. 5.1, considered in depth 4A_248/2019, 25 August 2020, para. 5.2, confirmed in 4A_406/2021, 14 February 2022, para. 8 and 4A_618/2020, para. 3.4.

With respect to human rights instruments, it is foundational SFT case law that these instruments cannot be directly relied upon to challenge an arbitral award. Specifically, neither the safeguards of the ECHR, nor of the Swiss Constitution, can be invoked autonomously, nor do they *eo ipso* amount to a breach of one of the listed grounds (see next sub-section). The extent to which the decision rendered by the ECtHR in *Semenya v. Switzerland* might warrant future adjustments to that jurisprudence is discussed in this chapter's conclusion.

2.2 Human Rights Jurisprudence Leaking Into SFT Decisions

In spite of the SFT's refusal to expand its scope of review, human rights, and specifically the ECHR, can and do play a role in its decisions. Indeed, they may be taken into consideration to concretize the concepts involved in the grounds listed in Art. 190(2) SPILA, in particular procedural or substantive public policy.

There has been a noticeable increase in recent years of occurrences in which the SFT called on the jurisprudence of the ECtHR in applications to set aside a CAS award. This increase correlates with the significant rise in sports arbitration matters adjudicated by the ECtHR since 2018, probably compounded by the fact that ECtHR rulings, with the exception of the lack of public hearing at the CAS sanctioned through *Mutu and Pechstein*, have so far supported the features of the Swiss system, thus forming welcome references for countering subsequent attacks. Prior to 2019, references to the jurisprudence of ECtHR in arbitration matters remained exceptional, and not specific to rulings of the ECtHR regarding sports matters.[16] Nevertheless, some SFT decisions included extensive references to scholarly writings on the ECHR and arbitration.[17]

So far, most references to ECtHR jurisprudence in SFT decisions appear inserted with the purpose of countering challenges to the SFT's limited power of review, or confirming the status of CAS as institutionally independent and impartial. It thus comes as no surprise that *Mutu and Pechstein* is the most frequently cited ECtHR decision [Table 1]. The decisions are also used to highlight the ECtHR's recognition of the legitimate interests in regulating sports in major areas touching on fairness and health, in particular the fight against doping, and of the appropriateness of a uniform dispute resolution system in international sports.

It remains to be seen how the SFT will address the ECtHR *Semenya* ruling (see Sect. 3.3.2), which is the first to truly encroach upon Switzerland's margin of appreciation with respect to the depth of control that the SFT should exert over the merits of a CAS award. Undoubtedly, the precedent will be used in the near future in

[16] 4A_238/2011, 4 January 2021 (commercial arbitration), para. 3.2. (citing ECtHR *Suda v. Czech Rep*); 4A_620/2009, 7 May 2010, para. 4.3.2 (citing ECtHR *Scoppola v. Italy*).

[17] E.g. 4P_172/2006, 22 March 2007, para. 4.3.2.1; 4P.105/2006, 4 August 2006, para. 7.3.

Table 1 References to ECtHR Case Law in SFT Decisions related to Sports Arbitration since 2019

• 4A_10/2022, 17 May 2022 : *Platini v. Switzerland; Mutu and Pechstein v. Switzerland; Bakker v. Switzerland*;
• 4A_564/2021, 2 May 2022: *Ali Riza v. Switzerland*; *Mutu and Pechstein v. Switzerland*;
• 4A_406/2021, 14 February 2022: *FNASS et al. v France;*
• 4A_600/2020, 27 January 2021: *Mutu and Pechstein v. Switzerland; Ali Riza v. Turkey; Platini v. Switzerland;*
• 4A_248/2019, 25 August 2020: *Mutu and Pechstein v. Switzerland; Platini v. Switzerland; Bakker v. Switzerland; FNASS et al. c. France; Suovaniemi et al. v. Finnland; Tabbane v. Switzerland; Ali Riza v. Turkey;*
• 4A_486/2019, 17 August 2020: *Mutu and Pechstein v. Switzerland;*
• 4A_268/2019, 17 October 2019: *Mutu and Pechstein v. Switzerland, Tabbane v. Switzerland*

applications to set aside CAS awards, forcing the SFT to take a position on that matter. In fact, in high-profile cases over the past years, applicants seem to routinely add arguments under the ECHR and/or Swiss Constitution when they invoke a breach of public policy under Art. 190(2) SPILA.

In *Sun Yang v. FINA*, the swimmer who had been sanctioned for refusing a doping test, under the heading of breach of substantive public policy, alleged a breach of several substantive safeguards of the ECHR (Art. 8), of UNO Pact II (17 (1)) and of the Swiss Constitution (10(2) and 13), arguing that the award was in breach of his private life and his right to health.[18] In *Leeper v. World Athletics* (IAAF), the athlete Blake Leeper who was refused participation in athletic competitions for excessive height of the blade prosthesis he had elected to compete with, equally included in his argument related to substantive public policy the claim of discrimination within the meaning of Art. 14 ECHR, as well as incompatibility with human dignity.[19] In *Semenya v. World Athletics*, the SFT was asked to look at the matter in terms of prohibition of discrimination and human dignity as components of substantive public policy.[20] In *ROC v. IPC*, regarding the ban of Russian athletes from participating in the Paralympic Games, the Russian Olympic Committee invoked various rights in relation to protection of disability (Art. 8(4) Swiss Constitution, UN Convention on the Rights of Persons with Disabilities).[21]

Needless to say, the arguments were rejected in all instances. At this point, one may suspect that most claims based on the ECHR are brought in strategically before the SFT to anticipate a subsequent request before the ECtHR, and avoid risk of forfeiture under Art. 35 ECHR for not having made the relevant arguments before national courts, rather than in hope of a genuine prospect of succeeding before the SFT. The SFT judges themselves describe the refusal to treat safeguards under the Swiss Constitution or the ECHR as autonomous grounds for challenging an

[18] 4A_406/2021, 14 February 2022, para. 7.4.

[19] 4A_618/2020, 2 June 2021, para. 5.

[20] 4A_248/2019, 25 August 2020, para. 9.2.

[21] 4A_470/2016, 3 April 2017, para. 4.2.

Table 2 Refusal to consider claims based on 'human rights' instruments as standalone grounds

4A_184/2023, 5 June 2023, para. 6.1.4: Cst and ECHR
4A_528/2022, 13 March 2023, para. 5: Art. 6 ECHR specifically
4A_10/2022, 17 May 2022, para. 5.1: Art. 6 ECHR specifically
4A_564/2021, 2 May 2022, para. 4.1: ECHR
4A_406/2021, 14 February 2022, para. 7.2 & 7.5: Cst and ECHR
4A_166/2021, 22 September 2021, para. 5.2.1: ECHR
4A_476/2020, 5 January 2021, para. 4.1: ECHR
4A_248/2019, 25 August 2020, para. 9.2: Cst and ECHR
4A_486/2019, 17 August 2020, para. 4.1: Art. 6 ECHR specifically
4A_268/2019, 17 October 2019, para. 3.4.3: ECHR
4A_114/2018, 14 August 2018, para. 2.2: ECHR
4A_384/2017, 4 October 2017, para. 4.2: Cst and ECHR
4A_80/2017, 25 July 2017, para. 2.2: Cst, ECHR, or 'other international treaties'
4A_342/2015, 26 April 2016, para. 4.1.2 (commercial arbitration) : ECHR
4A_246/2014, 15 July 2015, para. 7.2.2: ECHR
4A_178/2014, 11 June 2014, para. 2.4: Cst, ECHR, or 'other international treaties'
4A_198/2012, 14 December 2012, para. 3.1: ECHR
4A_404/2010, 19 April 2011, para. 3.5.3: Cst, ECHR, or 'other international treaties'
4A_43/2010, 29 July 2010, para. 3.6.1: Cst, ECHR, or 'other international treaties'
4A_320/2009, 2 June 2010, para. 1.5.3: Cst, ECHR, or 'other international treaties'
4A_370/2007, 21 February 2008, para. 5.3.2: ECHR
4P.105/2006, 4 August 2006, para. 7.3: ECHR

international award as 'established jurisprudence' (*ständige Rechtsprechung*).[22] However, according to the federal judges, "the approach taken by the SFT does not have the effect of depriving athletes of the opportunity to complain of a breach of fundamental safeguards of the ECHR, since these can, indirectly, be taken into account to concretize the safeguards resulting from Art. 190(2) SPILA".[23] Decisions of the SFT have been remarkably consistent in that regard from 2000–2023 [see Table 2].

Where the applicants do not attempt to invoke human rights safeguards as autonomous grounds,[24] arguments have also been put forward under the ground of improper composition of the arbitral tribunal (Art. 190(2)(a) SPILA),[25] and of

[22] 4A_476/2020, 5 January 2021, para. 4.1.

[23] 4A_10/2022, 17 May 2022, para. 5.1 (our translation): "l'approche suivie par le Tribunal fédéral n'a pas pour effet de priver les athlètes de la possibilité de se plaindre de la violation des garanties fondamentales de la CEDH, puisque celles-ci peuvent être prises, indirectement, en considération aux fins de concrétiser les garanties déduites de l'art. 190 al. 2 LDIP".

[24] E.g. 4A_10/2022, 17 May 2022, para. 5.1; 4A_486/2019, 17 August 2020, para. 4.1; 4A_476/2020, 5 January 2021, para. 4.2.

[25] See e.g. 4P.267/2002, 23 May 2003, para. 3.

violation of the right to be heard (Art. 190(2)(d) SPILA).[26] However, a majority of pleadings invoking provisions of the ECHR are made under the heading of public policy (Art. 190(2)(e) SPILA), in its procedural[27] or substantive aspect.[28] The following sub-sections hence focus on human rights claims in the context of public policy.

2.3 *Procedural Requirements of Fair Trial According to Art. 6 ECHR*

The SFT has variously insisted that the fair trial requirements of the ECHR (specifically Art. 6 ECHR) do not rule out the institution of arbitral tribunals to adjudicate certain disputes among private parties,[29] adding that the ECtHR itself recognizes that there is a legitimate interest for disputes in professional sport, especially those that have an international dimension, to be submitted to a specialized judicial body that can render a decision in a time- and cost-efficient manner.[30]

Decisions pre-dating the ECtHR ruling in *Mutu and Pechstein* lacked a clear-cut, consistent, line of reasoning with respect to the relevance of Art. 6 ECHR in challenges against CAS awards. The position in sports arbitration matters appeared to follow the parallel jurisprudence in commercial matters that parties may choose to bypass state courts and assign the resolution of their dispute to an arbitral tribunal, and that making that choice precludes subsequent complaints to the SFT that the arbitrators breached the ECHR.[31] In earlier decisions, arguments relying on Art. 6 ECHR were also brushed away with generic statements whereby the provision "is not applicable to voluntary arbitration proceedings",[32] or "Art. 6(1) ECHR does not pertain to the proceedings before an arbitral tribunal",[33] although decisions already made the (theoretical) concession that the principles underpinning Art. 6 ECHR may be used to concretize the grounds listed in Art. 190(2) SPILA.[34] In short, reliance on Art. 6 ECHR safeguards was curtailed by the SFT treating submission to CAS arbitration as 'voluntary' in nature.

---

[26] E.g. 4A_618/2020, 2 June 2021, para. 4.1.

[27] E.g. 4A_486/2019, 17 August 2020, para. 4.

[28] 4A_184/2023, 5 June 2023, para. 6.2.1.

[29] 4P.64/2001, 11 June 2001, para. 2.d.aa.

[30] 4A_248/2019, 25 August 2020, para. 5.2.4.

[31] 4A_246/2014, 15 July 2015, para. 7.2.2; also 4A_444/2009, 10 February 2010, para. 4.2 (commercial matter); 4P.176/2001, 16 October 2001, 2c.aa (commercial matter).

[32] 4A_320/2009, 2 June 2010, para. 2 ("auf Verfahren der freiwilligen Schiedsgerichtsbarkeit nicht anwendbar" (our translation)); 4P.105/2006, 4 August 2006, para. 7.3.

[33] 4P.64/2001, 11 June 2001, 2.d.aa (our translation) : "L'art. 6 par. 1 CEDH ne se rapporte pas à la procédure devant un tribunal arbitral".

[34] 4P.105/2006, 4 August 2006, para. 7.3.

The landmark decision *Cañas v. ATP* in 2007—in which the SFT struck down a waiver of the right to challenge a CAS award before the SFT, ruling that such a waiver cannot, in principle, be opposed to an athlete in disciplinary proceedings, even when the waiver satisfies the formal requirements of Art. 192(1) SPILA – is the only decision in which the SFT observed *sua sponte* that a waiver of fair trial safeguards in a situation in which "an athlete had no other choice than to accept the waiver to be authorised to participate in competition would also seem questionable under the angle of Art. 6(1) ECHR".[35] While this observation seems to have carried no repercussions for subsequent SFT decisions it contained the germs of rationales that led to the ECtHR findings in *Mutu and Pechstein.*

After the ECtHR decision in the *Mutu and Pechstein* case, one can hardly question that CAS panels, respectively CAS in combination with the SFT, are required to fulfil the requirements of Art. 6 ECHR *in extenso* whenever submission to arbitration (e.g., an athlete agreeing to an international federation's regulations) must be regarded as 'forced'; such as when there is no "free, lawful and unequivocal" consent to arbitration (see Sect. 3.2.1).[36]

Nevertheless, the *Mutu and Pechstein* decision appears to have had little tangible impact on the jurisprudence of the SFT overall, at least insofar as altering outcomes of CAS awards or sanctioning the CAS in procedural matters is concerned.[37] The SFT maintains, in the post-*Mutu and Pechstein* era, that Art. 6 ECHR is no autonomous ground of challenge.[38] In particular, a breach of the ECHR "is not necessarily to be equated per se to a contradiction with public policy within the meaning of Art. 190(2)(e) SPILA".[39] It is therefore incumbent on the party to show how the alleged violation of Art. 6 ECHR is incompatible with procedural public policy.[40]

If anything, the ECtHR ruling seems to have strengthened the CAS' position in the jurisprudence of the SFT, in that it 'crowned' the CAS as an independent and impartial tribunal established by law, and gave the SFT support to counter

---

[35] 4P.172/2006, 22 March 2007, para 4.3.2.1 (our translation): "athlète qui n'a eu d'autre choix que d'accepter la renonciation au recours pour être admis à participer aux compétitions apparaît également sujet à caution au regard de l'art. 6 par. 1 CEDH".

[36] 4A_600/2020, 27 January 2021, para. 5.5.2: SFT citing the ECtHR's findings in *Mutu & Pechstein v. Switzerland* whereby, in case of 'forced' arbitration, the arbitral tribunal must offer the safeguards enshrined in Art. 6 para. 1 ECHR, in particular those regarding independence and impartiality.

[37] The same can be said of other procedural safeguards invoked, e.g. Art. 13 ECHR (right to an effective remedy: 4A_10/2022, 17 May 2022, para. 6; already invoked in 4A_406/2021, 14 February 2022, para. 8.

[38] 4A_528/2022, 13 March 2023, para. 5.

[39] 4A_10/2022, 17 May 2022, para. 5.1 (our translation): "Toute violation du droit conventionnel n'étant pas nécessairement per se assimilable à une contrariété à l'ordre public au sens de l'art. 190 al. 2 let. e LDIP".

[40] 4A_10/2022, 17 May 2022, para. 5.1; 4A_486/2019, 17 August 2020, 4.1; 4A_644/2020, 23 August 2021, para. 5.1.

subsequent attacks on the CAS institution.[41] Thus, challenges seeking to rely on the dissenting opinion in the ruling to challenge selected aspects of the CAS mechanics (modalities of appointment of the panel chair in CAS appeal arbitration) have been categorically dismissed with the argument that, "the CAS' independence was definitively confirmed by the ECtHR",[42] so that it would be futile to "attempt to reopen the debate" on those questions.[43]

Ironically, the only instance in which the *Mutu and Pechstein* ruling has been used to put boundaries on non-consensual arbitration concerns a commercial arbitration case, where the SFT, citing the ECtHR ruling, denied that a third party be bound by the arbitration clause based on a criterion 'as blurry as' (*critère aussi flou que*) their interest in the performance of the contract, considering that taking such a step would hardly be consistent with the ECtHR requirement of free, lawful and unequivocal consent.[44]

If one takes a more granular look at recent SFT decisions, the sentiment is that the SFT has thus far been able to avoid elaborating on the implications of Art. 6 ECHR for sports arbitration after *Mutu and Pechstein*. Some arguments based on Art. 6 ECHR were dismissed due to the applicants seeking to put forward the provision as an autonomous ground, or failing to incorporate sufficient demonstration of breach of one of the grounds listed in Art. 190(2) SPILA.[45] In some instances, the SFT was able to circumvent the issue because the particulars of the dispute did not amount to a case of 'forced' arbitration,[46] or the case otherwise fell outside the scope of the ECHR.[47] In other instances, the applicants did not show (or did not argue), to the satisfaction of the federal judges, that they had been denied the benefit of a procedural safeguard and had made the argument in a timely manner in the proceedings.[48] Finally, in further instances the SFT deemed the argument in any event

[41] E.g. 4A_600/2020, 27 January 2021, para. 5.5.2 & 5.6; 4A_644/2020, 23 August 2021, para. 4.3.2.

[42] 4A_10/2022, 17 May 2022, para. 5.3.4 (our translation): "l'indépendance du TAS avait été définitivement confirmée par la CourEDH dans l'affaire Mutu et Pechstein".

[43] 4A_644/2020, 23 August 2021, para. 4.3.2 (our translation): "Aussi est-ce en vain que la recourante tente de rouvrir le débat sur la question de l'indépendance du TAS, laquelle a été définitivement tranchée par la CourEDH".

[44] 4A_64/2022, 18 July 2022, para. 6.6.

[45] E.g. 4A_10/2022, 17 May 2022, para. 5.1.

[46] 4A_476/2020, 5 January 2021, para. 4.2 (the player was actually given a choice between CAS and civil courts in his employment contract); 4A_600/2020, 27 January 2021, para. 5.6 (SFT questioned whether a dispute between two clubs both claiming the right over use of the same name can be considered 'forced arbitration' within the *Mutu & Pechstein v. Switzerland* meaning).

[47] 4A_486/2019, 17 August 2020, para. 4.2 (applicants not considered affected in their right or obligations of a civil nature, as mere informants).

[48] 4A_54/2019, 11 April 2019, para. 3 (applicant had not shown that she had requested a public hearing before CAS); TF, 4A_268/2019, 17 October 2019, para. 3.4.3 (applicant had not argued that the Algerian arbitral tribunal for sports disputes had been a forced arbitration).

unfounded or misdirected based on a hypothetical application of Art. 6 ECHR,[49] or left the issue undecided since the CAS arbitrators had *de facto* considered the principles invoked.[50]

The general takeaway from SFT jurisprudence since the ECtHR *Mutu and Pechstein* decision on matters related to fair trial and Art. 6 ECHR, is that the ECtHR ruling has had the paradoxical effect of supporting the Swiss system and the CAS institution, rather than of challenging it. There has yet to be a case in which the applicants obtained the setting aside of a CAS award based on the ECtHR ruling that CAS arbitration must fulfil the requirements of Art. 6 ECHR when it is to be regarded as 'forced'.

2.4 Application of Substantive Safeguards of the ECHR

Beyond the fair trial requirements of Art. 6 ECHR, the SFT has been asked on various occasions to explore the extent to which the merits of a CAS award should be subjected to judicial scrutiny based on substantive human rights safeguards. This question is again entwined with the SFT's interpretation of public policy. SFT jurisprudence acknowledges that claims directed at the substance of an international arbitral award are considered through an extremely narrow prism. One decision, in a commercial matter, recalled that a party who waived their right to access to court—a right that has both a constitutional (Art. 30 Swiss Cst) and a conventional (Art. 6 ECHR) basis—was entitled to expect an arbitral panel with sufficient independence and impartiality, and one that will respect the procedural agreement of the parties: "[I]t is only subject to this condition that one may confront them with an award that they will not truly be able to challenge on the merits, save from the very restrictive angle of substantive public policy".[51]

Indeed, while the definitions of substantive public policy have varied in the jurisprudence of the SFT, and specifically depending on the language of the decision, broadly speaking, the assessment of a claim only breaches public policy when it "is in violation of fundamental substantive law principles, to an extent that is no

[49] 4A_486/2019, 17 August 2020, para. 4.3 (even if there were a right to a public hearing within the meaning of Art. 6 ECHR, the CAS panel had sufficiently justified, in light of the ECtHR's jurisprudence, why an exception was warranted and the public hearing to be rejected *in casu*); 4A_384/2017, 4 October 2017, para. 4.2.1 (failure to demonstrate any encroachment upon privacy and impact on the compliance with appeal deadline).

[50] 4A_386/2010, 3 January 2011, 9.3 (left open for ne bis in idem, highlighting that the principle is enshrined in international law (Art. 14 para. 7 UN Pact II; Art. 4 para. 1 Protocol 7 to the ECHR, since the CAS arbitrators themselves had applied the principle).

[51] 4A_282/2013, 13 November 2013, para. 4 (our translation): « qu'on peut lui opposer une sentence qu'il ne sera pas véritablement en mesure d'entreprendre sur le fond, sinon sous l'angle très restrictif de son incompatibilité avec l'ordre public matériel ».

longer compatible with the relevant legal order and system of values".[52] The SFT has repeatedly insisted that it would be impracticable to provide an exhaustive list of principles and rights covered by the concept of public policy.[53] A number of aspects are, however, categorically excluded, such as the interpretation of contracts, including sport governing bodies' by-laws, erroneous application of rules of law, or evaluation of the evidence.[54]

In particular, rules on the allocation of proof are not considered part of substantive public policy.[55] An extremely consistent line of jurisprudence in that regard relates to the functioning of the World Anti-Doping Code in its aspects of strict liability, fault, and related proof, in disciplinary doping cases initiated by private SGBs.[56] The SFT has repeatedly found that the rule, whereby doping is presumed to have occurred upon the reporting of a prohibited substance in an athlete's sample, is not in breach of public policy.[57] More specifically, general principles derived from criminal law, such as the presumption of innocence, respectively *in dubio pro reo*, are irrelevant "within the realm of private law, including when the assessment is aimed at disciplinary measures of private sports associations", and including when the measure is imposed by an association with a monopoly.[58] These private measures cannot be assessed under safeguards derived from the ECHR either.[59] The SFT has taken the same position on challenges related to the standard of proof applied,[60] as well as the absence of requirement of fault (*Verschuldensprinzip*), or the absence of requirement of performance enhancement.[61] Arguments of this kind were

[52] 4A_10/2022, 17 May 2022, para. 5.2.1 (our translation): "Une sentence est contraire à l'ordre public matériel lorsqu'elle viole des principes fondamentaux du droit de fond au point de ne plus être conciliable avec l'ordre juridique et le système de valeurs determinants"; for decisions in German, see e.g. the definition in 4A_362/2013, 27 March 2014, para. 3.1.2: "Die materielle Beurteilung eines streitigen Anspruchs verstösst nur gegen den Ordre public, wenn sie fundamentale Rechtsgrundsätze verkennt und daher mit der wesentlichen, weitgehend anerkannten Wertordnung schlechthin unvereinbar ist".

[53] 4A_564/2021, 2 May 2022, para. 6.1.1; 4A_260/2017, 20 February 2018, para. 5.1.

[54] 4A_184/2023, 5 June 2023, para. 6.1.1; 4A_260/2017, 20 February 2018, para. 5.1.

[55] 4A_304/2013, 3 March 2014, para. 5.2.3; see already 4A_458/2009, 10 June 2010, para. 4.4.4.

[56] We treat this illustration as a case of substantive safeguard rather than procedural, since under the Swiss law system the allocation of the burden of proof is regarded as a substantive issue (Art. 8 CC), even though the parallel argument of human rights is frequently brought under the heading of Art. 6 ECHR.

[57] 4A_528/2022, 13 March 2023, para. 4.3.1.

[58] 4A_528/2022, 13 March 2023, para. 4.3.3 (our translation): "Dieser Vorgang ist im Anwendungsbereich des Privatrechts - auch wenn Disziplinarmassnahmen privater Sportverbände zu beurteilen sind - nicht an strafrechtlichen Prinzipien wie der Unschuldsvermutung beziehungsweise des Grundsatzes "in dubio pro reo" zu messen".

[59] 4A_612/2009, 10 February 2010, para. 6.3.2; 4A_80/2017, 25 July 2017, para. 2.2; 4A_470/2016, 3 April 2017, para. 3.4; 4A_178/2014, 11 June 2014, para. 5.2.

[60] 4A_362/2013, 27 March 2014, para. 3.3; 4A_612/2009, 10 February 2010, para. 6.3.2.

[61] 4P.105/2006, 4 August 2006, para. 8.2, with references.

described as “mere appellatory criticism of the decision of the CAS on the merits”.[62] With respect to the disciplinary sanction, adequacy of the sanction to fault is an issue of appreciation, which the SFT cannot review, and does not belong to public policy.[63]

In spite of this restrictive approach, SFT jurisprudence in matters of international sports subsumes under the heading of public policy a number of principles that are traditionally found in human rights instruments, although none have thus far led to setting aside a CAS award: prohibition of torture and inhuman treatments;[64] prohibition of forced labour;[65] human dignity;[66] abuse of rights;[67] protection of the incapacitated;[68] non-discrimination;[69] bribery;[70] and confiscatory measures.[71] A further component of public policy that is frequently invoked and cited in recent decisions concerns personality rights under the Swiss Civil Code (Art. 27 et seq. CC). Given the broad contents attributed to personality rights in the context of elite sport, consideration of egregious breaches of personality opens a reasonable door for SFT judges to grant protection to individuals subjected to decisions of private sports federations (this will be expounded upon in the next section).

An additional difficulty that the application of substantive safeguards involves in the context of the regulation of international sports, is that it presupposes the horizontal application of human rights to international federations as private (non-state) entities. The Swiss legal system does not, as a rule, recognize the horizontal application of constitutional or conventional rights among private parties.[72] This has led the SFT to question the relevance of substantive safeguards of the ECHR or the Swiss Constitution, “which first and foremost protect the individual towards the State”, where regulations or measures by private sports federations are at stake.[73] Contrary to what is often assumed, this is not to say that there is no jurisprudence of the SFT on arguments related to fundamental rights and principles in sports arbitration matters. Wherever possible, rather than to discard *ex ante* human rights claims, the SFT’s preference is to conduct the assessment and

[62] 4P.105/2006, 4 August 2006, para. 9 (our translation): “ist blosse appellatorische Kritik am Sachentscheid des TAS”.

[63] 4P.64/2001, 11 June 2001, para. 2.d.ee.

[64] 4P.64/2001, 11 June 2001, para. 2.d.cc.

[65] 4A_260/2017, 20 February 2018, para. 5.1.

[66] 4A_248/2019, 25 August 2020, para. 11; mentioned also in 4A_458/2009, 10 June 2010, para. 4.4.3.3, 4A_260/2017, 20 February 2018, para. 5.1.

[67] 4A_458/2009, 10 June 2010, para. 4.1.

[68] 4A_612/2009, 10 February 2010, para. 6.1.

[69] 4A_370/2007, 21 February 2008, para. 5.4; 4A_458/2009, 10 June 2010, para. 4.1.

[70] 4A_564/2021, 2 May 2022, para. 6.1.1; 4A_362/2013, 27 March 2014, para. 3.1.2.

[71] 4A_458/2009, 10 June 2010, para. 4.4.7: “Mesures spoliatrices”.

[72] 4A_248/2019, 25 August 2020, para. 9.4.

[73] 4A_458/2009, 10 June 2010, para. 4.4.3.3 (for Art. 6 and 8 ECHR, our translation): “qui protègent au premier chef la personne vis-à-vis de l'Etat”; 4A_248/2019, 25 August 2020, para. 9.4 (for non-discrimination and Art. 8 Cst).

decide that no breach occurred, either *obiter dictum*, or in order to leave the issue of the horizontal application to private SGBs undecided.[74]

In both *Caster Semenya* and *Blake Leeper*, the SFT thus expressed doubt as to whether the prohibition of discrimination should be covered by the restrictive notion of public policy when the alleged discrimination emanates from a private entity and affects relations among private parties.[75] In both cases, however, SFT judges explicitly refrained from further investigating that question, since they were able to reach the conclusion that the award did not, *in casu*, ratify a discrimination contrary to substantive public policy.[76] Even though the ECtHR, in the meantime, has deemed the depth of the SFT's assessment for *Caster Semenya* insufficient (see Sect. 3.3.2), these examples show that the concept of public policy does not categorically prevent the SFT from conducting an appropriate assessment of human rights claims, provided that they are properly substantiated and submitted in due form and time.

Indeed, one justification that the SFT frequently advances for its restrictive approach to human rights, is that the arguments are far-fetched and poorly substantiated, so that the SFT has an easy task dismissing them. The SFT regularly highlights the fact that applicants put forward generic claims, without trying to argue how these would fit into the public policy ground, or without making a demonstration of how the relevant human rights safeguards have been breached *in casu*.[77] The generic character of the arguments proved fatal to the applicants' case in several decisions, in which the argument amounted to little more than an enumeration of constitutional or ECHR provisions.[78] In some instances, the SFT commented on the boldness of the applicants invoking fundamental safeguards for their protection, for circumstances remote from the seriousness of the situations for which these fundamental safeguards were designed.

In a case relating to professional football, the SFT highlighted that the applicant was merely submitting to the SFT broad principles and reasoning of a theoretical nature, adding that, given the annual salary (1,140,000 EUR) at stake, invoking the prohibition of forced labour and human dignity with respect to that player appear

---

[74] 4A_184/2023, 5 June 2023, para. 6.3.2 / 6.3.3 (no discrimination nor violation of human dignity *in casu*); 4A_524/2009, 5 March 2010, para. 5.2.1 / 5.2.2 (no violation of *nulla poena sine lege in casu*); 4A_620/2009, 7 May 2010, para. 4.2 (whether *lex mitior* and non-retroactivity belong to substantive public policy left open since sports rules at stake deemed procedural in nature).

[75] Older cases in which discrimination was discussed: 4A_370/2007, 21 February 2008, para. 5.4; 4P.12/2000, 14 June 2000, para. 5a.aa.

[76] 4A_618/2020, 2 June 2021, para. 5.3.1; 4A_248/2019, 25 August 2020, para. 9.4; confirmed in 4A_184/2023, 5 June 2023, para. 6.3.2.

[77] 4A_458/2009, 10 June 2010, para. 4.4.3.3; 4A_370/2007, 21 February 2008, para. 5.4; 4P.64/2001, 11 June 2001, para. 2.d.dd; 4A_384/2017, 4 October 2017, para. 4.2.1; 4A_132/2016, 30 June 2016, para. 3.2.2.

[78] 4A_43/2010, 29 July 2010, para. 3.6.1; 4A_458/2009, 10 June 2010, para. 4.4.1; 4A_612/2009, 10 February 2010, para. 6.3.3.

"rather audacious".[79] In another case, the judges called the description of a refusal by a sports association to contract, for a period of six months, with a professional player who breached its rules as representing 'torture or inhuman or degrading treatment' "manifestly frivolous".[80]

This overview shows that the concept of public policy could, in principle, leave ample latitude for the Swiss federal judges to incorporate human rights into their review, and intervene where necessary to sanction breaches of these rights without having to abandon their strict adherence to the limitative grounds of Art. 190(2) SPILA contemplated by the Swiss legislator. A legal conundrum to solve remains the applicability of human rights safeguards to private entities, such as international sports federations. While the ECtHR in *Semenya v. Switzerland* tackled the issue from the angle of the positive obligations of the Swiss state, the protection of personality under Swiss law offers another tool that is at the immediate disposal of the SFT, *de lege lata*, to protect individuals from intrusive regulations or measures in international sport.

2.5 Personality Rights as a Counterpart to Human Rights in Private Relationships

While human rights do not apply horizontally in Switzerland, the Swiss legal order incorporates personality rights (Art. 28 CC) as their counterpart among individuals and private entities, and imposes limits on the extent to which individuals may contractually restrict their freedom with respect to those rights in private-law relationships (Art. 27(2) CC). In sports arbitration matters, the SFT has described personality rights as the realization, in private-law relationships, of the constitutionally guaranteed protection of the individual. At the level of the Constitution, this protection is reflected, in particular, in the right to personal freedom (Art. 10 Swiss Constitution): "However, a protection of personal fulfilment does not only exist towards infringements on part of the State, but also towards encroachments from private parties (cpre Art. 27 et seq. CC, which in Switzerland enshrines personal freedom in private law)".[81] Not every violation of personality rights in this context qualifies for a breach of public policy, however: "A contradiction with public policy

[79] 4A_116/2016, 13 December 2016, para. 4.3.3 ("plutôt audacieux"); see also, the argument in 4A_612/2009, 10 February 2010, para. 6.3.3, where the applicant invoked a breach of public policy based on disregard of her human dignity (Art. 7 Swiss Cst) because one of the experts testifying in her case had training in veterinary medicine.

[80] 4.64/2001, 11 June 2001, para. 2.d.cc ("manifestement téméraire").

[81] 4A_558/2011, 27 March 2012, para. 4.3.1 (our translation) : "Ein Schutz der freien persönlichen Entfaltung besteht jedoch nicht nur gegenüber Beeinträchtigungen von Seiten des Staates, sondern auch gegenüber Eingriffen Privater (vgl. Art. 27 f. ZGB, die in der Schweiz die persönliche Freiheit im Privatrecht konkretisieren)".

can only be assumed, where the sanction represents an obvious and severe infringement of personality".[82]

SFT judges create a functional parallel between fundamental rights and personality rights. A recent case series in French-speaking decisions describes the degree of severity of a breach of personality rights required to affect public policy through the prism of violation of a 'fundamental right' (*droit fondamental*), although without ever elaborating on the implications of this terminology.[83] Thus, SFT jurisprudence recognizes that breaches of personality rights are among the fundamental principles covered, in certain circumstances, by the concept of public policy.

In fact, the first and only instance of a CAS award being set aside for breach of substantive public policy applied personality rights. In *Matuzalem v. FIFA*, FIFA had imposed a ban on a football player for an indefinite period of time until he settled a debt.[84] The SFT reasoned that the limits to the extent to which private parties can voluntarily restrict the exercise of their personality rights apply also to statutes and by-laws of international sports federations.[85] Regarding the player, Matuzalem, the threat of a prohibition to exercise his professional activities as a way of enforcing a fine put the foundation of the player's economic existence at risk, without this being justified by an overriding interest of FIFA or its members.[86]

Given the context of the dispute, the decision in *Matuzalem* focused on situations in which the personality right encroached upon is economic freedom. Most case law in international sports arbitration related to an alleged breach of Art. 27-(2) CC involves pecuniary arguments (e.g., a loss of earnings due to an ineligibility period or after an employment dispute) and therefore is primarily concerned with this aspect of economic freedom. Over time, the SFT has considered and rejected arguments of a breach of public policy based on Art. 27 CC in a number of situations, including: restrictions due to the FIFA ban on Third Party Ownerships

[82] 4A_528/2022, 13 March 2023, para. 4.3.4 (our translation) : "kann eine Ordre-public-Widrigkeit nur angenommen werden, wenn die Sanktion eine offensichtliche und schwerwiegende Persönlichkeitsverletzung darstellen würde".

[83] "Selon la jurisprudence, la violation de l'art. 27 al. 2 CC n'est toutefois pas automatiquement contraire à l'ordre public matériel; encore faut-il que l'on ait affaire à un cas grave et net de violation d'un droit fondamental" (see e.g. 4A_184/2023, 5 June 2023, para. 6.3.1; 4A_406/2021, para. 7.3; 4A_260/2017, 20 February 2018, para. 5.4.2). It appears that this terminology was initially introduced through SFT decisions citing a scholarly opinion (4P.64/2001, 11 June 2001, para. 2. b.aa, 4P.12/2000, 14 June 2000, para. 5.b.aa). The expression was then reproduced in subsequent decisions without a discussion of its rationale and origins. In decisions issued in German, SFT judges typically use instead the expression "manifest and severe violation of personality" ('*offensichtliche und schwerwiegende Persönlichkeitsverletzung*'), see most recently: 4A_528/2022, 13 March 2023, para. 4.3.4; 4A_470/2016, 3 April 2017, para. 4.1; 4A_362/2013, 27 March 2014, para. 3.1.2; 4A_558/2011, 27 March 2012, para. 4.3.2. For an exception: 4A_320/2009, 2 June 2010, para. 4.4: "vielmehr ist ein solcher nur im Falle einer offensichtlichen und schwerwiegenden Grundrechtsverletzung denkbar".

[84] 4A_558/2011, 27 March 2012, para. 4.3.5.

[85] 4A_558/2011, 27 March 2012, para. 4.3.3.

[86] 4A_558/2011, 27 March 2012, para. 4.3.5.

and resulting fine for breach of the regulations;[87] proportionality of a two-year doping sanction for a professional wrestler;[88] five-year prohibition of football-related activities for a breach of the rules on the regulation of match-fixing;[89] termination of a professional football contract after a positive test for cocaine.[90]

Art. 27 CC, however, is also aimed at preventing commitments that are excessive in terms of their object, meaning commitments related to personality rights the importance of which is such that no one can commit for the future in their regard.[91] The SFT has also mentioned that it would apply the same reasoning, *mutatis mutandis*, to Art. 20 para. 1 Swiss Code of Obligations (CO), which targets agreements that have an object that is unlawful or against *bona mores*.[92]

Personality under Swiss law thus embraces a wide range of different aspects, as the SFT clarified in identical wording in *Sun Yang*,[93] and *Caster Semenya*:[94]

> In matters of elite sport, the Federal Tribunal recognises that personality rights (art. 27 et seq. Swiss Civil Code [CC; RS210] include the right to health, to physical integrity, to honour, professional consideration, sports activity and, with respect to professional sport, the right to development and personal fulfilment.

Two high profile cases illustrate the broader potential of personality rights for challenges in international arbitration. In *Sun Yang v. FINA*, in order to justify his refusal to submit to doping control which had led to him being declared ineligible for an anti-doping rule violation, the swimmer made allegations of being exposed to the arbitrariness of the DCO with regard to the choice and qualifications of collection personnel during doping control. The SFT rejected the argument, finding no severe and clear case of violation of a fundamental right, adding that the circumstances did not make it legitimate for the swimmer to resort to 'self-justice' by tearing up the doping control form and actively participating in the destruction of his blood samples.[95]

The most serious candidate to a 'Matuzalem II' type ruling, however, may be *Semenya v. World Athletics*, in which the SFT made an assessment of various infringements related to her personal freedom, privacy, and physical integrity, in particular under the angle of Art. 27(2) SPILA. Although the SFT found that the

[87] 4A_260/2017, 20 February 2018, para. 5.4.2.

[88] 4A_528/2022, 13 March 2023, para. 4.3.4

[89] 4A_362/2013, 27 March 2014, para. 3.4

[90] 4A_458/2009, 10 June 2010.

[91] 4A_458/2009, 10 June 2010, para. 4.4.3.2.

[92] 4A_458/2009, 10 June 2010, para. 4.4.3.2.

[93] 4A_406/2021, 14 February 2022, para. 7.3 (wording identical to 4A_248/2019 below).

[94] 4A_248/2019, 25 August 2020, para. 10.1 (our translation): "En matière de sport de haut niveau, le Tribunal fédéral reconnaît que les droits de la personnalité (art. 27 s. du Code civil suisse [CC; RS 210]) incluent le droit à la santé, à l'intégrité corporelle, à l'honneur, à la considération professionnelle, à l'activité sportive et, s'agissant de sport professionnel, le droit au développement et à l'épanouissement économique".

[95] 4A_406/2021, 14 February 2022, para. 7.6.

restrictions induced by the regulations fell short of representing a violation of personality rights so severe that substantive public policy was breached—such that the violation would weigh heavier *in casu* than the interests put forward by World Athletics for protecting fairness in the female category in international competitions—the argument ultimately failed at the stage of the proportionality analysis of the measures by the Swiss federal judges, and not on a principled refusal to consider discrimination claims. That proportionality analysis has now been challenged by the recent ruling of the ECtHR, but the case demonstrated that even extremely delicate issues affecting the participation of intersex athletes in sport could be adequately dealt with via personality rights.

In sum, the SFT has conceded little ground to those advocating the consideration of human rights enshrined in either the ECHR or the Swiss Constitution as autonomous grounds for challenging an international CAS award. While an assessment is possible, *de lege lata*, and indeed conducted in certain instances, successful challenges under the heading of public policy are (close to) non-existent in practice. Given that the only exception, *Matuzalem v. FIFA* concerned personality rights, and considering the broad scope of application of personality rights with respect to sports practice recognized by the SFT, these rights should be considered in all instances for their potential to at least force the SFT into a proper balance of interests and proportionality assessment.

3 The CAS at the ECtHR

The SFT's lenient review of CAS awards has been subjected to challenges before the ECtHR since the early 2000s.[96] Indeed, the two protagonists of one of the most important decisions by the SFT regarding the CAS,[97] Larisa Lazutina and Olga Danilova, where the first to submit an application to the ECtHR against Switzerland (in 2003).[98] While they withdrew their application in 2007 after waiting four years for the court to act—leading to a decision to remove the case from the roll in 2008—they were precursors in thinking of mobilizing European human rights law, and in particular the ECHR, to challenge the SFT's endorsement of the CAS. Because the seat of the CAS is in Lausanne, and the ICAS is a Swiss foundation, its awards can only be challenged before the SFT, so it is Switzerland, as a signatory of the ECHR, which is always the state defendant in cases involving the CAS and its awards. In recent years, the ECtHR has addressed a number of judgments and decisions

[96] The first challenge was submitted by Larisa Lazutina and Olga Danilova in November 2003, see *Lazutina and Danilova v. Switzerland* Appl No 38250/03 (ECtHR, 3 July 2008).
[97] 4P.267/2002, 27 May 2003.
[98] *Lazutina and Danilova v. Switzerland* Appl No 38250/03 (ECtHR, 3 July 2008).

concerning the CAS,[99] which have set a new framework for the review of the work of sports arbitrators in light of the ECHR.

3.1 *The Road to Strasbourg: Switzerland's Responsibility for the CAS*

The CAS is managed by the ICAS, a Swiss foundation; it is therefore not a public body within the Swiss state or an organization resulting from an international agreement. This raises an important legal question, which the ECtHR had to resolve from the outset, which is whether the international responsibility of Switzerland could be engaged over human rights violations stemming from the operation of a private arbitral tribunal. In *Mutu and Pechstein*, the ECtHR answered this question positively, justifying this by pointing at the jurisdiction of the SFT in reviewing CAS awards, and more specifically in "giving the relevant awards force of law in the Swiss legal order".[100] Accordingly, the Court concluded that "the impugned acts or omissions [of the SFT] are thus capable of engaging the responsibility of the respondent State under the Convention".[101] In particular, the ECtHR "has jurisdiction ratione personae to examine the applicants' complaints as to the acts and omissions of the CAS that were validated by the Federal Court".[102] The latter holding implies that the SFT's (almost systematic) condoning of CAS awards is sufficient to trigger the competence of the ECtHR vis-à-vis Switzerland in cases in which it is alleged that a CAS award or the process before the CAS is incompatible with the ECHR.

Thus, the ECHR becomes relevant at the CAS through the 'Midas touch' of the Swiss court, which offers the necessary backing to ensure the existence of the CAS and the finality of its awards.[103] This approach to the competence of the ECtHR towards CAS awards has been maintained in all cases decided by the Court since.[104] Further, in the recent *Semenya* ruling, the ECtHR "saw no reason to depart from its previous findings in other cases related to sports arbitration", and insisted that,

[99] *Mutu and Pechstein v. Switzerland* Appl No 40575/10 and 67474/10 (ECtHR, 2 October 2018); *Bakker v. Switzerland* Appl No 7198/07 (ECtHR, 3 September 2019); *Platini v. Switzerland* Appl No 526/18 (ECtHR, 11 February 2020); *Ali Riza v. Switzerland* Appl No 74989/11 (ECtHR, 13 July 2021); *Semenya v. Switzerland* Appl No 10934/21 (ECtHR, 11 July 2023).

[100] *Mutu and Pechstein v. Switzerland* Appl No 40575/10 and 67474/10 (ECtHR, 2 October 2018), para. 66.

[101] Ibid., para. 67.

[102] Ibid.

[103] On the central role of Switzerland in the operation of the CAS, see Duval (2024).

[104] *Bakker v. Switzerland* Appl No 7198/07 (ECtHR, 3 September 2019), paras 28–29 and *Platini v. Switzerland* Appl No 526/18 (ECtHR, 11 February 2020), paras 36–38.

> [t]he fact that the IAAF was a Monegasque private-law association with its seat in Monaco, and not a Swiss private-law association (like FIFA – Platini v. Switzerland (dec.), and the ISU – Mutu and Pechstein v. Switzerland) made no difference as regards the Court's jurisdiction ratione personae and loci, especially since [the Court's] examination would focus on the proceedings before the CAS and the Federal Court.[105]

In its response to an argument raised by the Swiss government based on the limited scope of review of the SFT in the context of international awards, the ECtHR pointed out that even within such a limited scope the SFT was considering rights protected under the ECHR.[106] Moreover, it clearly distinguished the situation of the CAS from two previous cases in which the ECtHR had denied its competence *rationae personae*, involving the Andorran courts and the International Criminal Tribunal for the Former Yugoslavia (ICTY), emphasizing the fact that in both cases the national courts of the signatories had no involvement in reviewing the decisions issued by these courts.[107] Finally, and most importantly, the ECtHR stressed that,

> the only remedy available to her [Caster Semenya] had been a request for arbitration to the CAS, followed by an appeal against the refusal of arbitration to the Federal Court [. . .] if the Court were to find that it did not have jurisdiction to examine this type of application, it would risk barring access to the Court to an entire category of individuals, that of female athletes, which would not be in keeping with the spirit, object and purpose of the Convention.[108]

In spite of a dissenting opinion of three of the seven judges challenging the basis for jurisdiction of the ECtHR – and subject to a different evaluation by the Grand Chamber in the referral currently pending – the *Semenya* judgement should put to rest any resistance that Switzerland may oppose to the competence *rationae personae* of the ECtHR in cases involving the CAS. While the ECtHR has shown its willingness to embrace the advantages of a single global judicial institution to resolve transnational sporting disputes, finding it necessary to maintain the coherence and uniformity of the transnational governance and regulation of sport,[109] it is also willing to draw on the lack of alternatives to the CAS to justify the need to ensure that it is not used to bypass the guarantees afforded by the ECHR and the competence of the Court.

If this position is endorsed by the Grand Chamber, the specter of an application to the ECtHR will always loom over CAS arbitrators and SFT judges.[110] Yet as will be discussed in the next section, the severity of this threat depends on the parties

---

[105] *Semenya v. Switzerland* Appl No 10934/21 (ECtHR, 11 July 2023), para. 107.

[106] Ibid., para. 108.

[107] Ibid., paras 109–110.

[108] Ibid., para. 111.

[109] *Semenya v. Switzerland* Appl No 10934/21 (ECtHR, 11 July 2023), para. 111 and *Mutu and Pechstein v. Switzerland* Appl No 40575/10 and 67474/10 (ECtHR, 2 October 2018), para. 98 ['Recourse to a single and specialised international arbitral tribunal facilitates a certain procedural uniformity and strengthens legal certainty; all the more so where the awards of that tribunal may be appealed against before the supreme court of a single country, in this case the Swiss Federal Court, whose ruling is final.'].

[110] See Shinohara (2022).

involved and the issues raised in each case. In any event, future applicants will need to invoke the application of the ECHR before the CAS and the SFT in order to lodge an application before the ECtHR.[111]

3.2 *Assessing the Compatibility of CAS Proceedings with the ECHR: The Mutu and Pechstein Judgment*

The resolution of the essential preliminary question of the competence of the ECtHR to entertain applications against Switzerland in matters concerning CAS awards has enabled the Strasbourg judges to weigh in on the compatibility of CAS arbitration with the ECHR. In the *Mutu and Pechstein* judgment,[112] the Court had to consider whether CAS proceedings were compatible with Article 6(1) ECHR. This institutional question was already at the heart of the first application involving the CAS, lodged by Larisa Lazutina and Olga Danilova.[113] Yet the application was ultimately withdrawn in October 2007, and the question of the compatibility of the CAS itself with Article 6(1) ECHR would only be answered a decade later.

The preliminary issue raised in the *Mutu and Pechstein* case was whether CAS proceedings should be considered of a criminal or civil nature. While it was common ground to regard the contractual dispute between Adrian Mutu and his football club as a civil dispute, the question whether an anti-doping disciplinary sanction would amount to a criminal or civil matter was less clear. Ultimately, the Court considered that the latter involved "a disciplinary procedure before the professional bodies and in the context of which the right to carry on an occupation is at stake", and, therefore, that "there is no doubt as to the 'civil' nature of the rights in question".[114] Accordingly, even in disciplinary proceedings, the ECHR compatibility of the arbitral process must be assessed on the basis of Article 6(1) ECHR.

3.2.1 The CAS Arbitration Clause as an Insufficient Waiver of the Safeguards of Article 6(1) ECHR

In its *Mutu and Pechstein* judgment, the ECtHR had to decide whether the applicants' acceptance of the jurisdiction of the CAS constituted a valid waiver of the

[111] See Article 35 ECHR. This admissibility requirement is interpreted relatively loosely by the Court, as exemplified by its Platini decision in which Platini had failed to invoke Article 8 ECHR before the SFT. In its Decision, the Court was satisfied by Platini's reference in his appeal to the SFT to his Personality Rights under the Swiss Civil Code (see Sect. 1 above) and more generally to his economic freedom, see *Platini v. Switzerland* Appl No 526/18 (ECtHR, 11 February 2020), para. 51.

[112] Much has been written already on this ruling, see Maisonneuve (2019).

[113] *Lazutina and Danilova v. Switzerland* Appl No 38250/03 (ECtHR, 3 July 2008).

[114] *Mutu and Pechstein v. Switzerland* Appl No 40575/10 and 67474/10 (ECtHR, 2 October 2018).

safeguards provided by Article 6(1) ECHR, as argued by Switzerland. In other words: is Article 6(1) ECHR applicable at all to CAS proceedings, or have the applicants validly waived their rights under this provision through their decisions to appeal to the CAS? In order to answer this question, the Court argued that it had to "determine whether that acceptance was the result of a 'free, lawful and unequivocal' choice".[115] The judgment pointed out that Claudia Pechstein had to choose "between accepting the arbitration clause and thus earning her living by practising her sport professionally, or not accepting it and being obliged to refrain completely from earning a living from her sport at that level".[116] Accordingly, "[h]aving regard to the restriction that non-acceptance of the arbitration clause would have entailed for her professional life, it cannot be asserted that she had accepted that clause freely and unequivocally".[117] Hence, "the acceptance of CAS jurisdiction by the second applicant [Claudia Pechstein] must be regarded as 'compulsory' arbitration",[118] and the CAS proceedings "therefore had to afford the safeguards secured by Article 6 § 1 of the Convention".[119]

Regarding Adrian Mutu, however, the Court came to the conclusion that he had freely committed to the CAS arbitration clause included in his labour contract, as he could not show that he was, like Claudia Pechstein, deprived of any choice in terms of the content of his contract in order to pursue a career as a professional football player.[120] However, the judges did not consider his choice unequivocal, as Mutu had challenged one of the arbitrators during the proceedings;[121] he could, therefore, also rely on the safeguards of Article 6(1) ECHR. By emphasizing in the Pechstein situation the forced nature of CAS arbitration, the Strasbourg judges denied Switzerland the ability to invoke the consensual basis of the jurisdiction of the CAS to limit the applicability of Article 6(1) ECHR. Instead, the CAS must fully abide by the due process safeguards offered by this provision. In particular, it must be an independent and impartial institution and must provide the opportunity for the publicity of CAS hearings.

3.2.2 The Independence and Impartiality of the CAS

In *Mutu and Pechstein*, the Strasbourg judges considered first whether the CAS was sufficiently independent and impartial as required under Article 6(1) ECHR. In particular, Pechstein challenged unsuccessfully the independence of the CAS from

[115] *Mutu and Pechstein v. Switzerland* Appl No 40575/10 and 67474/10 (ECtHR, 2 October 2018), para. 103.
[116] Ibid., para. 113.
[117] Ibid., para. 114.
[118] Ibid., para. 115.
[119] Ibid.
[120] Ibid., para. 118–120.
[121] Ibid., para. 122.

the SGBs, especially the members of the Olympic Movement. First, the ECtHR brushed aside the claim that the financing of the CAS, which is mostly provided by the Olympic Movement, would taint its independence. Indeed, the ruling concluded that by analogy to national courts, "the CAS cannot be said to lack independence and impartiality solely on account of its financing arrangements".[122]

The Court also rejected Pechstein's arguments related to the selection process of arbitrators at the CAS, which she considered to be structurally imbalanced in favor of the federations.[123] The judges recognized that the process was largely at the discretion of the ICAS, acknowledging "the existence of a certain link between the ICAS and organisations that might be involved in disputes with athletes before the CAS".[124] Furthermore, the judgment also noted the discretionary power of the ICAS on the selection and removal of arbitrators.[125] Yet the ECtHR argued that Pechstein failed to adduce "any factual evidence such as to cast any general doubt on the independence and impartiality of [the CAS] arbitrators", or the three members of the Panel that decided her case.[126] Thus, while the Court declared itself "prepared to acknowledge that the organisations which were likely to be involved in disputes with athletes before the CAS had real influence over the mechanism for appointing arbitrators", it refused to

> conclude that, solely on account of this influence, the list of arbitrators, or even a majority thereof, was composed of arbitrators who could not be regarded as independent and impartial, on an individual basis, whether objectively or subjectively, *vis-à-vis* those organisations.
>
> In the Court's view, therefore, there are insufficient grounds for it to reject the settled case-law of the Federal Court to the effect that the system of the list of arbitrators meets the constitutional requirements of independence and impartiality applicable to arbitral tribunals, and that the CAS, when operating as an appellate body external to international federations, is similar to a judicial authority independent of the parties. [127]

The Court also rejected Pechstein's attempt to argue that the power to make formal rectifications to the arbitral award of the CAS Secretary General (now Director

[122] Ibid., para. 151. This view is strengthened in *Ali Riza and others v Turkey* Appl No 30226/10. 5506/16 (ECtHR, 28 January 2020), para. 214 ['The Court reiterates that in *Mutu and Pechstein*, it found that, by making an analogy with the national courts which are always financed by the State budget, the CAS cannot be said to lack independence and impartiality solely on account its financial arrangements (cited above, § 151). In the present case, the Court sees no reason to depart from its findings in *Mutu and Pechstein*. The fact that members of the Arbitration Committee receive remuneration for each deliberation they attend and have their expenses reimbursed by the executive body of the TFF, the Board of Directors, is not in and of itself sufficient to conclude that the Arbitration Committee lacks independence and impartiality.'].

[123] *Mutu and Pechstein v. Switzerland* Appl No 40575/10 and 67474/10 (ECtHR, 2 October 2018), para. 152–156.

[124] Ibid., para. 154.

[125] Ibid., para. 155.

[126] Ibid., para. 157.

[127] Ibid.

General) was damaging the independence of the CAS due to a lack of evidence that such power was used in her case.[128]

The ECtHR's decision to endorse the structural independence of the CAS from the SGBs of the Olympic Movement is a consequential one, especially in the context of a compulsory arbitration system. It allows the CAS to continue to operate in its current institutional structure. In fact, this decision was already invoked by a number of courts at the national and European level in support of the CAS.[129] The ECtHR itself has systematically referred to it in its recent rulings involving the CAS.[130] Nonetheless, this conclusion is not uncontroversial, as illustrated by the strongly argued dissent by Judge Keller and Serghides under the decision. Their doubts regarding the independence of the CAS are supported by numerous authors and grounded on a number of institutional features of the CAS that point at it being captured (or at least at risk of appearing as captured) by the Olympic Movement.[131]

Finally, it is notable that in its appraisal of the structural independence of the CAS, the ECtHR did not consider the central role of the President of the Appeal Division in the nomination process of the President of a Panel (or Sole Arbitrator) in appeal arbitration cases—those involving challenges to decisions rendered by the SGBs, which constitute an overwhelming share of the CAS caseload and generally entail a forced arbitration. This might offer a future opening for claimants aiming to challenge anew the independence of the CAS before the ECtHR. In fact, in its *Ali Riza* judgment the Court already showed its willingness to challenge the independence of an arbitral body in the sporting context, specifically when the nomination process of the arbitrators is susceptible of leading the parties to believe that they are systematically biased.[132]

3.2.3 The Publicity of CAS Hearings

The *Mutu and Pechstein* judgment is important because it affirmed the fact that a CAS arbitration clause did not constitute a valid waiver of the safeguards of Article 6(1) ECHR. The impact of this finding was immediately demonstrated insofar as the publicity of CAS hearings is concerned. During the CAS proceedings, Claudia Pechstein had requested that her hearing be held in public; this request was denied

---

[128] Ibid., para. 158.

[129] See for example, CJEU, *International Skating Union v European Commission*, T-93/18, 16 December 2020, para. 156.

[130] *Platini v. Switzerland* Appl No 526/18 (ECtHR, 11 February 2020), para. 65 and *Semenya v. Switzerland* Appl No 10934/21 (ECtHR, 11 July 2023), para. 172.

[131] See Downie (2011), Vaitiekunas (2014), Hewitt (2014), Frumer (2016), Lindholm (2021). See as well the recent report by Grit Hartman, Tipping the scales of justice—The sport and its "supreme court", Play The Game, November 2021, available at https://www.playthegame.org/media/fmxi0jgx/tipping-the-scales-of-justice-the-sport-and-its-supreme-court.pdf.

[132] *Ali Riza and others v Turkey* Appl No 30226/10 and 5506/16 (ECtHR, 28 January 2020), paras 219-220. On this point, see the case notes by Frumer (2020) and Gemalmaz (2019).

by the CAS panel and the denial later endorsed by the SFT. In contrast, the Strasbourg Court found,

> that the questions arising in the impugned proceedings – as to whether it was justified for the second applicant to have been penalised for doping, and for the resolution of which the CAS heard testimony from numerous experts – rendered it necessary to hold a hearing under public scrutiny.[133]

In particular, it noted that "the facts were disputed and the sanction imposed on the applicant carried a degree of stigma and was likely to adversely affect her professional honour and reputation".[134] The Court therefore reached the conclusion that "there has been a violation of Article 6 § 1 of the Convention on account of the fact that the proceedings before the CAS were not held in public".[135]

Unlike with the independence of the CAS, the ECtHR's intervention triggered limited institutional changes at the CAS. Firstly, on the question of the publicity of hearings, through the introduction of a specific provision to this effect for appeal arbitration,[136] even though the CAS and the SFT have interpreted this requirement narrowly.[137] Secondly, and more broadly, the intervention of the ECtHR on this issue has likely contributed to greater administrative transparency at the CAS, with the release of an Annual Report since the end of 2021 that includes relevant information on the financial situation of the CAS and its caseload. Undoubtedly, the Strasbourg judges have influenced, through their application of Article 6(1) ECHR to the CAS, its institutional structure and thus the organization of the transnational judicial system of the Olympic Movement.

3.3 Assessing the Compatibility of CAS Awards with the ECHR: The Platini and Semenya Cases

The ECtHR's judgment in Mutu and Pechstein was focused on the compatibility of the CAS as an institution with the requirements of the ECHR, but the role of the Court vis-à-vis the CAS does not stop at the institutional level. In recent years, the Court has been called upon in a number of cases to decide whether CAS awards, and

---

[133] *Mutu and Pechstein v. Switzerland* Appl No 40575/10 and 67474/10 (ECtHR, 2 October 2018), para. 182.

[134] Ibid.

[135] Ibid., para.183.

[136] Art. R57 CAS Code: "[. . .] At the request of a physical person who is party to the proceedings, a public hearing should be held if the matter is of a disciplinary nature. Such request may however be denied in the interest of morals, public order, national security, where the interests of minors or the protection of the private life of the parties so require, where publicity would prejudice the interests of justice, where the proceedings are exclusively related to questions of law or where a hearing held in first instance was already public. [. . .]".

[137] See Duval (2020b).

their endorsement by the SFT, had violated the substantial provisions of the ECHR.[138] The central threshold for engaging the responsibility of Switzerland in this regard has been whether adequate institutional and procedural safeguards were provided at the CAS and the SFT to protect the rights of the applicants.[139] In the *Platini* decision, the ECtHR found that such safeguards were indeed present, while in *Semenya* it reached the opposite conclusion. Of note, the judgment in *Semenya* has been referred by Switzerland to the Grand Chamber, so that the ruling has not yet become final.

3.3.1 The Platini Decision: Granting Switzerland a Broad Margin of Appreciation in Its Review of CAS Awards

Michel Platini, the former French football star and UEFA and FIFA executive, contested the ECHR compatibility of the CAS award and SFT judgment upholding in part a decision of the FIFA Ethics Committee to exclude him from football activities.[140] The ECtHR recognized that the sanction, despite originating in Platini's professional life, had reached the threshold of severity required to engage Article 8 ECHR.[141] The judges noted the impact of the ban on Platini's ability to earn a living, especially due to FIFA's monopoly over professional football; its interference with Platini's "possibility of establishing and developing social relations with others", in light of the breadth of the activities covered by FIFA's sanction; and the negative reputational impact (stigmatization) Platini suffered.[142] In the decision, the Court then set the threshold for future assessments of the compatibility of CAS awards with the ECHR; as the CAS award did not constitute a state measure, it was examined in terms of the Swiss state's positive obligations and margin of appreciation.[143]

Before engaging in its assessment, the Court noted the specificity of the career path chosen by Platini as a football professional, stressing that while such a career brought with it certain privileges and advantages, it also came with some contractual

[138] See *Platini v. Switzerland* Appl No 526/18 (ECtHR, 11 February 2020), and *Semenya v. Switzerland* Appl No 10934/21 (ECtHR, 11 July 2023). The Valcke case (Appl No 57476/19) remains pending at the time of writing.

[139] *Platini v. Switzerland* Appl No 526/18 (ECtHR, 11 February 2020), para. 62 ['Il convient, en particulier, de vérifier si le requérant disposait en l'espèce des garanties institutionnelles et procédurales suffisantes, soit un système de juridictions devant lesquelles il a pu faire valoir ses griefs, et si celles-ci ont rendu des décisions dûment motivées et tenant compte de la jurisprudence de la Cour (*Obst*, précité, §§ 45-46).'].

[140] See CAS 2016/A/4474 Michel Platini c. Fédération Internationale de Football Association, Award of 16 September 2016. For a detailed commentary of the CAS award, see Beffa (2017) and of the ECtHR judgment, see Rietiker (2022).

[141] *Platini v. Switzerland* Appl No 526/18 (ECtHR, 11 February 2020), para. 58.

[142] Ibid., para. 57.

[143] Ibid., para. 60.

limitations on individual rights, which are acceptable if freely consented to.[144] Furthermore, the judges stressed that contrary to Claudia Pechstein, Platini did not claim that he was forced to consent to CAS arbitration. Instead, he expressly accepted the competence of the CAS by signing its procedural order.[145]

The ECtHR's assessment of the compliance of Switzerland with its positive obligations under the ECHR focused primarily on the coherence of the CAS award and the quality of the justifications advanced to support the arbitrators' decision. In this regard, the judges noted that the CAS had responded to the applicant's complaints in an "exhaustive and comprehensive manner", and that it delivered "a sufficiently detailed award" and "convincingly weighed up the interests at stake".[146] Additionally, the ECtHR found that the CAS had considered that the four-year ban was proportionate to the aim pursued, which was to impose a sufficiently harsh (and deterrent) sanction for the breach of the FIFA Code of Ethics, and to restore the reputation of football and FIFA.[147] It was also of the view that Platini's personal antecedents, his "outstanding services to football", had not been overlooked by the arbitrators.[148] Instead, the CAS arbitrators have given "due regard to the applicant's senior position in the highest football bodies at the time of the offences of which he stood accused, and also to his lack of remorse".[149]

Regarding the review exercised by the SFT, the Strasbourg judges considered that the Swiss court had "upheld the CAS award on the basis of plausible and convincing reasoning".[150] The judgement specifically highlighted the fact that the SFT had not considered the duration of the ban imposed to be manifestly excessive and had concluded that the CAS had not disregarded any material circumstance in deciding on that duration.[151] Hence, the ECtHR ruled that Platini had "been afforded adequate institutional and procedural safeguards through a system of adjudicatory organs, first private bodies then a State court, which had properly weighed up the interests at stake and had addressed all of the applicant's complaints in duly reasoned decisions".[152] Moreover, it held that the decisions of the CAS and the SFT "did not appear arbitrary or manifestly unreasonable, and pursued not only the legitimate aim of punishing breaches of the relevant rules by a high-ranking official of FIFA, but

[144] Ibid., para. 63 ['Si une telle carrière offre sans doute de nombreux privilèges et avantages, elle implique en même temps la renonciation de certains droits (voir, dans ce sens, *Fernández Martínez*, précité, §§ 134–135). De telles limitations contractuelles sont acceptables au regard de la Convention lorsqu'elles sont librement consenties (*ibidem*, § 135).'].

[145] *Platini v. Switzerland* Appl No 526/18 (ECtHR, 11 February 2020), para. 63.

[146] Ibid. 66.

[147] Ibid., para. 67.

[148] Ibid.

[149] Ibid.

[150] Ibid., para. 69.

[151] Ibid.

[152] Ibid., para. 70.

also the general-interest aim of restoring the reputation of football and of FIFA".[153] Finally, the Decision stressed the "broad margin of appreciation"[154] afforded to Switzerland, to come to the conclusion that the state had not failed to fulfil its positive obligations.

Platini points to the ECtHR's reluctance to engage in a detailed review of the substance of a CAS award, at least when Article 8 ECHR is involved. In *Platini*, the Strasbourg judges focused on a procedural check, highlighting the general coherence of the reasoning used in the award, as well as its sheer length. The final reference in the Decision to standards such as arbitrariness or the manifest unreasonableness of the contested decisions seems to support the impression that the ECtHR was unwilling to intervene in cases involving the CAS unless the challenged CAS or SFT decisions are manifestly deficient. Moreover, unlike in the *Semenya* judgment discussed in the next section, in *Platini* the judges did not consider whether the CAS or the SFT had referred to the ECHR, and relied on the ECtHR's jurisprudence in their decisions.

3.3.2 The Semenya Judgment: Limiting the Scope of Switzerland's Margin of Appreciation in Cases of Discrimination

The *Semenya* judgement, rendered by the Third Section/Chamber of the ECtHR on 11 July 2023 marks a clear departure from the deferent approach to the substantial review of CAS awards adopted in the *Platini* decision. The case is a controversial *cause célèbre* involving the regulations imposed by World Athletics to regulate the participation of athletes with differences of sex development (DSD) in its competitions.[155] In particular, the DSD Regulations led to the ineligibility of Caster Semenya, the dominant South African female runner and Olympic Gold medalist, from competing on her favorite distance, the 400m.

In its judgment, the Strasbourg Court recognized that the DSD Regulations were affecting the private life of Caster Semenya.[156] In particular, it deemed that the findings of the CAS regarding Caster Semenya's belonging to the female category for the purpose of athletics competitions were susceptible to directly affect her personal identity, and fell under the scope of Article 8 ECHR. Furthermore, the judges held that her personal autonomy was limited due to the dilemma she faced:

> either she took the medication, which was likely to cause her physical and mental harm, in order to decrease her testosterone level and to be able to practise her profession, or she

---

[153] Ibid.

[154] Ibid.

[155] There is an extensive literature on the case, see for example: Holzer (2020), Krech (2021), Winkler and Gilleri (2021); Leibee (2022), Cooper (2023).

[156] *Semenya v. Switzerland* Appl No 10934/21 (ECtHR, 11 July 2023), paras 121–127.

> refused to take it, with the result that she would have to renounce her right to compete in events of her choosing, and therefore her right to practise her profession.[157]

Accordingly, both Semenya's right to practice her profession and her right to protection from physical and mental harm were affected by the DSD Regulations, and their endorsement by the CAS, and thus the case fell within the ambit of Article 8 ECHR.[158] Moreover, the DSD Regulations "are also likely to have major 'consequences' for the enjoyment by the applicant of her right to respect for her private life, in particular, her reputation, private sphere and dignity".[159] Caster Semenya could invoke Article 8 ECHR to trigger the application of Article 14 ECHR.[160]

As the DSD Regulations stemmed from a Monégasque private-law association, the ECtHR had to determine whether Switzerland "was required, and if so to what extent, to protect the applicant from any discriminatory treatment [...] arising from the adoption of the DSD Regulations, which the CAS and the Federal Spreme Court held to be necessary, reasonable, proportionate and non-arbitrary".[161] The main question was whether the applicant had

> sufficient institutional and procedural safeguards available to her, in the form of a system of courts to which she could submit her complaints, in particular her complaint under Article 14, and whether those courts had delivered reasoned decisions which took account of the Court's case-law.[162]

In conducting this evaluation, the Court drew a clear difference between Semenya's situation and Platini's. It stressed that unlike the latter, Semenya had no real alternative to consenting to a CAS arbitration clause if she wished to pursue a professional career in athletics.[163] Moreover, the Court noted that differences of treatment based exclusively on sexual characteristics or his/her status as an intersex person required "very weighty reasons", "particularly serious reasons" or "particularly weighty and convincing reasons" in order to be justified.[164] Where "a particularly important facet of an individual's existence or identity is at stake", the discretion of the state is restricted.[165]

The ECtHR then assessed the CAS award and its reasoning. While the judges acknowledged the extent of the proceedings before the CAS and the many experts heard, they emphasized the fact that the CAS had failed to consider the relevance of Article 14 ECHR or the case-law of the ECtHR in its lengthy award.[166] Regarding

---

[157] Ibid., para. 124.

[158] Ibid.

[159] Ibid., para. 125.

[160] Ibid., para. 127.

[161] Ibid., para. 165.

[162] Ibid., para. 166.

[163] Ibid., para. 167.

[164] *Semenya v. Switzerland* Appl No 10934/21 (ECtHR, 11 July 2023), para.169.

[165] Ibid.

[166] *Semenya v. Switzerland* Appl No 10934/21 (ECtHR, 11 July 2023), para. 174.

the role of the SFT, the ECtHR noted its limited power of review in the present case.[167] Importantly, it found that such a limited scope of review is problematic in the area of sports arbitration, in which individuals face very powerful sports organizations and are not freely consenting to arbitration.[168] In particular, the majority "sees no reason why professional athletes should be afforded a lesser legal protection than that afforded to people practising a more conventional profession".[169] The judges also noted some serious scientific doubts expressed by the CAS on a variety of points, which were not lifted by the SFT, and considered that both the CAS and the SFT had failed to conduct an in-depth assessment of the motives supporting the objective and reasonable justification underpinning the Regulations.[170] Furthermore, regarding the potential side effects of the medication imposed on Caster Semenya in order to comply with the DSD Regulations, the judgment criticized the fact that the SFT simply assumed that she had a real choice between medicating or giving up her profession, and did not address her personal dilemma.[171] This resulted in the Court concluding that in order to comply with the Convention, the SFT should have considered the issue of the side effects much more seriously.[172]

Finally, the judgment criticized the SFT for failing to consider that the prohibition of discrimination by private entities would fall under the notion of public policy, and for refusing to assess the compatibility of the DSD Regulations with the Swiss Constitution and the European Convention.[173] Regarding the latter point, it must be highlighted that in reality the SFT *did* look into the merits of the arguments raised by *Semenya* and found no unlawful discrimination *in casu*.[174] Nevertheless, the Court concluded that the SFT had failed to satisfy the requirements of its jurisprudence, which imposes on States Parties to the Convention a duty to prevent and remedy effectively discriminatory acts, even when they emanate from private individuals or entities.[175]

Contrary to the *Platini* decision, the ECtHR came to the conclusion that Switzerland had overstepped the narrow margin of appreciation afforded to it in the present case by failing to provide a thorough institutional and procedural review of the CAS award.[176] Hence, the Strasbourg judges were "unable to find that the application of the DSD Regulations to the applicant's case could be considered a measure that was objective and proportionate to the aim pursued".[177] The same considerations as those

---

[167] Ibid., para. 175.
[168] Ibid., para. 177.
[169] Ibid., para. 178.
[170] Ibid., paras 179–184.
[171] Ibid., para. 187.
[172] Ibid., para. 190.
[173] Ibid., para. 194.
[174] SFT, 4A_248/2019, 25 August 2020, para. 9.4.
[175] *Semenya v. Switzerland* Appl No 10934/21 (ECtHR, 11 July 2023), para. 195.
[176] Ibid., para. 200.
[177] *Semenya v. Switzerland* Appl No 10934/21 (ECtHR, 11 July 2023), para. 201.

raised in the framework of the assessment of Article 8 and 14 ECHR led to the finding that Article 13 ECHR, enshrining the right to an effective remedy, had been violated for a lack of sufficient institutional and procedural safeguards afforded to Caster Semenya. The *Semenya* judgment refines the position of the ECtHR regarding the positive obligations of Switzerland in the context of CAS awards and the extent of its margin of appreciation in the review of such cases. First, it makes an important distinction between individuals, such as Platini, who have a certain latitude in subjecting themselves to the rules of the SGBs and the CAS, and international athletes who can only continue to exercise their sport professionally if they subject themselves to those same Regulations and arbitral clauses, such as Caster Semenya (or Claudia Pechstein).

In *Platini*, Switzerland enjoyed a wider margin of appreciation and the ECtHR's review of the quality of the CAS and SFT's reasoning was less meticulous. Contrariwise, in *Semenya*, the Strasbourg judges lambasted both the CAS and the SFT for failing to engage in a thorough balancing of the interests at play in light of the ECtHR's jurisprudence. The difference in approach is also linked to the issue at the heart of the controversial CAS awards. Unlike in *Platini*, where the issue was affecting solely the right to privacy enshrined in Article 8 ECHR, *Semenya* turned on a matter involving a discrimination on the basis of sexual characteristics. In the latter instance, the Court concluded that Switzerland enjoyed a narrow margin of appreciation and reviewed to a much more exacting standard the compatibility of the reasoning of both the CAS and the SFT with the ECHR's requirements.

In sum, the ECtHR's intensity of review of the compatibility of CAS awards with the ECHR, and of the compliance of the SFT's review of the awards with Switzerland's positive obligations stemming from the Convention, will vary depending on the complainants involved as well as the ECHR rights interfered with. Unless the Grand Chamber rules otherwise, Switzerland will not, unlike what might have been thought after the *Platini* case, systematically enjoy a wide margin of appreciation when the SFT reviews CAS awards. Instead the Swiss court, and therefore the CAS itself, will have to grapple in a much more detailed and systematic way with the compliance of the transnational regulations of sport with European human rights law.

4 Conclusion

The increasing importance of the CAS as the central judicial body that resolves disputes in international sports has gone hand in hand with increasing attention on its effects on human rights; with great judicial power has come great(er) human rights responsibility. This chapter has shown how the SFT progressively integrated human rights considerations in their review of the CAS and its awards. While it has proven reluctant to consider a violation of the ECHR as a self-standing ground in order to challenge CAS awards, it has increasingly considered human rights in its assessment of the compatibility of an award with Swiss public policy. This has been particularly true in recent years, a dynamic most likely driven by the latest decisions of the ECtHR. Yet, until now, this human rights control through the backdoor of Swiss public policy has not led to many awards being overturned. In other words, from the SFT's point of view, the CAS and its awards have not posed evident human rights problems.

The ECtHR does not seem to share this optimistic point of view regarding the human rights alignment of the CAS. While its first intervention in matters involving the CAS only dates back five years to the *Mutu and Pechstein* judgment, it has already upended the SFT's narrow interpretation of the application of European human rights law to the CAS. First by considering CAS arbitration, at least in appeal proceedings involving disciplinary cases, as forced arbitration, which must, therefore, fully comply with the strictures of Article 6(1) ECHR. Though the ECtHR endorsed the independence of the CAS, it did conclude as well that CAS's habit of deciding cases behind closed doors, even in the face of a request for a public hearing from one of the parties, was incompliant with the ECHR and should have been deemed as such by the SFT. Interestingly, a few years before, the CAS itself had considered the same question and found the practice fully compatible with the ECHR.[178] On the compatibility of the substance of CAS awards with the ECHR, the Court's first decision in the *Platini* case was rather deferent to the CAS and the SFT's assessment, but it became more critical in its latest *Semenya* judgment. It might be prudent not to read too much into these diametrically opposed outcomes in light of the context-sensitivity of the assessment in two cases involving different fact-patterns, individuals and rights. Nonetheless, the *Semenya* judgment is a stark reminder that the Strasbourg judges are not willing to sign a blank check to the CAS and the SFT.

In the future, CAS arbitrators and Swiss judges will have to carefully consider claims based on the ECHR and the jurisprudence of the ECtHR if they wish to escape the shame of being blamed by the Strasbourg Court. In addition, the claimants will likely see greater benefits in mobilizing human rights arguments and harnessing human rights expertise when pleading before the CAS and the SFT. Ultimately, the CAS and the SFT will probably be able to adapt relatively quickly to the need to engage with the ECHR and its interpretation by the ECtHR. As matters stand, however, the SFT seems to demonstrate little eagerness to engage with the implications of the *Semenya* judgment until the Grand Chamber issues its ruling, as it recently made clear in a doping case.[179] It is, therefore, not a given that more vigorous engagement with the ECHR will dramatically change the CAS' reluctance

---

[178] CAS 2014/A/3561 & 3614, *International Association of Athletics Federation (IAAF) & World Anti-Doping Agency (WADA) v. Marta Domínguez Azpeleta & Real Federación Española de Atletismo (RFEA)*, award of 19 November 2015, para. 207.

[179] 4A_488/2023, 23 January 2024, para. 3 (our translation from French): "To the extent that the Applicant relies on the decision of the European Court of Human Rights (ECtHR) [. . .], and based thereon invokes a violation of Art. 13 ECtHR, one must point out that this ruling has been challenged before the Grand Chamber and therefore has not yet become final as per Art. 42 et seq. ECtHR. The related arguments are of no avail".

to interfere with the SGBs' decisions, and the SFT's habit to endorse CAS awards, but only time will tell.[180]

References

Beffa L (2017) CAS 2016/A/4474 *Michel Platini v. Fédération Internationale de Football Association*, Award of 9 May 2016. In: Duval A, Rigozzi A (eds) Yearbook of international sports arbitration 2016. Yearbook of international sports arbitration. T.M.C. Asser Press, The Hague

Cooper J (2023) Protecting human rights in sport: is the Court of Arbitration for Sport up to the task? A review of the decision in *Semenya v IAAF*. Int Sports Law J 23:151–175

Downie R (2011) Improving the performance of sport's ultimate umpire: reforming the governance of the Court of Arbitration for Sport. Melbourne J Int Law 12(2):315–344

Duval A (2015) The court of arbitration for sport and EU law: chronicle of an encounter. Maastricht J Eur Comp Law 22(2):224–255

Duval A (2020a) *Not in my name!* Claudia Pechstein and the post-consensual foundations of the court of arbitration for sport. In: Ruiz Fabri H, Nunes Chaib A, Venzke I, von Bogdandy A (eds) International judicial legitimacy. Nomos Verlag, Baden Baden, pp 169–202

Duval A (2020b) Time to go public? The need for transparency at the Court of Arbitration for Sport. In: Duval A, Rigozzi A (eds) Yearbook of international sports arbitration 2017. The Hague, T.M.C. Asser Press, pp 3–27

Duval A (2021) Seamstress of transnational law: how the court of arbitration for sport weaves the lex sportiva. In: Krisch N (ed) Entangled legalities beyond the state. Cambridge University Press, Cambridge, pp 260–288

Duval A (2022) Lost in translation? The European Convention on Human Rights at the court of arbitration for sport. Int Sports Law J 22:132–151

Duval A (2024) Embedded *Lex Sportiva*: the Swiss roots of transnational sports law and governance. In: Duval A, Kruger A, Lindholm J (eds) The European Roots of the Lex Sportiva. Hart Publishing

Frumer P (2016) L'arbirage sportif, la lutte contre le dopage et le respect des droits fondamentaux des sportifs professionnels: une incertitude peu glorieuse. Revue Trimestrielle Des Droits De L'homme 108:817–853

Frumer P (2020) Carton rouge pour l'arbitrage de la Fédération turque de football: (obs. sous Cour eur. dr. h., arrêt *Ali Rıza et autres c. Turquie*, 28 janvier 2020). Revue trimestrielle des droits de l'Homme 124:991–1010

Gemalmaz HB (2019) Applicability of human rights standards in Turkish football arbitration: the contribution of the European Court of Human Rights. Int Sports Law J 19:38–58

Hewitt M (2014) An unbalanced act: a criticism of how the court of arbitration for sport issues unjustly harsh sanctions by attempting to regulate doping in sport. Indiana J Glob Legal Stud 22(2):769–787

Holzer L (2020) What does it mean to be a woman in sports? An analysis of the Jurisprudence of the Court of Arbitration for Sport. Human Rights Law Rev 20(3):387–411

Krech M (2021) "Sport Sex" before the European Court of Human Rights. Völkerrechtsblog, 22.03.2021, https://doi.org/10.17176/20210322-151035-0

Leibee S (2022) Talking T at the European Court of Human Rights: the human rights case against testosterone restrictions for female athletes and how the sports community should respond. Transnl Law Contemp Probl 32:169–195

[180] Pointing at the importance of structural and institutional factors, rather than normative one, see Duval (2022).

Lindholm J (2021) A legit supreme court of world sports? The CAS(e) for reform. Int Sports Law J 21:1–5

Maisonneuve M (2017) Le tribunal arbitral du sport et les droits fondamentaux des athlètes. Revue des droits et liberté fondamentaux, n°09

Maisonneuve M (2019) Le Tribunal arbitral du sport et le droit au procès équitable: l'arbitrage bienveillant de la Cour européenne des droits de l'homme: (obs. sous Cour eur. dr. h., arrêt *Mutu et Pechstein c. Suisse*, 2 octobre 2018). Revue trimestrielle des droits de l'Homme 119:687–705. https://doi.org/10.3917/rtdh.119.0687

Rietiker D (2022) 9 Football-related corruption as a human rights issue: the case of Michel Platini v. Switzerland before the European Court of Human Rights (Inadmissible, 11 February 2020). In: Hague yearbook of international law. Brill | Nijhoff, Leiden, The Netherlands

Shinohara T (2022) Which states parties should be held responsible for the implementation of positive obligations under the ECHR in sports-related disputes? Int Sports Law J 22:332–342

Vaitiekunas A (2014) The court of arbitration for sport: law-making and the question of independence. Stämpfli Verlag, Berne

Winkler M, Gilleri G (2021) Of athletes, bodies, and rules: making sense of Caster Semenya. J Law Med Ethics 49(4):644–660

Antoine Duval is Senior Researcher at the Asser Institute in The Hague, where he coordinates the Asser International Sports Law Centre. He has widely published on the transnational regulation and governance of sports and, in particular, the Court of Arbitration for Sport.

Marjolaine Viret is a Swiss-qualified attorney at the Geneva bar, and a researcher in sport and health at the University of Lausanne Institute of Sport Sciences (Switzerland). Her practice includes assisting individuals and organizations of the sports sector in a range of regulatory and litigation matters, in particular before the Court of Arbitration for Sport and the Swiss Federal Tribunal. She is a lecturer for various academic programs and author of numerous publications in sports law, including the book "Evidence in Anti-Doping at the Intersection of Science & Law" (T.M.C Asser/Springer). Current research centers on the use of scientific evidence and expertise as a basis for policy-making and judiciary decisions in international sports.

Conceptualizing the Right to Sport: Why Should *Trivial* Participation in Sport Be Regarded as a Human Right?

Antonio Di Marco

Contents

Abstract Considering its extraordinary capacity to be a vehicle of rights, and to give meaning to reality, sport is among the most important *trivial* subjects in the world. Discriminated groups, which are denied (or substantially limited) access to the practice of sport, demand not only their right to participate in sporting activities but also the recognition of this claim as valid by society and public authorities. This chapter proposes the idea that expanding the catalogue of human rights, by including the right to sport, is supported by the existing body of international human rights law. It would reinforce the protection of human rights in sporting contexts by enhancing the unity of fragmented claims founded on a plurality of legal instruments. Taking into consideration the thesis that inclusive and non-discriminatory access to sporting activities would be an amalgamation of several treaty-based rights, the legal foundations of the right to sport are explained and evaluated. By verifying the legal relationship between access to sporting activities and sport's social functions, the beneficiaries of such a right are investigated, and the obligations for national and sporting authorities are explored. By arguing that the right to pursue personal development would play a central role, while the right to health and education would be complementary, this chapter strives to answer the essential ethical question of why the *trivial* participation in sport should be considered an

A. Di Marco (✉)
University of Strasbourg, Strasbourg, France
e-mail: a.dimarco@unistra.fr

V. Boillet et al. (eds.), *Sports and Human Rights*, Interdisciplinary Studies in Human Rights 10, https://doi.org/10.1007/978-3-031-56452-9_12

inherent right of the human being, cutting through the considerable confusion surrounding the right to sport.

1 Introduction: The Distinction Between Cultural Tool and Legitimate Claim

> When we call anything a person's right, we mean that he has a valid claim on society to protect him in the possession of it, either by the force of law, or by that of education and opinion. [. . .] To have a right, then, is, I conceive, to have something which society ought to defend me in the possession of. (Mill, *Utilitarianism*, 1861, 54)

To have a right means, theoretically, to "have a claim against someone whose recognition as valid is called for by some set of governing rules".[1] From this perspective, defining sport as a right is a complex task, since sport itself is of an ambiguous nature.[2] Considering that 'sport' as a concept includes a great variety of physical activities and actors, which in turn vary in relation to the social and economic context, it is not clear what exactly the *claim* is.[3] In addition, there is no consensus on the 'government regulations that recognize this right as valid'. According to Giummarra and Lubrano, for example, the claim to access sport is essentially founded on the right to health, and on the freedom of peaceful assembly and association; other fundamental rights are taken into account as complementary or supporting sources.[4] Latty and Maniatis, as well as Stelitano and Pensabene Lionti, have instead focused on the right to education.[5] Other authors looked at these fundamental rights through the prism of the rights of some vulnerable categories; Colliver and Doel-Mackaway pay attention to the children's right to play;[6] Weston considers the claim to access sport in the light of the right of people with disabilities to participate meaningfully in all aspects of society.[7] The right to sport appears to be an emblematic case of what we can refer to as an 'incompletely generalized agreement', in which there is no consensus on its foundations, although

---

[1] In these terms see, for instance: Feinberg (1970), pp. 243, 249, and 270; Brett (1997), p. 3; Campbell (2006); Hart (1961), p. 2.

[2] On the different definitions of sport see, for instance: Holowchak (2002), p. 16; Salardi (2019), p. 3.

[3] On the lack of consensus on sport definition see, in addition to the authors mentioned in the previous note: Burghardt (2011), pp. 9–10; Göncü and Vadeboncoeur (2017), p. 422; Tobin and Lansdown (2019), p. 1204.

[4] Giummarra (2012); Lubrano (2020), pp. 234–272.

[5] Maniatis (2017), pp. 178–191; Latty (2013), p. 1885; Stelitano (2011), pp. 205–221; Pensabene Lionti (2012), p. 415.

[6] Colliver and Doel-Mackaway (2021), pp. 566–587.

[7] Weston (2017), pp. 2–36.

there appears to be loose agreement on the recognition of some of its components.[8] Regarding sport as a right would be a controversial theoretical exercise, which could foster the traditional concern about an illegitimate and uncontrolled expansion of new human rights.[9] The protection of sportspeople's claims should therefore be tied to existing rights, which can be given a particular color according to the evolution of social needs.

Sport has traditionally been regarded as a cultural tool to promote a democratic society, rather than a legally enforceable right. The United Nations (UN) has underlined in several occasions that sport is "a tool of peace and sustainable development".[10] The Council of Europe (CoE) has habitually described sport as "a vehicle of rights",[11] and the European Union (EU) has regarded it as "a source of, and driver for active social inclusion".[12] Several authors have addressed the complex relation between sport and human rights, by highlighting that sport is essentially a *means* to guarantee other important rights;[13] while others have argued that the right to sport could not be regarded as a stand-alone right.[14] However, the International Olympic Committee (IOC) emphatically affirms that "the practice of sport is a human right";[15] and the International Charter of Physical Education, Physical Activity and Sport (ICPEPA), adopted by the UN Educational, Scientific and Cultural Organization (UNESCO), states that "every human being has a fundamental

[8]The reference is to the Cass Sunstein's theory of incomplete theorised and specified agreements, which relies on the idea that, in diverse societies, people may reach agreements about certain outcomes despite the fact that they disagree deeply on the foundations of such outcomes and that they can reversely agree on some basic principles without agreeing on their implementation. On this theory see: Sunstein (1995), p. 1736.

[9]On the traditional concern against proliferation, inflation, or dilution of human rights, able to erode the very idea of human rights, see, *inter alia*: Alston (1984), p. 607; Ignatieff (2001); Buchanan (2013); Posner (2015); Hannum (2016), pp. 409–451.

[10]United Nations General Assembly (UNGA), *Sport for development and peace: building a peaceful and better world through sport and the Olympic ideal*, A/RES/74/18 (2019); UNGA, *Sport as a means to promote education, health, development and peace*, A/RES/69/6 (2014); UNGA, *Promoting human rights through sport and the Olympic ideal*, A/RES/24/1 (2003).

[11]CoE, *Recommendation on the principles of good governance in sport*, CM/Rec (2005)8 (2005), at 1.

[12]In these terms see, for example: European Commission (EC), *White Paper on Sport*, COM(2007) 391 final (2007); European Parliament (EP), *Resolution on an integrated approach to Sport Policy: good governance, accessibility and integrity*, 2016/2143(INI) (2017); EP, *Resolution on the European dimension in sport*, 2011/2087(INI) (2012); EP, *Resolution on the role of sport in education*, 2007/2086(INI) (2007); Council of European Union (CoEU), *Conclusions on the role of sport as a source of and a driver for active social inclusion*, 2010/C 326/04 (2010).

[13]In these terms, in addition to the authors mentioned in the notes 4–7, Weatherill (2014), p. 245; Gardiner et al. (2009); Depré (2007), p. 453; Bastianon (2009), pp. 391–411.

[14]Ireland-Piper (2014), pp. 1–24.

[15]IOC, Olympic Charter, Fundamental Principles of Olympism, in force from 17 July 2020, point 4, at 11.

right to physical education, physical activity and sport".[16] The CoE, in turn, has recently revised the European Sport Charter (ESpC),[17] by introducing the principle that "all human beings have an inalienable right of access to sport".[18] The need to regard sport as a human right emerges from this recent activity.

The ancillary and functional nature of sport ends up blurring the traditional division between 'cultural tool' and 'legitimate claim'. The UN High Commissioner for Human Rights (OHCHR) notes, "while sport is often an instrument for promoting peace, development, solidarity and human rights, [it] is often characterised by inequality and discrimination within and across national borders".[19] Around the world ethnic and religious minorities,[20] persons with disabilities,[21] women,[22] and the LGBTQ+ community[23] are in many cases still *de facto* and *de jure* denied access to sport (or have severely limited access). These groups demand not only their right to participate in sporting activities, but also the recognition of this claim as valid by society and public authorities. Fragmented legitimate claims, potentially founded on a plurality of legal instruments, would converge in questioning the uncertain status of human rights in sport.[24] From this perspective, expanding the catalogue of human rights, by including the right to sport, could enhance sportspersons' protection. By introducing the universal principles of gender equality, non-discrimination, and social inclusion in and through sport, it could be assumed that the right to sport would have an instrumental and hermeneutical function in relation to the implementation of existing rights in the sporting context according to the evolution of social needs.

By moving from the idea that the claim to participate in sport is a derivative treaty right, this chapter aims to describe, explain, and evaluate the legal foundations of the right to sport. Taking into account sport's social functions, which appear constant

---

[16] UNESCO, *International Charter of Physical Education, Physical Activity and Sport*, SHS/2015/PI/H/14 REV, Article 1. The ICPEPA, adopted on 1978, was revised on November 18, 2015, during the 38th session of the UNESCO General Conference.

[17] CoE, *Recommendation on the Revised European Sports Charter*, CM/Rec(2021)5, (2021). This is the second revision of the ESpC adopted in 1975; the first revision was adopted on 24 September 1992.

[18] ESpC, Article 10. In the previous version of the Charter, revised in 1992, sport was essentially regarded as a cultural tool to promote a democratic society (Article 6) and a sustainable development (Article 10).

[19] Human Rights Council (HRC), *Intersection of race and gender discrimination in sport*, A/HRC/44/26 (2020), para 51. This report was submitted under the HRC resolution 40/5, *Elimination of discrimination against women and girls in sport*, A/HRC/RES/40/5, 44/26 (2019).

[20] Verma and Douglas (2022).

[21] Smith and Sparkes (2019).

[22] Holzer (2020), p. 387.

[23] See, for instance, the reports of the European Gay and Lesbian Sports Federation (https://www.eglsf.info, last accessed 8 October 2022).

[24] On the uncertain and contested status of human rights standard in sporting context, due to the private nature of Sporting Organisations (SOs) and the transnational dimension of sport legal order, see, for instance: Di Marco (2022).

over time, independent of the dominant values in a specific period, it is possible to detect *existing rights* upon which the general claim to participate in sport could be based. By analyzing the legal relationship between access to sporting activities and sport's social functions, we can thus define *who* can effectively enjoy the right to sport, and under which conditions; to what extent the instrumental nature of sport can support a legitimate claim regarded as an *enforceable right*; and which obligations would be provided for national and sporting authorities in order to guarantee the *effectiveness* of this emerging right. Generally, by regarding sport as a right, rather than as a cultural tool, this chapter strives to answer the essential ethical question of why, and to what extent, the *trivial* participation in sport should be considered an inherent right of the human being, cutting through the considerable confusion surrounding the right to sport.

In order to answer to this essential ethical question, with the aims described above, the legal derivation's method will be applied to the main international and European law instruments potentially affecting sportspeople.[25] Particular attention will be focused on the ICPEPA, the ESpC, the activity of the relevant Committees of the International Covenant on Economic, Social and Cultural Rights (ICESCR), the European Convention on Human Rights (ECHR), and on case law from the European Court of Human Rights (ECtHR). Reference to the ECtHR is particularly relevant in light of its emerging jurisdiction on the Court of Arbitration for Sport (CAS) case law.[26]

The chapter will first analyze the legal sources of the right to sport, supporting the thesis that this right is a derivative treaty right (Sect. 2), and then explore the legal relationship between access to sporting activities and sport's social functions, as its natural contribution to human health (Sect. 3), its historical educational value (Sect. 4), and its important identity-social function (Sect. 5). It will finally illustrate to what extent the right to sport is a functional/derivative right, legally enforceable, and why the *trivial* participation in sport should be considered a human right for all (Sect. 6).

2 Sources of the Right to Sport: Sport as a Derivative Treaty Right

In the ICPEPA and the ESpC, UNESCO and the CoE, respectively, enshrined the right to sport at the international level. They followed a state practice including provisions on the right to sport in their laws, whether at the constitutional level or

[25] This method is a part of treaty interpretation imposed by the broad wording of human rights and their evolutionary nature. On the role of the treaty interpretation in the evolution and implementation of human rights see, *inter alia*: Abi-Saab (2019), and in particular see the Part III 'Evolutionary interpretation in human rights and environmental law', and the Gaggioli and Dörr's contributions.

[26] Di Marco (2021).

ordinary law.[27] It would be not a state practice to identify an international custom, as required under Article 38(1)(b) of the Statute of the International Court of Justice (ICJ).[28] The lack of consensus on the real nature and existence of a right to sport, highlighted in the previous section, suggests that constitutional recognition of the right to sport does not have identifiable practices amounting to a "constant and uniform usage" or an "extensive and virtually uniform behaviour considered as binding".[29] However, by starting from an approach based on the deduction from statements rather than on the induction of state behavior,[30] it could be assumed that this emerging constitutional practice would reflect an arising *opinio juris*, composed of a combination of *lex ferenda* (what the law should be) and *lex lata* (the law as it exists). This would reinforce and support the idea that sport could be a derivative treaty right.

The ancillary nature of sport, its functional and instrumental dimensions for the protection of human rights, allows it to be considered as a derivative right. Indeed, fundamental human rights generate claims regardless of their instrumental value in realizing or protecting other rights. By contrast, derivative or non-fundamental rights generate claims because they contribute to, or are pre-conditions for, safeguarding or implementing fundamental rights.[31] From this perspective, the derivative right should be inferred from other rights, with which it must logically share legal features (i.e., civil and political rights could only create civil and political rights, while socio-economic rights can only generate socio-economic rights).[32]

---

[27] The first Country that expressly introduced in its Constitution the right to sport and physical activities is the Soviet Union in 1936 (article 126). In 1976, it was recognised by the Cuban Constitution (Article 52) and the Portuguese Constitution (Article 79); in 1978 it was the turn of the Spanish Constitution (Article 43). In general terms, a right to access to sport is foreseen, for example, by the Constitutions of the following States: Brazil, Article 217; Mexico, Article 44; Venezuela, Article 111; Bolivia; Articles 104-105; Nicaragua, Article 65; China, Article 21; Cambodia, Article 65; Nepal, Article 39; Philippines, Article XVII; Laos, Article 26; Suriname, 37; Georgia, Article 5; Kyrgyzstan, Article 45; Turkmenistan, Article 15; North Macedonia, Article 47; Turkey, Article 59; Moldova, Article 50; Egypt, Articles 81–84; Mozambique, Article 93; Morocco, Article 26; Gambia, section 217, n 7; Ghana, Article 37(5); Tunisia, Article 43; Zimbabwe, Article 32; Ethiopia, Article 41; Uganda, Article XVII; Burkina Faso, Article 18; Cameroon, Article 56; Kenya, Articles 185–187. On the right to sport in the different national constitutions, see for example, Melica (2022); Maniatis (2017), pp. 178–191; Giummarra (2012).

[28] As known, pursuant to Article 38(1)(b) of the Statute of the ICJ, international custom requires two distinct elements: a general practice (*consuetudo*) and the conviction that this practice is accepted as law (*opinio juris sive necessitatis*).

[29] It is worth remembering that the ICJ has specified on several instances that the actual practice of States (termed the "material fact") should cover various elements, including the duration, consistency, repetition, and generality of a particular kind of behaviour by States. On this point, see *inter alia*: D'Amato (1971), pp. 89–90, and p. 160; Roberts (2001), p. 757.

[30] On this approach, see Simma and Alston (1992), pp. 82–108; De Schutter (2014), p. 64.

[31] In these terms, see Scolnicov (2016), pp. 194–214.

[32] On this point, in addition to the author mentioned in the previous note, see: Sinnott-Armstrong (2002), p. 231. However, it should be noted that the relations between civil and social rights are

While sources of soft law that lack the capacity to directly create international law, ICPEPA and ESpC provide the primary interpretative backbone for the development of the right to sport. As UN institutions and CoE bodies make constant reference to these documents, they are a useful starting point for defining the normative content of the right to sport.[33] Under the ICPEPA, the claim of the right to sport is expressly linked to the right to health (Articles 1.2 and 2) and to education (Articles 1.7, 4 and 5). According to the broader approach of the ESpC, the recognition of a valid claim to exercise sport is called for by "the rights to health, education, culture and participation in the life of the community" (Article 10). ICPEPA and ESpC both point to health and education as the source rights for the right to sport. As derived from these two treaty-based rights, the right to sport would essentially be a socio-economic right.

However, the scope and content of such a right to sport appear, *prima facie*, extremely large and generic. According to the ICPEPA, the claim of the right to sport should be generic access to "physical education, physical activity and sport" (Article 1.1). In more precise terms, the ESpC defines sport as "all forms of physical activity which, through casual or organized participation, are aimed at maintaining or improving physical fitness and mental well-being, forming social relationships or obtaining results in competition at all levels" (Article 2). The scope of the right to sport potentially covers a large variety of physical activities and actors, from the most expensive (e.g. skiing), and in part contested (e.g. hunting), to the most socially institutionalized (e.g. physical education in school systems), and collectively organized (amateur or professional sporting events). It may also include activities that are not physical (e.g. chess), or physical activities that are not necessarily regulated by sporting authorities or social conventions and customs (e.g. surfing or yoga). In relation to this wide scope, ICPEPA and ESpC have introduced at the international and regional level the universal principle of gender equality, non-discrimination, and social inclusion in and through sport. The right to sport would entitle everyone to "inclusive, adapted and safe opportunities to participate in physical education, physical activity and sport" (ICPEPA, Article 1.3; ESpC, Article 1.1).

This lack of clarity inevitably raises doubts as to the validity of the legal derivation under analysis. It would be a source of uncertainty and inaccuracy from a legal perspective, lending support to those who warn against proliferation, inflation, or dilution of human rights. Furthermore, considering that sport is a heterogeneous phenomenon, with pronounced divergences regarding its organization or social impact, it could be argued that its legal/social/anthropological foundation may be different; accordingly, the *link* with the basic rights should be verified on a case-by-case basis for all kinds of sporting activities potentially covered by the

more fluid and "open". It can be argued that some social rights are basic and functional for the enjoyment of other civil rights. See Gavison (2003), pp. 23–55; Cismas (2014), pp. 448–472.

[33] As known, the cross-reference by international organisations contributes to attributing to soft law acts the role of "introductory" elements in the creation of international law. On the controversial role of soft law in the corpus of international law-making, see *inter alia,* Boyle (2018), p. 119.

ICPEPA and the ESpC. In order to avoid an ever-expanding list of new human rights, which would erode the very idea of these rights, it should be verified to what extent the "inclusive, adapted and safe opportunities to participate in physical education, physical activity and sport" would contribute to the realization of the source rights. This should allow a more accurate definition of the scope and legal effects of the right to sport.

Thielbörger argues that "[if] a derivative right is *a conditio sine qua non* for the realization of the source right, there can be no objection to the derivative right's creation; otherwise the recognition of the source right itself would become void";[34] this would be a case of 'indispensable derivation'.[35] By contrast, if it is merely favorable for the implementation of the source right, the justification should meet the criteria elaborated by Philip Alston,[36] and the guidelines adopted by the UN General Assembly (UNGA) in developing international instruments in the field of human rights.[37] Namely, pursuant to UNGA guidelines, the emerging right to sport should,

> be consistent with the existing body of international human rights law; be of fundamental character and derive from the inherent dignity and worth of the human person; be sufficiently precise to give rise to identifiable and practicable rights and obligations; provide, where appropriate, realistic and effective implementation machinery, including reporting systems; attract broad international support.[38]

We can assume that the right to sport would be a case of *favorable derivation*, as theoretically, there are several conceivable ways in which the source rights (i.e., to health or education) can meaningfully exist even without "inclusive, adapted and safe opportunities to participate in physical education, physical activity and sport". The recognition of sport as a derivative right would be one option that maximizes implementation and guarantee of the source right. Accordingly, in light of the UNGA guidelines mentioned above, it should be noted that the right to sport has attracted international support from international organizations, such as CoE and

---

[34] Thielbörger (2015), p. 231.

[35] Ibid. See also Sinnott-Armstrong (2002), p. 233, according to which the legal derivation of constitutional rights is regarded as "necessary condition derivation" when a right is inferred because without its derivation, the source right would become "less meaningful or secure".

[36] Philip Alston is a legal scholar and the first Rapporteur for the Committee on Economic, Social and Cultural Rights (CESCR)—he has also chaired the committee from 1991 to 1998. By starting from the concept of quality control, he has argued that if a norm is to be considered for formal recognition as a human right, it should meet the following seven criteria: (1) reflect a fundamentally important social value; (2) be relevant, inevitably to varying degrees, throughout a world of diverse value systems; (3) be eligible for recognition on the grounds that it is an interpretation of [U.N.] Charter obligations, a reflection of customary law rules or a formulation that is declaratory of general principles of law; (4) be consistent with, but not merely repetitive of, the existing body of international human rights law; (5) be capable of achieving a very high degree of international consensus; (6) be compatible or at least not clearly incompatible with the general practice of states; and (7) be sufficiently precise as to give rise to identifiable rights and obligations. See Alston (1984), p. 607.

[37] UNGA, *Setting International standards in the field of human rights,* A/RES/41/120E (1986).

[38] Ibid., para 4.

UNESCO, and by international sporting federations (ISFs), like the IOC. Nevertheless, its consistency with the existing body of international human rights law, as well as its fundamental character inherent to human dignity, and especially its ability to give rise to identifiable and practicable rights and obligations, are largely untested.

We can see above that only some of the key criteria are met for treating access to sport as a human right. However, its capacity to contribute to the implementation of basic rights—by establishing identifiable and practicable rights and obligations, and the ability to define its scope and legal effects—could be verified by taking into account some of the fundamental functions of sport. Here we are discussing the structural features of sport, which appear constant over time, independently of the dominant values of a specific period. For example, the inherent relationship between sport and health.

3 The Natural Relationship Between Sport and Health: The Right to Achieve Psycho-Physical Integrity

The link between sport and health is evident and has been underlined by the World Health Organization (WHO) on several occasions.[39] Sport's contribution to health was recognized during the COVID-19 pandemic by the UN[40] and the Parliamentary Assembly of the Council of Europe (PACE).[41] The WHO has also signed several agreements with ISFs to promote health through sport and physical activity, confirming the important role of Sporting Organizations (SOs) to contribute to the health of people.[42] This is an essential function of sport emphasized during different periods, which has often been used for the benefit of the state and its ideology. For example, the promotion and prescription of therapeutic exercise during the Greek and Roman ages,[43] or the mass regimentation of people in SOs by totalitarian

[39]See, *ex multis*, the followings WHO's recommendations: *Governance: Development of a draft global action plan to promote physical activity*, Geneva, 2018; *Global strategy on diet, physical activity and health. Physical activity and young people*, Geneva, 2018.

[40]UN, Department of Economic and Social Affairs Social Inclusion, *The impact of COVID-19 on sport, physical activity and well-being and its effects on social development* (available at https://www.un.org/development/desa/dspd/wp-content/uploads/sites/22/2020/05/PB_73.pdf - last accessed 10 April 2022).

[41]PACE, *Sports policies in times of crisis*, Doc. 15426 (2022), paras 33–40.

[42]See, for example, the agreement signed with the IOC (https://www.who.int/news/item/16-05-2020-who-and-international-olympic-committee-team-up-to-improve-health-through-sport - last accessed 12 February 2022).

[43]Berryman (1992), pp. 1–56.

regimes in Europe.[44] In the "age of rights",[45] the natural relationship between sport and health has been addressed with regard to the implementation of the right to health, as suggested by several recommendations of the CoE,[46] the PACE,[47] and the UN.[48] The UN has underlined that,

> healthy lifestyles have not traditionally been viewed as a rights issue, but their adoption is integral to realisation of the right to health. Sport and physical activity are a vital part of healthy lifestyles, and States and other actors incur important obligations to maximize individual capacity to exercise and to live healthfully.[49]

The "inclusive, safe, and adapted" access to sport would be an underlying determinant of the right to health, enshrined in Article 25 of the Universal Declaration of Human Rights (UDHR),[50] Article 13 ICESCR,[51] or Article 11 of the European Social Charter (ESC).[52] As noted by the Committee on Economic, Social and Cultural Rights (CESCR), the "right to health is an inclusive right, covering a wide range of factors that can help us lead a healthy life".[53] Furthermore, it should be interpreted "as an inclusive right extending not only to timely and appropriate health care but also to the underlying determinants of health".[54] Considering the broad definition of health in the WHO Constitution—"a state of complete physical, mental and social well-being and not merely the absence of disease or infirmity"[55]—access to sporting activities could be regarded as part of the right to achieve or maintain psycho-physical integrity. It would be a new addition to the list of the

[44] During fascism in Italy, for instance, sport was regarded as an important means to pursue the "hygiene of the race", the "health of the race", and the "physical strengthening of the Italian race". On this point see, for instance: Landoni (2016).

[45] The reference is clearly to Henkin (1990).

[46] See, *ex multis*, CoE, *Principles for a policy of sport for all*, CM/Rec(76)41 (1976), point 3.

[47] See, for example: PACE, *Sport for all: a bridge to equality, integration and social inclusion*, PACE/Res. 2131 (2016).

[48] See, *ex multis*, UNGA, *Sport as an enabler of sustainable development*, A/RES/73/L24 (2018), paras 8 and 12.

[49] UNGA, *Report of the Special Rapporteur on the right of everyone to the enjoyment of the highest attainable standard of physical and mental health*, A/HRC/32/33 (2016), para 96.

[50] Pursuant to the Article 25 UDHR, "everyone has the right to a standard of living adequate for the health and well-being of himself and of his family" (UNGA Res 217 A/III).

[51] According to the Article 12 ICESCR, "The States Parties to the present Covenant recognize the right of everyone to the enjoyment of the highest attainable standard of physical and mental health" (UNGA Res. 2200A/XXI-).

[52] The ESC, adopted on 18 October 1961, has been revised on 3 May 1996 (European Treaty Series - No. 163).

[53] CESCR, *General Comment No. 14: The Right to the Highest Attainable Standard of Health (Art. 12)*, 11 August 2000, E/C.12/2000/4, paras 11 and 12. On this point see: Lougarre (2015), pp. 326–354; Tobin (2012); Karagiannis (2012), pp. 1137–1212; Toebes (1999).

[54] CESCR, *General Comment No. 14: The Right to the Highest Attainable Standard of Health (Art. 12)*, para 12.

[55] World Health Organisations Constitution, *Off. Rec. Wld Hlth Org*., 2, 100.

underlying determinants of health indicated by the CESCR;[56] another case of the emerging trend of defining derivative rights based on the right to health.[57]

In light of the therapeutic function of sport, it could be argued that the emerging right to sport would theoretically cover all sports, even those that do not involve physical activity (e.g., chess), which contribute to psycho-physical well-being. From this perspective, dangerous sports, which may have detrimental effects on the health of people, should be excluded.[58] Further, it could be assumed that the right to health would only partially cover sporting activities carried out for economic and professional purposes, where the therapeutic function is marginal. For example, in the famous case of the athlete *Semenya*,[59] the rules of athletics that set a limit for the natural levels of testosterone for female runners in order to be admitted into women's competition have been strongly contested from the point of view of respect for the right to health,[60] and for the principle of non-discrimination.[61] While considering "forced medical examinations and treatment [...] the very essence of a claim of violation of Article 3 of the Convention",[62] the ECtHR did not assess the appellant's exclusion from the sporting competitions in the light of this Article, considering that the "*seuile de gravité*" had not been reached to take account of this provision.[63] Moreover, it should be noted that the Court did not explicitly reject the objective of

[56] CESCR, *General Comment No. 14: The Right to the Highest Attainable Standard of Health (Art. 12)*, para 11.

[57] On this trend see, for instance: Marks (2016), pp. 97–142.

[58] It could be noted that dangerous sports - such as boxing, horseracing, auto racing, mountaineering, etc - have triggered a heated debate in many countries. Some people argued that dangerous sport should be banned, or extremely limited. In addition, it may be noted that the definition of "dangerous sports" is uncertain. On this point see, for example: Walin (2012), p. 3690.

[59] ECtHR, Semenya c. Suisse, 11.07.2023.

[60] The regulations from the International Association of Athletics Federations (IAAF) requiring that women athletes with specific differences in sex development to medically reduce their natural blood testosterone level, if they wish to continue racing as women in a few restricted events, was strongly contested by the World Medical Association (WMA). According to the WMA the testosterone rules would be 'contrary to international medical ethics and human rights standards' (https://www.wma.net/news-post/wma-urges-physicians-not-to-implement-iaaf-rules-on-classifying-women-athletes/, last accessed 11 October 2022). The IAAF changed its name to "World Athletics" in October 2019. As this chapter considers events occurring prior to this name change, it refers to the federation as the IAAF and not as World Athletics.

[61] The OHCHR has argued that "the implementation of female eligibility regulations denies athletes with variations in sex characteristics an equal right to participate in sports and violates the right to non-discrimination more broadly" (HRC, *Intersection of race and gender discrimination in sport*, para 34).

[62] ECtHR, Semenya c. Suisse, 11.07.2023, § 215 (translation of the author - judgment only available in French).

[63] Ibid., § 216. The Court pointed out that the applicant had not *de facto* undergone the medical treatment and that it was for this reason that the *seuile de gravité* has not been reached. It should be noted that this position was not unanimously shared by the judges of the Court (*Opinion en partie concordante, en partie dissidente du Juge Serghides*, §§ 21-44).

World Athletics to guarantee equal opportunities in women's competitions, which was the basis for the exclusion of the appellant.[64]

If the emerging right to sport is simply considered to be an underlying determinant of health, it could still be argued that the exclusion from a given competition may be regarded as "necessary, reasonable and proportionate" to ensure fair competition in women's sport.[65] The athlete's right to health would not be compromised, since there are several conceivable ways to achieve this right, even without the participation in specific sporting events. By contrast, a specific medical practice that may have detrimental effects on health should be banned. Non-state actors and SOs should guarantee access to sport in a safe environment, at both the professional and amateur level.[66] They should have the obligation to protect the health of their members and of those that *already* take part in their events.[67]

Accordingly, by taking into account the therapeutic function of sport, the right to sport would cover mainly (non-dangerous) amateur sports. Nevertheless, it could be regarded as a new emerging derivative human right since it theoretically meets all five criteria of the guidelines endorsed by the UNGA. The 'natural' contribution of access to sport to achieve or maintain psycho-physical integrity would confirm its fundamental character inherent to human dignity. National authorities would comply

[64] Ibid., *Opinion concordante du Juge Pavli*, § 24.

[65] This is the position of the Court of Arbitration for sport (CAS) in the Semenya v. IAAF & CAS case (CAS 2018/O/5794 Mokgadi Caster Semenya v. International Association of Athletics Federations & CAS 2018/O/5798 Athletics South Africa v. International Association of Athletics Federations, 30 April 2019). The CAS arbitration tribunal, while agreeing that the IAAF's policy was discriminatory against athletes with different sexual development (DSD) such as Semenya (paras 544 et seq), accepted the IAAF's argument based on scientific studies according to which high testosterone levels in female athletes confers significant advantages in size, strength and power from puberty onwards, and therefore stated that the policy was "necessary, reasonable and proportionate" to ensure fair competition in women's sport (paras 544 et seq.). These aspects were not substantially addressed by the ECtHR, as emphasised in the joint dissenting opinion of the Judges Grozev, Roosma and Ktistakis (ECtHR, Semenya c. Suisse, 11.07.2023, *Opinion dissidente commune aux juges Grozev, Roosma et Ktistakis,* p. 122).

[66] ICPEPA, Articles 8 and 9; ESC, Articles 1(1), lett. b), 10(1), and 15; UNGA, *Report of the Special Rapporteur on the right of everyone to the enjoyment of the highest attainable standard of physical and mental health*, paras 84–91. This would be a general obligation suggested, for instance, by the European Convention on an Integrated Safety, Security and Service Approach at Football Matches and Other Sports Events (St. Denis Convention), which is called to gradually replace the 1985 European Convention on Spectator Violence and Misbehaviour at Sports Events. The Convention of St. Denis was opened for signature on 3 July 2016 at the Stade de France in Saint-Denis, near Paris, on the occasion of the UEFA EURO 2016 tournament.

[67] ICPEPA, Article 10; ESpC, Articles 8(1), lett. a), and 16(2). This would be a general obligation affirmed, for example, by the Conventions against doping in sport. The Anti-Doping Convention of the CoE, adopted in 1989 and followed by an additional protocol in 2002, underlines in its Preamble that "public authorities and the voluntary sports organisations have complementary responsibilities to combat doping in sport, notably to ensure the proper conduct, on the basis of the principle of fair play, of sports events and to protect the health of those that take part in them". The same terms are reproduced in the UNESCO Convention against doping in sport, entered into force on 1 February 2007.

with the traditional obligations to fulfil this right, which require that states take positive actions to ensure the implementation of human rights.[68] The right to sport should be recognized in national political, budgetary, and legal systems, implying the adoption of a national physical activity policy for its realization.[69] On the basis of the obligation to respect and protect the right, all people should have access to state-run sporting facilities on an equal basis, with particular attention to vulnerable minorities.[70] Public authorities should be responsible for setting framework conditions, concerning sporting facilities and, where appropriate, legal requirements necessary to guarantee access to sporting activities.[71]

The right to sport, as a derivative right, logically shares the legal features and limits of the right to health. It would mainly imply general programmatic and interpretative obligations typical of socio-economic rights, which need to be implemented by national authorities[72] to achieve their progressive realization "to the maximum available resources".[73] In this sense, it could be noted that according to the CESCR, "the right to health is not to be understood as a right to be healthy";[74] instead it "must be understood as a right to the enjoyment of a variety of facilities, goods, services and conditions necessary for the realization of the highest attainable standard of health".[75] Access to sport activities would be connected to the right to the enjoyment of a variety of sporting facilities; it would play an important role in public policymaking, and in particular regarding the most vulnerable groups for whom sport can have a therapeutic function.

However, the right to sport would not necessarily imply an obligation of admission to sporting competitions; it would then cover a limited part of the large scope defined by ICPEPA and ESpC. For this reason, the right to health cannot completely justify the right to sport. Judged exclusively on this basis, the nature of sport as a derived right could not be established, at least in the terms in which it is presented by ICPEPA and ESpC. The contribution of sport to other 'basic rights' must then be

---

[68] CESCR, *General Comment No. 14: The Right to the Highest Attainable Standard of Health (Art. 12)*, paras 36-37. On this point see, also: Krennerich (2017), pp. 23–54; Tobin and Barrett (2020), pp. 67–88.

[69] In addition to CESCR's General Comment No. 14 and the authors mentioned in the previous note, see the UNGA, *Report of the Special Rapporteur on the right of everyone to the enjoyment of the highest attainable standard of physical and mental health*, para 25.

[70] ICPEPA, ESC, and UNGA report focused on the obligation to facilitate, promote, and provide, taking into account problems and needs of key populations and groups. The UNGA report appears particularly rich in indications (paras 16–84).

[71] ICPEPA, Article 3, and ESC, Articles 3 and 15.

[72] Bothe (1979), pp. 14–34; Lakehal (1991); Murphy (2013).

[73] The reference is to the doctrine, elaborated by the CESCR, concerning the specific meaning of the obligation of States to achieve the progressive realization of the full content on economic, social and cultural rights "to the maximum available resources". On this doctrine see, for instance: Uprimny et al. (2019), pp. 624–653.

[74] CESCR, *General Comment No.* 14: *The Right to the Highest Attainable Standard of Health (Art. 12)*, para 8.

[75] Ibid., para 9.

considered. The next section will address the right to education, the implementation of which could be improved by the pedagogical value of sport.

4 The Pedagogical Value of Sport: The Right to Physical Education

Sport's educational-pedagogical value is at the core of the resolutions and acts adopted by the UN,[76] the CoE,[77] and the EU mentioned in the previous discussion.[78] As noted by the CoE,

> sport has become more than just a leisure pursuit. It is a recognised social phenomenon. Sport offers a common language and a platform for social democracy. It creates conditions for political democracy and is instrumental to the development of democratic citizenship. Sport enhances the understanding and appreciation of cultural differences, and it contributes to the fight against prejudices. Finally, sport plays its part in limiting social exclusion of immigrant and minority groups.[79]

The international organizations would have recognized the sport's pedagogical value emerged throughout history, dating back to the ancient Greek understanding of sport as giving meaning to reality[80] and encouraging adherence to rules of behavior.[81] Cultures have ludic elements which influence human beings' interpretation of life, and their conception of good.[82] Sporting values have some influence on societies' values, and for this very reason sport appears as "the most important of the trivial subjects in the world".[83] In the light of its extraordinary capacity to educate and to be

[76] See the UNGA resolutions mentioned in the note 10.

[77] See the CoE resolutions mentioned at the notes 11, 46 and 47.

[78] In addition to the EU acts mentioned in the note 12, see: EP, *Resolution on the role of sport in education* (2007/2086(INI), 2007); and the Case C-325/08 *Olympique Lyonnais c. Bernard*, EU: C:2010:143, where the specific notion of the social function of sport elaborated by the CoE has been partially recognized by the ECJ, through its definitive inclusion within the conceptual framework of the imperative reasons of overriding public interest.

[79] CoE (2000), p. 67.

[80] On the function of ancient Greek sports, the literature is vast. See, for example: Miller (2003), pp. 197–292; Reid (2011).

[81] This aspect is particularly pointed out in relation of the role of ancient games in Sparta. In this sense see: Christen (2012), pp. 193–255. It could be also noted that this sport function is the core idea of the pedagogical proposal called "muscular Christianity", elaborated in the nineteenth Century for introducing sports in schools—Putney (2001); Hall (1994); idea that was embraced by Pierre de Coubertin to create our modern Olympic Games - Watson and Parker (2014), pp. 44–62.

[82] Huizinga (2005).

[83] Tollener and Schotsmans (2013), pp. 21–43, and in particular at 21.

vehicle of values, sport has been largely regarded as "an inspirational force for good".[84]

Accordingly, the governing rules recognizing the right to sport as valid could also be connected to the right to education, as provided by Article 26 of the UDHR or Article 13 ICESCR. In Article 13 ICESCR, there is clear evidence of the traditional binomial sport/education, considering that both sport and education activities are envisaged as a means of enabling "all persons to participate effectively in a free society, promote understanding, tolerance and friendship among all nations and all racial, ethnic or religious groups". As argued by the CESCR, within the "educational objectives which are common to Article 26 (2) of the UDHR and Article 13 (1) of the Covenant, perhaps the most fundamental is that education shall be directed to the full development of the human personality".[85] From this perspective, it could be argued that sport is an underlying determinant of educational objectives, and therefore, it would be part of the right to education. This has been implicitly affirmed by the UNESCO resolution that established the Statutes of the Intergovernmental Committee for Physical Education and Sport (CIGEPS),[86] and expressly admitted since the first International Conference of Ministers and Senior Officials Responsible for the Physical Education and Sport (MINEPS).[87] These are the two international bodies that have carefully examined the new version of the ICPEPA and elaborated the notion of "global education",[88] which includes physical education, and is enshrined in the International Convention on the Rights of the Child (ICRC).[89]

By affirming the right of the child to education (Article 28), the ICRC establishes that "the education of the child shall be directed to [t]he development of the child's personality, talents and mental and physical abilities to their fullest potential" (Article 29). As argued by the UN Committee on the Rights of the Child (CRC), Article 29

> insists upon a holistic approach to education which ensures that the educational opportunities made available reflect an appropriate balance between promoting the physical, mental,

---

[84]Munro (2016), pp. 3–11.

[85]CESCR, *General Comment No. 13, The right to education (article 13 of the Covenant)*, 8 December 1999, E/C.12/1999/10, para 4. On this point see, for example: De Beco et al. (2019), p. 5; Ferenci (2012), pp. 328–332.

[86]UNESCO, *III Programme for 1979-1980*, 20 C/Resolution 1/5.4/3, 5-10 Avril 1976. The establishment of the CIGEPS was justified on the basis of the achievement of Objective 5.4 (Improvement of educational content, methods and techniques). Ibid. (p. 30).

[87]UNESCO, *Première Conférence internationale des ministres et hauts fonctionnaires responsables de l'éducation physique et du sport*, Paris, 5-10 Avril 1976, para 28.

[88]UNESCO, *The Role of physical education and sport in the education of youth in the context of life-long education*', Paris, 5-10 Avril 1976, ED.76/CONF.205/COL.4.

[89]International Convention on the Rights of the Child (ICRC), adopted on 20 November 1989 (UNGA Res 44/25).

> spiritual and emotional aspects of education, the intellectual, social and practical dimensions, and the childhood and lifelong aspects.[90]

Further, the right to (global) education is reinforced by the "children's right to sport activities" enshrined in Article 31 ICRC, according to which, "States Parties recognize the right of the child to rest and leisure, to engage in play and recreational activities appropriate to the age of the child and to participate freely in cultural life and the arts". The CRC has considered the implementation of children's right to play as "essential to achieving compliance with the right provided for in Article 29".[91] Indeed, the Committee emphasized the positive impact of the rights under Article 31 on children's educational development, arguing that "inclusive education and inclusive play are mutually reinforcing [. . .], [and that] research has shown that play is an important means through which children learn".[92]

The ECtHR has also recognized the pedagogical value of sport by underlining the importance of physical activities as an underlying determinant of educational objectives. In the case *Osmanoğlu and Kocabaş v. Switzerland*,[93] the applicants alleged that the obligation to send their daughters (who were minors at the time) to mixed swimming lessons was contrary to their religious convictions, arguing that "swimming was only one element of sports education and that an exemption neither called into question any education content nor threatened the attainment of a school certificate or subsequent professional opportunities".[94] The applicants' arguments, however, were rejected by the Court, according to which,

> sports education, of which swimming is an integral part in the school attended by the applicants' daughters, is of special importance for children's development and health. That being said, a child's interest in attending those lessons lies not merely in learning to swim and taking physical exercise, but above all in participating in that activity with all the other pupils, without exception on the basis of the child's origin or the parents' religious or philosophical convictions.[95]

Treated in this way, sport has a fundamental educational role, which goes far beyond physical well-being. The possibility of attending private swimming lessons was regarded as irrelevant by the Court, because what was important to the children was "above all the fact of learning together and taking part in that activity collectively".[96]

---

[90] CRC, *General Comment No. 1: (2001) Article 29 (1): The aim of education*, 17 April 2001, CRC/GC/2001/1, para 12.

[91] CRC, *General Comment No. 17: (2013) on the right of the child to rest, leisure, play, recreational activities, cultural life and the arts (art. 31)*, 17 January - 1 February 2013, CRC/C/GC/17, para 27.

[92] Ibid.

[93] ECtHR, Osmanoğlu and Kocabaş v. Switzerland, 10.012017.

[94] Ibid., § 56.

[95] Ibid., § 98.

[96] Ibid., § 100. It should be noted that in this case the ECtHR held that there had been no violation of Article 9 (freedom of thought, conscience and religion) of the Convention, finding that by giving precedence to the children's obligation to follow the full school curriculum and their successful integration over the applicants' private interest in obtaining an exemption from mixed swimming

On the basis of the pedagogical role of sport, it could be argued that the emerging right to sport—treated as an underlying determinant of the right to education—would be enforceable in relation to educational and schooling activities, with specific reference to formal and informal educational systems. The Declaration of Berlin, where MINEPS V invited the Director-General to consider a revision of the Charter,[97] focused on the persisting inequalities in sport by certain categories of vulnerable people (such as children, women, and persons with disabilities).[98] In particular, the Ministers were committed to "ensure quality and inclusive physical education classes, as a mandatory part of primary and secondary education";[99] to "improve the conditions for physical education and sport at school";[100] to "foster the important role of inclusive extracurricular school sport in early development and educating children and youth";[101] and to "provide opportunities for traditional sport and games as a means for wider inclusion".[102] The other stakeholders (i.e., the SOs) were called upon to support the broad-based anchoring of sport in school and in all other educational institutions, recommending a generic review of sport governance in order to ensure equal opportunities to participate in sport at all levels.[103]

From the ICPEPA perspective, the claim of the right to sport would essentially concern participation in physical education classes and extracurricular school sports. Pursuant to the ESpC, the obligation to safeguard and promote the right to sport should be "guaranteed, both within the educational system and in other aspects of social life".[104] However, the "other aspects of social life" remain largely undefined, with the only concrete references to educational systems and programs. Therefore, there would not be a general right to participate, for example, in professional or amateur sporting events organized by private associations; perhaps with the exception of those organized in cooperation with formal and informal educational institutions.

With this in mind, a restrictive interpretation of the right to sport seems to be in part supported by the international instruments of hard law that expressly recognize the right to sport for certain vulnerable categories. In order to implement the children's right to play, for example, the CRC has argued that "[e]ducational environments should play a major role in fulfilling the obligations under Article

---

lessons for their daughters on religious grounds, the Swiss authorities have nevertheless offered the applicants very flexible arrangements, in that their daughters were allowed, among other concessions, to wear a burkini to the swimming lessons. On this case see, for example, du Plessis (2018), pp. 503–525.

[97] Declaration of Berlin, adopted by 600 participants from 121 countries, as an outcome of the 5th World Conference of Sport Ministers (28-30 May 2013), SHS/2013/PI/H/8 REV.

[98] See the Annex "Commission I Access to Sport as a Fundamental Right for All", points 1.1.–1.12.

[99] Ibid., point 1.15.

[100] Ibid., point 1.16.

[101] Ibid., point 1.17.

[102] Ibid., point 1.18.

[103] Ibid., points 1.19–1.29.

[104] ESpC, Article 10, para 3.

31", offering the educational system detailed indications.[105] The Convention on the Elimination of All Forms of Discrimination against Women (CEDAW),[106] in Article 10, foresees that,

> States Parties shall take all appropriate measures to eliminate discrimination against women in order to ensure them equal rights with men in the field of education and in particular to ensure, on a basis of equality of men and women [. . .] the same opportunities to participate actively in sports and physical education.

Considering the limited scope supported by the right to education, the right to sport appears as an emerging and "incomplete theorised right", in the sense that the emphatic affirmation of the principle (the access to sport for all) would reveal limited agreement as to how this principle should be implemented.[107] On the basis of the right to education, the access to physical activity and sport would be an enforceable right only for pupils within informal or formal educational systems. The right to access sport *for all* would be a right *for a few* categories, and in relation to very restricted contexts. Expanding the catalogue of human rights by including a *general* right to sport could lead to an illegitimate and uncontrolled expansion of new human rights, and would clearly be a source of uncertainty and inaccuracy from a legal perspective, which would not be sufficiently (and generally) supported by the existing body of international human rights law.

Finally, the educational role of sport suggests the idea that sport promotes the emergence of a pluralist, dynamic, and cohesive society. In this sense, the claim to participate to sport should be supported, in addition to the right to health and education, by the right to culture and participation in the life of the community, as indicated by the ESpC (Article 10). In this regard, sport would exercise an identity-social function suggesting an extensive interpretation of the emerging right to sport, as the following discussion will demonstrate.

---

[105] CRC, *General Comment No. 17: (2013) on the right of the child to rest, leisure, play, recreational activities, cultural life and the arts (art. 31)*, para 58(g).

[106] Convention on the Elimination of All Forms of Discrimination against Women (CEDAW), adopted on 18 December 1979 (UNGA Res 34/180).

[107] An "incomplete theorised right" represents the third type of incompleteness proposed by the Cass Sunstein's theory of incomplete theorised and specified agreements mentioned in the note 8. According to the author, this third category regards "incomplete theorised agreements on particular outcomes, accompanied by agreements on the low-level principles that account for them. [. . .] What is critical is that [people] agree on how a case must come out and on a low-level justification. [This incompletely specified agreements would fail to produce] depth—full accounts of the foundations of a decision, in the form of attempts to find ever deeper reasons behind the outcome' and width—that is, they do not try to rationalize the law by showing how an outcome in one case fits coherently with particular outcomes in the full range of other cases" (Sunstein (1995), pp. 1740–1742).

5 The Identity-Social Function of Sport: The Right to Participate in Cultural Life

The identity-social function of sport is closely linked to its ability to create, strengthen, and maintain over time social and interpersonal relationships between sportspeople, as well as with spectators.[108] As Silvia Salardi argues, this "minimal social function", grounded in a motivational force towards aggregation based on emotions more than rationality, would be the "constitutive definitional element of sport allowing its use to support very different models of civil and social coexistence".[109] From this perspective, the inclusive participation to physical activity and sport could maximize the implementation of the right to culture and the right to participate in the life of the community.

The reference to the right to culture and participation in the life of the community, provided by Article 27 UDHR and Article 15 ICESCR, is based on the anthropological notion of culture in international human rights, according to which "culture is to be understood as the way of life of a person or a group".[110] Since the first report on cultural rights, adopted by the Human Rights Council, culture is defined as "a broad, inclusive concept encompassing all manifestations of human existence, [...] *inter alia*, [...] sport and games".[111] Sport would be covered by this extensive notion of culture, and it would be an important part of the cultural life of the community.

Access to sport activities would therefore be closely linked to the right to freely construct one's personality, which is a key right of the post-war UDHR.[112] As argued in the 'General Discussion on the Right to Take Part in Cultural Life',

---

[108] On the identity-social function of sport, see Keys (2006); Lavermore (2004), pp. 16–21; Polley (1999).

[109] Salardi (2019), p. 5.

[110] On the "anthropological" notion of culture in international human rights, see *inter alia*, Donders (2007), p. 235.

[111] Human Rights Council (HRC), *Report of the independent expert in the field of cultural rights, Ms. Farida Shaheed, submitted pursuant to resolution 10/23 of the Human Rights Council*, 22 March 2010, A/HRC/14/36, paras 6 and 9. This report specifies that culture "encompasses, *inter alia*, ways of life, language, oral and written literature, music and song, non-verbal communication, religion or belief systems, rites and ceremonies, sport and games, methods of production or technology, natural and man-made environments, food, clothing and shelter and the arts, customs and traditions through which individuals, groups of individuals and communities express their humanity and the meaning they give to their existence, and build their world view representing their encounter with the external forces affecting their lives" (ibid.). The same definition is foreseen in the CESCR, *General Comment No. 21, Right of everyone to take part in cultural life (art. 15, para. 1 (a), of the International Covenant on*, 20 November 1999, UN Doc. E/C.12/GC/21, para 13.

[112] Article 22 of the UDHR clearly states: "Everyone, as a member of society, has the right to social security and is entitled to realization, through national effort and international co-operation and in accordance with the organization and resources of each State, of the economic, social and cultural rights indispensable for his dignity and the free development of his personality". This right is further underlined in Art. 29, according to which "Everyone has duties to the community in which alone the free and full development of his personality is possible".

organized by the CESCR in 1992, "participation in cultural life, at the very core of which lay a person's duties and responsibilities towards the common good, gives the individual a sense of belonging and reinforces his/her sense of identity".[113] While defining culture as all activities "through which individuals, groups of individuals and communities express their humanity and the meaning they give to their existence",[114] the CESCR underlined the fundamental role of the access to cultural life in the construction of identity, since it includes those meanings and values in which people find the references to make sense of the world around them. This link is particularly emphasized where the right to participate in cultural life is regarded as fundamental for "the transmission [...] of common cultural and moral values in which the individual and society find their identity".[115]

The idea that the claim to exercise sport should be founded, *inter alia*, on the rights to culture and participation in community life, is supported by international instruments of hard law that expressly recognize the right to sport for some vulnerable categories. For instance, Article 30 (5) of the Convention on the Rights of Persons with Disabilities (CRPD) establishes the right to participate "in cultural life, recreation, leisure and sport", and provides a general obligation to support "the participation, to the fullest extent possible, of persons with disabilities in mainstream sporting activities at all levels.[116] The "children's right to play", enshrined in Article 31 ICRC, is supported by the obligation of the States Parties to "respect and promote the right of the child to fully participate in cultural and artistic life and shall encourage the provision of appropriate and equal opportunities for cultural, artistic, recreational and leisure activity".[117] This right is expressly linked to the right to culture and participation in the life of the community; CRC has emphasized that "children reproduce, transform, create and transmit culture through their own imaginative play, songs, dance, animation, stories, painting, games, street theatre, puppetry, festivals, and so on".[118] The access to sports activities would be an essential part of the "[i]nvolvement in a community's cultural life [, which] is an important element of children's sense of belonging".[119]

The right to play would simply not be addressed in the educational system context. The CRC recommends fostering the right to play outside of overly structured and programmed schedules:

---

[113] CESCR, *General discussion on the right to take part in cultural life as recognized in article 15 of the Covenant*, 7 December 1992, UN Doc. E/C.12/1992/SR.17, para 17.

[114] CESCR, *General Comment No. 21, Right of everyone to take part in cultural life (art. 15, para. 1 (a), of the International Covenant on*, 20 November 1999, UN Doc. E/C.12/GC/21, para 13.

[115] Ibid., para 26.

[116] Convention on the Rights of Persons with Disabilities (CRPD), adopted on 13 December 2006 (UNGA Res 61/106).

[117] ICRC, Article 31, para 2.

[118] CRC, *General Comment No. 17: (2013) on the right of the child to rest, leisure, play, recreational activities, cultural life and the arts (art. 31)*, para 12.

[119] Ibid., para 11.

> children are entitled to time that is not determined or controlled by adults, as well as time in which they are free of any demands – basically to do nothing, if they so desire. Indeed, the absence of activity can serve as a stimulus to creativity. Narrowly focusing all of a child's leisure time into programmed or competitive activities can be damaging to his or her physical, emotional, cognitive and social well-being.[120]

The CRPD and the ICRC suggest that the right to sport would also be supported by the right to leisure, provided by Article 24 of the UDHR.[121] The right to rest and leisure is indeed a structural component of the right to participate in collective life, the implementation of which would contribute to personality development and to a sense of belonging to a community.[122] In general terms, it could be argued that leisure is a medium through which other rights and related benefits can be exercised, including: the physical, mental, emotional, and social development of people through play; support for family life; personal expression and development; sustaining the cultural life of the community; and the promotion of physical and mental health through sport and cultural engagement. Conversely, the denial of time for beneficial leisure activity can have serious consequences for the well-being of individuals and societies. According to this interpretation, the right to sport should then be understood holistically, both in terms of its constituent parts and also its relationship with the implementation of the different basic rights. Each element of the right under analysis would be mutually linked and reinforced, and when realized, would contribute to enriching people's lives. From this perspective, participating in sport activities is essential to one's health, well-being, and education, as well as improving the community's cultural life, by contributing to personality development and to a sense of belonging to a community.

The reference to the right to participate in cultural life broadened the scope of the emerging right to sport, which should be expressly guaranteed "both inside and outside school settings".[123] It would therefore cover both amateur and professional sports, and even dangerous sports would not immediately be excluded to the extent that they contribute to the definition of personal identity and to the feeling of belonging to a community. Furthermore, drawing on international indications concerning access to culture, the right to sport would emphasize more affordable activities, paying special attention to the poorest in society.[124] On the basis of the general principle of gender equality, non-discrimination and social inclusion in and through sport, enshrined in the ICPEPA and ESpC, national and sporting authorities should offer equal access to sporting opportunities, especially concerning vulnerable

---

[120] Ibid., para 42.

[121] Pursuant to the Article 24 UDHR, "everyone has the right to rest and leisure, including reasonable limitation of working hours and periodic holidays with pay".

[122] On this point see, for example: Tobin and Lansdown (2019), p. 1195; Morsink (2021), p. 152.

[123] ESpC, Article 10.

[124] By analogy, see, for instance: *Recommendation on Participation by the People at Large in Cultural Life and their Contribution to It* (adopted on 26 November 1976) UNESDOC, Records of the General Conference, 19th Session, I para 14 (b) UNESCO doc 19C/Resolution, I, 29 (Participation by the People at Large Recommendation).

groups of people, such as persons with disabilities,[125] the elderly,[126] or children. The emerging right to sport would support the claim of everyone to participate in all traditional contexts of sporting activities.

It could thus be argued that the 'minimal social function' of sport would be regarded as a right to participate and be part of a community. This idea is implicitly affirmed, for instance, in the EU legal order. The identity-social function of sport has gained momentum in the European project since 'Adonnino Report',[127] and was explicitly recognized by the Amsterdam intergovernmental conference. The conference "emphasise[d] the social significance of sport, in particular its role in forging identity and bringing people together", with "special consideration [...] to the particular characteristics of amateur sport".[128] Richard Parrish notes that "sport was identified as a tool through which the EU could strengthen its image in the minds of Europe's citizens";[129] it was "intended to be used as the means of creating a common will of Europe and help the awareness of Union citizenship to increase".[130] In *TopFit e.V. and Daniele Biffi v. Deutscher Leichtathletikverband e.V.*,[131] the Court of Justice of the EU (CJEU) affirmed the right of all EU citizens to participate in sporting competitions of the state in which they are residents; this includes the possibility of winning the title of national champion and representing the host Member State at the international level, on the basis of their right to be integrated in the host state.[132]

---

[125] By analogy, see, *inter alia*: *CESCR General Comment No 5: Persons with Disabilities*, 11th session (9 December 1994), UN doc E/1995/22, para 36 (Gen Comm No 5).

[126] By analogy, see, for example: CESCR *General Comment No 6: The Economic, Social and Cultural rights of Older Persons*, 13th session (24 November 1995), UN doc E/1996/22, para 39.

[127] As known, the Adonnino Report has put forward a number of measures to encourage the sense of belonging of European citizens: the adoption of the European flag with twelve stars, a European driving licence, a European anthem, postage stamps with European emblems, standardised postal rates within the Community and the removal of the customs' signs at internal frontiers (Communication by the Commission to the Council of 29 March 1985, *A people's Europe,* COM(84) 446 final, Reports from the *ad hoc* Committee). On the contribution of Adonnino report to the role of sport in the European project see, for instance: Bogusz (2007), p. 159; Tognon (2009), p. 6; Colantuoni (2009), p. 12.

[128] Treaty of Amsterdam, Declaration on sport (n. 29), p. 136.

[129] Parrish (2003), p. 5.

[130] See Gardiner et al. (2006), p. 158.

[131] CJEU, C-22/18, *TopFit e.V. Daniele Biffi v Deutscher Leichtathletikverband*, EU:C:2019:497.

[132] It should be noted that this case represents a seismic CJEU ruling on sport, able to overturn the Members States practice on the participation of non-nationals in national championships. As the Advocate general noted, there is no uniform rule or practice shared by the Member States on this topic; however, in general terms, the participation of non-nationals is largely limited and the attribution of a national record to foreigners is basically precluded (opinion of Advocate General Tanchev, 7 March 2019, C-22/18, *TopFit e.V. Daniele Biffi v. Deutscher Leichtathletikverband*, EU:C:2019:181, paras 45–47). For an interpretation of the *Biffi* case as the recognition of the right to participate to sport activities and manifestations as a specific implementation of the right to be integrated and to be part of a community see, for example: Di Marco (2020), pp. 598–614.

For signatories of the ECHR, the emerging right to sport would also be supported by Article 8 ECHR, concerning the right to respect for private and family life. This protects a right to personal development, and the right to establish and develop relationships with others and the outside world.[133] In the case *Friend and Countryside Alliance v. the United Kingdom*,[134] for instance, the applicants alleged that some national acts banning hunting constituted an interference with their private life.[135] The Court recognised that "the hunting of wild mammals with hounds had a long history in the United Kingdom; that hunting had developed its own traditions, rituals and culture; and, consequently, that it had become part of the fabric and heritage of those rural communities where it was practised".[136] The ECtHR focused on the significant role played by a sport/leisure activity (hunting) in relation to the identity of a person or a community, accepting that "hunting provides hunters opportunities for establishing interpersonal relations, for carrying out outdoor activities and being entertained".[137] The Court finally stated "that it cannot be qualified as an identity feature of a hunters",[138] finding "hunting to be too far removed from the personal autonomy of the applicants, and the interpersonal relations they rely on to be too broad and indeterminate in scope, for the hunting bans to amount to an interference with their rights under Article 8".[139] Nevertheless, this statement could be interpreted, *a contrario*, to argue that a specific sport or leisure activity *does define* the identity of a specific social group, so as to challenge a national measure capable of interfering with private life. As Bestagno argues,

> Following the European Court of Human Rights argument in *Friend and Countryside Alliance*, the applicants would have to prove that the activity at stake does not only amount to a pastime they share with other people, but that it is a traditional practice of the community they belong to, or, in other terms, an essential element of their identity.[140]

This interpretation is partly supported by the recent *Semenya* case, where the exclusion of the appellant from sporting competitions was considered discriminatory in light of Article 8 ECHR.[141] Although the sporting activity's contribution to the

---

[133] See, for instance: ECtHR, Niemietz v. Germany, 16.12.1992, § 29; ECtHR, Pretty v. the United Kingdom, 29.04.2002, §§ 61 and 67; ECtHR, Oleksandr Volkov v. Ukraine, 09.01.2013, §§ 165-167; ECtHR, El Masri v. the former Yu-goslav Republic of Macedonia [GC], 13.12.2012, §§ 248–250.

[134] ECtHR, Friend and Countryside Alliance v. the United Kingdom, 24.11.2009.

[135] Ibid., §§ 36–39.

[136] Ibid., § 40.

[137] Ibid., § 43.

[138] Ibid., § 44.

[139] Ibid., § 43.

[140] Bestagno (2018), pp. 327–336, and in particular at 334.

[141] ECtHR, Semenya c. Suisse, 11.07.2023, § 205.

athlete's *social identity* was not particularly emphasized,[142] Judge Serghides, in his opinion, partly dissenting and partly concurring, stressing how the appellant's "identity is linked to her ability to compete and succeed like the elite athlete she is".[143]

The identity-social function potentially appears as the main feature of sport able to support the claim to participate in professional and/or amateur sporting activities. The essential condition is that the sporting activity supports the definition of personality and identity; this is not conditional on belonging to specific categories or restricted contexts. Indeed, this could support a 'complete' legal conceptualization of the right to sport, leading to the development of a 'complete theorized right'.

6 Conclusion: Conceptualizing the Human Right to Sport

This chapter has developed the thesis that sport could be regarded as a human right on the basis of its fundamental social functions. The claim to take part in sporting activities and events should be recognized as valid because sport contributes to the development of identity and social relations, and fosters psycho-physical integrity. This argument emerged by analyzing sport's natural-born relationship with human health, its pedagogical value, and its identity-social function. The innate features of sport suggest that the right to sport should be understood as an amalgam of several (rather than a single) treaty-based rights.

As shown in the previous sections, sport should be a treaty-based right because access could be regarded as an underlying determinant of the right to health, education, and to participate in cultural life. It would be a case of *favorable derivation*, as theoretically there are several ways in which the source right could meaningfully exist, even without "inclusive, adapted and safe opportunities to participate in physical education, physical activity and sport", which would define the right to sport (ICPEPA, Article 1.3; ESpC, Article 1.1). However, it would be an option that maximizes the implementation and guarantee of the source rights, and this is a position that has attracted significant international support. According to the Alston criteria and the UNGA guidelines in developing international instruments in the field of human rights, this would reflect an important social value attributed to sport, relevant throughout a world of diverse value systems.

This chapter has also argued that guaranteeing inclusive, adapted, and safe opportunities to participate in sport is consistent with the existing body of international human rights law. Sport's natural contribution to achieve or maintain psycho-physical integrity further confirms its fundamental character inherent to human

---

[142] This aspect is expressly invoked by the applicant (ibid., § 203), but essentially neglected by the Court, which focuses on the exercise of professional activities as elements of the right to respect for private and family life enshrined in Article 8 (ibid., § 125).

[143] Ibid., *Opinion en partie concordante, en partie dissidente du Juge Serghides*, § 24.

dignity. In addition, the basic rights of the emerging right to sport allow to detect practicable rights and obligations. These could potentially be covered by realistic and effective implementation machinery, including reporting systems; indeed, it could be argued that the access to physical activities and sport as a *right* has been implicitly protected by the ECtHR and the CJEU in the cases mentioned in the text, and it is essentially monitored by certain international bodies, such as the Enlarged Partial Agreement on Sport (EPAS).[144]

Obligations and rights inferred from each basic right suggest that the treaty-based rights would be considered as interdependent and essential elements of the legal construct of the right to sport. Every treaty-basic right, considered separately, would partially contribute to guaranteeing access to sport. As an extension of the right to health, this chapter contends that the right to sport would imply obligations traditionally foreseen for the implementation of the right to health. There would be a general obligation for public authorities to maximize individual capacity to exercise and to live healthfully, with particular attention on groups that sport could have a therapeutic function; this would cover the traditional general programmatic commitments for a progressive realization "to the maximum available resources". Sporting authorities would be required to guarantee the safety and health of sportspeople who *already* have access to SOs' activities or competitions.

The right to education, in turn, would mainly concern participation in physical education classes and extracurricular school sport. The potential contribution of sport to the right to education would not imply a general right to participate, for example, in professional or amateur sporting events organized by private associations (except, perhaps, those organized in cooperation with formal and informal educational institutions). A *general* right to sport therefore would not be sufficiently supported by the right to health and education. The right to access sport *for all* would be a right *for few* categories, and in relation to restricted contexts.

The right to participate in cultural life, by contrast, would support a *general* claim of access to sporting activities, to the extent that it contributes to defining personal autonomy and interpersonal relations. However, it would not involve the same obligations of political and economic intervention, and planning as associated with the right to health.[145] Taking separately into account the treaty-based rights, the right to sport would be an "incomplete theorized right". The emphatic affirmation of the principle (access to sport for all) would reveal limited agreement as to how this

[144] The EPAS has been established in May 2007 by the CoE, in order to give fresh momentum to pan-European sports cooperation and address the current challenges facing sport in Europe. It uses CoE sports standards such as the ESpC and the Code of Sports Ethics as the basis for carrying out standards, monitoring them and helping with capacity building and the exchange of good practice. On the EPAS' activity see: https://www.coe.int/en/web/sport/epas/ (last access 11 October 2022). In addition, in the same direction, the PACE has proposed the adoption of a Convention on sport with a proper monitoring and compliance assessment system (PACE, *Towards a Framework for Modern Sports Governance*, res. 2199, adopted on 24 January 2018, point 9).

[145] On the different obligations provided by the right to participation in cultural life see, for instance: Romainville (2015), pp. 405–436.

principle should be implemented, which implies the difficulty of efficiently guarantee the right, and could lead to a case of illegitimate and uncontrolled expansion of new human rights. The right to sport should therefore be understood holistically, both in terms of its constituent parts, and also its relationship to the implementation of the different basic rights. As argued in the previous section, each element of this emerging right would be mutually linked and reinforced, and when realized, would contribute to enriching the lives of people. Playing and participating in sport activities would be understood as essential to the health, well-being, and education of society. Nevertheless, it could be placed in the more general context of the community's cultural life, by contributing to personality development and the sense of belonging to a community.

The problem of treating sport as a right does not seem to be its legal existence, or the possibility of regarding it as a human right; it would, rather, be the definition of its scope that would be generic and essentially undetermined. Some authors have argued that the lack of a clear universal definition of sport has contributed to children's right to play being referred to as "the forgotten article of the ICRC".[146] Without a clear definition of the preconditions and characteristics of sport as a human right, it is difficult for public and sporting authorities to ascertain whether participation in sporting activities is functional to the implementation of the basic rights. Similarly, without consensus on a definition, or agreement on universal criteria of sport as a human right, it is difficult for public and sporting authorities to know whether the right to sport is being upheld. Having clear and operational criteria that universally separate sport as a human right from other non-sporting pastime activities is crucial to ensure that public and sporting authorities uphold the right to sport. It is also essential to avoid a dangerous inflation of rights, according to the warning expressed by Philip Alston almost 40 years ago against conjuring up an ever-expanding list of new human rights.[147]

This chapter has argued that the notions of personal autonomy and interpersonal relations—which emerged in the *Friend and Countryside Alliance v. the United Kingdom* case—may be used as fundamental criteria to define the scope of sport as a human right. In the 'age of rights', recognition of the claim to "inclusive, adapted and safe opportunities to participate in physical education, physical activity and sport" would be regarded as 'valid' by moving from the 'minimal social function' of sport indicated in the previous discussion. While the right to health could be implemented in several other ways, participating in particular sporting activities can be seen as essential to the definition of one's identity. In this sense, it can be argued that the right to participate in cultural life, regarded as the right to freely construct one's personality, would play a central role in defining the right to sport. The right to education and health would be complementary or supporting in nature; the right to education would be complementary in relation to the scope of the right to

[146] Colucci and Wright (2015), p. 97; Colliver and Doel-Mackaway (2021), p. 572.

[147] Alston (1984), p. 607.

sport, sharing with the right to participate in cultural life the fundamental aim of the full development of the human personality.

Pursuant to this approach, it could be deemed that all sportspeople who are (or would like to be) members of SOs, should enjoy the right to sport; considering that membership of an association, and participation to activities collectively, could affect personal autonomy and interpersonal relations. Vis-à-vis the sporting authorities, every sportsperson would be entitled to demand respect of the principle of non-discrimination and protection of their health and safety; the right to freely construct one's personality would be of capital importance. For example, in the aforementioned case of the athlete *Semenya*, this chapter emphasized that taking into account the right to health, the exclusion from a given competition may be regarded as "necessary, reasonable and proportionate" to ensure fair competition in women's sport. The athlete's right to health would not be compromised, since theoretically there are several other ways in which this right can be achieved even without participation in particular collective sport events. By contrast, moving *prima facie* from the right to participate in cultural life, in order to assess the claim of the athlete to participate in sporting events, it could be argued that her right to freely construct her personality would be irremediably compressed; without taking unjustified medication and maintaining the essential characteristics that define her identity, it would preclude her to participate in events which have given an important meaning to her existence.[148]

For sportspeople that practice in a casual and individual way, evaluating on a case-by-case basis is all the more necessary. According to the reasoning of the ECtHR in the *Friend and Countryside Alliance v. the United Kingdom* case, we could assume that, for example, amateur and non-professional skiers, who do not participate in competitions organized by traditional SOs, would not enjoy the right to sport. Skiing would not be a sporting activity that may be regarded as a human right, because it is "too far from the personal autonomy", and the interpersonal relations that it implies are "too broad and indeterminate in scope".[149] Public and sporting authorities would clearly have the obligation to guarantee safety and health of sportspeople practicing this sport, however, derived from the right to health, skiers could not expect a right to enjoy this sport. It could be noted that this example is open to a different interpretation if we consider, in a separated way, the right to health as a basic right: we could argue that skiing is a sport that contributes to mental and physical wellbeing, and accordingly, public and sporting authorities should be 'obliged' to plan and provide ski facilities. This interpretation is extremely generic and inaccurate from a legal perspective, and indeed lends support to those who warn against the proliferation, inflation, or dilution of human rights. This would also

[148] It should be noted that Semenya was not allowed to defend her title at the Tokyo 2020 Olympics due to the DSD Regulations.

[149] By analogy see the mentioned case: ECtHR, Friend and Countryside Alliance v. the United Kingdom, § 43.

confirm the idea that the basic rights of the emerging right to sport should not be considered separately in order to recognize a specific claim as valid.

It could also be argued that the recognition of the right to sport appears particularly significant to guarantee the effective legal protection of human rights in a sporting context. The several violations related to access to sport, mentioned in the introduction of this chapter, are in part linked to the uncertain and contested status of human rights standards in sporting contexts, due to the private nature of SOs and the transnational dimension of the sport legal order. This has resulted in a situation of legal uncertainty and different degrees of protection, and led to an inadequacy in sportspeople's protection. By enhancing the unity of fragmented claims founded on a plurality of legal instruments, it could be assumed that the right to sport might have the legal status of the 'right of rights', since it would provide the means whereby sportspeople could ultimately enact and uphold all their other rights. In situations where the application of human rights standards are contested, the right to sport would provide a direct legal source for their application. If the claim to participate in specific physical and sporting activities is recognised as a valid human right, enshrined in the Olympic Charter, we could assume that international and European fundamental standards should also be applied in such a situation (in particular, the universal principle of gender equality, non-discrimination, and social inclusion in and through sport).

The ESpC has significantly contributed to the recognition of sport as a human right, by including for the first time the right to culture among the essential elements of the legal construct of the right to sport. In its form of soft law, it "may facilitate reaching a political consensus, bring [the issue of sport as a human right] into the international agenda, define the area of international concern, and provide guidelines for behaviour that may generate the requisite practice for a rule of international law".[150] A topic as complex as the human right to sport deserves such a meaningful and clear recognition. However, if such recognition is to be granted, it must be legally sound. Only a legally justified right to sport can also be politically compelling. Finally, it should be noted that the criteria of personal autonomy and interpersonal relations require case-by-case evaluation, which is not immune to criticism and unclear points.[151] However, these criteria make it possible to answer the essential ethical question that underpins every human right; namely, why participation in sport should be considered an inherent right of the human being. Indeed, as Amartya Sen has argued, "human rights can be seen as primarily ethical demands",[152] and that they allow for "immediate use of the colossal appeal of the idea of human rights to confront intense oppression or great misery, without having to wait for the theoretical air to clear".[153]

---

[150] In these terms, with reference to the traditional function of soft law in the international human right law, see: Chinkin (2017), p. 92.

[151] Marshall (2008), p. 337.

[152] Sen (2004), pp. 315–356, in particular at 317.

[153] Ibid.

References

Abi-Saab G (2019) Evolutionary interpretation and international law. Hart, Oxford

Alston P (1984) Conjuring up new human rights: a proposal for quality control. Am J Int Law 78: 607

Bastianon S (2009) La funzione sociale dello sport e il dialogo interculturale nel sistema comunitario. Rivista italiana di diritto pubblico comunitario:391–411

Berryman JW (1992) Exercise and the medical tradition from Hippocrates through Antebellum America: a review essay. In: Berryman JW, Park RJ (eds) Sports & exercise science: essays in the history of sports medicine. University of Illinois Press, Champaign, pp 1–56

Bestagno F (2018) Regulation of sport activities and right to respect to private life under the European Convention on Human Rights. Eur Pap 3(1):327–336

Bogusz B (2007) Commercial freedom and sport: has sport lost is sporting edge?. In: Bogusz B, Cygan A, Szyszczak EM (eds) The regulation of sport in the European Union. Edward Elgar, Cheltenham, p 159

Bothe M (1979) Les concepts fondamentaux du droit à la santé: le point de vue juridique. Académie de droit international de La Haye, 14–34

Boyle A (2018) Soft law in international law-making. In: Evans M (ed) International law. Oxford University Press, Oxford, p 119

Brett A (1997) Liberty, right, and nature. Cambridge University Press, Cambridge

Buchanan A (2013) The heart of human rights. Oxford University Press, Oxford

Burghardt G (2011) Defining and recognizing play. In: Nathan P, Pellegrini A (eds) The Oxford handbook of the development. Oxford University Press, Oxford, p 9

Campbell T (2006) Rights: a critical introduction. Routledge, London

Chinkin C (2017) Sources. In: Moeckli D, Shah S, Sivakumaran S, Harris D (eds) International human rights law. Oxford University Press, Oxford, p 92

Christen P (2012) Athletics and social order in Sparta in the classical period. Class Antiq 31(2): 193–255

Cismas I (2014) The intersection of economic, social, and cultural rights and civil and political rights. In: Riedel E, Giacca G, Golay C (eds) Economic, social, and cultural rights in international law: contemporary issues and challenges. Oxford University Press, Oxford, pp 448–472

CoE (2000) Diversity and cohesion: new challenges for the integration of immigrants and minorities. Council of Europe Publishing, p 67

Colantuoni L (2009) Diritto sportivo. Giappichelli, Torino

Colliver Y, Doel-Mackaway H (2021) Article 31, 31 years on: choice and autonomy as a framework for implementing children's right to play in early childhood services. Human Rights Law Rev 21:566–587

Colucci E, Wright L (2015) Moving children's participation forward through Article 31 - the right to play. Can J Children's Rights 294:97

D'Amato A (1971) The concept of custom in international law. Cornell University Press, New York

De Beco G, Quinlivan S, Lord J (eds) (2019) The right to inclusive education in international human rights law. Cambridge University Press, p 5

De Schutter O (2014) International human rights law. Cambridge University Press, Cambridge

Depré S (2007) Les droits fondamentaux et le sport. In: Andersen R, Déom D, et al (eds) En hommage à Francis Delpérée: itinéraires d'un constitutionnaliste. Bruylant, Bruxelles, p 453

Di Marco A (2020) Amateur sport and Union citizenship in the Biffi case: towards a European sporting citizenship. Maastricht J Eur Comp Law 27(5):598–614

Di Marco A (2021) Athletes' freedom of expression: the relative political neutrality of sport. Human Rights Law Rev 21(3):620–640

Di Marco A (2022) Human rights in olympic movement: the application of European Standards to the *Lex Sportiva*. Neth Q Human Rights 40(3):244–268

Donders Y (2007) The legal framework of the right to take part in cultural life. In: Donders Y, Volodin V (eds) Human rights in education, science and culture: legal developments and challenges. Routledge, London, p 235
du Plessis G (2018) The European struggle with religious diversity: *Osmanoğlu and Kocabaş v.* Switzerland. J Church State 60(3):503–525
Feinberg J (1970) The nature and value of rights. J Value Inq 4:243
Ferenci B (2012) Right to education. In: Nowak M, Januszewski KM, Hofstatter T (eds) All human rights for all. Intersentia, Cambridge, pp 328–332
Gardiner S et al (2006) Sports law. Cavendish, New York
Gardiner S, Parrish R, Siekmann R (2009) EU, sport, law and policy: regulation, re-regulation and representation. Springer, Berlin
Gavison R (2003) On the relationships between civil and political rights, and social and economic rights. In: Coicaud JM, Doyle MW, Gardner AM (eds) The globalization of human rights. United Nations University Press, Tokyo, pp 23–55
Giummarra S (2012) Les droits fondamentaux et le sport: contribution à l'étude de la constitutionnalisation du droit du sport. PU Aix-Marseille, Aix-Marseille
Göncü A, Vadeboncoeur JA (2017) Expanding the definitional criteria for imaginative play: contributions of sociocultural perspectives. Learn Behav 45:422–431
Hall D (1994) Muscular Christianity: embodying the Victorian age. Cambridge University Press, Cambridge
Hannum H (2016) Reinvigorating human rights for the twenty-first century. Human Rights Law Rev 16:409–451
Hart H (1961) The concept of law. Oxford University Press, Oxford
Henkin L (1990) The age of rights. Columbia University Press, New York
Holowchak MA (2002) Philosophy of sport: critical readings, crucial Issues. Pearson, London
Holzer L (2020) What does it mean to be a woman in sports? An analysis of the jurisprudence of the Court of arbitration for sport. Human Rights Law Rev 20:387
Huizinga J (2005) Homo ludens. Gallimard, Paris
Ignatieff M (2001) Human rights as politics and idolatry. Princeton University Press, Princeton
Ireland-Piper D (2014) Is there a 'right' to sport? Sports Law Gov J 1(1):1–24
Karagiannis S (2012) Le droit à la santé dans certains textes internationaux et constitutionnels: entre généreuse utopie et mesquin pragmatisme? Journal du droit international 4:1137–1212
Keys BJ (2006) Globalising sport. National rivalry and international community in the 1930s. Harvard University Press, Cambridge
Krennerich M (2017) The human right to health: fundamentals of a complex right. In: Klotz S, Bielefeldt H, Schmidhuber M, Frewer A (eds) Healthcare as a human rights issue: normative profile, conflicts and implementation. transcript Verlag, Bielefeld, pp 23–54
Lakehal M (1991) Prévologie: du droit aux soins au droit à la santé. Dunod, Paris
Landoni E (2016) Gli atleti del duce. In: La Politica Sportiva del Fascismo 1919-1939. Mimesis, Milano
Latty F (2013) Sport. In: Thouvenin JM, Trebilcock A (eds) Le droit international social. Droits économiques, sociaux et culturels. Bruylant, Bruxelles, 1885
Lavermore R (2004) Sport's role in constructing the "Inter-state" Worldview. In: Lavermore R, Budd A (eds) Sport and international relations. Routledge, London, pp 16–21
Lougarre C (2015) What does the right to health mean?: the interpretation of Article 11 of the European Social Charter by the European Committee of Social Rights. Neth Q Human Rights 33(3):326–354
Lubrano E (2020) Il diritto allo sport come diritto fondamentale in prospettiva anche costituzionale. Dirittifondamentali.it 2:234–272
Maniatis A (2017) El derecho al deporte. Anuario da Facultade de Dereito da Universidade da Coruña 21:178–191
Marks SP (2016) Normative expansion of the right to health and the proliferation of human rights. George Wash Int Law Rev 49(1):97–142

Marshall J (2008) A right to personal autonomy at the European Court of Human. Rights Eur Human Rights Law Rev 337–256
Melica L (2022) Sport e "diritti" in Italia e nel mondo. Bologna University Press, Bologna
Miller SG (2003) The organization and functioning of the Olympic games. In: Philips DJ, Pritchard D (eds) Sport and festival in the ancient Greek world. Classical Press of Wales, Cardiff, pp 197–292
Morsink J (2021) Article 24. Rights to rest and leisure'. In: Morsink J (ed) Article by article: the universal declaration of human rights for a new generation. University of Pennsylvania Press, Philadelphia, p 152
Munro B (2016) Sport as a force for good. In: Transparency international, global corruption report: sport. Routledge, London, pp 3–11
Murphy T (2013) Health and human rights. Hart Publishing, Oxford
Parrish R (2003) Sports law and policy in the European Union. Manchester University Press, Manchester
Pensabene Lionti T (2012) Il diritto allo sport: tra esigenza socialmente rilevante e interesse fondamentale della persona. Diritto Amministrativo 3:415
Polley M (1999) Moving the goalposts: a history of sport and society since 1945. Routledge, London
Posner EA (2015) The twilight of human rights law. Oxford University Press, Oxford
Putney C (2001) Muscular Christianity: manhood and sports in Protestant America, 1880-1920. Harvard University Press, Cambridge
Reid HL (2011) Athletics and philosophy in the ancient world: contests of virtue. Routledge, London
Roberts AE (2001) Traditional and modern approaches to customary international law: a reconciliation. Am J Int Law 95:757
Romainville C (2015) Defining the right to participate in cultural life as a human right. Neth Q Human Rights 33(4):405–436
Salardi S (2019) Lo sport come diritto umano nell'era del post-umano. Giappichelli, Torino
Scolnicov A (2016) Human rights and derivative rights: the European Convention on human rights and the rights of corporations. In: Kahana T, Scolnicov A (eds) Boundaries of state, boundaries of rights: human rights, private actors, and positive obligations. Cambridge University Press, Cambridge, pp 194–214
Sen A (2004) Elements of a theory of human rights. Philos Public Aff 32:315–356
Simma B, Alston P (1992) The sources of human rights law: custom, jus cogens, and general principles. Aust Yearb Int Law 12:82–108
Sinnott-Armstrong W (2002) Two ways to derive implied constitutional rights. In: Goldsworthy JD, Campbell T (eds) Legal interpretation in democratic states. Ashgate, Farnham, p 231
Smith B, Sparkes AC (2019) Disability, sport and physical activity. In: Routledge handbook of disability studies. Routledge, pp 391–403
Stelitano A (2011) Il diritto allo sport: evoluzione del concetto di diritto allo sport negli atti internazionali rilevanti. In: Tognon J, Stelitano A (eds) Sport, Unione europea e diritti umani: il fenomeno sportivo e le sue funzioni nelle normative comunitarie e internazionali. CLEUP, Padova, pp 205–221
Sunstein CR (1995) Incompletely theorized agreements. Harv Law Rev 108(7):1736
Thielbörger P (2015) Re-Conceptualizing the human right to water: a pledge for a hybrid approach. Human Rights Law Rev 15(2):225–249
Tobin J (2012) The right to health in international law. Oxford University Press, Oxford
Tobin J, Barrett D (2020) The right to health and health-related human rights. In: Gostin LO, Meier BM (eds) Foundations of global health and human rights. Oxford University Press, Oxford, pp 67–88
Tobin J, Lansdown G (2019) Article 31: the right to rest, leisure, play, recreation, and participation in cultural life and the arts. In: Tobin J (ed) The Convention on the rights of the child: a commentary. Oxford University Press, Oxford, p 1204

Toebes BCA (1999) The right to health as a human right in international law. Intersentia, Cambridge
Tognon J (2009) L'Unione Europea e sport: evoluzioni e sviluppi di un rapporto "particolare". In: Tognon J (ed) Diritto comunitario dello sport. Giappichelli, Torino, p 6
Tollener J, Schotsmans P (2013) Self, other, play, display and humanity: development of a five model for the analysis of ethical arguments in the athletic enhancement debate. In: Tollener J et al (eds) Athletic enhancement, human nature and ethics. Springer, Netherlands, Heidelberg, pp 21–43
Uprimny R, Chaparro Hernandez S, Araujo A (2019) Bridging the gap: the evolving doctrine on ESCR and 'Maximum Available Resources'. In: Sen A, Young K (eds) The future of economic and social rights. Cambridge University Press, Cambridge, pp 624–653
Verma GK, Douglas SD (2022) Winners and losers: ethnic minorities in sport and recreation. Routledge
Walin A (2012) Extreme sports: are they worth the risk? J First-Year Stud Res Writ 3690
Watson NJ, Parker A (2014) Muscular Christianity and sports ministry. In: Watson NJ, Parker A (eds) Sport and the Christian religion: a systematic review of literature. Cambridge Scholars Publishing, Cambridge, pp 44–62
Weatherill S (2014) Sport as culture in EC law. Springer, TMC Asser Press, The Hague, p 245
Weston MA (2017) The international right to sport for people with disabilities. Marq. Sports Law Rev 28(1):2–36

Antonio Di Marco Teaching professor in International and European law at the University of Strasbourg, former agent at the Council of Europe, PhD in European law at the University *Alma Mater* of Bologna, PhD in public law at the University of Strasbourg, PhD in international law at the University of Catania.

As agent at the Council of Europe, he worked on sporting issues at the Committee Culture, Science, Education and Media of the Parliamentary Assembly, and as expert at the Enlarged Partial Agreement on Sport (EPAS). Recent publications on sporting topics included: *Sporting antinomies and systemic aporia: the duty to co-operate (and the right to be involved) of Sporting Organisations* (Eunomia 2023); *Human Rights in Olympic Movement: the Application of the International and European Standards to the Lex Sportiva* (Netherland Quarterly of Human Rights 2022); *Sports Economy and Fight Against Corruption: which Limits for the Sporting Organisations Autonomy?* (European Business Law Review 2021); *Athletes' Freedom of Expression: the Relative Political Neutrality of Sport* (Human Rights Law Review 2021); *Amateur sport and Union citizenship in the Biffi case: towards a European sporting citizenship* (Maastricht Journal of European and Comparative Law 2020); *Conflicts of interest in sport: a comparative analysis of International and European remedies* (European Journal of Comparative Law and Governance 2020); *The internal governance of sporting organisations: international convergences on an idea of democracy* (The International Sport Law Journal 2019).

MIX
Papier aus verantwortungsvollen Quellen
Paper from responsible sources
FSC® C105338

If you have any concerns about our products,
you can contact us on
ProductSafety@springernature.com

In case Publisher is established outside the EU,
the EU authorized representative is:
Springer Nature Customer Service Center GmbH
Europaplatz 3, 69115 Heidelberg, Germany

Printed by Libri Plureos GmbH
in Hamburg, Germany